D0539261

Law, Values, and the Environment

A Reader and Selective Bibliography

edited by
Robert N. Wells, Jr.

The Scarecrow Press, Inc.
Lanham, Md., and London

SCARECROW PRESS, INC.

Published in the United States of America
by Scarecrow Press, Inc.
4720 Boston Way
Lanham, Maryland 20706

4 Pleydell Gardens, Folkestone
Kent CT20 2DN, England

British Cataloguing-in-Publication Information Available

Library of Congress Cataloging-in-Publication Data

Law, values, and the environment : a reader and selective bibliography / edited
by Robert N. Wells, Jr.
p. cm.
1. Environmental law, International. 2. International cooperation. I. Wells,
Robert n.
K3585.6.L39 1996 341.7'62—dc20 95–52588 CIP

ISBN 0–8108–3134–1 (cloth : alk. paper)

⊖™ The paper used in this publication meets the minimum requirements of
American National Standard for Information Sciences—Permanence of
Paper for Printed Library Materials, ANSI Z39.48–1984.
Manufactured in the United States of America.

To Anne and Frank Piskor

with sincere appreciation for their
support and encouragement

Contents

Copyright Acknowledgments

Deihl, Colin. "Antarctica: An International Laboratory," *Boston College Environmental Affairs Law Review*, v. 18, spring 1991, 423–56, is reprinted with the permission of the *Boston College Environmental Affairs Law Review*.

Glode, Mark L. and Glode, Beverly Nelson. "Transboundary Pollution: Acid Rain and United States-Canadian Relations," *Boston College Environmental Affairs Law Review*, v. 20, no. 1, 1993, 1–35 is reprinted with the permission of *Boston College Environmental Affairs Law Review*.

Grotta, Daniel and Sally. "Antarctica: Whose Continent Is It Anyway?" *Popular Science*, January 1992, 62–67, 90–91, is reprinted with permission from *Popular Science* Magazine, © 1992, Times Mirror Magazines, Inc., Distributed L.A. Times Syndicate.

Hackman, Sandra. "After Rio: Our Forests, Ourselves," *Technology Review*, v. 95, no. 7, October 1992, 32–40, is reprinted with the permission of *Technology Review*.

Hirsch, M. and Housen-Couriel, D. "Aspects of the Law of International Water Resources," *Water Science and Technology*, vol. 27, no. 7–8, 213–221, 1993, is reprinted with the permission of *Water Science and Technology*, Elsevier Science Ltd., Pergamon Imprint, Oxford, England.

Keller, Suzanne. "Ecology and Community," is reprinted from the *Boston College Environmental Affairs Law Review*, v. 19, no. 3, spring 1992, 623–34, with permission of the *Boston College Environmental Law Review*.

Lenssen, Nicholas. "The Ocean Blues," *World Watch* Magazine, v. 2, no. 4, July-August 1989, 26–35 is reprinted with the permission of the Worldwatch Institute, Washington, D.C. 20036–1904.

Massignon, Nicole. "The Urban Explosion in the Third World," *The OECD Observer*, no. 182, June-July 1993, 18–22, is reprinted with the permission of the *The OECD Observer*.

Myers, Norman. "Biodiversity and the Precautionary Principle," *Ambio*, v. 22, no. 2–3, May 1993, 74–79, is reprinted with the permission of *Ambio* and the Royal Swedish Academy of Sciences.

Whittle, R., Jessiman, B., and Raphael, R. "Hazardous Waste Management: An International Perspective, Summary Report," 5th Conference on Toxic Substances, April 1-2, 1992, Montreal, Canada, is reprinted here with the permission of Health and Welfare Canada, Ottowa, Ontario, Canada.

Treaties

Air Pollution

1979   Geneva Convention on Long Range Transboundary Air Pollution, The. (1985, 1988, and 1991 Protocols on sulfur emissions, nitrogen oxide emissions, and volatile organic compounds)

1985   Helsinki Protocol on the Reduction of Sulphur Emissions or Their Transboundary Fluxes by at Least 30%

Antarctica

1958   Antarctic Treaty

1980   Convention on the Conservation of Antarctic Marine Living Resources, Canberra Convention

Climate

1985   Vienna Convention for the Protection of the Ozone Layer

1987   Montreal Protocol for Substances that Deplete the Ozone Layer (as amended in 1990)

1992   Climate Change Convention (Rio)

Land Degradation

1971   Convention on Wetlands of International Importance (Ramsar Convention)

1994   Paris Convention on Desertification

Species

1946   International Convention for the Regulation of Whaling

1972   Convention Concerning the Protection of the World Cultural and Natural Heritage (World Heritage Convention) IUCN/IWRB

1973   Washington Convention on Trade in Endangered Species

1979   Convention on Conservation of Migratory Species of Wild Animals

1992   Biodiversity Convention

Toxics

1989   Basel Convention on the Control of Transboundary Movements of Hazardous Wastes

1989   Vienna Conventions on the Notification and Assistance in the Event of a Nuclear Accident

1991   Bamako Convention, Bans Waste Imports to the African Continent

Water Pollution

1909   Boundary Waters Treaty between Canada and the United States

1954   Convention for the Prevention of Pollution of the Sea by Oil (OILPOL I)

1972   London Convention on the Prevention of Marine Pollution by Dumping of Waste and Other Matter

1972   Oslo Convention to Curtail North Sea Dumping

1973   International Convention for the Prevention of Pollution from Ships and the Protocol of 1978 Relating Thereto with Annexes (MARPOL 73/78)

1974   Helsinki Convention to Curtail Baltic Sea Dumping

1974   Paris Convention, Placed Restrictions and Controls on Land-Based Sources of Pollution

1976   Barcelona Convention for the Protection of the Mediterranean Sea Against Pollution and Related Protocols

1976   Bonn Convention on the Protection of the Rhine River Against Chemical Pollution and Against Chloride Pollution

1978   Kuwait Region Convention for Co-operation on the Protection of the Marine Environment from Pollution

1981   Convention for the Co-operation in the Protection and Development of the Marine and Coastal Environment of the West and Central African Region

1981   Convention for the Protection of the Marine Environment and Coastal Area of the South-East Pacific

1982   United Nations Convention on the Law of the Sea, UNCLOS III

1983   Regional Convention for the Conservation of the Red Sea and Gulf of Aden Environment

1983   Convention for the Protection and Development of the Marine Environment of the Wider Caribbean Region

1985   Convention for the Protection, Management and Development of the Marine and Coastal Environment of the Eastern African Region

1986   Convention for the Protection of the Natural Resources and Environment of the South Pacific Region

1990   International Convention on Oil Pollution Preparedness, Response and Co-Operation-IMO

Preface

Pollution and environmental degradation don't recognize international borders and cannot be prevented by national laws and regulations alone. We have learned that the most common environmental problems are global in nature and require the cooperation of the world community to resolve. What we have yet to learn is how one hundred and ninety sovereign states can cooperate to protect the environment and draft agreements which curtail transboundary pollution and environmental degradation. This halting process began with the 1972 Stockholm Conference on the Human Environment and continued with the Rio Conference on Environment and Development, particularly with two documents emanating from that conference: *Agenda 21* and *The Rio Declaration.*

Law emerges out of a societal consensus on values and norms. At the international level this lawmaking function lacks these core elements which underpin domestic law. Consequently, efforts to forge international responses to world problems, such as the environment, are halting and often lack general acceptance. For example, there exists a wide gulf between the developed countries and the developing Third World on environmental issues and their resolution. These differences were dramatically displayed during the 1992 Rio Conference. They emerged again at the 1995 Berlin Conference on the Climate.

In this anthology it is my goal to acquaint the reader with the scope of worldwide environmental problems and suggested means to resolve them. Since the field of international environmental law and regulation is relatively new, traditional approaches to lawmaking have had to be augmented by innovative approaches to curbing transboundary environmental pollution. UNEP, the United Nations Environmental Program, has been a leader in developing new ways to reduce environmental pollution and degradation. However, the range of environmental problems and UNEP's modest status within the United Nations bureaucracy limit its leadership role and overall effectiveness. As an alternative, environmental nongovernmental organizations (Greenpeace, Worldwatch, World Wildlife Fund, and the like) have come forward to press the environmental agenda and pressure governments to cooperate on such critical matters as ozone depletion, acid rain, greenhouse gases, ocean and freshwater pollution, and land degradation.

We are far from developing an international environmental regime which would forthrightly address the environmental agenda. Although there has been acknowledged progress on limiting CFCs that deplete atmospheric ozone, acid rain, carbon emissions, ocean pollution and toxic dumping, population growth, land degradation, species depletion, deforestation, and pesticide damage remain largely unregulated. The rapidity with which international environmental disasters occur leaves little margin for error and even less time to organize to respond to potential crises. Hopefully, this reader on international environmental law will provide direction as to how the international community can organize to protect the environment and reduce harmful substances which degrade it.

I am indebted to my students who have participated in my environmental law and politics seminars for encouraging my interest in this area—an interest which led to the edition of this anthology. Having an environmental studies program at St. Lawrence University has provided me with colleagues and students who have honed my skills and broadened my perspective on environmental questions, particularly those which threaten the international commons. Mollie Crowe and Kevin Todd, my student research assistants, were invaluable in assembling this book. Sheila Murphy and Bonnie Enslow were ever available to provide editorial assistance and manuscript typing. The index was prepared by Carolyn G. Weaver of Weaver Indexing Service, Bellevue, WA. Laurie Olmstead prepared the entire manuscript for the publisher and her editorial assistance and manuscript preparation were, as always, invaluable.

I would like to acknowledge my gratitude to the authors who so kindly allowed me to include their articles in this anthology on international environmental law. I would like to thank St. Lawrence University which has supported me financially and otherwise in this enterprise.

Robert N. Wells, Jr.
Munsil Professor of Government
St. Lawrence University

1

From Stockholm to Rio: The Evolution of International Environmental Law

Robert N. Wells, Jr.

The 1992 Stockholm Conference on the Human Environment is generally regarded by scholars and practitioners as the one event most responsible for the development of international environmental law. In addition to creating UNEP (United Nations Environmental Program) the conference laid the groundwork for a wide range of initiatives to protect the world's environment. Between Stockholm and its successor environmental conference, Rio 1992, fifteen major international treaties and protocols on the environment were negotiated and signed. Beyond this, national regimes created environmental departments or ministries and enacted laws regulating land use, water purification, air quality, and toxins and pesticides.

However, this increased state activity at the national and international level to protect the environment should be placed in perspective. While a growing emphasis on the environment was emerging, so was a continuing degradation of the planet's natural resources and ecological systems. Population increase continued, particularly in areas of the world less able to sustain additional people. Scientists detected breaks in the ozone layer which surrounds the earth and protects us from ultraviolet rays. Pollution of the seas, and atmosphere and land degradation emerged as major environmental problems worldwide. Acid rain blighted the forest lands and lakes of North America and northern Europe. Even the heavens were affected by the pollution of our reach into space; seven thousand pieces of space junk are currently circulating the planet.

Unlike other branches of international law, international environmental law lacks an evolutionary basis, supported by custom and state compliance. Treaties and other international agreements which serve as the other principal source of international law do not begin to appear in the environmental field until the second half of the twentieth century. The 1909 United States-Canada Boundary Waters Agreement and the Trail Smelter Arbitration (1940) stand out as early efforts to regulate cross-boundary air and water pollution. The development of an environmental consciousness at the international level had to await the impact of modern technology, expanding industrialization and major environmental disasters, such as the Torrey Canyon oil spill.

Despite these limitations, the evolving field of international environmental law has developed its own modus operandi in setting standards and regulation of transborder environmental pollution. Prominent in this role is the work of UNEP and its panels of scientific and technical experts. Although UNEP lacks political power within the United Nations system, its professionalism and expertise within the environmental community is highly respected. The UNEP Regional Seas Program is a model of environmental cleanup and restriction. Moreover UNEP has provided the leadership in identifying principal environmental problems and organizing the international community to respond to them. It played a singularly prominent role in the preparatory meetings leading to the 1992 Rio Summit.

Many of these novel approaches in developing international environmental law are discussed by Geoffrey Palmer in his article, "New Ways to Make International Environmental Law" in Chapter 24. Prominent among these approaches is what is called "soft law" which includes UNEP Regulations, General Assembly resolutions, standards set by United Nations and regional organizations, and the most recent enactments of the 1992 Rio Conference on the Environment and Development: *The Rio Declaration* and *Agenda 21*.

Major credit for awakening international awareness must go to non-governmental organizations (NGOs) and the media which has selected the environment as a central topic for coverage. Much like the NGOs in the field of human rights, the environmental NGOs provide the information, expertise, involvement, monitoring, and lobbying to identify and bring environmental issues to the world agenda. Concurrent with the 1992 Rio Summit was a parallel meeting of NGOs and environmental organizations which numbered approximately 10,000 persons.

Differences between North and South (developed-developing countries) present real problems to a comprehensive approach to world environmental problems. These differences include financing environmental programs, responsibility for existing environmental damage, impact of environmental protection on economic development, and divergent perceptions of the environmental problem. These issues were prominent during the 1992 Rio Summit and consistently arise when regional and international conferences on the environment are convened to address a particular matter of environmental concern. These issues are thoroughly discussed by Edith Brown Weiss in her article, "International Environmental Law: Contemporary Issues and the Emergence of a New World Order," Chapter 25.

These North-South issues were prominent in the agenda for the Rio Summit. To begin with, the developing countries insisted that the conference focus be on development as well as the environment. A forest treaty was not included on the conference agenda due to the opposition of lumber exporting countries and major international lumber producers. The Climate Treaty, the international agreement to reduce earth warming, contained differential emission standards for both North and South, taking into consideration financial cost and emission levels produced. The Biodiversity Treaty was opposed by the United States because it was believed to infringe on American patent rights. Both *The Rio Declaration* and *Agenda 21* evidenced important compromises and concessions to developing countries. The conference produced a definition of "sustainable development" which allowed just about everyone to accept it.

Currently there are a number of environmental matters which require international attention. The failure to arrive at a forest treaty leaves unresolved the critical issue of rain forest destruction. Failure to achieve a system of rain forest protection affects both climate and biodiversity. The rain forests of the south are our primary providers of natural pharmaceutical and herbal medicines. In the absence of any international protection, governments and environmental action groups have come forward with "debt for nature" swaps which seek to forgive Third World debt for rain forest protection.

Although the United States adopted strict standards on the use of pesticides and certain chemical-based fertilizers as early as 1972, few, if any, restrictions on their production and exportation to developing countries exist. These toxic materials poison the animal and bird life in developing countries and are a major source of land degradation and water pollution. Strong lobbying interests oppose restrictions or importation of pesticides or chemical fertilizers. Major chemical firms and agribusiness interests support their continuance and developing countries depend on them to support cash crops and agriculture in general. Although the United States banned DDT almost a quarter century ago, the long-term impact of its residue still plagues us.

Perhaps the largest NIMBY (Not in My Backyard) opposition group is the anti-nuclear movement. It opposes nuclear power, nuclear waste disposal, and other commercial uses of nuclear materials which pose a threat to the environment. Three Mile Island and Chernobyl have graphically demonstrated the potential and real hazards of nuclear power. In response, the Swedish population voted to denuclearize Sweden by the year 2000. Other countries are certain to follow the Swedish example. Equally important is the matter of nuclear waste from both nuclear power plants and nuclear weapons production and now disarmament. Currently there is no safe way to dispose of or seal highly radioactive nuclear waste which is the by-product of nuclear power production, research, and nuclear weapons grade plutonium. Although IAEA (International Atomic Energy Agency) has concluded a treaty on nuclear accident warning and state responsibility, there is no international legislation on the disposal and safe encasement of highly radioactive nuclear waste. In the meantime, this volatile waste product continues to pick up in temporary storage centers.

Environmental disasters, such as the Torrey Canyon, the Exxon Valdez, Chernobyl, the Pennex oil blowout, and Kuwaiti oil fires, present a distinct challenge to the world community. In one way or another, each of the above disasters has something to do with energy production. As long as we continue to be so dependent on fossil fuels, particularly oil and gas, and nuclear energy, there is both environmental risk and harm involved. OILPOL I and II, conventions dealing with oil spills, address the matters of responsibility and liability, but do not attempt to grapple with the risk and harm such disasters pose. Both UNCLOS III (United Nations Conference on the Law of the Sea) and IMO (MARPOL convention) seek to limit ocean pollution and the frequency of oil spills through preventive measures and monitoring of shipping lanes. Certainly one area of international environmental law which needs strengthening is enforcement of minimum standards to prevent such disasters, assign liability, and award compensation on the basis of risk, harm, and "due diligence."

In 1975, the Convention on International Trade in Endangered Species (CITES) was approved. The United States Congress passed the Endangered Species Act in 1973. These instruments, along with the wake of IUCN (International Union for the Conservation of Nature), have been principally responsible for slowing, but not halting, the extinction of endangered species. The illicit trade in "exotic" mammals, birds, fish, and plants continues because states are either unwilling or unable to halt it. The present convention needs means to insure greater compliance and enforcement. Currently the treaty is self-enforcing and no international machinery exists to insure state compliance. Since many of these endangered species live in wildlife habitats, it has been suggested that they be brought under the protection of World Parks or nature preserves established under the provisions of the 1972 World Heritage Convention.

Beginning with the United Nations Water Conference in Mexico City there have been dire predictions regarding the availability of fresh, clean water if present use trends continue. The anticipated fresh water crisis stems from the fact that current use patterns either pollute or misuse water which must be protected for human and species consumption. Large scale irrigation, lack of sanitation, and non-source agricultural pollution, render water unsuitable for drinking and domestic use. Rivers and freshwater lakes are often not exclusively resources of one country. Little international regulation or protection exists for ground or surface water outside Europe and North America. Both of these regions experienced serious pollution and water quality problems before they began joint efforts to protect fresh water. Moreover, there is little international agreement as to what constitutes riparian water rights. This dilemma is discussed in Chapter 9, "Aspects of the Law of International Water Resources."

In 1994, the Paris Convention on Desertification was signed. This is the first international agreement which seeks to address land degradation. Population increases, poor land management practices, urbanization, over grazing, lack of crop rotation, and deforestation contribute to desertification and land degradation. The American dust bowl of the 1930s, Russian agriculture failures in the 1950s Virgin Lands experiment, and large-scale Chinese land mismanagement during the Great Leap Forward are but three examples of colossal societal failures in land management. Serious efforts of reforestation and soil conservation are underway worldwide to stem the tide of desertification, but national land use policies, systems of land tenure and land pressure, caused by swelling populations, seem to nullify any gains. Climate change, the attacks on rain forests, and the destruction of wetlands and savannas compound the problem of the disappearance of useable land.

Pollution knows no frontiers as demonstrated by the environmental concerns raised about Antarctica and outer space. Neither the 1959 Antarctic Treaty or the 1980 Canberra Convention on the Conservation of Antarctic Marine Living Resources were sufficient deterrents to halt the efforts to open up Antarctica to mining exploration. Such activities would be devastating to the ecology of the continent. The Antarctic shelf is home to a varied ecosystem, including mammals, fish, crustaceans, and plankton and more than fifty species of birds which feed on them (Switzer, 330). A 1988 treaty to permit limited exploration of mineral resources (CRAMRA) was put on hold in 1993, when a fifty-year moratorium on mining was established for Antarctica. Tourism, military activities, scientific activity, and construction pose threats to the fragile habitat of our most pristine continent. Environmental groups have proposed that Antarctica be declared an international commons and be protected in the same manner as World Heritage Parks.

Little has been done to protect the environment of outer space since the signing of the Outer Space Treaty in 1967. Subsequent treaties deal with the registration of space objects, rescue of astronauts, responsibility of space objects, and the application of space law to the moon. Two major environmental problems are the presence of space junk, seven thousand space objects, and pollution by orbiting space vehicles and their crews. When the Outer Space Treaty comes up for renewal in 1997, the environmental protection of outer space and limiting space activity which pollutes and contaminates outer space should be a key agenda item. Bernard Schaefer's article, "Solid, Hazardous and Radioactive Wastes in Outer Space: Present Controls and Suggested Changes" (Chapter 21) outlines a program of environmental protection for outer space.

Any further developments in international environmental law will entail the cooperation of both the developed and developing worlds. Currently, the level of trust and understanding is not sufficient to forge ahead and develop comprehensive international regimes which protect the atmosphere, land base, species, oceans, and fresh water. Third World leaders have strong doubts as to developed countries' commitment to environmental protection and view calls for greater environmental concern on their part as a way to stall their development and frustrate their trade. For these reasons, mechanisms such as the GEF (Global Environmental Facility), which was established by the Rio Summit to provide funds for Third World countries to undertake environmentally sustainable development, are very important in building trust between North and South.

Other approaches such as differential environmental standards, debt relief, technical assistance to raise hygiene levels in developing countries, and support of agricultural production will encourage Third World leaders to view environmental programs in a more positive way. With abject poverty, overpopulation, land pressure, food scarcity, and disease as principal problems for developing countries, the environment constitutes but one additional concern to be addressed. It is for this reason that when the North engages the South on environmental issues, which will be increasingly the situation, it needs to recognize both the South's limits and priorities. Environmental policy at the international level for the foreseeable future will be linkage policy involving both environment and issues central to the South's agenda.

It is with this recognition that I have assembled this anthology on international environmental law. Important strides have been made since the 1972 Stockholm Conference with the passing of the cold war and the winding down of the arms race. The issue of global environmental protection has taken center stage along with poverty, famine, development, and human rights. The crafting of international environmental law has been unique and creative which has made possible the enactment of improved standards sooner than traditional approaches to making international law. Hopefully, the articles included in this anthology will both illustrate this approach to lawmaking and inform the reader of the principal issues of the international environment and how states have and have not gone about resolving them.

Bibliography

Akerman, Nordal ed. *Maintaining a Satisfactory Environment: An Agenda for International Environmental Policy.* Boulder, CO: Westview Press, 1990.

Birnie, Patricia W. and Alan E. Boyle. *International Law and the Environment.* New York, NY: Clarendon Press, Oxford, 1992.

1994 Environmental Almanac. World Resources Institute. New York, NY: Houghton Mifflin Company, 1993.

French, Hilary F. *After the Earth Summit: The Future of Environmental Governance.* Worldwatch Paper 107, March 1992, Washington, DC:

Worldwatch Institute, 1992.

Imber, Mark F. *Environment, Security and U.N. Reform.* New York, NY: St. Martin's Press Inc., 1994.

Porter, Gareth and Janet Welsh Brown. *Global Environmental Politics.* Boulder, CO: Westview Press, 1991.

Rifkin, Jeremy. *Biosphere Politics.* New York: Crown, 1991.

Switzer, Jacqueline U. *Environmental Politics: Domestic and Global Dimensions.* New York, NY: St. Martin's Press, Inc., 1994.

Environmental Ethics and the Emergence of a Global Community

As the environmental problems of this planet approach the point of crisis, a trend toward valuing nature is emerging. The value is of varying degrees, but nonetheless there is a group of people who are beginning to recognize that humans have a vested interest in preserving the Earth, not only for us and future generations of humans, but also for the thousands of other species that inhabit this planet.

Humans often suffer from ethnocentrism. In terms of the environment, this ideology takes the form of envisioning the superiority of the human species above all others. This mentality grants us the freedom to exploit the resources, flora, and fauna of the planet without guilt for, according to the ideology of ethnocentrism, these things exist for the benefit of the human race.

This ideology functions well under the economic theory of capitalism and free enterprise, where development and individual success are the principal goals. However, in a world that cannot sustain a global system of this kind, a new ideology emerged.

Beginning in the early part of the 1970s, a new philosophy developed called "Deep Ecology." Among its principles are the ideas that all species have an equal right to exist and flourish on this planet and that diversity among humans and among all species should be valued. This ideology does not tolerate human ethnocentrism, nor does it allow for the total exploitation of nature for the good of the human race.

The idea of development can be modified to be compatible with the new environmental ethic. Sustainable development and environmentally sound development that can be maintained over the long term without depleting the environment and its resources, is quickly becoming the target for new development.

It is also important to recognize in these new environmental ethics the value placed on the "global commons." The environment is not divided along national boundaries and cannot be legislated and protected along those lines. As a global community, humans have a responsibility to preserve the environment. The new ethics call for international cooperation in protecting the flora, fauna, and their habitats.

—RNW

2

Ecology and Community

Suzanne Keller

Introduction

What do the following dates have in common: August 4, 1978; March 28, 1979; December 3, 1984; and April 26, 1986? Each refers to a humanly caused environmental disaster that stunned the world. It would be easy to criticize, with retrospective wisdom, the obvious failures that each incident represents, but that is not my goal. My objective is to see what these calamities can teach us about individual and collective responses to environmental crises.

The Lessons of Experience

At first glance, Love Canal, Three Mile Island, Bhopal, and Chernobyl would seem to have little in common, differing as they do in region, culture, and history. As one examines the record, however, striking similarities stand out in regard to not only the traumas that occurred in these places, but also the impact of the incidents on local residents, the response of the authorities, and the views of the experts.

The post-accident reactions of government authorities are typically slow and evasive. In these four cases, deceit and denial were prevalent, as were false reassurances, patronizing attitudes, and frequent resort to scientific jargon that obscured rather than enlightened. The first official response in each case was to discount the magnitude of the accident and thereby minimize the human suffering that it engendered.

Another characteristic that these environmental disasters shared was the experts' overconfidence in technical infallibility: an attitude that blocked any immediate, human response to the panicked population. A

1975 report by General Electric articulated this attitude, stating flatly that the chances of a severe accident at a nuclear reactor "were one in a million years." (Gould 1990: 139) At Three Mile Island, both industry representatives and federal regulators previously had officially dismissed the likelihood of multiple system failure as preposterous. (Walsh 1988: 34) As a result, during the first day after the accident, "utility and [Nuclear Regulatory Commission (NRC)] officials played down its seriousness, insisting there was no threat of radiation releases into the atmosphere." (Walsh 1988: 35)

Because we do not anticipate such accidents, we cannot effectively prepare for them or respond to them. The assumption of technological infallibility, not surprising in a technocratic civilization, prevents not only the policymakers but also the actors at the scene from anticipating a breakdown. In a crisis, their first response is to decry the danger, if not cover it up altogether, and cite statistical probabilities that deny the events that have occurred. In this way, technological overconfidence can lull even responsible officials into a refusal to heed evidence. Confident in their formulas, the experts refuse to believe that these or the machinery they generated might fail. Thus, at Chernobyl, the engineers, many of whom would later die in agony, did not believe the readings of the very instruments they had created, the radiation monitors.

Yet technology did and often does fail. It fails because of designs that are "not forgiving of mistakes" (Marples 1988: 22), because of human error, or because of too vast a distance between centralized policymakers and on-site managers. In the aftermath of Chernobyl, for example, Moscow did not grasp the full impact of the disaster until it dispatched a team of experts to the site to see for themselves. Only after the experts' return did the Soviet government sound a general alarm.

What Chernobyl and other major environmental accidents clearly indicate is that self-managing technology does not yet exist. Even more important, it has become clear that technology never "acts" on its own, for human fallibility can overcome any design and human error undermine any safeguard. (Haynes & Bojum 1985: 203) To underscore this point, we should note that all the major accidents at civilian nuclear facilities to date have been the result of human error: a category that contains a wide range of Pandoran ills including outright negligence, irresponsibility, overwork, fatigue, insufficient training, carelessness, and managerial neglect. Take poor management. At Chernobyl, the plant's deputy director fled right after the accident, and shockingly, the electrical engineer in charge of one experiment had had "no training in nuclear engineering." (Bethe 1991: A25)

In addition to institutional failings, there are moral delinquencies. Reports of deceit and bribery both of and by safety inspectors, equipment monitors, and government officials appear again and again in the dossiers. Still, no one seems to make any allowance for these in developing large-scale projects or implementing advanced technologies. Eventually all of these factors—the experts' overconfidence, human error, moral limitations, and official blind spots—prove extremely costly to both scientists and citizens.

The Devastation

A select, powerful few may formulate policy in the world's inner sanctums, but environmental disasters affect many thousands and tens of thousands of ordinary people in local communities. The Love Canals and Chernobyls have an overwhelming impact on the regions and populations that bear the brunt of miscalculation, mismanagement, and malfeasance by those in charge.

In addition to physical damage and danger, there is the pervasive disruption of life, habitat, and home that follows an environmental disaster. After the Three Mile Island accident, about 144,000 people within a fifteen-mile radius from the nuclear power plant abandoned their houses for several days, not because of a government order but because of the panic that rumor and speculation generated. In Pripyat, near Chernobyl, fifty thousand people—eventually to number about 135,000—were evacuated a few days after the explosion by 1100 buses to "nowhere."

Moreover, long after the initial crisis has passed, its aftermath lingers. There is the gnawing anxiety over one's health, the health of one's family, and, given the typically regional impact of such disasters, the health of one's neighbors. Deeper and more insidious is the erosion of confidence in Science, Authority, and Expertise and, at times, in life itself. For example, after the scope of the crisis at Love Canal became evident, and officials closed the local schools, the area's residents became frantic. Their whole world threatened to collapse. The word "home" suddenly aroused fear rather than security. (Levine 1982: 184) Because they could neither sell their houses nor just leave, residents felt trapped and overcome by a sense of irreparable loss. Individuals felt abandoned, with nowhere to go to. They became desperate for information as they waited for announcements that never came, and felt unable to protect their children or take care of their families. What is more, as is true for certain illnesses that make people shy away from contact with the afflicted, friends and neighbors now hesitated to visit. As suspicion grew, the flow of community and neighborhood life was permanently disrupted. (Barringer 1991: 28-39, 74)

Perhaps the most serious consequence of major environmental accidents, from a sociological viewpoint, is the ensuing decline in respect for authority in science and politics. Survivors of these accidents discredit the scientific elite for both its technical failures and its self-righteous arrogance. They resent the political authorities for their incompetence, deception, and disparagement of the public. Typically, there is outrage at the long delays by officials in responding to the emergency. Moreover, what the officials finally offer is generally too little and too late. Gorbachev made a terse official statement forty-three hours after the accident at Chernobyl and went on national television with a fuller statement a full sixteen days later. At Love Canal, the state government dismissed the newly formed citizens' groups with these words: "We deal with physical facts, not with social and political matters." (Walsh 1988: 34)

When the authorities fail to respond, it increases the collusion that citizens perceive exists between scientists and governments. The perception of collusion is bolstered by the secrecy that generally surrounds the nuclear power industry: a near-silence that engenders rumor, speculation, and profound distrust among members of the public. At Three Mile Island, for example, both the utility company and NRC officials tried to diminish the seriousness of the accident and withheld important information from the public. (Walsh 1988: 34) These dynamics create feelings of abandonment, of having been forsaken. The ensuing tension stokes residents' already high stress levels, which the authorities, although apprehensive about the possibility of collective panic, do little to alleviate. Eventually, fear and despair mobilize the citizens for intense political action.

Grassroots Political Action

Official mishandling of an environmental disaster and its aftermath has led to a political awakening in many a previously apathetic population. Three months after the crisis at Love Canal, about six hundred residents formed the Love Canal Homeowners Association. In their eyes, they were but "blameless victims of the disaster" who had to "stick together and take care of ourselves." (Levine 1982: 177) In this way, the residents recreated that "confidence that holds a society together." (Gould 1991: 137)

Local political activism takes two basic forms. On one hand, it may consist of a series of defensive maneuvers, expressed as a communal turning inward or a closing of ranks against outsiders. On the other hand, it may result in political outreach and the creation of networks and programs addressed to the wider society.

NIMBY: The Turning Inward

Environmental disasters tend to engender a special kind of "Not in My Back Yard" (NIMBY) response. NIMBY usually refers to a rejection of undesirable would-be neighbors. Postdisaster NIMBYs, however, refer to the rejection of perceived sources of danger such as landfills, hazardous waste disposal sites, microwave towers, nuclear power plants, and a wide range of other stigmatized facilities. (Edelstein 1988: 170) NIMBY represents an obverse of the "tragedy of the commons," in which private interests override and destroy the common good. The so-called "reverse commons effect" sees the common good served at the expense of those groups compelled to bear a disproportionate share of toxic risk. (Edelstein 1988: 185) In this context, a community's refusal to cooperate attests to the powerful role that psycho-social factors play in decisions with environmental implications. At stake is not just the community's physical integrity but its image and its reputation as safe or dangerous. (Edelstein 1988: 6)

Stigma thus plays a dual role, initially as a source of a sense of isolation and abandonment and subsequently as a source of community cohesion. Whatever the other bases of community—geographical, political, or social—"the discovery of a toxic threat provides a basis for a new and shared identity that effectively defines a community of interest among those residing within the boundaries of contaminations." (Edelstein 1988: 6)

In this regard, it is interesting to consider the difference between natural and humanly caused disasters. Both create victims, and both leave stress, loss, and disruption in their wake. In humanly caused disasters, however, it is the loss of control over a technology heretofore trusted that proves unnerving—whereas natural disasters are seen as unpredictable acts of God, unfathomable and beyond human control. (Edelstein 1988: 7) In the case of humanly caused disasters, then, people can fiercely blame the agents they consider responsible. Moreover, whereas religion may help people cope with natural disasters by offering shared explanations and perceptions, technological failings lack a place in this common framework and thus allows conflicting perceptions to hold sway. This fragments not only the explanations of what has occurred, but individuals' means of coping with it. All of this plays a role in the possible mobilization of local public opinion.

Political Outreach: The Mobilization of Local Residents

Environmental disasters make people aware and frustrated but usually are not sufficient to promote a widespread mobilization. (Walsh 1988: 58-60) Such organizing requires, in addition, a notable collective distrust and resentment of government authorities and technical experts, and support from leaders in business, religion, and the media. In the four cases that this paper examines, residents of the affected areas came to view the disastrous events not simply as unfortunate corporate or political mistakes but as "injustices" that had to be put right.

As is generally true for grassroots movements, the leaders in those cases came from unexpected places. At Love Canal, for example, it was a young mother, inexperienced and even disinterested in politics, who took the lead. She soon was joined by several hundred others who worked day and night for two and a half years to obtain justice. Perhaps because of their experience with community, women are often central actors in local environmental activism. Many come to display leadership skills they never knew they possessed. It is also interesting to note that evacuees are much more likely to become activists than those who remain in the polluted or endangered area. These new activists enlist their followers in town meetings, rallies, public debates, and political campaigns. In time, separate constituencies develop, each with its own special agenda: old versus young, renters versus owners. Overall, however, one unifying theme pits the people against the powers, the Davids against the Goliaths: the attainment of a safe and healthy environment.

Thus do local communities become critical forums for citizens' protests. One novel twist on the more traditional form of community activism is that environmental activism on the local level focuses not on deprived or marginal groups, but on advanced technologies and those scientists and political officials who in reality are responsible for making globally significant decisions. (Walsh 1988: 1) In addition, a split between citizens and scientists often polarizes many communities. The two operate with very different assumptions and definitions of environmental risk—scientists tend to view risk in narrower, technical

terms, whereas citizens usually emphasize its broader, moral dimensions. Citizens also anticipate possible failures of design, whereas
scientists generally expect their designs to perform as planned. In this
way, a sense of technological powerlessness may fuel a powerful
ecological grassroots movement.

Inequitable access to technical information is another divisive force.
This is true even in democracies, where citizens' limited access to the
information they need to make intelligent judgments about, for example,
the siting of a chemical plant in their community, renders their formal
options and choices something of a sham. (Walsh 1988: 62) The
hierarchy that places the minority of experts over the citizen majority
puts citizens at a distinct disadvantage, most visibly after a calamity. It
is not by chance, then, that after the Bhopal disaster, Congress enacted
the Emergency Planning and Community Right to Know Act of 1986,
42 U.S.C. 11001 *et seq.*, despite intensive lobbying against it. The law's
sponsors stated that its aim was to support citizens' "absolute, fundamental right to know what goes into the air their kids breathe, the water
they drink, and the ground they play on." (Schneider 1991: 65)

Knowledge and access to essential information are central tenets of
the social movements that ecological crises have spawned. Grassroots
ferment has accelerated despite civil lawsuits to discourage citizen
protest and rearguard actions by corporations unwilling to bear their
share of environmental responsibility—responsibility mandated, for
example, by the Comprehensive Environmental Response, Compensation, and Liability Act of 1980 or "Superfund" law. (Bishop 1991: B9)
Indeed, grassroots activism culminated in the most powerful political
protest movement of the postwar era: the Greens.

The Greens' conspicuous success, first in Germany, has inspired
citizens to compel local and national establishments to take notice in
many countries. In essence the Greens and their offspring worldwide
have sought to make economics subordinate to ecology. They aspire to
a postmaterial ethos of decentralization, nonviolence, limits on growth,
and ecological balance. (Graff 1983: 56) Most fervently, they proclaim
the need for a new philosophy of life, one based on respect for long-
term vitality rather than immediate comforts and profits. In this, the
Greens clearly collide with traditional goals of capitalist development.
They propose taking the "soft path" in energy use, including phasing out
fossil fuels; reducing consumer demand, one of the mainstays of late
capitalism; and banning ecologically destructive projects such as

constructing and operating airports and superhighways because of their heavy demands on natural resources. (Graff 1983: 59)

Accordingly, making tradeoffs has become a fundamental issue for local communities. Which is to have top priority: protection from the risk of contamination or unemployment, higher taxes or a lower standard of living? To those who say that contamination is the price we must pay for "the good life" twentieth-century style (Edelstein 1988: 193), the Greens reply that individuals in the developed world must examine the philosophy by which they live. They must acknowledge that theirs is a consumer society driven by materialism and a venality too reluctant to acknowledge the ecological price of technological advances. Even the victims of disaster continue to think not in terms of deeper values but in terms of technical "quick fixes" and of how to manipulate the system rather than rethink and restructure it. An ethic of self-interest, however, ultimately leads to an acceptance of pollution.

Conclusion

Just before coming to this conference, I attended a discussion on national environmental regulations and the petrochemical industry in Louisiana. One remark in particular has stayed in my mind. A local oil industry worker asserted that what happens at the national level with regard to environmental policies and regulations has virtually nothing to do with what happens out in the field. Why not? Because the oil industry fights environmental legislation tooth and nail, and because the workers see waste and pollution as less of a threat than unemployment and reduced profits. They do not deny the existence of pollution, but they accept the "engineering fallacy" that it simply needs to be cleaned up. This conventional wisdom—that pollution is fundamentally a technological problem—supports the collusion that sustains our wasteful society. (Edelstein 1988: 193) Focusing on cleanups, health testing, and economic compensation for victims avoids challenging the system's propensity to toxicity and thus avoids change. That, however, is what must happen. The real goal should not be NIMBY but NIABY—Not in *Anyone's* Back Yard. (Edelstein 1988: 196)

Therefore, in addition to various concrete proposals to help preserve the environment—tax rebates, incentive plans, and regulatory measures—we need to reconsider the philosophies by which we live. For the long run, nothing short of a new, collective ethic is needed. For the short run, some practical policies already are taking effect to mitigate the worst environmental abuses and safeguard nature for the generations to come.

Silent Spring, the influential book by Rachel Carson, signalled the existence of the current emergency thirty years ago. A decade later the Club of Rome sounded another alarm world-wide. Such alarms have become commonplace, but remedies remain elusive, and Faustian dilemmas proliferate. For example, the New York Times recently carried the following offer: $4.2 million in benefits to any rural community in upstate New York, the benefits to include a new town park as well as funds for the library, the fire department, road improvements, and higher education. Add to this the approximately $1.5 million per year in new taxes and fees that would result, and the lure should prove irresistible. Ah, but there was a tradeoff—in return for accepting this offer, the town would have to agree to be home to a dump for low-level radioactive waste. Given the current financial crunch, authorities from several towns expressed interest. Their populations, however, were up in arms and polarized almost at once, with one group urging "yes to progress" to the other group's "just say no": pitting friend against friend and neighbor against neighbor.

Such dilemmas are likely to multiply in the future as environmental controls become unavoidable. For example, every state in the United States now is under a federal mandate to find room for storing its waste within its borders. Courts increasingly are assessing the respective liabilities of industry, municipalities, and citizens, with cities and towns arrayed against industrial firms and governmental agencies in the battle over who is to pay what for past transgressions. Progress, however, is slow. Only sixty-three of the thousands of waste sites across the United States have been cleaned up in the past eleven years, at a cost of about $11.2 billion.

We must view these facts too in a broader context. As long as we define the problems as the responsibility of others, to be avoided by the clever manipulation of available loopholes, there will be no comprehensive framework to guide this vast undertaking. Moving on to solutions and implementation rather than stopping at diagnosis, here are my modest suggestions. The next steps must occur at three levels: the legal-political, the technological innovation-related, and the psycho-cultural.

The legal-political dimension should draw on new legislation, regulatory measures, fines, and incentives not to abuse the environment. The technological dimension must look to the development of more advanced technologies that would be not only more efficient, reliable, and "smarter" but also more ecologically sensitive and aware. The scientist Freeman Dyson would divide technology into "gray" and "green." "Gray technology" is the familiar one of motors, circuits, and mechanics, while "green technology" involves engineering to restore ecosystems, grow food, and create new environments. Dyson expects green technological predominance within fifty years. Such environmentally advanced technologies will be able to repair and renew the earth and put a halt to ozone depletion, the destruction of forests, the spread of deserts, and the erosion of the elemental bases for life and growth. Finally, the psycho-cultural aspect, although critical, is the most elusive, for it targets the most difficult changes of all: changes in values, belief systems, and perspectives on life and its perceived necessities.

To move from Not in *My* Back Yard to Not in *Anyone's* Back Yard is no mere play on words. It demands a new ethic, an ethic of concern for one's neighbor as one's self, and the recognition that there is no poisoning of just one well. As poet Andrei Voznosesky sensed in *Thoughts on Chernobyl,* "[w]hen the robot failed to switch off tragedy, / a man stepped into that radiant block. / Because of that man, we both stayed alive, / you and I . . . ."

References

Axelrod, H.R. *Gorbachev and the Chernobyl Disaster* (1986).

Barringer, Felicity. "Chernobyl," *New York Times Magazine,* April 14, 1991, 28–39, 74.

Bethe, Hans A. "Chernobyl: It Can't Happen Here," *New York Times,* May 2, 1991, A25.

Bishop, Katherine "Developers and Others Use New Tool to Quell Protests by Private Citizens," *New York Times,* April 26, 1991, B9.

Capra, Fritjof, and Charlene Spretnak. *Green Politics* (1984).

Diamond, Stuart. "The Disaster in Bhopal: Lessons for the Future," *New York Times,* February 3, 1985, A1.

Edelstein, Michael R. *Contaminated Communities: The Social and Psychological Impacts of Residential Toxic Exposure* (1988).

Gould, Peter. *Fire in the Rain: The Democratic Consequences of Chernobyl* (1990).

Haas, Peter M. *Saving the Mediterranean: The Politics of International Environmental Cooperation* (1990).

Haynes, Victor, and Marko Bojum. *The Chernobyl Disaster* (1988).

Houts, Peter S. *The Three Mile Island Crisis: Psychological, Social, and Economic Impacts on the Surrounding Population* (1988).

Kelly, Petra. *Fighting for Hope* (1983).

Gordon, Adeline Levine. *Love Canal: Science, Politics, and People* (1982).

Marples, David R. *The Social Impact of the Chernobyl Disaster* (1988).

Olson, Robert L. "The Greening of High Tech, *Futurist,* May-June 1991, 28–34.

Passell, Peter. "A New Commodity to be Traded: Government Permits for Pollution," *New York Times,* July 17, 1991, A1, A4.

Reilly, William K. "The Green Thumb of Capitalism," *Policy Review,* fall 1990, 16–21.

Schneider, Keith. "For Communities Knowledge of Polluters is Power," *New York Times,* March 24, 1991, E5.

————. "Industries and Towns Clash Over Who Pays to Tackle Toxic Waste," *New York Times,* July 18, 1991, A14.

Verhovek, Sam Howe. "Town Heatedly Debates Merits of a Nuclear Waste Dump," *New York Times,* June 28, 1991, B1, B5.

Walker, Martin. *The Waking Giant* (1986).

"Big Corporations Hit by Superfund Cases Find Way to Share Bill," *Wall Street Journal,* April 2, 1991, 1.

Walsh, Edward J. *Democracy in the Shadows* (1988).

3

The Global Commons
Harlan Cleveland

A Global Commons Trusteeship Commission is needed to guide our
use of the oceans, Antarctica, the atmosphere, and outer space.

The poor and the rich, we are cooperating to destroy—in different
but mutually reinforcing ways—the environment we share. It is the acts
of individuals that produce the pervasive threat to the global environment; the problem is precisely the behavior of innocent voters unwilling
to tax pollution, innocent peasants cutting down trees, innocent couples
having more babies than they can raise to be healthy and productive,
innocent citizens thinking that government regulation and corporate
responsibility are not matters for "people like us."

We are dealing now with a new class of problems: They are *global*,
and they are also *behavioral*. Global, because answers will be found
only by widening our world view, changing our minds about the scale
and dimension of what we face. Behavioral, because they require
literally hundreds of millions of people—not just rooms full of experts
and political leaders—to do something or stop doing something.

We need to treat the global environment not as a series of separable
puzzles in corporate strategy or national policy, but as parts of an
integrated Global Commons, with hundreds of millions of people
responsible for its health because its health is the key to their own.

Earth, Sea, and Sky

Four enormous environments, still mostly unexplored, are already
treated in international law and custom as parts of a Global Commons.

21

Outer space, the atmosphere, the oceans, and Antarctica are geophysically and biochemically related to one another, but each has its own history of human relations.

Oceans have the longest association with humans. Because they were accessible to a few courageous seafarers but a dangerous mystery to most land-dwellers, the oceans have long been an unregulated highway for those with the technological prowess to travel it.

The most recent Law of the Sea Treaty, completed in the 1980s, declares the deep ocean and its seabed to be "the common heritage of mankind." As useful marine resources were discovered and perceived to be scarce, nations have tried to make up rules for their exploitation. The difficulty of regulation increases with distance from the shoreline (offshore oil, seabed minerals) and mobility of the resource (fish). One of the resulting absurdities was an unenforceable edict by the U.S. Congress that salmon spawned in western U.S. rivers carry their American citizenship with them as they travel the wide Pacific Ocean.

Under the Treaty, large chunks of ocean space out to 200 miles from the world's shorelines are reserved as "exclusive economic zones." But even in these zones, the resources are to be managed by the states that happen to be nearby, as a kind of trust for the rest of humanity.

The Outer Space Treaty, with its parallel "Common Province" concept, assumes that human exploration outward from Earth will be unique, establishing a kind of monopoly in which human decisions will be definitive.

Some such decisions have been made. Nuclear weapons deployed in orbit and anti-ballistic missiles have been banned by treaty. In the 1980s, research by both the U.S. and Soviet governments on space-based military operations made the earlier demilitarization of outer space a fragile concept. Beyond the discouraging military applications, other decisions are urgently needed, such as how to deal with space debris and allocate fairly the most popular orbits. The best low-Earth orbits are a finite resource; at geosynchronous orbit, there is already a "parking problem."

Weather and climate have not been claimed as the exclusive province of any nation. Clouds, winds, and storms, unlike human artifacts such as aircraft and balloons, move through "national air space" without picking up any of the attributes of national sovereignty. The World Weather Watch was put together without provoking a single claim that the weather belongs to anyone.

Atmospheric pollution is obviously everybody's business. An Environmental Modification Treaty blocks "hostile" changing of the atmosphere. Some short-term weather can be modified at human command, but even where that has been done for many years (for example, Israel's cloud-seeding in the Eastern Mediterranean, which enhances rainfall not only in Israel but in Syria and Jordan), it has not yet produced international conflict.

Antarctica was established as a special kind of commons when in 1959 a dozen nations (most of which had laid claim to pie-shaped slices of the empty continent) signed the Antarctic Treaty; a few others have since joined the still-exclusive club.

Any nation with the technical capacity can conduct scientific research, or just explore, anywhere on the icy continent. Military operations are not allowed, and nuclear weapons are banned. You don't need a visa to visit Antarctica, but you do need plenty of help to get there and survive.

The Treaty came up for review in 1991. None of the original members defected or tried to press their former territorial claims. Some outsiders wanted to hedge against the discovery of valuable minerals under the ice or just offshore, but that seemed such a far-out contingency that agreement was reached to ban commercial minerals exploration for 50 years.

These four huge environments are for practical purposes indivisible: They are bounded by each other, affect each other's behavior, must take each other into account. No person, corporation, or nation can establish exclusive ownership of the oceans, outer space, the global atmosphere, or the Antarctic continent.

It *is* possible for a person, corporation, or nation to try to control some of the resources these commons environments may contain—not information, which is bound to leak, but fish, krill, oil, hard minerals, energy vents, upwelling cold water, induced rain, gravity-free manufacturing, solar energy, or hydrogen and other humanly useful elements. But to establish and hang on to rights to use or abuse the commons depends, like any consensus decision, on the acquiescence of those who care and the apathy of those who don't.

Responsibility for the Commons

The responsibility of nations and of their citizens for the health of the global environment is a clear enough global consensus now. The Earth Summit in Rio de Janeiro last year was, for example, the first time forest management had been put firmly on the international political agenda. It will take much scientific analysis, countless national and international consultations, many treaties and rules and regulations, and above all widespread knowledge conveyed by near-universal education to translate general responsibilities into specific behaviors—by governments and corporations and individuals—in every part of this endangered globe.

More than 5 billion human beings are not Nature's prime change-agent. "Every person on Earth is part of the cause, which makes it difficult to organize an effective response," wrote then-Senator Albert Gore in his book, *Earth in the Balance.* "But every person on Earth also tends to suffer the consequences, which makes an effective response essential and ought to make it possible to find one—once the global pattern is widely recognized."

The net result of the Earth summit, an 800-page paper, was essentially a tract about what national governments should consider in making environmental policy. The Rio outcome was flawed in its assumption, so common to U.N. agreements, that the only real actors in international affairs are "states." But most of the world's past pollution has been caused, and most future environmental actions will be taken, by *non*governments, from individual peasants to large business firms. In the next round, corporations, their executives and their governing boards, had better be brought early and often into the conversation; they are the people who can do the most to carry out the talkers' intentions.

Monitoring and environmental assessment were also treated as something "states" should do. But in the twenty-first century, keeping track of the global environment will be quintessentially a task for *global* concepts, technologies, and institutions. And the Global Commons doesn't belong to "states."

The Trouble with "Sustainable"

Our purpose in the global environment should be not just to keep it from further degradation at human command, not just to protect it from ourselves. Certainly we have to protect ourselves and each other from letting the Global Commons become humanity's littered backyard, its waste-disposal dump. But the present "tragedy of the commons" is that we are not yet using what it freely provides. The marvels of space satellites and information technology have not yet been used to narrow the gap between rich and poor; they mostly enable the affluent to work more efficiently with—or against—each other.

We are wasting most of the sun's beneficent rays by not converting them into usable energy. We are neglecting the power still locked in the temperature differences between the tropical sea surface and the ocean deeps. We are not yet stretching our biotechnological talent to use for development the resources that could make "poor" countries rich—their own dense biomass and solar radiation.

The idea of *sustainability* bids us conserve whatever environment we have left. That's not nearly a dynamic enough idea to generate a worldwide push for growth with fairness.

The Management of Global Behavior

The problem is not "management of the Global Commons." It is the management of human behavior in the Commons. "Eco" serves as prefix to both economics and ecology. The road ahead is littered with ethical choices, to reconcile what's efficient with what's prudent and fair:

What claim do future generations have on today's decision makers? The traditional way to take our grandchildren into account is to "discount" them. But shouldn't today's products be priced at their full social cost, including what we're borrowing from those very grandchildren? Should today's poor be favored over tomorrow's descendants of the affluent? Who, in decisions made today, can act as ombudsman for the yet-unborn?

Rates of consumption are another name for rates of pollution. Can we stop subsidizing inefficiency (as in energy), surpluses (as in food), and toxic waste? China expects to double its gross product in a few years, using soft coal and emitting carbon dioxide that will warm up the world, which the rest of humanity shares with the Chinese. Would it make sense, as a measure of global environmental protection, for the rest of us to help China make its 750,000 boilers fuel-efficient?

The world's people will number 6.3 billion by the year 2000. Whether world population can be stabilized at 8 billion or 11 billion or 14 billion is the biggest single question about the global environment. Who should be doing what about this, and why aren't they?

In a dramatic failure of market economics, private-sector companies have mostly stopped trying to sell contraceptives around the world—for fear of litigation and trouble with their own governments. The ironic consequence is a sharp increase in the use of abortion as a means of birth control.

If the Global Commons environments are not to be further polluted by human choice, who sets the outer bounds of human behavior in the Commons? Only those with the technical prowess to despoil Antarctica, foul the oceans, damage the ozone layer, spew out global-warming gases, and sprinkle debris in outer space? Or some agreed surrogate for the "everybody" that owns the Commons?

The two-tier principle of organization clearly applies here: One tier is needed to establish the rules and another to apply them. The Commons systems, and the dangers of degradation and conflict that arise from them, require the establishment of universal norms, standards, "rules of the road." Their conservation and use can then be handled by public, private, and mixed enterprise, within the framework of the agreed norms and standards—a framework that the operating people have had a consultative role in framing.

Who can fashion the rules of such a game? It has to be a club that credibly speaks for "all mankind," the plural owners of the Global Commons. The club that takes on such a responsibility has to be of manageable size, yet it must also represent the people who can do something about the problems that beset the Commons—those who pollute global air and water, chop down tropical forests, leave debris orbiting in outer space, and litter the icy wasteland of Antarctica. If they don't agree on what's to be done, it won't get done. The important thing is not to debate blame but to organize remedies.

An organization should be created to protect and supervise "the common heritage of mankind." Such an organization could be a revitalized version of the United Nations Trusteeship Council, a major Charter organ (parallel to the General Assembly and the Security Council), which the success of decolonization has now left without a function. The name is just right. A body acting for humanity should be a *trustee* for our four great surrounding environments.

The now-dormant Council could readily form a special Trusteeship Commission on the Global Commons, consisting of those countries most able to protect and preserve "the common heritage of mankind." This would include not only the traditional "great powers," but great nations such as Brazil with a special stake in the Commons, plus some rotating members, as in the U.N. Security Council.

This Global Commons Trusteeship Commission would negotiate norms, standards, and guidelines for exploring and exploiting the Global Commons and would keep the health of the Commons environments under open and continuous review. The Commission's role could only

be advisory, and it should make room in its work for major nongovernments (corporations, environmental groups, human-rights advocates,
scientific academies, and other professional associations) that can bring
to the Commission the fruits of technical and policy analysis—and the
assurance that, having been consulted about norms and standards, they
will be more disposed to be guided by them in their own day-to-day
actions.

While not itself engaging in operations, the Global Commons
Trusteeship Commission might be empowered to ask other international
agencies, nongovernments, or individuals to serve as "centers of
initiative" on particular problems in the Commons, as the United
Nations Environment Programme did so well on both the Mediterranean
cleanup and the Ozone Treaty.

Within the policy frame established by such a norms-and-standards
Commission, there are roles aplenty for many different kinds of
nongovernments—and indeed for public and private groups not usually
considered as participants in international relations—in heightening
awareness and educating whole populations about needed changes in
individual and group behavior as it affects the Global Commons.

Practitioners of world-scale policy analysis are to be found in some
think tanks, universities, environmental agencies, medical and health
associations, and research laboratories. They can help design the norms
and standards and help explain them to those who are supposed to be
guided by them. They can disseminate authoritative insights about how
to use the Commons without degrading it.

There is also a role for business leaders in regulating their own eco-
behavior—and explaining to their stockholders and customers why that
is so necessary. There is, of course, a role for the communications
media in generating public interest and projecting relevant metaphors.

Perhaps most important of all, there is a role for educators in
making sure that children in all cultures grow up with, and their parents
develop, a "feel" for the new global/behavioral issues and relate them
constructively to their own cultural identities and traditions. Education
about the Global Commons, from preschool to adult learning, should be
aimed at patterns of behavior and value systems consistent with a
sharing environment. Not only the schools, but the media, political
leaders, and nongovernments of many kinds will have to be teachers
about human conduct compatible with life in a shared commons.

The Remedy Is Us

The vast, distant, mysterious Commons—outer space, the atmosphere, the oceans, Antarctica—has contracted a degenerative but not irreversible disease. The impulsive actions of human beings now clearly outpace the slower evolution of Nature in the global scheme of things. The diagnosis is increasingly clear, and the remedy is us.

It's true that whenever we touch the Commons we tweak in unknowable ways what millions of years have wrought. Lao Tsu's cautionary question 2,500 years ago is still worth pondering: "Do you think you can take over the universe and improve it?" The "wilderness" approach, driven by a paralyzing sense of our own ignorance, would say "Don't touch," but as a practical matter the Commons won't be left alone. So the problem is to organize world consensus, place by place and case by case, in ways that balance our appetite for adventure and our civilizing mission with a healthy respect for the "foul-up factor" in every human enterprise.

Let's say it again: Global change is now being produced, more than any factor, by what hundreds of millions of individuals (and couples) are doing. Its pace and direction will only be changed by what hundreds of millions of individuals (and couples) do or stop doing.

Since the new *genre* or problems depends on such wide participation, reaches into so many technical and professional fields, and touches so many economic interests and political sensitivities, it is not to be expected that any one system of governance would "work." The Global Commons will be governed pluralistically or not at all.

Biodiversity

The World Charter for Nature, adopted by the U.N. General Assembly in 1984, states that all species merit respect regardless of their usefulness to human beings. This was the beginning of international cooperation and recognition of the value of diversity among species. It recognized that each individual species played an important role in the ecosystem and therefore deserved protection from destruction.

Some scientific studies estimate that up to 25 percent of all the world's species could become extinct in the next few decades. The causes of rapid extermination of species are numerous, but most result from environmental destruction as a result of human action.

Habitats, such as forests and wetlands, are being destroyed in order to create room for agricultural, razing, or industrial land. By destroying the ecosystems, the species occupying those areas are also lost. For example, one-half of the Earth's species inhabit the tropical forests, which only account for 6 percent of the total land base. With rapid deforestation, the rate of species extinction will continue to increase dramatically.

A great proportion of the species in existence have yet to be discovered and identified by scientists. Even those known to scientists may not be fully understood. Therefore, it is environmentally wisest to practice what is known as the "Precautionary Principle." This principle states that because the ecological role of an organism within an ecosystem may not be fully understood, no action should be taken that would threaten the survival of the species.

Not only is the value of species within their ecosystems not clearly understood, also the value of known and unknown species to humans is also unclear. Most of our medicines stem from plant remedies. Perhaps lying in the rain forest is a plant that could cure cancer or AIDS. Once again, it is wisest to preserve.

With all of these ideas in mind, The International Convention on Biological Diversity was presented at the Rio Convention. Its stated function is to conserve biological diversity for the benefit of present and future generations and for its intrinsic value. It calls for a greater emphasis on research and education, training and scientific cooperation. It calls for inventories to be done on the species of the world so there is a greater awareness of the vastness of diversity and the need for preservation. It stresses the value of local and indigenous knowledge in the pursuit of biological diversity preservation. Finally, it recognizes the need for increased financial support to accomplish its goals of biodiversity.

By recognizing the value of a variety of species and by dedicating the world community to preserving those species and their habitats, the chances of having diverse and healthy ecosystems are greatly increased. With scientific study and awareness, the diversity of life on this planet may in fact survive.

—RNW

4

CITES: The ESA and International Trade

Carlo A. Balistrieri

One of the greatest delusions in the world is the hope that evils in this world are to be cured by legislation.

—Thomas B. Reed
Address to the House of Representatives (1886)

The twentieth anniversary of the Endangered Species Act (ESA), 16 U.S.C. 1531–44 (1988), being celebrated this year, is shared by a little known but equally important international conservation measure known as the Convention on International Trade in Endangered Species of Wild Fauna and Flora (CITES). The signing of CITES in 1973 culminated over a decade of formal international discussion that began at the 1960 meeting of the general assembly of the International Union for Conservation of Nature and Natural Resources (IUCN). The concern at that time was that high levels of trade in wild animals, along with alarming loss of habitat, threatened the survival of many species. In 1963 the IUCN passed a resolution calling for the adoption of an international convention to regulate trade in endangered wildlife species. Several draft resolutions for that purpose were prepared between 1963 and 1972, when a recommendation was formulated at the United Nations Stockholm Conference on the Human Environment. In response to that recommendation, eighty-eight countries met in early 1973 to discuss a proposal for a convention. In March 1973—nearly ten years after the IUCN resolution—twenty-one countries signed CITES, which is also known abroad as the Washington Convention. Two years later,

31

on July 1, 1975, CITES was enacted after ten nations internally ratified the actions of their conference representatives.

First, the origins of CITES and its major provisions are explained; then some of the problems the signatory countries have experienced with CITES and this relationship to the ESA are addressed. Issues are identified in connection with administration and enforcement of the treaty that need to be resolved if its overreaching objectives are to be achieved.

CITES and Domestic Legislation

While the world was discussing international trade in endangered species, the United States was examining ways to protect endangered and threatened species with domestic legislation. Congress enacted laws in 1966, 1969, and 1973, which, along with their subsequent amendments, disclosed an evolving national attitude toward endangered species that prompted the United States' subsequent involvement in CITES.

The history of United States legislation concerning the protection of endangered species is an important first step in understanding CITES and the means by which the federal government interprets and enforces the convention. Because the ESA is the enabling legislation for CITES, its language and history are important tools for examining U.S. policy on international endangered species protection and U.S. involvement in CITES' regulation of trade in endangered wildlife.

The Endangered Species Preservation Act of 1966 afforded limited protection to endangered wildlife. The "First Endangered Species Act," as it is often referred to, directed the Secretary of the Department of the Interior (DOI) to "carry out a program in the United States of conserving, protecting, restoring and propagating selected species of native fish and wildlife." It was intended to protect those species of *native* wildlife that were "threatened with extinction."

The Endangered Species Conservation Act of 1969 expanded the application of the first statute and, in response to concerns of over-exploitation and the IUCN's 1963 resolution, called for the convening of an international ministerial meeting to create a "binding international convention on the conservation of endangered species." In addition, the 1968 Act required that the Secretary's determination be "based on the best scientific and *commercial data* available" (emphasis added), thus reinforcing the notion that trade could be a contributing factor to the problems faced by many species. Significantly, this statute also created an exemption to the general prohibition against the importation of endangered wildlife by authorizing importation "for zoological, education, and scientific purposes" and "for . . . propagation . . . in captivity for preservation purposes."

The Endangered Species Act of 1973 was meant to be much more comprehensive than either the 1966 or 1969 statutes. The 1973 ESA recognized that *threatened and* endangered species of wildlife and plants "are of aesthetic, ecological, educational, historical, recreational, and scientific value to the Nation and its people." This statute was the first to refer to flora. Part of its purpose was to provide a program for the conservation of threatened and endangered species. The Act prohibits the importation, taking, export, and sale of interstate or foreign commerce of any listed species. In addition the 1973 ESA required the United States to participate and cooperate in international efforts to protect endangered species and, as such, became the enabling legislation for CITES.

CITES (1973)

Simply stated, the purpose of CITES is to protect endangered and threatened species from overexploitation by international trade. To achieve this objective, the treaty creates a system of permits and certificates to restrict trade and allows it to be monitored by regulating authorities.

CITES is relatively short in length considering the wide scope of its provisions. It contains twenty-five brief Articles that can be grouped conveniently into five categories discussed below.

Introduction

CITES begins with a preamble that states its purpose and the rationale that lead the community of nations to adopt it. Article I defines terms that are central to the document. Unfortunately it is far from complete; many significant terms, critical to the operation and proper understanding of CITES, should have been included but were not. They can only be found by searching through the voluminous proceedings of the biannual conferences held to administer and implement the treaty.

The means by which plant and animal species and their parts and derivatives are brought within the ambit of CITES are explained in

Article II. It creates three appendices upon which species may be listed. Appendix I includes "all species threatened with extinction which are or may be affected by trade." It provides a strict prohibition against trade for "commercial purposes," which is defined broadly.

Appendix II includes species that, although not now threatened with extinction, may become so unless trade is subject to "strict regulation in order to avoid utilization incompatible with (a species') survival." It also includes species that must be regulated (e.g., because of problems with identification) so that trade of those species that could become endangered is controlled effectively.

The third appendix is composed of species that meet two requirements: First, a party must have identified them as subject to regulation within its jurisdiction. Second, the cooperation of other parties is needed to control trade and prevent or restrict exploitation. Parties are not allowed to trade any specimen of a species listed in Appendix I, II, or III except in accordance with the CITES provisions.

Regulation

The core of CITES is contained in Articles III–VII, which establish the regulatory structure and permit system for trade. They address regulation for each of the species identified by the appendices, permits and certificates, exemptions, and other special provisions contained in CITES.

These articles provide different layers of protection according to where species are listed in the appendices and have been the basis for most of the criticism leveled at CITES.

Duties

Articles VIII–X deal with the responsibilities of the parties to the treaty, Article IX requires each party to designate management and scientific authorities to fulfill the purpose of CITES within stated boundaries. Article X allows member parties to accept comparable documentation from nations which are not signatories of CITES.

Parties are mandated by Article VIII to take appropriate measures to enforce the CITES provisions. Although the article spells out several measures which must be included in enforcement efforts of each nation, it falls far short of establishing a coherent, uniform system for interpreting and enforcing CITES.

Several resolutions dealing with enforcement have been passed since the adoption of CITES. Among other things, they acknowledge the political, economic, and philosophical rifts that exist between developed and developing countries. Although the resolutions urge better implementation and enforcement, none press for uniform application of treaty provisions.

As is often the case, what is missing from CITES may be more significant than what is embodied in it. The resolutions are carefully crafted to avoid any implication of a usurpation of sovereign rights. No attempt is made to urge nations of the world to set aside concerns of sovereignty in the interest of preserving the environment or to further the purpose of the treaty. This is true even though 118 nations are now parties to CITES.

The net result is that each party has its own implementation and enforcement policies and priorities. In addition some multilateral trading blocs—including the European Community—have proposed regulations on trade in wildlife that incorporate CITES, and thus create additional layers of regulation and interpretation. For example, draft EC regulations published recently for comment are, in some ways, even more restrictive than the CITES provisions. Moreover, many countries have little or no enforcement system in place, and of those systems that are in place, none are identical. Accordingly, great care must be taken to determine the permit requirements of both the importing *and* exporting countries before any trade can be conducted between nations.

Administration

Much of the treaty (Articles XI–XVIII) is devoted to matters of an administrative nature. A secretariat is created to manage the day-to-day affairs of the treaty and coordinate the activities of the parties. A "Conference of the Parties," the governing body responsible for the implementation and enforcement of CITES, is required to meet at least once every two years. (The next meeting is scheduled to take place in the United States in fall 1994.) Procedures are provided for amending CITES and its appendices. Parties with disputes are required to engage in negotiations; if a satisfactory resolution cannot be achieved the parties may, by agreement, submit the dispute to binding arbitration.

Article XIV addresses the effect of CITES on domestic legislation and international agreements. In general, the treaty does not affect the right of member nations to adopt stricter domestic measures or participate in regional or multilateral trade agreements (e.g., the North American Free Trade Agreement (NAFTA). Current drafts of NAFTA, however, incorporate CITES provisions rather than seek more restrictive regulation.

Treaty Formalities

The final seven articles of CITES (Articles XIX–XXV) deal with treaty formalities. Among other things, a procedure is established for parties to take "reservations" to specific listings. (A reservation allows a party to continue trading in that species with other reserving parties.) Nations wishing to join or leave CITES have to comply with the procedures outlined in these articles. Switzerland is designated as the depository government and charged with responsibility for original documents.

Does It Work?

CITES is a working, dynamic document similar to a constitution. Almost 8,000 pages of proceedings from the Conference of the Parties is ample evidence that not all questions about the treaty can be answered by the document itself. Issues of major importance to those concerned with the protection of threatened and endangered species, and those trading in wildlife or wildlife products, are being discussed on an ongoing basis. Significant problems of implementation and enforcement are continually being addressed and new resolutions (referred to as "soft-laws") on all aspects of the treaty and its operation are being added to the body of international wildlife trade law.

It is difficult to point to specific successes of CITES. The treaty's high expectations and narrow purpose make it difficult to identify species whose continued existence is due primarily—if not solely—to CITES. Nonetheless, two general observations can be made. First, CITES has improved monitoring of the massive trade (over $5 billion) in wildlife and wildlife production. Although the data collected is suspect, a much better picture of the extent and flow of this trade is now available. Second, from the original ten ratifying countries that brought CITES into force in 1975, there are now 118 nations agreeing to its terms. These countries have seen a need for the regulation imposed by CITES and concluded that even with its flaws it is a step in the right direction.

Despite CITES' promise to serve as a tool for protection of the earth's biodiversity, it has its shortcomings. Many deal with the minutiae of treaty administration, implementation, and enforcement.

Several of these problems cut to the core of the treaty and its basic purpose.

The primary goal of CITES is to preserve threatened and vulnerable species in the wild by regulating international trade. A parallel objective, implicit in the treaty's purpose, is to allow some, presumably sustainable, level of exploitation of those species. The apparent conflict in these objectives creates the central tension in the treaty and impacts virtually every consideration of its provisions. Often CITES appears to forget or ignore its own narrow purpose. For example, despite evidence of little or no trade, the entire hummingbird family was listed on Appendix II; all orchids, some 30,000 species, are included in CITES even though only a small fraction of that number are currently in trade. Professor Kevin Hill perhaps identified the nature of the paradox best when he noted that "[t]he theoretical foundation of CITES is classically political. The convention attempts to balance the vague intuitive notion that the preservation of species is good, against commercial demands for exploitation. The stress between these competing interests is the core of the structural weakness of the convention." *Hill Convention on International Trade in Endangered Species: Fifteen Years Later,* 13 LOY, L.A. INT'L. & COMP. L.J. (1990).

As alluded to earlier, definitional problems also plague the treaty. Even the world scientific community cannot agree on a definition of "species." The determination of what constitutes a species needing protection under CITES creates additional dilemmas. Listing decisions often appear to be made more on political than biological and trade grounds. Even where rarity or endangered status is capable of being ascertained to some reasonable scientific degree, a listing under the treaty should only occur when it is clear that the species is threatened by international trade.

The treatment of man-made hybrids and artificially propagated specimens is the subject of much discussion and debate. They are not "*species of wild* fauna and flora." Nonetheless they are included in CITES regulation because of the use of CITES-listed species as parents or the inability of the authorities to distinguish these "man-made" individuals from wild specimens. Still another sore point for many is the treaty's proposed treatment of plants. Despite their importance to all life as well as international trade, plants have never been accorded an equal footing with animals and continue to receive perfunctory attention from the secretariat and the Conference of the Parties. As a consequence, plants are often regulated by analogy to animal rules and proposals for plants are generally examined only to be certain that no loophole is created for animal specimens.

Aside from the relatively recent creation of a Plants Committee and appointment of a Plants officer, the plant world has been regulated only by a framework of rules created for animals and reflecting little of what makes the plant kingdom unique. There is no indication that a separate system of regulation was ever contemplated for plants. At present the best the conference can do is to pass generic resolutions aimed at improving "implementation for plants."

One consequence of CITES being an international treaty is that it had no "binding" effect on nations that do not accept it; participation is voluntary. Even for those who do become parties, the binding effect of the treaty is questionable. Each party implements and enforces the treaty on its own and may take reservations on any listings that are not to its liking. Adherence to, and compliance with, the resolutions of the conference is a highly individual matter and trade sanctions are imposed infrequently, and then only for the most egregious of violations.

One hundred eighteen parties means that at least as many management authorities (sometimes combined with scientific authorities) are involved with the treaty but very few of these countries' views on implementation and enforcement of CITES coincide. This lack of uniformity is the problem most often mentioned by those who have to deal with the treaty on a business basis. The fact that requirements and documentation vary from country to country means that traders must make themselves aware of the rules in any country in which they export or import. More than one border confrontation has resulted from one country's refusal to accept paperwork that would have been approved in another.

CITES requires reporting and tabulating mountains of data at various levels. Permit applications and shipping documents from individuals, annual reports from management authorities, and sundry data from other entities are used to monitor the trade that CITES regulates. Despite the collection of all this data, CITES relies rather heavily on significant trade studies prepared by outside organizations (often under contract to the secretariat). The resulting studies, although accurately presenting the data collected, are of questionable value. Across the board, compliance with reporting requirements, and the data generated, are poor. Even among CITES management authorities participation is at unacceptably low levels. The quality of the data collected is flawed from the beginning by its incomplete nature and the way that it is obtained. The independent reports are also suspect because of unarticulated assumptions that may be built into its collection and interpretation.

Despite these problems there is a sufficient volume of data created to swamp the ability of the administrators to digest and use it in any meaningful way. Staffing and budget constraints severely limit the capability of even the best endowed of the world's management authorities to use this information to monitor trade effectively.

Compliance with the substantive terms of the treaty is equally poor. Innumerable illegal shipments make it through the system undetected, even in the so-called enlightened countries. Penalties amount to no more than a slap on the wrist; they are not costly enough to deter violators from illegal trading, and are often considered just another cost of doing business.

In addition, the treaty has no provisions for extraordinary situations. Every system of regulation has the potential for outcomes that shock moral or ethical sensibilities. Such a result may be antithetical to the ultimate goals and objectives of the regulation. Most systems set up some mechanism for exceptional circumstances. CITES does not. This leaves CITES enforcement authorities in the untenable situation of either following the letter of the law or ignoring it entirely. There is no middle ground.

This leads to another important paradox of CITES. The treaty is set up and enforced as a "zero-tolerance" measure. No level of noncompliance is acceptable to the regulators. Consequently, the deliberations of the conference result in ever-stricter regulation. Often this appears to create outcomes that are inconsistent with the treaty's conservation objectives.

There is some hope. Most of the problems with CITES are correctable. No one disagrees that protection of truly endangered species from overexploitation through international trade *is* an appropriate objective. Where reasonable minds begin to differ is how that objective can best be achieved.

Both the regulators and those regulated can be forces for change. Those regulated by the treaty, besides improving compliance with its terms, can make useful contributions toward the improvement of its operation. The regulators, by taking an enlightened and pragmatic approach to their duties, can avoid situations where blind adherence to theoretical constructs obscures practical consideration of the facts and circumstances that constitute everyday life under CITES.

CITES and the ESA

CITES interacts with the ESA in several important ways. Unfortunately, the listing of threatened and endangered species is not one of them. Each law maintains a separate list of such species. This can be explained in part by geographic reach and because the ESA is not concerned primarily with international trade. All species listed on CITES gain a measure of protection in the United States because of the ESA's incorporation of CITES. But the converse is not true; species listed under the ESA, while protected from domestic trade, do not necessarily carry that same protection with them across national boundaries. While each law deals with endangered and vulnerable species, they do so with different methods and goals.

CITES does have an important impact on the ESA regulatory authorities responsible for its administration. In the United States, the management and scientific authorities are the same agency responsible for much of the administration of the ESA: the Fish and Wildlife Service. Enforcement responsibilities belong to the Department of Agriculture. CITES imposes substantial burdens on these already strained staffs and resources.

Finally, CITES brings many businesses under the jurisdiction of the ESA. Any business incorporating plant or animal material in its products should be aware of the treaty and its requirements. As habitats shrink and native populations of plants and animals are reduced, more species will be protected by CITES. Many companies in apparently unrelated fields may be surprised to find themselves responsible for complying with CITES. The recent listing of Brazilian rosewood created unforeseen consequences for the musical instrument industry. Proposed listings of mahogany species were opposed vigorously by wood-working interests concerned that the woods would become unavailable for furniture building, veneer, cabinetry, carving, and household products.

The high level of participation in CITES makes it the world's most widely accepted international treaty and, arguably, the most successful of all international treaties concerned with the conservation of wildlife. It plays an important role in the protection of the earth's biodiversity. While it remains problematic on many fronts, increasing numbers of plants and animals are enjoying protection under its terms. As the visibility of the treaty is increased, its value as a monitor of international trade will become more apparent. Increased compliance by those regulated and those doing the regulating should increase CITES' effectiveness and the accuracy of the data it generates.

Although the regulation of trade is considered by some to be of little importance in the overall effort to preserve endangered species, it is an effective means of raising awareness. It is universally agreed that degradation of habitat is the most important contributing factor to the extinction of plant and animal species. Because it restricts our use of plants and animals and the products containing them, CITES has a more direct impact than laws like the ESA, which regulates the taking of creatures we may never see.

5

Biodiversity and the Precautionary Principle
Norman Myers

The precautionary principle is becoming an established guideline for policymakers tackling environmental problems. In salient respects, it applies to biodiversity more than to any other environmental problem. This is because the mass extinction gathering force will, if it proceeds unchecked, not only eliminate half or more of all species, but will leave the biosphere impoverished for at least 5 million years—a period twenty times longer than humankind itself has been a species. Present society is effectively making a decision on the unconsulted behalf of perhaps 100 trillion of our descendants, asserting that further generations can certainly manage with far less than a full planetary stock of species. Yet despite the ostensible certainty we display in making this decision, the biodiversity issue is attended by exceptional uncertainty, notably as concerns the adverse repercussions—biological, ecological, and economic among others—of mass extinction. Thus, there is a super-premium on applying the precautionary principle to the biotic crisis in a manner expansive enough to match the scope and scale of the problem. Policy implications have received all too little attention. Far from supplying the right answers, we are hardly at a point where we are asking all the correct questions.

Introduction

The precautionary principle is becoming established as a public policy guideline for environmental issues. It is specially relevant to the biodiversity problem, taken here to refer to the mass extinction of species underway. *Biodiversity is a broader concept than just species,*

42

but this paper confines itself to species and their extinctions insofar as this is the main manifestation of the biodiversity problem. In essence, the precautionary principle asserts that there is a premium on a cautious and conservative approach to human interventions in environmental sectors that are (a) unusually short on scientific understanding, and (b) unusually susceptible to significant injury, especially irreversible injury. The approach is all the more pertinent as humans expand their capacity to exert disruptive impacts on the planetary ecosystem.

The Conference on Sustainable Development, Science and Policy in Bergen in May 1990 was largely given over to the precautionary principle concept, urging its widespread application. The Ministerial Declaration concluding the Second World Climate Conference in Geneva in November 1990 asserted that *Where there are threats of serious or irreversible damage, lack of full scientific certainty should not be used as a reason for postponing cost-effective measures to prevent such environmental degradation.* The International Conference on an Agenda of Science for Environment and Development into the 21st Century in Vienna in November 1991 stated as its main recommendation that *Highest priority should be given to reducing the greatest disturbances to planet Earth,* especially those that are inadequately understood scientifically and may impose undue harm environmentally. *It's a case of If we live as if it matters and it doesn't matter, it doesn't matter. If we live as if it doesn't matter, and it matters, then it matters.*

So widely proclaimed is the principle's rationale that it has been the subject of a good number of pioneering papers (1–9). They all conclude that the burden of scientific proof should lie on would-be environment disrupters to demonstrate that their actions will not result in unacceptable damage to ecosystems.

This is particularly pertinent in the case of biodiversity and its progressive depletion. Our planet is subject to many other environmental problems besides biodiversity loss, notably acid rain and other forms of local pollution, soil erosion and desertification among other forms of land degradation, deforestation especially in the tropics, excessive drawdown of water stocks, thinning of the ozone layer, and global warming. Fortunately, all these environmental problems are inherently reversible.

Extinction of species is different. When a single species is gone, it is gone for good. Yet we are into the opening phase of a species-extinction spasm with capacity to eliminate a sizeable share of Earth's biodiversity. True, evolution will eventually come up with replacement species in numbers and variety to match today's array. But so far as we can discern from episodes of mass extinction and the subsequent recovery periods in the prehistoric past, the time required will be at least 5 million years, possibly several times longer (10–12). If we allow the present mass extinction to proceed unchecked, we shall impoverish the biosphere for a period equivalent to at least 200,000 human generations, or 20 times longer than humankind itself has been a species. As an illustration of our responsibility to future generations—a key component of the rationale for the precautionary principle—the biodiversity issue is in a league of its own.

Since mass extinction would amount to an unmatched degradation of the biosphere, it is worthwhile to engage in a brief review of the evidence and an exploratory analysis of the phenomenon's implications. There is much uncertainty associated with our basic biological understanding of the issue, i.e. what we partially know, what we don't know but know we don't know, and what we possibly don't even know we don't know, and how far it all matters.

Species Extinction Rate

A strong consensus of biologist opinion (11, 13–19) believes a mass extinction of species is underway. It has been calculated that we are losing at least 27,000 species per year in tropical forests alone (11, 14, 19, 20). Biodiversity is being reduced in other biomes as well, notably coral reefs, wetlands, islands, and montane environments. These areas put together do not remotely match tropical forests in terms of numbers of species disappearing, but they push the current extinction total beyond 30,000 species per year. This contrasts with the natural rate of extinctions before the advent of the human era, reckoned to be an average of one species every four years or so (12, 21). So the present rate is at least 120,000 times higher. In the future, and in the absence of greatly expanded conservation efforts, a number of independent analyses (14, 15, 19, 22, 23) propose that we face the prospect of losing 20 percent of all species within 30 years and 50 percent or more by the end of the next century. All these estimates are explicitly conservative.

There are biological, ecological, genetic, evolutionary, economical, aesthetic, and ethical reasons for us to regret the loss of any species (15, 19, 24–28). The U.S. National Academy of Sciences and the British Royal Society declared in July 1992 that "The failure to sustain biodiversity (is) a matter of great concern, locally, regionally and internationally" (29). Above all depletion of biodiversity will leave an impoverishing impact on the biosphere many times longer than all our other environmental problems put together.

The Question of Uncertainty: Big-Picture Aspects

Regrettably, the biodiversity, or rather, the biodepletion issue is clouded with much uncertainty. We have only a rough grasp of how fast species are disappearing today, let alone how many are likely to disappear during the next century. Amidst our lack of adequate knowledge, however, and with regard to our uncertainty about how we should respond to the situation, let us bear in mind that we are dealing with the *irreversible* loss of *unique* life forms.

This brings up a key question as concerns the mass extinction issue. What is *legitimate scientific caution* in the face of uncertainty as concerns the true extinction rate—given that the figures above are no more than best estimates and subject to many qualifications? Uncertainty can cut both ways. Some observers object that in the absence of conclusive evidence and analysis, it is appropriate to stick with low estimates of species extinctions on the grounds that they are more *responsible*. What if a low estimate, ostensibly *safe* because it takes a conservative view of such limited evidence as is at hand in documented detail, fails to reflect the real situation just as much as does an *unduly* high estimate, and is more of a best-judgment affair based on all available evidence with varying degrees of demonstrable validity? In a situation of uncertainty where not all parameters can be quantified to conventional satisfaction, let us not get hung up with what can be counted if that is to the detriment of what primarily counts. Conventional caution can be unwitting recklessness; and as in other situations beset with uncertainty, it will be better for us to find we have been roughly right than precisely wrong.

This is all the more pertinent in light of several other uncertainties, plus associated risks, of biodepletion (30). The ultimate outcome could be far worse than the prospect delineated above, both in terms of numbers of species eliminated and in the detrimental repercussions. We should at least identify and define some further possible consequences, even if we are far from being able to quantify and evaluate them.

Further Uncertainties and Risks

Human Appropriation of Plant Growth

Species are being eliminated today almost entirely through the direct effects of human activities. But, in future, many species could be made extinct through impacts of more indirect sort. Consider, for instance, the present and prospective reduction of plants' net annual growth. Already humans engage in so much exploitation, diversion, waste, and other significant misuse of plant growth that they are effectively appropriating 40 percent of all such growth on land each year, leaving 60 percent for the millions of other species (31). What will happen when human numbers double, as is projected within another few decades? Even if this means that human impact on plant growth merely doubles, it is likely to be still more as people demand more products from plants. The remainder of Earth's species could hardly survive with only 20 percent of plant growth per year.

What would be some likely consequences? Species communities would become grossly reduced in their populations. In turn, they would become ecologically unstable at best and far less able to maintain homeostasis. In addition, ecosystems would lose much of their biomass and energy flow, hence would become less efficient at mobilizing the most basic natural resource of all, sunlight. There would also be a decline in communities' resilience to other forms of ecological disruption and environmental degradation (32–33). There could then ensue an upsurge in the rate of species fallout from impoverished ecosystems (34–35). How great an upsurge is impossible to say in even rough terms. All we can assert is that the phenomenon itself is quite probable; only its detailed dynamics are subject to significant uncertainty.

Pivotal Linkages in Ecosystems

A similar prospect applies with regard to species known as keystone mutualists, rare species which are likely to suffer differentially high rates of extinction (36). There will certainly be many associated extinctions as a result of these species' demise, though how many more is far from certain. Consider, for instance, the Brazil nut tree, widely harvested in Amazonia as a source of cash. The tree is pollinated solely by a euglossine bee, which also pollinates orchids and many other plants. These other plants often supply prime sources of food to sundry other insects, which pollinate further plants, and so on. In this crucial sense, the bees serve as a *mobile link* species, and their plant host, by virtue of supplying food to extensive associations of mobile links, serves as a *keystone mutualist* (34, 37–39).

These pivotal linkages within tropical forest ecosystems are manifested by thousands of plants that through their nectar, pollen, and fruits supply critical support for multitudes of insects, mammals, and birds: for example, figs, with their several hundred species, and epiphytes with their thousands of species. If, as a result of human disturbance of forest ecosystems, a keystone mutualist is eliminated, the loss can often lead to that of several other species. In certain circumstances, these additional losses can then trigger a cascade of linked extinctions. Eventually, an entire series of forest food webs can become unravelled, developed as they are through the co-evolution of plants and animals that have sustained each other through ever-more complex relationships (40). They can steadily become destabilized from start to finish of their workings, with *shatter effects* throughout their ecosystems. But how the precise dynamics will work out, and how many more species will disappear as a result, is impossible to say, except that the total will be far from trivial and could be more than significant.

Habitat Fragmentation

Yet another certainty/uncertainty factor arises as concerns habitat fragmentation. In the long run, many species will be eliminated not through outright destruction of habitats but through the fragmentation of extensive habitats into small isolated patches that are too limited to maintain their erstwhile species stocks into the indefinite future (19, 41–46). In Amazonia, for instance, if deforestation continues until the forest cover is ultimately reduced to those areas set aside as parks and reserves by the mid-1980s, we would find that 66 percent of plant species would eventually disappear, together with almost 69 percent of bird species and similar proportions of other major categories of animal species (47).

True, the processes of ecological equilibration, with their delayed fall-out effects, will take an extended period to exert their full depletive impact. In some instances, it will be decades and even centuries before species eventually disappear. But the ultimate upshot will be the same.

Dynamic Inertia of Environmental Degradation

Dynamic inertia is a factor in processes of environmental degradation, especially degradation that has already occurred. Through dynamic inertia, this degradation will continue to exert an increasingly adverse effect for a good way into the future, no matter how vigorously we try to resist the process. An obvious example is acid rain, which will keep on inflicting injury on biotas by reason of pollutants already deposited though not yet causing apparent harm (48). Similarly, many tropical forests will suffer desiccation through climatic changes induced by deforestation that has already taken place (49–50). Desertification will keep on expanding its impact through built-in momentum (51). Ozone-destroying CFCs, now in the atmosphere, will continue their work for a whole century even if we cease releasing them forthwith (1). There is enough global warming in store through past greenhouse-gas emissions to cause significant climate change no matter how much we seek to slow it, let alone halt it (52).

Stressed Biotas

Still another way in which the mass extinction ahead could turn out to be greater than is anticipated through direct human impact lies with the possibility that many of Earth's biotas are stressed after events of the late Pleistocene. If this is the case, certain communities of species may prove to be unduly prone to extinction insofar as they lack *ecological resilience or survival capacity* of the long-term sort.

Major life forms seem to have expanded in numbers for hundreds of millions of years (53) until a marked decline set in just 30,000 years ago, extending until about 1000 years ago. Whether through human over-hunting or climatic change or both, the large mammal fauna of North and South America, Oceania, and Madagascar among other large regions lost more than 100 genera, including 70 percent of large North American mammal species (54). The demise of outsize herbivores must have led to deep-seated changes in associated vegetation communities, ostensibly with reduced niche partition and less diversified plant assemblies, and with all the detrimental effects that would have implied for survivor communities of animals (37).

Following this mini-extinction spasm, there has been continuing elimination of vertebrate species and some plant species, albeit not on such a spectacular scale as the late-Pleistocene episode. It has persisted right up until the onset of the present mass extinction episode starting roughly in the middle of this century, these recent eliminations being almost entirely due to human activities. We have no idea how many associated species, notably invertebrate species, have likewise been lost during the past 30,000 years.

Today's biodiversity has already become depauperate and many of the survivor species has been left stressed well before the arrival of the unprecedentedly severe human impact from around 1950 onwards. Many extant biotas have been adversely affected along the way, at least through depletion of their sub-species and populations (55). Large numbers of species must have lost much of their genetic variability,

hence of their ecological adaptability, a process leaving them all the
more vulnerable to summary extinction.

So much for five indirect sources of species extinction. There are
many other sources (19, 56). In order to assess the overall outcome, let
us engage in a brief thought experiment. Suppose that in the year 2000
the whole of humankind were to be removed from the face of the Earth
in one fell swoop. Because of the many extinction pressures already
imposed or in the pipeline, with their impacts persisting for decades if
not centuries, widespread environmental impoverishment would persist
and thus serve to eliminate further large numbers of species for an
extended period ahead (11).

Adverse Repercussions of Mass Extinction: Uncertainty of Matchless Scope

Whether in biological, ecological, environmental, or economic
terms, mass extinction will clearly constitute an irreversible impoverishment of the Earth and of the world. That much is certain; the rest is
uncertain.

How many species can we afford to lose biologically and ecologically? Plainly there is much redundancy built into nature (57–58). Most
countries of Europe have long since lost the wolf and several other top-
carnivore species without any apparent ill effects to the dynamics,
stability, and other attributes of their ecosystems. Worldwide we have
probably lost hundreds of thousands, conceivably a million or more,
species during the last few decades without apparent harm. But
redundancy itself could be a functional attribute insofar as it supplies
adaptability and *buffering capacity* to ecosystems. How much redundancy is enough, ecosystem by ecosystem? Or, to put the question more
concisely, how much can it be reduced before ecosystem injury ensues,
and when does the injury become significant, serious, crucial, critical,
or catastrophic? Biologists still have difficulty in framing the question
correctly, let alone providing the right answer.

In order to exercise proper caution, we must stick with a stance of
saying that in bio-ecological terms the optimum number of species to
preserve is the maximum number. At first glance, this seemingly simple
answer is akin to saying that in a situation of such uncertainty that we
do not know how much uncertainty there is, the prudent path is to
practice complete caution at every turn. But that response is not simple,
it is simplistic. We cannot realistically seek to preserve every last
species. Occasions will arise, though far less often than some observers

suppose, when a clash of interests, e.g. wildland habitat versus agricultural needs, will be so acute and unavoidable that on political grounds we must acknowledge that we cannot even aim to save all species. Hubristic heresy as this may sound to some conservationists, it is a fact of life of the world we live in. We may prefer the world to be different, but we have to live in the world we live in. We should seek to save as many species as we possibly can, but to save all of them is impossible.

As for economic values, the issue is similarly characterized by vast uncertainty. Much is made of the rosy periwinkle, the source of two anticancer drugs with annual economic benefits to American society alone of at least $400 million. Some of the most promising leads for potential therapies against AIDS have been derived from tropical forest plants. The present commercial value of all plant-derived drugs and pharmaceuticals can be roughly reckoned to be at least $40 billion per year worldwide (59–60). While the plant components make up only a small part of the products, they are an essential ingredient. But even if all 250,000 plant species were to prove to be sources of valuable drugs, would we need all those drugs? Today we manage in the main with just a few hundred. There is clearly a question of overlap and substitutability.

Of course, one can riposte that we do not know what new diseases and other public-health needs will arise during the millions of years required by evolution to generate replacement species. But so far as we can discern right now, medicinal economics does not offer justification for seeking to save all species. The economics argument is certainly weighty, but equally certainly it is not conclusive. At the same time, and in the face of great uncertainty about which species to save on medicinal grounds, we are left with the same path of prudence; try to save as many species as we can.

Much the same applies to other economic sectors, notably agriculture and industry, that are assisted by materials, research templates, and other supports supplied by species.

However, a crucial consideration keeps raising its head. Our analyses reflect no more than the situation as we see it today. How about the trillions of tomorrows before evolution can make good the loss of mass extinction? All we know for certain is that we do not remotely know what new needs, biological, ecological, economic, whatever, will arise in the fullness of time for a proper planetary complement of species. In this sense, the biodiversity issue is subject to more uncertainty than any other environmental problem, all of which can be resolved by fixing the problem within a matter of 100 thousand tomorrows at most.

Right now, we are effectively asserting that we can *afford* to allow large numbers of species to become extinct on the grounds that we cannot economically deploy the funds and other conservation resources necessary to save a good share of vulnerable species. The corollary of this stance is that we are implicitly deciding that at least 200,000 future generations can certainly do without large numbers of species, and that we feel sufficiently certain we know what we are talking about when we make that decision on their unconsulted behalf.

This must be the most far-reaching decision ever taken on behalf of such a large number of people in the whole course of human history (5.5 billion people alive today, and perhaps 100 trillion likely to live during the course of the next 5 million years if Earth's population maintains an average of 2.5 billion people with a 25-year generation time). The precautionary principle is construed to address the needs and rights of future generations, but generally to the extend of only the conventionally foreseeable future of a few generations; 10 generations equates to 250 years, at most. The best writings on intergenerational equity (61–62) give scarcely a nod to the prospect of a future extending for thousands, let alone millions, of years.

Our Policy Responses

If ever there is a case for applying the precautionary principle, and in a form expansive enough to match the scale of the problem, biodiversity must be that case. So what policy measures can we fashion in response? We need to apply the precautionary principle with full rigor and urgency in light of massive uncertainty of multiple sorts. As we have seen, there is a number of prominent factors about which we know there is much uncertainty; and it is all but certain there are further factors at work or waiting in the wings with capacity to precipitate still more extinctions, yet we know little if anything about them, i.e. our uncertainty is so great, that even Hamlet would be hard pressed to give them a local habitation and a name.

Support for Research on *Unknown Unknowns*

The reader might object that *unknown unknowns* are a contradiction in terms: how can we know what we do not know? But consider; while we know all too little about global warming, and still less about the time when it will arrive in full scope and with whatever regional variations, we know for all practical intents and policy purposes that it is on its way sooner or later. The same with acid rain; we do not know how much acid rain damage is in the pipeline, especially with regard to its impact on tropical forests. But there is enough evidence to make its eventual emergence a virtual certainty. These, then, are known knowns, even if there is much we do not know about them (63).

Until recently, however, we did not know of their very existence. What new unknown unknowns are building up in our environments, and with particular respect to biodiversity, poised to leap out on us at some indeterminate stage of the future? Can we not identify some at least, or hazard guesses at what form they might take? This ranks as one of the greatest challenges of the entire biodiversity sphere. We are pretty good at analyzing problems when we recognize their existence, but less skilled at reaching out to entirely new problems before they reach out to us. If we could do a better scientific job on this front, we could sometimes launch a preemptive strike and prevent certain biodiversity problems becoming super problems.

Where should we look for some of these unknown unknowns? What frontiers of conservation biology should we probe with a greater sense of exploratory foresight? We could make a start with a thematic area that will probably become prominent in our environmental future, yet remains almost entirely known. It lies with the question of synergisms, or the reinforced result that occurs when two or more processes interact so that the product of their effects is greater than the sum of their separate effects (64–65). We know all too little about environmental synergisms. Ecologists cannot even identify many of their natural manifestations, let alone document their impacts. If we discern possible synergisms in the biotic crisis ahead, we shall be better able to anticipate, and even contain, some of their adverse repercussions.

Consider, for instance, acid rain in tropical forests. As we have noted, these forests are so rich in species that if we manage to safeguard most of the remaining biome, the mass extinction ahead could be reduced by half or even more. Several large tracts of tropical forests are threatened by acid rain. Already it is a recognizable problem in forests of southern China (66–67), and it appears set to shortly affect several forest sectors in other parts of the humid tropics, totalling as much as 1 million square kilometers (68). Stresses on tropical forests such as slash-and-burn cultivation and over-logging markedly enhance the forests' susceptibility to injury from acid rain; damaged trees are more prone to pollution damage. Conversely, acid rain on undisturbed forests greatly increases their vulnerability to slash-and-burn cultivation and over-logging; many trees will be dying or dead, leaving them easier to clear for agriculture or to fell for commercial timber. The two problems together, working in amplificatory accord, could cause greatly increased degradation and destruction of species' habitats and life-support systems in tropical forests, leading to a further pulse of extinctions.

There are multiple potential synergisms available given the number of environmental assaults on the biosphere. They deserve to rank as *all but unknown* unknowns. A first policy response of precautionary-principle type for biodiversity is to mount a research effort of character and extent to match the synergisms problem and thus to clarify an area of major import and exceptional uncertainty. In many respects, this will prove to be a new sort of scientific endeavour. It will require a shift from developing more knowledge about what we already know in essence, to attempting to know something about what is almost entirely an unsuspected black hole of biology. With the correct conceptual framework of science policy in support, which is all too often lacking for nebulous or mushy issues such as this, the challenge should prove eminently manageable.

Support for Research on *System Tolerances*

We know next to nothing about *system tolerances* in the mass extinction field, and with particular respect to tolerances of two sorts. The first is biological, the second political. In biological terms, we face the fact that because of ongoing destruction of species' habitats, we shall willy-nilly lose a good many species. The relevant question here is not how many can we afford to lose, but which concentrations of species can we least afford to lose. We know from the hot-spots analyses (14, 20) that a full 20 percent of all plant species, and a still higher proportion of all animal species, are at severe risk in just 0.5 percent of Earth's land surface. These hot-spot areas also feature biogeological processes that are central to the planet's functioning, notably tropical forests and coral reefs, and estuaries and other wetlands. They perform many vital environmental services through their contributions to climate and nutrient recycling. They reveal less biological tolerance in global terms than do other areas, and warrant special attention through application of the precautionary principle. We need to identify and research these crucial areas with all due despatch.

Secondly, political tolerances. Not all countries view biodiversity with the same value; and of those that do, not all can devote adequate conservation resources. Which ones most deserve support from the community of nations, and which ones can put outside support to best use? Again, the question needs urgent research with respect to ways for us to mobilize the precautionary principle with the most positive payoff.

Saving Biodiversity Means Saving the Biosphere

Fortunately, there is much complementarity between our policy responses to the biodiversity problem and our responses to other environmental problems. It is becoming clear that the established mode of protecting species, viz. setting aside more parks and reserves, is falling far short of meeting our needs. For one thing, the present network of protected areas safeguards only a limited proportion of species at risk, and as we have seen, the fragmentation effect means that most such areas will prove incapable of preserving more than a modicum of their species in the long run.

More important, protected areas are increasingly subject to threats that even the best managed areas cannot resist. These threats are not only conventional, viz. multitudes of landless and destitute peasants, a problem that seems set to grow worse. As many as one-third of developing-country parks and reserves are already being overtaken by agricultural encroachment. The new threats stem too from land-degradation processes such as desertification and decline of water supplies, and problems originating in areas well outside parks and reserves. They further stem from even more distant and diffused problems, e.g., as atmospheric pollution in the form of acid rain and global warming.

These various types of threats can be countered only by remedial measures that achieve much more than protection of wildland habitats. The measures include efforts to slow, halt, and even reverse desertification, deforestation, overuse of water supplies, acid rain, and global warming. They also include population planning, relief of peasant poverty, and a host of other development activities. In other words, we can save biodiversity only by saving the biosphere; and we can save biodiversity by doing many other things that need to be done for many other cogent reasons. There need be few special policy provisions in support of biodiversity.

An Ultra Degree of Precaution

In the biodiversity sphere and with reference to the precautionary principle, unique values are at stake, the irreversible injury to which these values are prone, and the exceptional length of time that a mass extinction will impoverish the biosphere for hundreds of trillions of people to come. On grounds of justice of unique character and extent, this urges application of the precautionary principle to an exceptional if not extreme degree. We should even think of a version exceeding what is known as the Strict Precautionary Principle, formulated for cases where very heavy environmental damage may occur with very heavy costs to people affected. So should we also think of an Ultra-Strict variation for biodiversity?

In practical terms, this would often entail a basic shift in the onus of responsibility in situations where species' habitats can be degraded or destroyed by exploiters of natural-resource stocks. An obvious example arises with tropical forests, where a marked asymmetry of evaluation has been at work. To date, a commercial logger has felt free to exploit timber stocks without regard for his impact on biodiversity. It has been up to conservationists to make the entire running by demonstrating that his actions would be significantly detrimental to biodiversity. How about shifting the burden of proof, requiring the logger to show why he cannot gain his timber by harvesting trees in areas with no particular importance to biodiversity, or, better, taking his timber from plantations established on deforested lands? The same applies to cattle ranchers, road and dam builders, and others who currently are in a position to exploit tropical forests with indifference to biodiversity interests. A fundamental adjustment of this sort would change the rules of the game from the start, which is the proper point for policy interventions.

Some people might respond that this is all very well in principle but how would it work in practice? One approach would be to apply an assurance-bonding system as proposed by the imaginative analysis of Constanza and Cornwell (4). In summary, the forest exploiter would have to post an assurance bond with value equal to our best present estimate of the largest future environmental damage and loss, including, though not limited to, biodiversity loss. The bond would be held in an interest-bearing escrow account. The forest exploiter would receive back part of his bond, plus interest, when he proves that he has not caused any worst-case damage, or that it will be less than originally assessed. Any other damage that he imposes will either be made good, or will be compensated for from the bond account. A forced saving system along these lines would serve a major pragmatic purpose. It would shift any costs arising from uncertainty with respect to biodiversity among other forest values, away from those who benefit from an intact forest and onto the resource exploiter. The exploiter would then face strong incentive to reduce the damage of his exploitation activities, or to gain his forestland products (timber, beef, etc.) from alternative sources.

A related approach lies with what has long been known as the *safe minimum standard of conservation* (69–72). This postulates that when we are confronted with the threatened degradation, depletion, or outright destruction of a natural resource, and when there is much uncertainty about how large the loss will be to society, it is the prudent path for us to take all due measures to safeguard the resource provided those measures do not impose unacceptable costs on society. This approach applies specially to species since extinction represents the irreversible loss of a unique resource; whether an actual or potential resource is not germane. During the past decade the approach has been accepted in principle, though with many deficiencies in practice, through the U.S. Endangered Species Act.

Conclusion

There is unprecedented need for the precautionary principle to be applied with unprecedented stringency to the biodiversity question. Given our limited experience of the principle at work in other environmental spheres, we have scant idea how to formulate a suitably-scaled version of the principle, together with policy initiatives, to meet the demands of the biodiversity crisis. Indeed, we may suppose that experience in other spheres would hardly be apposite to the particular exigencies of biodiversity: we need to devise a policy framework of a specially expansive sort to cater to the unique needs of biodiversity. An approach of *the same as before only more so and better so* would avail little: the biodiversity problem is qualitatively different. Herein lies a sizeable challenge for life scientists and social scientists alike who grapple with policy responses to biodiversity (73).

References and Notes

1. Benedick, R. 1991. Environmental risk and policy response. In: *Resources, Environment and Population.* Davis, K. and Bernstam, M.S. (eds). Oxford University Press, New York, 201–203.
2. Bodansky, D. 1992. Commentary: the precautionary principle. *Environment 34*, 4.
3. Cameron, T. and Abouchar, J. 1991. The precautionary principle: a fundamental principle of law and policy for the protection of the global environment. *Boston College International and Comparative Law Review* 14, 1–27.

4. Costanza, R. and Cornwell, L. 1992. The 4-P approach to dealing with scientific uncertainty. *Environment 34*, 12–17, 40–42.
5. Maler, K. G. 1989. *Risk and the Environment: An Attempt at a Theory.* Stockholm School of Economics, Stockholm.
6. O'Riordan, T. 1992. The precaution principle in environmental management. In: *Sustainable Development in Industrial Economies.* Simonis, U.E. and Ayres, R.U. (eds). United Nations University Press, Tokyo.
7. Pearce, D.W., Barbier, E., Markandya, A., Barrett, S., Turner, R.K., and Swanson, T. 1991. *Blueprint 2: Greening the World Economy.* Earthscan Publications, London.
8. Perrings, C. 1991. Reserved rationality and the precautionary principle: technological change, time and uncertainty in environmental decision making. In: *Ecological Economics: The Science and Management of Sustainability.* Costanza, R. (ed.). Columbia University Press, New York, 153–166.
9. Young, M.D. 1993. *For Our Children's Children: The Practical Implications of Inter-Generational Equity, the Precautionary Principle, Maintenance of Natural Capital and the Discount Rate.* CSIRO Division of Wildlife and Ecology, Lyneham, Australia.
10. Jablonski, D. 1991. Extinctions: a Palaeontological perspective. *Science* 253, 754–757.
11. Myers, N. 1990. Mass extinctions: what can the past tell us about the present and the future? *Glob. Plan. Change* 82, 175–185.
12. Raup, D.M. 1991. *Extinction: Bad Genes or Bad Luck?* W.W. Norton, New York.
13. Ehrlich, P.R. and Ehrlich, A.H. 1981. *Extinction.* Random House, New York.
14. Myers, N. 1990. The biodiversity challenge: expanded hot-spots analysis. *The Environmentalist* 10, 243–256.
15. Raven, P.R. 1990. The politics of preserving biodiversity. *BioScience 40.* 769–774.
16. Soule, M.E. 1991. Conservation: tactics for constant crisis. *Science* 253, 744–750.
17. Western, D. and Pearl, M. (eds). 1989. *Conserving Biology for the Next Century.* Oxford University Press, New York.
18. Wilson, E.O. 1988. *Biodiversity.* National Academy Press, Washington, D.C.
19. Wilson, E.O. 1992. *The Diversity of Life.* Belknap Press, Cambridge, Massachusetts.
20. Myers, N. 1988. Threatened biotas: "hot spots" in tropical forests. *The Environmentalist 8*, 198–208. (For an analysis that concentrates on specific localities within tropical forests.)
21. Raup, D.M. 1991. A kill curve for Phanerozoic marine species. *Palaeobiology 17*, 37–48.

22. Myers, N. 1993. Questions of mass extinction. *Biodiversity and Conservation 2*, (in press).
23. Diamond, J.M. 1989. The present, past and future of human-caused extinction. *Philos. Trans. R. Soc. London B325*, 469–478.
24. Ehrlich, P.R. and E.O. Wilson 1991. Biodiversity studies: science and policy. *Science 253*, 758–762.
25. Morowitz, H. J. 1991. Balancing species preservation and economic considerations. *Science 253*, 752–754.
26. Myers, N. 1986. *Tackling Mass Extinction of Species: A Great Creative Challenge*. The Horace M. Albright Lecture in Conservation, University of California, Berkeley.
27. Norton, B.G. 1987. *Why Preserve Natural Variety?* Princeton University Press, Princeton, New Jersey.
28. Norton, B. 1992. *Toward Unity Among Environmentalists*. Oxford University Press, New York.
29. Press, F. and Atiyah, M. 1992. *Joint Statement on Biodiversity*. National Academy of Sciences, Washington D.C., and British Royal Society, London.
30. Note that uncertainty is to be distinguished from risk; the concept of risk implies an acceptably precise knowledge of what is at stake, how probable is the prospect that it will be depleted or eliminated, and what will be the consequences, especially the costs, of its loss. Alternatively stated, risk, being statistical uncertainty, is an event with known probability; whereas uncertainty, being indeterminacy, is an event with unknown probability. Many environmental problems feature either uncertainty, or risk, or both.
31. Vitousek, P.M., Ehrlich, P.R., Ehrlich, A.H. and Matson, P.M. 1986. Human appropriation of the products of photosynthesis. *BioScience 36*, 368–373.
32. Ehrlich, P.R. and Roughgarden, J. 1987. *The Science of Ecology*. Macmillan, New York.
33. Odum, E.P. 1989. *Ecology and Our Endangered Life-Support Systems*. Sinauer Associates, Sunderland, Massachusetts.
34. Gilbert, L.E. 1980. Food web organization and the conservation of neotropical diversity. In: *Conservation Biology: An Evolutionary-Ecological Perspective*. Soule, M.E. and Wilcox, B.A. (eds). Sinauer Associates, Sunderland, Mass., 11–13.
35. Terborgh, J. 1992. *Diversity and the Tropical Rain Forest*. W.H. Freeman, New York, 11–33.
36. Terborgh, J. 1986. Keystone plant resources in the tropical forest. In: *Conservation Biology: The Science of Scarcity and Diversity*. Soule, M.E. (ed.). Sinauer Associates, Sunderland, Massachusetts, 330–344.
37. Owen-Smith, N. 1988. *Megaherbivores: The Influence of Very Large Body Size on Ecology*. Cambridge University Press, Cambridge.

38. Pimm, S.L. 1991. *The Balance of Nature?* University of Chicago Press, Chicago.
39. Terborgh, J. 1988. The big things that run the world. *Conserv. Biol.* 2, 402–403.
40. Gilbert, L.E. and Raven, P.H. 1975. *Coevolution of Animals and Plants.* University of Texas Press, Austin.
41. Case, T.J. and Cody, M.L. 1987. Testing theories of island biogeography. *Am. Sci.* 75. 402–411.
42. Heaney, R. and Paterson , B.D. 1986. *Island Biogeography of Mammals.* Academic Press, New York.
43. MacArthur, R.H. and Wilson, E.O. 1967. *The Theory of Island Biogeography.* Princeton University Press, Princeton, New Jersey.
44. Shafer, C.L. 1991. *Nature Reserves: Island Theory and Conservation Practice.* Smithsonian Institution Press, Washington, D.C.
45. Wilcove, D.S. 1987. From Fragmentation to extinction. *Nat. Areas J.* 7, 23–29.
46. Williamson, M. 1981. *Island Populations.* Oxford University Press, New York.
47. Simberloff, D. 1986. Are we on the verge of a mass extinction in tropical rain forests? In: *Dynamics of Extinction.* Elliott, D.K. (ed.). Wiley, New York, 165–180.
48. McCormick, J. 1989. *Acid Earth.* Earthscan Publications, London.
49. Nobre, C.A., Sellers, P.J. and Shukla, J. 1991. Amazonian deforestation and regional climate change. *J. Climate 4*, 957–988.
50. Salati, E. and Vose, P.B. 1984. Amazon Basin: a system in equilibrium. *Science 255*, 129–138.
51. United Nations Environment Programme. 1991. *Status of Desertification and Implementation of the United Nations Plan of Action to Combat Desertification.* United Nations Environment Programme, Nairobi, Kenya.
52. Houghton, J.T., Callender, B.A. and Varney, S.K. (eds). 1992. *Climate Change 1992: The 1992 Supplementary Report to the IPCC Scientific Assessment.* Cambridge University Press, Cambridge.
53. Signor, P.W. 1990. The geologic history of diversity. *Ann. Rev. Ecol. Syst. 21*, 509–539.
54. Martin, F.S. and Klein, R.G. (eds). 1984. *Quaternary Extinctions Events in Earth History.* Springer-Verlag, New York.
56. Ehrlich, P.R. 1986. *The Machinery of Nature.* Simon and Schuster, New York.
57. diCastri, F. and Younis, T. 1990. Ecosystem function of biodiversity. *Biol. Int. 22* (special issue).
58. Solbrig, O.T. 1991. *From Genes to Ecosystems: A Research Agenda for Biodiversity.* International Union of Biological Sciences, Paris.
59. Myers, N. 1983. *A Wealth of Wild Species.* Westview Press, Boulder.

60. Principe, P.P. 1987. *The Economic Value of Biological Diversity Among Medicinal Plants.* OECD, Paris.
61. Rawls, J. 1971. *A Theory of Justice.* Harvard University Press, Cambridge, Massachusetts.
62. Weiss, E.B. 1988. In: *Fairness to Future Generations: International Law, Common Patrimony, and Intergenerational Equity.* Transnational Publishers, New York.
63. Myers, N. 1990. Facing up to the lack of interface. In: *Sustainable Development, Science and Policy.* Norwegian Research Council for Science and Humanities, Bergen, Norway, 513–521.
64. Myers, N. 1987. The extinction spasm impending: synergisms at work. *Conserv. Biol. 1,* 14–21.
65. Myers, N. 1993. Environment and development: the question of linkages. *BioScience.* (in press).
66. Galloway, J.N. 1989. Atmospheric acidification projections for the future. *Ambio 18,* 161–166.
67. Zhao, D. and Sun, B. 1986. Air pollution and acid rain in China, *Ambio 15,* 2–5.
68. Rodhe, H. and Herrera, R. 1988. *Acidification in Tropical Countries.* Wiley, Chichester.
69. Bishop, R.C. 1978. Endangered species and uncertainty: economics of a safe minimum standard. *Am. J. Agric. Econ. 57,* 10–18.
70. Ciriacy-Wantrup, S.V. 1968. *Resource Conservation: Economics and Policies.* University of California Division of Agricultural Sciences, Agricultural Experiment Station, Berkeley, California. For a specific application of the safe minimum standard to biodiversity.
71. Norton, B.G. 1987. *Why Preserve Natural Variety?* Princeton University, Princeton, New Jersey.
72. Norton, B.G. 1991. *Toward Unity Among Environmentalists.* Oxford University Press, New York.
73. I thank Dr. David Duthie, Professor Bryan Norton, and Professor Tim O'Riordan for helpful comments on an interim version of this article.

6

Biodiversity: The Legal Aspects

Wolfgang E. Burhenne

From the legal point of view, there are two facets to the future of biodiversity: one is the international law dimension, the other the national law aspects. They are, of course, complementary.

According to scientific sources, "the term biological diversity is commonly used to describe the number, variety and variability of living organisms, and it has become a widespread practice to define biological diversity in terms of genes, species and ecosystems, corresponding to three fundamental and hierarchically-related levels of biological organisation."

Taking this as a starting point, to determine the law applicable to biological diversity necessitates identifying those legal instruments which deal with the variety of species in given areas; the variety of genetic variations within any species; and the variety of ecosystems.

At the outset, it can immediately be said that—even if the concept was not used—neither national nor international law in the field of biodiversity is new; in the former case it has existed for centuries, in the latter case for decades.

It is naturally at the national level that the need to establish legally based constraints for the conservation of species and ecosystems has first been felt; conservation has to be understood here as a scale of measures ranging from protection to rational (or now sustainable) use of living resources and the ecosystems of which they are a part.

Starting with legislation to regulate the taking or harvesting of specimens (collecting, hunting, fishing) used by a community, or to set aside areas of special biological importance, such legislations have

61

evolved into rather sophisticated tools, at least in the developed world. I will come back to this aspect later on.

Consonant with the sovereignty of States over natural resources, these national measures were for a long time considered sufficient.

With increased pressures on the natural environment, it became more and more apparent that these national measures, even if good *per se*, were totally inadequate in several instances, namely: when the resource is situated wholly outside any national jurisdiction (high sea fishing); when the resource is located in such a way that it may be affected by action in several countries (shared resource or resource which may be affected by transboundary interferences); and when a threat cannot be controlled without an effort on the part of several States concurrently (international trade; ozone).

In those cases, conservation cannot be achieved without international agreements, and the evolution of conservation treaties is a testimony of this recognition.

It started with agreements toward the maintenance of a resource economically important for several partners; these treaties have naturally remained restricted in their geographical scope, and number of Parties (user-oriented treaties).

For nonharvested species, a similar trend can be detected. The range of the species considered have determined the scope of the treaties, which also naturally have tended to become regional: Western Hemisphere, Africa, Europe, South Pacific, and ASEAN.

Treaty obligations evolve, and reflect albeit belatedly, the evolving science of conservation: as of 1970 (roughly), the regulation or prohibition of taking is no longer considered sufficient, and obligations to conserve habitats and habitat types appear, followed by attention being given to ecological processes within ecosystems. The most recent conservation conventions (ASEAN, ALPS) tend to take into consideration the management of the natural environment as a whole.

Until recently, only very few conservation conventions were of global scope. Four global conventions have been concluded on matters directly relevant to biological diversity: Ramsar—on one type of life support systems; World Heritage—on sites of world importance; CITES—on one threat (international trade) to species; Migratory Species—on one type of species (moving across borders).

The two first bear an early imprint of globalism. In both cases the accent is put on the international importance of the areas dealt with.

It took another twenty years after Ramsar for the international community of States to recognise that this puzzle of measures would not add to saving species and ecosystems on a global basis, let alone biodiversity. What is required is a global effort, i.e. obligations and commitments on the part of each State of this planet, toward its own biological diversity.

This evolution happens in the wake of the recognition that for a series of environmental problems, the global level is the only one which may provide appropriate action or remedy: the oceans (Law of the Sea), the atmosphere (long-range pollution; ozone layer), and climate change.

The Convention on Biological Diversity was adopted in Nairobi on May 22, 1992, and signed in Rio on June 5. As of July 1992, it has been signed by 157 States and the EC.

The Convention is a landmark from many points of view:

1. It is the first time that biodiversity as such is addressed in an international instrument; as we have seen, the picture at international level until then can be compared to an incomplete jigsaw puzzle. Further, the genetic level of biodiversity had never been taken into consideration before in an internationally binding instrument.

2. It is the first time that biodiversity is considered as of common concern to the global community of States—a recognition that, in spite of the sovereignty of States over its elements, the goal of conservation cannot be achieved without coordinated, parallel, national measures.

3. It recognises that, because the burden of conservation is unequally spread between the nations of the world, and the burden greater in the South, financial transfers will have to be made to support action in the South.

4. It gives a prominent place to sustainable use, rather than preservation, as a recognition of the fact that species and ecosystems can only be conserved if people have an interest in maintaining them.

5. It is a give and take between the developed world, keen to obtain conservation commitments by the developing countries, and the developing world, keen to obtain access to technology and benefits deriving from genetic resources over which they have sovereignty.

The Convention holds promises for both camps, and only because of that was it concluded.

In fact, Article 1 of the Convention says it all: "The objectives of this Convention are the conservation of biological diversity, the sustainable use of its components, and the fair and equitable sharing of the benefits arising out of the utilisation of genetic resources . . . ."

Conservation obligations mandate, inter alia, for each Party: to develop national strategies, plans and programmes for the conservation and sustainable use of biological diversity; to identify components of biological diversity important for its conservation and sustainable use; establish a system of protected areas where special measures need to be taken to conserve biological diversity; and most importantly, regulate or manage biological resources important for biological diversity whether within or outside protected areas with a view to ensuring their conservation and sustainable use.

These are only a few of the conservation obligations, which contain specific articles on *in situ* and *ex situ* conservation, sustainable use, important assessment, incentives research, and training.

The Convention, when compared, for instance with the climate change instrument, is a much more detailed document, and entails a considerable number of fairly precise conservation obligations.

Next come the obligations related to access and transfer of technology. Parties undertake to provide or facilitate access to, and transfer of technologies that are relevant to the conservation and sustainable use of biological diversity, or make use of genetic resources; and provide this access and transfer to developing countries under fair and most favorable terms; where the technology is subject to patents and other intellectual property rights, the Convention states that the transfer must be on terms consistent with such protection.

Of major importance to the South are the obligations related to biotechnology and deriving benefits; they require to provide effective participation in biotechnological research to Parties, especially developing countries providing the genetic material; and to promote priority access to the same countries to the results and benefits deriving from biotechnologies based on genetic resources which they provide.

These obligations are carefully crafted not to ask the impossible, but it is quite clear that the developing world is not prepared to see them remain on paper; they are part and parcel of the package. In order to stress this point, the article on Access to Genetic Resources is entirely new law: access is made subject to the prior informed consent of the country where the collection takes place *in situ,* and must be on mutually agreed terms.

Mutually agreed terms may mean, for instance, participation in the benefits of products derived from such resources.

In order to make things even clearer, it is explicitly stated in the treaty that the "extent to which developing country Parties will effectively implement their commitments under the Convention will depend on the effective implementation by developed country Parties of their commitment under the convention related to financial resources and transfer of technology."

This indicates how crucial the clauses on the financial mechanism and their acceptability by developed nations are. The mechanism created is to operate under the authority of the Conference of the Parties; its function is to provide financial resources to developing country Parties for purposes of the Convention. This provision has been the subject of considerable dissent and reluctance on the part of the developed countries: read in conjunction with another stating the financial needs at stake (incremental costs of developing countries) it may be interpreted as requiring a blank check from the North. Statements for the records by nineteen nations during the signature of the Final Act aim at preventing such an interpretation.

The Global Environmental Facility (GEF) is designated as interim financial mechanism, until the Conference of the Parties decides otherwise. This, also, was highly controversial, and the developing countries delayed acceptance until the very last minute, subjecting it to the restructuring and democratization of the Facility.

It was difficult to conclude the Convention; it will, perhaps, be more difficult to implement it meaningfully. One thing is certain: if the developed world does not honor what it has (reluctantly) agreed to, the Convention will remain a paper tiger. We should do all we can to make a success of this unique chance to view biological diversity globally.

The first reactions will be seen during the ratification process, and the speed at which the Convention will enter into force will be an indicator of its future: thirty ratifications are required.

Assuming that the Convention enters into force, national legal instruments will be needed to implement it. No Convention is completely self executing—this one, as a framework convention, even less so than others.

What does this mean?

There are two main sectors where legislation will be needed: the "conservation aspects," and the "access" aspects.

The latter is rather new: Parties, particularly developing countries, will have to enact legislation submitting access to genetic resources to a permit system, and provide the general conditions for the issuance of such permits. As this is new, no model exists. One of those conditions should be access to the benefits of inventions which might derive from this material. It would also be useful to specify that the fees received (for collection or from benefits) constitute a National Fund for Biodiversity Conservation.

Such a legislation will only function if the "others" play the game fairly, as collection can easily be done unnoticed.

Thus, it is important that Parties, particularly developed ones, enact legislation to deter (penalize) unlawful activities in the countries of collection; also, transparency regarding the origin of the material used might well be made compulsory.

The same Parties (developed), if faithfully implementing their obligations under the Convention, will have to consider how to transfer, or facilitate the transfer of technology relevant to the conservation or sustainable use of biodiversity. There are two basically different cases here: either the technology is accessible because in the public domain (for instance, if resulting from government-supported research), or it is in private hands. In the first case, no legal problem (but a lot of practical problems!); in the second instance, no real legal problem either, because the Convention safeguards intellectual property rights.

To "facilitate" the transfer of such technology, there are several possibilities: acquisition by the State (unlikely); acquisition through the Funding mechanism under the Convention; volunteer measures on the part of the industry; or a mixed system (incentives to make technology available).

The recent proposal of the Austrian Prime Minister is relevant here: an international "Fund" constituted not by money, but by know-how and technology. This idea could also be retained at national level.

The conservation aspects are more well known. A large number of countries already have legislation which serves the purpose of biological diversity conservation.

Usually, this legislation is still divided between those provisions relating to species, and those related to the protection/conservation of areas. Virtually all legislations permit the regulation or taking of harvested and endangered species, and the establishment of protected areas.

Much more sophisticated instruments have evolved in some jurisdictions, mainly in developed countries. The necessity to conserve habitats generated these. Two techniques are used in this regard: firstly, the obligation to protect the habitat (at least the critical habitat) of a protected species as one of the attributes of this protection; second, the protection of habitat types (prohibiting modifications without a permit). The essential difference between this and a classical protection tool is that no designation is required (non-site-specific protection).

But novelties have also appeared in the field of site-specific protection. The most interesting ones are the constitution of larger planning units where conservation is the main goal (so-called nature parks), and are administered separately from the rest of the territory this facilitates the cohabitation of economic uses compatible with the conservation of the area with stricter controls in certain parts of it; the taking into account of conservation concerns in the "normal" planning process (e.g. building prohibitions along the coast or in flood plains); and, the promotion—through legislation—of voluntary conservation by landowners; of special importance here are incentives in the form of reduced taxation. Contracts also play an increasingly important role: leases and easements management agreements provide opportunities to secure the management of the land for conservation purposes while providing a financial incentive to the owner.

These tools provide a remarkable panoply of possibilities for the implementation of the conservation obligations of the Convention.

But let me finish by a note of caution, and a call for reflection: the legislation which is needed to conserve biological diversity must be attuned to the conditions of each individual country. No general recipe is available, not only because of the difference between the various legal systems, but also because of the different socioeconomic conditions. In this connection, in many instances sophisticated models will be inadequate. What is needed is an effort for the legislation to provide simple tools which provide local populations with an incentive to live in harmony with nature.

Protecting the Oceans and Fresh Water Sources

Water pollution is a major problem confronting the global community today. Fresh water poses problems of availability as well as contamination. Oceans are polluted and exploited for their resources. Because the sources of these problems cannot be pinpointed to a single guilty party and due to the international nature of bodies of water, finding a solution is a matter for the world as a whole.

Fresh water makes up just 2.59 percent of all of the Earth's water supply and much of this is frozen in ice and snow in the polar regions. Useable fresh water is a limited resource that needs to be regulated and protected. Unfortunately, reserves are polluted through industrial and municipal wastes, by agricultural runoff and pesticide use, and through acidification from acid rain. The little fresh water available is being threatened.

What little available fresh water that does exist must be distributed. Equitable distribution of fresh water poses difficulties due to the unevenness of natural water distribution on the planet, as well as differing power relationships in nations around the world. As the world population expands, the distribution of fresh water will become even more problematic.

Oceans present another range of problems. Seventy percent of the Earth's surface is covered by oceans. The ocean is a rich source of resources and for this reason, among others, sixty percent of the world's population lives in coastal regions.

The widespread use of the oceans has led to environmental problems. Ocean dumping, oil spills, and depletion of fish populations due to over-exploitation have damaged the marine ecosystem.

The international community passed the Law of the Sea Convention in 1982, which outlines the rights and responsibilities of coastal nations, with special attention given to the control of pollution from cities, agricultural runoff, hazardous waste, deep sea mining, oil exploration, and ocean dumping.

The United Nations Regional Seas Program is also playing an important role in protecting international bodies of water. It has led to the signing of treaties for the protection of ten seas, including the Mediterranean Sea, the North Sea, and the Baltic Sea.

The waters of this planet are part of an increasingly recognized "global commons." International cooperation to protect and regulate these resources is essential for their health and survival.

—RNW

7

The Ocean Blues
Nicholas Lenssen

*They are the source of food, livelihood and meteorological balance,
but the oceans are reeling from human assault.*

The last two years have been rough on the oceans. Hundreds of beaches along the Italian Adriatic were off-limits due to an infestation of algae. Medical waste washing ashore closed beaches in many areas of the eastern United States. Thousands of seals died in the North Sea, possibly due to a combination of disease and pollution. A similar fate befell dolphins off the U.S. Atlantic coast. And in Alaska, a supertanker hit a reef and dumped a quarter million barrels of oil into one of the world's richest fishing grounds.

Once thought to be so vast and resilient that no level of human insult could damage them, the oceans are now crying out for attention. While the public eye is periodically turned to large disasters such as the ones mentioned above, it is routine assaults that most threaten the marine environment. Daily chemical and biological pollution is damaging the oceans at a frightening rate, while ongoing coastal development and overfishing hamper their ability to recuperate.

Gone with pristine waters are futurists' dreams of a world fed by the sea's abundance. In their place is the reality of stagnating oceans; shrinking wetlands, coral reefs, and mangroves; and falling fish catches that jeopardize a key source of protein for the world's poor. Unless we act soon, reversing these worsening conditions will only become more difficult.

Too Much of a Good Thing

One of the chief oceanic pollutants is human sewage. Properly handled on land, human waste makes a good fertilizer that has a balanced complement of nutrients to promote plant growth. Flushed into streams and rivers, these same nutrients can lead to eutrophication—the overenrichment of water. Additional nutrients wash into the sea from fertilized farmland and from acid rain, which contains nitrogen compounds released in fossil-fuel combustion. Algae feed on this windfall of nutrients and multiply at an incredible rate until they form what are called "blooms."

As these tiny organisms decompose, they leave surrounding waters oxygenless and lifeless. In Australia, Chile, Nigeria, Pakistan, the Soviet Union, and the United States, the story is the same: Nutrient overload has left beaches unusable and large areas of water temporarily dead.

Even worse, there is a growing epidemic of algae blooms that are toxic. These "red tides" can poison marine life and throw whole ecosystems off balance. Until recently, scientists thought red tides were entirely natural events. Theodore Smayda of the University of Rhode Island and Donald Anderson of the Woods Hole Oceanographic Institution now have found a strong correlation between the occurrence and location of these blooms and increased nutrient levels.

European waters are in particularly bad shape. Nearly half of the Baltic Sea's bottom waters have become oxygenless; algae blooms in the Adriatic Sea killed fish in areas as large as 400 square miles; and the North Sea coasts of Denmark and Germany experienced a 400–percent increase in major blooms.

Last May, a particularly devastating toxic algae bloom dominated the Skagerrak, which connects the North Sea to the Baltic Sea, killing nearly all marine life to a depth of 50 feet, including fish valued commercially at $200 million. Norway's Bergen Scientific Center found that the bloom was caused at least in part by urban and agricultural pollution. It warns that as long as such nutrient discharges continue, similar blooms can be expected.

Red tides were once rare events along the East Coast of the United States, but since 1972 waters from Massachusetts to North Carolina have been plagued by six major toxic blooms. A bloom of the algae *Ptychodiscus brevis*, normally found in the Gulf of Mexico, struck near Cape Hatteras, North Carolina, in October 1987, inflicting $25 million in losses on the fishing and tourist industries. This bloom created a political uproar when a government report implicated it in the deaths of 3,000 dolphins, many of which had washed up on public beaches along the eastern seaboard. Some scientists and members of Congress remain skeptical about the causes of the dolphin deaths, contending that extremely high levels of PCBs and pesticide residue found in the dead mammals were a contributing factor.

The increase in blooms and their toxicity has created problems for fishers and consumers of sea products. Guatemala and the Philippines have reported deaths from bloom-contaminated shellfish, an event unknown until this decade.

Sewage discharges can lead to health problems even when blooms don't occur. In Shanghai, nearly 300,000 people came down with hepatitis A in a three-month stretch last year, due to contaminated clams; 47 victims died. Industrial countries generally have better controls that keep contaminated seafood from the market, which means that at any one time one-third of the U.S. shellfish beds are closed because of pollution.

Oil and Water Don't Mix

The wreck of the supertanker *Exxon Valdez* in Alaska's Prince William Sound on March 24th was the most dramatic oceanic disaster in recent memory. By mid-May, crude oil covered more than 730 miles of wilderness coast, in some places three feet deep. The spill created an environmental disaster that will linger for decades, for oil does not break down as fast in Alaska's cold climate as it does in warmer regions. Also, since much of the oil either fell to the bottom of Prince William Sound or dissolved into the water, diseases or damage to animal reproduction will occur irregularly as hydrocarbons seep out and move up the food chain.

Amidst the bungled cleanup effort, Exxon executive Don Cornett claimed the spill was "just another cost of doing business." For the oil industry, with its vast economic resources, this may be true, but not so for the Alaskan fishing and tourist industries, whose losses could approach $250 million. Fishing is a $130–million-a-year business in Prince William Sound, and the spill's effects on salmon, herring, shrimp, and other populations will be felt for years to come.

The Alaska spill caps an extremely messy year for the oil industry. Antarctica's coast was fouled by two petroleum spills in a month and oil has coated shorelines in Belgium, the Netherlands, Florida, Hawaii, and on Washington State's Olympic Peninsula. Recent research findings from Panama show that oil in warmer, tropical waters has a far greater impact than previously thought; it now is seen as particularly deadly to coral reefs and mangroves.

Although large spills get media attention, far more oil silently finds its way into the oceans via street runoff, ships flushing their tanks, and effluent from industrial facilities. A 1985 U.S. National Research Council (NRC) study, *Oil in the Sea,* estimated that 21 million barrels of oil annually enters the seas this way, many times more than the 600,000 barrels accidentally spilled on average each year this decade. The NRC also warned that there is a special concern for areas suffering chronic exposure, since as little as one part of oil for every 10 million parts of water has serious effects on the reproduction and growth of fish, crustaceans and plankton.

A petroleum derivative—plastic—also takes a heavy toll on marine life. Each year, 30,000 northern fur seals die as they become entangled in plastic bags or lost fishing nets, as do hundreds of thousands of other marine mammals, seabirds, and fish. It's estimated that up to a half million plastic containers are dumped into the seas from merchant ships every day and that untold miles of fishing gear—including whole nets—are accidentally set adrift.

A Thin Layer of Death

Chemical pollutants constitute another assault on the marine environment, especially in the uppermost layer of water. The tiny phytoplankton and zooplankton that form the base of the oceanic food chain congregate in the microlayer, which is 1/100th of an inch thick, as do certain fish and shellfish in early stages of their lives.

Unfortunately, that's not all that concentrates there. John Hardy, a biologist at Oregon State University, has found toxic chemicals and such heavy metals as copper, lead, and zinc in the microlayer in concentrations 10 to 1,000 times greater than in the rest of the water. Scientists are trying to determine what role the contaminated microlayer has in diminishing fish and shellfish populations in coastal waters.

These chemicals come from a variety of sources—industries, airborne pollutants, shipping accidents, pesticide runoff, mine tailings, and waste incineration. Once toxics enter the marine environment, it's very hard to get them out, since they seep into the sediments, enter the food chain, or simply flow with the currents. More than 2.1 million tons of liquid chemical waste is poured into the North Sea alone each year, and the shipboard incineration of more than 100,000 tons of hazardous wastes adds an unspecified amount of toxic ash. The intergovernmental North Sea Scientific Commission has found that although several opportunistic species have thrived under these conditions, the overall diversity of marine organisms is reduced by these discharges.

Over the past year, 17,500 seals in the North and Baltic seas died mysteriously, worrying citizens and politicians in bordering countries. While scientists have blamed a new virus for the epidemic, the role the poisoned waters has played in wiping out three-quarters of the North Sea's seal population is hotly debated. Marine biologists agree, however, that chemicals will impede the recovery of the seals, as up to 80 percent of female seals in the Baltic are believed to be sterile due to polychlorinated biphenyls (PCBs).

Chemical pollutants are doing damage in other bodies of water as well. High levels of PCBs, DDT, mercury, cadmium, and other chemicals are blamed for the collapse of beluga whale populations in Canada's St. Lawrence River. Autopsies of 72 dead whales have found tumors, ulcers, respiratory ailments, and failed immune systems. Joseph Cummins, genetics professor at the University of Western Ontario, believes that the "beluga is the most polluted mammal on earth" and that marine mammals around the world face extinction from PCBs.

These chemicals move through the food chain and can also end up in humans. Between 1953 and 1968, some 649 residents of Minamata, Japan, were killed after they consumed seafood contaminated by industrial mercury. Seafood from Minamata Bay still cannot be eaten. In the United States, lobsters containing up to 20 times the allowable limit of PCBs have been caught off the Massachusetts coast. Fish with tumors from unknown causes also are being caught with greater frequency along the eastern seaboard of the United States, as are fish in Florida with high levels of mercury.

Robbing the Cradle

As chemical threats grow, the marine habitats that nurture ocean life are disappearing. That's bad news for the future of the oceans, since coral reefs, mangroves, and sea grasses are the "nurseries" and feeding grounds for much of marine life, supporting as they do the sea's richest areas of biological diversity and productivity.

Coral reefs are home to an estimated one million species—including 2,000 fish species—and are considered the tropical rain forests of the oceans. They also happen to be the ecosystems most sensitive to changes in temperature and light. Healthy coral reefs are becoming hard to find. Rivers choked with sediment from deforested lands or eroded agricultural fields cloud coastal waters and kill reefs by blocking sunlight. Along Costa Rica's Caribbean coast, sediments from local rivers have killed 75 percent of the reefs. Local fishers in Indonesia, Kenya, and elsewhere add to the damage by using dynamite to kill and collect fish that hide in coral reefs. Also, reefs throughout the world are mined for construction material or ornamental pieces.

By 1981, 70 percent of the reefs in the Philippines had been damaged, many beyond recovery, by the cumulative effect of poisoning from cyanide, mine tailings, pesticides, and erosion. Particularly damaging is the use of cyanide in collecting tropical fish for the commercial aquarium business. Fishers squirt sodium cyanide into reef hideaways to stun valuable species. Even though the cyanide is not intended to kill the fish, it frequently does. It also kills the coral.

The natural and economic losses from this destruction are vast. More than 100,000 jobs, as well as $80 million in potential fish catches, are lost each year as coral reefs disappear, estimates Don McAllister, curator of the National Museums of Canada and director of the International Marinelife Alliance (IMA). "Due to lowered fish production from destroyed coral reef, more than five million Filipinos do with less than enough seafood; many starve," says McAllister. Already between one-fourth and one-half of the children living in coastal settlements in the Philippines are malnourished. The continuing loss of coral reefs and fish will only increase this figure. Encouragingly, IMA and the Philippine Ministry of Agriculture, with funding from the Canadian government, have initiated programs to assist fishers in returning to sustainable harvesting methods.

The salt-tolerant mangrove trees that inhabit low-lying areas of the tropics and subtropics are also threatened. Even richer breeding, nursery, and feeding grounds than coral reefs, mangrove forests are nonetheless being rapidly cut to make charcoal and pulp and to clear the way for salt-making and aquaculture ponds. Between 1963 and 1977, almost half of India's mangroves were cut down; one-third of Ecuador's mangroves have been converted to ponds for a rapidly growing shrimp-farming industry; and 10 years is all Philippine mangroves are given before aquacultural expansion wipes them out. On a positive note, Tanzania recently banned the destruction of its remaining 200,000 acres of mangroves.

Bounty of the Sea

Along with pollution, overfishing threatens the future productivity of the seas, warned Edouard Saouma, director general of the United Nations Food and Agriculture Organization (FAO) in April. Paradoxically, his statement came as the worldwide commercial catch reached a record level of 84.5 million tons in 1987, up from 21 million tons in 1950. Fish account for more than 40 percent of the animal-protein supply for two billion people in the developing world, although only 24 percent for the world as a whole. Fish supplies are not unlimited, however; after nearly doubling between 1950 and 1970, the per capita fish catch of 40 pounds has advanced little since.

The global commercial fish catch is nearing the maximum sustainable yield of 100 million tons that FAO scientists think the oceans can produce. Indeed, the total catch may exceed that level, since subsistence fishers net another 24 million tons. Trends in particular fish species confirm this. Of the 280 fish stocks monitored by the FAO, only 25 are considered slightly to moderately exploited. Meanwhile, at least 42 stocks are already overexploited or depleted.

The recent upswing in catches is attributed to the use of more-efficient fishing techniques and the increased exploitation of less desirable species in the herring and sardine family. Also, the world's fishing fleets have intensified their exploitation of remote regions in the southern Pacific Ocean. As fisheries decline, family income and even food intake will head downward for the more than 100 million people who depend on the oceans for their livelihood. In Costa Rica, the Philippines, and elsewhere, hunger is driving fishing families away from the sea, adding to bulging urban populations.

Fore more than two decades, scientists and policymakers have worked to better manage fishing, particularly that by long-range trawler fleets, through stronger national responsibility and management of fish stocks. A potential solution was agreed to during negotiations on the United Nations Conference on the Law of the Sea in the seventies. The treaty extended national economic boundaries out to 200 miles from the shoreline—an area that yields more than 90 percent of the ocean's fish catch.

Although more than 70 countries have declared these "exclusive economic zones" (EEZs), that in itself is not enough to protect national fisheries. Developing nations with small navies or coastal patrols are having an especially difficult time enforcing stringent controls on fishing. Vlad Kaczynski, a research associate at the University of Washington's Institute for Marine Studies, finds that West African countries, such as Guinea, Mauritania, and Senegal, are unable to police the predatory trawlers from South Korea, Spain, the Soviet Union, and others. Indonesia hopes to discourage foreign poaching through its recent announcement that illegal fishers will be tried for treason, a crime that carries the death penalty.

Beyond the 200–mile zones, huge trawlers are catching up, reducing, and moving on from one fish species to another. In the northern Pacific, more than 700 Japanese, South Korean, and Taiwanese fishing boats equipped with 20– to 40–mile-long drift nets sweep an area of sea the size of Ohio each night. These vessels ostensibly fish for squid, but all marine life, including fish, mammals, and birds, gets tangled in the nets.

Scientists blame driftnetters for last year's crash in the Alaska pink salmon fishery, in which only 12 million fish of an expected 40 million were taken by Alaskans. The vast reach of driftnet ships is also being felt in the southern Pacific, where it is expected that albacore tuna's sustainable yield will be surpassed by as much as 600 percent this year.

What happens in the open seas can foil even the best efforts to protect native fisheries. When Canada declared an EEZ in 1977, it hoped to regulate a sustainable harvest of Atlantic cod, a species that accounts for nearly one-third of the country's total catch. Since the cod's migration takes it outside Canadian waters, however, foreign fishers continued to prey on the fish, leading to a steep drop in its population. Past errors in estimating the cod's mortality rate haven't helped matters. To compensate, the Canadians have ordered cuts in their own cod catches for this year; they expect further reductions in the future.

With cod supplies down, Pacific Ocean pollock will face more pressure from the Canadian fleet, but that fish already is showing signs of stress from overfishing, particularly in the international waters of the Bering Sea. There, the catch has increased from 100,000 tons in 1984 to 1.3 million tons in 1988—a level that marine scientists think is unbearable.

Fish is becoming a more expensive food source as supply falls behind demand. In the United States, fish prices have more than doubled in real terms since the mid-sixties, while beef and pork have held constant and chicken has declined. Higher prices in the industrial world can and probably will lead to higher prices in, and more exports from, developing countries. In fact, between 1974 and 1987, the volume of fish exported from cash-starved, protein-deficient developing countries nearly quadrupled.

For a world with limited fish stocks, a growing population that needs more protein, and a rising demand for fish in the industrial world, more protein malnutrition among the fish-dependent poor becomes inevitable.

As if that Weren't Enough

Decreased global stratospheric ozone—and an anticipated 5– to 20–percent increase in ultraviolet radiation over the next 40 years—poses another threat to marine life. Too much ultraviolet radiation slows down photosynthesis and growth by phytoplankton and can alter their genetic makeup. Globally, a 2–percent decrease in ozone has occurred, but the Antarctica "ozone hole" gives us an idea of what future losses will lead to. Last year, Antarctica suffered a 15–percent loss of ozone and a 15– to 20–percent decline in the population of surface phytoplankton. While negligible declines in phytoplankton numbers were recorded below 35 feet, scientists expect impacts as deep as 100 feet in the future.

At stake is the oceanic food chain itself. As ultraviolet radiation increases, changes in the species of algae are bound to follow, with ultraviolet-resistant strains gaining and less resistant strains disappearing. The most severe consequences are predicted for tropical and subtropical regions, where the high angle of the sun will allow more ultraviolet radiation to enter.

The seas will also be affected by another global environmental threat—the greenhouse effect. The seas now act as a brake on global warming because they absorb much of the excess heat produced by this phenomenon and capture much of the carbon dioxide that drives it. They store more than 90 percent of the planet's actively cycling carbon, and are thought to absorb 45 percent of the carbon dioxide—the prime agent of warming—emitted by the burning of coal and oil. However, scientists are concerned that predicted changes in climate could warm the oceans and eventually alter their circulation and currents, which, in turn, would alter global climatic patterns.

The oceanic influence on planetary health goes even deeper. A decrease in plankton productivity could accelerate the warming. Via photosynthesis, plankton capture carbon dioxide that otherwise would contribute to the greenhouse effect; they split the carbon molecule from the oxygen, use it as food, and then sink it to the ocean bottom when they die.

The ocean's ability to absorb carbon dioxide already is diminishing, due to increased saturation of surface waters with the gas and to warmer oceanic temperatures. In fact, the U.S. government released findings in April showing that the oceans warmed at a far faster rate in the eighties than previously anticipated. The greenhouse effect will also cause the seas to expand and rise, creating a five- to seven-foot increase in sea level by the end of the next century that threatens to flood important estuary and coastal habitats.

Stewards of a Shared Resource

The steady deterioration of the world's oceans stems largely from the fact that these waters are a huge commons that individual citizens and nations have little incentive to protect. Like the village commons that is overgrazed because it is shared property, the oceans could lose their vitality if governments and international bodies don't soon develop rules and regulations that encourage people to become stewards of a shared resource, rather than plunderers of a common frontier.

The world is in the early stages of a fundamental transition in the way it views and treats the oceans. Since the seventies, a growing array of local, national, and international laws has been adopted to protect the marine resource base. While not all of these efforts have met with immediate success, they have formed an important groundwork for progress in the next decade.

In the United States, several state governments have taken action to improve the health of coastal waters. In 1987, Maryland, Pennsylvania, Virginia, and the District of Columbia committed themselves to an ambitious and comprehensive program to cut the nutrient discharge into Chesapeake Bay by 40 percent by 2000. The four governments that jointly pollute the Chesapeake have pledged to work toward a toxic-free bay and to achieve an increase in wetland habitats in the region.

Some industrial-country governments are also moving to protect marine habitats. The U.S. Congress, for example, has adopted a goal of "no net loss" of wetlands. The Japanese government, meanwhile, has decided not to construct a controversial airport runway atop the largest blue coral reef in the world.

In developing countries, the connection between marine habitats and the health of fisheries is still being realized, but such awareness could be accelerated with the encouragement of development agencies. In Ecuador, Sri Lanka, and Thailand, for example, the U.S. Agency for International Development is training scientists and fishers to manage wild shrimp stocks and slow the destruction of coastal resources as economic development continues.

One of the most important steps in protecting the oceans is for individual nations to gain better control of their waste streams. As with land-based waste problems, polluted oceans will not become clean until less garbage is produced and the recycling of sewage and other wastes is encouraged. Banning ocean dumping of all wastes by the year 2005 would be a first step.

The International Challenge

The world is also moving to adopt international agreements that manage the oceanic commons. To date, 39 nations have ratified an international treaty known as Annex V of MARPOL, which bans the discharge of plastics by ships. The ban went into effect this January. The London Dumping Convention, signed in 1972, has led to a ban on the dumping of extremely hazardous materials, including radioactive wastes, heavy metals such as cadmium and mercury, and synthetic materials, in the oceans. Last year, 63 signatories of the London accord also approved a ban on ocean incineration of toxic substances by 1994.

The eight countries bordering the North Sea agreed in 1987 to reduce nutrient and toxic discharges by half by 1995. The Netherlands, West Germany, and Norway are moving ahead to finance improvements in sewage treatment and reduce the agricultural runoff of nitrogen fertilizers. A similar accord has been signed by the seven Baltic Sea nations.

To make these agreements effective, it may be necessary to provide an international transfer of financial resources. The Nordic Investment Bank, for example, is considering providing credits to Poland for reducing discharges of industrial and municipal pollutants into the

Baltic. This precedent could be carried over to developing countries, which have been severely constrained in their ability to pay for pollution prevention measures.

In protecting fisheries, the problem of the commons is particularly evident, since migrating fish move freely between various countries' national waters. The advent of exclusive economic zones offers a promising start at controlling overfishing, since it gives national governments clear responsibility for their own fisheries.

EEZs are a necessary but insufficient condition of fishery regulation, since many governments have failed to enforce compliance with existing controls on fishing. However, governments seem to be taking fishery management more seriously now and the U.S. government has even threatened trade sanctions against Asian countries that allow their fleets to intercept migrating salmon.

"The most significant initial action that nations can take to protect the ocean's threatened life-support system is to ratify the Law of the Sea Convention," says the U.N. World Commission on Environment and Development. Completed in 1982, the Law of the Sea offers an integrated management regimen, or "constitution," for the world's oceans. It was negotiated with the belief that the seas are "the common heritage" of humanity. Besides the 200–mile exclusive economic zones that entrust most fisheries to national governments, this constitution includes provisions on seabed mineral resources, the protection of the marine environment, and navigation rights.

Yet, of the 159 countries that have signed the treaty, only 40 have ratified it, leaving 20 to go before it can enter into force. Particularly crucial is the support of key nations such as the United States, the United Kingdom, and West Germany, which have so far refused to sign or ratify the convention. There is, however, a good chance that recent maritime crises will increase support for the Law of the Sea and lead to new efforts to make it work.

If government leaders do not respond soon, popular concern for the health of the sea may become more strident. Citizens the world over are beginning to demand changes. Last year, 30,000 people formed a 25–mile chain in Sylt, West Germany, to protest North Sea pollution; 40,000 volunteers cleaned up beaches in the United States; and up to 100,000 Estonians, Lithuanians, and Latvians linked hands along the Baltic Sea to call for a cleaner environment. In the United States, an organized campaign has led thousands of consumers to mail their

EXXON credit cards back to the company following this spring's oil spill.

These public events demonstrate a growing political backing for better protection of the oceans and a dissatisfaction with the weak policy measures of the past. It's time for governments to hear the message and act.

8

WEST AFRICAN STATES: The Marine Pollution Problem: Some Lessons from UNCLOS

G.A. Sarpong

Introduction

Marine pollution[1] is a global problem of several dimensions; it affects the quality of the oceans in all parts of the world; and most states contribute to some aspects of the problem. Pollutants know of no national frontiers so that even when pollution is localized, the effects of winds, currents, and waves almost invariably result in a spread of these pollutants to other areas. Traces of DDT have been located in remote areas of Antarctica illustrating the global nature of oceanic pollution.[2] Pollution has dire consequences for marine life: wild birds, fisheries, and marine flora all suffer in varying degrees. Pollution could also affect human health. The carcinogens ingested by fisheries in polluted waters could get concentrated in the food chain. These agents become a hazard to man through the consumption of fish. There is also the problem of physical and aesthetic damage. These include the tainting of nets and fishing gear, the contamination of yachts, harbour works, beaches, and coastlines with consequent losses to the tourist industry.[3] And yet the picture has not changed despite various attempts to control the problem. Indeed it has lately assumed a wider dimension in some developing states like those of the West African subregion[4] whose marine environments have become dumping grounds for toxic and other wastes from industrialized states. UNCLOS provides, *inter alia*, for a 12–mile Territorial Sea (TS); a 200–mile Exclusive Economic Zone

(EEZ), and the concept of the common heritage of mankind as a basis for the exploitation of the resources of the area. In addition, it makes a significant contribution to the solution of the marine pollution problem; and in fact devotes over 45 articles to the subject.[5] Most states of the West African subregion have ratified UNCLOS.[6] An examination of their national legislation, however, reveals certain lapses which have serious implications for marine pollution enforcement in the light of UNCLOS: whereas most of these states adhere to the limits prescribed for the extent of the territorial sea and the EEZ, a few others exceed these limits; some of these states, in apparent reaction to dumping and other acts of pollution in their environment, have enacted legislation whose penalties for violations far exceed the conventional limits; yet for others, their legislations are bereft of content as to the necessary regulatory standards prescribed by UNCLOS, while others have outmoded and/or outdated legislation dealing with the subject.[7]

The object of this paper is to establish that UNCLOS provides a sufficiently effective framework for dealing with the marine pollution problem; particularly in the enforcement of standards. It is thus in the interest of the states of the subregion to enact and/or harmonize their national legislation in conformity with UNCLOS' texts so as not to violate their obligations assumed under international law. In this regard the article further examines some of these national legislations in the light of UNCLOS and other related issues; and draws out some lessons for states of the subregion.

UNCLOS and the Marine Pollution Problem: Standard Setting and Enforcement

Standard Setting

UNCLOS imposes a positive obligation on states to protect and preserve the environment.[8] It acknowledges the right of states to exploit their natural resources. This must, however, be in accordance with their duty to protect and preserve the environment. UNCLOS upholds the customary law principle that states are to conduct their activities in such a way that pollution arising from incidents or activities under their jurisdiction or control does not spread beyond areas of national jurisdiction.[9] On the basis of sources of origin, pollution under UNCLOS is classified as land-based; by dumping; from vessels; from activities in the area; and from or through the atmosphere.[10] States are obliged to take measures to deal with all these sources of pollution.[11] In recognition of the global nature of marine pollution, UNCLOS enjoins states to cooperate on a global basis, and as appropriate, on a regional basis in formulating and elaborating international rules, standards, and recommended practices and procedures for the protection and preservation of the marine environment, taking into account characteristic regional features.[12] UNCLOS further enjoins the international community to cooperate either directly or through competent international organizations in the provision of scientific, technical, and educational assistance in marine environmental protection matters to developing states such as those of the West African subregion. Developing states are to be granted preferential treatment in the allocation of funds, technical assistance, and the utilization of specialized facilities for marine environmental protection.[13]

UNCLOS also enjoins states to enact appropriate legislation to deal with the various types of marine pollution. It draws, however, a distinction between the permissible levels and/or extent of competence in the TS and that of the EEZ; both in terms of standard setting and enforcement:[14] in the territorial sea, UNCLOS permits coastal states to enact legislation on the preservation of the environment and the prevention, reduction, and control of pollution thereof.[15] Thus any act of serious and wilful pollution of the TS is deemed a violation of the regime of innocent passage established under the Convention.[16] However, such legislation shall not apply to the design, construction, manning, or equipment (DCME) of foreign ships unless they are giving effect to generally accepted international rules or standards.[17] Furthermore, imprisonment as a penalty may only be imposed with respect to violations committed by foreign vessels in the TS only in cases of wilful and serious acts of pollution.[18] In all other instances, only monetary penalties may be imposed. In the EEZ however, only monetary penalties may be imposed in all cases.[19] Furthermore, all legislation that may be enacted for dealing with pollution be it DCME, discharge, or otherwise, shall conform to, and give effect to generally accepted international rules and standards established through the competent international organization or general diplomatic conference.[20] In the case of vessel source pollution[21] where the international rules and standards prescribed are inadequate to meet the circumstances of the particular state, special measures may be enacted to deal with the situation only after prior consultation with, and approval by, the competent international organizations.[22] UNCLOS does not expressly state what this "competent international organisation" is. However, with regard to vessel-source pollution and dumping the International

Maritime Organization (IMO) is acknowledged as the organization concerned. Indeed, one delegation stated in an informal negotiating group of the Third Committee that the applicable international rules and standards for the prevention of pollution from vessels refer to existing and future IMO Conventions. This was not contradicted.[23] This view also has the support of jurists.[24] Thus the IMO rules constitute the standard-setting norms under UNCLOS.

The first of these IMO norms is the 1954 Convention on the Prevention of Pollution of the Sea by Oil (OILPOL 54)[25] which has been superseded by the International Convention for the Prevention of Pollution by ships (MARPOL 73/78) as subsequently amended. MARPOL 73/78's objective is the elimination of all forms of marine pollution from vessels other than dumping. The technical measures designed to achieve the Convention's objectives are contained in five annexes dealing with oil, noxious substances carried in bulk, harmful substances carried in packages, sewage, and garbage. In terms of standard setting, MARPOL 73/78 is widely acknowledged as capable of combatting vessel source pollution.[26] As of December 31, 1991, MARPOL 73/78 had 70 contracting state parties, the combined merchant fleet of which constitutes approximately 90 percent of the gross registered tonnage (grt) of the world's merchant fleet.[27] There are other IMO Conventions concluded in response to the need to ensure safety at sea. There is no doubt that a major cause of vessel source pollution is discharges from substandard vessels or those that lack the requisite safety devices or adequate and/or trained personnel to man them with resultant accidents. Hence measures aimed at ensuring vessel safety at sea through maintenance of CDME standards indirectly assist in pollution control in the marine environment. There are several such generally accepted IMO conventions which can be briefly touched upon in a work of this nature: There is the international Convention on Loadlines (LL 1966) as amended; with 124 states parties the combined merchant fleet of which constitutes approximately 98 percent of the grt of the world's merchant fleet; the International Convention for the Safety of Life at Sea (SOLAS 74) as amended by its protocols of 1978, 1988, and 1989; with 116 states parties the combined merchant fleet of which constitute approximately 97 percent of the grt of the world's merchant fleet; the Convention on the International Regulation for Preventing Collisions at Sea (COLREG 72) with 113 states parties the combined merchant fleet of which constitutes approximately 96 percent of the grt of the world's fleet; and the Convention on Standards of

Training Certification and Watch-keeping for Sea Farers (STCW 1978) with 89 states parties the combined merchant fleet of which constitutes approximately 83 percent of the grt of the world's merchant fleet.[28]

On dumping, there is the Global Convention on the Prevention of Marine Pollution by Dumping of Wastes and Other Matter, 1972 as amended (LDC 1972) with 67 contracting state parties.[29] LDC 1972, *inter alia*, bans outright the dumping of such harmful and/or toxic compounds as organohalogens, mercury, cadmium, and plastics as well as crude fuel, heavy diesel, and lubricating oils.

A feature of these generally accepted IMO standards is their universal applicability: state parties to UNCLOS are obliged to enact the necessary laws and legislation incorporating them.[30] This would appear to offend the *pacta tertii nec nocent nec prosunt rule;*[31] although it is arguable that these IMO standards constitute customary international law. Indeed it has been argued that the environmental provisions of UNCLOS as a whole, in view of the nearly complete consensus by which they were arrived at, could be customary rules on the matter.[32] Thus the IMO rules, especially MARPOL 73/78, become the norm or benchmark by which the validity of any national standard may be assessed. State parties to UNCLOS would thus have to change, modify or even adapt, as the case may be, their national legislations to be in conformity with these IMO standards.

Standards Enforcement

The pre-UNCLOS scheme of enforcement[33] of marine pollution standards was based primarily on flag state competence. This had its genesis from the Grotian concept of the freedom of the seas.[34] Owing to the inability, unwillingness, and/or lack of interest on the part of many flag states, this scheme of enforcement was ineffective.[35] The problem was acute with flags of convenience states[36] that had no genuine links with vessels flying their flags; and also lacked the necessary power and administrative machinery to impose regulations on these vessels. UNCLOS deals with land-based or other sources of pollution in general terms but provides a rather comprehensive enforcement mechanism for vessel source pollution[37] incorporating the IMO standards as a basis for enforcement. UNCLOS marks a shift from the reliance on flag-state enforcement outside the TS. In addition to flag-state jurisdiction, UNCLOS provides for coastal and port-state enforcement, and hence a three-pronged assault on the marine pollution problem.

Flag-State Enforcement under UNCLOS

Since the main burden of enforcement action should occur before a vessel commits violation of pollution laws,[38] much emphasis is still placed on flag-state enforcement under UNCLOS. It is this idea, and in particular, the right of pre-emption (discussed below) accorded flag-states that has raised doubts about the enforcement regime under UNCLOS. Professor Bernhardt for example has commented:

"The practical effect of [flag state pre-emption] is to make flag State enforcement the lowest common denominator of mandatory enforcement under the vessel-source pollution chapter, notwithstanding the elaborate machinery which has been established for port State and coastal State enforcement. *Given the poor record of flag State enforcement, this scheme is not likely to be effective* (emphasis added)."[39]

A contrary view, however, is presented in this article. Admittedly the flag-state enforcement record in the past has been poor. However, flag-state jurisdiction under UNCLOS is radically different from the 1958 Geneva provisions: UNCLOS follows the Geneva texts on nationality and the requirement for a "genuine link" between a vessel and the state of its registry. In addition it goes beyond the mere requirement for a state to exercise its jurisdiction and control in administrative, technical, and social matters over ships flying its flag (as provided by the 1958 Geneva provisions), by detailing certain specific obligations in connection with these requirements: UNCLOS provides specifically that states maintain a register of vessels containing the names and particulars of vessels flying their flag, and to assume jurisdiction under their internal laws in respect of masters, crew, and other administrative and social matters connected with these vessels; Article 94 (3) further requires states to take appropriate measures to ensure safety at sea with regard to: the construction, equipment and seaworthiness of ships; the manning of ships, labor conditions, and the training of crews, taking into account the applicable international instruments; the use of signals, the maintenance of communications, and the prevention of collisions.

Furthermore, such measures shall include those necessary to ensure that each ship, before registration and thereafter at appropriate intervals, is surveyed by a qualified surveyor of ships, and has on board such charts, nautical publications and navigational equipment and instruments as are appropriate for the safe navigation of the ship; that each ship is in the charge of a master and officers who posses appropriate qualifications, in particular in seamanship, navigation, communications, and marine engineering, and that the crew is appropriate in qualification and numbers for the type, size, machinery, and equipment of the ship; that the master, officers and, to the extent appropriate, the crew are fully conversant and required to observe the applicable international regulations concerning the safety of life at sea, the prevention of collisions, the prevention, reduction, and control of marine pollution, and the maintenance of communication by radio.

These measures are not exhaustive and must conform to generally accepted international regulations. These are the IMO Conventions already discussed. Article 217 further imposes an obligation on flag-states to ensure compliance by their vessels, of international rules and standards established by the IMO for the prevention, reduction, and control of vessel-source pollution. In this connection, they are to adopt laws and regulations including measures for their implementation. The measures include ensuring that ships are prohibited from sailing until they can comply with these international standards, periodical inspections, the carrying on board of international certificates, and immediate investigation of, and where necessary, institution of proceedings in respect of violations irrespective of where they occurred. The outcome of these proceedings must be promptly communicated to either the coastal state or the IMO in cases where such proceedings are instituted at their request. Penalties in the event of convictions are to be "adequate in severity to discourage violations wherever they occur."[40] The requirement by the flag-states to inform states and the IMO of the outcome of proceedings being now an overriding obligation imposed by UNCLOS, is not likely to be ignored. This is because governments do not want to have a reputation for illegal or irresponsible behavior. The recording, publication, and discussion of enforcement records could thus put a substantial pressure on states to act.

UNCLOS does not provide for sanctions in the event of non-compliance by flag-states with these provisions as certain delegations and some publicists would have wished.[41] However, in spite of lack of sanctions states are unlikely to ignore positive obligations assumed for the protection and preservation of the marine environment under UNCLOS owing to the harm that pollution does to the marine environment. The point has been fully brought home to states following catastrophic vessel accidents such as the *Torrey Canyon*, the *Argo Merchant* and the *Amoco Cadiz*; the activities of various environmental pressure groups and international fora such as the Stockholm Conference on the Environment, the IMO, Third U.N. Conference on the law of the Sea (UNCLOS III), and more recently the UN Conference on Environment and Development (UNCED); as well as unilateral action by states such as Canada and Iran. Further, unlike the 1958 High Seas Convention that was not widely ratified, a majority of states was in total agreement with UNCLOS texts on environmental preservation.[42] It may be recalled that it was through the initiative of states such as the United States and the United Kingdom that the pollution enforcement regime was devised at UNCLOS III. The refusal of these states to sign UNCLOS is not because of the marine environment provisions, which in fact were the first to be negotiated, but rather due to their non-acceptance of the sea-bed provisions.

Flags of Convenience

The problem, however, is with flag of convenience states. These, as noted, lack effective administrative, technical, and other institutional structures to ensure compliance by their vessels of antipollution standards. Even with these vessels as the Liberian example shows,[43] there could be a way of enforcement. The issue, however, is not particularly important in practice; the main flag of convenience states—Liberia and Cyprus—are parties to the IMO regulatory conventions; and Panama to all except STCW 1978.[44] The issue of their control and enforcement under UNCLOS is further resolved by coastal and port state enforcement. Under these, substandard vessels could be denied entry into ports, detained, or even prosecuted for noncompliance with prescribed international standards.[45] The United Nations has also concluded a convention on the subject. It is designed to fill the gap in international maritime law by defining the minimum elements of a genuine link that should exist between a ship and the state whose flag it flies.[46] Ultimately then, the significance of flags of convenience vessels from the point of view of safety and protection of the marine environment would pale into insignificance.

Port States Enforcement

Besides, the enforcement regime provided by UNCLOS must not be viewed solely in terms of flag-state enforcement. It is a tripartite scheme involving as well, coastal and port-states, together with adequate checks and balances to ensure an effective and viable system. Port-state jurisdiction, in a strict sense, is not new. States in the past have had the right to set conditions for entry into and exit from their ports. Also certain IMO Conventions, in particular, MARPOL 73/78, incorporated the concept of port-state enforcement even to the extent of enforcing the discharge violation standards on the vessels of nonstate parties. However, this jurisdictional question was not fully resolved. MARPOL 73/78 also does not allow prosecutions by port-states.

Under UNCLOS, in addition to powers of inspection and investigations, port-states have powers to prosecute vessels that violate the established international standards. UNCLOS recognizes the right of states to set conditions for the entry into their ports subject to the requirement of due publicity. Further, it goes beyond this by providing for port-state enforcement (including prosecutions) of international discharge violations up to and including the high seas when a vessel is voluntarily within its ports.[47] Those violations occurring outside a coastal state's own internal waters, TS sea, or EEZ must however, be enforced at the request of a state damaged or threatened by the discharge violation or unless the violation has caused or is likely to cause pollution in the maritime zones of the coastal state concerned. UNCLOS limits states in-port inspections to the examination of documents issued under the IMO Conventions.[48] Further in-port inspection may be carried out only after an inspection of these documents and when there are clear grounds for believing that the condition of the vessel does not correspond substantially with the particulars of these documents, the contents of such documents are not sufficient to confirm or to verify a suspected violation, or the vessel is not carrying valid certificates and records. Where an investigation reveals a violation of international standards, the vessel, pending proceedings, should be promptly released on the posting of a bond or other financial security. This provision is aimed at preserving a balance between environmental protection and rights to navigation. However, the release of such a vessel may be refused, whenever it would present an unreasonable threat of damage to the marine environment . . . or made conditional upon proceeding to the nearest repair yard.[49]

This provision should enable port-states to prevent substandard vessels from polluting the marine environment. Article 218 refers to discharge violations. However, Article 219 provides a basis for the enforcement of construction, design, manning, and equipment (CDME) standards as well. Article 218 is couched in permissive terms ("may" instead of "shall") and this has been criticized by Professor Bernhardt. He argues that given that port-state enforcement was formulated as the viable compromise solution between the conflicting modes of coastal-state and flag-state enforcement, the failure to insist that it be mandatory seems an unnecessary sacrifice of environmental interests.[50]

The provision, however, is designed so as not to place obligation on states; especially the developing ones that may lack the necessary technical and other institutional structures to carry out such obligations under MARPOL 73/78. There is, however, every incentive for such states as well as the developed ones, to exercise this right of enforcement. This is more so in view of the harm that pollution does to marine life in the TS and the EEZ over whose resources these states enjoy sovereign rights. Besides, a coastal state is under the general obligation to take the necessary measures to protect and preserve the marine environment, and this includes the requirement to legislate to give effect to international rules.

Port-state enforcement is quite significant in many respects: it should reduce the incentive of coastal states to extend unilaterally their powers over broad areas of the sea. Coastal states may be induced to relinquish some of their power by allowing port states to conduct their enforcement proceedings. This is largely motivated by safety and economic considerations; coastal states would be able to reduce their policing of coastal waters and the boarding at sea of vessels suspected of violating pollution standards. The port state has an incentive to accept its enforcement role because it may later wish to request similar assistance from other states.[51]

Hence it is to the reciprocal advantage of both the coastal state and the port state to assign enforcement powers to the port states.

The issue is whether this reciprocal advantage is sufficient enough an inducement for states to spend time and scarce resources on the enforcement of pollution regulations for violations occurring in other states jurisdiction. Contrary to doubts expressed on the matter, it appears that states are prepared to do this.[52] Thus, contrary to fears expressed by certain jurists, port-state enforcement is in fact a viable institutional mechanism for dealing with vessel-source pollution.

Port-state enforcement should provide an alternative means of enforcement, especially for developing states that lack the necessary technical and manpower requirements to police vast expanses of their maritime zones. This is because many of the vessels that navigate through these zones usually call at ports.[53] The technical and manpower limitations are not with developing states alone. The cost of regular air and sea patrols is such that many developed states have had to rely almost completely on reports of aircraft and vessels engaged in other duties. Even the United States Coast Guard engages in little surveillance outside the harbors. Similarly, Canadian enforcement in the EEZ is limited to the Department of National Defence (DND) surveillance flights.[54] Port-state enforcement underlies the global nature of pollution and the need for international means to combat it. For without it, even if a state could eliminate pollution within its TS and EEZ by effective standards and enforcement measures, it could not protect itself from discharges occurring, just beyond these zones that are carried landwards by winds and currents.

Coastal State Enforcement

Article 220 provides for coastal state enforcement: When a vessel is voluntarily within a port or at an off-shore terminal of a State, that State may, subject to section 7 (discussed below), institute proceedings in respect of any violation of its laws and regulations adopted in accordance with UNCLOS or applicable international rules and standards for the prevention, reduction, and control of pollution from vessels when the violation has occurred within the TS or the EEZ of that State.

This provision, like that on port-state enforcement, is couched in permissive and not mandatory language. The criticisms and comments on port-state enforcement regime, thus apply *mutatis mutandis* to this enforcement regime. Coastal state enforcement involves surveillance, inspections, investigations, and prosecutions. Inspections and investigations are to be carried out as provided under port state enforcement. UNCLOS' limitation of acts of innocent passage to cases of serious and wilful pollution in the TS has been criticised.[55] The provision it is submitted, does not prevent a coastal state from taking the necessary measures for the preservation of its environment or to enforce same in terms set out above. The significance of the provision lies in the form of sanctions—monetary penalties—that may be imposed. Coastal-state enforcement power for the violations in the EEZ is limited to information gathering and inspections; the latter action under stated conditions. There must be "clear grounds" for believing that the vessel has violated international rules and standards governing vessel-source pollution. Further, the violation must have resulted in "substantial discharge causing or threatening significant pollution of the marine environment." In addition, inspection is justified only when the vessel has refused to give information or "if the information supplied is at variance with the evident factual situation and if the circumstances of the case justify such inspection."[56]

After inspection, and where violations are established, the coastal state may either await the arrival of the vessel in its ports so as to commence proceedings, or transmit the necessary evidence to the next port of call for necessary action. In this connection, article 220(3) allows the coastal state to require information regarding the identity and port of registry, the last and next port of call, and other relevant information required to establish whether a violation has occurred. As observed, UNCLOS requires port states to act as far as practicable on this request. Flag-states are also to adopt laws and regulations and to take measures to ensure that vessels flying their flags comply with such requests (article 220(4)).

Admittedly, the success of the system depends on cooperation between states, but, in view of the global nature of the pollution problem, there is every incentive for states to act collectively against it; and also in fulfilment of their convention obligations. In addition, coastal states have other stronger powers of enforcement in the EEZ: Where there is "clear objective evidence" that a violation has resulted in "discharge causing major damage or threat of major damage" to the coastline, related interests or resources of the TS, or the EEZ, the coastal state may institute proceedings including detention of the vessel in accordance with its laws (article 220(6)). In this connection, it may exercise the right of hot pursuit.

UNCLOS does not define "clear grounds," "objective evidence," or "substantial discharge." Presumably it leaves that for the determination of coastal states. In view of the rights that these states have over their maritime resources, and in spite of the circumscribed nature of coastal state enforcement powers, there is immense potential for coastal states to determine these standards in such a manner as to enable them to exercise greater enforcement powers than UNCLOS' stipulation in the name of resource conservation.

Other Areas of Enforcement

UNCLOS also provides for enhanced coastal state enforcement with regard to dumping, rights of intervention as well as enforcement in "special" and "Arctic areas."[57] At the conference that adopted LDC 72, delegates were unable to agree on the extent of coastal states' jurisdiction outside the TS. Article 216 provides an answer to this jurisdictional problem by providing for coastal state enforcement of this antidumping law in the TS, the EEZ, and the continental shelf.[58] Article 211 also provides for a much broader and enhanced coastal state right of intervention in the event of maritime casualties. Article 211(6) on special areas, as noted, enables coastal States to adopt "special mandatory measures" of enforcement in areas of its EEZ where international standards are inadequate. This is an improvement on MARPOL 73/78 which is limited to discharge violations mainly in the Baltic, Gulf, and Mediterranean Seas areas.

The Safeguard Provisions

Both coastal and port-State enforcement are subject to the safeguard provisions of UNCLOS.[59] These provide guidelines on enforcement. They are also aimed at protecting international navigation from abuse and thus help ensure that careful balance required between coastal States rights and navigational interests. UNCLOS provides for the observance of the "due process" requirement in proceedings; that enforcement may only be exercised by states' officials, warships, military aircraft, or other ship or aircraft marked and identifiable as being on government service; that enforcement should not cause hazard to vessels or their crew; and that a vessel should be promptly released on the posting of a bond. It is also provided, in addition, that states shall not delay a foreign vessel longer than necessary. Inspections are limited generally to those documents required under the IMO Conventions. Furthermore, enforcement is to be exercised in a nondiscriminatory way, and except for violations in the territorial seas as noted, only monetary penalties may be imposed upon foreign vessels. A three-year period of limitation for proceedings as well as a "double jeopardy" clause are also provided for under the provisions. The most important and also the most controversial of the safeguard provisions is the flag-state pre-emption clause. This provision[60] enables flag-states to suspend proceedings instituted by coastal or port-states, within six months of the institution of such proceedings, and to undertake its own proceedings. This provision must, however, not be viewed as detracting from the effectiveness of the enforcement regime. The rationale behind the rule is that before allowing coastal or port-states to take proceedings and impose penalties on foreign vessels, the flag-state should be given reasonable opportunity to exercise its enforcement rights and carry out its obligations which are directly derived from the relation of the ship to this state.[61]

As formulated, the provision is not an immutable precept that allows flag-states to pre-empt proceedings anyhow. The right or pre-emption applies only in respect of violations beyond the TS; it also does not apply in the case of "major damage." What amounts to a major damage is not defined. Hence, a coastal state could deny a flag-state pre-emption rights on the ground that the polluting vessel's damage amounts to "major damage."

Furthermore, it does not apply where a flag-state has repeatedly disregarded its enforcement obligations. A flag-state that "pre-empts" proceedings without imposing any sanctions on its vessels could find itself being denied this right in subsequent proceedings involving its vessels. This is more so since flag-states are obliged to inform coastal or port-states of the outcome of such proceedings. Above all, state parties would have to ensure that their legislations conform with UNCLOS' texts. So long as the rules, especially penalties, are uniform, flag-state pre-emption pales into insignificance.

Sovereign Immunity

UNCLOS' environmental protection and preservation provisions are made subject to the "Sovereign immunity" provision under article 236.[62] The issue of immunity for warships and other government vessels was not much discussed at UNCLOS III. The Convention merely follows the example of other pre-existing conventions by granting immunity to such vessels, on the basis of the restrictive immunity doctrine.[63]

Thus a polluting vessel confronted in the TS or EEZ of a coastal state cannot just raise a claim of sovereign immunity on the ground of being on government noncommercial service. The matter would initially have to be determined in the municipal forum with consequent loss of time and expense. That in itself is enough a deterrent. Above all, the immunity is from arrest and prosecution and not immunity from liability.[64] Consequently, all vessels are legally obliged to observe the environmental pollution regulations; UNCLOS reiterates this by enjoining government vessels to act in a manner consistent with the convention.[65]

UNCLOS and the Marine Pollution Problem: Concluding Remarks

UNCLOS crystallizes the 12–mile TS and the 200–mile EEZ concepts as norms of international law. Within these regimes, it prescribes the IMO standards as the basis for standard-setting in pollution control. Further, UNCLOS provides for an effective enforcement mechanism of these IMO standards through the tripartite flag, coastal- and port-states enforcement. The universal nature of port-state enforcement, in particular, is a welcome inroad into the enforcement system. For, apart from acting as a check on flag-state enforcement it should provide a viable alternative basis of enforcement, especially for States that lack the required technical and manpower requirements to police their maritime zones. UNCLOS provides an effective tool for dealing with the marine pollution problem. It remains to be seen to what extent states of the West African subregion conform to UNCLOS' provisions on the subject. In the subsequent chapter an attempt will be made to ascertain this through a selective examination of some of the national legislation in the subregion on the subject.

The West African Subregion, UNCLOS, and the Marine Pollution Problem

The coastal states[66] of the subregion front the Atlantic ocean, which has its fair share of the world's shipping routes. Apart from vessel source pollution, the area suffers from pollution from land based sources like rivers as well as industrial wastes, although not to the same extent as in such highly industrialized regions as the Baltic. Nevertheless, the recent spate of dumping of toxic and other wastes in the region's marine environment has heightened awareness about environmental pollution in the area; and one of the states, Nigeria, has enacted legislation dealing specifically with the subject.[67] With the exception of Benin, Liberia, and Sierra Leone, all these states are parties to UNCLOS.[68] However, an analysis of the maritime legislation of these states reveals certain inconsistencies with UNCLOS' texts: Whereas Côte d'Ivoire, Gambia, Ghana, Guinea, Guinea-Bissau, Mauritania, Nigeria, and Senegal claim 200–mile EEZ, the non-parties Benin, Liberia, and Sierra Leone each claim 200–mile TS. Even amongst the 200–mile EEZ claimants, some states assert jurisdiction beyond the permissible 12–mile limits prescribed for the TS by UNCLOS. Thus Nigeria and Togo each claim 30–mile TS. Since the nature and/or regulatory competences for states in the TS and the EEZ are not the same for pollution control, the effect of extending legislation beyond 12 miles for the TS is to assert in the EEZ certain regulatory competences not permitted under UNCLOS. For example, imprisonment for violations can only be imposed for infringement of standards in the TS and not the EEZ.[69] With regard to the 200–mile TS claimants, it can now be asserted that the 200–mile EEZ represents customary international law; so that even in the absence of binding treaty obligation imposed by UNCLOS, they are still obliged to conform to the 200–mile EEZ concept.[70]

Further, some of these states such as Ghana, Togo, Mauritania, Guinea, and Guinea-Bissau,[71] even though they have proclaimed EEZs, are bereft of any specific legislative competences to be exercised for pollution control in the zone apart from restating UNCLOS article 56 jurisdiction with regard to the protection and preservation of the marine environment, in spite of a positive obligation imposed by UNCLOS on all parties to enact specific legislation dealing with all sources of marine pollution.[72] This situation is rather unsatisfactory. In Ghana, for example, the only existing piece of legislation on marine pollution[73] is based on OILPOL 54 which has for almost two decades now been superseded by MARPOL 73/78. Even for states like Nigeria and Côte d'Ivoire that have specific enactments dealing with the subject, their provisions in certain respects offend the relevant provisions of UNCLOS.

As a reaction to the dumping of toxic wastes at its Western port of Koko, Nigeria enacted the Harmful Wastes Decree to deal with the subject. The Decree makes it an offense punishable by imprisonment for life if without lawful authority any person, *inter alia*, "carries, deposits, dumps or cause to be carried, deposited or dumped, or is in possession for the purpose of dumping any harmful waste on any land or in any territorial waters or contiguous zone or Exclusive Economic Zone of Nigeria or its inland waters," or "transports or causes to be transported or is in possession for the purpose of transporting any harmful waste."[74] The Decree cannot be faulted for prescribing imprisonment for life in respect of violations on land and the TS; but certainly not with respect to violations in the EEZ.[75] Furthermore, it is possible to envisage a situation where a maritime vessel transporting harmful wastes through Nigerian EEZ could be arrested, tried, and convicted for committing an offense under the Decree.[76] This is rather far-fetched and would run counter to UNCLOS provisions on freedom of navigation.[77] Another aspect of the Harmful Wastes Decree is its total disregard for the rules on diplomatic immunity: diplomatic agents caught for violating the law are subject to arrest, trial, and punishment-imprisonment for life.[78] As Gye Wado rightly points out, the anxiety in trying to deal with a deadly phenomenon can be appreciated, but this anxiety should not be explained in such a synthesis that disregards certain international obligations freely entered into.[79] This provision of the law ought therefore to be expunged from the statute. For, as noted, immunity granted under UNCLOS is in respect of arrests and prosecutions and not from liability. Recourse can thus be had through diplomatic channels, in the event of violations, for reparation in the event of infringement of the law by diplomatic agents. Similarly, the Ghanian legislation establishing the EEZ, inasmuch as it prescribes the punishment of imprisonment for violations in the zone, also offends international law.

On the subject of toxic wastes, it is noteworthy that the Lome IV Convention signed on December 15, 1989 between the EEC and the African, Caribbean, and Pacific (ACP) states (including all states of the West African subregion) integrates environmental protection into the cooperation agreement. Amongst other things, article 39(1) of Lome IV specifically requires the EEC to prohibit all direct or indirect exports of such wastes to ACP countries while the latter agree to prohibit the direct or indirect import into their territory of such waste from the Community or any other country.[80] Thus, Lome IV should help combat the toxic waste menace in the subregion and elsewhere.

Apart from substantive provisions, the residual powers asserted by some states in the subregion offend the relevant UNCLOS provisions on the subject. For example, La Côte d'Ivoire,[81] apart from asserting jurisdictional rights over resources along the lines prescribed by article 56[82] of UNCLOS also claims in its article 6 the "right to take any measures and to undertake any action to prevent, reduce or control pollution of the marine environment." With regard to pollution, it is MARPOL rules that govern the subject. Besides, only financial penalties may be imposed under UNCLOS for violations in the EEZ. Thus any attempt to assert jurisdiction in excess of that prescribed by UNCLOS would amount to a violation of international law. In this regard, it is worthwhile ascertaining to what extent states of the subregion have ratified the IMO rules which, as parties to UNCLOS, they are legally obliged to do.[83]

Of the 11 states, only Liberia is a party to all the generally accepted IMO Conventions on the subject.[84] As a flag of convenience state, the ratification by Liberia of those IMO Conventions is quite significant in that it enables other states to enforce standards on Liberian vessels through the port-state enforcement regime even though Liberia has not ratified UNCLOS. Of the remaining ten states, four—Côte d'Ivoire, Gambia, Ghana, and Togo have ratified MARPOL 73/78;[85] eight have ratified SOLAS 74;[86] ten have ratified LL 1966;[87] eight have ratified

COLREG 1972; six have ratified STCW 1978;[88] and only two states—Côte d'Ivoire and Nigeria—have ratified LDC 72. Apart from the ratification by states of these IMO standards, UNCLOS further enjoins state parties to enact same in their domestic legislation.[89] Ghana, for example, has not enacted any of these ratified IMO Conventions into domestic legislation. The issue is, however, very important because it is these IMO rules that are to be the basis of enforcement of pollution standards in the respective states under UNCLOS' port-state regime. Once the states of the West African subregion adopt domestic legislation in conformity with these prescribed IMO standards, there would be consistency and uniformity in their national legislation. This in turn would engender a much more efficient and effective regime of enforcement since, as in the European example,[90] it would be easier for states to cooperate on the matter. Reliance on international standards is highly desirable; it makes for simple and more efficient ship management to know exactly where a ship stands legally at any given time and situation thus removing uncertainty or confusion over local law.[91] The implementation of the port-state enforcement regime by states of the subregion must be viewed as a matter of great importance since each of the states on its own lacks the necessary technical and manpower requirements to police the vast expanses of their maritime zones. The idea of cooperation in the fight against pollution is not new to the states of the region; indeed prior to the conclusion of UNCLOS, there was an institutional medium established under the auspices of UNEP as part of one of its regional seas programmes to deal with the subject: the Action Plan for the Protection and Development of the Marine and Coastal Environment of the West and Central African region (WACAF).[92]

Regionalism, WACAF, and the Marine Pollution Problem

As observed,[93] article 197 of UNCLOS enjoins states to cooperate on a global and as appropriate on a regional basis in formulating and elaborating international rules, standards, practices, and procedures for the protection and preservation of the marine environment taking into account characteristic regional features. This is an endorsement of regional pollution control arrangements like WACAF which antedated the conclusion of UNCLOS. More significantly, by employing the mandatory "shall" on the subject in article 197,[94] UNCLOS imposes a positive obligation on states to cooperate on the subject. The effect of article 197 is that state parties to UNCLOS in the West African subregion are all legally obliged to be members of WACAF. This in fact is the case although not all the states have ratified the conventions concluded under WACAF.[95] WACAF is currently administered by UNEP's regional coordinating unit. Its objectives are to consolidate and expand pollution monitoring and control, promote national environmental legislation, increase ability to respond to pollution emergencies, promote integrated coastal zone management to prevent erosion, adopt protocols on hazardous waste and pollution, and expand public awareness.[96] Under WACAF,[97] a convention and a protocol have been concluded to deal with the marine pollution problem.[98] The Government of la Côte d'Ivoire has been designated as the depository for the Abidjan Convention and the protocol.[99] Currently seven of the states of the subregion have each ratified the Abidjan Convention and the protocol. The Abidjan Convention is a framework agreement for the protection and management of the marine and coastal areas of the state parties to the Convention. It identifies the sources of pollution from vessels; from land-based sources; from exploration and exploitation of the Sea; and from or through the atmosphere.[100] The Abidjan Convention, however, deals with these matters in general terms; and to that extent, state parties to WACAF would have to rely on the UNCLOS provisions on the subject. The Abidjan Convention also identifies environmental management issues for which cooperative efforts are to be made: coastal erosion, specially protected areas, combating pollution in cases of emergency; environmental impact assessment; scientific and technological cooperation; and liability and compensation.[101] The protocol addresses the issue of marine emergency[102] and the required emergency plans[103] and response[104] to deal with such emergencies. Under the protocol state parties are obliged to cooperate in all matters concerning the protection of their coastlines from marine emergencies. To this end, they are required to adopt laws, regulations, and cooperative measures on the subject.[105]

The Abidjan Convention also makes provision for the required institutional means for its implementation and that of the protocol. It designates UNEP as the Convention's secretariat and further provides for the appointment of national coordinators[106] with a regional coordinating unit to be established in Abidjan.

In the decade and more of its existence, WACAF has chalked some successes; for example, its training activities have produced scientists from national institutions who are actively participating in the monitoring of pollution in the marine environment of the subregion.[107] However, WACAF currently faces problems: the program is in serious financial crisis. Owing to the low level of national contributions, its financial resources are inadequate for any meaningful large-scale environmental action in the region; the rate of ratification of the Abidjan Convention is rather slow (only ten ratifications/accessions out of twenty-one states) with consequent limited national involvement in WACAF. As a result of WACAF's financial crisis, the establishment of the Regional Coordinating Unit in Abidjan has been delayed. This is rather unfortunate; for apart from the several advantages and benefits which regionalism offers in the fight against pollution,[108] the establishment of the coordinating unit in Abidjan would offer a boost to the implementation of the port-state enforcement regime by providing a focal point for coordinating in the subregion. Indeed, article 197 of UNCLOS on regional cooperation was formulated with regional institutions like WACAF in mind. Hence, UNCLOS and WACAF should become joint partners in marine environmental protection in the subregion. Support from the international community would thus be worthwhile; and would underscore the global nature of the marine pollution problem. Above all, however, WACAF's success to a large extent also depends on the state parties themselves. They have to devote more attention and resources to the problem of marine pollution which WACAF seeks to address; and which is a problem with several dimensions. For instance, WACAF states have recently concluded a convention on fisheries cooperation[109] which addresses environmental protection concerns;[110] thus confirming the widely unacknowledged view that the idea of integrating environmental protection and economic development holds the key to development in the region.

Concluding Remarks

1. UNCLOS provides for a 12–mile TS and 200–mile EEZ. The former is a zone of absolute sovereignty for coastal states subject only to the regime of innocent passage whilst the EEZ is a functional zone of jurisdictional competence that allows a two-fold utilization of the seas: it grants coastal states sovereign rights to the resources therein whilst allowing all other states to exercise the traditional high seas freedoms like navigation and overflight with the exception of fisheries. Hence, the competences that may be exercised by coastal states in the TS are not the same as those in the EEZ: coastal states may impose the punishment of imprisonment for violations in cases of wilful and serious pollution in the TS but may only impose monetary penalties in the case of

violations in the EEZ. Thus states parties to UNCLOS in the West African subregion will have to amend their legislation in conformity with UNCLOS' prescribed 12– and 200–mile limits respectively, for the TS and the EEZ. Even for the few nonstate parties the preponderant state practice on the subject has led to the establishment of a customary rule on the subject; thus requiring a similar compliance like state parties to the subject.

2. UNCLOS prescribes the IMO standards as the basis for standard-setting in pollution control. States of the subregion thus have to follow the Liberian example and ratify these conventions since the IMO standards are now the norms or benchmarks by which the validity of any national pollution enforcement standard may be assessed. Indeed, UNCLOS imposes a positive obligation on state parties to enact these IMO rules into national legislation.

3. UNCLOS provides for an effective tripartite scheme of flag, coastal, and port-state enforcement. The port-state enforcement regime in particular, is a welcome inroad into the enforcement system for states in the subregion which lack the requisite technical and manpower requirements to police their individual maritime zones. The successful implementation of the scheme calls for, *inter alia*, harmonization of national legislation by states of the subregion in line with the relevant UNCLOS texts on the subject.

4. UNCLOS endorses regionalism as a means of dealing with the marine pollution problem. Thus by becoming parties to UNCLOS, states of the subregion assume further obligations to cooperate to achieve the objectives of WACAF. They should thus systematically work towards the elimination of the problems currently facing WACAF which, together with UNCLOS, are inseparable links in the protection and preservation of the marine environment. In this regard financial, technical, and other support from developed states would be worthwhile: marine pollution is a problem of global dimensions and virtually all states contribute to it. Above all, the integration of environmental concerns into development programs holds the key to the subregion's rapid socioeconomic development. UNCLOS provides an effective mechanism for dealing with the marine pollution problem. By ratifying UNCLOS, states of the subregion accept a positive obligation to protect and preserve the environment. They should strive to achieve this; and WACAF offers a good institutional base for the attainment of this objective.

Notes

1. Pollution of the Marine Environment is defined under the United Nations Convention on the Law of the Sea (hereafter UNCLOS) rep. in 21 International Legal Materials (I.L.M.) art. 1(4) as "the introduction by man, directly or indirectly, of substances or energy into the marine environment including estuaries, which results or is likely to result in such deleterious effects as harm to living resources and marine life, hazards to human health, hindrance to marine activities, including fishing and other legitimate uses of the sea, impairment of quality for use of sea water and reduction of amenities."

2. Oscar Schachter and Daniel Sewer, "Marine Pollution, Problems and Remedies," 65 A.I.I.L. 84 (1971); Erick P. Eckholm, *Down to Earth* 79 (New York, 1982).

3. See M'Gonigle and Zacher, *Pollution, Politics and International Law* chap. 2 (Berkeley, 1979); The Sea: Prevention and Control of Marine Pollution, U.N. Doc. E/5003 May 1, 1971 para. 45; D.W. Abecassis, *The Law and Practice Relating to Oil Pollution from Ships* 133 (London, 1978); *Pollution: An International Problem for Fisheries* (FAO Rome, 1971).

4. Reference to states of the West African subregion denotes state parties to the treaty of Economic Community of West African States (ECOWAS) namely Benin, Burkina Faso, Cape Verde, Côte d'Ivoire, Gambia, Ghana, Guinea, Guinea Bissau, Liberia, Mali, Mauritania, Niger, Nigeria, Senegal, Sierra Leone, and Togo. Burkina Faso, Mali, and Niger are landlocked states. Emphasis is on the coastal states of the region.

5. See UNCLOS, n. 1. *supra* arts 3; 55; 136 and 192–237.

6. The only two exceptions are Liberia and Benin. On state parties and dates of ratification of UNCLOS in the subregion, see Barbara Kwiatkowska, *Ocean Affairs and the Law of the Sea in Africa: Towards the 21st Century.* Inaugural lecture delivered on the occasion of her appointment as Professor of the International Law of the Sea, October 14, 1992 (Martinus Nijhoff, 1992) (hereafter inaugural lectures).

7. These issues are fully discussed in part 11 of this article, p. 21 below.

8. UNCLOS *supra* art. 192.

9. Arts. 192–194.

10. See arts. 207–212. These, however, are not mutually exclusive. Vessels for example, are employed as means for dumping.

11. Art. 194 provides that the measures to be adopted shall include those designed to minimize to the fullest possible extent the release of toxic, harmful, or noxious substances, especially those which are persistent, from land-based sources, from or through the atmosphere or by dumping; pollution from vessels, in particular measures for preventing accidents and dealing with emergencies, ensuring the safety of operations at sea,

preventing intentional and unintentional discharges, and regulating the design, construction, equipment, operation, and manning of vessels; pollution from installations and devices used in exploration or exploitation of the natural resources of the sea-bed and subsoil, in particular measures for preventing accidents and dealing with emergencies, ensuring the safety of operations at sea, and regulating the design, construction, equipment, operation and manning of such installations or devices, pollution from other installations and devices operating in the marine environment, in particular measures for preventing accidents and dealing with emergencies, ensuring the safety of operations at sea, and regulating the design, construction, equipment, operation, and manning of such installations or devices. In taking measures to prevent, reduce, or control pollution of the marine environment, States shall refrain from unjustifiable interference with activities carried out by other States in the exercise of their rights and in pursuance of their duties in conformity with UNCLOS. Furthermore, the measures taken shall include those necessary to protect and preserve rare or fragile ecosystems as well as the habitat of depleted, threatened, or endangered species and other forms of marine life.

12. Art. 197. The measures to be adopted include notification to the States concerned of accidents of imminent or actual damage to the marine environment and the development and promotion of contingency plans for responding to pollution incidents in the marine environment; as well as studies, research programs and exchange of information and data on the subject: see arts. 198–201. The subject of regionalism and marine control in the West African subregion is discussed in part IV of this article.

13. See arts. 202, 203.

14. Enforcement is discussed separately below.

15. Art. 21(f).

16. See art. 19(2)(h).

17. Art. 21(2).

18. See art. 230.

19. *Id.* Art. 56(1)(b) grants coastal state jurisdiction with regard to the protection and preservation of the marine environment.

20. See arts. 207(4); 210(4); 211(5); 212(3).

21. "Vessel source pollution" denotes pollution mainly arising out of operational and accidental discharges from ships. A ship is any sea-going vessel of any type whatsoever and any floating craft, but does not include an installation or device engaged in the exploration and exploitation of the resources of the sea-bed and the ocean floor and the sub-soil thereof. See art. 11(2), Int'l Convention relating to intervention on the High Seas in cases of Oil Pollution Casualties, 1969 (Intervention 69), 9, I.L.M., 25 (1970); of art. 2(4), Int'l Convention for the Prevention of Pollution from Ships 1973 (MARPOL 73/78) as amended, 12 I.L.M., 13 19 (1973). For

an excellent treatment of the subject see M'Gonigle and Zacher, *Pollution, Politics and International Law*, *op. cit.* n. 3 esp. parts 1 and 2.

22. Art. 211 6(a) on the subject provides:

(a) Where the international rules and standards referred to in paragraph 1 are inadequate to meet special circumstances and coastal States have reasonable grounds for believing that a particular, clearly defined area of their respective exclusive economic zones is an area where the adoption of special mandatory measures for the prevention of pollution from vessels is required for recognised technical reasons in relation to its oceanographical and ecological conditions, as well as its utilisation or the protection of its resources and the particular character of its traffic, the coastal States, after appropriate consultations through the competent international organisation with any other States concerned, may, for that area, direct a communication to that organisation, submitting scientific and technical evidence in support and information on necessary reception facilities. Within 12 months after receiving such a communication, the organisation shall determine whether the conditions in that area correspond to the requirements set out above. If the organisation so determines, the coastal States may, for that area, adopt laws and regulations for the prevention, reduction and control of pollution from vessels implementing such international rules and standards or navigational practices as are made applicable, through the organisation, for special areas. These laws and regulations shall not become applicable to foreign vessels until 15 months after the submission of the communication to the organisation.

(b) The coastal States shall publish the limits of any such particular, clearly defined area.

(c) If the coastal States intend to adopt additional laws and regulations for the same area for the prevention, reduction and control of pollution from vessels, they shall, when submitting the aforesaid communication, at the same time notify the organisation thereof. Such additional laws and regulations may relate to discharges or navigational practices but shall not require foreign vessels to observe design, construction, manning or equipment standards other than generally accepted international rules and standards; they shall become applicable to foreign vessels 15 months after the submission of the communication to the organisation, provided that the organisation agrees within 12 months after the submission of the communication.

The international rules and standards referred to in this article should include *inter alia* those relating to prompt notification to coastal States, whose coastline or related interests may be affected by incidents, including maritime casualties, which involve discharges or probability of discharges.

23. W. van Reenen, "Rules of Reference in the new Convention on the Law of the Sea, in particular in connection with the Pollution of the Sea by Oil from Tankers, 12 Neth. Yr. Bk. Int'l L.21 (1981).

24. See for example J.D. Kingham and D.M. McCrae, "Competent International Organisations and the Law of the Sea," 3 Marine Policy 106 (1979); R.R. Churchill, "The Role of IMCO in Combating Marine Pollution," in Douglas (et. al eds.), *The Impact of Maritime Pollution* 73 (London, 1980); Mario Valenzuela, "International Maritime Transportation: Selected Issues of the Law of the Sea," 23 L. Sea Inst. Proc. 197 (1990); Louis B. Sohn, "Implications of the Law of the Sea Convention Regarding the Protection and Preservation of the Maritime Environment," 18 L. Sea Inst. Proc. 103 (1984).

25. Rep. in *New Directions in the Law of the Sea* (Documents) Vol. 11, (hereafter "New Directions") 557. OILPOL 54 completely banned operational discharges of oil from ships except where the total discharge on a ballast voyage did not exceed 60 litres per mile travelled by the ship. OILPOL 54 also prohibited discharge of oil from cargo spaces of tanks within 50 miles of the nearest land: and introduced a new form of oil record book designed to show the movement of cargo oil and its residue from loading to discharging, on a tank-to-tank basis. Finally, for other ships, OILPOL 54 placed a limit on rate of discharge at not more than 60 litres per mile being travelled by the ship. With regard to the oil content of any bilge water discharged from ships, it was not to be less than 100 parts per million. The 1971 amendments to OILPOL 54 provided greater protection to the Great Barrier Reef of Australia and also limited the size of tanks on oil tankers, thereby minimizing the amount of oil that could escape in the event of an accident. See L.J.H. Legault, "Freedom of the Seas: A Licence to Pollute?" 21 U. of T.L.J. 211 (1971).

26. The oil pollution regulations apply to all tanks and ships of 150 and 400 gross tons and above respectively. MARPOL 73/78 imposes an absolute prohibition on oil discharge in special areas. The Convention also requires state parties to provide adequate facilities for the reception of oily mixtures in places like loading terminals and ports. In addition, it provides that oil tankers must be equipped with facilities like slop tanks, oily water separating equipment, or filtering systems for the discharge of machinery, space bilges, and oil monitoring devices. The latter helps detect the amount of oil discharged by vessels upon inspection. MARPOL 73/78 also retains the limitations on tank size imposed by the 1971 amendment to OILPOL 54. Furthermore, it requires new oil tankers of 20,000 tons dead weight and above to be provided with segregated ballast tanks (SBTS) of sufficient capacity to enable them to operate on ballast voyages without using cargo tanks for ballast purposes; and since SBTS

are not used for carrying oil, there are no oily mixtures and hence no pollution. Provision is also made for crude oil washing (COW) as an alternative requirement in SBTS on existing tankers, and is an additional requirement for new tankers. Under COW, tanks are washed with crude oil and not with water. The crude oil's solvent action makes cleaning process far more effective than when water is used. Besides, there is no mixture of the oil and water that caused so much operational pollution in the past. The system, however, poses operational dangers because of the attendant build-up of explosive gases in cargo tanks. It is for this reason that the SOLAS 74 protocol prescribes the use of inert gas systems on such vessels.

To ensure that tankers in the event of accidents survive bottom damage, MARPOL 73/78 has introduced new subdivision and stability requirements based on ships lengths. There is the requirement for an initial survey before a ship is put into service or before an IOPCC is issued, as well as periodical surveys of vessels at intervals not exceeding five years.

The application of MARPOL 73/78's technical requirements to "new tankers" has meant that most vessels ordered since December 1975 have incorporated the requirements of MARPOL 73/78: IMO News 4 (1982); IMO News 7 (1983).

27. On MARPOL 73/78 and other IMO Conventions on the subject and their status, see *"Status of Multilateral Conventions and Instruments in respect of which the International Maritime Organisation or its Secretary-General performs depositary or other functions"* as at December 31, 1991, IMO Doc. U2735/Rev. 6; (hereafter "Status Document"); Marlo Valenzuela, *supra* n. 25.

28. See "Status Documents" *supra* pp. 73–122; 143–175; 9–34 and 361–374 for MARPOL 73/78; LL 66; SOLAS 74 and STCW 78 respectively.

29. Status Documents *ibid* at 416. Art. 5(a) of the Convention defines "Dumping as any deliberate disposal of wastes or other matter from vessels, aircraft platforms or other man-made structures at Sea; The definition does not cover discharges from vessels. However, in as much as vessels as carriers are employed in dumping, the enforcement measures discussed in this article although centering around vessel source pollution include dumping as well."

30. See L.B. Sohn; Mario Valenzuela, *supra* n. 25 at 109; 195 respectively.

31. As emphasised by the I.C.J. in the North Sea Continental Shelf Cases (Fed. Rep. of Germany-Denmark; Fed. Rep. of Germany-Netherlands) (1969) I.C.J. Rep. 4, a Convention is in force for any individual state only insofar as having signed it within the time limit provided for that purpose that State has subsequently ratified it; or not having signed within that time limit, has subsequently acceded to the Convention.

32. L.D. Guruswamy, "Environmental Protection and the United Nations Convention on the Law of the Sea," 4 Lloyd Mar. Comm. L.Q. 705 (1983).

UNCLOS' provisions on the protection and preservation of the marine environment were concluded as part of the package deal in the Third Committee in May 1978. Indeed, the provisions were the first concluded item on the agenda of UNCLOS III negotiations.

In these negotiations, an earnest effort was made to keep a viable balance between ecological considerations and the legitimate demands of international navigation; between national legislation and enforcement measures on the one hand and international rules standards and regulations on the other; between coastal and flag state jurisdiction; and between the interests of developed maritime powers and developing states.

That the marine environmental provisions were the first to be concluded is due partly to the fact that marine environmental issues had been the subject of discussion in previous international forums such as the IMO and Stockholm Conferences. Thus, compared to issues like seabed mining, it was not new to delegates, many of whom had participated in these international conferences. With regard to vessel source pollution, there already existed technical rules on the matter. What was required was the necessary jurisdictional framework to allow the technical expertise of the IMO to be brought to bear on these measures. Even on the question of jurisdiction, issues such as port state enforcement and enhanced coastal-state competence outside the territorial seas had been the subject of intense discussion in previous conferences. The consensus and compromise approach to the negotiations also facilitated proceedings; and port-state enforcement emerged as the main basis of this enforcement. See Committee III Chairman's Report, UNCLOS off. Rec. vol. X, 99.

33. In the general context of marine pollution, enforcement denotes the process by which legislative or other acts aimed at combating pollution are made effective or the process designed to compel obedience to such rules. Enforcement may be either *lato sensu* or *stricto sensu*. *Lato sensu* enforcement covers measures for the application of anti-pollution rules including the punishment of violations, intervention on the high seas in the event of accidents, cleaning up operations, and the establishment of physical conditions for the application of the rules. On the other hand enforcement *stricto sensu* refers to the punishment for violations of the rules. The Convention's provision on enforcement which deals mainly with vessel source pollution are concerned with *stricto sensu* enforcement.

There are, however, two exceptions; namely flag-state enforcement and intervention on the high seas in case of emergency.

Enforcement *stricto sensu* is a continuous and inseparable process and entails in practice, the following stages: the reporting or the discovery of the violation which involves measures such as inspection and surveillance; the investigation involving the collection of all evidence and material surrounding the violation; the judgment which involves the evaluation of such evidence and the determination of sanctions and finally, the process of giving effect to the sanction determined (enforcement of the judgment). A related process is the obtaining of security in advance for the purpose of facilitating the enforcement of the judgment. Security is usually obtained by the arrest of the ship or its subsequent release upon depositing adequate bond. Arrests or detentions in some cases also serve investigation purposes: Timagenis, *International Control of Marine Pollution* (Dobbs Ferry, N.Y., 1980) at 57, 58, 615.

34. In the era of small populations and limited technologies, problems of congestion or over-exploitation rarely occurred. The principal ocean activities of fishing and navigation could be pursued with little concern for the impact on other interests. The legal regime that periodically prevailed under these conditions came to be known as freedom of the seas. One of the foremost exponents of the rule was Hugo Grotius. In his *Mare Liberium*, he wrote: "The sea is common to all because it is so limitless that it cannot become a possession of anyone, and because it is adapted for the use of all, whether we consider it from the point of view of navigation or fisheries. . . . Therefore, the sea can in no way become the private property of anyone, because nature not only allows, but enjoins its common use."

The principle of the freedom of the seas was, however, not without an initial opposition. There were those who adhered to the doctrine of *mare clausum* or the closed seas which was the opposite of the Grotian view. Indeed, Anaud describes the history of the Law of the Sea as the story of the vicissitudes through which the doctrine for and against the freedom of the seas has gone through the ages.

It was freedom of the seas that eventually won the day. This was confirmed by the Geneva Convention on the High Seas: "The high seas being open to all nations, no state may validly purport to subject any part of them to its sovereignty. Freedom of the high seas . . . comprises *inter alia*, both for coastal and non-coastal states: 1) Freedom of navigation, 2) Freedom of fishing, 3) Freedom to lay submarine cables and pipelines, 4) Freedom to fly over the high seas. . . ."

The freedom of the high seas are, however, made subject to the consideration that they shall be exercised by all states with reasonable regard to the interests of other states. Freedom of the seas does not, therefore, mean the high seas are a lawless area of vacuum. The "reasonable regard" clause requires the maintenance of juridical order on the seas as states engage in various activities on the seas; and flag-state competence developed as a corollary of the freedom of the seas: See Ann L. Hollick, *U.S. Foreign Policy and the Law of the Sea* 4 (Princeton, N.J., 1981); James Brown Scott (ed.), *The Freedom of the Seas (Mare*

Liberium): A Dissertation by Hugo Grotius (Washington, D.C., 1962); John Selden, *Of the Dominion or Ownership of the Sea* (Leonard Silk ed.) (New York, 1972); R.P. Anaud, *Origin and Development of the Law of the Sea* (The Hague, 1982); Geneva Convention on the High Seas 1958, "New Directions" vol. I, 257; B.A. Boczek *Flags of Convenience* 92 (Harvard, 1962).

35.	Marine pollution prior to UNCLOS had been dealt with on treaty basis by way of OILPOL 54. This was aimed primarily at pollution resulting from routine tanker operations which at the time was the greatest cause of pollution from ships. In time with the prevailing doctrine of the freedom of the seas, OILPOL 54's enforcement: inspections, investigations, and prosecutions for violations on the high seas was left to the flag-state. Coastal-state enforcement was limited to violations occurring in the internal waters and territorial seas. For its enforcement, OILPOL 54 had serious limitations. Detection of oil discharges was difficult and could be achieved only at the expense of visual surveillance which in itself was difficult in view of the vast amount of areas to be policed and the rapidity with which oil slicks break up into smaller particles. Furthermore, since prosecution of offenses beyond the territorial seas was the exclusive competence of flag-states, in the event that they were disinclined to prosecute, such vessels could effectively escape control. This was the case in many instances; for almost invariably, the pollution did not affect the flag-state's territory, but that of some other coastal-state. Besides, all states encountered difficulties in getting the necessary evidence to prosecute. OILPOL 54's enforcement record was thus very poor. Many flag-states refused to prescribe penalties against their offending vessels as provided under the Convention. For example, in a ten-year period ending 1977, of the eighty violations what were recorded by Canadian authorities and reported to the offending vessel's flag-states, almost half of the violations received no comment at all, and in only slightly over twenty percent of the reported violations did convictions result. Similarly, of the seven reported violations referred to flag-states from 1969 to 1972 by the United States authorities, only two violators received penalties. A United Kingdom (U.K.) delegate at UNCLOS III also disclosed, in the Third Committee, that the U.K. authorities had found it difficult to obtain sufficient evidence for successful prosecutions. Over the previous five reporting years it had been possible to link with particular vessels 203 of the 900 spillages occurring off U.K. Coasts, but there had been only eighteen successful prosecutions: See Ted L. McDorman (et al.) *The Marine Environment and the Caracas Convention on the Law of the Sea.* 16 (Halifax; 1981); Richard A. Legatsi *"Port State Jurisdiction over Vessel Source Marine Pollution,"* Harv. Envt'l L. Rev. 449 (1977); statement by Sir Roger Jackling (U.K.) UNCLOS off. Recs., vol. IV at 8.

36. The term refers to the registration and operation under flags of States like Cyprus, Liberia, Panama, and Honduras, of vessels that are beneficially owned and controlled by nations of other states, are manned usually by foreign crews, and hardly ever put in at their ports of registry. The registration is done under conditions convenient and opportune to persons registering these vessels, in particular, lower operating costs: comparatively lower wages are paid to the seamen on these ships, and the laws regarding labor regulations, crew composition, and manning can be avoided. Registration in the convenience states also provides other advantages, such as low tax liability, secrecy, and greater mortgage security.

The growth in the number of flags of convenience vessels, in particular in the period after World War II, has thus been largely owing to the specific competitive advantage which these vessels possessed over others. The ship owners of certain European states, like Greece, also resorted to registration in convenience states for fear of nationalization.

The features of the flags of convenience posed two problems: firstly, the danger of unfair competition resulting from their special economic advantages, and secondly, the threat to the maritime community as a whole in view of their inadequate standards and ineffective enforcement. In the present study, concern is focused on the latter with its associated dangers of maritime pollution.

On flags of convenience see Boczek, *op. cit.* n. 36; "OECD Study on Flags of Convenience," 4, J. Mar. L. Comm. 231 (1973); Sally A. Meese, "When Jurisdictional Interests Collide: International, Domestic, and State Efforts to Prevent Vessel-source Oil Pollution," O.D.I.L. 71 (1982); Ebere Osieke "Flags of Convenience Vessels: Recent Developments," 73 A.J.I.L., 604 (1979); L.L. Herman, "Flags of Convenience-New Dimensions to an Old Problem," 24 McGill L.J. 1 (1978); A.H.E. Popp, "Recent Developments in Tanker Control in International Law," 18 Can. Yr. Bk. Int'l 3 (1980).

37. Land-based pollution, originating as it does from land, is an area where the notion of national sovereignty is particularly strong. States are not willing to accept international limitations on issues of vital interest that might result in a slowing down of their development. Pollution control from land-based sources has thus largely been a subject of national competence. There is, however, a trend towards regionalization on the matter. Different considerations apply to vessels. Being movables, the harm from them may affect their states more directly. Further, although subject to flag-state competence, vessels may be often found in other coastal areas subject to other states' jurisdiction. Vessel-source pollution thus has peculiar jurisdictional implications. Besides, vessel accidents and in particular those from tankers resulting in large spills, often have dramatic and devastating consequences, and they are certainly spectacular

media events. International action has thus been focused largely on the control of vessel-source pollution through the IMO: See M.W. Holdgate (*et al* eds.) UNEP Report *The World Environment, 1972-1982* 105 (Dublin, 1982); Gr. T. Timagenis, *Marine Pollution and the Third United Nations Conference on the Law of the Sea: The Emerging Regime of Marine Pollution* 5 (London, 1977).

38. See statement by Sir Roger Jackling (U.K.) Off. Recs. vol. IV *supra* n. 37.

39. J.P.A. Bernhardt, "A Schematic Analysis of Vessel Source Pollution: Prescriptive and Enforcement Regimes in the Law of the Sea Conference," 20 Va. J.Int'l. L. 265 (1979) at 298.

40. UNCLOS *supra*, art. 217 (8).

41. This is a feature of international law which, among other things, has no police force to ensure compliance with its rules but defers to states to ensure such compliance. In this regard, article 300 of UNCLOS requires states to fulfil in good faith the obligations under the Convention and to exercise the rights, jurisdiction, and freedoms recognized in it in a manner that would not constitute an abuse of rights. This is a codification of the *pacta sunt servanda* rule.

Provision of sanctions for noncompliance with conventional obligations is likely to be frowned upon by states as inconsistent with their sovereignty. This does not mean that without this states will not comply with the rules provided by the Convention. For, as Henkin has stated: violations of law attract attention and the occasional important violation is dramatic; the daily, sober loyalty of nations to the law and their obligations is hardly noted. It is probably the case that almost all nations observe almost all principles of international law and almost all of their obligations almost all of the time.

Despite the lack of sanctions, there are other equally compelling reasons for state observance of the rules of international law: that international law will be generally observed is an assumption built into international relations. Nations have a common interest in keeping the society running and keeping international relations orderly. . . . Every nation's foreign policy depends substantially on its "credit," maintaining the expectation that it will live up to international mores and obligations. Governments do not like to be accused or criticized. They know that violations will bring protest, will require reply, explanations, etc.; and may be brought before the U.N. Few Governments would face that prospect with equanimity: see, Louis Henkin, *How Nations Behave* 31–39 (N.Y., 1968).

42. UNCLOS is not yet in force. It enters into force twelve months after the 60th ratification. As of December 31, 1991, 51 states had ratified UNCLOS: see E. Riddell-Dixon, "The Preparatory Commission on the International Sea-bed Authority: New Realism," *Int'l. Journ. of Estuarine*

and Coastal Law (vol. 7 no. 3) 197. The environmental preservation component of UNCLOS however is widely acknowledged as constituting customary international law.

43. Most of the vessels registered under the Liberian flag seldom call at its ports. Liberia has, therefore, instituted a system of vessel inspection abroad. It has set up a Marine Division made up of inspectors and qualified surveyors and requires its vessels to undergo a periodic inspection once a year. For convenience, owners or masters may request their annual inspection at a port convenient for the ship's purpose. The inspector's report could result in an investigation and eventual prosecution for an offense or a revocation of license. Liberia has also updated its procedures in respect of inquiries in connection with vessel accidents. These usually turn up navigational and other offenses and thus help to ensure that standards are maintained in the future. These developments in Liberia are quite significant since about 21.3 percent of the recorded 28.9 percent of the registered world shipping tonnage sailing under flags of convenience are registered in Liberia: David W. Abecassis, *The Law and Practice Relating to Oil Pollution from Ships* 56 (London, 1978); UNEP Report, *op. cit.*; This article however does not take into account the effects, if any, of the recent events in Liberia on the subject.

44. See Mario Valenzuela; status documents, *supra* n. 25 and 29, respectively.

45. For purposes of enforcement, a "port state" is a state in which a vessel which has violated a relevant rule in a sea area not under the jurisdiction of such state enters port. The term "Coastal State" is used when the violation takes place in a sea area which falls under the jurisdiction of this state regardless of whether or not the vessel violating the rules enters port. "Flag-state" is the state of registry of a vessel. See W. van Reenen, *supra* n. 24.

46. The Convention on conditions for registration of ships (CCRS 86); 26 I.L.M. 1236 (1986) C.C.R.S. 86 provides standards of responsibility and accountability for the world's shipping industry and attempts to harmonize state action concerning the registration of ships. It provides, *inter alia*, that flag states shall implement the applicable international rules and standards concerning the safety of ships and persons on board and the prevention of pollution of the marine environment. CCRS 86 further enjoins flag states to ensure the compliance of these rules by the vessels flying their flags.

47. UNCLOS, *supra*, art. 218.

48. Such as the International Oil Pollution Prevention Certificate (IOPPC) under MARPOL 73/78, the Cargo Ship Safety Construction Certificate (CSSCC), and Cargo Ship Safety Equipment Certificate (CSSEC) under SOLAS 74, as amended. These certificates are issued by Classification Societies. To ensure the bona fides of these, MARPOL 73/78 requires state parties to furnish the IMO with the details of Classification Societies

which they authorize to issue these documents to their vessels. See
UNCLOS art. 226; M'Gonigle and Zacher *op. cit.* n. 3.

49. UNCLOS, *supra* art. 226.

50. Bernhardt, *supra* n. 41 at 266.

51. Legatsi, *supra* n. 37 at 467.

52. Indeed, the Helsinki Convention and Bonn agreement dealing with marine
     pollution by oil on a regional basis in Europe have adopted port-state
     enforcement.

     The Helsinki Convention is a formal and comprehensive inter-
     governmental arrangement on marine pollution, including both East and
     West European states. For vessel source pollution, the Convention follows
     MARPOL 73/78 and the relevant IMO recommendations on the subject.
     These have been adopted and largely implemented especially by the
     Scandinavian countries.

     Under the Bonn Agreement, states bordering the North Sea are
     responsible for surveillance, reporting, and combating of oil spills on the
     basis of geographical zones of responsibility, and for providing mutual
     assistance when required. To strengthen this Agreement, the parties
     decided to turn it into an instrument for a regional "port state"
     enforcement system for vessel-source pollution as envisaged in the
     MARPOL Convention of 1973/78 and UNCLOS. The Paris Memorandum
     of Understanding on Port State Control was concluded in July 1982.
     During the first year of operation, a total of 8839 vessels from 108
     different states were inspected by authorities in the 14 states which signed
     the Memorandum. These arrangements are as a result of the Stockholm
     Conference on the Environment and the deliberations at UNCLOS III.
     The agreements include the Bonn Agreement for Cooperation in Dealing
     with the Pollution of the North Sea by Oil (Bonn Agreement), the Oslo
     Convention for the Prevention of Pollution by Dumping from Ship and
     Aircraft (Oslo Convention), the Paris Convention for the Prevention of
     Marine Pollution from Landbased Sources (Paris Convention), and the
     Helsinki Convention on the Protection of the Marine Environment of the
     Baltic Sea Area (Helsinki Convention): Sonia Boehmer-Christiansen,
     "Marine Pollution Control in Europe: Regional Approaches, 1972–80," 8
     Marine Policy 44 (1984).

53. It is estimated that 96 percent of vessel traffic in U.S. waters call at U.S.
     ports. Similarly majority of vessels navigating through Canadian waters
     end up in Canadian ports: Meese *supra* n. 38; M'Gonigle & Zacher *op.
     cit.* n. 3 at 234.

54. *Id.*

55. UNCLOS attempts to give content to the meaning of innocent passage by
     providing a list of activities that are considered prejudicial to the peace,
     good order, or security of a coastal state. These include "any act of wilful
     and serious pollution (art. 19(h))." This provision is said to be

unsatisfactory as it detracts from the pre-existing customary international rules on the matter; for irrespective of the polluter's state of mind, pollution alone may constitute a sufficient threat to coastal states' vital interests to demand the retention of the state's unfettered legal authority to protect those interests. The view has thus been expressed that such a measure may not endure time and state practice and will only contribute to an eventual erosion of respect for the Convention: Brian Smith "Innocent Passage as a Rule of Decision, Navigation v. Environmental Protection," 21 *Col. J. Transnational L.* 49 (1982).

56. UNCLOS, *supra* art. 220(5).
57. UNCLOS, *supra* arts. 211, 234. 58. Art. 216 provides:
     1. Laws and regulations adopted in accordance with this Convention and applicable international rules and standards established through competent international organisations or diplomatic conference for the prevention, reduction and control of pollution of the marine environment by dumping shall be enforced:
     (a) by the coastal State with regard to dumping within its territorial sea or its exclusive economic zone or onto its continental shelf;
     (b) by the flag State with regard to vessels flying its flag or vessels or aircraft of its registry;
     (c) by any State with regard to acts of loading of wastes or other matter occurring within its territory or at its off-shore terminals.
     2. No State shall be obliged by virtue of this article to institute proceedings when another State has already instituted proceedings in accordance with this article.
59. UNCLOS, *supra*, s.7 (arts. 223–233).
60. Art. 228. It provides:
     1. Proceedings to impose penalties in respect of any violation of applicable laws and regulations or international rules and standards relating to the prevention, reduction and control of pollution from vessels committed by a foreign vessel beyond the territorial sea of the State instituting proceedings shall be suspended upon the taking of proceedings to impose penalties in respect of corresponding charges by the flag State within six months of the date on which proceedings were first instituted, unless those proceedings relate to a case of major damage to the coastal State or the flag State in question has repeatedly disregarded its obligation to enforce effectively the applicable international rules and standards in respect of violations committed by its vessels. The flag State shall in due course make available to the State previously instituting proceedings a full dossier of the case and the records of the proceedings, whenever the flag State has requested the suspension of proceedings in accordance with this article. When proceedings instituted by the flag State have been brought to a conclusion, the suspended

proceedings shall be terminated. Upon payment of costs incurred in respect of such proceedings, any bond posted or other financial security provided in connection with the suspended proceedings shall be released by the coastal State.

2.   Proceedings to impose penalties on foreign vessels shall not be instituted after the expiry of three years from the date on which the violation was committed, and shall not be taken by any State in the event of proceedings having been instituted by another State subject to the provisions set out in paragraph 1.

3.   The provisions of this article are without prejudice to the right of the flag State to take any measures, including proceedings to impose penalties, according to its laws irrespective of prior proceedings by another State.

61.   Timagenis *op. cit.* n. 35 at 622.

62.   Article 236 reads:

The provisions of this Convention regarding the protection and preservation of the marine environment do not apply to any warship, naval auxiliary, other vessels or aircraft *owned or operated by a State and used, for the time being, only on government non-commercial service.* However, each State shall ensure, by the adoption of appropriate measures not impairing operations or operational capabilities of such vessels or aircraft owned or operated by it, that such vessels or aircraft act in a manner consistent so far as is reasonable and practicable, with this Convention (emphasis added).

63.   For a long time, absolute immunity remained the rule. However, with states' entry into commercial or other private law transactions there developed a theory of restrictive immunity that distinguishes between acts *jure imperii* and acts *jure gestionis* recognizing immunity in the former, and denying it in the latter. With regard to vessels, a related problem is the identification of such vessels. As to warships, naval, or auxiliary vessels, there is not likely to be a problem. For, usually such vessels have identification marks. The problem is, however, determining vessels owned or operated by a state and used only on government noncommercial service within the meaning of article 236. Stated differently, the problem is how to draw a distinction between acts *jure imperii* and acts *jure gestionis*. For as Lauterpacht concludes from a study of the subject, in a real sense all acts *jure gestionis* are acts *jure imperii*—in modern conditions, the distinction between acts *jure gestionis* and acts *jure imperii* cannot be placed on a sound logical basis: see Lauterpacht, "The problem of jurisdictional immunity of foreign states," 28 B.Y.B.I.L. 220 (1951) at 224. The problem is further compounded by state legislation on the matter that fails to provide satisfactory definitions as to what constitutes commercial activity. This is, however, important, for if the plea of immunity is accepted anytime it is raised, the restrictive theory

would cease to have any content and trading relations as to state-owned ships would become impossible. Legislatures have thus shifted the determination of the issue to the courts. An attempt has been made by the English House of Lords to provide guidelines on the matter. In the *Congreso case*, [1981] 2 ALL E.R. 1064 at 1074 the court said (per Lord Wilberforce) that faced with such a situation it has to characterize the activity into which the defendant state has entered. It should then be for the defendant state to make a case that the act complained of is outside that sphere and within that of sovereign action. In so doing, the existence of a governmental purpose or motive will not convert what would otherwise be an act *jure gestionis* or an act of private law into one done *jure imperii*.

64. See UNCLOS, *supra* arts. 194, 195.

65. *Id.* art. 236.

66. In this article emphasis is on the eleven coastal states of the region namely Benin, Côte d'Ivoire, Gambia, Ghana, Guinea, Guinea Bissau, Liberia, Mauritania, Nigeria, Sierra Leone, and Togo. On those states and their maritime legislation see Barbara Kwiatkowska, "Inaugural lecture," *supra* n. 6; "The Law of the Sea"—National Legislation on the Exclusive Economic Zone, the Economic Zone and the Exclusive Fishery Zone (United Nations, New York, 1986); Lawrence Juda, "The Exclusive Economic Zone: Compatibility of National Claims and the U.N. Convention on the Law of the Sea," 16 *O.D.I.L.* (vol. 1).

67. The Harmful Waste (Special Criminal Provisions) Decree no. 42 of 1988 (hereafter Harmful Waste Decree). For a detailed discussion of the law see Onje Gye-Wado, "Nigerian Law and the Toxic Waste Question: Another Dimension of the Limits of International Law?" *Nigerian Journal of International Affairs,* vol. 16 no. 2, 1990, 61–85 (hereafter "Toxic Waste Question").

68. See Barbara Kwiatkowska, "Inaugural lectures," *supra* n. 6 at 37–39.

69. See UNCLOS art. 230.

70. See for example Continental Shelf (*Tunisia/Libyan Arab Iamahariya*), judgment [1982] *I.C.J. Rep.* 18 para. 100.

71. Ghana: Maritime Zones (Delimitation) Law (PNDCL 159); Togo: Ordinance No. 24 Delimiting the Territorial Wastes and creating a protected Economic Maritime Zone of 16 August 1977; Mauritania: Law No. 78.043 establishing the Code of the Merchant Marine and Maritime Fisheries of 28 February 1978; Guinea: National limits of Jurisdiction Decree No. 336/PRG of 30 July 1980; Guinea Bissau; Law No. 3/78 on the Extension of the Territorial Sea and the Exclusive Economic Zone of 19 May 1978. On these see "The Law of the Sea," *supra* n. 69, 289, 175, 126, and 127 respectively for legislation on Togo, Mauritania, Guinea, and Guinea-Bissau.

72. See UNCLOS *supra* arts. 192; 194; 207–234.

73. The Oil in Navigable Waters Act (Act 234). See G.A. Sarpong, "Ghana's Fisheries Laws: The AJAX Case and the United Nations Convention on the Law of the Sea," vol. 17 *Review of Ghana Law.*

74. Harmful Wastes Decree n. 70 *supra* 5.1.

75. Gye-Wado (n. 70 *supra* at 74) takes the view that imprisonment for violations in the EEZ is consistent with international law. Certainly this is not so in view of art. 230(1).

76. *Id.* at 68.

77. See for example arts. 58, 87 of UNCLOS which restate the traditional rule of the freedom of navigation in the EEZ. Merely transporting toxic waste through an EEZ without more should not constitute an offense.

78. Under S.9 of the Decree, the immunity from prosecution conferred on certain persons by or under the Diplomatic Immunities and Privileges Act 1962 (which re-enacts The Vienna Convention on Diplomatic Relations) shall not extend to any crime committed under this Decree by any of those persons.

79. See n. 67 *ante.*

80. Diana Shelton and Alexandra Kiss, *International Environmental Law* 53–54 (New York; 1991). Many of the ACP states including those of the subregion have not signed the Basel Convention on Transboundary Movement of Hazardous Waste owing to lack of punitive sanctions against those engaged in the trade. Instead African States have sought to draft an African Convention on the Control of Transboundary Movement of all Forms of Hazardous Wastes in the Region. *Id.*

81. See Law No. 77–926 Delimiting the maritime zones placed under the national jurisdiction of the Republic of Ivory Coast of November 17, 1977 (hereafter Law of 17 November).

82. UNCLOS art. 56 provides:
    1. In the exclusive economic zone, the coastal State has:
    (a) sovereign rights for the purpose of exploring and exploiting, conserving and managing the natural resources, whether living or non-living, of the waters superjacent to the sea-bed and of the sea-bed and its subsoil, and with regard to other activities for the economic exploitation and exploration of the zone, such as the production of energy from the water, currents and winds;
    (b) Jurisdiction as provided for in the relevant provisions of this Convention with regard to:
    (i) the establishment and use of artificial islands, installations and structures;
    (ii) marine scientific research;
    (iii) the protection and preservation of the marine environment;
    (c) other rights and duties provided for in this Convention.
    2. In exercising its rights and performing its duties under this Convention in the exclusive economic zone, the coastal State shall

have due regard to the rights and duties of other States and shall act in a manner compatible with the provisions of this Convention.

83. See n. 31; 32 *ante.*

84. On state parties and extent of ratification of these IMO Rules see "Status Documents," *supra* n. 28.

85. *Id.* at 79. Ghana has not as yet acceded to annexes iii, iv, and v of the convention.

86. Benin, Côte d'Ivoire, Gambia, Ghana, Guinea, Nigeria, and Togo. Of these four states—Côte d'Ivoire, Ghana, Nigeria, and Togo have ratified the 1978 Solas protocol in addition.

87. *Id.* at 51. Benin, Côte d'Ivoire, Gambia, Ghana, Guinea, Nigeria, Senegal, and Togo.

88. Benin, Côte d'Ivoire, Gambia, Ghana, Nigeria, and Togo.

89. See UNCLOS *supra* art. s. 207–212.

90. See n. 55 *ante.*

91. Abecassis, *op.cit.* n. 45 at 24.

92. On WACAF see "UNEP: The West and Central African Action Plan: Evaluation of its development and achievements, UNEP Regional Seas Reports and Studies," No. 101 UNEP, 1989 (hereafter, "UNEP Report").

93. See n. 13 *ante.*

94. Article 197 of UNCLOS provides: "States shall co-operate on a global basis and, as appropriate, on a regional basis, directly or through competent international organisations, in formulating and elaborating international rules, standards and recommended practices and procedures consistent with this Convention, for the protection and preservation of the marine environment, taking into account characteristic regional features."

95. WACAF comprises not only states of the subregion fronting the Atlantic Ocean but those in central and southern Africa as well. These are Angola, Benin, Cape Verde, Congo, Equatorial Guinea, Gabon, Zambia Ghana, Guinea, Guinea-Bissau, Côte d'Ivoire, Liberia, Mauritania, Namibia, Nigeria, Sao Tome and Principe, Senegal, Sierra Leone, Togo, United Republic of Cameroon, and Zaire; see Barbara Kwiatkowska, Inaugural lecture, *supra* n. 6 at 40.

96. *Id.* at 9–10.

97. WACAF is one of UNEP's Regional Seas Programmes where action plans are operative or under development. These are the Mediterranean (1975); the Kuwait Action Plan Region (1978); the East Asian Seas Region (April 1981); the South-East Pacific Region (1981); the Red Sea and Gulf of Aden (1982); the South-West Pacific (1982); the East African Region, and the South-West Atlantic (1983). Although the specific activities for any region are dependent on the needs and priorities of that region, all action plans are similarly structured and have the following components: Assessment, Management, Legal, Institutional, and Financial components. On these see UNEP document on "Convention for Co-operation in the

Protection and Development of the Marine and Coastal Environment of the West and Central African Region and Protocol concerning Cooperation in Combating Pollution in Cases of Emergency (United Nations, New York, 1981) p. 2. Hereafter, "UNEP Doc."

98. The convention for cooperation in the Protection and Development of the Marine and Coastal Environment of the West and Central African Region and the Protocol in Combating Pollution in Cases of Emergency; rep. in UNEP Doc. (Hereafter referred to as "The Abidjan Convention" and "the protocol," respectively).

99. The twelve states are Benin, Congo, Gabon, Zambia, Ghana, Guinea, Côte d'Ivoire, Liberia, Mauritania, Nigeria, Senegal, and Togo. See UNEP Doc. *supra* n. 100 Appendix.

100. The States are Côte d'Ivoire, Zambia, Ghana, Guinea, Nigeria, Senegal, and Togo. Benin, Liberia, Guinea Bissau, and Mauritania have not each ratified either the Convention or the protocol. In addition Cape Verde, Equatorial Guinea, Sao Tome and Principe, Namibia, and Zaire, the other WACAF States, have not ratified either the Convention or the Protocol: information from UNEP.

101. *Id.* arts. 10–15.

102. Defined as any incident, occurrence, or situation, however caused, resulting in substantial pollution or imminent threat of substantial pollution to the marine and coastal environment by oil or other harmful substances and includes in particular collisions, strandings, and other incidents involving ships including tankers, petroleum production blowouts and the presence of oil or other harmful substances arising from the failure of industrial installations: art. 1(2) of protocol n. 101 *supra* at 17.

103. Marine emergency contingency plan denotes a plan prepared on a national, bilateral, or multilateral basis to deal with pollution and other adverse effects on the marine and coastal environment, or the threat thereof resulting from accidents or other unforeseen events. 11 art. 1(3).

104. Marine emergency response means any activity intended to prevent, reduce, combat, and control pollution by oil or other harmful substances or threat of pollution resulting from marine emergencies and includes the cleanup of oil slicks and recovery or salvage of packages, freight containers, portable tanks, or road and rail wagons, *id.* art. 1(4).

105. Protocol arts. 4–10.

106. Abidjan Convention, *supra* n. 101 art. 16.

107. On the details, see UNEP Report, *supra* n. 95 at 3.

108. Regionalism provides for a decentralized implementation of marine programs which allows for greater participation and wider responsibility of states in the program. On this and other benefits of Regionalism, see C.O. Okidi, "Protection of the Marine Environment through Regional Arrangements," 23 1. *Sea lust. Proc.* 478 (1990); and Commentary by Salvano Briceno, *id.*

109. On this see Barbara Kwiatkowska, "The Dakar 1991 Convention on Fisheries Co-operation Among African States Bordering the Atlantic Ocean" 7 *Int. Journal of Estuarine and Coastal Law* 147–64 (1992).

110. *Id.* art. 12 of the Dakar Convention provides that the parties "shall intensify their efforts at the national regional and international levels directly or with the assistance of competent regional or international organisations to ensure the protection and preservation of the marine environment. . . . To this end they shall promote the strengthening of bilateral, subregional and international co-operation mechanisms dealing with the protection and preservation of the environment . . . taking into account the relevant international standards and regulations on the subject." The references includes WACAF and UNCLOS.

9

Aspects of the Law of International Water Resources

M. Hirsch and D. Housen-Couriel

Abstract

As a result of the nature of lakes, rivers, and aquifers, which ignore national boundaries, states are often presented with the problem of how to share and manage these limited resources. The role of law is to clarify the rights and responsibilities of states in such situations. Two aspects of the law of international water resources will be explored in this article. The point of departure for the analysis is public international law itself, which contains principles and guidelines for the utilization and management of water resources by the states which share them. The international legal regime applying to surface water will first be discussed. The second part of the article will consist of a comparison of several treaty regimes which presently apply in a situation of shared water resources between states.

Keywords
Water Resources—International Law—International Rivers—Treaty Regimes—Jordan River Basin

Introduction

As a result of the physical nature of lakes, rivers, and aquifers, which ignore political and national boundaries, states are often presented with the problem of effective common utilization of these limited

122

natural resources. The role of law is to clarify the rights and responsibilities of states in such situations. Although the international law of water resources has not yet reached the level of maturity and sophistication which is perhaps desirable given the urgent nature of world water problems, important basic principles and rules have evolved. It is our underlying assumption that elucidation of these norms and their application to the water problems of the Jordan River Basin has the potential for assuring reasonable and efficient resource management there, and may also help to avoid serious conflict in the future.

Two aspects of the law of international water resources will be explored in this article. The international legal norms applying to international rivers will first be discussed. The second part of the article will consist of a review of the lessons which can be learned from the comparison of existing treaty regimes for the sharing of international water resources. Some ramifications of the legal analysis for the Jordan River Basin will be explored in the conclusion.

International Rivers Law

The law regulating the rights and obligations of riparian states of international rivers is one of the oldest branches of public international law. This section will focus on international customary law, namely, the law which binds all states, regardless of their acceptance of these rules, by international agreement. International customary law has two constitutive elements: a. the general practice of states; b. their recognition that this practice is required by law (Schwarzenberger, 1976; Brownlie, 1990; and Shaw, 1991).

The General Doctrines

The general doctrines applying to international rivers are of great importance for the determination of the specific rights and duties of riparian states, and especially for resolving the questions of apportionment, utilization, and conservation of the waters flowing in these rivers. The four general doctrines are: a. absolute territorial sovereignty; b. absolute territorial integrity; c. limited territorial sovereignty; d. community of co-riparian states.

On one end of the scale we find the extreme doctrine of absolute territorial sovereignty, according to which a riparian state has the freedom to do whatever it chooses with the waters flowing in its territory, regardless of the adverse effects on other states. It is indisputable that this doctrine does not reflect the contemporary international law (Griffin, 1959; Batstone, 1959; Lipper, 1967; Barberis, 1986; and Naff and Matson, 1989). On the other end of the scale stands the doctrine of absolute territorial integrity. According to this doctrine one riparian state is not allowed to use the waters flowing in its territory in a way which will alter its course, flow rate, volume of water, or its quality, in the territory of another state. This doctrine was rejected by the Nile Commission and it is not part of international customary law (Nile Commission Report, 1929; Lipper, 1967; Barberis, 1986; and Batstone, 1959). Between these two extreme doctrines there are two other intermediate theories, which are pragmatic and take into account the interests of all the watercourse states. It is not surprising that one of these intermediate doctrines is at present the prevailing theory in international law, namely the doctrine of limited territorial sovereignty.

The doctrine of limited territorial sovereignty provides that a watercourse state is not allowed to utilize the waters of an international river in a way which will cause significant harm to reasonable utilization by other watercourse states. This doctrine is undoubtedly a principle of international customary law and it is supported by decisions of international tribunals, state practice, numerous treaties, resolutions of international organizations, and an overwhelming majority of international jurists (Griffin, 1959; Institute de Droit International, 1961; International Law Association, 1966; Lipper, 1967; Barberis, 1986; International Law Commission, 1987; Doherty, 1965; and Caponera, 1978). The second intermediate doctrine, "community in waters," takes us one step further and proposes to develop an integrated program for the entire watercourse system without the limits of political borders. This doctrine, unquestionably, could achieve the optimal utilization of the waters; however, it does not constitute binding customary rule in contemporary international law (Lipper, 1967).

Allocation of the Waters of International Rivers

One of the crucial questions in regard to utilization of international rivers concerns the allocation of their waters among the riparians. The customary test of allocation does not direct us to one parameter, but rather to the multiple and flexible test of "equitable and reasonable" share (International Law Commission, 1987; International Law Association, 1966; Lipper, 1967; and Griffin, 1959). Similar tests of equity have been applied in relation to other environmental resources located in lakes, groundwaters, and some marine areas (Schachter, 1991; and Kiss, 1986). The criterion of equitable and reasonable share requires taking into account many factors pertaining to a specific international watercourse, and some influential international institutions have formulated lists defining the principal factors involved (International Law Commission, 1987, International Law Association, 1966; and Griffin, 1959). Here we shall briefly present the modern version of the International Law Commission, which elaborated the following factors: natural physical factors—such as geographic, hydrographic, hydrological, and climate factors; water-related social and economic needs of the watercourse states; the effects of the use on other watercourse states; the existing and potential use; conservation, protection, development and economy of use of waters; and the availability of alternatives, their corresponding value, and their costs.

In this connection, a few remarks should be made. First, neither the list mentioned above nor any other is meant to present an exhaustive list of the relevant factors. Second, no factor has a fixed weight, but the weight given to each factor will change in accordance with the other factors relevant to a specific case. There is some dispute whether to accord some priority to the factor of existing use. It seems that international law considers this factor to be one of the most important ones, though not necessarily outweighing the others (Lipper, 1967; Griffin, 1959; Bourne, 1965; International Law Association, 1966; and International Law Commission, 1987). Additionally, it is accepted that international customary law does not contain any rule to prohibit the watercourse states of diverting the waters of international rivers outside of the drainage basin (Doherty, 1965; and International Law Association, 1986).

Utilization Projects

By "utilization projects" (or planned measures) we refer to any project planned or executed by one of the watercourse states in order to utilize the rivers' waters, e.g. building hydroelectric plants, dams, or desalination projects. The major principle, derived from the general doctrine of equitable and reasonable utilization, is that a watercourse state is not allowed to implement such a project, which may entail appreciable adverse effects on other watercourse states, without genuinely attempting to negotiate with the other riparians in order to ensure their equitable share in the waters to them. This general principle includes the obligation to notify the other riparians of the planned measures, accompanied by adequate information. If the notified state does not respond within a reasonable period of time, the planning state may legally proceed with the implementation of the project. However, this right to proceed with the planned project does not exclude the obligation imposed upon all the watercourse states not to harm the lawful interests of the other riparian states (Griffin, 1959, Institute de Droit International, 1961; International Law Commission, 1987; and The World Bank, 1989).

If one of the watercourse states communicates its objection to the implementation of the planned measure, the obligation to negotiate in good faith is put into operation (Institute de Droit International, 1961; International Law Commission, 1987; Barberis, 1986; and Lake Lanoux Arbitration, 1957). Here arises an important question concerning the power of the affected state during the negotiations. In the absence of agreement between the disputed parties, does the affected state have a 'veto power' to block the implementation of the project? The answer provided by international customary law is negative. The question arose in the dispute between France and Spain in 1953 concerning the diversion of the river Carol's waters, planned by France. The international arbitration tribunal ruled that there is no mandatory requirement of prior agreement between the interested states (Lake Lanoux Arbitration, 1957). While international customary law does not confer upon the watercourse state the right to veto planned undertaking, where a project will cause substantial harm to the equitable and reasonable use by other riparians, the implementing states may be held internationally responsible for violating the lawful rights of the other states (Bourne, 1965; Griffin, 1959; and Institute de Droit International, 1961).

Pollution

The general principle in international customary law is that states are not allowed to pollute the waters of international rivers, thereby causing substantial harm to other riparians. This principle, which is derived from the doctrine of limited territorial sovereignty, involves the obligation upon a state not to permit the use of its territory in such a manner as to cause such pollution (Lammers, 1984; International Law Commission, 1988; International Law Association, 1966; Salmon, 1986; Institute de Droit International, 1979; Ando, 1981; and Lester, 1967).

There is some difference of opinion among international lawyers whether the responsibility of states is conditional upon the existence of some fault (negligence) or intention on the part of those who commit the violation of international law (objective versus subjective responsibility). This important topic exceeds the limits of this paper, however. It seems, however, that at least with respect to the state's obligation not to allow others (e.g. its nationals) to pollute the international river from its territory, the obligation is of due care or due diligence and not objective (Lammers, 1984; International Association, 1966; and Lester, 1967). In the case of violation of this obligation, the state responsible will be required to cease the wrongful conduct and compensate the other riparian state for the injury caused to it (International Law Association, 1966; and Lester, 1967).

International Legal Treaty Regimes for the Sharing of International Water Resources

Important lessons can be learned from the comparison of treaty regimes for the sharing of international water resources which are currently in operation. In this brief survey, we will attempt to highlight the most salient of those.

The critical unit of analysis for international lawyers, as well as hydrologists, is now that of the "international drainage basin," which has been defined in Article 2 of the 1966 Helsinki Rules as ". . . a geographical area extending over two or more states determined by the watershed limits of the system of waters, including surface and underground waters, flowing into a common terminus." Although the International Law Association, the body responsible for having drafted these Rules, has recently proposed an augmentation to Article 2, the general definition of the basin has been preserved. Thus, the term has replaced other concepts such as "international lakes and rivers" and "international water resources." In the words of a United Nations study from the 1970s, "The drainage basin is an indivisible hydrological unit which requires comprehensive consideration in order to achieve maximal management and development of any part of the water region" (United Nations, 1975). Some problems with this concept include the exclusion of atmospheric water and the influence of nonwater resources on basin management, although space does not permit elaboration of these points.

There are approximately 200 international drainage basins in the world, 20 of which cover more than 1 million square kilometers; 71 cover an area between 100,000 and 1 million square kilometers (United Nations, 1975). For the sake of comparison, the Jordan River Basin extends over only 50,000 square kilometers, and is thus to be considered relatively small. Factors which characterize individual basins include climate, soil use, flora and fauna, navigability, irrigation and other water works, industrial installations, and the need for pollution control.

The types of problems dealt with by legal regimes for international water management are, naturally, quite varied and depend on the physical characteristics, yet some common strands do run through those examined. First, there are the obvious issues of the sharing arrangements between two or more countries, joint planning and supervision, and environmental quality control. More complex issues include the extensive technical background work involved before the legal regime can come into force, compensation for losses incurred by division of water resources, mechanisms for controlling water flow and flood prevention, the assignment of binding authority to a joint body which will manage the basin, the establishment of investigatory and dispute resolution procedures, and the determination of political boundaries.

The role of international law in setting up efficient legal regimes is crucial. Broadly speaking, there are several principles which bind states as part of the general international law. These include the principle of *sic utere tuo ut altenum non laedas* (the obligation to use one's property in a manner which will not cause injury to others), the requirement to settle disputes peaceably, responsibility of the state for damages attributable to it, and reasonableness in interpreting states' rights and duties (Brownie, 1991; Shaw, 1991; and Akehurst, 1990). Specific legal norms which apply to the use of surface waters in any international drainage basin have been discussed above, particularly the requirement of equitable distribution. The question of whether these last norms are binding at present fades into the background when one examines treaty regimes which have been established, since such regimes unquestionably bind signatories, and tend to build extensively on prior examples of successful basin management. Thus, a dependence on legal and managerial precedent appears to be inherent in the process of establishing new water regimes. And rightly so: water resources are too precious to gamble with, and planners cannot usually afford the luxury of radical experimentation (Elliot, 1991). Thus, we would suggest that the self-reinforcing nature of the hundred or so treaty regimes which have been established in international drainage basins may at some point in the relatively near future give rise to binding norms of customary law on the international plane.

We will now turn to a brief survey of three treaty regimes for the sharing of water resources in international drainage basins: the

Columbia River Treaty between Canada and the United States (1961); the La Plata Basin Agreement between Paraguay, Uruguay, Argentina, Bolivia, and Brazil (1969); and the Indus Waters regime between India and Pakistan (1960). These regimes have been chosen for their diversity, and represent varying degrees of success in basin management.

The Columbia River Treaty

This treaty, signed in January 1961, represents one of the success stories of international regimes for the co-utilization of water resources, although significant problems needed to be overcome before the treaty could be concluded. A two hundred-year-long history of negotiation over water rights along the Canada-U.S. border preceded the 1961 treaty, including an important agreement between the British and the Americans in 1909 regarding the boundary waters between the two countries and the establishment of a joint commission for dealing with water issues. The present regime applies the principle of equitable distribution of joint water resources, and adds to it important innovations in the field of joint planning and the settlement of disputes.

The La Plata Basin Treaty

The five basin states (Paraguay, Uruguay, Argentina, Bolivia, and Brazil) signed a treaty for the establishment of a common legal regime on April 23, 1969, and it entered into force the following year. The huge land area watered by the five major rivers of the basin encompasses one-sixth of the South American continent, and the river system covers a major percentage of the territories of the basin states. Thus, the rivers of the basin possess major strategic importance as factors in national planning, especially for purposes of navigation and communication.

In summary, although the La Plata Basin enjoys a relative abundance of water resources and the basin states are willing to cooperate in managing them for mutual benefit, technical problems in implementing the agreement have held back the development of the region's rivers.

The Indus River Basin

This basin represents an especially complex example of co-utilization of international water resources. In fact, the two hostile basin states have "agreed to disagree" regarding the utilization of the six major rivers of the basin by dividing the rights to their use in an absolute manner, without actual sharing arrangements.

The agreement which establishes the present legal regime is the Indus Waters Treaty of 1960 between India, Pakistan, and the World Bank. Two additional operating and development agreements were concluded between the latter two parties. All three treaties are the fruit of such technical background work and laborious negotiations which commenced in the early 1950s under the auspices of the World Bank.

Under the present agreement, the six rivers which feed the vast irrigational system of the Indus Basin have been divided as follows: the Ravi, Beas, and Sutlej are controlled by India, and the Indus, Jhelum, and Chenab by Pakistan. Although the basin has in effect been divided into areas of national influence, the Indus Waters Treaty is widely perceived as applying the principle of equitable apportionment as eventually formulated in the Helsinki Rules.

Our brief examination of three treaty regimes only begins to illustrate the importance of such comparative studies for basin states wishing to initiate their own arrangements for basin management. Of chief importance to the success of future regimes is the inclusion of guiding legal principles for the distribution of water resources, presumably on an equitable basis; a mechanism for resolution of disputes which is binding on all basin states; a body invested with sufficient authority for effective implementation of the treaty provisions; and thorough joint technical work which can serve both as a stable basis for treaty negotiations and an ongoing framework for cooperation. Finally, we would point out the importance of flexibility in the implementation of the treaty and sufficient economic backing (whether internal or external) to ensure its success.

Conclusion

From the foregoing analysis, several conclusions may be derived which may apply in the Jordan River Basin: (1) the prevailing doctrine in international customary law—the principle of limited territorial sovereignty—prescribes that none of the Jordan's riparians are permitted to utilize its waters in a way which will cause significant harm to the river's reasonable utilization by other riparians; (2) each riparian is entitled to an equitable and reasonable share of the water resources according to the parameters set by international customary law; (3) a riparian planning a utilization project must notify other riparians and negotiate with them in good faith in order to ensure their equitable share in the waters; (4) the most efficient and equitable division of the benefits accruing from utilization of the Jordan's waters can be achieved only by an international treaty between all riparians; (5) such a future agreement should address issues such as apportionment, water quality, monitoring, technical and scientific cooperation, and settlement of disputes.

References

1. Akehurst, M. (1990). *A Modern Introduction to International Law*, 6th ed., George Allen and Unwin, London.
2. Ando, N. (1981), "The Law of Pollution Prevention in International Rivers and Lakes," in R. Zacklin and L. Caflisch (eds.), *The Legal Regime of International Rivers and Lakes*, Nijhoff Pub., The Hague, 331–370.
3. Barberia, J.A. (1986), "International Rivers," in R. Bernhardt (ed.), *Encyclopedia of Public International Law*, vol. 9, 212–214.
4. Batstone, R.K. (1959), "The Utilisation of the Nile Waters," *International and Comparative Law Quarterly*, vol. 9, 523–558.
5. Bourne, C.B. (1965), "The Right to Utilize the Waters of International Rivers," *Canadian Yearbook of International Law*, vol. 3, 187–264.
6. Bourne, C. (1990). "Columbia River," in R. Bernhardt (ed.), *The Encyclopedia of Public International Law*, vol. 12, North-Holland, Amsterdam-New York-London, 73–74.
7. Brownlie, I. (1990). *Principles of Public International Law*, 4th ed., Clarendon, Oxford.
8. Caponera, D. and Alheritiere, D. (1978), "Principles for International Groundwater Law," *Natural Resources Forum* D-C 749, United Nations, New York.
9. Doherty, K.B. (1965), "Jordan Waters Conflict," *International Conciliation*, No. 553 (May 1965), Carnegie Endowment for International Peace, New York.
10. Elliot, M. (1991). "The Global Politics of Water," *The American Enterprise*, Sept-Oct., 27.
11. Griffin, W.L. (1959), "The Use of Waters of International Drainage Basins Under Customary International Law," *American Journal of International Law*, vol. 53, 50–80.
12. Hayton, R. (1967), Lester, A. (1967), and Lipper, J. (1967). "The La Plata Basin," "Pollution," and "Equitable Utilization," in A. Garretson et al. (eds), *The Law of International Drainage Basins*, Oceana, Dobbs Ferry, N.Y.
13. Hummer, W. (1984). "La Plata Basin," in R. Bernhardt (ed.), *The Encyclopedia of Public International Law*, vol. 6, North-Holland, Amsterdam-New York-London, 237.

14. The Indus Water Treaty of 1960 between the Government of India, the Government of Pakistan and the International Bank for Reconstruction and Development, 419 *UNTS* 125 (1962).
15. Institute de Droit International (1961), *Annuaire*, vol. 49 II, 381–384.
16. Institute de Droit International (1979), *Annuaire*, vol. 58 II, 197–203.
17. International Law Association (1966), *Report of the Fifty-Second Conference*, Helsinki, 477–533.
18. International Law Association (1986), *Report of the Sixty-Second Conference*, Seoul, 231–250.
19. International Law Commission (1987), *Yearbook*, vol. 2, part 2, 24–38.
20. International Law Commission (1988), *Report to the General Assembly*, Official Records: Forty-Third Session, Supp. No. 10 (A/43/10), United Nations, New York, 45–139.
21. Kiss, A. (1986), "The International Protection of the Environment," in Macdonald, R. St. J. and Johnston, D.M. (eds.), *The Structure and Process of International Law; Essays in Legal Philosophy, Doctrine and Theory*, Nijhoff Pub. Dordrecht, 1069–1093.
22. Lake Lanoux Arbitration (1957), International Law Reports, 24, 101–142.
23. Lammers, J.G. (1984), *Pollution of International Watercourses*, Nijhoff Pub., Dordrecht.
24. Naff, T. and Matson, R.C. (1989), *Water in the Middle East: Conflict or Cooperation?* Westview Press, New York.
25. Salmon, J.J. (1986), "International Watercourses; Pollution," in R. Bernhardt (ed.), *Encyclopedia of Public International Law*, vol. 9, 220–222.
26. Schachter, O. (1991), *International Law in Theory and Practice*, Nijhoff Pub., Dordrecht.
27. Schwarzenberger, G. (1967), *A Manual of International Law*, 6th ed., Professional Books, U.K.
28. Shaw, M. (1991). *International Law*, 3rd ed., Grotius, Cambridge.
29. Treaty Between Great Britain and the United States of America Relating to Boundary Waters and Questions arising along the Boundary between Canada and the United States and the Establishment of an International Joint Commission, January 11, 1909, 102 *BFSP* 137 (1908–9).
30. Treaty of the River Plate Basin, Brasilia, April 23, 1969, 875 *UNTS* 3 (1973).
31. Treaty Relating to the Cooperative Development of the Water Resources of the Columbia River Basin, January 17, 1961, 542 *UNTS* 302 (1965).
32. *Management of International Water Resources: Institutional and Legal Aspects*, United Nations, New York, 1975.
33. World Bank (1989), Operational Directive No. 7.50, in: *International Rivers and Lakes*, No. 14, May 1990, 6–7.

International Efforts to Protect the Tropical Rain Forests

The world's environmental focus has been on deforestation in recent years. It is a problem that merits this kind of attention, since the world's forest land is being lost at a rate of 17 million hectares per year. This loss is of global concern due to its impact on the world's climate as well as on biodiversity.

Forests are being cleared for a variety of economic reasons. Land is cleared to create grazing land for cattle. It is being cleared to create more space for agricultural production. Forests are cut to provide fuel and timber. Trees are also dying as a result of the acidification of the soils caused by air pollution.

As forests are lost, so are the species that populate them. There is much talk of preserving biodiversity, but in order to do so the habitats of the many endangered species must also be preserved.

Flora and fauna are not the only organisms that rely on the forests for their survival. Human civilizations also depend on the survival of forests, particularly the tropical rainforests. Indigenous populations inhabit the forests and have done so for thousands of years. Their lives and cultures depend on their continued ability to populate these habitats.

Loss of forests is a major cause of global climate change. Trees serve to remove carbon from the atmosphere during photosynthesis. With fewer trees to do this work, more carbon is left in the atmosphere. Carbon forms with oxygen as carbon dioxide, a leading greenhouse gas.

Tree cover protects the soil from the elements that degrade it. As forests are cleared, the soil is no longer protected and the soil is eroded. The eroded soil ends up in bodies of water as silt, a deposition which alters the marine ecosystem.

International efforts are needed to protect remaining forests and to plan and manage reforestation efforts in areas where deforestation has already taken place. The world community must make a firm commitment to protecting this vital part of the Earth environment. An international agreement protecting the world's forests must rank as a high priority in environmental conservation.

—RNW

10

Saving the Tropical Forest: Needs and Prognosis

Jerome K. Vanclay

Attempts to reverse deforestation in the tropics have failed because they addressed symptoms rather than causes. Many pressures come from outside the forest, so a multisectoral approach is needed. The real causes and some possible solutions are examined. Whilst there is scope for further research, many problems can be overcome through increased community participation, better communication, more effective management and the implementation of a few simple guidelines.

Introduction

Tropical forests have the interest of the public and the attention of the media. Unfortunately, reference to tropical rainforests in the popular press is often simplistic and ill-informed. Nonetheless, much support has been mobilized, and the controversy surrounding rainforests and "old-growth" forests has influenced elections and government policies in several countries. This paper reexamines some issues, attempts to clarify some areas of confusion, and examines the prognosis for the tropical forests.

Significance of the Rainforest and the Timber Trade

Any attempt to rectify the problems in the tropical forests must discriminate between symptoms, problems, and other issues. Too much effort has been misdirected because the real issues and problems were not identified.

The Wet and Dry Tropics

Not all tropical forests are rainforests. Much of the tropics is arid and only 40 percent is forested (Table 1). About half the tropical forest is rainforest; the remainder comprises seasonal forests, savannah woodland, and other forms of open forest. *Tropical moist forest* is the collective term for rainforest, seasonal or monsoon forest, and mangroves (1).

Table 1. Forest area relative to land area with the tropics (in percent).				
Forest type	America	Africa	Asia	Overall
Total forest	50	30	40	40
Moist forest	40	10	30	25
Rainforest	30	5	20	20

Although the tropical moist forest has the limelight, tropical woodlands are also of great importance. These forests may be under the greatest threat of overuse, through the gathering of fuelwood and fodder, through grazing, and from the resulting soil erosion. This is not just an ecological disaster, but a human tragedy. Many people suffer malnutrition not only because of food shortages, but also because of a shortage of fuel needed for cooking.

Fuelwood is a major forest product. Of the total tropical wood supply, 83 percent is consumed as fuelwood, 13 percent is consumed locally as timber, and only 4 percent is exported to the international timber trade (2). Sustainable production of industrial timbers is only part of the solution; efficient production and consumption of fuelwood are also essential. Sustainable production of all forest products will be difficult to attain. The international timber trade is a more tractable problem, with only a few dominant players: 70 percent of the timber originates in Malaysia and Indonesia, and 80 percent is destined for Japan, the EEC, and the USA (2).

Carbon Dioxide and Climate Change

CO_2 levels in the atmosphere are higher than at any other time in the past 160,000 years are still increasing at an alarming rate, and will have a significant impact on our climate (3). We should not expect a benevolent warming, bringing the Mediterranean to the Baltic; the implications are more serious (4). Consider the slight warming of the Pacific that triggered the El Niño Southern Oscillation, and influenced the weather not only in the Pacific, but from India to the Amazon, causing floods, droughts and other extremes (5).

The tropical forest cannot compensate for the current reckless consumption of fossil fuels. Estimates are plagued by unreliable data and assumptions, but it seems that the destruction and burning of all the tropical moist forest would cause a comparatively small increase in atmospheric CO_2 levels (3,6); fossil-fuel contributions less than this century. Sustainable timber production should be CO_2-neutral or beneficial, since durable products store carbon and vigorous regeneration has higher net photosynthesis. Carbon dioxide is a problem for the industrialized nations and it is imperialistic to assume otherwise. Nor will plantations solve our dilemma. Offsetting current CO_2 output may require over a billion hectares of well-managed plantations (7), several times the existing worldwide plantation area and half as much as the remaining area of natural tropical forest worldwide (8). If trees were efficient at fixing carbon, we would use wood instead of fossil fuels. To solve the CO_2 problem, the industrialized nations simply have to reduce emissions; we could begin by examining road and rail subsidies (9). There are, however, other reasons for saving the tropical forests.

Biodiversity

Tropical rainforests are rich in plant and animal species, and may contain 50 to 90 percent of the world's species. But this is of little relevance for the management of these and other forests. A balanced conservation strategy is necessary for all habitats; people need to eat, and conservation schemes need local support if they are to succeed. Contrary to popular belief, many rainforests are not so fragile, and their species richness provides some resilience. Well-managed forests may retain most of the diversity of the primary forest, both in terms of numbers and diversity of species, and may support animals that cannot survive in small isolated primary forest reserves (10–13).

Who are the real beneficiaries of biodiversity? Few species, often from secondary forest, satisfy most needs of the local communities. Some species attract tourists, but diversity itself is rarely an attraction. Plant-based pharmaceuticals from 90 plants may account for 25 percent of prescription drugs and $40 billion in sales each year, but the statistics do not indicate the potential value of the other 250,000 plant species. Biodiversity offers a potential for enhancing the productivity of domestic plants, animals, and new pharmaceuticals, but who will benefit and when? How great is the potential: pharmaceutical firms don't own much rainforest. The current custodians of the forest have more pressing problems than the possibilities for curing cancer and AIDS, and history suggests that the industrialized nations will be the major beneficiaries. Equitable ways of sharing the costs and benefits of this unrealized potential need to be found (14). Until they are, developing countries will have little incentive for conserving rainforests for their biodiversity.

Loss of the Tropical Moist Forest

Rate of Deforestation

Some 17 million hectares of tropical forest are destroyed each year (15). Africa has the highest rate of destruction, (1.7 percent per year), but the largest deforested area is in tropical America. About half the area deforested becomes shifting cultivation, whilst the remainder is converted to permanent agriculture, grazing, plantations, and other uses. Although agriculture accounts for more than 75 percent of all deforested areas, commercial timber extraction is also significant.

Before the turn of the century, half the people in developing countries will have insufficient fuelwood, and only 10 out of the present 33 timber exporting nations will remain timber exporters. Apart from the loss of invaluable resources, this will have a serious impact on the balance of trade of these nations. Deforestation is inevitable when profits are easily reaped and costs remain undefined; this is the tragedy of the commons (16), and may only be moderated by community loyalty (17). Estimates of the value of rainforests and alternative land uses are convenient for politicians and other decision makers, but convincing valuations of intact forest and sustainable harvests are not yet available. Some analyses vary as much as 100–fold in their assessments of sustainable production of forest products (18–20).

Causes and Symptoms

It is not easy to discriminate between causes and symptoms of deforestation, or to identify the real causes. Too often, symptoms rather than causes are given and attempts to alleviate the problems are thus misdirected. The real problems often originate outside the forest, and may be intractable; but hiding the symptoms does not cure the problem. Table 2 summarizes some symptoms and causes of rainforest destruction. Although discretely tabulated, they are all interrelated. It is important to recognize several items as symptoms rather than causes (e.g., shifting cultivation), to focus on the real causes. Many presumed causes of deforestation are, like unsustainable logging practices, merely symptoms of more serious and more difficult problems. To solve the deforestation crisis, we need to recognize and understand the true causes; only then will we find solutions.

Table 2. Symptoms and causes of rainforest destruction.

SYMPTOMS	CAUSES	SOLUTIONS
Erosion, flooding, and landslides	Poverty and overpopulation	Education, training, and information
Species extinction	Corruption and greed	Cooperation
Destructive logging	Imperialism	Social security
Shifting cultivation	Bureaucracy	Land tenure
Migrants and squatters	Ignorance and carelessness	Boost in agricultural production
Industrial monocultures	International trade policy	Land rehabilitation
		Economic stability
		Broad outlook

Erosion, Flooding, and Landslides

Erosion is one obvious outcome of unsustainable land use, and may be caused by forestry, agriculture, and other land uses. Erosion may cause flooding and landslides, and may create problems far downstream (21). However, good land husbandry can minimize erosion and reduce flooding and landslides. Logging and other forest operations need not have adverse hydrological effects (22). Logging was blamed for and banned following disastrous floods in Thailand in 1988 (and elsewhere), but it was only one factor (23). The torrential rain also triggered landslides in natural forest, and clearing for rubber plantations and other crops contributed to the problem (24, 25).

Endangered Species

It is unfortunate, but inevitable, that many species will become extinct as a result of land-use changes in the tropics. Even if all tropical forest destruction could be arrested immediately, fragmentation and invasion by exotic species already condemns many primary forest species to extinction (26). The tree species *Calvaria major* is threatened because germination apparently depended upon the dodo (27), which was exterminated centuries ago. Some theories have indicated the approximate number of species that may be lost, but we cannot yet identify them. The rare and endangered species may not be the most vulnerable; several species have fallen from abundance to extinction in a few years (e.g., carrier pigeon). However, species dependent upon large areas of forest, those that require undisturbed primary forest, and some epiphytes may be susceptible. This doesn't mean preserving all the big tracts of remaining primeval forest. On the contrary, the protection, consolidation, and rehabilitation of fragmented, degraded, and secondary forest may be critical to the survival of some species. We need to reappraise the status of both existing reserves and disturbed areas, before the latter are further degraded.

The best way to ensure the survival of plant and animal species is to reserve representative areas that are protected from artificial disturbance and buffered with managed forest. Within such a system, and when confined to the buffer areas, timber harvesting may not threaten species. A selection-harvesting system is preferred within the buffer area to maintain a seminatural habitat; plantations are no alternative (28). Sensitive management of buffer areas for timber and other forest products may be the best way to preserve the integrity of reserves and balance conflicting demands for production and preservation. Currently, about 5 percent of the tropical forest is protected in national parks and other reserves. This is insufficient to ensure the survival of many species. The management of the land surrounding these protected areas will, ultimately, determine the fate of many species.

Logging Practices

Is logging a cause or an artifact of deforestation? Why does timber harvesting often lead to degradation and deforestation? Sometimes the objective is to deforest the land, and logging is simply an accessory. Often lack of interest, investment, supervision, and training, lead to poor harvesting practices. The sociopolitical environment and the conditions of the concession may promote a short-term outlook and hamper investment in better training, equipment, and practices. If these real problems can be identified, then sustainable timber production can be achieved through a few simple guidelines (29,30).

Shifting Cultivators and Squatters

Timber harvesting and *landless poor* often work in concert to deforest. The loggers provide access roads and remove the big trees, while the poor destroy the remaining vegetation and begin subsistence cultivation. But is logging the cause? Without loggers and logging roads, people still need to eat, and would continue to occupy what they see as underutilized land. If the loggers merely provide the path of least resistance, then stopping the timber harvest will neither cure the problem nor stop the deforestation.

The *landless poor* includes traditional forest dwellers and migrants. The forest dwellers may be shifting cultivators or hunter-gatherers, whose territorial claims may or may not be recognized. The Penan conflict in Sarawak is largely an issue of land rights and community involvement, rather than opposition to timber harvesting *per se*, and harvesting of timber and other forest products could be compatible with their lifestyle and aspirations (31). Shifting cultivation by traditional forest dwellers may be sustainable where it occurs at subsistence level, uses hand tools, involves limited cash cropping, and supports a stable population; under these circumstances it may not encroach on primary forest. Deforestation may occur when populations increase, cash cropping escalates, or when power tools are used for clearing and cultivating. Traditional forest dwellers may want their forest to be logged, to simplify agricultural clearing, to bring a road to their village, or to obtain *de facto* title to the land (32). In all cases, harmonious timber harvesting requires participation by local communities in planning, conducting, and receiving benefits from all operations.

Migrants may be transient or permanent, legal or illegal. Legal transients include the families of the forest workers, who may establish a house and garden close to forest operations, especially if a forest sawmill is involved. The impact and duration of subsistence gardens may be small, but they may convey the initial impression of a stream of landless poor following logging roads into the depths of the jungle.

The permanence of illegal migrants or squatters may depend primarily on their detection and eviction by the authorities. Such migrants may be landless or poor from nearby or from abroad, or they may be speculators, neither landless nor poor. Eviction of the true landless poor is counterproductive, as they will simply move to another underutilized area of forest and start again, and the chance of detection may be small. Eviction may exacerbate deforestation, but granting tenure invites a rush of speculators. If the flow of migrants cannot be stopped at its source, one solution may be to grant limited tenure subject to an agreed cultivation system (e.g., agroforestry or trees-with-crops). However, this approach relies on mutual trust. Farmers may uproot trees, fearing that their land will be depossessed when the trees mature. Part of the problem lies in the perception that forests are underutilized, and thus part of the solution is greater participation and better use of nontimber products.

Permanent legal migrants include the victims of transmigration schemes that move people from overpopulated to underpopulated regions, in an attempt to improve the economies of both regions. This may be futile, as it seldom addresses the problems at the source, and may create additional problems at the destination. It may simply be colonialism, exporting the unwanted from their home territory to strengthen territorial claims over insecure colonies. It is unfortunate for the victims and land alike; there are usually good reasons for underpopulated lands, including diseases and limited land capabilities. Preventive medicine, soil amelioration through drainage and fertilizers, and new plant varieties may overcome some of these problems, but many remain. Foremost among the problems is the fact that many migrants are simply not equipped for the new problems they face. Regrettably, many of these lands are doomed to be degraded and abandoned.

Industrial Agriculture

Agricultural cash crops at both the industrial and family scale have led to the destruction of vast areas of tropical forest. Sugarcane, coconut, rubber, oil palm, coffee, cocoa, tea, many spices, and other crops are produced on land that once supported rainforest; and encroachment continues. These crops are eagerly sought by the same nations who would ban timber harvesting, and they also provide an important source of employment and income. Substitutes or alternatives may be available, but may have other undesirable ecological consequences, and substitution by consumers may simply force a substitution by producers—and a switch to a crop with lower return may lead to increases in cultivated area.

Real Causes of Deforestation

The most important issues for tropical forest management are often omitted from forestry textbooks and training courses. Temperate forestry in industrial nations is comparatively easy; most causes and effects are internal to the forest. In the tropics, the external forces are more important than silviculture.

Poverty and Overpopulation

The cycle of poverty and population is probably the most pressing problem in the world today (33). Poverty will remain until populations stabilize, and populations will grow until poverty is alleviated. Condoms are not enough. The link between population and poverty is clear. In the developed countries, most people want children for self-fulfillment or companionship; in developing countries children provide support in old age. Those with social security, pension schemes, and aged-care, need not fear old age without a family. For most people, children are the only form of security and aged-care. Until we can change this the population problem will not be solved.

Nepal has one of the highest population growth rates, not despite, but because of its high infant mortality. Because child mortality is high, many children are necessary to ensure that some may be around when parents get old. Infant mortality, immigration, and lack of social security all contribute to high population growth, to deforestation, and to a shortage of resources.

The world's human population consumes 40 percent of terrestrial primary productivity, and this figure may double within 40 years (34). We need to choose between quantity and quality of life. Those with security have the choice: children in the developed world consume ten times more resources than those in developing countries. Instead of big families, we need extended families. We retain the right to have many children, but it is our responsibility (and capability) to limit our fecundity. To provide appropriate social security in the Third World, we must stimulate social, political, and economic development by establishing social, political, and economic links through trade and cultural exchanges.

Corruption and Greed

The wealthy landowners, influential elite, and multinational corporations are instrumental in shaping the future of the forest. Their influence is rarely visible, but occasionally the extent and nature of this influence become evident.

During the late 1980s, a political dispute in Papua New Guinea (PNG) led to a Commission of Inquiry with unprecedented powers, including ability to seize documents and subpoena witnesses, to investigate the timber industry. The report by Justice Barnett is lengthy and not readily available, but some summaries have been published (35, 36). Many politicians, several community leaders, and most logging companies were exposed as corrupt. One revelation was that companies were transferring profits to tax havens, e.g., Singapore, by falsely declaring amounts and values of log exports and equipment imports, thus depriving the PNG people of their share of the benefits. While not all countries or companies are corrupt, we may assume that the PNG industry is characteristic of many operations in the tropics (37,38).

Education and information could help people recognize the value of forest resources, learn how to participate in land-use planning, and better understand democracy and the responsibilities it demands of both politicians and constituents.

Imperialism and Bureaucracy

Imperialism takes many forms and still remains in the dual standards which permit destructive harvesting. It is the right and the responsibility of every nation to set the minimum standard, but this can and should be improved upon. If, for example, Japan imposed the same stringent environmental requirements on Japanese operations in Malaysia as it does on operations in Japan, there would be little opposition to their role in Sarawak and elsewhere (39).

Inefficient, understaffed, and ill-equipped forest services invite corruption. The PNG situation was exacerbated by the limited capability of the Provincial Forest Services, many having insufficient staff and resources. Staff rely on logging firms for transport, cannot arrive unannounced, and have limited opportunities to inspect operations (40). Low staff turnover and little peer review limits innovation and contributes to corruption. Throughout the tropics, forest services are sufficient to facilitate but are unable to control exploitation.

Ignorance and Carelessness

Sustainable timber harvesting relies heavily on the skill and the will of machine operators, but training and incentives for these operators are often neglected (30,41). This is inexcusable, as this responsibility lies wholly within the forestry sector, is cost effective, and may enable a major reduction in the environmental impact of operations. For example, damage to remaining trees can be reduced if the chainsaw operators control the direction in which trees fall. Erosion, soil, and nutrient losses can be minimized when the tractor driver is skilled and understands the consequences. Training may increase profitability of logging operations, as fuel consumption decreases, breakage of timber and equipment is reduced, and productivity is enhanced. Careful harvesting may save contractors $8 per meter^3 harvested, and may increase the value of future harvests by 30 percent (42). It also saves lives and reduces injuries. The current fatality rate among loggers in Sarawak is 21 times higher than in Canada.

International Trade Policies

Trade and tax policies also have an impact on the rainforest. Efforts to influence domestic prices also influence prices and production worldwide, and so shape the destiny and behavior of farmers in the tropics. Changes in policy may be worse than the *status quo*, as increased prices or demand may stimulate new clearing for industrial agriculture and cash cropping. Reduced prices and diminished markets may deprive many of their incomes and force them to cultivate a bigger area of a less productive crop, or to abandon their farms to the loan-sharks and start subsistence cultivation in the forest.

Links between rainforests and agriculture policy may be far-reaching. The Netherlands imports fodder for livestock; tapioca from Thailand and soybeans from Brazil are cheaper than European alternatives. Almost 4 million tonnes of tapioca a year are imported, mostly from Thailand, from 700,000 hectares of cultivation (43). Over 3 million tonnes of soybeans come mainly from Brazil, and correspond to almost 2 million hectares of cultivated land. The total area of soybean production in Brazil is about 10 million hectares, much of which was once forested land. Would import restrictions help? Could the EC duties on tapioca, which amount to $40 million a year, be deployed to boost sustainable production? Could Thailand produce livestock and meat products to keep the nutrients, e.g., nitrogen pollution in Netherlands, employment and added value in Thailand?

Popular Solutions

Although there is scope for some technical research on the problems of tropical rainforest deproduction and deforestation (44), much of the solution lies in the application of a few simple and well-established principles. The principles are simple, but their application may not be. Successful implementation of any solution will require patience, understanding, and the cooperation of many individuals and institutions.

Plantations

Critics of rainforest harvesting advocate that the world's timber should be drawn from fast-growing plantations established on deforested land, rather than from the natural forests. Unfortunately, there are several practical difficulties. Rarely is sufficient land available, in suitable tracts, for efficient plantation management. Where land areas are sufficient, soil and rainfall may not promote fast growth. Fast growth usually means monocultures, fertilizers, pesticides, and cultural practices that diminish other values. Plantations also incur considerable financial risks and environmental hazards. There is certainly a place for plantations, but we should consolidate better management of existing plantations before we advocate increased plantation areas.

Technology and human needs change rapidly compared to tree growth, and flexibility is necessary. Future markets for plantation timber are uncertain, so plantations should first satisfy local needs such as fuelwood and construction materials. High value timbers may be a better prospect than fast-growing species for fiber.

Portable Sawmills

The portable sawmill enables the conversion of logs in the forest, may reduce soil disturbance and road-construction costs, and increase benefits from local processing. Unfortunately, these benefits may not be realized. Like the chainsaw, the portable sawmill is just a tool, that can be used wisely or destructively. Many portable sawmill operations create too much soil disturbance, leave piles of sawdust and debris, and obtain a lower recovery than conventional sawmills. The only certain benefit is, probably, the reduction in transport costs between the forest and the market.

Tropical Timber Bans

Boycotts on tropical timber have been promoted as one way to save the tropical rainforest, and have been effected by many authorities (25). Although no governments have yet implemented such bans, they are under consideration by several nations. Would they help to reduce the loss of rainforest? To answer this question, we need to examine three scenarios: a total ban, a ban effected by some consumers, and a ban effected on some producers.

Although unattainable, it is instructive to consider the effect of a total ban by all consumers on all producers of tropical timbers. Would it save the rainforest? If effected, it would stop the international trade in tropical timber in its present form (it might continue in a less recognizable form such as paper pulp), but domestic consumption would continue. Exporting nations would suffer a loss of foreign earnings, a trade imbalance, and unemployment. The natural forest would become worthless and might be converted to more productive forms of land use. Detrimental side effects of such a ban would probably outweigh the benefits. However, the scenario is unlikely to arise.

It seems improbable that a simultaneous ban could be effected, and it is more likely that the EC would support a ban while Japan would not. The message to producers would be that future markets were doubtful and that they should "make hay while the sun shines." The remaining consumers, as astute entrepreneurs, would offer lower prices. The result would be an escalating harvest with diminished returns to the producer countries. In the rush to realize profits before the opportunity ceased, some countries would further neglect environmental guidelines and supervision. By itself, a ban will be counterproductive. While calls for bans remain, we must deliver a clear message that we will continue to purchase, and pay a premium for, timber produced in a sustainable way. One difficulty is that few sustainable harvesting operations currently exist, and this may appear bluff (45). In the short term, we must grant some producers this recognition, even if they do not presently reach the ultimate standard. We need to devise clear criteria for sustainability, to show all producers where they stand, and to help them reach the required standard.

The third scenario bans nonsustainable production while supporting sustainable production, to minimize negative implications of limited participation. The difficulty lies in assessing what constitutes sustainability and in defining the time frame necessary to achieve it. Criteria and procedures for assessing sustainability have recently been proposed, but no field operations have yet been assessed in this way (46,47). Few existing operations will satisfy these provisions, so interim standards may be necessary. Excessive haste in demanding compliance may trigger economic and social difficulties with detrimental effects on the forest, e.g., subsistence agriculture. This scenario offers the best solution, but care and understanding will be necessary for effective implementation.

Labelling

In theory, labelling of timber would enable consumers to exert their preference for sustainable products. Unfortunately, the validity of labels is hard to control. Regional labelling may enable species-level controls but may penalize a country for its neighbor's indiscretions. National, and concession-based, labelling pose considerable difficulties in tracing timber, and create opportunities for importing and reexporting through green-certified ports. The challenge is to provide reliable labelling at a modest cost. Although, most tropical timbers could command higher prices, the extra revenue should accrue to the country of origin and be invested in better forest management, rather than to a monitoring bureaucracy. Some illegitimate labels may be an acceptable price to pay for a realistic ceiling on monitoring costs. Accreditation schemes also must include plantations to minimize pressure for conversion of natural forests to plantations and other land uses.

Sustainable Timber Production

Is sustainable timber production from rainforests possible? What constitutes sustainable production? Is it relevant to the survival of the rainforests? After all, it is human nature to use available resources, irrespective of sustainability. We should strive for *wise use* of these resources, but strict sustainability may be hard to ascertain. However, as long as we achieve *wise use*, does it matter if some external inputs are necessary to maintain the system? Why are we so insistent that rainforest management is sustainable, when little else in developing countries works well, and when our agricultural systems and energy consumption are clearly unsustainable?

These questions are relevant. Many agricultural projects on rainforest soils have failed, but similar examples exist for every ecosystem. Clearly, there is a limit for every ecosystem but, provided we stay within that limit, sustainable production should be possible. Although precise definition of the limit may be complex, effective operational guidelines are easy to define. Harvesting of timber and other products may be sustainable provided that few nutrients are lost, both directly by harvesting, and indirectly through erosion; that soil disturbance and erosion are minimized; and that natural habitats and processes are not disrupted (30). Sustainable management of tropical forests is feasible. The Queensland (41,48–50) and CELOS (51,52) systems are well documented examples of sustainable timber-production systems, and other examples also exist (53–55).

Alternative Solutions

These forest sector initiatives are only part of the solution. The population-poverty cycle remains a major obstacle needing major social, political, and economic reform. It cannot be solved by the forestry sector alone, but requires a concerted and sustained multisectoral effort. To be effective, such reform efforts must be supported internally, but opportunities to initiate and influence reform are available. The developed nations can do much to create a favorable economic environment by fostering trade and tourism, and to stimulate new ideas through education and cultural exchanges.

Land Tenure

Land reform is a prerequisite for eliminating deforestation. Land and resources are rarely distributed equally, but in many developing countries the inequality is extreme; the poorest own nothing, and have nothing to loose by destroying the forest. In Brazil, for example, 4.5 percent of landowners have 81 percent of the farmland whilst 70 percent of rural families are landless (56). Unless these landless have satisfactory employment, they have little choice but to clear the forest.

Secure tenure may also limit deforestation. Some deforestation occurs because the harvesting agreement provides a *de facto* title deed. Elsewhere, traditional landowners may clear lands not immediately required for agriculture because they feel they have a more secure claim on cleared lands. Official recognition of ownership and efficient resolution of disputes over all lands regardless of land use may prevent such deforestation.

Many timber-harvesting concessions are short-term agreements, and may not be renewed. Companies have little incentive to do a good job if their concessions may be lost to less conscientious competitors within a few years. Thus, one necessary incentive for sustainable management is secure tenure for concessionaires, conditional upon good performance.

Agricultural Production

Improved production from existing agricultural lands and existing timber plantations through higher yields and less degradation will relieve the pressure on the remaining natural forests. Agroforestry offers the potential to provide fuelwood, fodder, and other benefits from agricultural lands without reducing agricultural yields (57). It may be possible to modify agricultural systems to provide great conservation values and less of a barrier to migration between remaining forested areas.

Information

Good policy and management rely on efficient provision of information to politicians and constituents, to policy makers and land managers, and to the public in both developed and developing countries. Policy makers are rarely given substantiated facts on the costs of deforestation and degradation. People need to know the value of forests, the rate of deforestation, and the economic and ecological consequences of their loss.

In many countries, women are the main users of the forest, and the main victims of deforestation. For example, fuelwood is usually collected by women, for whom deforestation means more work. Many obstacles restrict input by women during community consultation and planning, and one solution may be more women foresters. Most forest services and training centers are male-dominated, both in developed and developing countries, and incentives for the recruitment of women may be helpful. Many forestry schools are located in the forest, away from other centers of learning, and offer little opportunity for forestry trainees to broaden their communications skills across disciplines.

Stability and Outlook

Political and economic stability is a prerequisite for long-term corporate investment in sustainable timber production. Stability in trade policies and commodity prices may avoid the destructive "boom and bust" that destroys much rainforest, for timber as well as for farmland. Progressive reform in the tropical timber trade, and in other areas, needs a broad outlook to see both sides of the issues, and to appreciate possible unintended consequences of our reforms, protectionism, and policies.

Research

While there is considerable scope for forest research in the tropics, a lot can be done by implementing existing knowledge. Many forest services have much potentially useful information languishing as unpublished reports, and the collation and dissemination of this material could be cost-effective. Many trial plots and experiments could provide useful data for species selection and silviculture; documented failures provide as much information as successes. Consolidating such information may not have the appeal of a new experiment, but it eliminates the long wait for growth plots to reach a useful age.

Taxonomy is essential to support research in the tropical rainforest; it is a prerequisite for documenting and communicating results. Most forest services have species lists with undescribed taxa, known only by a local name or specimen number. The silvicultural characteristics of many species remain unknown, little is known about nutrient cycling in most forests, few species have been screened for useful compounds, and efficient techniques for processing and utilizing the less common species are unknown. Some species may have a pivotal or keystone role in providing food during lean times and in acting as vectors for the dispersal of seed (58,59). We need to know the identity of these species and more about their roles. Processing of forest products in the tropics is often primitive and dangerous; considerable scope exists to improve safety and efficiency of timber extraction and processing, and other forest products (41,60). Most forest services have insufficient or inadequate growth data from the natural forest, thus, growth models and simulation studies cannot be made, and we can only guess the sustainable timber yield.

Shaping the Future of the Rainforests: What Can We Do?

What can we, as individuals, organizations, and nations, do to effect solutions? There is much to be done with limited resources, so we should interact with, rather than duplicate, existing initiatives such as the Tropical Forestry Action Plan of the United Nations Food and Agriculture Organization (61), the ITTO (International Tropical Timber Organization) Action Plan (62), and the new Centre for International Forest Research (CIFOR) of the Coordinating Group for International Agricultural Research (CGIAR) (63).

Reform Starts at Home

Direct action may feel good, but do little to help the cause. Buy labor-intensive goods manufactured in developing countries to boost employment and wealth. Be selective and thrifty with timber, and ask your supplier how it was produced, about the royalties paid, and where it was processed. Choose sustainable tropical timber first, as it needs support. Don't simply switch to temperate timbers or plastics, but apply the same criteria for sustainability to all the goods you consume.

Lobby for reform in trade policies to stimulate trade with developing countries in manufactured goods rather than primary products. Existing trade barriers cost developing countries over $100 billion a year in income foregone, a figure half as large again as total foreign aid, and more than enough to service the debt to outside creditors. About half the Third World debt is owed by 27 counties with 97 percent of the tropical forest, countries with a net deficit whose debt is increasing every year.

Training in Communication and Management

Foresters in many tropical countries are well trained in forestry and may hold higher degrees from prestigious universities in Europe and North America. Unfortunately, these achievements have often not been translated into good forest management, perhaps because of overemphasis on technical training instead of management. Sustainable forestry is like a major civil engineering undertaking: it involves land-use plans, community consultation, the timely involvement of many individuals from many different disciplines, quality control over all operations, and efficient accounting and revenue collection. But how much training is devoted to management, accounting, public relations, and communication? Ph.D. students may choose to study in prestigious technical areas such as gene transfer, micropropagation, and mycorrhiza, but return to management and administration positions. It may be better to provide on-the-job exchanges to give hands-on management experience in efficient organizations. The Barnett Report suggests that emphasis on accounting is essential (36).

Provide Information

Tropical forestry is hampered by both too much and too little information, much of which in unavailable to key players. Many forest services lack current information, and receive few foreign scientific journals. It is easy to support institutions with journal subscriptions, but few aid agencies want such small projects.

Much of the important information on tropical forestry does not appear in journals, but in the "grey literature" of various aid agencies. It doesn't appear in *Current Contents, Forestry Abstracts,* or on-line databases, and isn't available to many potential readers. Whilst confidentiality between donors and recipients requires some restrictions, it is unfortunate that so much information has such a limited audience.

Many forest services lack good maps and reliable area estimates of their forest estates, and these deficiencies can be overcome using satellite technology. Satellite data have proven utility for forest management and mapping, and Global Positioning Systems offer the possibility of efficient forest surveying (64). Support, cooperation, and training in these technologies may provide a cost-effective way to improve information for forest management.

Foster Social, Political, and Economic Stability

How can we stimulate reform? How do people develop higher expectations of their political and social systems? Many factors are involved, but experiences and expectations of individuals are key factors. Bans may hasten reform, but isolation may not be productive, and increased social and economic links may also stimulate reform. How much aid should be reward and how much should try to influence reform and development? What role can and should the timber trade play in influencing human rights? There are no easy answers, but open discussion of these topics may lead to a more satisfactory conclusion for all parties.

In Summary

We won't save the tropical forest overnight, but there is much we can do to improve the prognosis for these forests and the people dependent upon them. We should not get carried away with reactive and emotive solutions, but should try to identify and alleviate the real causes. Much can be achieved locally, by exerting consumer preference, providing information, asking questions, and lobbying politicians. What is most important is to begin.

Notes

1. Whitmore, T.C. 1984. *Tropical Rainforests of the Far East*, 2nd ed. Clarendon Press, Oxford.
2. Anonymous. 1991. *Tropical Forest Report by the Government of the Federal Republic of Germany, with Special Regard to Tropical Moist Forests*. Press and Information Office, Bonn.
3. Houghton, J.T., Jenkins, G.J., and Ephraums, J.J. (eds). 1990. *Climate Change: The IPCC Scientific Assessment*. Cambridge University Press.
4. Rotmans, J., and Swart, R.J. 1991. Modelling tropical deforestation and its consequences for global climate. *Ecol. Model. 58*, 217–247.

5. Goreau, T.J. 1990. Balancing atmospheric carbon dioxide. *Ambio 19*, 230–236.
6. Glynn, P.W. 1990. *Global Ecological Consequences of the 1982–83 El Niño-Southern Oscillation*. Elsevier Oceanography Series Volume 52. Elsevier, Amsterdam.
7. Schroeder, P. 1992. Carbon storage potential of short rotation tropical tree plantations. *For. Ecol. Mgmt 50*, 31–41.
8. Evans, J. 1982. *Plantation Forestry in the Tropics*. Oxford University Press, Oxford.
9. Schneider, C. 1991. The politics of prevention. *Clim. Change 19*, 257–261.
10. Sayer, J., McNeely, J.A., and Stuart, S.N. 1990. The conservation of tropical forest vertebrates. In: *Vertebrates in the Tropics*. Peters, G. and Hutterer, R. (eds). Museum Alexander Koeinig, Bonn, 407–419.
11. Johns, A.D. 1992. Vertebrate responses to selective logging: implications for the design of logging systems. *Phil. Trans. R. Soc. Lond. B 335*, 435–442.
12. Lambert, F.R. 1992. The consequences of selective logging for Bornean lowland forest birds. *Phil. Trans. R. Soc. Lond. B 335*, 443–457.
13. Johns, Λ.D. 1985. Selective logging and wildlife conservation in tropical rain-forest: problems and recommendations. *Biol. Conserv. 31*, 355–375.
14. Joyce, C. 1991. Prospectors for tropical medicines. *New Sci. 1791*, 36–40.
15. Lanly, J.P., Singh, K.D., and Janz, K. 1991. FAO's 1990 reassessment of tropical forest cover. *Nat. Resour. 27*, 21–26.
16. Hardin, G.J. 1968. The tragedy of the commons. *Science 162*, 1243–1248. (Reprinted in Hardin, G.J. 1972. *Exploring New Ethics for Survival*. Viking, NY).
17. Cox, S.J. 1985. No tragedy on the commons. *Environ. Ethics 7*, 49–61.
18. Peters, C.M., Gentry, A.H., and Mendelsohn, R.O. 1989. Valuation of an Amazonian rainforest. *Nature 339*, 655–656.
19. Schwartsman, S. 1989. Extractive reserves in the Amazon. In: *Fragile Lands of Latin America: Strategies for Sustainable Development*. Browder, J.G. (ed.). Westview Press, Boulder, 150–163.
20. Godoy, R., and Lubowski, R. 1992. Guidelines for the economic valuation of nontimber tropical-forest products. *Curr. Anthropol. 33*, 423–433.
21. Hodgson, G., and Dixon, J.A. 1988. Logging versus fisheries and tourism in Palawan. *Occasional Papers of the East-West Environment and Policy Institute, Paper No. 7*.
22. Bruijnzeel, L.A. 1992. Managing tropical forest watersheds for production: where contradictory theory and practice co-exist. In: *Wise Management of Tropical Forests*. Miller, F. (ed). Forestry Institute, Oxford, 37–75.
23. Hamilton, L. 1992. Storm disasters—has logging been unfairly blamed? *IUCN Forest Conservation Programme Newsletter*, No. 12:5.
24. Rao, Y.S. 1988. Flash floods in southern Thailand. *Tiger Paper 15*, 1–2.

25. Hamilton, L.S., 1991. Tropical forests: identifying and clarifying issues. *Unasylva 42*, 19–27.

26. Sayer, J.A., and Whitmore, T.C. 1991. Tropical moist forests: Destruction and species extinction. *Biol. Conserv.* 55, 199–213.

27. Jacobs, M. 1981. *The Tropical Rain Forest.* Springer Verlag.

28. Laurance, W.F. 1991. Ecological correlates of extinction proneness in Australian tropical rain forest mammals. *Conserv. Biol. 5*, 79–89.

29. International Tropical Timber Organization. 1990. ITTO guidelines for the sustainable management of natural tropical forests. *ITTO Technical Series 5.* ITTO, Yokohama.

30. Vanclay, J.K. 1992. Environmentally sound timber harvesting: Logging guidelines, conservation reserves and rehabilitation studies. In: *Restoration of Tropical Forest Ecosystems.* Lieth, H. and Lohmann, M. (eds). Kluwer Academic. (In press).

31. Lamb, D. 1991. Combining traditional and commercial uses of rain forests. *Nat. Resour. 27*, 3–11.

32. Lamb, D. 1990. *Exploiting the Tropical Rain Forest: An Account of Pulpwood Logging in Papua New Guinea.* Man and the Biosphere Series, vol. 3. UNESCO/Parthenon, Paris.

33. Ehrlich, P.R. and Ehrlich, A.H. 1990. *The Population Explosion.* Simon & Schuster, Sydney.

34. Vitousek, P.M., Ehrlich, P.R., Ehrlich, A.H., and Matson, P.A. 1986. Human appropriation of the products of photosynthesis. *BioScience 34*, 386–373.

35. Marshall, G. 1990. The political economy of logging: The Barnett inquiry into corruption in the Papua New Guinea Timber Industry. *The Ecologist 20,* 174–181.

36. Marshall, G. 1990. *The Barnett Report.* Asia-Pacific Action Group, Hobart.

37. Sarawak Study Group. 1989. Logging in Sarawak: the Belaga experience. In: *Logging Against the Natives of Sarawak.* INSAN, Petaling Jaya, 1–30.

38. Anonymous. 1992. *Plunder in Ghana's Rainforest for Illegal Profit.* Friends of the Earth, London.

39. Nectoux, F., and Kuroda, Y. 1989. *Timber From the South Seas.* WWF, Gland.

40. Flint, A. 1992. Rainforest logging in PNG. *Inst. For. Aust. Newsl. 33,* 25–30.

41. Crome, F.H.J., Moore, L.A., and Richards, G.C. 1992. A study of logging damage in upland rainforest in north Queensland. *For. Ecol. Mgmt 49,* 1–29.

42. International Tropical Timber Organization, 1990. *ITTO Action Plan: Criteria and Priority Areas for Programme Development and Project Work.* ITTO, Yokohama.

43. Elliott, C. 1991. *Tropical Forest Conservation.* WWF Position Paper 7, September 1991. WWF, Gland.

44. Vanclay, J.K. 1991. Research needs for sustainable forest resources. In: *Tropical Rainforest Research in Australia: Present Status and Future Directions for the Institute for Tropical Rainforest Studies.* Goundberg, N. and Bonell, M. (eds). ITRS, Townsville, 133–143.

45. Poore, D., Burgess, P., Palmer, J., Rietbergen, S., and Synnott, T. 1989. *No Timber Without Trees: Sustainability in the Tropical Forest.* Earthscan, London.

46. International Tropical Timber Organization. 1992. Criteria for the measurement of sustainable tropical forest management. *ITTO Policy Development Series Paper No. 3.* ITTO, Yokohama.

47. Ussach, I. 1992. *Draft Principles and Criteria for the Forest Stewardship Council, May 15, 1992.* Forest Stewardship Council, Gland.

48. Vanclay, J.K. 1990. Effects of selection logging on rainforest productivity. *Austral. For. 53,* 200–214.

49. Vanclay, J.K. 1993. *Lessons from the Queensland Rainforests: A Century Striving for Sustainability.* IUFRO Centennial Conference, Berlin. Forest Research Institute, Malaysia.

50. Vanclay, J.K. 1993. Sustainable timber harvesting: simulation studies in the tropical rainforests of north Queensland. *For. Ecol. Mgmt.* (In press).

51. Anonymous. 1992. The CELOS management system: treading softly in the forest. *ITTO Forest Management Update 2,* 4–6.

52. van Bodegom, A.J., and de Graaf, N.R. (eds). 1992. *The CELOS Management System: A Provisional Manual.* IKC-NBLF, Wageningen.

53. Buschbacher, R.J. 1990. Natural forest management in the humid tropics: ecological, social and economic considerations. *Ambio 19,* 253–258.

54. Anderson, A.B. (ed). 1990. *Alternatives to Deforestation: Steps toward Sustainable Use of the Amazon Rain Forest.* Columbia University Press, New York.

55. Finegan, B. 1992. The management potential of neotropical secondary lowland rain forest. *For. Ecol. Mgmt 47,* 295–321.

56. Sawyer, J. 1990. *Tropical Forests.* WWF, Switzerland.

57. Nair, P.K.R. (ed). 1989. *Agroforestry Systems in the Tropics.* Kluwer, Dordrecht.

58. Howe, H.F. 1977. Bird activity and seed dispersal of a tropical wet forest tree. *Ecology 58,* 539–550.

59. Terborgh, J. 1986. Keystone plant resources in the tropical forest. In: *Conservation Biology: the Science of Scarcity and Diversity.* Soule, M.E. (ed). Sinauer, Sunderland, 330–344.

60. Jagels, R. 1990. Notes on responding to those concerned about perception and reality. IV. Alternatives to boycotting. *J. For. 88,* 30–31.

61. Committee on Forest Development in the Tropics, 1985. *Tropical Forestry Action Plan.* FAO, Rome.

62. ITTO. 1990. *ITTO Action Plan: Criteria and Priority Areas for Programme Development and Project Work.* ITTO, Yokohama.

63. Center for International Forestry Research (CIFOR). 1992. *Strategic Planning Thematic Papers: Issues Contributing to Program Development.* ACIAR, Canberra.

64. Sader, S.A., Stone, T.A., and Joyce, A.T. 1990. Remote sensing of tropical forests: An overview of research and applications using non-photographic sensors. *Photogramm. Eng. Remote Sensing 56,* 1343–1351.

65. First submitted April 9, 1992, accepted for publication after revision November 11, 1992.

11

After Rio: Our Forests, Ourselves

Sandra Hackman

Nongovernmental organizations both foreign and domestic are helping countries such as Brazil link environmental and social issues.

Brazil is a land of extremes. The most populous and largest nation in Latin America, it contains one-fifth of the planet's freshwater and its most extensive rainforest. The country's GNP grew at a yearly clip of 7 percent during the "miracle years" of the 1960s and 1970s, and though that rate has slowed considerably, Brazil still boasts one of the largest economies in the developing world. Yet despite its abundant natural resources and considerable wealth, the nation's income distribution is among the world's most skewed. One-third of its people live in poverty while 4 percent of the population owns half the land. Millions of people live in squatter settlements on the outskirts of cities such as Rio de Janeiro, their numbers swelling daily as cattle ranchers, loggers, and miners encroach on the country's rural expanses and dispossess local inhabitants.

Brazil's willingness to host the U.N. Conference on Environment and Development (UNCED) in Rio this past June thus seems appropriate. Billed as the largest global meeting ever convened, the Earth Summit aimed to reconcile intensifying international pressure to protect the world's natural inheritance with a mandate to address the devastating poverty endemic to much of the Third World. Yet in its focus on long-term environmental questions, the conference failed to address the needs of people who must daily cope with degraded conditions that threaten their lives.

157

"UNCED avoided dealing with the pressing problems that we know already exist," says Jesse Ribot, professor of urban planning at MIT. In cities such as São Paulo, for example, only 50 percent of the population has access to sewage systems, and much of the drinking water is contaminated. "Safe drinking water is the single biggest threat to public health worldwide," according to Jonathan Fox, MIT political science professor.

Participants in the Global Forum, a gathering in Rio of nongovernmental organizations (NGOs) of the North and South—or "haves" and "have nots"—attempted to address such questions during the summit. Negotiations at this parallel conference, which included international environmental and grass-roots groups alike, reflected a growing realization that even deforestation and other large-scale ecological threats affect the lives of local residents as much as the long-term health of the planet. "Deforestation needs to be stopped not only because of global warming but because people live in the forests and depend on them," says Ribot. "By not paying attention to people, we are undermining both people and trees."

The Amazon, where widespread burning has prompted much of the outcry over rainforest loss, is a case in point. "The Amazon is not a sanctuary but an inhabited area, home to 17 million people," says Antônio Rocha Magalhães, a former secretary of planning for the Brazilian state of Ceará. While "long-term climate change is the hook by which people from the North can focus on problems in the South, regional impacts from burning, including declining rainfall and rising temperatures, are more immediate and severe."

Recognizing this, Northern scientists and funders have joined rainforest residents in an innovative attempt to combine social benefits with environmental protection in the Brazilian Amazon. In areas called extractive reserves, these NGOs are forging a link between efforts to manage natural resources and alleviate poverty.

Sustainable Development in the Rainforest

In the reserves, the Brazilian government guarantees land rights to long-time residents of the forest such as rubber trappers and Indian tribes. The inspiration of Brazil's National Council of Rubber Tappers, which sought to protect the traditional way of life of people who harvest latex, the reserves aim to allow residents to live off the Amazon's bounty without destroying its ecological integrity. Before 1988, when the government created the first such region, the idea of establishing an inhabited conservation area had no legal precedent. Now 19 reserves—covering some 8.3 million acres—allow shared ownership of land among rubber tappers and Indians and restrict encroachment by cattle ranchers and squatter farmers. (President Fernando Collor de Mello announced the creation of the five newest reserves, some outside the rainforest, just before the summit.)

Convincing the government to establish the reserves—a significant achievement in a country that has long subsidized clearcutting and encouraged rainforest immigration—was a first step. The hard part—"setting up an infrastructure to make the idea work"—is now the focus of local inhabitants assisted by Northern funders, says José Roberto Borges, director of Brazilian programs for the Rainforest Action Network, based in San Francisco.

A one million-acre reserve in Acre, on the upper Juruá River, one of the major tributaries of the Amazon, is the site of many efforts to create a long-term infrastructure. Until 1987 the area was completely dominated by *seringalistas*, rubber barons who forced destitute migrants from the Northeast to work in the forest essentially as slaves. Today NGOs such as the Rainforest Action Network and Cultural Survival, based in Cambridge, Mass., provide technical assistance and funding to the Union of Indian Nations and the National Council of Rubber Tappers, which manage the reserves and sell fruit pulp, nuts, and tropical oils to distributors. Cultural Survival requires buyers of rainforest products to share a percentage of their profits with native suppliers. And to bring more of the processing and thus the profits under local control, the organization has helped set up a community-owned factory in Acre to shell Brazil nuts before they are shipped.

The income from such sales is being used to hire health workers, establish schools, monitor violence against rubber tappers and Indians by ranchers, and purchase cooperatively owned boats to ship supplies into the region and goods out. Digitizing maps of the Amazon is another important joint project mounted by Cultural Survival and CEGI, the country's largest human-rights group. Computers scanning the maps against Landsat photos can detect illegal incursions into the reserves in a matter of weeks or months, says Cultural Survival research director Jason Clay.

Northern groups such as Oxfam and the Ford Foundation have also helped support the Center for Indian Research and Training, which combines schooling in Western biology and law with traditional techniques for sustainably harvesting the forest's trees, animals, and fruits. The National Council of Rubber Tappers and the Union of Indian Nations are now attempting to secure funding for a computer network that would link the groups' dispersed branches with environmental and human-rights organizations in Brazil and abroad.

Northern NGOs are also assisting residents of sensitive areas outside the reserves. In Mato Grosso, a savannah that is home to thousands of landless people, the Rainforest Action Network is funding small cooperatives of residents who make and sell adobe bricks as an alternative to cutting nearby forests for salable wood. In the northern state of Pará, landless peasants are collaborating with agronomists from the Gaia Foundation, established in England by former Brazilian environmental secretary José Lutzenberger, to develop high-yielding strains of native crops that thrive in marginal soils.

Rainforest residents aim to use such efforts to change the way both government and outsiders look at environmental questions. "The rubber tappers have forged a link between social issues and large-scale problems such as deforestation, says Yale University anthropologist Margaret Keck. "They are not just saying that Brazil should stop cutting down trees because it's bad for the world; they are saying that we should be treating populations differently."

Stephan Schwartzman, an anthropologist with the Environmental Defense Fund, sees an expanding awareness among environmental groups such as EDF, which have long pursued a purely conservation-oriented approach, that deforestation is basically a human-rights issue. "Extractive reserves are the first grass-roots alternative to the kind of top-down, outside-in development debacles that have destroyed much of the Amazon," Schwartzman says. "The idea has succeeded where broader initiatives to 'save the rainforest' have failed."

Frances Spivy-Weber of the Audubon Society, which has established branches in countries such as Mexico, Guatemala, El Salvador, and Venezuela, agrees that the focus of environmental groups is changing: trying to keep people out of ecologically sensitive land no longer works as a long-term strategy even in the United States. Working on site, Audubon and its sister organizations of the North can contribute experience in environmental advocacy while learning about the needs of local residents as well as of the land, she says.

Despite the promise of extractive reserves, both Southern and Northern activists say they have yet to prove their long-term viability. Producing commodities in quantities that supply the international market can actually disrupt the local economy and put more pressure on the forests than they can bear, says Glenn Switkes, producer of the documentary *Amazonia: Voices from the Rainforest.* "People don't yet know what sustainable development in the Amazon really means."

EDF's Schwartzman adds that resolving land rights is only one measure of success in the Amazon: "Rainforest residents also want long-term access to education and health care, services that most citizens expect the government to provide." Meanwhile, he fears the effects of fickle demand for forest products—especially if international interest in saving the Amazon wanes. In fact, the region has a history of boom and bust, with U.S. and European demand for commodities such as rubber, chicle gum, and lumber attaining feverish levels and then cooling off.

According to Schwartzman, long-term stabilization of the region will require examining pressure produced by unsustainable development in the rest of the country. "Many of the people who are panning for gold or cutting the Amazon to farm, including migrants from other parts of the country, are desperate—they need real options."

Urban Prospects

Because many people lack such options, most of the Third World's population is becoming urbanized, says Henrique Rattner, professor of political science at São Paulo University. In Brazil, hundreds of thousands of people have been evicted from their land by the mechanization of agriculture and a push to grow sugarcane for gasohol, while some two-thirds of the people who once inhabited the Amazon rainforest have left for the cities. Cândido Gryzbowski of the Brazilian Institute for Social and Economic Analyses (IBASE) says that even Curitiba, a city in the relatively wealthy state of Paraná often cited for its ambitious public transportation and recycling program, is sustaining an influx of rural refugees that is straining its ability to provide services.

Although Northern NGOs often focus on the problems of rural areas, local NGOs and neighborhood groups are convincing many Brazilian cities to address the needs of poor residents, says Herbert de Souza, president of IBASE. Neighborhood groups have been particularly effective in monitoring local officials for corruption, which is much less severe than at the federal level, he maintains. Provisions in the 1988 constitution, adopted after 21 years of military rule, have funneled money from the federal to the local level and encouraged urban dwellers to press for better housing, schools, and water supplies.

To address a crisis of homelessness in urban areas throughout Brazil, many community groups have focused on expanding the supply of permanent housing, says Gryzbowski. In Goiânia, a city near the capital of Brasilia, a federation of some 24 organizations has constructed modest dwellings for 80,000 families using the labor of residents and some funds from local government. The cities of Rio de Janeiro and São Paulo have benefitted from similar efforts to build houses on land occupied by recent immigrants.

Residents of São Gonçalo, dormitory city for Rio de Janeiro and one of Rio State's poorest municipalities, have mobilized to secure a safer water supply. Home to one million people, the city endures one of the country's highest rates of immigration. CEPIA, an NGO established in 1990, has been encouraging women to join forces to pressure local officials for basic services. "Women are the key to the struggle to provide potable water for their families," explains Jacqueline Pitanguy, one of the group's founders and former head of the National Council for Women's Rights. As a result of CEPIA-sponsored debates on the connection between the neighborhood's quality of life and women's health needs, municipal authorities have begun to upgrade the sewage system and are funding a program to provide reproductive care.

In Santos, a major southern port with half a million residents, an enterprising group of mothers formed an NGO in 1990 to reclaim the area's polluted beaches, which suffered from decades of illegal sewage and industrial-waste disposal from several nearby cities. With support from businesspeople, students, and other citizens, SOS Praias convinced state and local officials to fund new waste-treatment plants and crack down on illegal dumping, generating much-needed jobs in the process. Santos is also working with neighborhood groups to install a sanitation system in densely populated poor communities, and to set up a program to collect household waste formerly dumped into nearby ravines. Recycled wastepaper has been used to supply schoolchildren with 200,000 notebooks.

Urban areas often suffer from environmental degradation of the surrounding countryside. Roberto Klabin, president of SOS Mata Atlântica (the nation's largest environmental organization), says that the few remaining stands of timber along the industrialized southern coast must be protected to prevent landslides that crush impoverished communities clinging to steep land. In the town of Iguape in São Paulo State, Klabin's group has established an agricultural school and experiment station to promote sustainable harvesting of *caixeta*, a tree that inhabitants cut and sell to manufacturers of products such as pencils. Working with the U.S.-based Nature Conservancy and Conservation International, the group is also fostering sustainable oyster production among coastal communities so that residents are not forced to cut the dwindling forest.

Cetesb, a publicly owned environmental company in São Paulo State, has enlisted the help of neighborhood groups in tackling oppressive air pollution in Cubatão. NGOs in the city, known as the Valley of Death and site of some of the country's worst air quality, have claimed a link between emissions from petrochemical and steel plants, as well as factories owned by multinationals such as Union Carbide and Monsanto, and high incidence of serious birth defects. In the late seventies, the World Bank established a line of credit to enable companies to install pollution-control equipment. But not until a gas pipeline exploded in 1983, killing up to 200 people, did Cetesb gain enough clout to convince the companies to act.

Holding neighborhood seminars and encouraging residents to use a hotline to report noxious fumes, the agency pressured the companies to buy the new equipment. The result was a significant cut in emissions—although María Carmen Lemos, a Brazilian graduate student in political science at MIT, cautions that the gains have improved conditions only "from horrible to bad." Still, Cetesb has been asked to help other states reproduce its results. And the experience may draw a second look from national and local leaders who maintain that dealing with pollution cannot be a priority amid other pressing concerns.

NGOs Look Ahead

To have a lasting effect, rural and urban NGOs must forge a common platform—a task that participants hoped the recent Global Forum would facilitate. According to Yale's Keck, conference preparations accelerated contacts within Brazil among usually fractious environmental groups, women's groups, and unions. Gryzbowski, of IBASE, says the summit also prompted discussion among many Brazilians about the link between deteriorating environmental conditions and widespread poverty. "People realize that if poor citizens build slum housing on sensitive land, it's because they have been excluded from the mainstream economy." He credits the rubber tappers with bringing home this connection.

Such realizations are important because the impact of Agenda 21—the nonbinding blueprint for sustainable development signed by governments attending the summit—will depend on domestic politics in Brazil and elsewhere. Says former planning secretary Magalhães, now head of an NGO that hopes to bring responsible development to the arid Northeast, "If you don't have local conditions in each country that encourage sustainable development, then outside funds and treaties won't work."

Such conditions may be building in Brazil. Political science professor Rattner sees a growing realization that "the current world economic model based on the validity of the market and ruled by the international banking system has brought Brazil to a stalemate, producing a polarized society based on waste." He cites the tentative efforts at self-management led by NGOs as evidence of a deep desire for change, and sees a movement among small-business leaders, mid-level government employees, and people active on the local level to create a new model of development.

Magalhães points to progress at even the top levels of government in rethinking a model of development that excludes huge segments of the population while putting untenable stress on natural resources. A recent article on sustainable development written by President Collor "would have been impossible only two years ago," he says, while Brazil's report to the summit highlights public participation as essential in overcoming poverty and preserving the environment.

The Earth Summit itself reflected an accelerating influence of NGOs on the national and international level. "UNCED's emphasis on community involvement was unprecedented," says Audubon's Spivy-Weber, with smaller grass-roots organizations as well as major environmental groups participating in two years of preparatory meetings. "It's hard to find a page of Agenda 21 that doesn't refer to some aspect of community."

While NGOs looked to the Global Forum to help cement their widening national and international contacts, EDF's Schwartzman cautions that one event cannot instantly enable NGOs to make common cause. Governments have had 50 years to organize forums to address UNCED's agenda, he says—civilian groups are just beginning to set up their own such forums. To help maintain the momentum, U.S. environmental groups are meeting to devise a joint strategy for "doing what Rio failed to do," says Liz Barratt-Brown of the Natural Resources Defense Council, and to promote sustainable development in the United States. Such joint efforts will be particularly valuable in monitoring compliance with the summit treaties, she maintains, especially since the newly established U.N. Sustainable Development Commission will rely partly on reports from NGOs.

While applauding the NGO influence on the summit agenda, she laments that some of the major players were missing from the official conference. UNCED chief Maurice Strong's original vision included participation by corporations as well as governments and NGOs. But the Rio Declaration—the summit's general statement on sustainable development—and Agenda 21 omit any reference to multinationals. This despite the recommendation of the Business Commission for Sustainable Development that the U.N. adopt a version of U.S. right-to-know laws and Toxic Release Inventory, which mandate disclosure of hazardous substances. Wastefully high military expenditures were another glaring omission from the UNCED agenda, says Barratt-Brown.

Yet for all its flaws and uncertain long-term effects, both the main summit and the Global Forum put the important issues on the table, maintains Magalhães—and those were not limited to natural resources alone. "The lesson we are all learning is that development has to be constrained by both social equity and the environment. The focus has to become one of improving *human* resources."

The Impact of Population Growth
on the Environment

The population of the Earth is growing at a rate of one billion people every eleven years. With this increase comes added pressures on the already vulnerable environment.

Population growth is not evenly distributed throughout the world. Ninety-five percent of population growth will occur in the developing nations; nations that can least afford the cost of supporting more people. As the population in these nations increases, the need for resources also grows.

This increased demand leads to deforestation and subsequent species extinctions. It also leads to land degradation due to increased demands on agricultural land. The abuse of agricultural land has a "snowball" effect. As overuse leads to the degradation of an area of land, people are forced to seek out more productive land to fulfil the needs of the population. The new land is eventually degraded and the search begins for more arable land from a shrinking amount of available fertile land.

Increases in population also place greater demands on the supply of freshwater resources. Humans require water for survival and as the population grows, more water is required for human consumption. Increased agricultural production requires greater supplies of fresh water for irrigation. All of this places a demand on a limited resource that, as the population grows, is increasingly threatened with population.

As the rural environment is degraded and resources become scarce, people migrate to urban areas. The populations of cities skyrocket. This change in demographics places a high demand on resources in a small area. It also creates a high concentration of pollutants and waste.

The solution to population growth is complex, but is integrally linked with a more equitable distribution of wealth and environmentally sound development opportunities.

—RNW

12

Carrying Capacity: Earth's Bottom Line
Sandra Postel

As a society, we have failed to discriminate between technologies that meet our needs in a sustainable way and those that harm the earth.

It takes no stretch of the imagination to see that the human species is now an agent of change of geologic proportions. We literally move mountains to mine the earth's minerals, redirect rivers to build cities in the desert, torch forests to make way for crops and cattle, and alter the chemistry of the atmosphere in disposing of our wastes. At humanity's hand, the earth is undergoing a profound transformation—one with consequences we cannot fully grasp.

It may be the ultimate irony that, in our efforts to make the earth yield more for ourselves, we are diminishing its ability to sustain life of all kinds—humans included. Signs of environmental constraints are now pervasive. Cropland is scarcely expanding any more, and a good portion of existing agricultural land is losing fertility. Grasslands have been overgrazed and fisheries overharvested, limiting the amount of additional food from these sources. Water bodies have suffered extensive depletion and pollution, severely restricting future food production and urban expansion. And natural forests—which help stabilize the climate, moderate water supplies, and harbor a majority of the planet's terrestrial biodiversity—continue to recede.

These trends are not new. Human societies have been altering the earth since they began. But the pace and scale of degradation that started about mid-century—and continues today—is historically new. The central conundrum of sustainable development is now all too

167

apparent: population and economies grow exponentially, but the natural resources that support them do not.

Biologists often apply the concept of "carrying capacity" to questions of population pressures on an environment. Carrying capacity is the largest number of any given species that a habitat can support indefinitely. When that maximum sustainable population level is surpassed, the resource base begins to decline; sometime thereafter, so does the population.

The earth's capacity to support humans is determined not just by our most basic food requirements but also by our levels of consumption of a whole range of resources, by the amount of waste we generate, by the technologies we choose for our varied activities, and by our success at mobilizing to deal with major threats. In recent years, the global problems of ozone depletion and greenhouse warming have underscored the danger of overstepping the earth's ability to absorb our waste products. Less well-recognized, however, are the consequences of exceeding the sustainable supply of essential resources, and how far along that course we may already be.

As a result of our population size, consumption patterns, and technology choices, we have surpassed the planet's carrying capacity. This is plainly evident by the extent to which we are damaging and depleting natural capital. The earth's environmental assets are now insufficient to sustain both our present patterns of economic activity and the life-support systems we depend on. If current trends in resource use continue, and if world population grows as projected, by 2010 per capita availability of rangeland will drop by 22 percent and the fish catch by 10 percent. Together, these provide much of the world's animal protein. The per capita area of irrigated land, which now yields about one-third of the global food harvest, will drop by 12 percent. And cropland area and forestland per person will shrink by 21 and 30 percent, respectively.

The days of the frontier economy, in which abundant resources were available to propel economic growth and living standards, are over. We have entered an era in which global prosperity increasingly depends on using resources more efficiently, on distributing them more equitably, and on reducing consumption levels overall. Unless we accelerate this transition, powerful social tensions are likely to arise from increased competition for the scarce resources that remain. There likely will be, for example, a surge in hunger, cross-border migration, and conflict—trends already painfully evident in parts of the world.

The roots of environmental damage run deep. Unless they are unearthed soon, we risk exceeding the planet's carrying capacity to such a degree that a future of economic and social decline will be impossible to avoid.

Driving Forces

Since mid-century, three trends have contributed most directly to the excessive pressures now being placed on the earth's natural systems—the doubling of world population, the quintupling of global economic output, and the widening gap in the distribution of income. The environmental impact of the world's population (now numbering 5.5 billion) has been vastly multiplied by economic and social systems that strongly favor growth and ever-rising consumption over equity and poverty alleviation; that fail to give women equal rights, education, and economic opportunity, and thereby perpetuate the conditions under which poverty and rapid population growth persist; and that do not discriminate between means of production that are environmentally sound and those that are not.

Growing Inequality in Income

Of the three principal driving forces, the growing inequality in income between rich and poor stands out in sharpest relief. In 1960, the richest 20 percent of the world's people absorbed 70 percent of global income; by 1989 (the latest year for which comparable figures are available), the wealthy people's share had climbed to nearly 83 percent. The poorest 20 percent, meanwhile, saw their share of global income drop from an already meager 2.3 percent to just 1.4 percent. The ratio of the richest fifth's share to the poorest's thus grew from 30 to 1 in 1960 to 59 to 1 in 1989 (see table 1).

This chasm of inequity is a major cause of environmental decline. It fosters overconsumption at the top of the income ladder and persistent poverty at the bottom. People at either end of the income spectrum are often more likely than those in the middle to damage the earth's ecological health—the rich because of their high consumption of energy, raw materials, and manufactured goods, and the poor because they must often cut trees, grow crops, or graze cattle in ways harmful to the earth, merely to survive from one day to the next.

Families in the western United States, for instance, often use as much as 3,000 liters of water a day—enough to fill a bathtub 20 times. Overdevelopment of water there has contributed to the depletion of

Table 1 Global Income Distribution, 1960-89			
	Share of Global Income Going to		Ratio of Richest to Poorest
Year	Richest 20%	Poorest 20%	
	(percent)		
1960	70.2	2.3	30 to 1
1970	73.9	2.3	32 to 1
1980	76.3	1.7	45 to 1
1989	82.7	1.4	59 to 1

Source: United Nations Development Programme, *Human Development Report 1992*, Oxford University Press, 1992.

rivers and aquifers, has destroyed wetlands and fisheries, and, by creating an illusion of abundance, has led to excessive consumption. Meanwhile, nearly one out of every three people in the developing world (some 1.2 billion people in all) lack access to a safe supply of drinking water.

Disparities in food consumption are revealing as well (see table 2). As many as 700 million people do not eat enough to live and work at their full potential. The average African, for instance, consumes only 87 percent of the calories needed for a healthy and productive life. Meanwhile, diets in many rich countries are so laden with animal fat as to cause increased rates of heart disease and cancer. Moreover, the meat-intensive diets of the wealthy usurp a disproportionately large share of the earth's agricultural carrying capacity, since producing one kilogram of meat takes several kilograms of grain. If all people in the world required as much grain for their diet as the average American does, the global harvest would need to be 2.6 times greater than it is today—a highly improbable scenario.

Economic Growth

The second driving force—economic growth—has been fueled in part by the introduction of oil onto the energy scene. Since mid-century, the global economy has expanded fivefold. As much was produced in two-and-a-half months of 1990 as in the entire year of 1950. World trade, moreover, grew even faster. Exports of primary commodities and manufactured products rose elevenfold.

Table 2 Grain Consumption Per Person in Selected Countries, 1990	
Country	Grain Consumption Per Person (kilograms)
Canada	974
United States	860
Soviet Union	843
Australia	503
France	465
Turkey	419
Mexico	309
Japan	297
China	292
Brazil	277
India	186
Bangladesh	176
Kenya	145
Tanzania	145
Haiti	100
World Average	323

Sources: Worldwatch Institute estimate, based on U.S. Department of Agriculture, *World Grain Database* (unpublished printout), 1992; Population Reference Bureau, *1990 World Population Data Sheet*, 1990.

Unfortunately, economic growth has most often been of the damaging variety—powered by the extraction and consumption of fossil fuels, water, timber, minerals, and other resources. Between 1950 and 1990, the industrial roundwood harvest doubled, water use tripled, and oil production rose nearly sixfold. Environmental damage increased proportionately.

Population Growth

Compounding the rises in both poverty and resource consumption in relation to the worsening of inequality and rapid economic expansion, population growth has added greatly to pressures on the earth's carrying capacity. The doubling of world population since 1950 has meant more or less steady increases in the number of people added to the planet each year. Whereas births exceeded deaths by 37 million in 1950, the net population gain in 1993 was 87 million—roughly equal to the population of Mexico.

The U.N. median population projection now shows world population reaching 8.9 billion by 2030, and leveling off at 11.5 billion around 2150.

The Resource Base

The outer limit of the planet's carrying capacity is determined by the total amount of solar energy converted into biochemical energy through plant photosynthesis minus the energy those plants use for their own life processes. This is called the earth's net primary productivity (NPP), and it is the basic food source for all life.

Prior to human impacts, the earth's forests, grasslands, and other terrestrial ecosystems had the potential to produce a net total of some 150 billion tons of organic matter per year. Stanford University biologist Peter Vitousek and his colleagues estimate, however, that humans have destroyed outright about 12 percent of the terrestrial NPP and now directly use or co-opt an additional 27 percent. Thus, one species—*Homo sapiens*—has appropriated nearly 40 percent of the terrestrial food supply, leaving only 60 percent for the millions of other land-based plants and animals.

It may be tempting to infer that, at 40 percent of NPP, we are still comfortably below the ultimate limit. But this is not the case. We have appropriated the 40 percent that was easiest to acquire. It may be impossible to double our share, yet theoretically that would happen in just 60 years if our share rose in tandem with population growth. And if average resource consumption per person continues to increase, that doubling would occur much sooner.

Perhaps more important, human survival hinges on a host of environmental services provided by natural systems; for example, forests regulate the hydrological cycle and wetlands filter pollutants. As we destroy, alter, or appropriate more of these natural systems for ourselves, these environmental services are compromised. At some point, the likely result is a chain reaction of environmental decline—widespread flooding and erosion brought on by deforestation, for example, or worsened drought and crop losses from desertification, or pervasive aquatic pollution and fisheries losses from wetlands destruction. The simultaneous unfolding of several such scenarios could cause unprecedented human hardship, famine, and disease. Precisely when vital thresholds will be crossed, no one can say. But as Vitousek and his colleagues note, those "who believe that limits to growth are so distant as to be of no consequence for today's decisionmakers appear unaware of these biological realities."

How have we come to usurp so much of the earth's productive capacity? In our efforts to feed, clothe, and house ourselves, and otherwise satisfy our evergrowing material desires, we have steadily converted diverse and complex biological systems to more uniform and simple ones that are managed for human benefit. Timber companies cleared primary forests and replaced them with monoculture pine plantations to make pulp and paper. Migrant peasants torched tropical forests in order to plant crops merely to survive. And farmers plowed the prairie grasslands of the United States' Midwest to plant corn, thereby creating one of the most productive agricultural regions in the world. Although these transformations have allowed more humans to be supported at a higher standard of living, they have come at the expense of natural systems, other plant and animal species, and ecological stability.

Continuing along this course is risky. But the flip side of the problem is equally sobering. What do we do when we have claimed virtually all that we can, yet our population and demands are still growing?

Cropland

Cropland area worldwide expanded by just 2 percent between 1980 and 1990. That means that gains in the global food harvest came almost entirely from raising yields on existing cropland. Most of the remaining area that could be used to grow crops is in Africa and Latin America; very little is in Asia. The most sizable near-term additions to the cropland base are likely to be a portion of the 76 million hectares of savanna grasslands in South America that are already accessible and potentially cultivable, as well as some portion of African rangeland and forest. These conversions, of course, may come at a high environmental price, and will push our 40-percent share of NPP even higher.

Moreover, a portion of any cropland gains that do occur will be offset by losses. As economies of developing countries diversify and as cities expand to accommodate population growth and migration, land is rapidly being lost to industrial development, housing, road construction, and the like. Canadian geographer Vaclav Smil estimates, for instance, that between 1957 and 1990, China's arable land diminished by at least 35 million hectares—an area equal to all the cropland in France, Germany, Denmark, and the Netherlands combined. At China's 1990 average grain yield and consumption levels, that amount of cropland could have supported some 450 million people, about 40 percent of its population.

In addition, much of the land we continue to farm is losing its inherent productivity because of unsound agricultural practices and overuse. The "Global Assessment of Soil Degradation," a three-year study involving some 250 scientists, found that more than 550 million hectares are losing topsoil or undergoing other forms of degradation as a direct result of poor agricultural methods (see table 3).

On balance, unless crop prices rise, it appears unlikely that the net cropland area will expand much more quickly over the next two decades than it did between 1980 and 1990. Assuming a net expansion of 5 percent (which may be optimistic), total cropland area would climb to just over 1.5 billion hectares. Given the projected 33-percent increase in world population by 2010, the amount of cropland per person would decline by 21 percent (see table 4).

Pasture and Rangeland

Pasture and rangeland cover some 3.4 billion hectares of land, more than twice the area in crops. The cattle, sheep, goats, buffalo, and camels that graze them convert grass (which humans cannot digest) into meat and milk (which they can). The global ruminant livestock herd, which numbers about 3.3 billion, thus adds a source of food for people that does not subtract from the grain supply, in contrast to the production of pigs, chickens, and cattle raised in feedlots.

Much of the world's rangeland is already heavily overgrazed and cannot continue to support the livestock herds, and management practices that exist today. According to the "Global Assessment of Soil Degradation," overgrazing has degraded some 680 million hectares since mid-century. This suggests that 20 percent of the world's pasture and range is losing productivity and will continue to do so unless herd sizes are reduced or more sustainable livestock practices are put in place.

During the 1980s, the total range area increased slightly, in part because land deforested or taken out of crops often reverted to some form of grass. If similar trends persist over the next two decades, by 2010 the total area of rangeland and pasture will have increased 4 percent, but it will have dropped 22 percent in per capita terms. In Africa and Asia, which together contain nearly half the world's

Table 3 Human-Induced Land Degradation Worldwide, 1945 to Present						
Region	Over-grazing	Defores-tation	Agricultural Misman-agement (million hectares)	Other[1]	Total	Degraded Area as Share of Total Vegetated Land (percent)
Asia	197	298	204	47	746	20
Africa	243	67	121	63	494	22
South America	68	100	64	12	244	14
Europe	50	84	64	22	220	23
North & Central America	38	18	91	11	158	8
Oceania	83	12	8	0	103	13
World	679	579	552	155	1,965	17

1 Includes exploitation of vegetation for domestic use (133 million hectares) and bioindustrial activities, such as pollution (22 hectares).

Sources: Worldwatch Institute, based on "The Extent of Human-Induced Soil Degradation," Annex 5 in L.R. Oldeman et al., World Map of the Status of Human-Induced Soil Degradation (Wgeningen, Netherlands: United Nations Environment Programme and International Soil Reference and Information Centre, 1991).

rangelands and where many traditional cultures depend heavily on livestock, even larger per capita declines could significantly weaken food economies.

Fisheries

Another natural biological system that humans depend on to add calories, protein, and diversity to human diets is our fisheries.   The annual catch from all sources (including aquaculture) totaled 97 million tons in 1990—about 5 percent of the protein humans consume. Fish account for a good portion of the calories consumed overall in many coastal regions and island nations.

The world fish catch has climbed rapidly in recent decades, expanding nearly fivefold since 1950. But it peaked at just above 100 million tons in 1989. Although catches from both inland fisheries and aquaculture (fish farming) have been rising steadily, they have not offset

Table 4 Population Size and Availability of Renewable Resources, Circa 1990, With Projections for 2010				
	Circa 1990	2010	Total Change	Per Capita Change
	(million)		(percent)	
Population	5,290	7,030	+33	
Fish Catch (tons)[1]	85	102	+20	-10
Irrigated Land (hectares)	237	277	+17	-12
Cropland (hectares)	1,444	1,516	+5	-21
Rangeland and Pasture (hectares)	3,402	3,540	+4	-22
Forests (hectares)[2]	3,413	3,165	-7	-30

1 Wild catch from fresh and marine waters, excludes aquaculture.
2 Includes plantations; excludes woodlands and shrublands.
Sources: Population figures from U.S. Bureau of the Census, Department of Commerce, *International Data Base,* unpublished printout, November 2, 1993; 1990 irrigated land, cropland, and rangeland from U.N. Food and Agriculture Organization (FAO), *Production Yearbook 1991*; fish catch from M. Perotti, chief, Statistics Branch, Fisheries Department, FAO, private communication, November 3, 1993; forests from FAO, *Forest Resources Assessment 1990, 1992 and 1993.* For detailed methodology, see *State of the World* 1994, among other sources.

the decline in the much larger wild marine catch, which fell from a historic peak of 82 million tons in 1989 to 77 million in 1991, a drop of 6 percent.

   With the advent of mechanized hauling gear, bigger nets, electronic fish detection aids, and other technologies, almost all marine fisheries have suffered from extensive overexploitation. Under current practices, considerable additional growth in the global fish catch overall looks highly unlikely. Indeed, the U.N. Food and Agriculture Organization (FAO) now estimates that all seventeen of the world's major fishing areas have either reached or exceeded their natural limits, and that nine are in serious decline.

   FAO scientists believe that better fisheries management might allow the wild marine catch to increase by some 20 percent. If this could be achieved, and if the freshwater catch increased proportionately, the total wild catch would rise to 102 million tons; by 2010, this would nonetheless represent a 10-percent drop in per capita terms.

Freshwater

   It may be even more essential than cropland, rangeland, and fisheries; without water, after all, nothing can live. Signs of water scarcity are now pervasive. Today, twenty-six countries have insufficient renewable water supplies within their own territories to meet the needs of a moderately developed society at their current population size. And populations are growing fastest in some of the most water-short countries, including many in Africa and the Middle East. Rivers, lakes, and underground aquifers show widespread signs of degradation and depletion, even as human demands rise inexorably.

Water constraints already appear to be slowing food production, and those restrictions will only become more severe. Agricultural lands that receive irrigation water play a disproportionate role in meeting the world's food needs. The 237 million hectares of irrigated land account for only 16 percent of total cropland but more than one-third of the global harvest. For most of human history, irrigated area expanded faster than population did, which helped food production per person to increase steadily. In 1978, however, per capita irrigated land peaked, and it has fallen nearly 6 percent since then.

Forests and Woodlands

They are the last key component of the biological resource base. They contribute a host of important commodities to the global economy—logs and lumber for constructing homes and furniture, fiber for making paper, fruits and nuts for direct consumption, and, in poor countries, fuelwood for heating and cooking. More important even than these benefits, however, are the ecological services forests perform—from conserving soils and moderating water cycles to storing carbon, protecting air quality, and harboring millions of plant and animal species.

Today, forests cover 24 percent less area than in 1700—3.4 billion hectares compared with an estimated 4.5 billion about 300 years ago. Most of that area was cleared for crop cultivation, but cattle ranching, timber and fuelwood harvesting, and the growth of cities, suburbs, and highways all claimed a share as well. Recent assessments suggest that the world's forests declined by about 130 million hectares between 1980 and 1990, an area larger than Peru.

Redirecting Technology

Advances in technology—which is used broadly here to mean the application of knowledge to an activity—offer at least a partial way out of our predicament. In most cases, "appropriate" technologies will no longer be engineering schemes, techniques, or methods that enable us to claim more of nature's resources but, instead, systems that allow us to benefit more from the resources we already have. As long as the resulting gains are directed toward bettering the environment and the lives of the less fortunate instead of toward increased consumption by the rich, such efforts will reduce human impacts on the earth.

The power of technology to help meet human needs was a critical missing piece in the world-view of Thomas Malthus, the English curate whose famous 1798 essay postulated that the growth of human population would outstrip the earth's food-producing capabilities. His prediction was a dire one—massive famine, disease, and death. But a stream of agricultural advances combined with the productivity leaps of the Industrial Revolution made the Malthusian nightmare fade for much of the world.

Without question, technological advances have steadily enhanced our capacity to raise living standards. They not only helped to boost food production—the main concern of mothers—they also increased our access to sources of water, energy, timber, and minerals.

As a society, however, we have failed to discriminate between technologies that meet our needs in a sustainable way and those that harm the earth. We have largely let the market dictate which technologies move forward, without adjusting for its failure to take proper account of environmental damages. Now that we have exceeded the planet's carrying capacity and are rapidly running down its natural capital, such a correction is urgently needed.

In the area of food supply, it remains an open question whether technological advances will continue to raise crop yields fast enough to meet rising demand, and whether such gains will be sustainable. Given the extent of cropland and rangeland degradation and the slowdown in irrigation expansion, it may be difficult to sustain the past pace of yield increases. Indeed, per capita grain production in 1992 was 7 percent lower than the historic peak in 1984. Whether this is a short-term phenomenon or the onset of a longer-term trend will depend on what new crop varieties and technologies reach farmers' fields and whether they can overcome the yield-suppressing effects of environmental degradation. Another factor is whether agricultural policies and prices will encourage farmers to invest in raising land productivity further.

In many agricultural regions—including northern China, parts of India, Mexico, the western United States, and much of the Middle

East—water may be more of a constraint to future food production than land, crop yield potential, or most other factors. Developing and distributing technologies and practices that improve water management is critical to sustaining the food production capability we now have, much less to increasing it for the future.

Water-short Israel is a frontrunner in making its agricultural economy more water-efficient. Its current agricultural output could probably not have been achieved without steady advances in water management—including highly efficient drip irrigation, automated systems that apply water only when crops need it, and the setting of water allocations based on predetermined optimal water applications for each crop. The nation's success is notable: between 1951 and 1990, Israeli farmers reduced the amount of water applied to each hectare of cropland by 36 percent. This allowed the irrigated area to more than triple with only a doubling of irrigation-water use.

Matching the need for sustainable gains in land and water productivity is the need for improvements in the efficiency of wood use and reductions in wood and paper waste, in order to reduce pressures on forests and woodlands. A beneficial timber technology is no longer one that improves logging efficiency—the number of trees cut per hour—but rather one that makes each log harvested go further. Raising the efficiency of forest product manufacturing in the United States, the world's largest wood consumer, roughly to Japanese levels would reduce timber needs by about one-fourth, for instance. Together, available methods of reducing waste, increasing manufacturing efficiency, and recycling more paper could cut U.S. wood consumption in half; a serious effort to produce new wood-saving techniques would reduce it even more.

With the world's paper demand projected to double by the year 2010, there may be good reason to shift production toward "treeless paper"—that made from nonwood pulp. Hemp, bamboo, jute, and kenaf are among the alternative sources of pulp. The fast-growing kenaf plant, for example, produces two to four times more pulp per hectare than southern pine, and the pulp has all the main qualities needed for making most grades of paper. In China, more than 80 percent of all paper pulp is made from nonwood sources. Treeless paper was manufactured in forty-five countries in 1992, and accounted for 9 percent of the world's paper supply. With proper economic incentives and support for technology and market development, the use of treeless paper could expand greatly.

The Role of Trade

Consider two countries, each with a population of about 125 million. Country A has a population density of 331 people per square kilometer, has just 372 square meters of cropland per inhabitant (one-seventh the world average), and imports almost three-fourths of its grain and nearly two-thirds of its wood. Country B, on the other hand, has a population density less than half that of Country A and nearly five times as much cropland per person. It imports only one-tenth of its grain and no wood. Which country has most exceeded its carrying capacity?

Certainly it would be Country A—which, as it turns out, is Japan—a nation boasting a real gross domestic product (GDP) of some $18,000 per capita. Country B, which from these few indicators seems closer to living within its means, is Pakistan—with a real GDP per capita of only $1,900. By any economic measure, Japan is far and away the more successful of the two. So how can questions of carrying capacity be all that relevant?

The answer, of course, lies in large part with trade. Japan sells cars and computers, and uses some of the earnings to buy food, timber, oil, and other raw materials. And that is what trade is supposed to be about—selling what one can make better or more efficiently, and buying what others have a comparative advantage in producing. Through trade, countries with scarce resources can import what they need from countries with a greater abundance.

Imports of biologically based commodities like food and timber are, indirectly, imports of land, water, nutrients, and the other components of ecological capital needed to produce them. Many countries would not be able to support anything like their current population and consumption levels were it not for trade. To meet its food and timber demands alone, the Netherlands, for instance, appropriates the production capabilities of 24 million hectares of land—10 times its own area of cropland, pasture, and forest.

In principle, there is nothing inherently unsustainable about one nation relying on another's ecological surplus. The problem, however, is the widespread perception that all countries can exceed their carrying capacities and grow economically by expanding manufactured and industrial goods at the expense of natural capital—paving over agricultural land to build factories, for example, or clear-cutting forest to build new homes. But all countries cannot continue to do this indefinitely. Globally, the ecological books must balance.

Many economists see no cause for worry. They believe that the market will take care of any needed adjustments. As cropland, forests, and water grow scarce, all that is necessary, they say, is for prices to rise; the added incentives to conserve, use resources more productively, alter consumption patterns, and develop new technologies will keep output rising with demand. But once paved over for a highway or housing complex, cropland is unlikely to be brought back into production—no matter how severe food shortages may become. Moreover, no mechanism exists for assuring that an adequate resource base is maintained to meet needs that the marketplace ignores or heavily discounts—including those of vital ecosystems, other species, the poor, or the next generation.

Trade in forest products illuminates some of these trends. East Asia, where the much-touted economic miracles of Japan and the newly industrializing countries have taken place, has steadily and rapidly appropriated increasing amounts of other nations' forest resources. In Japan, where economic activity boomed after World War II, net imports of forest products rose eightfold between 1961 and 1991. The nation is now the world's largest net importer of forest products by far. Starting from a smaller base, South Korea's net imports have more than quadrupled since 1971, and Taiwan's have risen more than sevenfold.

Like technology, trade is inherently neither good nor bad. One of its strengths is its ability to spread the benefits of more efficient and sustainable technologies and products, whether they be advanced drip irrigation systems, nontimber products from tropical forests, or the latest paper recycling techniques. Trade can also generate more wealth in developing countries, which conceivably could permit greater investments in environmental protection and help alleviate poverty. So far, however, the potential gains from trade have been overwhelmed by its more negative facets—in particular, by its tendency to foster ecological deficit-financing and unsustainable consumption.

In light of this, it is disturbing, to say the least, that negotiators involved in the seven-year-long Uruguay Round of the General Agreement on Tariffs and Trade (GATT) seemed barely interested in the role trade plays in promoting environmental destruction. While the reduction of government subsidies and other barriers to free trade—the main concern of the GATT round—could make international markets more efficient and increase the foreign exchange earnings of developing countries, that offers no guarantee that trade will be more environmentally sound or socially equitable.

As part of the newly created World Trade Organization, a committee will probably be formed to address the trade/environment nexus more directly, although probably not as broadly as is needed. With short-term considerations such as slow economic growth and high unemployment taking precedence over long-term concerns, a coordinated effort to make trade more sustainable through cost-internalizing measures is not high on the agenda. If action is delayed too long, however, the future will arrive in a state of ecological impoverishment that no amount of free trade will be able to overcome.

Lightening the Load

Ship captains pay careful attention to a marking on their vessels called the Plimsoll line. If the water level rises above the Plimsoll line, the boat is too heavy and is in danger of sinking. When that happens, rearranging items on the ship will not help much. The problem is the total weight, which has surpassed the carrying capacity of the ship.

Economist Herman Daly sometimes uses this analogy to underscore that the scale of human activity can reach a level that the earth's natural systems can no longer support. The ecological equivalent of the Plimsoll line may be the maximum share of the earth's biological resource base that humans can appropriate before a rapid and cascading deterioration in the planet's life-support systems is set in motion. Given the degree of resource destruction already evident, we may be close to this critical mark. The challenge, then, is to lighten our burden on the planet before "the ship" sinks.

More than 1,600 scientists, including 102 Nobel Laureates, underscored this point by collectively signing a "Warning to Humanity" in late 1992. It states: "No more than one or a few decades remain before the chance to avert the threats we now confront will be lost and the prospects for humanity immeasurably diminished. . . . A new ethic is required—a new attitude towards discharging our responsibility for caring for ourselves and for the earth. . . . This ethic must motivate a great movement, convincing reluctant leaders and reluctant governments and reluctant peoples themselves to effect the needed changes."

A successful global effort to lighten humanity's load on the earth would directly address the three major driving forces of environmental decline—the grossly inequitable distribution of income, resource-consumptive economic growth, and rapid population growth—that would redirect technology and trade to buy time for this great movement. Although there is far too much to say about each of these challenges to be comprehensive here, some key points bear noting.

Wealth inequality may be the most intractable problem, since it has existed for millennia. The difference today, however, is that the future of rich and poor alike hinges on reducing poverty and thereby eliminating this driving force of global environmental decline. In this way, self-interest joins ethics as a motive for redistributing wealth, and raises the chances that it might be done.

Important actions to narrow the income gap include greatly reducing Third World debt, much talked about in the 1980s but still not accomplished, and focusing foreign aid, trade, and international lending policies more directly on improving the living standards of the poor. If decision makers consistently asked themselves whether a choice they were about to make would help the poorest of the poor—that 20 percent of the world's people who share only 1.4 percent of the world's income—and acted only if the answer were yes, more people might break out of the poverty trap and have the opportunity to live sustainably.

A key prescription for reducing the kinds of economic growth that harm the environment is the same as that for making technology and trade more sustainable—internalizing environmental costs. If this is done through the adoption of environmental taxes, governments can avoid imposing heavier taxes overall by lowering income taxes accordingly. In addition, establishing better measures of economic accounting is critical. Since the calculations used to produce the gross national product do not account for the destruction or depletion of natural resources, this popular economic measure is extremely misleading. It tells us we are making progress even as our ecological foundations are crumbling. A better beacon to guide us toward a sustainable path is essential. The United Nations and several individual governments have been working to develop better accounting methods, but progress with implementation has been slow.

In September 1994, government officials will gather in Cairo for the "International Conference on Population and Development," the third such gathering on population. This is a timely opportunity to draw attention to the connections between poverty, population growth, and environmental decline; and to devise strategies that simultaneously address the root causes. Much greater efforts are needed, for instance, to raise women's social and economic status and to give women equal rights and access to resources. Only if gender biases are rooted out will women be able to escape the poverty trap and choose to have fewer children.

The challenge of living sustainably on the earth will never be met, however, if population and environment conferences are the only forums in which it is addressed. Success hinges on the creativity and energy of a wide range of people in many walks of life. The scientists' "Warning to Humanity" ends with a call to the world's scientists, business and industry leaders, the religious community, and people everywhere to join in the urgent mission of halting the earth's environmental decline.

13

Population, Poverty, and Pollution
Sharon L. Camp

The speed of 20th century demographic growth is unprecedented. In fact, population growth has become an important force behind the increasing momentum of global environmental change.

In the 1,800 years between the birth of Christ and the beginning of the 19th century, human population probably only quadrupled, from about 250 million to one billion. During the 19th century, spurred on by the Industrial Revolution, population growth rates in some parts of the world may have reached 1.5 percent a year. World population thus doubled—from one billion to two billion—between about 1800 and 1930.[1] Most of this increase occurred in Europe and North America, where economies were expanding rapidly. Between 1900 and 1930, the rich open lands of North America absorbed more than 15 percent of this European population increase.[2]

Beginning about 1930, the pace of demographic change accelerated. The third billion was added to the world's population in just 30 years, between 1930 and 1960. The fourth and fifth billions were added in 14 years and 13 years, respectively.[3] And with an annual population increment of more than 90 million people, adding the next billion will take just 11 years.[4]

In contrast to all earlier demographic changes, more than 85 percent of world-population growth since 1960 has occurred among the poorest countries.[5] In the developing countries of Africa, Asia, and Latin America, the availability of antibiotics, vaccines, and insecticides, along with improved sanitation and nutrition since World War II, has caused death rates to plummet.

185

Although birth rates have begun to decline in most parts of the world, many developing countries still have population growth rates above three percent a year, at least twice the rate of growth in Europe during the Industrial Revolution.[6] Until recently, for example, Kenya's population was growing at the astounding rate of 4.2 percent a year, a growth sufficient to produce a doubling of population in just 17 years.[7]

As former Council on Environmental Quality head Russell Peterson told a recent meeting of U.S. governors,

> The quality of all life on earth is increasingly threatened by a powerful and growing ecological force. We humans are that force, ever more of us using ever more materials, assaulting the environment with ever more machines, chemicals, weapons, and waste.[8]

In Paul Ehrlich's characterization, population growth is creating a "crowded monoculture" of human beings.[9] He and others estimate that humanity has appropriated approximately two-thirds of the planet's land surface, converting at least one-third of natural ecological systems to human-dominated ones and impairing the life-supporting services performed by those natural systems. These services include absorbing atmospheric pollution, providing freshwater, generating fertile soils, controlling floods and droughts, and maintaining genetic diversity.

Many people would have us side-step the environmental impact of population growth by focusing on environmentally destructive technologies or on over-consumption by the industrialized countries. These problems are urgent and deserve immediate attention. But one need not minimize them to acknowledge that the more people there are, the more demand they put on natural systems for life-supporting services. The faster our numbers increase, the more difficult it is to adjust the technological systems or resource-consumption patterns that would reduce environmental impacts. At some point, there must be limits to the world's carrying capacity.

According to a projection by Robert Repetto of the World Resources Institute, if world population were to grow continuously at the 1987 rate of 1.67 percent, all of the earth's land area, excluding Antarctica, would be packed solid with 427 trillion, 384 billion people by the year 2667. The standing room on Antarctica would last another 5 years. Lest we consider 687 years from now too much like science fiction, Repetto asks us to remember that 687 years ago Marco Polo had just returned to Venice, and the cathedrals of Notre Dame and Chartres had been dedicated.[10] This projection, of course, suffers from what statisticians call "the fallacy of misplaced precision." But population projections are never meant to be predictions.

Nevertheless, the world is now on a demographic trajectory that would result in an eventual world population almost triple the current five billion, perhaps by the end of the next century.

One of the reasons that many people concerned about environmental issues ignore the urgency of population pressures is that these pressures manifest themselves most clearly at the local level and are easily missed at the global and sometimes even at the national level. The links between population pressure and environmental degradation also manifest themselves mainly among poor people in poor communities, and it is often women who bear the most adverse effects.

Agents and Victims

Low-income households in Africa, Asia, and Latin America are increasingly both the victims and the unwitting agents of ecological damage. In the rural areas of many developing countries, increasing numbers of poor families can stay alive only by destroying their own natural resource base. In their daily struggle for subsistence—for food, fodder, firewood, and water—they are rapidly changing local ecosystems and contributing, in some cases, to global environmental change.

1. Throughout much of the developing world, millions of low-income households in need of fuel or new farmland are cutting forests twice as fast as the trees can regenerate.[11] Every year 40 to 50 million acres of tropical forest—an area at least the size of Washington state—is lost.[12] In most developing countries, 80 percent of the wood harvested is used for firewood or charcoal.[13]

2. In dozens of countries, farmers forced onto marginal lands are cultivating highly erodible hillsides, thereby denuding the watersheds needed to prevent flooding and causing the erosion of topsoil during heavy rains—topsoil that took hundreds of years to form.

3. Growing human pressure on the natural environment has rendered ecosystems more vulnerable. As a result, more people are affected by natural catastrophes such as landslides, cyclones, earthquakes, and floods.[14]

4. Increasing populations of humans and their livestock are overcropping and overgrazing fragile soils. These trends contribute to desertification, which threatens to put up to 15 million acres

beyond hope of reclamation and takes 50 million more worn-out acres out of cultivation.[15] The poorest farmers cultivating the poorest lands are those most often affected.

5. In many areas, expanding demand for water is depleting freshwater supplies above and below ground. Although some waterways and coastal areas in the developed world are becoming cleaner, in developing countries they are becoming more polluted at great cost to human health. Human activities are invading sensitive coastal wetlands, the breeding grounds for many species of fish and fowl.

6. Women, who most often depend on the renewability of natural systems for family food, fuel, and water, must work harder to fulfill their traditional economic roles.

7. To escape deepening rural poverty, at least 10 million "environmental refugees" are now on the move, mostly from rural to urban areas where city services are collapsing under the weight of population growth and where pollution is an increasing threat to human health.[16]

Solutions are Expensive

There are, of course, solutions to these problems:

1. Alternative energy technologies and greater energy efficiency.
2. Massive reforestation and new, faster-growing trees.
3. Soil conservation practices, such as terracing, that help reduce erosion.
4. Land reforms and credit that help poor farmers invest in conservation.
5. New nitrogen-fixing or drought-resistant crops.
6. Pollution controls on industry and agriculture and new recycling techniques.

But many of these solutions require substantial investments over many years by developing countries already strapped for capital. And those investments—even with much more generous help from rich countries—will almost certainly be overwhelmed in most developing countries if populations triple or quadruple over the next 50 years.

Population Pressures and Poverty

As population pressures mount, the degradation of arable lands in wide areas of Africa, Asia, and Latin America increases. These trends may threaten future food production capacity. In Africa, food production has already declined 15 to 20 percent on a per capita basis since 1970, and many Africans do not have enough to eat to lead healthy, productive lives.[17]

Although population growth is not the major factor behind hunger, it has clearly aggravated the grinding poverty and, in some cases, the environmental destruction that has kept people from growing or getting enough to eat. Worldwide, a billion people are severely malnourished. The Food and Agriculture Organization estimates that without conservation, developing countries in Asia, Africa, and Latin America will experience an almost 30-percent decline in productivity by the end of the next century.[18]

Such patterns of soil degradation can be seen on every continent:

1. In Guatemala, 40 percent of the land's productive capacity has been lost through soil erosion.[19]
2. In Turkey, more than 50 percent of arable land is severely degraded.[20]
3. In Mexico, two-thirds is moderately to severely damaged.
4. In northern India, where domesticated animal populations exceed rangeland carrying capacity, desertification is also threatened.[21]
5. In the Sudan, the desert has moved south by some 100 kilometers in 17 years.[22]

The United Nations Environmental Programme (UNEP) estimates that one-third of the earth's land surface, on which almost one-fifth of humanity lives, is threatened with desertification. UNEP estimates $4.5 billion per year is needed to bring desertification under control.[23]

To understand the urgency of curbing population growth, let us look at some examples of the interaction of population growth, poverty, and the degradation of agricultural land.

Burkina Faso

Burkina Faso is one of seven countries that make up the semi-arid region of West Africa known as the Sahel. As in other semi-arid parts of Africa, severe environmental degradation is resulting from the interaction between changing land use and rising human and livestock populations in a sensitive ecosystem. As elsewhere, patterns of traditional land use (most importantly, long fallow periods) that sustained African populations for generations have been broken, leading to overcropping and overgrazing.[24]

Burkina Faso's 1989 population was estimated by the Population Reference Bureau at 8.7 million, growing at 2.8 percent a year. The average number of children per woman is 6.5. At current growth rates, the population will top 20 million in just 30 years. Approximately 18 percent of the nation's gross national product (GNP) is in foreign aid, reflecting Burkina Faso's status as one of the world's poorest countries. GNP per capita is $210 a year.[25]

The country's central plateau is already disastrously overpopulated, considering its natural resources and current levels of technology. In years of normal rainfall, local production meets 40 percent of food needs. The rangeland, like that in many parts of the world, is susceptible to degradation and now meets the forage needs of domestic livestock only one year in five. Firewood consumption is four-and-one-half times above levels of sustainable wood production. In the dry season, women must spend up to half their waking day collecting water for drinking, cooking, and bathing.

With increased populations, there is too little land to permit the fields to rest over long fallow periods, so soil fertility is declining. To compensate, farmers should use increasing amounts of fertilizer and soil builders. However, there is no money for chemical fertilizer, and animal manure is scarce because herders have been pushed further north. Crop residues that could be plowed under to build up the soil are needed for fuel and fodder.

Burkina Faso was one of the countries hardest hit in the 1984–85 African drought, in which one million people may have starved to death. As elsewhere in Africa, favorable rainfall during the 1950s and 1960s encouraged an expanding population to convert rangeland to cropland, forcing herds of domestic animals further north into marginal areas. When the rains stopped, the animals quickly stripped all vegetation. Millions of animals died, and much of the land turned to desert. In Burkina Faso, an estimated million people—one-sixth of the country's population—have migrated in search of work.[26]

Burkina Faso's story was told to *Earthwatch* magazine by a local farmer, Jean-Marie Sawadogo, who lost half his land to the desert:

> In my father's time, millet filled all the granaries and the soil was deeper than your body before you reached rock. Now, we have to buy food in all but the wettest years, and the soil is no deeper than my hand.

About deforestation, he said,

> When we were boys, the forest was all around us, too thick to penetrate. Gradually, more and more of it was cleared around

the compounds, until one clearing met the next and made the great openness you see now.[27]

Mali and Niger

Just to the north of Burkina Faso, in Mali and Niger, lies the great Niger River bend—one of the world's most extensive river systems—which one historian dubbed the "Great Brown Cod."

Because of deforestation around its headwaters near the coast (the Niger flows north, then east, then south) and all along its course, the Great Brown Cod is silting up, and waterflows downstream are dropping. In the country of Niger, firewood consumption substantially exceeds annual tree growth. Over much of the Niger River basin, covering vast areas in a half-dozen countries, tributaries are drying up; water is in short supply; and farmland dependent on river water is turning to desert. Some experts believe these trends have helped produce a drier local climate. In the last 20 years, the region has experienced significantly less rainfall than in the past.

East Africa

The Sahel is not the only part of Africa undergoing severe soil erosion. The vast rangelands of East Africa provide another compelling case, in part because the area's growing human and livestock populations compete for living space with the world's largest remaining concentrations of mixed plains wild game, including endangered species such as the African elephant and rhino. Of the many game reserves in East and Southern Africa, one of the best is Masai Mara in Kenya, which is now threatened by encroachment from the Masai tribe's cattle, sheep, and goats. The Masai herders have been challenged, in turn, by farmers moving onto the best pastureland.

The conversion of good quality rangeland to crops has denied Masai herds access to adequate food and water in the dry years and has concentrated the growing numbers of livestock onto too little land. Between 1969 and 1979, human and cattle populations doubled, and sheep and goat populations tripled.[28] Overgrazing has destroyed some of the most productive perennial grasses, allowing less nutritious grasses and woody vegetation to take over. This has lowered the carrying capacity of the land. In areas of severe overgrazing, wind and water have swept away the topsoil. Here sun and many hooves have packed the ground hard, impairing the land's ability to hold water. When the rains failed in 1983 and 1984, the Masai tribe lost 78 percent of its cattle.[29]

Population Pressure and Deforestation

Between 1850 and 1980, global cropland at least doubled. Much of the new farmland was cut out of the forest. The result: half the total reduction in forest cover since prehistoric times has occurred since 1850, and many forests that remain are less dense with fewer tree species.[30] Although forests in temperate zones have been stabilized, forests in tropical zones are disappearing at a rate of some 40 to 50 million acres a year.[31]

According to Food and Agriculture Organization data, the destruction of forest cover since 1850 has been greatest in North Africa and the Middle East—some 60 percent. The second most severely affected area is South Asia with a 43-percent loss.[32]

1. Throughout the Himalayan region, watersheds have become rapidly destabilized, and each year an estimated 1.5 billion tons of sediment wash into the Bay of Bengal.[33]
2. In the Andean range, Ecuador and Peru show major erosion on cultivated foothills.[34]
3. In Africa, the most outstanding example is Ethiopia, which was 40 percent forested at the beginning of this century. Forest cover is now only 4 percent.[35] Firewood consumption in Ethiopia exceeds tree growth by about 2.5 times.[36]

The World Resources Institute estimates that at current rates of deforestation, a quarter of the tropical forests that remained in 1980 will be gone by the year 2000.[37]

Forest cover is a critical renewable resource for the more than two billion people in developing countries who depend on firewood for heating and cooking.[38] Forests also provide an important global life-support service by absorbing excess carbon dioxide released into the atmosphere from burning biomass and fossil fuels. By reducing the earth's "lung capacity," net deforestation contributes to the buildup of greenhouse gases. In addition, when the forests are burned to make room for crops or livestock, the burning itself contributes substantially to the release of carbon dioxide in the atmosphere.

Tropical forests are treasure troves of genetic diversity, containing perhaps half the world's plant and animal species, including most of the thousands estimated to become extinct each year. This loss of genetic diversity may threaten future innovations in agriculture, industry, and medicine, given the contributions that wild species have made to previous progress in these fields.

Among the nine countries accounting for approximately 80 percent of remaining tropical forest, population doubling times range from 23 years for Zaire to 38 years for Colombia (where family planning programs are lowering fertility).[39] Although contraception has increased in most countries, the growing needs of still-growing populations for food, fuel, shelter, and foreign exchange will create enormous future pressures on remaining forests.

One of the countries where deforestation has done enormous local damage is mountainous Nepal, where some of the elaborate hillside terraces are crumbling as the rains, unencumbered by tree cover, race down the steep slopes. In the past 25 years, Nepal has lost more than 30 percent of its forest cover, mainly to firewood gathering and subsistence farming. Soil loss is now estimated at 108 million cubic yards a year.[40]

Nepal's 1989 population was 18.7 million, growing at 2.5 percent a year—a doubling time of 28 years.[41] Women in Nepal have six children each. As in most developing countries, Nepalese women are responsible for collecting firewood and fodder from the forest, along with their other agricultural and household responsibilities. The collection of forest products consumes about 40 percent of the workday.[42]

Deforestation means that for most women, the woodlands are sparser and farther away. In one recent study, Nepalese hill women were allocating, on average, an extra hour of their 10-hour workday just for firewood collection.[43] In areas of severe deforestation, 45 percent more time was needed. To meet firewood needs, the study showed, women reallocated work time away from farming and food preparation. This produced a diet both lower in total calories and in quality calories. In areas of severe deforestation, preschool children scored poorly on standard height and weight measures—an indication of poor nutrition.[44]

As in many developing countries, deforestation in Nepal also affects the urban poor by raising the price of wood and charcoal. In parts of Asia, Africa, and Latin America, the urban poor spend up to a quarter of their income on wood and charcoal—sometimes as much as they spend on food.

Haiti provides a similar example of environmental degradation driven by population growth and poverty. At the time of Columbus, the country was almost completely covered in forest. By 1987, forest cover was down to 2 percent. Although most of the clearing in colonial times was for large plantations, today an ever-expanding number of poor rural families are clearing steep slopes to make room for crops and to collect firewood.[45]

Haiti has one of the world's highest population densities on arable land. Much of Haiti's soil is already exhausted from overplanting, and each year more topsoil is swept away by wind and water. Four miles out to sea from the capital of Port-au-Prince, the water is stained brown with sediment. In one rainy season, floods deposited three feet of mud in the city.[46]

Haiti's population of 6.4 million is growing at 22.2 percent a year. Women have an average of 4.9 children each, and only about 7 percent use contraception.[47] In 30 years, the population is projected to reach 10.8 million. The U.S. Agency for International Development is funding a $27 million agroforestry project in which 7 to 9 million new trees are planted annually. However, 45 to 60 million established trees are lost each year to growing fuel consumption.[48]

Population's Impact on Pollution

Large portions of major cities in developing countries are squatter settlements without municipal water or waste disposal, often built on inaccessible hillsides or depressions prone to flooding. Slums also tend to proliferate around industrial zones, close to jobs but where air and water pollution may be aggravated by the lack of pollution controls on industries.

Urban migrants over time tend to upgrade their settlements, with or without help from government. But the rapid pace of growth ensures a constantly expanding fringe of newly arrived squatters. Investments in urban infrastructure can never catch up.

1. Mexico City had just over three million people in 1950. By the end of this decade, it will have 26 million.[49]
2. When its original water and sewer systems were being laid out in 1950, Cairo had 2.5 million people. In 10 years, it will have more than 11 million.[50]
3. New Delhi had 1.4 million in 1950 and will have more than 13 million in 2000.[51]
4. Nairobi had 140,000 in 1950 and will have 5.3 million in 2000.[52]

Since 1950, the world's urban population has tripled. Third World urban population has quadrupled. By the end of the decade, developing countries will need to build and manage urban infrastructures with 60 percent more capacity simply to avoid further degradation of water, sewage, and transportation services. These infrastructures are already stressed, and housing stocks are grossly inadequate.

The Indian government estimates that 2.5 million of its city dwellers live their entire lives in the streets. Of India's urban poor, 65 percent lack tap water and 50 percent have no sanitary waste disposal.[53]

Some two-thirds of Rio de Janeiro's shantytowns are built on steep slopes. In 1987, the government estimated it would cost $800 million to make the areas safe for habitation. In 1988, torrential rains produced a mudslide that claimed 275 lives and left 20,000 people homeless.[54]

Human and industrial waste in developing countries is rapidly polluting waterways and coastal areas. Worldwide, many saltwater marshes, estuaries, and coral reefs are being degraded because of the concentration of large populations along the coastlines, where half the world's population lives. In much of Southeast Asia, the rivers are virtually open sewers as they reach the sea. In metropolitan Manila, the rivers are biologically dead.[55]

In Indonesia, Jakarta Bay, rich in fish and shellfish 20 years ago, is brimming with millions of tons of untreated industrial and municipal waste. Parts of the bay are becoming eutrophic, and many spawning areas are already destroyed. Poor families living nearby suffer from chronic intestinal disorders because they have no choice but to fish in the bay and eat the catch.[56]

In the estuarial country of Bangladesh, water-borne pollution means children suffer repeated episodes of diarrhea and are sick many days out of the year.

Overall, at least three in four people in developing countries lack sanitary facilities and 25,000 deaths a day are due to water-borne diseases.[57] Every year, 4.6 million children under five years of age die of preventable, curable diarrheal diseases.[58]

The world's most revered river, the Ganges in India, is also one of the most polluted. India, the world's second largest country, grows by some 18 million people a year—more than all of Sub-Saharan Africa combined. An estimated 70 percent of India's surface water is polluted. Lining the banks of its sacred river are Calcutta and a half-dozen other major cities. It is estimated that only 12 of the 132 major industrial concerns pumping effluents into the river have waste-treatment plants in working order. Many cities and towns lack sewage treatment. The government estimates it would cost $195 million over five years just to begin the major cleanup needed to protect the health of millions of riverside residents.[59]

With current rates of urban growth in developing countries—60 percent the result of high urban birthrates rather than migration—municipal solid waste is expected to double in the next 10 to 15 years. During the next 30 to 40 years, the relative contribution that developed and developing countries make to air and water pollution, waste generation, and other environmental problems will change. Given projected population increases, this would be true even without substantial improvements in developing country living standards.

For example, Paul Shaw estimates that without any increase in incomes, developing countries would generate 60 percent of new waste between 1985 and 2025.[60] With an increase in average incomes from $750 to $1,500, they would account for more than 80 percent of new waste and would double their share of total world waste from 25 to 50 percent. Shaw estimates this modest increase in developing-country affluence would boost per-capita waste from .17 tons to .35 tons, compared to 1.6 tons per capita in industrialized countries in 1985. Thus, even small gains in living standards, laid over huge increases in population, have potentially huge environmental consequences.

Some of these consequences can be global, as in the case of climate change produced by increases in emissions of greenhouse gases. The unprecedented increase in world population probably has contributed to the increase in atmospheric concentrations of carbon dioxide over pre-industrial times, but population increases probably have played an even more direct role in the increase in methane concentrations. Two-thirds of methane emissions are tied directly to increasing human activities, including a tripling since 1950 of rice paddy production and a quadrupling of herds of large and small ruminants. Methane molecules trap 20 times as much solar energy as carbon dioxide.

To minimize global climate change resulting from the buildup of greenhouse gases, the world will need to reduce dramatically current levels of energy consumption based on fossil fuels, most of it now concentrated in developed countries. But in developing countries, population growth will help drive up energy demand, even at modest levels of economic growth. If present trends were to continue, by 2025 developing countries would emit some 16.6 billion tons of carbon dioxide annually—four times 1990 emissions by industrialized countries.[61]

A New Global Bargain

If developing countries are to reverse the mounting environmental degradation that threatens their future and ours, they must get off the population treadmill. There is no conceivable way for most developing countries to achieve resource-sustainable economic development if their populations continue to grow at unmanageable rates.

Because many forms of environmental degradation—such as air and water pollution—do not respect national boundaries, and because some natural systems—such as coastal wetlands and tropical forests—have important value for all peoples, wealthy industrialized countries owe it to themselves to help developing countries slow their population growth.

Industrialized countries cannot and should not ask the world's low-income countries to forego economic development to protect the global environment—certainly not while the rich nations are devouring the lion's share of the world's resources and, for now at least, emitting the lion's share of the world's pollutants.

But rich and poor counties can make a new global bargain based, in James Gustave Speth's words, on "a sense of shared responsibility and common destiny."[62] Rich countries must commit to reduce their rapacious demand for natural resources through conservation; they must revitalize natural systems; and they must make the substantial investments it will take to develop technologies that can support future world prosperity without damaging the environment. They also must greatly increase the flow to poor countries of both new financing and new technology for natural resource conservation and environmentally sound economic development.

Above all else, developed and developing countries must agree on the urgent need to stabilize the world's population at the earliest time and at the lowest level possible, under humane and voluntary measures.

With an enormous cooperative effort, world population growth could be stopped at between 9 and 10 billion people sometime in the next century. But this can be done only if all the world's governments act now to ensure that, by the end of this decade, family-planning messages and services reach every couple of childbearing age.

The price tag for universal family planning is small—between $9 and $11 billion annually by the year 2000.[63] The cost of not bringing population growth under control is incalculable: irreversible damage to the global environment; hundreds of millions of children doomed to live their entire lives in absolute poverty; and a growing gap between the world's rich and poor, with all that implies for global security.

The 1990s will be the most important decade in the history of human population growth. the actions we take or fail to take in this decade will largely determine whether human populations stop growing at double or triple their current number. If we dither away the next decade, we risk leaving our children a world far less habitable, prosperous, and peaceful than that left to us.

Notes

1. Thomas W. Merrick, "World Population in Transition," *Population Bulletin* 41 (April 1986): 10.
2. Population Crisis Committee, *Population Pressures Abroad, Immigration Pressures at Home* (Washington, D.C.: Population Crisis Committee, 1989), 2.
3. Robert Repetto, "Population, Resources, Environment: An Uncertain Future," *Population Bulletin* 42 (July 1987): 10.
4. Population Reference Bureau, *1990 World Population Data Sheet* (Washington, D.C.: Population Reference Bureau, 1989).
5. Repetto, "Population, Resources, and Environment," 10.
6. Merrick, "World Population in Transition," 12.
7. Kenyans challenge the view that their growth rate was ever this high. But many demographers agreed with the Population Reference Bureau (PRB) figure of 4.2 percent for 1986. See PRB, *Population Data Sheet* (Washington, D.C.: PRB, 1986).
8. Russell W. Peterson, "Bringing Environmental Concerns to the Forefront of the National Agenda," National Governors' Association winter meeting, February 27, 1990.
9. Paul Ehrlich, "Populations of People and Other Living Things," *Earth '88* (Washington, D.C.: National Geographic Society, 1988), 310.
10. Repetto, "Population, Resources, Environment," 7.
11. The Food and Agriculture Organization (FAO) estimated in 1983 that 1.5 billion people were cutting wood for fuel faster than forests could regenerate and that by 2000, 2.4 billion people could face a severe fuelwood crisis. FAO, *Fuelwood Supplies in Developing Countries*, Forestry Paper 42 (Rome: FAO, 1983), 6.
12. This new estimate made in 1990 and based on satellite photos is twice the level of previous estimates. World Resources Institute (WRI), *World Resource 1990–1991* (Washington, D.C.: WRI, 1990), 102.
13. FAO, *The Tropical Forestry Action Plan* (Washington, D.C.: FAO, in cooperation with WRI and United Nations Development Programme, 1987).
14. United Nations Conference on Trade and Development (UNCTAD), *Trade and Development 1989*, (Geneva: UNCTAD, 1989), 152.

15. Sandra Postel, "Land's End," *World Watch* (May-June 1989): 12; and Robin Clarke, "Sounds of Change: Why Land Becomes Desert and What Can Be Done About It," *UNEP Environment Brief* 2 (1987): 1.

16. Jodi L. Jacobson, *Environmental Refugees: A Yardstick of Habitability*, Worldwatch Paper 86 (Washington, D.C.: Worldwatch Institute, 1988); Maggie Black, "Population, Resources, and Environment: A New Assessment," *Earthwatch* 32 (1988): 2.

17. WRI, *World Resources 1990–91*.

18. FAO, *Land, Food, and People* (Rome: FAO, 1984), 20.

19. Repetto, "Population, Resources, Environment," 20.

20. Ibid.

21. Centre for Science and Environment, *The State of India's Environment—1984–85: The Second Citizen's Report* (New Delhi: Centre for Science and Environment, 1985), 7.

22. United Nations Population Fund (UNFPA), *The 1988 State of World Population: Safeguarding the Future* (New York: UNFPA, 1988).

23. United Nations Environment Programme (UNEP) estimates summarized in Robin Clark, "Sands of Change," 3, 5.

24. Analysis of Burkina Faso from Paul Harrison, "Pressures on the Margins," *Earthwatch* 33 (1988): 2–3.

25. Harrison, "Pressures on the Margins"; World Bank, *World Development Report* (New York: Oxford University Press, 1990), table 1.

26. Clarke, "Sands of Change."

27. Harrison, "Pressures on the Margins."

28. The classic discussion of these trends in Masai land from which this data comes is David J. Campbell, "The Prospect for Desertification in Kenya," *The Geographic Journal* 152 (March 1986): 44–55. See also Lee M. Talbot, "Demographic Factors in Resource Depletion and Environmental Degradation in East African Ranges," *Population and Development Review* 12 (September 1986).

29. Campbell, "Prospects for Desertification."

30. Repetto, "Population, Resources, Environment."

31. WRI, *World Resources 1990–91*, 102.

32. FAO data compiled in *World Resources 1990–91*, table 19.1.

33. El Swaily, et al., *Soil Erosion and Conservation in the Tropics* (Madison, WI: American Society of Agronomy, 1982), 8.

34. UNFPA, *The 1988 State of World Population*, 9.

35. Lloyd Timberlake, "Unlocking the Potential of Ethiopia," *Earthwatch* 19 (1984): 4.

36. World Bank draft report of 1984 cited in UNCTAD *Trade and Development Report 1989* (New York: UNCTAD, 1989), 151.

37. Estimate by World Resources Institute, May 1990.

38. Robin Clarke, "The Disappearing Forests," *UNEP Environment Brief* 3 (1988): 5.

39. PRB, *1990 World Population Data Sheet*.
40. UNFPA, *The 1988 State of World Population*, 10.
41. PRB, *1990 World Population Data Sheet*.
42. Shubh K. Kumar and David Hotchkiss, "Consequences of Deforestation for Women's Time Allocation, Agricultural Production, and Nutrition in Hill Areas of Nepal," *International Food Policy Research Institute Report* 69 (1988): 1–4.
43. Kumar and Hotchkiss, *Consequences of Deforestation*. See also for deforestation's impact on nutrition, Norman Myers, *The Primary Source: Tropical Forests and Our Future* (New York: W.W. Norton, 1984), 116; and FAO, *Tropical Forestry Action Plan*, 17.
44. Kumar and Hotchkiss, *Consequences of Deforestation*, 4.
45. Marcia D. Lowe, "Hope for Haiti's Barren Hills," *World Watch* 1 (May-June 1988): 66–67.
46. Lowe, "Hope for Haiti's Barren Hills." See also Lloyd Timberlake and Anders Wijkman, *Natural Disasters: Acts of God or Acts of Man?* (London: International Institute for Environment and Development, 1984).
47. PRB, *1990 World Population Data Sheet*.
48. Lowe, "Hope for Haiti's Barren Hills."
49. *Estimates and Projections of Urban, Rural, and City Populations, 1950–2025: The 1982 Assessment* (New York: UN DIESA, 1985), table A-12; and UNFPA, The 198 State of World Population.
50. Ibid.
51. Ibid.
52. Ibid.
53. For a discussion of India's urban problems, see Raj Changappa, "India's Urban Chaos," *World Press Review* (April 1988): 57.
54. UNFPA, *The 1988 State of World Population*, 7.
55. Don Hinrichsen, "Living on the Edge," *Earthwatch* 35 (1989): 2.
56. Don Hinrichsen, "Coping with Pollution Indonesia," *Earthwatch* 35 (1989): 4.
57. Robin Clarke, "Safeguarding the World's Water," *UNEP Environmental Brief* 6 (1988): 3.
58. UNEP, *The State of the Environment 1986: Environment and Health* (Nairobi: UNEP, 1986), 3.
59. UNFPA, *The 1988 State of World Population*, 12.
60. R. Paul Shaw, "Rapid Population Growth and Environmental Degradation: Ultimate versus Proximate Factors," *Environmental Conservation* 16 (Autumn 1989): 204.
61. UNFPA, *The State of World Population, 1990: Choices for the New Century* (New York: UNFPA, 1990), 2.
62. James Gustave Speth, "Coming to Terms: Toward a North-South Bargain for the Environment," *WRI Issues and Ideas* (June 1989): 4.

63. The Population Crisis Committee (PCC) global budget estimate for the year 2000 is $10.5 billion, based on an average couple cost of $16.00. See PCC's *1990 Report on Progress Towards Population Stabilization* (Washington, D.C.: PCC, 1990). The UNFPA *State of the World Population 1990* uses the range of $9 to $11 billion.

14

The Urban Explosion in the Third World
Nicole Massignon

Around one and a half billion people in the developing countries today live in cities, a figure which is expected to double in the next 20 years; in the 1950s, by contrast, fewer than 300 million people in the Third World were city-dwellers. Such rapid urbanisation, on such a massive scale, has never been encountered before. It brings with it the danger of disequilibria and strain, for the demands to be met are huge and the policies, infrastructure and services to cope with them are not yet in place.[1]

A comparison of the pace of urban and population growth in the developed world and in the developing countries brings home the unprecedented nature of the process of urbanization under way in the Third World. The developed countries are largely urbanized, with nearly three-quarters of their population now living in towns and cities. But the urban growth rate there is low (0.8 percent in 1990), and falling: the number of city-dwellers—some 880 million in 1990—is not expected to hit the billion mark before 2005.

In the developing countries urban growth has been sudden, swift, and massive, under the double impact of population growth and a drift from the land. Forty years ago a little fewer than 300 million people (17 percent of the population), or roughly one in five, lived in or near a city. Recent United Nations estimates[2] suggest this figure will reach 1.4 billion (34 percent), or one person in three. The latest forecast is for 2 billion (40 percent of the population) by the turn of the century and 4 billion (57 percent) in 2025. By 2015 in the Third World there will be more people living in towns than in the country. Within three generations the lifestyles of most people on the planet will have been radically transformed.

These figures, of course, contain a degree of uncertainty. In 1992 the United Nations—the principal source of demographic and urban statistics for the world as a whole—revised their 1990 projections, producing substantial differences for a small number of towns. For Mexico City, for example, the numbers were revised downwards after the most recent census, in 1990. These revisions don't change the wider trends, of course.

There are evidently wide variations between and within regions (table). Latin America is already heavily urbanized (72 percent of the population); it is Asia and Africa, where the proportion of city dwellers is still a little over 30 percent, that are feeling the full onslaught of the change. By the end of the century, nearly 600 million more inhabitants will have poured into Third World cities. And it is in Africa, particularly East Africa, that urban growth is most rapid. An increase of 120 million in the number of African city-dwellers between 1990 and 2000 is predicted (the equivalent of urban growth in the entire developed world between 1975 and 1990). In Asia, the urban population will have soared to 1.4 billion by the year 2000. In cities like Calcutta, Bombay, and New Delhi, it is shooting up by some 200,000 to 400,000 every year.

When the century draws to a close, there will be 21 cities with over 10 million inhabitants—17 of them in developing countries. São Paulo already has nearly 20 million inhabitants, Mexico City more than 15 million (less than an earlier estimate of more than 20 million in 1990), and Lagos, a medium-sized city (300,000) in the 1950s, had swollen to 8 million by 1990. Lagos, indeed, is expected to grow to accommodate 13 million people by the end of the century, many more than Paris (9.5 million by 2000). The forecasts for 2010 involve staggering sums, thanks to a high growth rate and the numbers in question. By contrast, the large cities of the West (London, New York, Paris) are not expected to grow much.

Urban and Rural Development

Any reversal, even slowing down, of the move to the cities simply won't occur for years, for three reasons: first, the rapid population growth expected—city-dwellers are young and of childbearing age (the estimates put over half the anticipated increase down to this factor);

Table Urban Population Growth, 1990–2000					
	1990		2000		1990–2000
	Urban Population *millions*	Urban Population/ Total Population %	Urban Population *millions*	Urban Population/ Total Population %	Growth *millions*
World	**2,282.4**	**43**	**2,962.1**	**48**	**679.7**
Developing Countries	**1,401.4**	**34**	**1,993.7**	**40**	**592.3**
Africa	**205.5**	**32**	**322.1**	**38**	**116.6**
Algeria	12.9	52	19.5	60	6.6
Ivory Coast	4.9	40	8.0	47	3.1
Egypt	23.0	44	30.0	46	7.0
Kenya	5.7	24	11.1	32	5.4
Nigeria	38.2	35	63.9	43	25.7
Zaire	10.5	28	15.8	31	5.3
Latin America	**315.5**	**72**	**400.6**	**77**	**71.1**
Bolivia	3.7	51	5.2	58	1.5
Brazil	112.1	75	140.8	82	28.7
Mexico	61.3	73	79.7	78	18.4
Peru	15.0	70	19.6	75	4.6
Asia	**974.3**	**31**	**1,370.0**	**37**	**395.7**
Bangladesh	18.7	16	33.1	23	14.4
China	302.2	26	451.7	35	149.5
India	216.1	26	290.9	29	74.8
Indonesia	53.1	29	79.5	37	26.4
Pakistan	37.8	32	58.6	38	20.8
Philippines	26.7	43	37.2	49	10.5
Thailand	12.1	22	17.7	29	5.6
Developed Countries	**880.9**	**73**	**968.4**	**76**	**87.5**
Australia	14.6	85	16.8	86	2.2
United States	188.1	75	213.3	78	25.2
Europe	373.4	73	401.4	77	28.0
Japan	95.3	77	101.1	79	5.8
Source: *World Urbanisation Prospects 1992*, United Nations, New York, 1993					

second, the transformation of rural areas, where modernization is forcing more and more farmers and farmworkers off the land to look for jobs in the cities; third, the increased likelihood of finding work in cities.

Cities have already been a driving force in economic development. According to the World Bank,[3] they already account for an average of 50 percent of GDP in the Third World, a proportion that may rise to two-thirds by the end of the century. Cities are major centers of production for industry, services, and trade and so generate resources and jobs. They have a two-edged effect on national budgets, bringing in tax revenue on the one hand and increasing the demands on revenue on the other. Conversely, urban activities rely heavily on macro-economic and sectoral policy decisions. Taxation, trade, structural adjustment, the location of industry—all have repercussions for urban areas. So the framing of macro-economic policies should give consideration to their implications for cities and, indirectly, for rural areas.

In the long run, urbanization ought to curb population growth, the birth-rate falling as standards of living and education rise and family planning is targetted on a more limited area. But in most developing countries the requisite conditions do not yet exist.

It is now accepted that urban and rural development, far from conflicting, are mutually reinforcing and ought to be pursued simultaneously. The idea that the various problems of urbanization can be solved through strategies designed to improve life in rural areas has to be abandoned. If the rural labour force does not turn to urban activities, it will, to be able to grow crops, have no choice but to destroy forests or move onto land that is environmentally sensitive or ill-suited to farming. That process is already well under way in a large and steadily increasing number of countries.

A city cannot be separated from its hinterland. So an all-inclusive national approach is required. Cities have to support agriculture by providing the inputs, equipment, services, and, above all, markets for farm produce; indeed, many smaller towns offer this very function. And for rural workers who cannot find employment, leaving the land offers the best hope of finding a job. They may be able to find work in the cities, particularly in the informal sector which sometimes accounts for two-thirds of all jobs.[4]

But if this interaction between town and country is to benefit both, cities have to continue to offer the right conditions for productive resources to be built up. Deficient infrastructure, inappropriate laws and regulations, and the weakness of municipal institutions in many developing countries mean that urban productivity cannot be raised, restricting growth in both urban and rural areas alike.

Cities and Poverty

If urbanization can thus take some of the pressure off the rural environment in developing countries, it is nonetheless putting ever-increasing pressure on the urban environment. Galloping urbanization, with its attendant congestion and pollution, and coupled with a lack of resources, has disastrous effects on living conditions: squalid and overcrowded housing, scarcity of clean water, no proper sewage or drainage systems, no services (schools, dispensaries), and no provision of law and order whatsoever. "Street children" (and there are 2 million of them in Latin America) often fall prey to organized crime, drugs, and prostitution. Poor neighbourhoods are often located in areas where the risks of soil erosion, water pollution, and natural disasters are higher than elsewhere.

Measures to alleviate poverty and protect the environment therefore have to be linked with the provision of better living conditions in the towns. Poverty, once more prevalent in rural areas, is now becoming a primarily urban problem. The number of people living in shanty towns on the outskirts of Third World cities is growing much faster than the population housed in modern residential areas. In the 1980s, in cities such as Addis Ababa, Bombay, and Cairo, between 60 and 80 percent of the population were reported to live in slums and informal settlements.

The World Bank states bluntly that poverty in urban areas could become one of the most explosive political problems of the 21st century.[5] And indeed, cities carry a lot of political weight because they have a high concentration of resources and institutions, and their inhabitants are better educated, better trained, and consequently have more political, economic, and cultural clout. Cities also draw young people in search of a better life. In most Third-World cities, over half the population is under 25. In sub-Saharan Africa, as much as a quarter of the population is aged between 15 and 25. And although young people can be a stimulus for entrepreneurship and initiative, they can also erupt into unrest and violence if they lose hope and feel alienated and marginalized.

Facing Up to Difficulties

These various factors should encourage lenders and investors to work out an effective policy to help Third-World cities. But it has to be said that (with the exception of the World Bank) they have so far been reluctant to do so. Why? Is it the enormity and complexity of the task?

Difficulty in perceiving what is required for balanced and sustainable urban development? Are there no clear models or policies for reference, even though cities in the developed countries also have their difficulties?[6] Are they unwilling to relinquish an approach that has hitherto given preference to rural development? Are the necessary structures and skilled staff not available?

In November 1992 the OECD Development Assistance Committee (DAC), taking up the challenge, held a meeting with the World Bank, the United Nations Centre for Human Settlements (Habitat) and the United Nations Development Programme (UNDP), jointly defining aid for urban development as encompassing all policies, programs, and projects that are designed to improve the management, infrastructure, and the quality of life in areas identified by the country concerned as urban and that also have a population of 20,000 or more. The joint definition also stresses the importance of quality (of policies, management, life) as well as quantity (of investment). It should also lead to progress in collecting statistics, which currently suffer both from problems of definition and from incompleteness.

Today there is a broad consensus on what aid policies for the urban sector ought to involve. The aid agencies emphasise that urban development ought to be economically efficient, socially just, and environmentally friendly.[7] A more comprehensive, coordinated approach to urban development should replace the narrow, sector-specific stance adopted hitherto. In the past, urban aid consisted basically of providing modern infrastructure. In the future, it will also have to take macroeconomic factors into account, as well as education, health (not least family planning), welfare, job-creation, and improving the environment for all city-dwellers, including those living on the outskirts. The new approach will also have to be flexible and pragmatic to accommodate innovation and adjustment.

Mobilizing Involvement

For decades to come, urban growth will call for huge investment if the shortcomings in infrastructure and services are to be put right—$100–150 billion a year, according to the World Bank. Aid will have to be the catalyst here, and technical assistance high on the list in finding solutions in each country. The task is so huge that it will require the combined efforts of central government, local authorities, public and private enterprise, trade and user associations, and NGOs.

Although central government does have a crucial role to play in the balanced and sustainable development of cities, lenders and investors have in the past focused too narrowly on that particular institution and overlooked three others, equally important: local authorities, the private sector and public/private sector partnerships, and individual inhabitants.

First, local authorities must be given more freedom of action and more say in developing the cities they run—in particular, more power to raise revenue and thus improve services. In return, they must be more readily accountable to both central government and to their citizens, while at the same time improving the services they provide and making their management more transparent. Allowing them to overspend will overburden the central-government budget. Lenders and investors should therefore plan on giving adequate technical assistance to allow the upgrading of technical and management skills. "Decentralised co-operation," involving twinning or cooperation agreements between towns and cities in developed and developing countries, could be encouraged—they would make for an exchange, particularly of experience. Partnerships between local authorities and NGOs working in development could also be fostered.

Second, it is crucial to give free rein to the initiative potential of private enterprise and the informal sector for the provision of urban services. It would be a mistake to underestimate the perverse effects of regulation. Red tape complicates land-use, and zoning rules, over-fussy building standards, and long and complicated industrial planning procedures discourage investors by pushing up costs. Aid organizations could encourage initiatives which require satisfactory and reliable service delivery so that investing firms can operate efficiently, which call for the reform of laws, rules, and administrative practices so that they help rather than hinder productive activities, harness market forces and competition, and which pay due attention to the requirement of the informal sector.

Third, experience has shown that allowing people to participate directly in urban-development projects makes for more efficiency and may even determine success. The providers of services should therefore forge closer links with their clients (NGOs, local action groups, neighbourhood and consumer associations) from the outset of a project and throughout its duration. Lenders and investors should support initiatives that encourage the flowering of a community spirit in the urban areas they are working in. The attitude of the relevant municipal services, and the way a project dovetails into municipal, even national, structures are also decisive. "Neighbourhood development projects" seem to be among the best ways of building effective partnerships. With projects on a larger scale, it may be advisable to base the approach on consultation rather than participation, or to link action by local office-holders with work done by other institutions (central government, city councils, and technical services).

The DAC also emphasises the importance of acknowledging gender in framing urban development projects and programs: staff in both donor and recipient countries have to be trained to deal with it. Men and women do have different requirements (particularly in infrastructure, services, and housing) because they play different roles in society and at home. On average, one-third of all households in developing countries are run by women (compared with 10–15 percent in OECD countries), and in the cities the proportion is probably higher still. So women should have more say, perhaps more decision-making power, than men in matters of housing design, spatial planning, and urban services, particularly transport. Law-and-order issues, too, are of vital importance to women.

Aid for urban development has suffered in the past not only from the weakness of the national institutions involved but also from the structural weaknesses of aid agencies when it comes to organizing tasks of such complexity, which transcend traditional ministerial and policy-area divisions.[8] A number of bilateral and multilateral agencies still have no department or unit working expressly on the urban sector; instead, urban projects are shunted between the services in charge of infrastructure and social affairs. Aid agencies do not always have access to the partners most closely involved with the city, the local authorities in particular. Another drawback is that few agency personnel have been trained to work in an urban environment.

The lack of coordination between central units, technical units, and the projects themselves, as well as among aid agencies, is sorely felt, too. Some agencies acknowledge that several projects have been under-taken in the same city without those in charge knowing about the others, simply because each was run by a unit of the agency concerned that dealt with a different area of policy. The main problem in the field appears to be the difficulty of linking infrastructure projects with social projects, and of coordinating the various policy-area components of each.

Whatever the differences between situations and resources, officials in both the developed and the developing countries must face up to the complexities of urban management. More and more city-dwellers are falling into poverty. The kind of urban development that has been so popular until now threatens the environment. Discussion and exchange of experience among officials and experts from North and South could help address these problems.

OECD Bibliography

Development Co-operation: 1993 Report, 1993.

Rémy Prud'homme, "City Limits," *The OECD Observer*, No. 181, April/May 1993.

Christopher Brooks, "Rethinking the City," *The OECD Observer*, No. 178, October/November 1992.

Development Co-operation: 1991 Report, 1991.

Raundi Halvorson-Quevedo, "The Growing Potential of Micro-Enterprises," *The OECD Observer*, No. 173, December 1991/January 1992.

Carl Wahren, "The Imperative of Population Control," *The OECD Observer*, No. 167, December 1990/January 1991.

Notes

1. *Development Co-operation: 1993 Report*, OECD Publications, Paris, 1993, includes a chapter on this subject.

2. *World Urbanization Prospects 1992*, United Nations, New York, 1993.

3. *Urban Policy and Economic Development: An Agenda for the 1990s*, World Bank, Washington D.C., April 1991.

4. Raundi Halvorson-Quevedo, "The Growing Potential of Micro-Enterprises," *The OECD Observer*, No. 173, December 1991/January 1992; see also Friedrich Kahnert, *Improving Urban Employment and Labour Productivity*, World Bank Discussion Paper, No. 10, May 1987.

5. Op. cit.

6. Christopher Brooks, "Rethinking the City," *The OECD Observer*, No. 178, Oct./Nov. 1992 (conference held at the OECD in Nov. 1992 on the economic, social, and environmental problems of cities); Rémy Prud'homme, "City Limits," *The OECD Observer*, No. 181, April/May 1993.

7. *Urban Policy and Economic Development*, op. cit.; see also *Cities, People and Poverty—Urban Development Co-operation for the 1990s*, UNDP Strategy Paper, UNDP, New York, 1991; Nigel Harris (ed.), *Cities in the 1990s: The Challenge for Developing Countries*, Overseas Development Administration, Development Planning Unit, UCL Press, London, 1992; and *Coopération française pour le développement urbain*, Ministère de la Coopération et du Développement and Caisse centrale de coopération économique, Paris, October 1990.

8. Isabelle Milbert, *Coopération et développement urbain—Politiques des agences d'aide bilatérales et multilatérales*, Swiss Development Co-operation (SDC). Geneva, second edition, November 1992.

The Challenge to Develop Clean Energy Sources

The world relies almost solely on fossil fuels to meet their energy needs. However, as these resources become more and more scarce and the evidence of the environmental damage caused by these materials mounts, it is becoming clear that the time has come to seek alternative sources to fulfill our energy needs.

Fossil fuels, by which we mean fuel sources such as coal, wood, and petroleum, have been the main source of energy for the world. They are used to heat our homes and businesses, run our automobiles, cook our food. . . . However, the burning of this type of energy source causes the release of carbon dioxide, sulfur oxides, nitrogen oxides, carbon monoxide, and particulate matters. These are the principle causes of air pollution, acid rain, and global warming. The burning of the fuels society depends so heavily on is bringing about its own destruction.

Fossil fuels are not only causing the pollution of air. They are also a principle cause of water pollution. Oil spills and effluents that leak from oil refineries and power plants leak hazardous waste into oceans and rivers. Mining the earth for coal causes the contamination of surface water and ground water.

Finally, the by-products of refining fossil fuels and their burning leave behind hazardous solid waste. This is waste that we cannot safely rid ourselves of.

Some turn to nuclear power as a source of clean energy. However, as with fossil fuels, nuclear waste is a by-product of nuclear power creation that cannot be safely disposed of and that is dangerous to the health and safety of humans and the environment.

All of these negative effects of the use of fossil fuels point to the need for new energy sources. Risk-free power can be obtained through solar and wind power. Another energy source, biomass, is also a possible clean source. The energy is released when the plant matter, biomass, is burned. Although carbon dioxide is released during the burning process, the biomass captures the carbon while it is living, causing no net change in carbon levels. Geothermal energy and hydroelectric energy are two other sources of energy that do little damage to the environment.

These are some of the most common clean energy sources that could reduce our dependence on environmentally destructive fossil fuels. It is worth the scientific effort needed to explore clean energy options such as these and others, that would reduce the damage done to the environment and provide us with sustainable cost-efficient fuel.

—RNW

15

World Energy Future: The Demand Side Challenge

Robert G. Skinner

Non-OECD countries will account for the greatest share of growth in future energy demand. Policymakers, in response to public concern that the continued use of fossil fuels could bring about global climate change have sought out policies which will reduce future energy demand. However, economic instruments which can do so, such as carbon taxes, provoke significant distributional and equity issues. Most OECD governments have set CO_2 reduction targets, but few of those targets are backed up by effective legislation and programs. Instead, most governments seem to count on increasing energy efficiency, seemingly 'spontaneously,' to bring about CO_2 reductions. Realization of OECD CO_2 reduction targets would be insignificant on a global scale, but they are nevertheless very ambitious when compared to recent changes in the OECD's energy-derived CO_2 emissions. Reliance on market forces alone may therefore not be enough.

The demand side of energy is receiving unprecedented attention in policy debates in most industrialized countries. For the first time since the 1960s, when the concept of an "energy policy" captured the imagination of governments. The USA, for example, has identified the increased efficiency of energy use as a leading goal in its national energy strategy.

The implications of this pendulum swing are significant: they are also extremely uncertain. By examining government policies and other analyses of their effects, this paper explores this duality, namely, the

212

potential for improved energy efficiency, the degree of political reliance on efficiency to achieve a host of economic, strategic, and environmental goals, as well as the uncertainty of their achievement, and the signal that this dilemma sends to the energy industry in trying to plan for the future.

World Energy Outlook

The International Energy Agency's (IEA) Energy Outlook[1] is a rather conventional view of the future, notwithstanding the fact that in some respects it is "outside the pack" of other projections. It was prepared in late 1989/early 1990 when oil prices were rising, the "magic" 85 percent OPEC capacity was being squeezed, OECD growth was still quite healthy, the full dimensions of the economic situation in Eastern Europe were not yet evident, and many governments had not yet declared their intentions in the area of environmental policy. While our "reference case," (based on oil prices rising in 1990 dollars from $23/bbl in 1991 to $35/bbl by 2000, and then flat to 2005) was in many ways a "business as usual" outlook, we did anticipate fairly rigorous attention to the demand-side, with a -1.3 percent per annum improvement in energy intensity in the OECD region. This would be better than the rate of energy intensity decline since 1985: so, it was not entirely "business as usual."

This conventional view saw world energy demand up by 40 percent by 2005; the shift in OECD:non-OECD energy demand ratio, already at 50:50 in 1990, to an increasingly greater share being consumed by non-OECD, the oil share of which would reach half of the globe's total oil consumption by the end of the century. While oil's share of fuel use drops, the world would still need a further 15–20 bbl x 10^6/day by 2005; meanwhile, natural gas's share increases, especially its use in power generation; and notwithstanding these shifts, the world would still face a future increasingly dominated by fossil fuels. The historical and prospective expression of these regional shifts in terms of energy-derived carbon emissions is shown in figure 1. This figure also conveys some other messages: the OECD region's carbon emissions dropped during periods of recession and during periods of rapid increases in energy prices. This point will be examined again later when looking at the intent of future environmental policies directed at the energy sector. Figure 1 also presents the key policy challenge: increasing dependence on fossil fuels in the non-OECD world. If CO_2 emissions are a global concern, what must be done to reverse this trend?

Figure 1. World energy-derived CO_2 emissions.

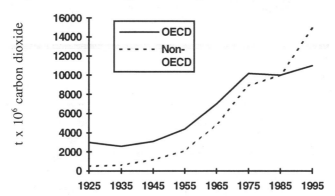

Key to any energy projection are the assumptions about oil prices. This is a treacherous minefield to venture into. Many do, with a dismal rate of failure.

The IEA does not make oil price forecasts. It follows the oil market closely and for the medium- to long-term, it simply 'tests' its outlook with different price assumptions. For the purpose of this paper, and more precisely, to set up the energy framework within which demand side issues can be examined, it might be useful to look at some of the forces seen as acting, or likely to act, on oil prices over the next decade.

While an upturn in OECD economic growth would add some demand-driven upward pressure on oil prices, the highest growth pressure is, and is expected to continue to be, in the Asia-Pacific region. Both production and demand in the former Soviet Union are falling. In 1991, production fell significantly faster, leading to a decrease in net exports. In recent months both demand and production appear to be falling at about the same rate. Over the longer term, however, the newly independent states (NIS) of the former Soviet Union can be expected to act as a downward force on oil prices as their production capacity increases. Finally, there is the persistent inevitability of a 'screw-up' or two which could cause prices to jump. In the short term, over the next few quarters (see the IEA's most recent *Monthly Oil Market Report*), while the likelihood of a perturbation is anyone's guess, it should be stressed that the historically low level of OECD stocks and the limited excess production capacity available would enhance the possibility that a perturbation would tighten prices. While the media and others seem convinced that the climate is getting warmer, very cold winters can still happen! A swing in temperature in the USA between the warmest and coldest winters (as recorded over the last 10 years) would result in an 18 percent difference in heating degree days; this would generate change in demand of about 500,000 bbl/day. Weather counts as a factor in oil prices.

Forces acting to keep oil prices down include continuing substitution for oil, improvements in efficiency, continued recession, along with environmental policies (which can also accelerate substitution and efficiency investments). There is potential for a significant increase in usable OPEC capacity in the medium term. Kuwait has announced that its production will again reach 2 bbl x 10^6/day by the end of the next year; Iran claims that its capacity will soon exceed 4 bbl x 10^6 and, at some stage, one can expect Iraq to again become an exporter of crude oil. As for non-OPEC production, it is doubtful whether it will increase much right away, but one cannot help but be impressed by the rapidity with which many countries are opening up to exploration and investment by foreign firms. The flight of drilling rigs from North America to non-OPEC countries would seem to confirm this trend. Perhaps non-OPEC production by the end of the decade could be more or less equal to that of OPEC today. Meanwhile, in the oil business, there is no truth like the truth of the drill-bit, and with only some 850 rigs currently operating worldwide (according to Salomon Brothers), not much 'truth' seems likely to be found by so few rigs. A recent PIW report (August 3, 1992), in reviewing published forecasts of surplus capacity, reported a spread of 0.5 to 7.9 bbl x 20^6/day global surplus capacity by 1995. No consensus here!

When one looks at the industry's scope for increasing investment in new supply, the short-term prospects are dim. The oil industry emerged from the 1974–75 and 1981–83 recessions in strong financial positions, ready to reinvest. Their position is certainly not as strong in today's recession. And there are many calls on their cash for "non-productive" capital expenditures (especially in the downstream); namely, to respond to new environmental requirements. In the upstream, there is oil to be developed—provided the terms reflect the costs and the political and geological risks. Governments, at least some, have a role in reducing political risk, and it is not in giving grants or soft loans directly or through international financing agencies. Rather, it is in creating systems of sound governance and an attractive climate for commercial investment, accompanied by the necessary legislation to provide the normal international standards of protection for investments.

Climate Change Policies: "A Walk on the Demand Side"

Since late 1988, the International Energy Agency has been actively engaged in the international debate and analysis related to global climate change. Our focus has been on identifying the linkages between energy use and greenhouse emissions, principally carbon dioxide, and on assessing the energy and economic implications of policies designed to reduce greenhouse gas emissions. Most of these policies are aimed at reducing the demand for fossil fuels, and energy generally.

The IEA, as an institution, is not in a position to debate the scientific basis for the claim that climate change is taking place or will occur owing to human activities. We do recognize, however, that energy is central to the climate change issue, that the greenhouse gas emissions derived from human activities are over 50 percent CO_2 and that, of this, up to 80 percent is believed to originate from the production, transport, and consumption of energy. The IEA's analyses have focused primarily on 24 OECD member countries, because they account for 45 percent of the world's energy-derived CO_2. Our timeframe is the next 15 years (the scope of the IEA's energy model and average span for member countries' energy policies). Sectorially, emphasis is given to transport and electricity which account for about 60 percent of energy-derived CO_2. These are also the two fastest growing demand areas and paradoxically, in many but different ways, the most difficult to address through government policies.

Governments of OECD member countries have reacted to the prospect of climate change with policy proclamations and other pronouncements, commitments, and programs. The IEA Secretariat has monitored these developments closely and has recently published a description of all OECD member countries' policies, as well as those of the major emitters of CO_2 among non-OECD countries. This is the only authoritative source of what governments are actually doing as opposed to saying or being characterized by others as doing. Table 1 summarizes those policies.

A review of OECD governments' policies reveals that, besides many of those policies being conditional on others taking parallel action, much reliance is being placed on energy efficiency and the increased use of low- or no-carbon fuels, such as natural gas, non-hydro renewables, and new energy technologies. While five countries

(Denmark, Finland, the Netherlands, Norway, and Sweden) have implemented carbon taxes ranging from $3-166/tonne carbon, there are many exemptions granted in most of these countries for carbon-intensive industries. Other countries and jurisdictions have implicitly implemented "carbon taxes" of sorts, without necessarily naming them as such, or intending them to have the effect of reducing CO_2 emissions. The best example is perhaps the UK's Non-Fossil Fuel Obligation. This in effect acts like a carbon tax but is applied only to electricity. Other electric utilities that collect price premiums to cover, for example, special nuclear costs, including those designated to cover the projected costs of decommissioning and spent-fuel disposal, or to include special renewable projects at marginal cost, can be interpreted as placing a cost burden on their subscribers for low- or no-carbon sources of electricity.

Table 1. Characterization of approach to commitments by OECD member countries.

Unilateral, unconditional commitments to targets (Austria, Canada, Iceland, Luxembourg, and Switzerland) of which two elaborated by funded plans of action and supported by carbon or CO_2 taxes (Netherlands and Denmark).

Unilateral, but preliminary nonbinding and/or conditional commitments to targets (Australia, Germany, Italy, New Zealand, and United Kingdom) of which two supported by carbon tax (Finland and Norway).

Target adjusted for need for economic growth (Spain).

Conditional targets based on per capita emissions (France and Japan).

Commitment to a set of policies which will stabilize emissions (USA).[*]

Regional targets balanced out by allowing economic-growth-adjusted targets of some countries to be offset by the more aggressive targets of other countries (the European Community).

Targets not specified but implicit in membership in European Community or EFTA (Belgium, Greece, Iceland, Ireland, and Portugal) of which one supported by carbon tax (Sweden).

[*]On April 22, President Clinton announced that the United States will aim to stabilize U.S. emissions at 1990 levels by 2000.

While not taxes *per se*, those programs amount to notional internalization of the costs of avoiding the use of carbon dioxide emitting sources. But this argument should not be taken too far because it calls for rather fanciful revision of motives!

The European Community has agreed to a regional target and the European Commission has launched the proposal for a community-wide energy-carbon (50:50) tax to reach $10/bbl ($42/tonne carbon for the carbon component of the tax) by 2000. This has generated much debate and it too seems relegated to the "conditional" category—"après vous Alphonse"—namely, it is applicable only if others, principally North America and Japan, also impose such a tax.

The IEA has analysed the market impact of these policy undertakings/targets relative to other policy interventions. In other words, if governments were actually implementing policies and programs to achieve their targets, what would be the implications in terms of CO_2 reductions, emissions, and energy markets?

Figure 2 shows the total effect on CO_2 emissions should all the commitments of OECD countries be fully attained by their target date (mostly 2000). They are shown as a wedge attaining 827 million tonnes of CO_2 off the top of total OECD emissions. Several points are evident from this figure. First, these policies, even if totally successful, would have little effect on global emissions. Based on the IEA's reference case, OECD emissions increase 22 percent by 2005 and the world's emissions increase about 40 percent; with these policies, world emissions still rise about 25 percent and the OECD's about 3 percent by 2000. While the global effect is small, they would significantly constrain growth in fossil fuel use in the OECD. Even though they are, as described, mostly policy statements rather than actual laws and programs, they nonetheless constitute an important investment signal for the fossil fuel industry.

This figure of 827 t x 10^6 CO_2 can be compared with experience and, theoretically, with other policy interventions modelled against the reference case. In this way one can attain some additional measure, if anything, of the political intent behind the current policy statements. In terms of the magnitude of CO_2 emissions, 827 t x 10^6 is about equivalent to twice the current total annual energy-derived CO_2 emissions for Canada (table 2). It is also in the range of the reduction in energy-related CO_2 emissions in the OECD between 1975 and 1985 (figure 1). Recalling this period, that drop in emissions accompanied major increases in oil prices, a fourfold increase in the contribution of

Figure 2. Effects of stated OECD policies on world CO_2 emission forecasts.

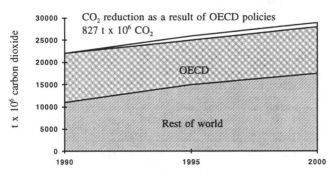

nuclear power and the attendant reduction in the use of oil in electricity generation, new vehicle efficiency improvements of up to 25 percent, and two significant recessions. This provides a sense of the relative magnitude of economic perturbations and structural change that might be implied by interventions sufficiently robust to achieve the OECD governments' CO_2 targets over the next ten years or less. Economically, of course, there are differences. Taxing to provide the necessary price signals (to replicate the sixfold increase in oil prices while perhaps achieving no net increase in overall taxes) would not have the same economic effect as did the increases in the price of imported energy. It is therefore instructive at this point to look closely at carbon taxes.

Carbon Taxes and Other Policy Interventions: Lessons From Models

IEA has modelled a number of policy interventions econometrically using its World Energy Model. As noted earlier, this model is being re-vamped, but the overall relative effects of policy interventions or excursions from the Reference Case are still instructive for this discussion. It is intended that they will be updated and refined by future analyses. Four scenarios are presented here:

1. Regulation of fuel use in order to force increased use of natural gas in electricity generation: "High gas" case;
2. Regulation of fuel use in order to force out fossil fuels from electricity generation: "Nuclear" case;
3. "Carbon tax" case ($130/tonne carbon applied at the point of consumption); and,
4. A combined ($130 carbon tax/nuclear) scenario.

Table 2. Climate change: key energy and CO_2 emissions data[a] for OECD countries (1990).

	TPES[a] Mtoe	TFC[c] Mtoe	TPES/ GDP ratio[b]	TFC/GDP ratio[b]	Energy-related CO_2 emissions (ktons CO_2)	Energy-related CO_2 emissions per capita[c]	Energy-related CO_2 emissions per unit GDP[d]	% of energy-related OECD emissions of CO_2[e]	% of energy-related world CO_2 emissions[f]	CO_2 emissions from biomass (ktons)	CO_2 from bunkers (ktons)
Australia	85.02	55.32	0.45	0.30	274 000	16.02	1.46	2.63	1.27	16 400	2 070
Austria	22.36	18.77	0.29	0.25	57 200	7.41	0.75	0.55	0.27	9 480	0
Belgium	51.81	38.39	0.55	0.41	124 000	12.40	1.32	1.19	0.57	949	13 300
Canada	202.43	151.32	0.50	0.38	435 000	16.35	1.08	4.18	2.02	33 500	2 010
Denmark	18.26	14.08	0.29	0.22	56 100	10.92	0.90	0.54	0.26	4 000	3 080
Finland	25.73	20.25	0.40	0.32	58 600	11.76	0.92	0.56	0.27	14 600	1 810
France	219.34	142.55	0.36	0.24	384 000	6.80	0.64	3.69	1.78	15 500	8 150
Germany	366.76	240.80	0.47	0.31	1 039 000	13.05	1.34	9.99	4.82	8 959	7 970
Greece	24.11	17.05	0.66	0.47	81 000	8.00	2.23	0.78	0.38	2 160	8 050
Iceland	1.43	1.13	0.44	0.34	2 450	9.57	0.75	0.02	0.01	0	0
Ireland	10.51	7.33	0.45	0.31	33 100	9.46	1.42	0.32	0.15	46	57
Italy	156.33	121.19	0.32	0.25	411 000	7.13	0.83	3.95	1.91	4 260	8 580
Japan	433.28	303.16	0.26	0.18	1 060 000	8.58	0.63	10.19	4.91	184	16 500
Luxembourg	3.54	3.37	0.83	0.79	10 300	27.10	2.42	0.10	0.05	97	0
Netherlands	77.12	63.26	0.54	0.44	183 000	12.22	1.27	1.76	0.85	792	35 000
New Zealand	13.55	9.71	0.59	0.42	26 800	9.45	1.39	0.26	0.12	1 420	1 020
Norway	21.07	17.51	0.34	0.28	31 900	6.33	0.43	0.31	0.15	3 740	1 450
Portugal	15.87	12.33	0.61	0.48	42 900	4.37	1.66	0.41	0.20	4 500	1 950
Spain	91.18	63.59	0.44	0.31	227 000	5.83	1.10	2.18	1.05	1 870	11 700
Sweden	42.83	28.74	0.38	0.26	55 300	6.47	0.50	0.53	0.26	21 000	2 130
Switzerland	24.19	19.46	0.23	0.18	44 400	6.53	0.42	0.43	0.21	3 310	58
Turkey	43.81	33.28	0.62	0.47	133 000	2.33	1.90	1.28	0.62	31 000	380
UK	212.15	149.48	0.40	0.28	589 000	10.26	1.11	5.66	2.73	1 530	8 000
USA	1 871.201	340.00	0.41	0.29	5 020 000	19.97	1.09	48.27	23.27	248 000	92 000
OECD Total	4 122.53	2 915.05	0.39	0.28	10 400 000	248.32	27.54	100.00	48.21	427 337	225 226
European Community	1 246.98	873.43	0.42	0.29	3 180 000	127.55	16.24	30.58	14.74	44 648	105 791

[a] All data are IPCC adjusted: including bunkers and peat, excluding biomass, and treating sequestered carbon as suggested in the IPCC/OECD methodology. [b] GDP in billion US$ 1985. TPES and TFC per GDP shows TPES and TFC per US$1 000 at 1985 prices. [c] CO_2 per person. [d] CO_2 per US$1 000 at 1985 prices. [e] OECD total CO_2 emissions = 10 400 000 ktons. [f] World total CO_2 emissions = 21 570 432 ktons.

Source: Climate Change Policy Initiatives; OECD/IEA, Paris 1992

These "interventions" were only applied to the OECD region. In other words, they simulated regional "go-it-alone" initiatives. Table 3 summarizes these cases and their principal effects. For a fuller discussion of market and sectoral effects, see Skinner and Smyser and Vouyoukas.

The central point for this discussion is that, when compared to these "interventions," the stated intentions of governments for 2000 are approximately in the same ballpark or "band" in terms of projected reductions of CO_2. This is shown in figure 3. In other words, the tenor of the political intent is very significant.

A "Demand Side" Case

It is possible to analyze changes in demand by changing the assumption about the rate of energy intensity improvement (which was assumed to be -1.3 percent per annum). However, to arbitrarily adjust this rate, say by doubling it (which is the highest rate encountered since 1970, and occurred between 1979 and 1982), would be simplistic, implying hundreds of assumptions about technology improvements and their rate of penetration into the marketplace, and perhaps implicitly, about government policies to make it happen (this will be further discussed). It should also be pointed out that the other half of energy intensity—GDP—is treated exogenously in the IEA Model.[2]

The "Natural Gas" Case

Most energy projections see a greatly expanded use of natural gas, perhaps doubling by 2005, even without the implementation of greenhouse gas reduction policies. While there would seem to be ample gas resources to meet this demand, the question remains: "at what price?" To examine this question, we assumed that the price of gas doubled by 2005. To more than triple the use of gas in electricity generation implies early retirement of other (probably coal) plants. Our country-by-country examination[3] of actual plant age and capacity would suggest an upper limit of doubling the share of gas in electricity of 2005, rather than, as forced in this case, tripling.

The question of the effects on gas prices of an increased reliance on natural gas requires further consideration, and it must be looked at from the perspective of different markets. For the European market, the costs of significant incremental supplies to Western Europe require re-examination. Doubtless, the NIS would be the major supplier but the forces on costs and prices along the gas system, from the well-head in

the former Soviet Union to the burner-tip in Western Europe, present a
picture of great uncertainty. First, costs are rising at the well-head.

Table 3. Four climate change policy cases.

Regulation of the use of natural gas in electricity. Tripling the projected
share of natural gas in power generation by 2005 (from 16 percent in 1990
to 85 percent rather than 26 percent) reduces the growth in OECD CO_2
emissions from 22 percent to 10 percent. Natural gas prices to industrial
consumers would rise by 140 percent over 1990 levels in real terms
compared with 70 percent in the Reference Case projection.

Regulation of nonfossil fuel use. In the Reference Case projection the share
of nonfossil fuels in electricity generation in the OECD decreases from 42
percent to 35 percent by 2005. If instead it were forced to increase to a 65
percent share, growth in OECD CO_2 emissions to 2005 would decline from
22 percent to 9 percent above 1990 levels.

Carbon taxes (a tax level of $130/tonne C applied only in the OECD). A
carbon tax of $130/tonne of carbon is equivalent to trebling current world
coal prices, doubling crude oil and gas import prices when added to all
existing energy taxes, including gasoline and diesel fuel taxes.
Approximately 70 percent of the effect of the carbon tax is to reduce
overall energy demand and the remainder is shifting fuel shares depending
on the carbon content of fuels. By 2005, a carbon tax of this magnitude
would reduce primary energy demand in the OECD area by some 9
percent below the Reference Case projection, roughly halving expected
growth in demand. By 2005, coal use would see a 26 percent reduction
from the Reference Case projection, petroleum use would be 7 percent
down and natural gas largely unaffected.

Combined tax and regulated nonfossil fuel use in electricity. A $130 per
tonne carbon tax combined with forced increase in nonfossil electricity, the
most draconian case, would reduce OECD emissions in 2005 below 1990
levels by 6 percent but world emissions would still grow by 27 percent
(rather than 40 percent).

Future investment will have to include foreign sources of capital. This
capital, in turn, will impose Western engineering standards and
reassurance criteria that will increase costs. Upgrading and improving
the transport system will also add costs. The economic aspirations of
transit jurisdictions such as the Ukraine, Slovakia, and the Czech lands
could lead them to seek higher fees. Meanwhile, in Western Europe, at

the consumer end, the initiatives of the European Commission to increase competition seem designed to reduce consumer prices. Finally, bearing in mind that it was the environmental chaos brought on by central planning and confirmed by Chernobyl, that motivated public support for the economic "revolution" in this region, natural gas' environmental premium will also be appreciated by post-Soviet Europe and by the Russians—either for their own use or for export to earn desperately needed foreign exchange. Therefore, the European gas market could become a seller's market for some time to come. The signal for European environmental policies, let alone national energy strategies, is only now beginning to register with governments in this part of the world.

Figure 3. Impact of various response options on OECD CO_2 emissions to 2005.

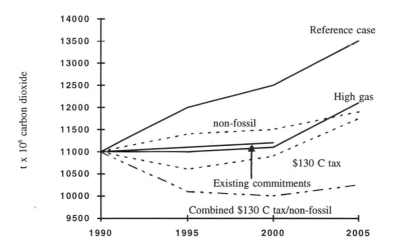

The "Carbon Tax" Case

It is assumed that the OECD coal industry is a lot smaller and more efficient than it used to be. It could perhaps even approach becoming a net coal exporter. Under the "carbon tax" case, the overall use of coal and oil would be less than otherwise expected, and its production would tend to concentrate in the lower cost regions. Because anticipating the response of the principal oil producers is impossible, this case assumed that crude oil prices would be unaffected by the imposition of a carbon tax. It is uncertain that this is realistic. Certainly to date, OPEC spokesmen have been very critical of proposals to impose carbon taxes, especially those of the European Commission.

Under the "carbon tax" case, the response to the carbon tax in the electricity sector is a 11 percent drop in demand from what it would otherwise be. Overall, 30 percent of the demand reduction in fossil fuel is due to fuel substitution—the remainder arises from increased efficiency of energy production and use. Oil use in road vehicles falls only 8 percent, essentially because substitution opportunities are limited (within the 15 years' timeframe of the study) and because the consumption of transport services is less price-responsive than is electricity. This is partly due to the relatively high taxes already in existence for transport fuels, especially in Europe. Intermodal shifts and transport fuel switching could reduce greenhouse gas emissions from the transport sector, but probably not significantly before 2005. Recent IEA full fuel-cycle analyses show that compressed natural gas and diesel fuel (in the OECD) release about 15 percent less greenhouse gases than does gasoline (figure 4).

Considerable attention has been given by economists to the analysis of carbon taxes. Given a choice of policy instruments to reduce greenhouse gases among the economic instruments, economists tend to favor taxes, because they are generally believed to be the most efficient. The OECD has recently analyzed the application and effects of carbon taxes using its new multi-sector, multi-region dynamic general equilibrium model (GREEN), and compared the results with those of other models, including the IEA's energy econometric model.[4] From this work, which is still underway, and from the above discussion, the following summary comments emerge relating to carbon taxes, both in terms of their effects and their modelling:

1. Different models can yield vastly different levels of taxes required for stabilization of emissions, depending on the assumptions made about such factors as population growth, GDP, and energy prices.
2. Fossil fuel exporting countries would be heavily affected if carbon taxes sufficiently high to achieve targets such as stabilization by 2000.
3. Different levels of tax are required between countries to get equal percentage reductions in CO_2.
4. Regional, go-it-alone taxes would have little effect on world emissions (confirming the need for global action; not necessarily

all countries taking the same action, but acting together); i.e. major actions nationally or regionally have little effect globally.

5. The availability of fuel diversification or substitutability is key to reducing cost, or the level of tax required.

6. Backstop or low or no carbon technologies are critical. Their availability places a cap on the level of tax required, otherwise a tax has to increase with time to be effective.

7. Assumptions about efficiency gains are critical, as are those relating to capital stock turnover—if a perfect policy world is assumed, where investors have adequate policy knowledge to make perfectly timed or sized investments.

8. Eliminating fossil-fuel price subsidies worldwide would significantly reduce CO_2 emissions with net social benefit.

Figure 4. LDV full fuel cycle greenhouse gas emissions OECD Europe base case in 2000.

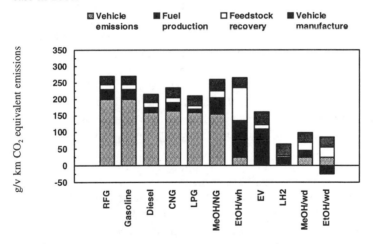

The last point—eliminating subsidies—deserves much greater attention. A review of energy subsidies, particularly outside the OECD, reveals large energy price differentials across regions. Price subsidies range from 15 percent for coal to 33 percent for natural gas. Their gradual removal by 2000 would result in a 7 percent drop in world CO_2 emissions (20 percent by 2050) [1]. While the political and social implications of removing subsidies are admittedly daunting, surely to do so would be preferable to imposing carbon taxes, given their uncertain effects and inevitable administrative complications and costs.

Energy Efficiency

As noted earlier, OECD governments are placing great reliance on significant improvements in energy efficiency to achieve their greenhouse gas reduction targets. Also, assessment of the costs and effectiveness of carbon taxes depends fundamentally on what one assumes about the availability, introduction, and rate of market penetration of efficient appliances, vehicles, and other energy-consuming equipment. Thus, assumptions about efficiency are central to any discussion of the future prospects for energy markets in general, and for the energy supply industry, in particular.

There is little doubt that considerable potential exists for energy efficiency gains worldwide. Recent work by the IEA[5] confirms that there is technical potential in some electricity end-uses, for unit reductions in electricity use exceeding 50 percent, perhaps up to 70 percent, in such areas as residential lighting. But how to translate this technical potential into a market reality remains a challenge. Moreover, as efficiency gains are made in some uses, new applications are discovered that, for example, result in switching from a fossil fuel to electricity. In places like Quebec with its reliance on hydro, this might reduce CO_2 emissions. This is not necessarily the case, however, in many parts of the USA. Even with greatly accelerated rates of efficiency improvement in the electricity sector (say 20 percent over and above current rates of improvement), overall OECD emissions from the electricity sector would still be 13 percent higher in 2005 than at present.

Similarly in the transport sector, great technological potential exists for efficiency gains, fuel switching, or intermodal shifts, but to achieve it will require concerted efforts by manufacturers, all levels of government and the fuel industry; changes in transport pricing policies; and a change in consumer attitudes and preferences. This has obvious political difficulties. Even if we could accelerate the rates of turnover for the road vehicle stock (through policy intervention) such that new vehicle efficiency could be improved 30 percent by 2005 (from 7.8 litres/100 km to 5.8 litres/100 km), and at the same time the share of diesel engines in the total OECD car park could be increased from 8 percent (today's estimate) to 20 percent in 2005, OECD CO_2 emissions would be 16 percent higher, rather than the 22 percent projected in the Reference Case.

If there is one major finding from the IEA's recent analyses of IEA member countries' policies and aspirations in the area of energy efficiency, it is that, for the most part, few have reliable information on the breakdown of energy demand; the availability, costs, and potential of efficient technologies; and their efficiencies relative to current stock. This lack of information is a serious deficiency, given their almost unanimous claim that accelerated energy efficiency will achieve member countries' environmental goals. It begs the question, "If governments do not know where they are today, how will they be able to monitor and measure their progress in the application of this policy tool?" As Casey Stengel said, "If you don't know where you're going when you start out, you may end up some place else!"

Conclusion

A fundamental message comes through from this brief review. If governments want to achieve their greenhouse gas production targets, specifically CO_2, reliance on market forces alone will not get them there. There is little doubt that considerable potential exists for increasing energy efficiency. But it must be asked: Is this a marketing opportunity overlooked, or a policy challenge shunned? OECD countries who hope to achieve their CO_2 targets by increased reliance on natural gas while hoping that their citizens become more "enercentric"—consciously making efficiency investments in all their energy purchases—may be disappointed. The dilemma is that OECD governments have had their share of bad experience with energy policy of an interventionist nature. So today's policymakers have a major challenge. Carbon taxes are nice in theory, but try that argument with a public who already feels over-taxed. Finally, the potential export trade implications of such taxes will need careful review.

Steps to assure an adequate gas supply will surely be needed, given this fuel's stature as the "right stuff" among energy sources. A commercial approach to the development of more open and competitive markets would ensure the exploration, development, and production of these resources. A stable investment climate, diversity of supplies, and long-term availability and security of energy sources are all important factors. Intergovernmental agreements to facilitate and maintain competitive markets, access to resources and transmission systems, and commercial contracts on a nondiscriminatory international basis are likely to be required before private capital can be mobilized to back very large, long-term gas development in remote parts of the world.

Governments face major policy dilemmas in reducing greenhouse gas emissions from electricity generation and transport. Growth in energy demand, especially for these two energy end-use areas, is a complex function of economic growth, technological change, increasing individual prosperity, changing consumer habits and lifestyle preferences, and socio-political trends which emphasize the pursuit of personal convenience and freedom of mobility. Technical realities compound the dilemma: transport is almost entirely oil-dependent, switching to alternative fuels or significantly improving vehicle efficiency is slow. It is probably safe to say that alternatives to oil for the transport sector will have little influence on reducing greenhouse gas emissions from this sector within the next 15–20 years.

Electricity generation, in the absence of the climate change issue, was headed for a future increasingly dependent on fossil fuels, especially coal. For electricity generation, if future access to nonfossil fuel options, such as hydro, other renewables, and nuclear were assured, OECD member countries could have some confidence in being able to sustain energy security, while greatly reducing their reliance on fossil fuels for environmental reasons, and especially to address heightened concerns about global climate change. But such assurance does not exist for most countries. Major hydro options are few, the nuclear option faces strong public opposition in most OECD member countries, and non-hydro renewables are insufficient to meet demand, even though their relative economics would improve under carbon taxes. As suggested by modelling of carbon taxes, if society rejects existing low or no-carbon technologies, it must be prepared to pay higher costs, either through higher carbon taxes if they are chosen, or the costs of yet-to-be-developed backstop technologies. Hence, any government actions designed to significantly reduce greenhouse gas emissions must reconcile these social, economic, and technical realities, while ensuring they do not run counter to those macroeconomic policies credited with stimulating the economic growth which is so essential, *inter alia*, to environmental improvement.

Greatly increasing the efficiency of energy use is a preferred option by most governments, but there remain major social and other barriers to doing so. The IEA's recent surveys of what governments are actually doing to accelerate efficiency gains in their energy sectors revealed a serious gap in most countries between their reliance on efficiency and their actual ability to assess its costs and achievability. Therefore, the question remains: how will they achieve their targets?

While specific policy elements will differ between countries, their effectiveness would be enhanced with some concordance in general approach and timing among countries; in other words, "different but together." Ensuring significantly greater access to nonfossil forms of energy over the long term, while in the short term reducing the barriers to greater efficiency in both the production and use of energy must remain the major directions of energy policy if it is to contribute to reducing greenhouse gas emissions. Moreover, eliminating existing subsidies of energy prices and especially of coal would make a significant contribution to reducing CO_2 emissions.

Notes

1. This paper draws on the IEA's World Energy Outlook summarized in *Energy Policies of IEA Countries: 1990 Review*, Paris OECD/IEA, 1991. Subsequent to finalization of this paper, a revised outlook was published in May 1993 (*The World Energy Outlook 2010*, International Energy Agency, OECD/IEA, 1993). It takes into account significant changes in the former Soviet Union, the availability of new energy data for non-OECD regions, as well as new assumptions on GDP and crude oil prices up to 2010. For additional information on the IEA model, and in particular its application to studying carbon taxes, the reader is referred to L. Vouyoukas, 1992, *Carbon Taxes and CO₂ Emissions Targets: Results from the IEA Model*, OECD Economics Department, Working Paper No. 114.

2. For the most recent (1993) version of the IEA's World Energy Outlook (ibid.) we "imposed" an arbitrary set of policy measures whose effect would be to improve the efficiency of energy use by 2010 through the forced adoption of commercially available technologies in the residential/commercial sector (20 percent more efficient than in the new reference case), industrial sector (7 percent more efficient) and the transportation sector (10 percent higher). The effects on CO_2 emissions relating to the new reference case are significant: 70 percent reduction of the projected increase in CO_2 emissions by 2010—almost as great as the effect of a \$300/tonne carbon tax.

3. IEA (1992), *Electricity Supply in the OECD*: OECD/IEA, 1992.

4. The reader is referred to a recent OECD publication. *The Economic Costs of Reducing CO₂ Emissions*, OECD Economic Studies, No. 19/Winter 1992, Special Issue, OECD, Paris. Containing a series of six papers, this report describes the GREEN model, compares its results with those of other models, explores the costs of international agreements to reduce CO_2 emissions, examines the effects of price distortions in energy markets, including existing energy taxes on a carbon basis, as well as trade aspects and the effectiveness of unilateral CO_2 abatement actions.

5. IEA (1991), *Energy Efficiency and the Environment*, OECD/IEA, Paris, 1991.

References

Burniaux, et al., OECD Economics Department Working Papers Nos. 115 and 116, 1992.

Dean and Hoeller, *Costs of Reducing CO₂ Emissions: Evidence from Six Global Models*, OECD Economics Department Working Paper No. 122, 1992.

Hoeller, et al., *New Issues, New Results, the OECD's Second Survey of the Macroeconomic Costs of Reducing CO₂ Emissions*, OECD Economics Department Working Paper No. 123, 1992.

IEA, *Energy Policies of IEA Countries—1990 Review*, OECD/IEA, Paris, 1991.

————, *Climate Change Policy Initiatives*, Paris OECD/IEA, 1992.

R. G. Skinner and C. Smyser, *Assessment of Policy Responses to Climate Change and their Likely Effects on the Energy Sector 1992.*

Limiting Transboundary Atmospheric Pollution

As the environmental crisis grows, there is an increasing acknowledgment that degradation of the Earth's air, water, and land resources is not a problem that can be solved within national boundaries. Because all nations on Earth share the same supply of air and many nations depend on the same bodies of water to meet their demands, pollution is a global problem that does not recognize political divisions and requires international cooperation to curb, and eventually solve, the problems.

The need for international efforts was first recognized politically at the beginning of this century. In 1909, the United States and Canada signed the Boundary Waters Treaty, created to address problems of the pollution of the Great Lakes and other waterways shared by the two nations. The treaty recognized the shared responsibility for the creation of the pollution and the subsequent need for cleanup, monitoring, and protection.

Other international agreements followed that contained similar ideas of cooperation. In 1972, the United Nations held the Conference on the Human Environment in Stockholm, which focused attention on the global nature of environmental problems created by industrialization. The Convention on Long-Range Transboundary Air Pollution followed in 1979, focusing more specifically on the international problem of Acid Rain. The Vienna Convention and the Montreal Protocol were important international responses to the global problem of ozone depletion.

While efforts to address international environmental pollution have made headway, the efforts are not without hurdles to cross. A major hurdle confronting international efforts is the lack of enforcement mechanisms. All of the international agreements depend upon the goodwill and cooperation of the participating nations to obey and sometimes that is not enough.

Despite the pitfalls, international efforts will become even more essential as more nations attempt to industrialize, increasing the already crucial problem of transboundary atmospheric pollution.

—*RNW*

16

Transboundary Pollution: Acid Rain and United States-Canadian Relations

Mark L. Glode
Beverly Nelson Glode

To every action there is always opposed equal reaction: or, the mutual actions of two bodies upon each other are always equal, and directed to contrary parts.

—Sir Isaac Newton (1642–1727)[1]

Introduction

Newton's third law of motion addresses the quid pro quo attributes of the physical universe.[2] Newton observed that action was inversely related such that advancement by one body obstructed the advancement of an opposing body to a similar degree.[3] Although Newton's law focused on motion, there is an even more fundamental principle embedded in the law: a change of any type, exerted upon a mass, will necessarily alter the state of other bodies juxtaposed to that mass.

Unfortunately, scientists did not discover the full impact of Newton's axiom and its relevance to the earth's ecosystem for many years. Scientists were slow to recognize the link between technological advancements and changes in the physical environment. Failing to recognize the quid pro quo attributes of nature, scientists did not anticipate that one of the ecosystem's reaction to industrialization would be acid rain. Instead of viewing the human race as caretakers of the earth's ecosystem, early industrialists acted as though the human race were separate and apart from that system. The result of their earlier

232

unenlightened use of the ecosystem is at the root of most, if not all, of our modern-day air pollution problems.

The Industrial Revolution began in England during an era known as the Age of Reason.[4] By changing the ratio of open fields to towns, encouraging population shifts and new social structure, the Industrial Revolution forever changed the face of England.[5] Sleepy hamlets turned into thriving villages. Prosperous villages became populous towns and giant chimney stacks, releasing the gaseous by-products of coal-burning furnaces, began to dominate the skyline.[6] The Industrial Revolution, once underway, swiftly moved across Europe and migrated to North America.

In 1863, shortly after the conclusion of the Industrial Revolution, England passed the first Clean Air Act.[7] The Act was aimed at reducing the local effects of air pollution on the environment and diminishing health risks for those residing in densely industrialized regions.[8] The term "acid rain" originated in 1872, to describe precipitation in and around England's heavily industrialized areas. By then, industrialization had reached a transcontinental level and a by-product of industrialization, acid rain, would present the international community with one of the most vexing problems of the twentieth century.[9]

This article explores the international law issues associated with transboundary air pollution. While the primary focus of this article is acid rain and its effect on the relationship between the United States and Canada, attention is also given to the development of international environmental law. This article first gives a brief description of the cause and effect of acid rain. Next, this article examines the existing principles of international law. Finally, this article explores the efforts of the United States and Canada to resolve transboundary pollution issues. The focus of the discussion will be on acid rain's effect on the relationship between the United States and Canada. This article concludes with an analysis of present efforts to resolve transboundary air pollution between the United States and Canada.

What is Acid Rain?

Burning coal releases sulfur which combines with the oxygen in the air to form sulfur dioxide (SO_2).[10] The amount of SO_2 created depends upon the combustion process and the sulfur content of the coal.[11] Coal's sulfur content varies with the location of the coal mine.[12] In the United States, power plants utilizing high sulfur coal generate about forty percent of the country's electricity.[13] Once released into the atmosphere,

SO_2 transforms into sulfuric acid.[14] Prevailing winds then transport the compound miles away from the source.[15]

Although the combustion process releases primarily SO_2, coal-burning plants also release nitrogen oxides (NO_x) and carbon dioxide (CO_2) into the air.[16] Additionally, emissions from motor vehicles and industrial combustion processes contribute NO_x gases to the atmosphere.[17] Finally, natural processes such as decomposition of organic material, forest fires, and volcanic eruptions release SO_2 and NO_x into the atmosphere.[18] Globally, emissions of SO_2 and NO_x by natural phenomena comprise significant portions of the volume of acid rain precursors.[19] In the more heavily industrialized regions such as Europe and North America, however, human activity contributes a much larger part of the total emissions.[20] About ninety percent of the total SO_2 production on the North American continent may originate from human activities.[21]

Acid rain is the result of complex chemical processes involving SO_2, NO_x, and atmospheric occurrences.[22] SO_2 and NO_x in the atmosphere are chemically changed into molecules of sulfate and nitrate.[23] In fact, these reactions occur fairly rapidly due to the presence of the various constituents of air pollution.[24] As an example, the transformation of SO_2 into sulfuric acid is facilitated by reaction with NO_x and other compounds in the air.[25] Prevailing winds transport these compounds hundreds of miles. The compounds return to earth in the form of acid precipitation, or dry particles that release sulfuric and nitric acid upon contact with water.[26] Thus, in some respects the phrase "acid rain" is a misnomer because acid rain encompasses dry deposition as well as snow, sleet, rain, and other forms of precipitation. The term "acid rain" in this paper refers to both wet and dry deposition.

Precipitation is "acid rain" when the precipitation has a pH lower than 5.6, the pH of pure rain.[27] It should be noted that because the pH scale is logarithmic, the difference in acidity between one pH value and the next is tenfold.[28] Consequently, rainfall with the pH of 3.6 is one hundred times more acidic than "pure" rain.[29] Precipitation in parts of Canada has averaged a pH value of 3.5 while precipitation in West Virginia had a pH of 1.5 on at least one occasion.[30]

Researchers have concluded that lake-water with a pH below 5.0 is detrimental to fish and other forms of aquatic life.[31] In much of the eastern United States, this situation is becoming widespread as precipitation routinely has pH values between 4 and 5.[32] Studies have linked forest decline in West Germany, Canada, and the United States to acid deposition in those countries.[33] Acid rain also destroys building materials and weathers historic monuments.[34] More important, evidence suggests that excessive inhalation of sulfates and nitrates contributes to human respiratory ailments and that other indirect human health threats may exist.[35] There have been incidents during the twentieth century in which fatalities have been directly linked to acute SO_2 exposure.[36] For example, in 1952, four thousand deaths were blamed on excessive SO_2 in the air in London coupled with an inversion layer which prevented dispersal of the pollutant.[37]

Scientists still have not discovered the total effect of acid rain. Thus far, scientists have linked SO_2 to diminished lung function and respiratory tract irritation in humans, reduced leaf and root growth in trees, and suppressed nitrogen fixation in symbiotic bacteria.[38] Scientists believe NO_x aggravates cardiovascular problems, nephritis, and respiratory tract ailments in humans, reduces plant growth, causes premature leaf drop, and facilitates release of metal ions in moist soil.[39] If a direct causal link between pollution and damage to local areas could be discerned, the magnitude of the acid rain problem may be lessened domestically. However, because prevailing winds do not stop at state or national boundaries, acid rain is an environmental problem of international concern. Consequently, the significant ecological, cultural, and political issues involved in abating acid rain are best addressed through international environmental policy-making processes.[40]

International Environmental Law Initiatives Recognizing Transboundary Pollution Problems

Can the international legal system, which is consensual by nature, resolve the issues raised by transboundary pollution? Many scholars do not believe that the international legal system has developed to the point where independent states will give prospective attention to global environmental concerns.[41] Critics claim that the slow process by which usage evolves into customary international law is too time-consuming, and further, that the obligations imposed on the parties in the process are not always clear.[42] Indeed, one writer has commented that the vague obligations of customary law may promote the use of "legal fictions" by encouraging parties in dispute to distort the facts so that an otherwise irrelevant custom will apply to their case.[43] Despite the doubt expressed by some commentators, traditional international law has demonstrated a respectable degree of success in addressing environmental problems.[44] As a result, a coherent body of international environmental law is emerging.[45] In fact, the progressive course of international environmental law initiatives directed towards abatement of air pollution clearly indicates that a solution to transboundary pollution is very close at hand.

Early Intervention Efforts

It is not surprising that England, the seat of the Industrial Revolution, showed the first signs of damage caused by acid rain.[46] To combat pollution problems and mitigate future damages, British industry built taller smoke stacks to disperse emissions over a larger area.[47] While the British solution relieved local pollution, taller smokestacks resulted in the dispersion of sulfate and nitrate molecules over the North Sea toward Europe.[48] The impact of the United Kingdom's local pollution abatement procedure gained international attention in the 1950s when pink snow was found on the hillsides of Norway facing England.[49] Evidence of acid rain moved across Europe, following the path of industrialization. When yellow snow appeared on slopes in Scandinavian countries windward of Germany, apprehension radiated throughout Europe.[50] These events set the stage for the first international conference addressing air pollution.

Stockholm Declaration

On June 5, 1972 the United Nations Conference on the Human Environment convened in Stockholm, Sweden.[51] With Scandinavian countries playing a primary role, the Conference directed the international community's attention to the need for international control of transboundary pollution.[52] Initiating an era of increased global awareness of international environmental issues, the Conference provided the theoretical basis for future international initiatives in the area of transboundary pollution.[53] Perhaps the Conference's most important product was the Stockholm Declaration, enunciating "principles to inspire and guide the peoples of the world in the preservation and enhancement of the human environment."[54]

The Stockholm Declaration begins with seven proclamations focusing on the relationship between mankind and the environment with recognition that industrialization has adversely affected the latter.[55] The Declaration's second part consists of twenty-six principles establishing pollution as a worldwide problem.[56] Even though the principles do not directly reference acid rain, Principle 6 is broad enough to encompass an array of pollution sources.[57] The Declaration's third, and final, part consists of an Action Plan that establishes an international assessment and environmental management program.[58] The Action Plan created systems for research, information exchange, training, monitoring, and evaluating environmental changes.[59]

The Stockholm Declaration reinforced and synthesized existing international law. The proclamations and principles contained in the Stockholm Declaration, however, are nonbinding to the extent that they do not reflect recognized principles of international law. Consequently, the Stockholm Declaration is a "soft" law document.[60] Such soft law declarations and resolutions by the United Nations and other international organizations may become *opinio juris*[61] if recognized by a significant number of nations.[62] Over time, internationally recognized declarations and resolutions evolve into rules of customary international law.[63]

Of significance, the Stockholm Declaration specifically addresses the issue of state sovereignty.[64] A fundamental principle of international law, sovereignty recognizes that independent states have an unfettered right of action within their own borders.[65] Although the Stockholm Declaration acknowledges the right of independent states to use their resources as they choose, the Declaration qualifies that right by restricting sovereigns' resource exploitation to those usages which have a negligible impact on the rights of other states.[66] Despite the fact that sovereignty is a keystone of international law, the signatory states viewed the restrictions on state action expressed in Principle 21 of the Declaration as a restatement of existing customary international law.[67]

On the whole, the Stockholm Declaration represented a significant first step towards addressing air pollution problems created by the Industrial Revolution. The Action Plan formulated at the United Nations Conference on the Human Environment led to the creation of the United Nations Environment Programme (UNEP).[68] UNEP was established in 1973 to initiate and monitor environmental programs, coordinate research, develop training programs, and oversee global environmental monitoring efforts.[69] UNEP represents an international effort to resolve global environmental problems through assessment and information exchange. Neither the Stockholm Declaration nor UNEP proposed that the international community take affirmative action to reduce air pollution.[70]

The 1979 Convention on Long-Range Transboundary Air Pollution

In an effort to address and control the European acid rain problem, an initiative requiring sovereign states to adopt measures to control pollution was introduced by the United Nations' Economic Commission for Europe (ECE) at the 1979 Convention on Long-Range Transbound-ary Air pollution held at Geneva, Switzerland.[71] The ECE Convention elicited a commitment from sovereign states to reduce and ultimately prevent air pollution by developing systems to control air quality.[72] The 1979 ECE Convention established joint research and cooperative programs between signatory states to monitor and address transboundary pollution problems.[73]

The 1979 Convention was the first international agreement with a primary focus on abating pollution caused by acid rain.[74] In 1985 a majority of the ECE states signed a protocol requiring a thirty percent reduction in sulfur dioxide emissions.[75] The Convention adopted a second protocol limiting nitrogen oxide emissions in 1988.[76] Yet, the 1979 Convention and its protocols are "soft" law documents that lack binding force. While the ECE Convention and its subsequent protocols establish limits on pollution levels no timetables or goals for reducing pollution levels were established.[77] Moreover, the Convention sought to balance the political, economical, and social interests of states with dissimilar levels of development and geographical conditions.[78] The problems associated with balancing competing states interests can frustrate international consensus.[79] As a result, the 1979 ECE Convention failed to address adequately the European acid rain problem because the agreement does not obligate signatory states to take affirmative steps towards abating transboundary pollution.

Modern Intervention Efforts

With a spotlight on the need for a more responsible approach towards the earth's ecosystem, the international community met in Montevideo, Uruguay to identify environmental issues affecting developing nations.[80] The meeting was organized by UNEP to identify global environmental law priorities.[81] Depletion of the earth's ozone layer was one of the Convention's priority concerns.[82]

Ozone in the earth's stratosphere serves to absorb ultraviolet radiation from the sun and thus is vital to the protection of human health and maintenance of the existing biological chain.[83] The ozone molecule consists of three oxygen atoms.[84] Ozone molecules are destroyed when chlorine causes separation of one of the oxygen atoms.[85] Chlorine is released into the atmosphere when chlorofluorcarbons used in aerosols disintegrate.[86] Scientists first discovered a hole in the ozone layer over Antarctica in 1985.[87] Since 1985 the hole has expanded and, in 1987, scientists estimated the hole to be the size of the continental

United States.[88] The rapid depletion of the ozone layer was the impetus for an international agreement specifically addressing the international community's shared responsibility for the earth's environment.[89]

The Vienna Convention

The Vienna Convention for the Protection of the Ozone Layer was an outgrowth of the 1981 meeting in Uruguay to identify significant global environmental concerns.[90] The Convention, using the Stockholm Declaration as the nucleus, established a framework for exchanging scientific and technical information, conducting cooperative research activities, and monitoring pollution with respect to the ozone layer.[91] The Convention, signed by sixty states including the United States and Canada, provided a procedure for adopting protocols and created a mechanism for mediating disputes concerning the interpretation of the Convention.[92] The Vienna Convention focused global attention on a documental environmental issue of major significance and universal impact.[93]

While the Vienna Convention provided a process for developing methods to control depletion of the ozone layer the Convention did not establish goals or timetables for achieving changes.[94] Like previous international environmental agreements, the Vienna Convention was a "soft" law document because the Convention imposed only general obligations upon signatory states.[95] Nevertheless, the Vienna Convention focused global attention on the ozone layer and reminded the international community that the earth has just one environment.[96] The Convention also led the way for the Montreal Protocol.

Montreal Protocol

Shortly after the Vienna Convention, fifty-six members of the United Nations, including the United States and Canada, gathered in Montreal to negotiate the terms of the Protocol on Substances that Deplete the Ozone Layer.[97] The Montreal Protocol obligated signatory nations initially to limit production of specific ozone-depleting substances to a level not exceeding ten percent of the state's 1986 production rate.[96] Signatories to the Montreal Protocol agreed to calculate their level of consumption of specified controlled substances on a twelve-month basis in order to establish the level at which they must freeze, and eventually reduce, chlorofluorocarbon emission.[99] The Montreal Protocol established guidelines and timetables for reducing and eventually eliminating emission of ozone-depleting substances.[100] Under the Protocol, developing nations have the ability to delay compliance with established control measures provided the annual calculated level of production of the controlled substance in the country does not exceed 0.3 kilograms per capita.[101]

In that the Montreal Protocol imposes specific duties on signatory states to gradually decrease ozone-depleting substances and provides for development of enforcement mechanisms to promote compliance, the Protocol has the force and effect of law. The Montreal Protocol is significant to the development of international environmental law in that it was the first international agreement to impose specific obligations on the signatory states to limit production of substances that are harmful to the environment.[102] Besides representing the first "hard" law in the area, the Montreal Protocol represents the first prospective effort to address a worldwide environmental threat by imposing strict pollution controls.[103]

The Montreal Protocol affirmed the role of traditional international law in bringing about solutions to transboundary pollution problems.[104] Analogously, the North American acid rain problem can be resolved through application of international environmental law. The Montreal Protocol provides a model of the type of agreement the United States and Canada must reach to abate the acid rain problem confronting the two nations. While this task is difficult it is not insuperable. The United States and Canada have entered agreements to resolve pollution problems in the past. Most notable are the 1972 and 1978 Great Lakes Water Quality Agreements.[105] On the other hand, many of the issues presented by the acid rain debate have sparked strong emotional reaction, in the United States and Canada, which has delayed and complicated resolution of transboundary air pollution between the two countries.

Acid Rain's Effect on United States and Canadian Relations

The United States and Canada have developed a tradition of resolving disputes without resorting to the use of force.[106] As neighbors, they share a boundary of 5,000 miles which passes through heavily industrialized and highly populated areas.[107] Despite the number of cultural, economic, and political issues that arise as a result of their proximity, Canada and the United States have maintained cordial relations as well as an unfortified border since the mid-nineteenth century.[108]

Even though the United States and Canada are both federal nations, there is an immense difference in the autonomy these federal governments grant to their states and provinces with respect to environmental issues.[109] Both governments provide for shared responsibility of matters affecting the environment.[110] Yet, while Congress clearly has authority to enact environmental legislation, the scope of Parliament's regulatory authority is not as clear.[111] Under the Canadian Constitution, the federal government may preempt provincial rule only "for the general advantage of Canada."[112] Further, Canada's federal regulatory powers with respect to environmental legislation are limited to those matters extending beyond provincial interests which are inherently of concern to the Dominion.[113] Consequently, the provinces argue that environmental legislation that regulates activities wholly within their boundaries exceeds the scope of federal authority.[114] Hence, although Parliament passed a Clean Air Act similar to that enacted by Congress, which withstood provincial challenge, the Canadian government uses its preemptive power sparingly in the interest of maintaining amiable federal-provincial relations.[115]

Besides enacting individual domestic air pollution measures, the United States and Canada committed to engage in joint research to resolve the acid rain problem under the 1980 Memorandum of Intent.[116] A group of concerned Americans even initiated litigation in an attempt to gain relief for themselves, and for Canadians, from the ravages of acid rain.[117] While none of these efforts were successful they laid the foundation for a 1991 agreement which promises to hold the answers to resolving the long-standing problem of acid rain between the United States and Canada.

A Look at Past Relations

Lakes Erie, Huron, Ontario, Superior, and well over a hundred lesser lakes and rivers form part of the water boundary between Canada and the United States.[118] With this large aqueous boundary, the United States and Canada have established formal methods of developing and managing their shared water resources.[119] The most notable of these systems is the International Joint Commission (IJC) which was created by the 1909 Boundary Waters Treaty.[120] Originally drafted by the United States and Canada to resolve navigation disputes and issues concerning diversion and use of waters, the Boundary Waters Treaty contains a reciprocity provision granting aggrieved parties access to the courts of the country wherein the incident giving rise to the dispute occurred.[121] Over the years, the IJC's responsibilities have extended to air and water pollution matters.[122]

The Boundary Waters Treaty reserved to Canada and the United States the exclusive right to control waters within their respective territories.[123] Management of the waters bisected by the international boundary between the two countries was delegated to the IJC.[124] The IJC is a six-member body with the United States and Canada each appointing three members.[125] Although the IJC engages primarily in technical work, the Commission has authority to resolve water disputes submitted by both nations and to make recommendations concerning diversions, obstructions, and new uses of waters bisected by the international boundary between the United States and Canada.[126] IJC recommendations concerning pollution-related matters carry less weight than those concerning water diversions and are not binding on the parties.[127] While the 1909 Boundary Waters Treaty grants the IJC binding authority over water diversions and obstructions, the Treaty does not confer enforcement power on the Commission with respect to pollution of boundary waters.[128] Nevertheless, the IJC has played a significant role in addressing pollution problems between the two nations.[129] In fact, the United States and Canada called upon the IJC to resolve a transboundary air pollution complaint against a smelter in Trail, British Columbia shortly after the Commission was created.

The effects of burning high sulfur coal in North America began to appear during the 1890s when farms surrounding a smelter in Northport, Washington reported property damage related to smoke.[130] Parties apparently resolved disputes locally.[131] A second smelter was constructed in 1896, across the border from Washington in Trail, British Columbia.[132] Although a new smelter had smoke stacks over 400 feet high, its emissions still caused significant damage to property in Washington.[133] Washington residents filed a formal complaint against the Canadian owners of the Trail smelter in 1926.[134] While the parties settled the initial claims, damage from the smelter continued to accrue.[135] By 1931, the IJC had become involved in the transboundary air pollution dispute.[136]

The IJC's first report in 1931 fixed current damages at $350,000.[137] The Commission ordered the owners of the Trail smelter to pay the damages that had accrued, with future damages to be assessed later.[138] By 1935, the United States and Canada agreed to submit the matter to arbitration because the two countries had not yet determined future damages.[139] The United States and Canada asked the arbitral panel to determine, *inter alia*, whether the smelter at Trail should be restrained from causing further damage in Washington.[140] In its report, the arbitral panel stated that under international law a state could not use or permit the use of its territory in such a manner as to cause injury by fumes to the territory of another state or to the properties or persons therein.[141]

While Trail Smelter is known for its restatement of the basic international principle of "good neighborliness"[142]—also referred to as the *sic utere* doctrine—it made other contributions to international environmental law.[143] Of special note, the Trail Smelter arbitral panel established a pollution control regime which fixed maximum emissions levels for the smelter.[144] Additionally, the Trail Smelter arbitration represents the earliest effort by an international tribunal to resolve a transboundary pollution problem.[145] The Trail Smelter arbitration also marked the beginning of what would become a long-term debate between the United States and Canada over transboundary air pollution.

The Present State of Affairs

SO_2 emissions in North America can be attributed primarily to coal-burning power plants and smelters.[146] The Ohio River Valley emits the greatest amount of acid-producing gases in the United States.[147] The primary source of SO_2 emissions in Canada are coal-burning smelters, particularly those located east of the Manitoba/Saskatchewan border.[148]

Transboundary pollution travels both ways between the United States and Canada.[149] Canada, however, is far more vulnerable than the United States to damage caused by acid deposition.[150] Besides enormous regions of extremely acid-sensitive spruce-fir forests, Canada's geology offers little protection from acidification.[151] Some areas in southeastern Canada lack certain compounds such as carbonates and bicarbonates of calcium and potassium which are helpful in neutralizing the incoming acids.[152] This absence of buffering quality renders Canadian lakes and rivers more susceptible to acidification.[153] In contrast, the United States is geologically well-protected, having relatively few regions—Wisconsin, Minnesota, New York, and the New England states—which are vulnerable to damage from acid rain.[154]

Not only is Canada more vulnerable than the United States to acid rain damage, it is also in a downwind position. Thus, Canada receives far more transboundary air pollution from the United States than it exports.[155] More than fifty percent of the air pollution in Canada originates in the United States.[156] Canadian sources generate less than twenty percent of the United States' total acid deposition.[157] For these reasons, it is not surprising that Canada is the complainant in the modern-day acid rain dispute.[158]

1980 Memorandum of Intent

Responding to the heightened interest of their constituents in transboundary air pollution issues, the United States and Canada established a bilateral research consultation group in 1978 to study the issue of long-range transport of air pollutants.[159] The group's report set the stage for further negotiations between the parties with the aim of developing a strategy to protect the environment from transboundary air pollution.[160] In 1979, the United States and Canada issued a Joint Statement on Transboundary Air Quality[161] which paved the way for the 1980 Memorandum of Intent between the Governments of the United States and Canada Concerning Transboundary Air Pollution.[162]

While the 1980 Memorandum of Intent represents "soft" law in that it does not impose binding legal obligations on the parties, a number of the Memorandum's accomplishments are noteworthy. For example, the 1980 Memorandum refers to the 1979 ECE Convention on Long-Range Transboundary Air Pollution and the 1972 Stockholm Declaration reinforcing their status as *opinio juris*.[163] Further, the Memorandum includes, for the first time, the term "acid rain" as a particular element of transboundary air pollution.[164] Also, the document provides for joint study groups to develop strategies for reducing air pollution, assess the cost and impact of implementing proposed abatement processes, conduct, atmospheric modelling, and draft documents to present the groups findings.[165] A bilateral oversight committee was created to coordinate the groups' work efforts and undertake preparatory discussions to formal negotiations for an agreement on transboundary air pollution.[166] Equally important, the 1980 Memorandum evinces a commitment on the part of both parties to develop a bilateral agreement to combat transboundary air pollution.[167] In the interim the parties pledged to take actions to address pollution while negotiating the agreement.[168]

The Memorandum work groups concluded their work in the early 1980s.[169] Negotiations for a bilateral agreement began shortly thereafter.[170] As an interim action, the United States and Canada agreed to develop domestic policies and strategies for abating air pollution.[171] Further, the nations agreed to exchange information on their individual programs to study the effects of acid rain on the ecosystem.[172] Finally, the United States and Canada agreed to continue cooperative efforts involving advance notification of actions which might have a significant environmental impact with respect to air pollution.[173]

Domestic Air Pollution Controls

Both the United States and Canada have enacted Clean Air Acts which set standards for air quality.[174] The Canadian Clean Air Act, however, is vastly different from the United States' Clean Air Act primarily because Canada has only six smelters and one utility as pollution sources.[175] Accordingly, Canada's Clean Air Act does not establish emissions standards comparable to those of the U.S. Clean Air Act.[176] Rather, the Canadian Clean Air Act sets guidelines for air quality and reserves to the provinces the method(s) of achieving and enforcing the federally instituted goals.[177] It should be noted, however, that the 1971 Canadian Clean Air Act does establish maximum emissions levels beyond which plants may not operate.[178]

In contrast, there are large number of pollution sources in the United States.[179] While the United States government enacted legislation to address the issue of air pollution as early as 1963, the United States did not pass a comprehensive Clean Air Act until 1970.[180] At the same time, the United States government created the Environmental Protection Agency (EPA) to regulate pollution activity.[181] Under the EPA's authority, the 1970 U.S. Clean Air Act,[182] and subsequent amendments, vest a great deal more power in the federal government than does its Canadian counterpart.[183] Most notable is the federal government's authority to establish air quality standards for certain regions of the country designated as Prevention of Significant Deterioration Zones (PSDs).[184] Also worthy of mention is the federal government's power to establish standards for future pollution sources.[185]

Under the U.S. Clean Air Act, state governments have the responsibility for administering and enforcing air quality standards promulgated by the EPA.[186] To this end, states must submit a State Implementation Plan (SIP) to the EPA for approval.[187] SIPs must detail how air quality standards will be met by preventing emissions from exceeding maximum pollution levels established by the EPA.[188] If a SIP is not stringent enough to achieve air quality standards, the EPA may require the state to revise its plan.[189] Under the United States Clean Air Act administrative powers are vested in the states while the federal government retains rule-making authority.[190]

When Congress enacted the 1965 amendments to the 1963 Clean Air Act, the legislature included, under section 102, language which could arguably be construed as providing aggrieved foreign states with a means of addressing transboundary air pollution originating from the United States.[191] The language of section 102 and the legislative history, however, fail to explain the conditions for obtaining relief.[192] Through amendments to the Clean Air Act in 1977, Congress clarified its intentions.[193] Section 115 of the amended Act provided, in part, that if the EPA Administrator received notice from an international agency that pollution originating from the United States endangered the public welfare of a foreign country, the Administrator must require the offending state(s) to submit a revised SIP addressing the problem.[194] In order to trigger this section of the Act, the injured foreign state must have provided the United States with reciprocal rights.[195]

In early 1981, EPA Administrator Douglas M. Costle publicly announced that "acid deposition is endangering public welfare in the United States and Canada . . . U.S. and Canadian sources contribute to the problem not only in the country where they are located but also in the neighboring country."[196] Costle stated that he based his findings on a report issued by the IJC.[197] A few years later, four environmental groups, four individual United States citizens with land in Canada, and six states armed with Costle's announcement filed suit in the United States District Court for the District of Columbia, to compel current EPA Administrator, Lee M. Thomas, to invoke the provisions of section 115 of the Clean Air Act and order any states contributing to Canada's air pollution to revise their SIPs.[198]

An Appeal for Judicial Relief

In *New York v. Thomas*, after determining that it had jurisdiction to hear the complaint and that the states, environmental associations, and individuals bringing the action had standing, the court proceeded to the merits of the case.[199] The court determined the issue to be whether the litigants had satisfied the requirements of section 115 and, if so, what action the statute required the Administrator to take.[200] Upon examination of the language in section 115, the court held that in order to invoke the provisions of section 115 the Administrator only need have "reason to believe that any air pollutant or pollutants emitted in the United States cause or contribute to air pollution which may reasonably be anticipated to endanger public health or welfare in a foreign country."[201] Further, the court found that the IJC report upon which Administrator Costle based his findings, constituted a report from an international agency sufficient to support a reasonable conclusion that pollutants from the United States endangered health and public welfare in Canada.[202]

As to the reciprocity requirements of section 115, the court found that the Canadian legislature had enacted a statute with similar language.[203] Under the Canadian Clean Air Act, the Minister of Environment was required to recommend emissions standards to abate pollution when confronted with "reason to believe that Canadian contaminants contribute to air pollution which may reasonably be expected to constitute a significant danger to the health, safety, or welfare of persons in another country."[204] Moreover, in order to remedy transboundary pollution, the Canadian legislation conferred upon the Minster of Environment the duty of consulting with provinces believed to be the source of the pollutants.[205] The court found this consultation similar to the EPA requiring a state to revise its SIP.[206] After concluding that EPA Administrator Costle had sufficient justification in 1981 to invoke section 115, the court acknowledged that there may be a need to review present circumstances.[207]

Next, the court proceeded to examine the question of what action the EPA Administrator must take, once the provisions of section 115 are met.[208] The Clean Air Act then compels the EPA Administrator to commence the process of requiring offending states to revise their respective SIPs.[209] Consequently, the court ordered EPA Administrator Thomas to provide the required notice to the Governors of the states responsible for the conditions revealed in the IJC report made public by Administrator Costle in 1981.[210]

On appeal, the United States Court of Appeals for the District of Columbia reversed the district court's decision in *Thomas*.[211] In the court's decision, written by Circuit Judge Scalia, the appeals court described the case as involving "an unusual statute executed in an unexpected manner."[212] Finding it unnecessary to address the merits of the case because administrative rule-making procedures were not adhered to, the appeals court concluded that Costle's findings could not serve as the basis for the judicial relief sought by the plaintiffs.[213] Thus, the circuit court never established conclusively whether section 115 of the Clean Air Act could serve as a means of resolving transboundary air pollution issues.[214]

Many scholars advocate a municipal law approach similar to *Thomas* to address the issues raised by acid rain despite the international nature of transboundary air pollution.[215] While *Thomas* was pending appeal, the plaintiffs' lead counsel prepared an eloquent discourse outlining the reasons why the Canadian government should join in any future litigation of the case.[216] While this approach is not without some merit, it presents complex questions from an international law perspective including whether becoming entangled in a foreign state's domestic affairs is good diplomatic policy.

Notwithstanding the question of sovereignty, Canada's intervention in the American legal system could possibly ignite similar action by the United States under the reciprocity provisions of the Canadian Clean Air Act. More important, by accepting the jurisdiction of the United States court system in the *Thomas* case, Canada would waive any immunity afforded by the act of state[217] and sovereign immunity doctrines against counterclaims for damages caused in the United States by Canadian pollutants.[218] These two possibilities are sufficient to make application of municipal law a less than desirable dispute resolution mechanism for addressing transboundary air pollution.

While the Canadian government elected not to intervene in *New York v. Thomas*, the Canadian government did prepare an amicus brief and requested that the State Department present the brief to the court.[219] The State Department refused to grant the request.[220] The State Department's refusal suggests that Canadian involvement was unwelcome. Not wanting to infringe on United States sovereignty, Canada may have declined to intervene in the *Thomas* appeal for diplomatic reasons. Regardless, the Canadian national government chose not to participate in the *Thomas* appeal and the circuit court's decision was reversed on procedural rather than substantive grounds. Thus, the issue of transboundary air pollution between the two countries remained unresolved.

A Bilateral View of the Issues

Historically, relations between the United States and Canada have been cordial, evincing a large degree of comity. In the past, the two countries have applied the principle of good neighborliness to resolve environmental issues.[221] The acid rain problem, however, raises issues which impinge upon the concept of territoriality.[222] Further, abatement of transboundary air pollution will require examination of the principles of absolute sovereignty and external liability.[223] While the United States and Canada have resolved disputes involving territoriality and reached agreement on sovereignty issues associated with marine areas, past negotiations never reached the level required for preliminary discussions to begin on resolving the problems of acid rain.[224] The complications inherent in achieving a balance between independence and interference, the required equilibrium for resolving transboundary air pollution, can have devastating effects on even the most congenial relations.

Considering the difficulty of the task, it is not astonishing that the United States and Canada suspended negotiations for a bilateral agreement on transboundary air pollution, which the United States and Canada committed to establish under the 1980 Memorandum of Intent, shortly after negotiations were initiated.[225] One reason for the breakdown in talks may be the differences in the Carter and Reagan Administrations' priorities.[226] While environmental concerns were of top priority to the Carter Administration, the Reagan Administration insisted on greater proof that acid rain was an environmental menace worthy of the expense necessary to abate the problem.[227] Canada did not receive this wait-and-see attitude of the Reagan Administration very well.[228]

Canada's Perspective

Canada recognized acid rain as a major environmental hazard during the 1970s.[229] Since that time, federal and provincial governments have taken steps to reduce domestic emissions.[230] The Canadian utility, Ontario Hydro, has experimented with technologies designed to reduce SO_2 emissions and has future plans to switch from coal to nuclear-powered electricity generation.[231] Smelters have reduced emissions by equipping plants with devices that capture sulfurous gases before they escape into the air.[232] Canada realized, however, that the ultimate solution to the acid rain problem required United States' commitment to a joint effort to improve air quality.[233] Understandably, the Canadians viewed the Memorandum of Intent as a significant step towards addressing the air pollution problem between the two nations.[234]

The Reagan Administration's position that more research on the effects of acid rain was necessary before meaningful abatement strategies could be undertaken infuriated Canada.[235] In response, the Canadian government launched a public awareness campaign designed to raise the consciousness of both American and Canadian citizens with respect to the effects of acid deposition on the earth's ecosystem.[236] Canada's willingness to engage in public debate in the United States over the damage caused by acid rain is a clear indication of the seriousness and depth of the Canadian government's concern over transboundary air pollution.[237] The Canadian government also unilaterally undertook to reduce domestic SO_2 emissions by fifty percent by the year 1994.[238]

In Canada, acid rain issues represented one of the few areas where political differences did not take precedence over progress.[239] Quebec, considered the most militant of the provinces with respect to the issue of provincial powers, advocated a stronger federal posture in addressing the United States-Canadian acid rain problem.[240] Moreover, Ontario and Quebec, galvanized by the effects of acid rain, took the unusual action of intervening in United States regulatory proceedings in an effort to block relaxation of the EPA's SO_2 emission limits.[241] Other Canadian provinces have evinced a heightened interest in overall air quality and many have enacted meaningful, and sometimes costly, environmental protection legislation.[242]

When the Canadian Parliament revised its Clean Air Act to provide legislation reciprocal to section 115 of the United States Clean Air Act, the Canadian Parliament intended to give the United States government a tool for invoking stricter emission controls on pollutant exporting states.[243] The effectiveness of the Canadian Clean Air Act and United States Clean Air Act, working in tandem to eliminate air pollution, has yet to be tested. The Canadian government, under Prime Minister Pierre Trudeau, vigorously promoted Canadian initiatives aimed towards acid rain abatement and supported proactive measures to ensure future environmental health.[244] Trudeau's successor, Prime Minister Brian Mulroney, placed a higher priority on negotiating a bilateral free trade agreement than on transboundary air pollution problems.[245]

Prime Minister Mulroney was far less vocal than Trudeau on environmental concerns which could impede trade talks.[246] As a result, Canada's international leadership on air pollution matters has diminished.[247] Meanwhile, the provinces and scientific community strive to maintain the commitments and level of environmental awareness created by the Trudeau government.[248] The proliferation of acid rain along the United States-Canadian border, however, did not diminish and, in 1986, the United States government finally admitted that the problem of acid rain was ripe for resolution.[249]

The American Opinion

After the work groups established under the Memorandum of Intent released their first reports in 1983, the U.S. scientists were not convinced that the environment was in imminent danger of irreparable harm as a result of acid rain.[250] Accordingly, U.S. scientists recommended further studies before acceptance of the Canadian conclusion that a fifty percent reduction in emissions was necessary to bring sulfate pollutants to a safe level.[251] In response, Canadian scientists accused American scientists of manipulating facts and figures to achieve desired results and deliberately releasing ambiguous information to the public.[252]

Although the United States spent more than $200 million on research, the effort failed to produce scientific evidence acceptable to the Reagan Administration proving that acid rain was responsible for the ecological decline of North American lakes and forests.[253] Furthermore, because individual states were basically in compliance with the Clean Air Act, stricter controls to curb acid rain would require additional legislation which, absent credible scientific evidence of necessity, would undoubtedly fail to garner sufficient support for passage.[254] Consequently, what Canadians perceived as the United States' lack of commitment could equally have been resignation to the fact that American industries required hard, scientific data before making costly reductions in SO_2 emissions beyond levels already in force.[255]

Unlike the period immediately following the Industrial Revolution, where the causal link between a bellowing smoke stack and local smog was obvious, the cause and effect relationship in the case of acid rain is not as clear.[256] The use of tall smoke stacks to disperse pollutants changed the nature of proof from demonstrative to speculative in long-range transboundary air pollution issues.[257] Consequently, investing in costly measures to alleviate acid rain, absent proof that it warrants immediate action, could be construed by Americans as poor public policy.[258] Nevertheless, even if a "leap of faith" were required to tie midwestern states to acid rain damage, the United States was committed to reducing air pollution.[259] This was evident when the Reagan Administration, which was somewhat indifferent to giving environmental issues priority, agreed in 1988 to restrict future NO_x emissions to 1987 levels.[260] The Reagan Administration's efforts cleared the way for progress towards a bilateral agreement specifically addressing long-range transboundary air pollution between the United States and Canada.

Preparing for the Future

The United States' reluctance to match Canada's efforts to abate transboundary air pollution must be weighed against the United States' efforts to improve air quality prior to the formation of the so-called "30% Club."[261] For example, the United States made significant movement towards reducing transboundary pollution prior to signing the 1979 Convention on Long-Range Transboundary Air Pollution.[262] In fact, the United States achieved a twenty-five percent reduction in SO_2 one year before the "30% Club" was formed.[263] In addition, by the turn of the century, the United States expected to realize nearly a fifty percent decrease in SO_2 emissions over 1980 levels.[264] Still, the United States recognized that current domestic efforts did not address adequately the issue of acid rain.[265] Accordingly, the United States sought to amend the Clean Air Act to accommodate transboundary air pollution concerns.[266] The United States recognized that any legislative action would have to be drafted to overcome regional differences while balancing public and private sector concerns.[267]

1990 United States Clean Air Act Amendments

Credit for finding a compromise solution to permit the enactment of legislation aimed directly at abating acid rain belongs to the Bush Administration, which pushed the innovative Clean Air Act Amendments of 1990 through Congress.[268] The amended Act is an international model for cost-effective environmental strategies and expected to stimulate development of low-cost technologies to reduce air pollution.[269] In addition, the Amendments call for a significant reduction of SO_2 and NO_x emissions.[270] While past attempts to regulate SO_2 emissions covered a multitude of diverse industries, Title IV of the 1990 Amendments focuses on coal-fired power plants, the chief contributors of sulfurous gases to the atmosphere.[271] Equally important, while the Amendments establish maximum emission levels, the method of obtaining compliance is left to the discretion of the individual utility plant.[272]

The real innovative feature of the Clean Air Act Amendments, however, is the emissions trading program.[273] Essentially, the new law creates a system under which individual power plants receive pollution allowances.[274] Pollution allowances represent the maximum SO_2 emission level at which the power plant may legally operate.[275] Plants reducing emissions below their allowance level may sell or trade the remainder of their pollution allowance to other utilities, emissions brokers, or any interested party.[276] Under this program, a utility taking the initiative to reduce pollution beyond the required level could recover part of the cleanup costs by selling its unused allowance. While the EPA required continuous monitoring devices be installed in the smoke stacks of utility plants to measure emissions, ultimately responsibility for monitoring the program rests with the states.[277]

It should be noted that Congress did not expect the 1990 Amendments to address the issue of acid rain fully.[278] Indeed, critics have described the legislation as representing "a patchwork of compromises, accommodating regional and economic interests that had defeated" prior legislative attempts.[279] Nevertheless, it is the first effort by the United States to address the acid rain problem specifically.

The 1991 Air Quality Agreement

Enactment of the 1990 Clean Air Act Amendments cleared the way for negotiations to commence on the bilateral agreement the United States and Canada committed to develop under the 1980 Memorandum of Intent. On March 13, 1991, less than six months after the Amendments were passed, President George Bush and Prime Minister Brian Mulroney met in Ottawa to sign the accord.[280] At the signing ceremony, Prime Minister Mulroney emphasized the importance of the pact to Canada.[281] The Prime Minister stated that he believed the document would make possible the elimination of acid rain as an environmental threat by the year 2000.[282] Prime Minister Mulroney expressed appreciation for American efforts in making the accord possible.[283] President Bush, after thanking all parties for their role in negotiating the agreement, pointed to the "treaty" as an indicator of the "seriousness with which both countries regard this critical environmental issue."[284]

To a large extent, the 1991 Air Quality Agreement merely reiterates existing policies and procedures between the United States and Canada regarding acid rain concerns.[285] The document is repetitive in its call for joint research efforts and the information exchange.[286] In addition, the Agreement provides that the parties are responsible for establishing their own objectives for reducing or limiting air pollutants.[287] Naturally, the United States selected standards identical to those achievable under Title IV of the 1990 Clean Air Act Amendments.[288] The document also incorporates language reflecting the parties' earlier agreement to give advance notice of projects or planned actions which would have an impact on air quality.[289]

Despite the reiteration of prior understandings, the 1991 Agreement adds a new dimension to the United States-Canadian effort to address acid rain and contributes to the rapidly growing field of international environmental law. The Air Quality Agreement broadens the role of the IJC as party advisor on issues related to the monitoring of air pollutants.[290] Further, the document creates a bilateral Air Quality Committee to review progress towards implementation of the Agreement's terms and provide public notice of the countries' efforts in the area of air pollution abatement.[291] The IJC is given responsibility for synthesizing public reaction to Air Quality Committee reports and for providing the countries with public feedback on their efforts.[292] The Agreement also establishes a mechanism for resolving disputes whereby the countries may submit any controversy arising under the document to the IJC in accordance with the applicable provisions of the 1909 Boundary Waters Treaty.[293] Finally, the Agreement requires that the two countries review the terms of the document every five years.[294]

While much of the Agreement restates existing understandings between the two countries, the Agreement does cover new ground. For example, the assessment provision addresses a common criticism of taking legally binding approaches to international environmental problems—the methods are too inflexible to permit revisions based on new scientific data or technologies.[295] By providing for regular review of the target levels for NO_x, SO_2, and the time frame for achieving the stated goals both countries can make adjustments dictated by time and new information.[296]

Clearly, the Air Quality Agreement between the United States and Canada embraces the generally accepted principle that international environmental law obligates nations to conduct activities within their jurisdiction so as not to cause environmental harm outside their territory.[297] Further, by including target emission standards and deadlines for achieving the stated levels in Annex 1 of the Agreement, the parties have created a binding obligation.[298] Detailing the obligations undertaken by the parties distinguishes the Air Quality Agreement from documents that are merely framework treaties—documents asserting obligations in broad terms to permit flexibility in application, interpretation, and enforcement.[299] The Agreement also provides dispute resolution machinery which either nation may trigger providing for third-party intervention if the countries are unsuccessful in reaching a resolution after consultations.[300] Thus, the Agreement not only regulates the behavior of the nations, it also provides a means of enforcing the obligations the countries have agreed to undertake.

The Air Quality Agreement between the United States and Canada is distinguishable from the 1980 Memorandum of Intent in that the former is more representative of "hard" international law because it imposes binding obligations upon the parties. Indeed, the document appears to have overcome most of the impediments cited as reasons for limiting environmental agreements to nonbinding expressions of general principles, such as the high costs of abatement techniques, uneven environmental impact, and political concerns.[301] Because the Canadians and Americans have successfully used the IJC to resolve boundary issues in the past, it is likely that expanding the IJC's role in transboundary air pollution disputes will hasten resolution of some of the controversies likely to arise under the Agreement. In fact, the structure of the Air Quality Agreement is very similar to that of the Great Lakes Water Quality Agreements of 1972 and 1978 which were fostered by the IJC.[302] Like the Air Quality Agreement, the Great Lakes Water Quality Agreements merely reiterated standards the United States was already statutorily obligated to achieve.[303]

On the other hand, decisions of the IJC under the dispute resolution machinery of the 1909 Boundary Waters Treaty are not binding on the parties.[304] The Commission can only intervene in disputes with the consent of both governments, and even then the Commission is constrained to act within the authority delegated to it by the parties of the dispute.[305] Further, even though IJC members pledge to perform their duties in an impartial manner, the members are political appointees.[306] In order to carry out its mission the Commission depends heavily upon the services of national officials from both countries.[307] Hence, it is most unlikely that the IJC would take a hard-line position and risk angering either country.

Nevertheless, in concluding the Agreement, President Bush referred to the document as a treaty.[308] How the President portrays an international agreement when presenting the document to the Senate for consent or during the signing ceremony must be taken into account when determining how the United States will carry out its obligation.[309] Therefore, the document may be perceived as having the full force and effect of a treaty. If the Air Quality Agreement is a treaty then the agreement is self-executing because there is no need for implementing legislation.[310] The agreement obligates the United States to do no more than what the United States must do under the Clean Air Act. However, even if the Agreement does not have the full force and effect of a treaty, it is still legally binding upon the United States by virtue of the statutory obligations incorporated in Annex 1 of the document.

Finally, the Air Quality Agreement contains lenient time frames for achieving emission reductions and some of the goals are unenforceable because they are so broadly written.[311] While the parties have committed to a long-range environmental cleanup program, there is no provision for recognition of responsibility for damages already incurred or that may be incurred while remedial efforts are undertaken. Nevertheless, the Air Quality Agreement between the United States and Canada represents an honorable beginning to recognizing and alleviating a serious environmental problem.

Conclusion

The Industrial Revolution was a precursor to dramatic, worldwide technological advancements and social change. As Sir Isaac Newton observed, however, for every action there is an equal opposing reaction. Acid rain is the ecosystem's reaction to the output from the billowing smoke stacks that symbolized the Industrial Revolution. Since the end of the Industrial Revolution, transboundary air pollution has received global attention. International environmental law initiatives aimed towards abatement of transboundary pollution represent one of the few areas where independent states have accepted softened definitions of sovereignty and territoriality.

The field of international environmental law has developed considerably since the beginning of the twentieth century. While international law is used primarily as a vehicle for expounding principles, particularly when addressing environmental concerns, the law can be used to resolve transboundary air pollution issues.[312] Adherence to principles and obligations can be enforced through dispute resolution machinery.[313] Further, the best method of creating binding obligations is to employ the most widely recognized method of creating international law—treaties.[314] The acid rain debate between the United States and Canada can be resolved through application of international environmental principles. The 1991 Air Quality Agreement contains the essential requirements for creating a binding agreement between the United States and Canada.

Notes

1. Sir Isaac Newton, "Mathematical Principles of Natural Philosophy," in *The Age of Reason* 108 (Louise L. Snyder ed., 1955).
2. See id.
3. Id.
4. See generally, id. (the period of enlightenment and achievement which later became known as the Age of Reason covers approximately the period 1650 to 1800).
5. See generally, Thomas S. Ashton, *The Industrial Revolution 1760–1830* (1964).
6. See id. at 58–93.

7.   Christian Cleutinx, "European Community Air Pollution Abatement Policy," 17 *U. Tol. L. Rev.* 113, 115 (1985).

8.   See id.

9.   See id.

10.   Ned Helme & Chris Neme, "Acid Rain: The Problem," 17 *E.P.A. J.*, Jan-Feb. 1991, at 18, 19.

11.   Id. In the U.S. high sulfur anthracite coal is produced by the lower midwestern states and northern Appalachia region. Low sulfur bituminous coal is more abundant in the West and East where there are also some high sulfur coal reserves. Id.

12.   Id.

13.   Id. One power plant, producing an average of 350 megawatts daily, emits approximately 28 metric tons of SO_2 and 8.6 metric tons of NO_x, daily. Walter E. Westman, *Ecology, Impact Assessment, and Environmental Planning* 271 (1985).

14.   Helme & Neme, supra note 10, at 19.

15.   Id.

16.   Id. NO_x includes nitrogen oxide (NO), nitrogen dioxide (NO_2) and dinitrogen oxide (N_2O). See John Kotz & Keith F. Purcell, *Chemistry and Chemical Reactivity* 824 (1987).

17.   Carol Garland, "Acid Rain over the United States and Canada: The D.C. Circuit Fails to Provide Shelter under Section 115 of the Clean Air Act while State Action Provides a Temporary Umbrella," 16 *B.C. Envtl. Aff. L. Rev.* 1, 4 (1988–1989).

18.   Id. at 4, n.16.

19.   *Acid Rain Information Book* 4 (David V. Bubenick, ed., 2d ed. 1984).

20.   See id.

21.   Id.

22.   Joseph M. Schwartz, Note, "On Doubting Thomas: Judicial Compulsion and Other Controls of Transboundary Acid Rain," 2 *Am. U.J. Int'l L. & Pol'y* 361, 363–64 (1987).

23.   Id. at 364, n.17.

24.   Stanley E. Manahan, *Environmental Chemistry* 331 (4th ed. 1990).

25.   Id.

26.   Id. SO_2 is 1300 times more soluble in water than is oxygen, therefore, SO_2 and water readily form a solution. Kotz & Purcell, supra note 16, at 736.

27.   Helme & Neme, supra note 10, at 20.

28.   Id.

29.   Id.

30.   Schwartz, supra note 22, at 365, n.22.

31.   See Garland, supra note 17, at 7 n.49.

32.   Manahan, supra note 24, at 345.

33. See Garland, supra note 17, at 8. SO_2 has been linked to inhibition of photosynthesis in some species, with deciduous trees and shrubs being more susceptible than evergreens. Westman, supra note 13, at 286–87. NO_2 has been cited as stimulating premature leaf drop. Id. at 287.

34. Garland, supra note 17, at 9.

35. Id. at 10, see also, Schwartz, supra note 22, at 366. Recent studies indicate that acidification enhances the ability of toxic metals to leach into the water supply. This has a potential impact upon the entire biological chain. For example, cadmium is released as a vapor emission during the smelting process. Cadmium contaminates surrounding soil and there is evidence to suggest that it leaches and may travel readily in the environment. Plants absorb and accumulate cadmium, which, therefore, passes through the food chain. Long-term exposure to low levels of cadmium can produce pulmonary disease and emphysema. Arsenic is also released during smelting, coal burning, and using pesticides. It bioaccumulates readily in some aquatic organisms, such as fish and crustaceans, notably crab and lobster. Arsenic's toxic effects include liver injury, vascular disease, skin cancer, and sensory impairment. *Casarett & Doull's Toxicology* 589–93 (Curtis D. Klaasen et al., eds., 3rd ed. 1986).

36. *Casarett & Doull's Toxicology*, supra note 35, at 802.

37. Id.

38. Westman, supra note 13, at 286–87.

39. Id. at 287.

40. See Lynton K. Caldwell, *International Environmental Policy: Emergence and Dimensions* 12 (1984).

41. Allen L. Springer, *The International Law of Pollution* 31 (1983).

42. Id.

43. Id. at 32.

44. Id.

45. Id.

46. Fitzhugh Green, "Public Diplomacy and Acid Rain," 17 *U. Tol. L. Rev.* 133, 133 (1985).

47. Id.

48. Id.

49. Id.

50. Id.

51. Declaration of the United Nations Conference on the Human Environment, June 16, 1972, 11 *I.L.M.* 1416, 1416 [hereinafter Stockholm Declaration].

52. Schwartz, supra note 22, at 370–71.

53. Id.

54. Barry E. Carter & Phillip R. Trimble, *International Law: Selected Documents* 709 (1991).

55. Margot B. Peters, Comment, "An International Approach to the Greenhouse Effect: The Problem of Increased Atmospheric Carbon Dioxide can be Approached by an Innovative International Agreement," 20 *Cal. W. Int'l L. J.* 67, 75–77 (1989–1990).
56. Id.
57. Id.
58. Id. at 78.
59. Id. at 78 n.82.
60. Irene H. Van Lier, *Acid Rain and Interntational Law* 94 (1980).
61. Barry E. Carter & Phillip R. Trimble, *International Law* 113 (1991). Customary international law is evidenced by a sense of legal obligation on the part of a state to adhere to or refrain from certain practices. *Opinio juris* refers to customs and habits that have gained the status of law. This occurs when states no longer feel legally free to deviate from a practice (*opinio juris sive necessitatis*). Id.
62. I. Van Lier, supra note 60, at 97.
63. Id.
64. Constance O'Keefe, "Transboundary Pollution and the Strict Liability Issue: The Work of the International Law Commission on the Topic of International Liability for Injurious Consequences Arising Out of Acts Not Prohibited by International Law," 18 *Den. J. Int'l. L. & Pol'y* 145, 162 (1990).
65. Id.
66. Id.
67. Id.
68. See Peters, supra note 55, at 78–79.
69. See id. at 78
70. See id. at 78–79.
71. Id.
72. Id.
73. O'Keefe, supra note 64, at 173.
74. David Rubin, Note, "Acid Rain in the European Community: A Hard Rain's A-Gonna Fall," 16 *Brook. J. Int'l. L.* 621, 627–30 (1990).
75. Id. at 627–28.
76. Id. at 628.
77. Id. at 627.
78. Id. at 628.
79. Springer, supra note 41, at 32.
80. Peters, supra note 55, at 79–80.
81. Id.
82. Id.
83. Id. at 79–81.
84. Id. at 79.
85. Id.

86. Id.
87. Id. at 80.
88. Id.
89. Id.
90. Id. See also "Vienna Convention for the Protection of the Ozone Layer," March 22, 1985, 26 *I.L.M.* 1516 (1987).
91. Peters, supra note 55, at 80.
92. Id. at 80–81.
93. Id.
94. Id.
95. Id.
96. Id.
97. Id. at 81. Montreal Protocol on Substances that Deplete the Ozone Layer, 26 *I.L.M.* 1541 (1987), 52 Fed. Reg. 47,489, was signed by the United States and Canada. Id. at 81 n.105.
98. Peters, supra note 55, at 81–82.
99. "Montreal Protocol on Substances that Deplete the Ozone Layer," supra note. 97, Art. 2(1) at 1552.
100. Peters, supra note 55, at 81–82.
101. Id.
102. Roberta Dohse, Comment, "Global Air Pollution and the Greenhouse Effect: Can International Legal Structures Meet the Challenge?" 13 *Hous. J. Int'l. L.* 179, 202–03 (1990).
103. Ved P. Nanda, "Trends in International Environmental Law," 20 *Cal. W. Int'l L. J.* 187, 192–94 (1989–1990).
104. Id. On May 2, 1989 eighty nations signed the Helsinki Declaration on the Protection of the Ozone Layer, 28 *I.L.M.* 1335 (1989), expressing an intent to cooperate in research, to exchange information, and to assist developing nations with costs associated with abatement procedures. Nanda, supra note 103, at 202.
105. See 1972 Great Lakes Water Quality Agreement, Apr. 15, 1972, U.S.-Can., 23 *U.S.T.* 301, and Great Lakes Water Quality Agreement of 1978, Nov. 22, 1978, U.S.-Can. 30 *U.S.T.* 1383.
106. Van Lier, supra note 60, at 172–174.
107. Id.
108. Erik K. Moller, Comment, "The United States-Canadian Acid Rain Crisis: Proposal for an International Agreement," 36 *UCLA L. Rev.* 1207, 1207 (1989).
109. Alastair R. Lucas, "Acid Rain: The Canadian Position," 32 *U. Kan. L. Rev.* 165, 172 (1983).
110. Id.
111. Moller, supra note 108, at 1213 n.40.
112. Lucas, supra note 109, at 172.
113. Id. at 173.

114. Id.
115. Id.
116. Garland, supra note 17, at 1–3.
117. Id.
118. Joel A. Gallob, "Birth of the North American Transboundary Environmental Plaintiff: Transboundary Pollution and the 1979 Draft Treaty for Equal Access and Remedy," 15 *Harv. Envtl. L. Rev.* 85, 112–16 (1991).
119. Id.
120. Id. The Boundary Waters Treaty, 36 Stat. 2448, T.S. No. 548, was signed Jan. 11, 1909 by the United Kingdom (on Canada's behalf) and the United States. Id. at 112, n.137.
121. Id. at 112–15
122. Id.
123. Id.
124. Id.
125. Id.
126. Id.
127. Id.
128. Id.
129. Id. at 116–18. For an example of the breadth of the IJC's involvement in pollution matters, see generally, David K. Wilson, Jr., "Cabin Creek and International Law—An Overview," 5 *Pub. Land L. Rev.* 110 (1984).
130. See Alfred P. Rubin, "Pollution by Analogy: The Trail Smelter Arbitration," 50 *Or. L. Rev.* 259, 259–60 (1971).
131. See id.
132. Id. at 260
133. See id.
134. Id.
135. See id.
136. See id.
137. See id.
138. Id.
139. See id.
140. Id. at 260, 262.
141. Id. at 267 (quoting Convention for Settlement of Difficulties Arising from Operation of Smelter at Trail, B.C. (U.S. v. Can.), 3 *R. Int'l Arb. Awards* 1905, 1965 (1941)).
142. Van Lier, supra note 60, at 108–109.
143. Id. at 108 (*sic utere tuo ut alienum non laedas*, loosely translates into "so, exercise your right in such a manner as not to injure others").
144. Gallob, supra note 118, at 120–21.
145. Caldwell, supra note 40, at 105.
146. Garland, supra note 17, at 4–6.
147. Id. at 4.

148. Id.   Ontario and Quebec Provinces contribute more than half the SO$_2$ produced in eastern Canada.
149. John E. Carroll, "The Acid Rain Issue in Canadian American Relations: A Commentary," in *International Environmental Diplomacy: The Management and Resolution of Transfrontier Environmental Problems* 141–46 (J. Carroll ed., 1988) [hereinafter *International Environmental Diplomacy*].
150. Id.   Geologically, Canada's foundation is primarily granitic shield bedrock which provides poor buffering protection from additional acid deposition.
151. Id. at 141–42.
152. Cecie Starr & Ralph Taggart, *Biology: The Unity and Diversity of Life* 738 (4th ed. 1987).
153. Id.
154. Carroll, supra note 149, at 142.
155. Id.
156. Id.
157. Id.
158. Id.
159. Scott A. Hajost, "Introduction: A Symposium on Acid Rain," 17 *U. Tol. L. Rev.* 107, 108 (1985).
160. Id. at 108–09.
161. Moller, supra note 108, at 1211.   See also, "1979 Joint Statement on Transboundary Air Quality Talks," reprinted in *Dep't St. Bull.*, Nov. 26, 1979, at 26.
162. Memorandum of Intent Concerning Transboundary Air Pollution, Aug. 5, 1980, U.S.-Can., 32 *U.S.T.* 2521.
163. Id. at 2521.
164. Id. at 2524.
165. Id. at 2529.
166. Id. at 2525.
167. Id. at 2524.
168. Id.
169. Hajost, supra note 159, at 108.
170. Id.
171. Marian Nash Leich, *Digest of United States Practice in International Law* 899–900 (1980).
172. Id.
173. Id.
174. Sydney G. Harris, "Canadian Positions, Proposals, and the Diplomatic Dilemma: Acid Rain and Emerging International Norms," 17 *U. Tol. L. Rev.* 121, 126 (1985).
175. Id.
176. Id.
177. Id.

178. Id. at 125–126.
179. Id.
180. Government Institutes, Inc., *Environmental Law Handbook* 259 n.1 (10th ed. 1989).
181. Id.
182. 42 U.S.C. §§ 7401–7642 (1982).
183. Moller, supra note 108, at 1215.
184. Id. at 1215 n.49.
185. See id. at 1215.
186. Id.
187. Schwartz, supra note 22, at 375 n.79.
188. Id.
189. Id.
190. Moller, supra note 108, at 1215.
191. John L. Sullivan, Note, "Beyond the Bargaining Table: Canada's Use of Section 115 of the United States Clean Air Act to Prevent Acid Rain," 16 *Cornell Int'l. L. J.* 193, 208, n.89 (1983).
192. Id.
193. Id. at 209–11.
194. Id. at 209.
195. Id. at 209–11.
196. Letter from Douglas Costle, Administrator of the E.P.A., to Edmund Muskie, Secretary of State (Jan. 13, 1981), reprinted in *New York v. Thomas*, 613 F. Supp. 1472, 1488 (D.D.C. 1985), rev'd, 802 F.2d 1443 (D.C. Cir. 1986).
197. Id. at 1476.
198. Id.
199. Id. at 1479–81.
200. Id. at 1481–82.

(a) Whenever the Administrator, upon receipt of reports, surveys or studies from any duly constituted international agency has reason to believe that any pollutant or pollutants emitted in the United States cause or contribute to air pollution which may reasonably be anticipated to endanger public health or welfare in a foreign country or whenever the Secretary of State requests him to do so with respect to such pollution which the Secretary of State alleges is of such a nature, the Administrator shall give formal notification thereof to the Governor of the State in which such emissions originate.

(b) The notice of the Administrator shall be deemed to be a finding under section 7401(a)(2)(H)(ii) of this title which requires a plan revision with respect to so much of the applicable implementation plan as is inadequate to prevent or eliminate the endangerment referred to in subsection (a) of this section. Any foreign country so affected by such emission of pollutant or pollutants shall be invited to appear at any public hearing associated with any revision of the appropriate portion of the applicable implementation plan.

(c) This section shall apply only to a foreign country which the Administrator determines has given the United States essentially the same rights with respect to the prevention or control of air pollution occurring in that country as is given that country by this section. 42 U.S.C. § 7415(a)-(c)(1982).

201. Id. at 1482.

202. *New York v. Thomas*, 613 F. Supp. at 1482–83.

203. See id. at 1483.

204. Id.

205. Id.

206. See id.

207. Id. at 1483–84.

208. Id. at 1484.

209. Id.

210. Id. at 1486.

211. *Thomas v. New York*, 802 F.2d 1443, 1448 (D.C. Cir., 1986).

212. Id. at 1446.

213. Id. at 1446–48.

214. Id. at 1448.

215. See generally, Sanford E. Gaines, "International Principles for Transnational Environmental Liability: Can Developments in Municipal Law Help Break the Impasse?," 30 *Harv. Int'l L. J.* 311 (1989) (suggesting that general liability principles of municipal law, when applied to issues involving transboundary pollution, will encourage reduction in environmental damage and facilitate development of theoretical environmental liability and compensation limits); cf. Garland, supra note 17, at 36–37 (proposing that state and provincial legislation be used to bridge the gap created by the decision in *Thomas v. New York*).

216. See David R. Wooley, "Acid Rain: Canadian Litigation Options in U.S. Court and Agency Proceedings," 17 *U. Tol. L. Rev.* 139 (1985). David R. Wooley was Assistant-Attorney General for the State of New York and represented the States of New York, Maine, Connecticut, Vermont, New Hampshire, and Rhode Island, the National Audubon Society, National Wildlife Federation, Sierra Club, Natural Resources Defense Council, three U.S. citizens owning land in Canada's Muskoka Lakes area, and then New York Congressman Richard Ottinger in their suit against the EPA. Id. at 139. n.1.

217. See generally, United States Foreign Sovereign Immunities Act of 1976, 28 U.S.C. § 1607(b)(1988); First Nat'l City Bank v. Banco Nacional de Cuba, 406 U.S. 759, 768 (act of state doctrine should not be applied by court when Executive Branch expressly indicates that such application would not advance American foreign policy interests) (1972).

218. See, Foreign Sovereign Immunities Act of 1976, 28 U.S.C. § 1607(b), reprinted in Carter & Trimble, International Law: Selected Documents 579, supra note 54, at 579.
219. Wooley, supra note 216, at 140, n.2.
220. Id.
221. Anthony Scott, "The Canadian-American Problem of Acid Rain," 26 *Nat. Resources J.* 337, 337 (1986).
222. Id. at 337–38.
223. Id. at 338.
224. Id. at 337–38.
225. Hajost, supra note 159, at 108.
226. Id. at 108–09.
227. Sullivan, supra note 191, at 202–03.
228. Id. at 203.
229. Id. at 202–03.
230. Id.
231. Harris, supra note 174, at 126–27.
232. Id. The devices capture SO_2 before the chemical enters the air and manufactures sulfuric acid. Kotz & Purcell, supra note 16, at 846–47. Approximately 40 million tons of sulfuric acid are produced annually in the United States for use in manufacturing fertilizer, treating industrial waste, and creating white pigment for use in paper, plastics, and paint.
233. Harris, supra note 174, at 128.
234. Id. at 128.
235. Id. at 129.
236. Id.
237. Id.
238. Id.
239. Lucas, supra note 109, at 168–170.
240. Id. at 178.
241. Id. at 169–170.
242. Sullivan, supra note 191, at 215–17. For example, Ontario imposed emission restrictions on International Nickel Company, a smelting complex, requiring a reduction from 5100 tons of sulfur dioxide per day to 700 tons. Later, the Ontario government ultimately revised the limit upward to 1950 tons per day. Id. at 215–16.
243. Commons Debates (Dec. 16, 1960) reprinted in 20 I.L.M. 762 (1981).
244. Carroll, supra note 149, at 144.
245. Id.
246. Id.
247. See id.
248. Id.
249. Id.

250. Lucas, supra note 109, at 167 (citing Impact Assessment Work Group I, United States Canada Memorandum of intent on Transboundary Air Pollution Final Report 21 (Jan. 1983)).

251. Id. at 167–68. Canadian scientists determined that the environment could tolerate a maximum annual sulfate level of eighteen pounds per acre before damage would occur. Id. at 167.

252. Id. at 168. Indicative of the level of trust with respect to the motives on either side, a 1984 publication suggested that the Canadians were secretly seeking to destroy the coal industry in the midwestern United States in order to open a wider market for the export of Canadian nuclear and hydro generated electricity. See James M. Friedman & Michael S. McMahon, *The Silent Alliance*, noted in Harris, supra note 174, at 130–31.

253. Green, supra note 46, at 136–37.

254. Id.

255. Michael S. McMahon, "Balancing the Interests: An Essay on the Canadian-American Acid Rain Debate," in *International Environmental Diplomacy*, supra note 149, at 147, 159–60.

256. Id.

257. Id.

258. Id.

259. Id.

260. Carter & Trimble, supra note 61, at 150.

261. See McMahon, supra note 255, at 156. The United States sought status as a "precursor" member of the "30% Club" in recognition of its efforts during the prior year. Id. Several signatories to the Geneva Convention on Long-Range Transboundary Air Pollution, including Canada, formed a "30% Club," by signing a protocol and pledging to reduce SO_2 emissions by thirty per cent from their 1980 levels. Armin Rosencranz, "The Acid Rain Controversy in Europe and North America: A Political Analysis," in International Environmental Diplomacy, supra note 149, at 173, 163–74.

262. See McMahon, supra note 255, at 156.

263. Id.

264. See id. at 157–58.

265. Gallob, supra note 118, at 134.

266. Id.

267. William K. Reilly, "The New Clean Air Act: An Environmental Mile-stone," 17 *E.P.A. J.*, Jan.-Feb. 1991, at 2, 3.

268. See id.

269. See id. at 4.

270. Eileen Claussen, "Acid Rain: The Strategy," 17 *E.P.A. J.*, Jan-Feb. 1991, at 21, 21.

271. Id.

272. Id.
273. See Elizabeth Corcoran, "Cleaning Up Coal," *Sci. Am.*, May 1991, at 106, 112.
274. Id.
275. Id.
276. Id.
277. Id.
278. See Gallob, supra note 118, at 135.
279. Id. at 135 (quoting Weisskopf, "Clean Air Measure Wins Hill Clearance," *Wash. Post*, Oct 28, 1990, at A16).
280. Brian Mulroney and George Bush, Remarks by the President and Prime Minister Brian Mulroney of Canada at the Air Quality Agreement Signing Ceremony in Ottawa (Mar. 13, 1991), in 27 *Wkly Compilation Pres. Doc.* 298, 298.
281. Id. at 299.
282. Id.
283. See id. at 299.
284. Id. at 300–01.
285. Agreement Between the Government of the United States of America and the Government of Canada On Air Quality, Mar. 13, 1991, art. III, 2(c), Mar. 13, 1991, 30 I.L.M. 676, 679. [hereinafter Air Quality Agreement]
286. Id.
287. Id., art. IV, at 680.
288. Id., Annex 1, at 685.
289. Id., art. V, at 680.
290. Id., art, VI (2), at 681.
291. Id., art. VII.
292. Id., art. IX, at 682.
293. Id., art. XIII, at 684.
294. Id., art. X, at 683.
295. See Allen L. Springer, "U.S. Environmental Policy and International Law," in *International Environmental Diplomacy*, supra note 149, at 44, 60.
296. Id.
297. Nanda, supra note 103, at 198–99 (referencing Principle 21 of Stockholm Convention).
298. Air Quality Agreement, supra note 285, at 677.
299. Patricia Birnie, "The Role of International Law in Solving Certain Environmental Conflicts," in *International Environmental Diplomacy*, supra note 149, at 101.
300. Air Quality Agreement, supra note 285, at 677.
301. Amy A. Fraenkel, "The Convention on Long-Range Transboundary Air Pollution: Meeting the Challenge of International Cooperation," 30 *Harv. Int'l. L. J.* 447, 459 (1989).

302. Sullivan, supra note 191, at 200–01. The 1978 Great Lakes Water Quality Agreement was the first bilateral agreement between the two parties to address transboundary air pollution. It specified that the parties would seek to develop a program to prevent air pollution from harming the Great Lakes. Id.

303. Compare Federal Water Pollution Control Act of 1972, Pub. L. No. 92–500, 86 Stat. 816 (1972); Marine Protection, Research and Sanctuaries Act, Pub. L. No. 92–532, 86 Stat. 1052 (1972); and 1977 Clean Water Act, Pub. L. No. 95–217, 91 Stat. 1566 (1977).

304. Gallob, supra note 118, at 114–15.

305. Van Lier, supra note 60, at 181–83.

306. Id.

307. Id.

308. See Mulroney & Bush, supra note 280, at 298.

309. Carter & Trimble, supra note 61, at 150.

310. Id.

311. Air Quality Agreement, supra note 285, at 677.

312. Birnie, supra note 299, at 100–106.

313. Id.

314. Id.

Land Degradation

The Earth's soils are threatened as increased demands placed upon them are causing their overuse and abuse. Overcropping, overgrazing, population growth, deforestation, and climate change are all contributing to a worsening land degradation problem.

As the population continues to increase, farmers must produce a greater amount of food. There is a demand for more intensive farming and grazing practices to meet the needs of the people. To meet the demands, farmers ignore the long-term effects of overfarming and over-grazing, excessive use of pesticides and fertilizers, and long-term exploitation of land without allowing for recovery of lost nutrients. Instead they engage in intensive farming that eventually destroys the soil.

Not only are demands placed on current agricultural land, but also on the world's forest land. People are seeking agricultural land through deforestation. Once forest land is cleared, much of the soil is eroded by rainfall and wind. The land becomes unsuitable for agricultural production, but the damage and loss of forest land cannot be easily erased.

In many of the drier areas of the world, degraded land becomes desert. Desertification effects six million hectares of productive agricultural land every year. As the amount of desertified land increases, the ability to produce food for the growing population decreases, threatening the sustainability of the human race. The problem does not disappear since as arable land is lost, greater demands are placed on remaining agricultural land, quickening the pace of its degradation.

One-quarter of the world's soil has fallen victim to serious land degradation. The cost of revival of this land is tremendous and will take an effort that, thus far, the world community has been unwilling to make. This is not a problem that can be ignored. Five hundred and fifty million people went hungry in 1990. As the population increases and the amount of cultivatable land decreases, the situation will only worsen. The international community must develop strong regulations to control the loss of productive soil. Countries must recognize the global nature of this problem and prepare to sacrifice a degree of sovereignty in exchange for the long-term survival of the environment and its inhabitants.

—RNW

17

Land's End

Sandra Postel

Each year desertification renders an area of land the size of West Virginia unusable for any purpose. Small-scale successes at keeping land alive show promise for a needed international rescue effort.

Farmers in the north African country of Niger know firsthand that the land they have farmed for decades is worn out. *Kasar mu, ta gaji,* they lament in their native Hausa. "The land is tired." Peasants in western parts of the country strike a more ominous chord in Zarma with *Laabu, y bu,* "The land is dead."

The phrases aptly depict land suffering from what scientists call desertification. While the term conjures up images of Saharan sand dunes engulfing new territories, its most worrisome aspects are less dramatic. Desertification refers broadly to the impoverishment of the land through overgrazing, overcultivation, deforestation, and poor irrigation practices. Under these pressures, land degrades gradually and insidiously toward a desert-like state.

Each year, desertification claims an estimated 15 million acres worldwide—an area the size of West Virginia lost beyond practical hope of reclamation. An additional 50 million acres annually become too debilitated to support profitable farming or grazing. Hundreds of millions of acres lie somewhere on the degradation continuum, between fully productive and hopelessly desertified. Unfortunately, much of this land is sliding down the diminishing productivity side of the scale.

Techniques to restore resilience and productivity to stressed lands exist, but so far the international commitment does not. The majority of

270

people affected are poor, disenfranchised farmers and pastoralists living at society's margins. A lasting victory over land degradation will remain a distant dream if there are not social and economic reforms that give rural people the security of tenure and access to resources they need to improve and protect the land. And, with degradation rooted in excessive human pressures, slowing population growth lies at the heart of an effective global strategy.

Unlike acid rain, toxic contamination or the nuclear weapons threat, desertification is difficult to rally around and adopt as a cause. Yet its consequences—intensified droughts and floods, famine, declining living standards, and swelling numbers of environmental refugees—could not be more real or packed with emotion.

A world of 5.1 billion people growing by nearly 90 million each year cannot afford to squander its food base. Without good land, humanity quite literally has nothing on which to grow.

How to Make a Desert

Spurred by the devastating drought that struck much of western and north-central Africa from 1968 through 1973, government representatives from around the world gathered in Nairobi, Kenya, during the summer of 1977 for a United Nations conference on desertification. It was the first time the world's attention was focused on the problems and prospects of fragile lands. Out of Nairobi came the plan of Action to Combat Desertification, which recommended 28 measures that national, regional, and international institutions could take to halt land deterioration.

Sadly, the action plan fell victim to inadequate funding and a lack of sustained commitment by governments. In 1984, when the United Nations Environment Program (UNEP) assessed progress in implementing the plan, it found not only that little had been accomplished during the past seven years, but that an already daunting problem was worsening rapidly.

According to UNEP, 11 billion acres—35 percent of the earth's land surface—are threatened by desertification and, with them, fully one-fifth of humanity. Three-quarters of this area has already been at least moderately degraded and an astonishing one-third has lost more than 25 percent of its productive potential.

These numbers point toward an unbalanced relationship between people and the land, a predicament all the more tragic because people are both degradation's victims and its unwitting agents. The four principal causes of land degradation—overgrazing on rangelands, overcultivation of croplands, waterlogging and salting of irrigated lands, and deforestation—all stem from human pressures or poor management of the land (see table 1).

Degradation of rangelands results from excessive grazing by the three billion cattle, sheep, goats, and camels that roam the world's pastures. As the size of livestock herds surpasses the carrying capacity of perennial grasses on the range, less palatable annual grasses and shrubs move in. Eventually, plant cover of all types begins to diminish, leaving the land exposed to the ravages of wind and water.

In the most severe stages, animal hooves trample nearly bare ground into a crusty layer no roots can penetrate and erosion accelerates. The appearance of large gullies or sand dunes signals that desertification can claim another victory. This process is most pervasive and visible in Africa, home to more than half of the world's pastoralists.

Similarly, cropland left without protective vegetative cover or situated on steeply sloping hillsides is subject to the erosive power of wind and rain. An inch of topsoil takes anywhere from 200 to 1,000 years to form; under the most erosive conditions, that same soil can be swept off the land in just a few seasons. Crop production suffers over the long-term, because those upper layers of soil contain most of the organic matter and nutrients that plants need to grow. Erosion also breaks down the soil's structure and diminishes its water-holding capacity, which is often erosion's most damaging effect, especially in drought-prone regions.

At least 825 million acres of rain-fed cropland—more than a third of the global total—are losing their productive potential in this way. If fertilizers cannot make up the loss, as is often the case among poor subsistence farmers, crop yields decline.

Ultimately, when pastoralists or subsistence farmers can no longer eke out an existence, they leave their homelands in search of more fertile fields or a better life in the already swelling slums and shantytowns of major cities. Nouakchott, the capital of Mauritania— among the countries most severely stricken by desertification—has grown from a population of 20,000 in 1960 to about 350,000 today. More than half these people migrated from the deteriorating countryside, leading some to call that city the largest refugee camp in the world.

Although irrigated lands are well-watered and protected from the ravages of drought, they, too, suffer from a special type of desertification. Over time, seepage from irrigation canals and overwatering of fields will cause the underlying water table to rise. If drainage is inadequate, the root zone eventually becomes waterlogged and inhospitable to plants. Farmers belonging to a large irrigation project in the Indian state of Madhya Pradesh have referred to their once-fertile fields as "wet deserts."

Table 1	Observations of Land Degradation in Selected Countries and Regions
Country/Source	**Observation**
Mali Patricia A. Jacobberger, geologist, Smithsonian Institution, 1986	"On the landsat maps, there is now—and there wasn't in 1976—a bright ring of soil around villages. Those areas are now 90 percent devoid of vegetation, the topsoil is gone, and the surface is disrupted and cracked."
Mauritania Sidy Gaye, *Ambio*, 1987	"There were only 43 sandstorms in the whole country between 1960 and 1970. The number increased tenfold in the following decade, and in . . . 1983 alone a record 240 sandstorms darkened the nation's skies."
China *Beijing Review*, interview with Zhu Zhenda, Chinese Acaemy of Sciences, 1988	"Unless urgent measures are taken, desertification will erode an additional 29,000 square miles . . . by the year 2000, more than twice the area of Taiwan."
Indonesia Ronald Greenberg and M.L. Higgins, USAID Jakarta, 1987	"Thirty-six watersheds . . . have critical erosion problems. . . . In Kalimantan, the silt load in streams has increased 33-fold in some logging areas."
Thailand D. Phantumvanit and K.S. Sathirathai, Thailand Development Research Board, 1988	"The pace of deforestation has been accelerating since the early 1900s, but it has moved into a higher gear since the 1960s. . . [Between 1961 and 1986.] Thailand lost about 45 percent of its forests."

In dry regions, the evaporation of water near the soil surface leaves behind a damaging residue of salt, a process called salinization. UNEP's assessment placed the irrigated area suffering from salinization at 100 million acres. About half of this area is in India and Pakistan, but the problem also pervades the Tigris and Euphrates river basins of Syria and Iraq, California's San Joaquin Valley, the Colorado River basin, China's North Plain, and Soviet Central Asia.

The consequences of desertification on irrigated lands are disproportionately costly. Irrigation represents a hefty investment that typically pays off because it boosts yields by two to three times over those of rain-fed cropland. Roughly a third of the world's food is grown on the 18 percent of cropland that is irrigated. So the destruction—and sometimes abandonment—of this land represents a heavy loss of investment, diminished food security, and further shrinkage of the planet's agricultural resource base.

The Roads to Ruin

While it is easy to ascertain desertification's direct causes, the conditions leading to these pressures are more varied and complex. Generally, they stem from population densities greater than what the land can sustain and, more fundamentally, from social and economic inequities that push people into marginal environments and unstable livelihoods.

In response to mounting concern about environmental deterioration in West Africa, the World Bank set up a special working group led by French agronomist Jean Gorse to study this troubled region in greater depth. Gorse's group focused on a band of seven countries in what are known as the Sahelian and Sudanian zones: Burkina Faso, Chad, The Gambia, Mali, Mauritania, Niger, and Senegal. In these countries, annual rainfall increases from north to south—from less than 8 inches in the northernmost zone to more than 30 inches in the southernmost— and so, consequently, does the number of people that can be supported by traditional farming and livestock practices.

Gorse's study found that in parts of the region the rural population in 1980 had already exceeded the number for which the land could sustainably provide sufficient food. Even more important, fuelwood emerged as the limiting factor in the carrying capacity of every zone in the region. Indeed, the 1980 population of the seven countries collectively exceeded the number of people the region's wood resources could support by 10.1 million.

Not surprisingly, this imbalance between what the land can yield and the number of people living on it has led to pervasive desertification. Virtually all the rangeland and an estimated 82 percent of the rain-fed cropland in those same seven countries is already at least moderately degraded. With a projected population in the year 2000 of 55 million—a 77–percent increase over the 1980 total—pressures on the land will increase markedly and land productivity is bound to fall even further.

Similarly, in India, where both the human and animal populations have doubled since 1950, the demand for fuelwood and fodder in the early eighties had exceeded supplies by 70 and 23 percent, respectively. The resulting overgrazing and deforestation have caused extensive degradation. Out of 657 million acres of potentially productive land, 232 million suffer varying degrees of assault from water erosion, wind erosion or salinization. More than 70 million of the nation's 185 million acres of "forestland" lack tree cover and an additional 25 million support only shrubs.

Next to population pressures, perhaps no other factors foster more degradation than the inequitable distribution of land and the absence of secure land tenure. In an agrarian society, the holding of a disproportionate share of land in the hands of a few forces the poorer majority to compete for the limited area left, severely compromising their ability to manage what land they do have sustainably. Since land is often needed as collateral, farmers without land titles have difficulty getting the loans they need to purchase seeds, fertilizer, equipment, and other items that can boost their land's productivity. As a result, many resort to abandoning worn-out fields for new land—and desertification spreads.

In many areas, these problems are aggravated by the denial of social and economic rights to women. For example, African women grow 80 percent of the food their families eat and, with their children's help, collect the water and wood needed for cooking and heating, yet rarely do they have property rights or even access to their husbands' incomes. Agricultural extension services and training programs are usually designed by and directed toward men, even though it is the women who till the fields. Because women lack the resources needed to improve their farms' productivity, the land—and the families living on it—suffers.

Unless the existing pattern of land distribution and land rights changes, the number of small landholders and landless families in the Third World will grow by nearly 30 percent by the year 2000—to a total of 220 million households. Without access to secure property rights, extension services and credit, these rural people will have no choice but to overuse the land and to farm areas that should not be cultivated.

Desertification Begets Drought?

The African Sahel had just gone through six dry years when, in 1975, Massachusetts Institute of Technology meteorologist Jule G. Charney put forth a disturbing idea. In dry regions, he posited, a reduction in vegetative cover might cause rainfall to diminish because of an increase in the albedo, the share of sunlight reflected back from the earth. Desert sands and bare rock, for example, have higher albedos than grassland, which in turn reflects more sunlight than does a dense forest.

According to Charney's hypothesis, less of the sun's radiation is absorbed at the earth's surface as albedo increases, so surface temperatures drop. This in turn fosters greater subsidence, or sinking motion, in the atmosphere. Since subsiding air is dry, rainfall declines. A degraded, higher-albedo area would therefore feed on itself, becoming more desert-like.

Tests of Charney's hypothesis using climate models generally confirmed its validity: large increases in albedo did indeed reduce rainfall. Less clear, however, was how smaller changes in reflectivity would affect rainfall and whether the patchy pattern of desertification could produce albedo changes sufficient to affect rainfall levels. Unfortunately, the global circulation models used in climate studies are not sufficiently fine-tuned to predict changes for specific locations.

Another worrisome link surfaced from the modeling studies Jagadish Shukla and Yale Mintz conducted at the University of Maryland. They examined the effects of changes in evapotranspiration on rainfall, which is the transfer of water vapor from the land to the atmosphere through evaporation or transpiration by plants. For this process to occur, the soil must be sufficiently moist and vegetation must be present to bring that moisture into contact with the air. Presumably, if evapotranspiration is an important source of atmospheric water vapor in a given locale, then rainfall levels would decline as it diminishes. Shukla and Mintz found just that, although, as with Charney's study, their conclusions pertained to changes on a large scale.

Meanwhile, Sharon Nicholson, a meteorologist at Florida State University at Tallahassee, was analyzing rainfall data from roughly 300 sites in some 20 African countries. She established a long-term average from data covering the years 1901 to 1974, and then calculated the annual percentage departures from that long-term average for the years 1901–84.

Between 1976 and 1984, these countries experienced 17 consecutive years of below-normal rainfall, by far the longest series of sub-par rains in the 84–year record. Annual rainfall in 1983 and 1984 fell more than 40 percent short of the long-term average. Interestingly, Nicholson also analyzed northern sub-Saharan rainfall levels according to three bands, each running east-west, and found that drought was most persistent in the northernmost, most arid band, where theoretically the albedo and low evapotranspiration feedbacks would be greatest.

The Well Gone Dry

Regardless of whether desertification can actually diminish rainfall, there is little doubt that the water cycle is greatly influenced by the land and its vegetative cover. When rainwater hits the surface, it either immediately runs off into rivers and streams to begin its journey back to the sea, soaks into the subsurface to replenish groundwater supplies, or returns to the atmosphere through evaporation or transpiration.

Land degradation shifts the proportion of rainfall following these pathways. Due to less vegetative cover and hard-packed soils, degraded land suffers from increased runoff and decreased infiltration into the subsurface. The resulting reduction in soil moisture and groundwater supplies worsens the effects of drought, while the increase in rapid runoff exacerbates flooding.

What appear, then, to be consequences and signs of meteorological drought—withered crops, falling groundwater levels, and dry stream beds—can actually be caused in large part by land degradation. Perhaps nowhere has this case been made more convincingly than in India, where a growing number of scientists now blame deforestation and desertification for the worsening of droughts and floods. Jayanta Bandyopadhyay of the Research Foundation for Science, Technology and Natural Resource Policy in Dehra Dun writes: "With an amazing rapidity, acute scarcity of water has grabbed the center stage of India's national life. . . . State after state is trapped into an irreversible and worsening crisis of drought, desertification and consequent water scarcity, threatening plant, animal and human life."

Water shortages plagued some 17,000 villages in the northern state of Uttar Pradesh in the sixties; by 1985, that figure had risen to 70,000. Similarly, in Madya Pradesh, more than 36,400 villages lacked sufficient water in 1980; in 1985 the number totaled more than 64,500.

And in the western state of Gujarat, the number of villages short of water tripled between 1979 and 1986, from some 3,840 to 12,250.

Ultimately, drought and desertification reinforce each other by preventing land from recovering from stress. Whereas healthy land will bounce back to its former productivity after a drought, degraded and abused land frequently will not. Areas plagued both by drought and degradation—including much of Africa and India—thus face the prospect of a downward spiral of land productivity, bringing even greater hunger and human suffering than these regions witnessed during the eighties.

Restoring Life to the Land

Halting the spread of desertification is no easy task. Populations are growing fastest in some of the regions most threatened by desertification. The challenge is to restore and protect the land while at the same time meeting the basic needs of growing numbers of people. Here and there—in villages, grass-roots organizations, research institutes, experiment stations, and development agencies—strategies are being devised, tried, and shown to have potential.

The most promising efforts center around measures that concentrate production on the most fertile, least erodible land; stabilize soils on sloping and other marginal land; and reduce rural people's vulnerability to crop failure by diversifying income-generating options at the village level.

One such effort is under way in China's Loess Plateau, a highly eroded area spanning some 150 million acres around the middle reaches of the Yellow River watershed (see "China Revives Lost Land," March/April, page 7). There, a partnership of scientists, villagers, political leaders, and international development agencies has dramatically altered the use of the land in selected villages, bringing soil erosion under control while at the same time raising living standards.

In the village of Quanjiagou, flat, fertile farmland created with soil-trapping dams and extensive terraces allowed crop production to increase 17 percent between 1979 and 1986, even though the area planted in crops was reduced by half. With the added value from cash-crop tree products and animal husbandry, the village's per-capita income more than doubled (see table 2).

Similar strategies are being tried in the drought-plagued, degraded highlands of Ethiopia. Simple structures called bunds, really just walls of rock or earth constructed across hillsides, catch soil washing down the slopes. As soil builds up behind the bund, a natural terrace forms that both diminishes erosion and enhances water infiltration, which has led to higher crop yields.

Table 2	Effects of Land Rehabilitation Strategy in Quanjiagou, Mlarhi County, 1979–86		
Effects	1979	1986	Change
Land Use	(acres)		(percent)
Cropland	578	289	- 50
Trees	149	274	+ 85
Pasture	40	205	+413
Crop Production	(tons)		(percent)
	250	293	+ 17
Per-capita Income	(yuan[1])		(percent)
	127	313	+146

[1]As of April, one yuan exchanged for U.S. $0.15.
Source: Shaanxi Control Institute of the Loess Plateau.

Between 1976 and 1985, through projects sponsored by the United Nations and various foreign aid agencies, Ethiopian farmers built nearly 373,000 miles of bunds and 292,000 miles of terraces to stabilize steep slopes. Although impressive, these efforts are but a start: just 6 percent of the threatened highlands are now protected.

Some Simple Solutions

Whatever strategy is devised, successful land reclamation hinges on simple techniques that add nutrients and moisture to the land while holding the soil in place. Work at the International Institute of Tropical Agriculture in Ibadan, Nigeria, has shown, for example, that applying a mulch of crop residues in amounts of 2.4 tons per acre (a very thin layer) can control erosion nearly completely on slopes of up to 15 degrees, making sustainable cropping possible. In field trials, yields increased over non-mulched plots by 83 percent for cowpeas, 73 percent for casava, and 23 percent for maize.

Alley cropping, in which food crops are planted between hedgerows of trees, holds promise for tropical regions. Hedgerow trimmings provide a good mulch for the crop and offer fodder for animals and fuelwood for cooking. Leguminous trees that fix nitrogen are especially useful since they improve and maintain soil fertility. Sudanese farmers who leave native *Acacia senegal* trees on their cropland have learned this over time and find they can grow millet continuously for 15 to 20 years, compared with three to five years if the trees are removed.

Another promising approach for fighting land degradation is planting a densely tufted, deep-rooted plant called vetiver grass. Native to India and known there as *khus*, vetiver grass can be put to work on erosive land for between 1 and 10 percent of the cost of bunds and earthen walls, and it requires no maintenance. When closely spaced along the contours of a hillside, vetiver grass forms a vegetative barrier that slows runoff, giving rainfall a chance to spread out and seep into a field. It also traps sediment behind it, gradually forming a natural terrace. Farmers only need to give up a 20–inch strip of cropland for each contour hedge of vetiver and, since yields typically increase by 50 percent, the conservation gains far outweigh the loss from the small amount of land taken out of production.

Unfortunately, successes in rehabilitating degraded rangelands and salinized irrigated lands make for a rather short list. Perhaps the clearest advance in rangeland restoration comes from the revival of the ancient "Hema" system of management in Syria. There, cooperatives are established that have sole right to graze demarcated sets of range. Families in a cooperative are then granted a license to graze only a certain number of sheep. By reducing overgrazing, the system has enabled the revegetation of 17 million acres of rangeland.

Among the countries most affected by salinization, Pakistan has perhaps tried hardest to tackle it, but has achieved only mixed results. In 1960, the government committed itself to draining salt-affected lands by installing vertical tube wells. Two decades and over 12,000 tube wells later, the area reclaimed still falls far short of the target. The Five Year Plan for 1983 to 1988 allocated an astonishing 43 percent of the total water budget to drainage activities and provided for credits and subsidies to foster more private development of tube wells.

In Egypt, a proposed drainage system covering only a small portion of the Nile Delta has been priced at $1 billion. Such high sums partly explain why governments tend to ignore the problem and why preventing salinization through careful water management is so crucial.

Sizing up the Opponent

Why, more than a decade after a global goal was set to stop desertification by the year 2000, are we losing more trees, more topsoil, and more grazing land than ever before? The easy answers are that governments fail to grasp the severity of the threat, lack the political will to give it priority, and underfund efforts to combat it.

But a more fundamental reason may lie in the very nature of "desertification control" itself. It crosses all traditional disciplinary and bureaucratic boundaries to tie in agriculture, forestry, water management, and pastoralism. Lasting solutions will be rooted as much in social and economic reforms as in effective technologies.

All the elements needed to halt land degradation exist, but they have not been joined effectively in the battle or given the resources needed to mount an adequate fight. In the United Nations Environment Program and its executive director, Mostafa Tolba, desertification control has a strategic headquarters and a strong, committed leader. But the amount of funding mobilized over the last decade has fallen far short of UNEP's estimated investment needs of $4.5 billion per year to bring desertification under control within 20 years. Several countries have developed the national plans of action called for by the 1977 Nairobi conference, but only three—Burkina Faso, Mali, and Tunisia— have drummed up sufficient support to begin implementing them.

While this top-down approach proceeds at a snail's pace, efforts starting at the village level have produced numerous, albeit small, successes. In western Kenya, 540 local organizations—mostly women's groups and primary schools—are working with the U.S.-based organization CARE to promote reforestation. CARE provides the materials needed to establish nurseries, as well as training and extension services, but local people do the planting. Each group plants between 5,000 and 10,000 seedlings a year, collectively amounting to nearly a third of the plantings the government estimates are needed.

Projects such as this demonstrate that the greatest hope for reversing land degradation lies in marrying the commitment and experience of organizations operating at the local level with stepped-up international support and technical guidance through United Nations agencies, bilateral and multilateral donors, and national governments.

UNEP has begun to recognize that community-based initiatives have higher success rates and more lasting impacts than top-down projects and is now strengthening its cooperation with nongovernmental organizations (NGOs). The agency currently supports several grassroots projects through the Nairobi-based African NGO Environmental Network and also has helped launch the Deforestation and Desertification Control NGO Network in the Asia-Pacific region. Among the groups that have benefited from UNEP's new approach is the "Millions of Trees Club," which has set up "people's nurseries" and training centers for reforestation in southern India. UNEP's infusion of $35,000 over two years helped local people plant more than two million trees and shrubs.

Credit Where It is Due

Until governments and donor agencies begin giving farmers the incentives they need to invest in land productivity, there is little hope of making more than a dent in desertification. As noted earlier, reforming land ownership and tenure policies and providing access to credit for small landholders is crucial to the reversal of land degradation. Special emphasis needs to be placed on the status of women—especially in Africa, where the disparity between the work women do and the rights they have is greatest.

Of the multilateral development organizations, the International Fund for Agricultural Development (IFAD) is heads above the others in more thoroughly incorporating these needs into its projects. This decade-old U.N. agency has now carried out some 190 projects and, in the words of IFAD president Idriss Jazairy, they are "people-oriented" and built upon the philosophy that development involves the "liberation of [people's] creative potential."

An IFAD project in Kenya, for example, operates through women's savings clubs and other community groups to enhance access to credit, farm supplies, and extension services. Another project in The Gambia works to uphold traditional female cultivation rights under a new land-distribution scheme and establishes day-care centers for children of women whose work loads have increased with the introduction of double-cropping. While the provision of child-care services may seem far removed from desertification control, freeing women to do the work of boosting land productivity could, in fact, be an essential first step.

More research into crop varieties and production systems appropriate for the lands and people at risk is also needed. With the high-yielding, "green revolution" package of technologies commanding the research limelight over the last several decades, efforts to improve the productivity of subsistence farming are just beginning to get the attention they deserve. Research on cowpeas, for example, an important legume grown in Africa, has led to varieties harvestable in 50 to 60 days instead of 90 to 100. That paves the way for double- or even triple-cropping in some regions, which would reduce pressures to extend cultivation to marginal lands.

Finally, with much of degradation stemming from excessive human pressures, reversing it will require a dramatic slowing of population growth. If current growth rates persist, Africa's worn-out lands will need to support an additional 263 million people by the year 2000— more people than currently live in the United States. India will grow by nearly 200 million people, or 24 percent, and the Philippines, with the fastest growth rate in Southeast Asia, by more than a third. No matter how much funding comes forth, how fast effective technologies spread, or how diligently governments implement land reforms, a lasting victory over land degradation will remain out of reach until population pressures ease.

International Toxic Waste Management

Disposal of wastes, both human and industrial, is an increasingly critical problem. As the world population increases and nations strive to develop, often leading to urbanization, waste production increases as well. Although the entire waste question is important, the disposal of hazardous and toxic wastes is most urgent due to the health and safety issues surrounding them.

The question of what to do with toxic and hazardous wastes has been controversial. Ideally, halting production of such wastes would eliminate the debate over their disposal and would be the most effective means of ridding ourselves of the problem. Other than this ideal scenario, there are several options. First recycling these toxic wastes back into the production process would keep the toxic materials out of the waste stream. Another option would be to recover some of the ingredients from the waste product to be reused and other ingredients to be treated to reduce the level of toxicity of the waste to be disposed. Finally, the current preferred option for waste disposal, the dispersal, dumping, or storing of toxic or hazardous wastes. This is the most ineffective and dangerous solution to the hazardous waste problem.

In order to control the damaging effects that toxic and hazardous substances have on both humans and the environment, the world community has taken steps to regulate, monitor, and control the transport and disposal of hazardous wastes.

In 1976, the UNEP established the International Register of Potentially Toxic Chemicals. The register collects information on over 800 hazardous chemicals, which it disseminates to raise awareness of national laws and regulations of their use. To further raise awareness, the WHO, UNEP, and ILO created the International Programme on Chemical Safety in 1980. The program assesses the risks that these chemicals pose to human and environmental health.

The international community has responded to the needs for management of toxic and hazardous wastes. The Basel Convention of 1989 controls the exportation of these wastes. Signatory nations must follow the "informed consent" principle, under which the exporting country must have permission from the importing nation before hazardous wastes can be transported.

In March of 1990, the European Community agreed to stop exportation of hazardous wastes to former colonies of E.C. members. The Organization of African Unity responded the following year by creating the African Convention on the Ban of Imports of All Forms of

Hazardous Wastes into Africa and the Control of Transboundary Movements of Such Wastes Generated in Africa.

There has been significant international action to control the transport of toxic and hazardous wastes. However, much work still needs to be done, both in this area and in the area of reduction of the creation of toxic and hazardous wastes.

—RNW

18

Hazardous Waste Management: An International Perspective: Summary Report

R. Whittle, B. Jessiman, and R. Raphael

Abstract

This presentation examines international hazardous waste legislation and waste management practices with the express purpose of providing additional and useful information for health and environmental agencies in Canada. Legislation and regulations drawn from a number of other countries and organizations are examined in relation to the restriction and/or promotion of various types of hazardous waste disposal (excluding reduction, reuse, and recycle) techniques. The role of the generator, transporter, and waste disposer ("cradle-to-grave") will be presented in order to critically examine the legal framework present in each country.

A review and analysis of international waste management practices illustrate contrasting priorities and utilization of alternate technologies. Considerations include availability of current and updated technology, the population density factor, land-mass considerations, the prevalent economic conditions of each country, and past hazardous waste management practices and trends; all of which tend to encourage the use of disparate practices and treatment techniques.

The Federal government, in the preparation of waste management strategies, seeks to develop more efficient methods of identifying, assessing and mitigating human health risks which may be associated with various options and practices. The incorporation of human health considerations in the selection of future waste management practices is a high priority to Canadians.

Introduction

This study paper examines international hazardous waste legislation and waste management practices, with the express purpose of providing additional and relevant information, for health and environmental agencies in Canada. Legislation and regulations are drawn from other countries and organizations in relation to the restriction, and/or promotion, of various types of hazardous waste disposal strategies. In effecting the above, the various responsibilities, obligations of generators, transporters, and waste disposers, in addition to the various treatment, storage, and disposal methods and techniques are presented in order to critically examine the contrasting legal framework present in other countries.

A review of international waste management practices will illustrate alternate priorities, and in some instances, contrasting technologies. The national implementation of a hazardous waste management system emanates from a multitude of considerations, which may, in certain instances, be unique to that particular country. Considerations range from past and current legislative practices, past hazardous waste management practices and trends, the prevalent social and economic conditions in each country, and geographic and land-mass considerations, in addition to population density factors—all which tend to encourage, or discourage, certain legislative, and/or treatment and disposal practices.

In Canada, the federal government, in relation to hazardous waste management strategies, seeks to develop and incorporate more efficient techniques for identifying, assessing, and mitigating potential health and/or environmental risks associated with various international waste management practices. The incorporation of health considerations into the hazardous waste management spectrum is, and will continue to be, a concern of all Canadians.

Approach and Methodology

Identification of waste management legislation and regulatory practices, classification systems, generator, transporter and waste disposer obligations, transfrontier waste movement policies, and various treatment, storage, and disposal practices undertaken in selected countries are presented. Information was obtained from disparate sources: books, periodicals, journals, conferences, and through contact with various government/organization officials. Selected legislation, policy, and disposal method/treatment practices were examined and assessed on the basis of how the federal government may endeavor to proceed during the upcoming decade in relation to the consideration and incorporation of new, or alternate, waste management legislation or disposal/treatment practices.

Options for Action in Respect to Hazardous Waste Legislation

Hazardous Waste Legislation

A wealth of international hazardous waste legislation and regulation has been enacted within the countries examined in this report and is extensive. Most assuredly, the actual implementation of a hazardous waste legislative and regulatory system emanate from a multitude of considerations, which in some instances are unique to that particular country. In consequence, therefore, no single legislative and regulatory approach selected from a country encompassed within this study paper is able to, or should, serve as a "model system." Clearly, the common element in relation to international hazardous waste management practices undertaken in the respective countries examined reflects an underlying concern for both human health and the environment. This examination of international hazardous waste legislation has illustrated the comparative features and divergences which are apparent.

Option for Action

First, in my view "different" cannot be construed as "better," or "worse," for that matter, so therefore, in the legislative and regulatory realm, this study has simply identified international hazardous waste legislation which has been implemented, the various regulatory bodies and agencies operating as implementary vehicles serving to enact the above-mentioned legislation in addition to the waste management regulation, and enforcement methods used in enacting and effecting actual legislation and regulation in the aforementioned countries. Clearly, however, a closer examination of the Organizations examined in this study paper—the Organization for Economic Cooperation and Development (OECD), the European Economic Community (EEC), and the United Nations Environment Programme (UNEP)—is necessary. It must be duly noted that these Recommendations, Decisions, and

Guidelines governing hazardous waste, are designed for adoption, yet the incorporation of these regulations on a uniform basis by member and/or nonmember countries have been governed by other criterion which has not allowed this to occur.

In the United States, the federal government, through the Environmental Protection Agency, develops and enforces programs designed to ensure the safe management and control of hazardous waste. American legislation, as mandated through the Resource Conservation and Recovery Act (RCRA), and the Comprehensive Environmental Response, Compensation, and Liability Act (CERCLA), endeavours to establish a regulatory framework to protect against the deleterious effects of solid or hazardous waste contamination and is extensive. The American legislation reflects both a formal and a structured approach. Although the RCRA defines hazardous wastes in rather broad terms by hazardous waste types in addition to the four characteristics of ignitability, corrosivity, reactivity, and extractive procedure toxicity. One source (Hughes, 1990), alludes to the RCRA omission of listing infectious wastes, municipal garbage, or ash from garbage incineration, in hazardous waste definition. Conversely, however, American legislation concerning abandoned hazardous waste disposal (with CERCLA) is extensive.

As is the case with American hazardous waste legislation, German hazardous waste legislation is highly structured, and utilizes statutory instruments which exhibit precise public and private regulatory responsibilities. In Germany, the federal government formulates hazardous waste law (which in Germany is the Waste Avoidance and Waste Management Act and represents the primary hazardous waste legislation) while the various states (the Lander), in cooperation with the counties (Kreise), and municipalities (Gemeinde), exert day-to-day control over hazardous waste management. The trend in respect to implementation of recent international hazardous waste legislation reflect an emphasis on incorporation of waste reduction and waste minimization strategies, and clearly, the updated Waste Avoidance and Waste Management Act is no exception, and represents an attempt to transform German legislation from a traditional waste disposal system into an environmentally conscious waste management system emphasizing waste reduction and minimization.

In the United Kingdom, the Control of Pollution Act and the recently enacted Environmental Protection Act, represent the framework for British legislative and regulatory policy. In general, British regulations emphasize flexibility through guidelines, recommendations, and informal persuasion taking precedence over statutory orders and prosecutions for the most part. The British waste management system, as does the German system, endeavors to leave the actual day-to-day waste management affairs in local hands, whereas hazardous waste legislation and regulation represents a National Act. In the United Kingdom, the Environmental Protection Act represents a legislative vehicle in an endeavor to incorporate waste minimizations and waste reduction measures into the hazardous waste realm.

The Law on Waste disposal and Recovery is the primary hazardous waste law in France. The law place the onus of proper disposal upon the generators of hazardous waste, and utilizes a "cradle-to-grave" method of control. In France, hazardous waste management appears to be highly administrative and bureaucratic, yet efficient. The French utilize an alternate method for implementing hazardous waste legislation, as the National Agency for Waste Recovery and Study (ANRED), a quasi-public, government-funded agency, implements hazardous waste law, whereas, the Ministere de la Culture et de l'Environment is responsible for legislation, national policy formation, and the establishment of National environmental standards. In some respects, French hazardous waste law is similar to American and Japanese legislation, as French law applies to wastes in general, in addition to "special wastes." The "Green Plan" initiatives in France constitutes legislative attempts at encouraging waste reduction and waste minimization.

In Japan, the Waste Disposal and Public Cleansing Law represents the primary hazardous waste law. The Ministry of Health and Welfare is authorized to establish standards for the collection, transportation, treatment, storage, and disposal of waste, and delegate to the Environment Agency authority in determining which wastes are deemed hazardous. The National government serves in the promotion, research, and development of waste treatment technology, in addition to dispensing technical and financial assistance to regional and local governments.

In the Netherlands, the Chemical Waste Act and the Soil Clean-Up Act represent the main Dutch hazardous waste laws. The former law is based on the "polluter pays" principle, and the onus of waste management is firmly placed on the waste generator. In addition, the

Chemical Waste Act incorporates a "cradle to grave" notification system which enables the government to identify abusers. In essence, The Netherlands has a plethora of hazardous waste dumpsites, as does the United States, and the Soil Clean-Up law is designed to effect remedial action over these waste dumpsites. The Netherlands, as does many other countries examined in this study paper—Canada, Germany, Japan, France, and the United Kingdom—defer actual waste management responsibility to the provincial, or local, governments. In addition, the actual cleanup of hazardous waste sites is essentially a central government endeavor.

In Denmark, the Disposal of Oil and Chemical Waste Act and the Environmental Protection Act, in addition to a multitude of notifications and circulars, constitute the primary laws in the hazardous waste realm. In Denmark, as is the case with many of the other countries examined in this study paper, local government exercises control over the enforcement of hazardous waste laws and regulations. A more recent piece of legislation, indicative of the trend in promulgating waste reduction and waste minimization endeavors in industrial nations, is the Recycling and Reduction of Waste Act which attempts to encourage process substitution.

Hazardous Waste Classification Methods

In relation to International hazardous waste classification methods, there is considerable variance between the countries examined within this study paper. At present, some countries have not yet incorporated a hazardous waste definition, notably the United Kingdom, Japan (which identifies "industrial" and not "hazardous" waste), and Denmark. The Netherlands classifies hazardous waste as "chemical waste." The United States and the United Kingdom endeavour to classify hazardous waste on the basis of criteria relating to chemical properties. The United States uses the published lists, or characteristics of hazardousness. The British approach defines "special waste" in relation to listed substances, allowing for flexibility, however. Clearly, all countries examined in this study utilize extensive lists. The National legislation for Germany classifies "chemical waste" by both type and source, listing over 800 waste types cataloged from waste groupings, whereas France and Denmark classify waste by type only, while the Netherlands classifies hazardous waste by origin on the basis of criteria based on potential harm, persistence, cumulative effects, and toxicity, in addition to arbitrary concentration limits (The Netherlands, 1984).

Option for Action

In relation to International hazardous waste classification methods, the necessity to implement uniform classification systems is real in consequence of the considerable variance between the countries examined within this study paper. The adoption of uniform classification procedures, utilizing the EEC or OECD as a vehicle for change should be examined.

Transporter Duties and Responsibilities

Many of the countries examined in this study paper maintain a reporting system for hazardous waste transportation, the United States utilizes a manifest system where notification to the EPA is not required (although some states require notification). Conversely, other countries such as Germany, the United Kingdom (on a shipment-by-shipment basis), and France (on a quarterly basis), utilize alternate methods of reporting hazardous waste shipment. Clearly, there are considerable differences relating to reporting procedures, and it is this lack of uniformity which constitutes the central problem concerning national or international hazardous waste movement (sometimes in advance of waste shipment). In most situations where hazardous waste shipment is required to be reported, notification procedures are effected prior to the waste shipment taking place. The United Kingdom and Germany utilize a combined reporting/manifest system, France uses a manifest system in addition to the quarterly notification system, while the United States uses a uniform manifest system. Generally, hazardous waste import and/or export, of hazardous waste is prohibited where the intended hazardous waste activity has not been licensed, where proper notification procedures have not been followed (if required), and/or where the manifest and transport documents have not been properly prepared. In addition, there are contrasting notification procedures regarding hazardous waste (not utilized in some countries, i.e. the United States), and while the United Kingdom and France exercise interfrontier control and regulation at the border, the United States notifies the importing country when the hazardous waste has been designated for export. It is these contrasting reporting methods which serve to make hazardous waste control that much more complex and difficult. Japan, unlike other countries examined in this study paper, does not utilize a manifest system to track waste from "cradle to grave." Only when the Waste Management Law is contravened will the government, again, reassert authority over the process. It is at this stage that the prefectural government may order the hazardous waste disposer to take the necessary requisite action to remedy the situation.

Option for Action

In my view, the entire process of hazardous waste shipment proves more effective in situations where notification takes place in advance, while acknowledging that exceptions to reporting requirements are apparent in several countries. As aforementioned, it is clear that the central problem in relation to transporter duties and responsibilities for hazardous waste is in respect to the lack of uniformity. International procedures, adopted by hazardous waste-producing countries, would go a long way towards remedying the situation. As one source notes (Van Veen, 1985), and I concur, the most effective method of hazardous waste control is through an internationally proposed, nationally implemented, combined manifest and notification document utilizing code-numbers. These code-numbers are designed to indicate the hazardous waste generator, waste type, the transporter, disposer, and disposal method. These code-numbers would be assigned by the competent authorities of each country.

Treatment, Storage, and Disposal Methods

In Europe, waste management practices, in contrast to that in North America, have evolved from an alternate perspective: a scarcity of land for disposal of hazardous waste away from population centers; a concern regarding groundwater contamination; a perpetuation of a World War II material scarcity and conservation ethic; and, an emphasis of the traditional government/industry cooperation in all areas of industrial policy and technological development (Davis, Huisingh, and Piasecki, 1987). Generally, as one source notes (Davis, Linnerooth, and Piasecki, 1987), European governments, unlike their North American counterparts, appear to play a larger role in supporting and subsidizing industrial development, and in consulting their industrial colleagues, to a greater degree, when it comes to the formulation of environmental policy. European countries have adopted a "low and non-waste technology" and "clean technology" attitude in respect to hazardous waste management, while "waste minimization" and "waste reduction" is emphasized in American programs (Davis, Huisingh, and Piasecki, 1987). European counties pioneered the concept of the integrated waste treatment facility during the 1960s. Clearly, there are distinct advantages apparent with this type of facility in the economic, managerial, and enforcement realm. Conversely, the physical siting of a large-scale facility, the longer transportation distances posed, the increased risk of accident, and the real, or threatened, public opposition regarding central facilities represent distinct disadvantages. In general, European nations utilize high-temperature hazardous waste incineration in the view that the risk to human health is low, although there is some concern expressed in relation to the incomplete combustion of chlorinated organics and heavy metal emissions. All European countries examined in this paper utilize at least one commercial centralized facility, and a greater number of in-house facilities. In addition, by and large, European countries have emphasized treatment and incineration over landfill disposal, although costs are borne by both public and industry, and, as indicated in this study paper, the incineration of hazardous waste is more expensive than land disposal (Davis, Linnerooth, and Piasecki, 1987). In Europe, during the first half of the 1980s, above-ground storage, and "controlled" burial, represented the most favored hazardous waste-management techniques, although sea disposal and recycling were also popular. At present, the trend in Europe indicates that although landfill of hazardous waste is still practiced, both landfill and sea disposal will fall into disfavor (OECD, 1991). In addition, the practice of ocean burning, at one time considered a progressive technology favored over ocean dumping and landfilling, is no longer considered as a viable solution. Advances in European hazardous waste management technologies have taken place, which provide waste generators with land-based options (Piasecki and Sutter, 1987). In essence, European countries have encouraged, and emphasized, the construction of expensive treatment and incineration facilities in order to minimize the direct land disposal of hazardous waste. In consequence, authorities have been assured a market for high-cost systems by requiring that all transported waste be delivered to these facilities, thereby de facto creating a public monopoly (Davis and Linnerooth with Piasecki, 1987). Centralized and fully-integrated facilities utilizing rotary kiln incinerators are primarily used for hazardous waste disposal, and in-house facilities primarily use liquid injection incinerators. North American hazardous waste policy, in contrast to that in Europe, illustrates that a greater reliance has been placed on the private market to provide a network of management facilities, with an emphasis on land disposal of hazardous waste (no public subsidies), has taken place, yet this situation may be changing. As one source notes (Davis, 1987), the trend indicates that the United States is turning to incineration for hazardous waste disposal, despite inherent concerns pertaining to incinerator air emissions, and as to whether this may simply constitute the trading of one type of hazard (groundwater pollution), for another of equal or possibly greater magnitude (toxic air emissions). Clearly, in a country such as the United States which disposes approximately 80 percent of hazardous waste, through landfill, this disposal method will clearly not solve the ongoing waste problem prevalent in the United States (Hughes, 1990). As aforementioned, international hazardous waste management practices, legislation, and regulation, has stemmed from a plethora of alternate considerations which transcend and preclude actual hazardous waste treatment and disposal practices.

Option for Action

In my view, the promulgation of central treatment facilities, despite a host of relevant concerns and alternate considerations, replete with incineration and chemical/physical treatment capabilities for treating hazardous waste, and landfill for the relatively minute and inert quantities of treated waste, represent the most viable, efficient, and complete hazardous waste treatment method (perhaps, however, not the least expensive, in addition to concerns pertaining to human health). Unfortunately, as aforementioned, alternate considerations has limited the incorporation of central facilities on a large scale. In general, most central facilities are publicly owned and managed in Europe, whereas in the United States hazardous waste facilities are by and large privately owned, and from a cost perspective, this treatment process has been beset by limitations. Recent initiatives in the United States has led some states to begin to investigate the establishment of central treatment facilities along German lines. Hazardous waste management in Denmark, which arguably utilizes the most complete waste management system, represents in some respects a "model system." The Danish waste management initiatives, however, it must be pointed out, work in a geographically small, and sparsely populated country. Therefore, geographically larger countries and/or countries with a greater population density factor, would find the Danish system unworkable, and/or unaffordable. Conversely, however, small population centers, such as provinces like Prince Edward Island and Nova Scotia, could find the Kommunekemi facility more palatable. In addition, the general trend in recent international legislative and regulatory initiatives have been attempts to incorporate reduce, reuse, and recycle methods pertaining to hazardous waste management disposal/treatment. The utilization of the new technologies mentioned above, in concert with waste minimization and waste reduction endeavors, would prove most beneficial in terms of human health and the environment.

Assessment of Current and Future Disposal Methods

Generally, European countries have emphasized construction of central treatment and incineration facilities in an endeavor to minimize direct land disposal. The physical/chemical treatment of hazardous waste, commonplace in Europe, utilizes multiple chemical processes in order to produce relatively inert, aqueous waste, which is acceptable for either sewer or surface water discharge, and/or a dewatered sludge or solid waste component acceptable for landfilling (a country such as Japan uses a disproportionately high number of plants for concrete solidification). The problem with physical/chemical treatment methods, although popular and efficient, relate to the fact that voluminous amounts of sludges are produced, and from a cost perspective are, at present, uneconomical to recover. In addition, essentially due to mounting discontent with the technology and performance history of European incinerating ships, European nations are focusing on other disposal technologies. Presently, the most popular method for managing hazardous wastes from a cost perspective in industrialized countries is through land disposal. This includes landfills, surface impoundments, land farming, and deep-well injection. In the United States, a variety of treatment methods are currently being used, as it appears that the country is turning to incineration of hazardous waste after a long embrace with landfill. The fluidized bed incineration method is also used in the United states, yet to a far-lesser degree. In addition, American hazardous waste management techniques include deep-well injection, surface impoundments, and landfills which account for 80-90 percent of the off-site disposal of hazardous wastes (Davis and Linnerooth with Piasecki, 1987). Clearly, however, the global trend indicates that hazardous waste landfill is becoming an increasingly restricted practice, essentially used to dispose of the residue from incineration or chemical treatment processes (Denmark, Germany, and the United States). The United Kingdom utilizes the co-disposal method of landfilling waste, mixing municipal refuse with hazardous waste, emphasizing a belief that co-disposal of waste results in far fewer problems in relation to contaminated sites than would an alternate policy of segregating and entombing the waste product. Conversely, in The Netherlands, the landfill of hazardous waste is essentially a prohibited (with certain exceptions) practice, with few acceptable sites for either hazardous or municipal waste landfill (a concrete landfill facility has been in operation since 1988). Japan, conversely, utilizes three different types of landfill, with distinguishable and varying degrees of protection. An alternative method of hazardous waste control is through use of surface impoundments, which for the most part, is a practice used by few countries, including the United States and the United Kingdom, and used in relatively limited fashion. The practice of ocean disposal, governed by the London Dumping Convention (worldwide), as well as the Oslo Convention (North Sea and the North East Atlantic), is essentially a restricted practice, requiring a license which must be obtained beforehand from the competent authority within the country of origin, and/or under the conditions of license. Internationally, most countries engage in limited shallow sea dumping with the United Kingdom representing an exception to this trend. In addition, ocean dumping of hazardous waste, as is the case with sea incineration, is becoming a restricted practice as most countries are halting this practice (Denmark 1982, Germany 1989, and recent EEC initiatives). During the early 1970s, in Europe the ocean burn of chlorinated hazardous waste was a preferred disposal method over ocean dumping and landfilling, however, this is no longer the case due to inherent operating and maintenance problems, in addition to the fact that ocean burning of hazardous waste does not allow for recovery of any waste components for recycling purposes (Piasecki and Sutter, 1987). Furthermore, the practice of ocean incineration has declined as a viable disposal method as exemplified by the fact that only 80,234 tons of hazardous waste was delivered for sea disposal, representing a 20 percent reduction from 1981 across all nations as early as 1983 (Piasecki and Sutter, 1987). In addition, essentially due to mounting discontent with the technology and performance history of incinerating ships, European nations are focusing on alternate disposal technologies. In the United States, a variety of thermal destruction technologies have shown promise. Other recent technologies include plasma arc destruction, infrared thermal processing, wet air oxidation, and supercritical water oxidation which tends to destroy organic waste more completely than does incineration, and in addition, promises greater efficiency and safety in return. In Germany, many hazardous waste treatment/disposal methods are utilized: incineration, physical/chemical treatment, and to a lesser extent, landfill, in addition to storage and export. In Germany, land-based incinerators have played only a minor role in that country's decision to terminate ocean burning, as most of Germany's wastes originally destined to maritime destruction are now managed by recycling, reuse, or waste reduction techniques (Piasecki and Sutter, 1987). The German approach represents an attempt to match the different chemical qualities of waste with distinct control strategies and land-based disposal options. The landfilling of hazardous wastes constitutes, by far, the most popular disposal technique used in the United Kingdom, although ocean disposal is also used extensively in concert with alternate methods. France, as is the case with Germany, utilizes a variety of treatment methods, yet, incineration and physical/chemical treatment are favored to a far greater degree than landfilling. The physical/chemical treatment techniques for hazardous waste are widely used in Japan, yet a significant amount of hazardous waste is landfilled. The Netherlands is a densely populated country and in consequence of a dearth of treatment/disposal facilities and a small landmass, designates large amounts of hazardous waste for export to other European countries. Finally, Denmark, which in essence may have the most fully integrated hazardous waste management system of all nations encompassed within this study paper, utilizes a central facility (Kommunekemi) to dispose of virtually all the hazardous waste produced in the country (yet in consequence of the low population and landmass of Denmark, this management system is efficient and workable). The Netherlands, a land-locked country, exhibits a definitive lack of a significant treatment and disposal infrastructure despite early legislative action and relatively precise and rigorous formal regulations. In consequence of the dearth of treatment, storage, and disposal facilities, the export of hazardous waste (including sea disposal: primarily halogenated organic incineration by ships) account for over 60 percent of the total (Wynne and Hortensius, 1987). The Netherlands, however, has rather ambitiously indicated that it will strive to endeavor to make contaminated land "agriculturally sound." In essence, most European nations have placed a heavy reliance on solid waste incineration, in a belief that it incorporates the best possible control strategy, for the low concentration of toxics found in residential waste streams. In Denmark, the 21 transfer stations are situated throughout the country so that no one waste generator is required to travel in excess of 30 miles to reach the nearest one. The transfer stations, operated by local municipalities, segregate both household and industrial wastes. Kommunekemi's treatment techniques utilize rotary kiln incineration, as well as various types of physical/chemical treatment processes. In addition, there is a landfill in close proximity to the central facility (approximately 12 miles away), which is utilized to dispose of Kommunekemi's incineration ash and treatment sludges, waste from oil and gas exploration and used batteries.

Options for Action

Central Treatment Facilities

Advantages. The integrated waste treatment facility offer distinct advantages in the economic, managerial, and enforcement realm. All European countries examined in this paper utilize at least one commercial centralized facility, and a greater number of in-house facilities. In essence, most European nations have utilized solid waste incineration, in the belief that it offers the best possible control mechanism to combat the lower concentration of toxics found in residential waste streams. European countries have, for the most part, emphasized treatment and incineration over landfill disposal (minimize direct land disposal). In relation to integrated and centralized facilities, rotary kiln incinerators represent the primary method used for hazardous waste disposal, and in-house facilities basically utilize liquid injection incinerators. Currently in France, financial incentives and legislation are being discussed, proposing the advancement of incineration as the primary disposal method over landfill (The Netherlands, 1990). In the United States, approximately 230 operational hazardous waste incinerators are in service, most being liquid injection units, while 40 are rotary kiln (Forester, 1987). In The Netherlands, a rotary kiln facility was established in 1973 and hazardous waste disposal is centralized. A company, ARV-Chemie CV, engages in high temperature incineration, controlled landfill, and small toxic waste management. The Netherlands incinerates, dewaters, and detoxifies over 50 percent of the hazardous waste produced in the nation. In Denmark, the Kommunekemi facility is estimated to destroy approximately 70 percent of the hazardous waste produced in the country.

Disadvantages. The actual physical siting of a large-scale facility, the longer transportation distances posed, the increased risk of accident, and the public opposition to these central facilities constitute distinct disadvantages. In addition, concerns have been expressed as to the incomplete combustion of chlorinated organics, and heavy metal emissions. Furthermore, incineration of hazardous waste is more expensive than are the various methods of land disposal (Davis, Linnerooth, and Piasecki, 1987).

Physical/Chemical Treatment

Advantages. This method utilizes multiple chemical processes in order to produce relatively inert, aqueous waste which is acceptable for either sewer or surface water discharge, and/or a dewatered sludge or solid waste component acceptable for landfilling. France, as is the case with Germany, utilizes a variety of treatment methods, yet incineration and physical/chemical treatment is a favored treatment process. Physical/chemical treatment techniques are widely used in Japan.

Disadvantages. There are problem areas related to the fact that voluminous amounts of sludges are produced, and are, from a cost perspective, at present uneconomical to recover.

Ocean Incineration

Advantages. None.

Disadvantages. There are disadvantages, as Europe, due to mounting discontent with the technology and performance history of European incinerating ships, have focused on other disposal technologies. In essence, the practice of ocean burning, once considered a progressive technology, utilized to a greater degree than either ocean dumping or landfilling, is no longer considered as a viable solution. Internationally, ocean incineration has declined as a viable disposal method. During the early 1970s, in Europe the ocean burn of chlorinated hazardous waste was a preferred disposal method over ocean dumping and landfilling, however, this is no longer the case due to inherent operating and maintenance problems of incinerating ships, in addition to the fact that ocean burning of hazardous waste does not allow for recovery of any waste components for recycling purposes (Piasecki and Sutter, 1987). In addition, many countries are outlawing the practice of ocean incineration of hazardous waste, including the United Kingdom, who announced in March 1990 that no further wastes would be licensed for marine incineration beyond year-end. The United Kingdom also outlines plans to terminate existing licenses for marine disposal of liquid industrial waste and fly-ash by 1992 (The Control of Hazardous Waste in Britain: Reference Fact Sheet, 1991).

Landfilling

Advantages. Presently, the most popular method for managing hazardous wastes from a cost perspective in industrialized countries is through land disposal. This includes landfills, surface impoundments, land farming, and deep-well injection. At present, the trend in Europe indicates that although landfill is still a utilized method of disposal, the practice will continue to fall into disfavor (OECD, 1991). Presently, the most popular method for managing hazardous wastes from a cost perspective in industrialized countries is through land disposal. The landfilling of hazardous wastes constitutes by far the most popular disposal technique in the United Kingdom, where approximately 85 percent of all hazardous wastes produced in the United Kingdom are disposed through landfill (Wynne, 1987). The United Kingdom practices co-disposal, emphasizing a belief that co-disposal of waste results in far fewer problems in relation to contaminated sites than would an alternate policy of segregating and entombing the waste product. Land farms, or disposal of hazardous waste mixed with soil, represents another seldom-used method in the country (Sierig, 1977). In Japan, a significant amount of hazardous waste is landfilled. Japan utilizes three different types of landfill with distinguishable and varying degrees of protection. An alternative method of hazardous waste control is through the use of surface impoundments which are, for the most part, used by few countries, namely the United States and the United Kingdom and used in relatively limited fashion. In The Netherlands, on the other hand, only 5 percent of hazardous waste is landfilled in The Netherlands.

Disadvantages. Clearly, the trend indicates that hazardous waste landfill is becoming an increasingly restricted practice, essentially being used only to dispose of waste residue from incineration or chemical treatment processes (Denmark, Germany, and the United States). Although, in contrast to other disposal methods, landfill is relatively inexpensive, the trend indicates that costs are increasing. In relation to North American hazardous waste policy, in contrast to European policy, a greater emphasis on land disposal of hazardous waste (no public subsidies) has taken place, yet this may be changing. In The Netherlands, the landfill of hazardous waste is essentially a prohibited (with certain exceptions) practice, with few acceptable sites for either hazardous or municipal waste (a concrete landfill facility has been in operation since 1988). The use of surface impoundments, such as pits, ponds, and lagoons, are utilized on an infrequent basis in Germany, and primarily for degraded sludges. In Germany, it is estimated that there are over 80,000 abandoned waste sites in the nation, over 20,000 abandoned landfills in France, over 6,060 contaminated sites situated in The Netherlands, and over 3,115 contaminated sites located in Denmark, with approximately 800,000 tonnes of contaminated soil requiring treatment (The Netherlands, 1990). Although co-disposal of "special waste," with conventional refuse, does take place in Germany and has been past practice, using a 5 to 10 percent special waste ratio to that of household waste, the system is no loner recommended. Similarly, in Denmark, the practice of co-disposal of hazardous waste in combination with conventional refuse (a popular method in the UK) is not permitted. In addition, land farms, or disposal of waste mixed with soils, is also not encouraged. In the United States, there are 200 landfills nationwide serving to dispose of approximately 3 million tons of hazardous waste (Forester, 1987).

Ocean Dumping

Advantages. Relatively inexpensive.

Disadvantages. The practice of ocean disposal governed by the London Dumping Convention (worldwide), as well as the Oslo Convention (North Sea and the North East Atlantic), is essentially becoming a restricted practice requiring a license which must be obtained beforehand from the competent authority within the country of origin, and/or under the conditions of license. Internationally, most countries engage in limited shallow sea dumping, with the United Kingdom representing an exception to this trend. Finally, ocean dumping of hazardous waste, as is the case with sea incineration, is quickly becoming a restricted practice as most countries are halting this practice (Denmark 1982, Germany 1989, and EEC initiatives).

Alternative Methods

Advantages. In the United States, a variety of thermal destruction technologies have shown promise. Other recent technologies include plasma arc destruction, infrared thermal processing, wet air oxidation and supercritical water oxidation, which tends to destroy organic waste more completely than does conventional incineration, and in addition, promises greater efficiency and safety in return. In Germany, wastes originally destined for maritime destruction are now managed by recycling, reuse, or waste reduction techniques (Piasecki and Sutter, 1987). The German approach is an endeavor to match the different chemical qualities of waste, with distinct control strategies and land-based disposal options. In addition, over 35,000 tons of cyanide salts, mercury sludges, chlorinated pesticides and concentrated PCB's are stored in the Herfa Neurode salt mine in Germany, a private facility owned by Kali and Salz which doubles as a producing salt mine (30,000 tonnes per day), using the room and pillar mining technique and working a three meters-thick potash deposit approximately 500 meters below the surface (Environment Canada, 1979). Over 1,000 tons of hazardous waste has been retrieved from the salt mine for detoxification and recycling purposes (Davis, 1987). The German salt mines represent another potential option for action, as a country such as Canada certainly has a number of abandoned mines! In the United Kingdom, improvements and advances in hazardous waste technology has led to implementation of three new treatment processes. The first process involves treatment of acid tar wastes, converting the waste into inert solid tar and aqueous organic effluent. A second process, known as "Vitrifix," converts fibrous asbestos into glass utilizing a high temperature furnace. Thirdly, an interesting process includes the pyrolysis of waste tires, which are converted into fuel products (a process also used in Germany), constitutes another process. In the United Kingdom (unlike Germany), waste exchange schemes are not popular. Current initiatives in Japan are in respect to the recycling of domestic and industrial waste, and the incorporation of more restrictive standards regulating waste disposal facilities which in turn serve to increase disposal costs, and thereby providing incentive for industrial waste recycling. In Japan, research and development on recycling technology with a focus on plastics, and hazardous waste and energy recovery, is apparent (The Netherlands, 1990). Clearly, as indicated, most countries have embarked on legislation, regulation, and other initiatives which emphasize waste reduction and minimization. Another option for action involves a policy of The Netherlands and Denmark which imposes a tax on the generation of hazardous waste. In The Netherlands, the tax is authorized under Dutch legislation (the Chemical Waste Act, 1976), and has been imposed upon those generators manufacturing certain products, or use chemical processes listed in regulation. The tax is imposed upon the treatment, storage, and disposal facility license (Davis, Hisingh, and Piasecki, 1987). Finally, in Denmark, the Kommunekemi treatment facility recovers heat from waste incinerators, which then serves to supply Nyborg's 18,000 residents with 35 percent of their heating needs

(Piasecki and Davis, 1987). The quantity of heat produced is equal to oil consumption of approximately 1.5 tonnes per hour (Muller, 1987).

Summary

This review has established a national selection of options through illustrating a multitude of international hazardous waste treatment and disposal methods and technologies, available to both federal and provincial government through this international study paper. This examination of international legislation and disposal methods/technologies offers a wealth of knowledge for competent authorities in the hazardous waste realm.

This review of international hazardous waste legislation and disposal technologies should aptly assist the federal government in the promulgation of future hazardous waste legislative and disposal methodologies in an endeavor to mitigate human health risks, and minimize the degradation of our environment associated with current waste practices.

References

Davis, G., Huisingh, D., and Piasecki, B., 1987. "Waste Reduction Strategies: European Practice and American Prospects." In *America's Future in Toxic Waste Management*, Piasecki, B., and Davis, G., 1987. Quorum Books, New York. 309 pp.

Davis, G., Linnerooth, J., with Piasecki, B., 1987. "Government Ownership of Risk: Guaranteeing a Treatment Infrastructure." In *America's Future in Toxic Waste Management*, Piasecki, B., and Davis, G., 1987. Quorum Books, New York. 309 pp.

Environment Canada 1979. *Environment Canada: Inventory of Hazardous Waste in Northwest Region*, Vol. 1, January 1979. W.L. Waldrop and Associates.

Forester, W.S., 1987. "Hazardous Waste Management in the United States of America." In *International Perspectives on Hazardous Waste Management*, Forester, W.S., and Skinner, J.H., (Eds.), 1987. Academic Press, London. 289 pp.

Hughes, E. "Toxic waste incineration at sea." In *The University of British Columbia Law Review*, Vol. 24, no. 1, 1990, 19–36.

Muller, K. 1987. "Hazardous Waste Management in Denmark." In *International Perspectives on Hazardous Waste Management*, Forester, W.S., and Skinner, J.H., (Eds.), 1987. Academic Press, London. 289 pp.

The Netherlands. 1984. Brief Survey of Legislation and Arrangements for the Disposal of Chemical Waste in a number of Industrialized Countries. Ministry of Housing, Physical Planning and Environment. October 1984.

Published by the Ministry of Housing, Physical Planning and Environment Central Department for Information and International Relations.

Organisation for Economic Co-operation and Development. 1991. The State of the Environment. OECD Publication Service, Paris, France.

Piasecki, B., and Davis, G., 1987. "Restructuring Toxic Waste Controls: Intrinsic Difficulties and Historical Trends." In *America's Future in Toxic Waste Management*. Piasecki, B., and Davis, G., 1987. Quorum Books, New York. 309 pp.

Sierig, G. 1987. "Hazardous Waste Management in the Federal Republic of Germany." In *International Perspectives on Hazardous Waste Management*. Forester, W.S., and Skinner, J.H., (Eds.), 1987, Academic Press, London, 289 pp.

Van Veen, F., 1987. "National Hazardous Waste Monitoring Systems." In *Transfrontier Movements of Hazardous Waste. Legal and Institutional Aspects, 1985*. The Organisation for Economic Cooperation and Development. Paris, France. 304 pp.

Wynne, B., and Hortensius D., 1987. "The Rationalities of Problem Definition: The Netherlands and Hazardous Waste Management." In *Risk Management and Hazardous Waste*. Implementation and the Dialectics of Credibility. 1987. Springer-Verlag, New York. 447 pp.

United Kingdom. February 1991. The Control of Hazardous Waste in Britain: Reference Fact Sheet. Foreign and Commonwealth Office, 10 pp.

International Efforts to Protect the Last Frontiers: Antarctica and National Parks

Antarctica is the last unspoiled wilderness continent. It is the world's largest wildlife sanctuary, a habitat of one hundred million birds, several species of seals and penguins, and fifteen species of whales which feed there in the summer. It is also a global scientific laboratory of significant value in the measuring of the Earth's weather, climatic patterns, and pollution levels. Within the polar icecap is contained historical information which allows us to understand and record the climatological history of the Earth.

Additionally, the polar regions are quite sensitive to the changes in the global environment and provide warming signals to atmospheric and oceanographic changes induced by environmental degradation, e.g. ozone depletion. For all of the above reasons it is important to protect, through international agreements, Antarctica. The 1991 Madrid Protocol to the 1961 Antarctica Treaty on Environmental Protection seeks to achieve an internationally protected status for Antarctica. The protocol proposes that Antarctica be designated a "world park" and protects its ecosystems, wilderness, and degradation values and status as an international scientific laboratory. Moreover, mining and all forms of mineral resource activities are banned for 55 years. The protocol is binding on signatories, however, several key countries have yet to sign and the goal of an internationally protected commons awaits broad-based ratification of the protocol.

Lewis and Sandra Hinchman argue that fragile ecosystems, biological diversity, and pristine wilderness areas are inherently valuable. As such, they need and deserve protection. However, the model of protection that is appropriate to conditions in wealthy countries like the United States is unlikely either to hold much appeal or to achieve its desired results in the impoverished and often overpopulated nations of the Global South. In many cases, established parks and reserves exist only on paper; more generally, nature protection is thwarted by various factors, including pressure by land-hungry peasants, greedy exploitation by local elites and multinational corporations, ill-conceived projects sponsored by international agencies, and simple neglect and lack of adequate funding by remote control governments. For nature preservation to succeed in the Global South, it must be part and parcel of a larger strategy that incorporates ecodevelopment and social justice. In particular, it is important that indigenous peoples not be displaced, that they be given an economic stake in preservation, and that their views be solicited and their traditions respected in any nature preservation initiatives. Furthermore, public education campaigns must stress the value of nature protection to the national welfare: the ways in which human society depends upon the integrity of nature's life support systems and the services they provide. The authors advance their argument by presenting numerous case studies that demonstrate what has worked, and what has not worked, worldwide.

—RNW

19

Antarctica: An International Laboratory
Colin Deihl

*May this continent, the last explored by humankind, be the first one
to be spared by humankind. Out of the errors of the past, may there
rise a dawn of respect and love for the free-living creatures and
pristine beauty of the last virgin land on Earth—Antarctica.*

Jacques-Yves Cousteau[1]

Section I: Introduction

In June 1988, the member nations of the Antarctic Treaty System[2]
signed, but did not ratify, the Convention on the Regulation of Antarctic
Mineral Resources Activities (CRAMRA).[3] CRAMRA's purpose is to
establish a regime governing the exploration and exploitation of
minerals in Antarctica while simultaneously preserving Antarctica's
pristine environment.[4] CRAMRA has generated criticism from environmentalists who believe that it would allow oil companies to begin test
drilling on the Antarctic continental shelf. These critics contend that
ratification of CRAMRA will lead to the continent's ruin. Largely
because of the environmentalists' criticism, CRAMRA probably never
will be ratified. At the most recent Antarctic Treaty system meeting in
December 1990, CRAMRA had lost most of its earlier support.[5] Only
Japan continued to support CRAMRA in its original form.[6] Consequently, CRAMRA did not have sufficient support to be introduced for
ratification.[7]

CRAMRA and the accompanying controversy over Antarctic oil
exploration deserve close examination. In many respects Antarctica

308

represents a microcosm of global environmental problems. No nation legitimately can claim sovereignty over the Antarctic continent; therefore, its environmental problems must be solved in the same manner that the world's environmental problems must be solved— through treaties and unilateral actions. As a result, Antarctica can serve as an accurate laboratory for international environmental law. The conflict over the future of Antarctica encapsulates many of the key political issues of the 1990s: environmentalism versus economic growth, the developing nations versus the industrial powers, and international cooperation versus unilateral action.

This article's purpose is to determine how Antarctica's environment best can be protected. Proponents of CRAMRA believe that the Antarctic Treaty members need to enter into a minerals regime in order to avoid an unregulated gold rush in Antarctica. They argue that only by ratifying a minerals regime will Treaty members be able to control and regulate mineral exploitation in Antarctica. Critics of CRAMRA advocate a complete ban on mineral exploration and exploitation. They propose that setting aside Antarctica as a World Park is the only way to protect Antarctica's environment.

This article examines both the World Park proposal and CRAMRA to determine which is better for the Antarctic environment. Although the article discusses geopolitical influences, it only looks at these influences as they affect environmental protection. Section II of this article describes Antarctic geography, geology, and politics, providing an introduction to the physical realities of Antarctica. Section III explains the Antarctic Treaty System and examines CRAMRA. To a large extent, CRAMRA has shaped the current controversy over Antarctica's future. Moreover, although CRAMRA has lost almost all of its supporters, it remains important since there is still a slight possibility that the Treaty members may decide to use it as the basis for a new minerals agreement. Section III also evaluates the concept, proposed by CRAMRA's critics, of a World Park. Section IV compares the views of those who support a minerals regime like CRAMRA with the views of those who support setting aside the continent as a World Park. The purpose of section IV is to analyze critically the two dominant perspectives shaping the debate over Antarctica and to determine which perspective, if adopted, would be protective of Antarctica's environment. This Article concludes that the best way to prevent the despoliation of Antarctica is to follow the recommendations of environmentalists and to prohibit minerals exploration in the Antarctic region permanently.

Section II: The Physical Continent

Geography

The isolation of Antarctica, combined with the harshness of its climate, must be considerations in any plan to drill for oil or mine for minerals. Antarctica's extreme environment makes minerals exploration there more difficult than anywhere else on earth. Moreover, the harsh Antarctic environment will magnify the environmental impacts of any mineral exploration.[8]

Of the seven continents, Antarctica is the least hospitable to human activities.[9] It is the coldest continent on earth.[10] Summer temperatures average about 0° centigrade along the coast and -20° centigrade in the interior. Winter temperatures average about -20° centigrade along the coast and -65° centigrade in the interior.[11] The average year-round temperature in the coastal regions is -15° centigrade.[12] The lowest temperature ever recorded on earth, -89.6° centigrade, was recorded on July 21, 1983, at the Soviet Union's Volstock station.[13] These extreme temperatures are aggravated by continual high winds with speeds often exceeding 200 kilometers per hour.[14] During a severe storm in 1960, scientists estimated that gusts exceeded 250 kilometers per hour (140 miles per hour).[15]

Anyone proposing minerals exploitation on Antarctica also must take into account the continent's magnitude. The Antarctic continent and its surrounding oceans cover an enormous area. It is the fifth largest continent, covering about 5.4 million square miles or approximately ten percent of the earth's surface.[16] Ninety-nine percent of Antarctica's area is covered in a layer of ice.[17] This icecap contains seventy percent of the world's fresh water and ninety percent of its ice.[18] On average, the icecap is 1600 meters thick.[19] If the icecap melted completely, it would raise the level of the world's sea level by fifty-five meters.[20] The icecap extends beyond the continent's coastline as ice shelves. The largest such shelf, the Ross Ice Shelf, is the size of France.[21] Occasionally, huge chunks of the ice shelf break away and float into the Southern Ocean, presenting enormous hazards to ships transiting the area.[22]

Antarctica is also isolated. South America is 1000 kilometers (620 miles) away across the roughest stretch of water in the world. Australia is 2500 kilometers (1550 miles) away, and Africa is 4000 kilometers (2500 miles) away.[23] The continent and its ice shelves are separated from the rest of the world by a barrier of shifting pack ice and a stormy Southern Ocean. The pack ice varies in size according to the seasons.

In summer, its ice shrinks and breaks apart, forming channels that can be kept clear for ships. In winter, it can extend as far north as Tierra del Fuego in South America. During severe winters its expansion can double the size of Antarctica's summer ice cover.[24]

Potential Mineral Resources

Despite the obvious difficulties associated with attempting any mineral extraction in such a harsh and remote continent, numerous countries and multinational corporations have expressed interest in exploring Antarctica for mineral wealth.[25] Although there are no known commercially valuable deposits of either hydrocarbons or hard minerals in Antarctica, many scientists believe that Antarctica may contain economically valuable mineral resources.[26] This belief is based on a geological theory known as plate tectonics.

According to plate tectonics theory, the earth is made up of rigid plates that move with respect to one another a few centimeters per year.[27] Approximately 200 million years ago, the continents of the Southern Hemisphere were joined together into a supercontinent known as Gondwanaland.[28] One way of accessing Antarctica's potential mineral wealth is by analogizing to the mineral wealth found on the continents that once were joined to Antarctica.[29]

According to geologists, Australia, India, and parts of southern Africa once were joined with eastern Antarctica. All of these areas contain Precambrian Shield rocks that hold some of the world's most valuable mineral deposits. Minimal exploration in Antarctica has revealed that the continent contains huge quantities of coal, as well as deposits of platinum, chromite, copper, molybdenum, gold, silver, and many other minerals.[30] Nevertheless, minerals experts think that the price of these minerals would have to rise substantially before they would become commercially exploitable.[31]

Currently, no one knows if any valuable hydrocarbon deposits exist. Nevertheless, interest in Antarctic oil has been building since a United States scientific drilling ship, the *Glomar Challenger*, discovered the presence of gaseous hydrocarbons in three out of four holes drilled in the Ross Sea continental shelf.[32] Although, the appearance of hydrocarbons does not indicate necessarily the presence of commercial oil or gas deposits,[33] scientists consider the Ross Sea area promising for future oil and gas exploration. According to current theories about Gondwanaland, the Ross Sea once adjoined the Gippsland basin of Australia.[34] In 1974 that area of Australia had proven reserves of 2.5 billion barrels of oil and 220 billion cubic meters of gas.[35]

Without more drilling, estimates of oil reserves are not likely to be accurate.[36] Nevertheless, estimates have been widely quoted.[37] In 1974 and again in 1983, the United States Geologic Survey studied Antarctica's mineral potential.[38] This research, known as the Wright-Williams Report,[39] estimated that the Ross Sea area contained forty-five billion barrels of oil, of which only fifteen billion barrels could be extracted.[40] This amount of oil is comparable to the amount of oil on the United States Atlantic continental shelf and less than the thirty to sixty billion barrels believed to be off the coast of Alaska.[41] Although these published estimates appear to be fueling the international quest for Antarctic minerals, there is no way to know the petroleum potential of the offshore basins without further study of the underlying geology.[42]

Commercial Viability

Drilling for oil in Antarctica may become technologically feasible. Recent scientific drilling demonstrates that offshore geologic surveys are possible using existing technology.[43] Furthermore, the past decade has witnessed the oil industry's entry into increasingly challenging environments such as the North Sea, the coast of Labrador, and the Beaufort Sea.[44] Proponents of Antarctic mineral exploration point to the success of oil drilling operations in the Arctic as an indication that such drilling will become technologically feasible in the Antarctic.[45]

Nevertheless, drilling will be more difficult in the Antarctic than in the Arctic. The Ross Sea differs from the Arctic in several ways. Most importantly, the waters off Antarctica are very deep. Experience in the Arctic, most notably in the Beaufort Sea, has been limited to shallow inshore waters.[46] Because of the pressures of high winds and ice, companies operating in the Beaufort Sea have used artificial gravel islands instead of the conventional drilling platforms. Such islands would be impossible in the Antarctic, where the water depth is an average of ten to twenty times deeper than that of the Arctic.[47] Furthermore, the waves in the Beaufort Sea are moderate compared to the waves of the Ross Sea.[48] Finally, the icebergs encountered in Antarctica are gigantic. Although crews operating off the coast of Labrador have developed methods to avoid icebergs while operating oil platforms, those methods are not applicable to the Antarctic due to the immense size of Antarctic icebergs.[49] The only existing option is to make the drilling rigs capable of quick evacuation.[50] These gigantic icebergs often scour the seabed in the Antarctic. As a result, sub-sea pipelines and wellheads will have to be buried below the depth of maximum scour to be protected.[51]

Even if technology could be developed that would allow operators to drill safely in the Antarctic, there would still be enormous problems associated with oil production. Because of the build-up of ice in the winter months, the whole production system would have to be below the surface and would have to function nine months of the year without surface maintenance.[52] Additionally, there would be tremendous problems designing and building a storage and export facility. There are no analogous oil producing areas anywhere in the world.

Antarctica's Significance

Antarctica's importance may not be immediately apparent. Antarctica is no person's home. Most of the continent is covered by a frozen ice sheet that supports very limited life forms. Although the surrounding ocean is home to a complex and varied ecosystem, it is separated from the rest of the planet, and consequently there is little danger that human life will be threatened. Nevertheless, the integrity of the Antarctic environment is important for at least three reasons. First, Antarctica is important to scientists. Second, it plays a major role in stabilizing the planetary environment. Finally, Antarctica is one of the last remaining wilderness areas on earth.

Scientific Value

Antarctica's importance as a scientific laboratory was recognized officially by the signing of the Antarctic Treaty in 1959.[53] Article II of the Treaty states that freedom of scientific investigation and cooperation shall continue.[54] Moreover, all scientific research is supposed to be shared.[55] As a result, Antarctica is host to some fifty science stations operated by twenty-one different countries. The largest such station, the United States' McMurdo Station, is home to approximately 1200 scientists during the summer months.[56]

Antarctica offers scientists ideal opportunities to study global environmental problems, including sea-level change, global climate, and global levels of atmospheric constituents such as ozone. In recent years, Antarctica's importance as a scientific laboratory increased due to greater awareness of these problems. Antarctica's isolation from the rest of the planet, combined with its harsh climate, makes it relatively unaffected by man. Therefore, it provides a base line for studies on global pollution of various kinds.[57]

Antarctica already has provided scientists with a number of important findings. Its snow and ice contain a history of the earth's pollution levels over the last few hundred thousand years.[58] The discovery of a hole in the ozone was made by Antarctic scientists.[59] Antarctic scientists are able to monitor global warming by measuring carbon dioxide levels in the otherwise unpolluted Antarctic atmosphere.[60] Theories about the impact of the greenhouse effect on the global sea level came from research in Antarctica.[61] By studying the West Antarctic Ice Sheet, scientists were able to determine that a temperature rise of five degrees centigrade will cause the ice shelves to disintegrate, leading to a rise of five meters in the world's sea level.[62] Antarctica's importance as a scientific laboratory depends on the existence of a relatively undisturbed ecosystem.[63] Negative impacts of mineral exploration might threaten the continent's scientific value.[64]

Global Significance

Scientists have just begun to understand Antarctica's importance in stabilizing the global environment. Antarctica represents the planet's thermostat. Even in mid-summer, the Antarctic atmosphere serves as a global heat sink, drawing warm air from other continents and thus keeping them cooler than they otherwise would be.[65] Furthermore, its volume of ice effectively controls world sea level.[66]

The seas surrounding Antarctica are also important. The Southern Ocean teems with tiny zooplankton called krill.[67] The principal Antarctic krill concentrations lie within 200 miles of the continent in an area geologists believe is promising for oil exploration.[68] Almost all the other species in the Southern Ocean depend on krill for survival. Many predator species, such as whales, migrate throughout the world. Thus, a decrease in the population of the Antarctic krill would cause a decline in whale species worldwide.[69]

Wilderness

Several environmental organizations argue that mineral exploration should be banned from Antarctica because of the continent's significance as one of the last undisturbed areas on the earth's surface.[70] In many ways this "wilderness argument" mirrors the two previous arguments. The argument from science stresses Antarctica's importance as a base line study area.[71] The argument about the Antarctic's importance in balancing the global environment stresses the vital role Antarctica plays in keeping the planet livable.[72] Both of those arguments emphasize Antarctica's benefit for human science and research.

The wilderness argument, in contrast to others, contends that the continent should be protected regardless of its scientific or global importance because it is important to preserve some areas of the planet from the influence of humanity.[73] Preserving the natural state of Antarctica could benefit humankind. For example, one could argue that Antarctica must be preserved so that future generations can experience what "true" wilderness is like. By keeping part of the planet unaffected by human intervention, future generations will be able to assess the changes that man has wrought to determine their relative value and harm. Nonetheless, at its root the wilderness argument is not based in utilitarianism. Rather, those who argue for preserving Antarctica as wilderness believe that some areas of the planet are sacred and should be left alone.

Section III: The Legal Regime

The Antarctic Treaty

The Antarctic Treaty was a natural outgrowth of the history of the continent. After a period of exploration, colonial powers began to claim parts of Antarctica. By the mid-1950s, seven countries—Argentina, Australia, Chile, France, New Zealand, and the United Kingdom—had laid claim to sections of the continent based upon the notions of discovery, occupation, geographic connections, and historic rights.[74] The claimants divided the continent into slices radiating from the South Pole.[75] The British, Chilean, and Argentine claims overlapped.[76] Five other countries—Belgium, Japan, South Africa, the Soviet Union, and the United States—operated in Antarctica, but refrained from making any claims of territory.[77] These five nations also refused to honor claims made by the others.[78]

In 1957–1958, the twelve nations active in Antarctica participated in a year of scientific cooperation and experimentation known as the International Geophysical Year.[79] This cooperation led to the negotiation of the Antarctic Treaty.[80] The Treaty protects the continent as a research preserve with nations freely exchanging scientific information. The Treaty applies to the area south of sixty degrees latitude, including ice shelves, but not to the areas of high seas, where the rights of international law controls.[81]

To ensure friendly relations, the Treaty parties agreed that "Antarctica shall be used for peaceful purposes only," and they banned "any measures of a military nature."[82] The Treaty also created the world's first nuclear-free zone.[83] To further the atmosphere of cooperation, the Treaty provides for the free exchange of scientific information, personnel, and observations.[84] It also provides for verification procedures, under which "all areas of Antarctica, including all stations, installations and equipment . . . and all ships and aircraft at points of discharging or embarking cargoes and personnel in Antarctica . . . shall be open at all times to inspection" by observers designated by any one Consultative Party.[85]

Article IV of the Treaty solved, at least temporarily, the deepest conflict between the Treaty parties—conflicts between those claiming sovereignty and those who refused to recognize those claims. Article IV states:

> Nothing contained in the present Treaty . . . nor acts or activities taking place while the Treaty is in force . . . shall prejudice the respective positions of the parties in regard to territorial claims or constitute a basis for asserting, supporting or denying a claim to territorial sovereignty in Antarctica or create any rights of sovereignty. . . ."[86]

Article IV helped to stabilize a web of competing national interests: among claimants; between claimants and nonclaimants; between the superpowers; and between rich nations able to maintain Antarctic presences and smaller ones, like Belgium and South Africa, which barely have done so.[87] By ignoring the sovereignty issue, the Consultative Parties were able to create a Treaty System.

The Treaty's most impressive achievement has been its durability. This durability is due largely to Article IX. Article IX calls for regular meetings "at suitable intervals and places, for the purpose of exchanging information, consulting together on matters of common interest pertaining to Antarctica and formulating, considering and recommending to their Governments measures in furtherance of the principles and objectives of the Treaty."[88] Because of Article IX, a series of meetings have been held since 1959. These meetings have resulted in a comprehensive system of rules and regulations known as the Antarctic Treaty System.[89] The Antarctic Treaty System includes three formal treaties that the Consultative Parties have negotiated, adopted, and ratified. It also includes numerous less formal agreements known as recommendations.[90] These additional recommendations and treaties fill gaps left by the original Treaty.

In 1964, the Consultative Parties adopted the first of these treaties, the Agreed Measures for the Conservation of Antarctic Fauna and Flora. The Agreed Measures protects native Antarctic mammals and birds and preserves several areas as off limits from human interference.[91] In 1972, the Consultative Parties adopted the second treaty, the London Convention for the Conservation of Antarctic Seals. This Convention prohibits the taking of some seal species and sets quotas on other species. Enforcement depends on self-policing by the signatory nations.[92] In 1980, in response to heavy fishing, the Consultative Parties adopted the Canberra Convention on the Conservation of Antarctic Marine Living Resources (CAMLR).[93] CAMLR calls for the conservation and management of all living resources within Antarctica's ecosystem. Like the Seal Convention, enforcement is left to the individual nations.

The Antarctic Treaty peacefully coordinated all the nations with interests in Antarctica. Unfortunately, it has several significant weaknesses. First, some observers contend that the Treaty creates an exclusive club giving the wealthier nations control over Antarctica.[94] Although Article VIII permits any member of the United Nations to accede to the treaty by ratifying it, a nation cannot become a voting member of the Treaty (a Consultative Party) unless it engages in "substantial scientific research activity."[95] Currently thirty-nine nations have acceded, of which twenty-two are Consultative Parties.[96] More than three-fourths of the world's population is now represented.[97] Nevertheless, to become a Consultative Party, a nation must be wealthy enough to undertake a scientific research program.[98]

A second weakness is the Treaty System's lack of enforcement mechanisms. Because the Treaty ignores territorial claims, it is difficult to determine which nations are responsible for environmental problems. Consultative Parties have been hesitant to criticize each other's environmental records. For example, in the early 1980s the French started to construct an airfield at Dumont d'Urville in an area they had claimed in the years before the Treaty.[99] While preparing the landing strip, they injured and killed many penguins and other birds and destroyed the habitat of others.[100] None of the Consultative Parties responded to the French actions.[101] The French government stopped the project only after Greenpeace put pressure on them.[102] The lack of any enforcement provisions in the Treaty can result in significant environmental damage before any international pressure is exerted.

CRAMRA

CRAMRA is the most recent treaty signed by the Consultative Parties. After it was negotiated, CRAMRA was heralded as "one of the strongest pacts of environmental protection that has ever been negotiated."[103] However, support for CRAMRA has waned. At the most recent Antarctic Treaty meeting held in Chile in December 1990, the Treaty members divided over the issue of future mineral exploitation in Antarctica.[104] Approximately ten nations wanted a permanent ban on mineral exploration.[105] Others, led by Britain and Japan, wanted to revive CRAMRA.[106] At the present time, CRAMRA does not have the votes it needs to be ratified and probably never will be revived.[107] Instead, a majority of the Consultative Parties support the World Park proposal.[108]

Despite its current lack of support, CRAMRA still represents one possible solution to dealing with future mineral exploitation conflicts. Moreover, it has been at the center of the current controversy over the future of Antarctica. Many nations, including the United States, supported CRAMRA until recently.[109] Some of these nations still support some kind of minerals regime. As a result, CRAMRA may be utilized by negotiators as a framework for any future minerals negotiations. CRAMRA presents a possible solution to the uncertainty about the validity of mineral prospecting in Antarctica.

CRAMRA's proponents contend that CRAMRA will protect the environment while easing tensions over mineral development. Furthermore, they argue that the World Park proposal is unrealistic in light of our global demand for scarce resources.[110] By addressing both environmental and mineral concerns, CRAMRA will allow the Treaty System to remain intact. Because CRAMRA is the result of years of negotiations, the Consultative Parties may have difficulty formulating such an agreement again.[111]

The history of minerals and negotiations supports the arguments of CRAMRA's proponents. When the Antarctic Treaty was negotiated in 1959, the minerals issue was so controversial that the subject of minerals exploration and exploitation was ignored. If it had been pursued, the parties would not have agreed to a Treaty at all.[112] Partially in response to concerns about minerals development, the original signatories to the Treaty agreed that the Treaty would run for only thirty years, at which time it would be open to review and renegotiation.[113] From 1959 until 1972, it was not even possible to discuss the subject of minerals exploitation at any of the Consultative Meetings.[114] The combination of the shock from oil shortages in the mid-1970s and the growing knowledge of the potential for oil in offshore Antarctic areas made it increasingly difficult for Treaty members to ignore the minerals issue.[115] Knowing that the Treaty would be open for renegotiation in 1991, and feeling increased international pressure from the developing world in the United Nations General Assembly, the Consultative Parties began to fear that if they did not address the minerals issue, the international community might make it more difficult for them to control Antarctic policy.[116] CRAMRA was negotiated in this political climate.[117]

The first real action on the minerals question was taken at the Ninth Consultative Meeting in London in 1977. At that time, the Consultative Parties were receiving criticism from the United Nations General Assembly for their domination of Antarctic matters. After the Law of the Sea Conference in 1974, the "Group of 77"[118] voted to establish a one-nation, one-vote organization to oversee deep-sea mining.[119] The Group of 77 then turned their attention to Antarctica. They argued that the continent should be incorporated into the Law of the Sea Conference as part of the common heritage of mankind.[120] The Group of 77 argued that the United Nations should govern Antarctica according to a one-nation, one-vote organization. The Group of 77's demands frightened the Consultative Parties into beginning serious minerals negotiations.[121] The Consultative Parties did not want the United Nations to assert any influence over the region and resisted any suggestion that the United Nations should act with respect to Antarctica.[122] As a result, the Consultative Parties adopted a policy known as "voluntary restraint."[123] Under this policy, they agreed to "urge their nationals and other States to refrain from all exploration and exploitation of Antarctic mineral resources while making . . . timely adoption of an agreed regime concerning Antarctic mineral resource activities."[124]

On June 2, 1988, after six years of negotiations, CRAMRA was adopted.[125] CRAMRA seeks to balance the Antarctic Treaty's interest in protecting the environment with creating a workable system for the development of mineral resources.[126] At the same time that CRAMRA was adopted, the Consultative Parties reaffirmed the "voluntary restraint" policy in an agreement known as the Final Act of the Fourth Special Antarctic Treaty Consultative Meeting on Antarctic Mineral

Resources (Final Act).[127] The Final Act explicitly continues the policy of voluntary restraint, but goes even further by prohibiting prospecting.[128]

Although all of the Consultative Parties signed and initialed CRAMRA, it cannot come into force until it is ratified by sixteen of the twenty parties.[129] The sixteen ratifying Consultative Parties must include five developing and eleven developed countries.[130] The regime set up by CRAMRA does not contain a detailed mining code. Rather, it sets basic standards for mineral exploitation and leaves the creation of more detailed guidelines to the new institutions established by the Convention.

CRAMRA Institutions

The first and most important institution of CRAMRA is the Antarctic Mineral Resources Commission (Commission).[131] The Commission is charged with the administration of possible mineral resource activities in Antarctica.[132] The Commission decides which areas in Antarctica should be opened up for possible mineral exploration and development.[133] It also is charged with designating areas where mineral resource activities will be prohibited.[134] The Commission has the authority to place environmental conditions and guidelines on areas it opens for exploration.[135] It is also responsible for all budgetary matters,[136] including all fees and levies,[137] and the disposition of all revenues.[138]

The Commission is the only decisionmaking body set up by CRAMRA to which all of the Consultative Parties belong. Along with the Consultative Parties, other parties to the Convention that either currently are engaged in substantial research relevant to mineral resource activities, or currently are sponsoring Antarctic mineral resource exploration or development, are also members of the Commission.[139] Therefore, voting membership in the Commission is open to all countries who have previously operated in Antarctica, as well as all those who have the resources to conduct substantial research or to engage in mineral resource activities.

On substantive matters, Commission decision are taken by a three-fourths majority vote.[140] A decision to identify an area for exploration and development and decisions on budgetary matters require consensus.[141] Under the Antarctic Treaty, consensus is defined as the absence of a formal objection.[142] Procedural questions are decided by a simply majority vote.[143] When a question arises as to whether a matter is one of substance or not, that matter is treated as one of substance unless otherwise decided by three-fourths majority of the members present and voting.[144]

If the Commission decides to open an area for exploration and development, the Commission will appoint a Regulatory Committee for that area.[145] Each Committee will consist of ten members selected from Commission members, four of which must be claimants and six of which must be nonclaimants.[146] Included on the Committee must be the members that have made claims in the area being considered,[147] as well as the United States and the Soviet Union.[148] Three of the ten members must be developing countries. In addition to these ten members, the Commission member that proposed opening the area is added as a member if it is not already chosen under the preceding guidelines.[149] The proposing member will remain a member until an application for exploration is lodged. Those parties that lodge application permits and those parties whose applications result in approved Management Schemes remain Committee members while they are operating in the area.[150]

A Regulatory Committee is responsible for overseeing its assigned geographical area.[151] It promulgates detailed requirements for exploration and development consistent with the guidelines of the Commission.[152] The Regulatory Committee is the primary manager of its assigned area and has the power to set the conduct of operators in its area,[153] to issue or deny exploration permits, to enter into contracts with developers, and to suspend, modify, or cancel contracts.[154] In many ways the decisions of the Committee are final because the Commission is limited in its ability to overturn Committee decisions.[155]

Three other institutions are envisioned by CRAMRA: The Special Meeting of Parties, the Secretariat, and the Advisory Committee.[156] These institutions do not make decisions, but nevertheless have some input into the decisionmaking process. The Special Meeting of Parties is composed of all parties to CRAMRA.[157] The Special Meeting's only purpose is to present its views about whether a particular area should be opened. It is designed to give input in decisions of the Commission to all those states acceding to CRAMRA.[158] A Secretariat may be established by the Commission as necessary to support the work of the other institutions of CRAMRA.[159] The Scientific, Technical, and Environmental Advisory Committee's purposes are to give expert advice to both the Commission and the Regulatory Committees on all technical questions.[160] Membership is open to all parties to CRAMRA.[161]

Operation of CRAMRA

There are three stages to the mineral exploitation process envisioned by CRAMRA: prospecting, exploration, and development.[162] As soon as CRAMRA enters into force, any party to CRAMRA may begin prospecting in Antarctica without prior approval.[163] CRAMRA effectively overrides the Final Act because it creates a mechanism through which mineral exploitation can begin.[164] A prospector's "sponsoring state" must ensure that the prospector meets the financial and technical requirements of the Convention.[165] The sponsoring state also is responsible for notifying the Commission of the planned prospecting and providing an environmental impact assessment.[166] The sponsoring state is the nation that petitions the Commission on behalf of an operator. Operators are strictly liable for any damage caused by their activities.[167] If a prospector obtains commercially valuable information, it can keep the information secret for at least ten years.[168] A prospector, however, does not automatically gain any right to the mineral resources it discovers.[169]

A prospector who determines that an area contains viable mineral deposits may ask its sponsoring state to ask the Commission for permission to engage in exploration. Exploration is defined as activities aimed at identifying and evaluating specific mineral resource occurrences to determine their nature and size.[170] The Commission must decide by consensus to open an area for exploration.[171] If an area is opened, the Commission will set up a Regulatory Committee for the area. The Regulatory Committee accepts applications from any interested operators and then either issues an exploration permit or denies exploration. If exploration is permitted, the Regulatory Committee develops a contract or "Management Scheme." The Management Scheme gives the chosen operator exclusive rights to exploration, as well as a presumptive right to development of the specified mineral resources at a specific site within an area.[172] The Management Scheme also defines the responsibilities of the operator.

The holder of an exploration permit may apply at any time for a development permit.[173] Development is defined as activities that take place after exploration and are aimed at exploitation of mineral resource deposits.[174] Before issuing a development permit, the appropriate Regulatory Committee determines whether the original contract needs modification.[175] The Regulatory Committee may revise the original contract only if the development application modifies the planned development previously envisioned or if the development would cause previously unforeseen impacts on the Antarctic environment.[176] Once the Regulatory Committee has reviewed and approved the development permit, the operator can begin development of the resource.[177]

World Park

CRAMRA is much more detailed than the preceding summary. The foregoing section, however, provides a glimpse of the proposed system and serves as a basis for further discussion. Before examining the problems of CRAMRA, this Article explains the World Park proposal. Those who have attacked CRAMRA because they thought it would be destructive to the Antarctic environment have generally supported the idea of creating a World Park. To facilitate the comparison of the two regimes, the following section briefly describes the World Park option.

The World Park idea originated at the Second World Conference on National Parks in 1972.[178] The Conference's participants unanimously voted to delimit the Antarctic as an international park.[179] Since that time, several environmental groups persistently have urged the Consultative Parties to set Antarctica aside as a World Park. Their World Park proposal would be easy to implement. The proposal advocated by Greenpeace is a prototype of the environmentalists' proposals.[180] Greenpeace contends that there is no need to replace the Antarctic Treaty System. As a result, Antarctica would remain demilitarized and free of nuclear activity. Scientific research would continue to be given top priority on the continent, and there would be even greater coordination of scientific programs. The Greenpeace proposal is essentially a continuation of the status quo with a ban on mineral exploration and development.[181]

To enforce the ban on mineral exploration and development, an Antarctica Environmental Protection Agency (AEPA) would be created.[182] The AEPA would undertake independent investigations and assessments of proposed scientific activities, conduct inspections of base facilities, monitor operations, and prepare environmental regulations for all activities taking place on the continent.[183]

Until recently, Greenpeace's proposal was supported only by a small group of environmental organizations.[184] In 1984, the Consultative Parties would not even consider the idea of a World Park.[185] In August 1989, however, France and Australia announced that they would support protecting the continent as a World Park.[186] Because ratification of CRAMRA required their support, their announcement indicated that CRAMRA was in trouble. Following their announcement, Senator

Albert Gore introduced in the United States Senate a resolution that rejected CRAMRA and called for a stronger Antarctic agreement that would preserve Antarctica as a global ecological commons that would be closed to the commercial exploitation of oil and mineral resources.[187] In October 1990, the United States House of Representatives approved a ban on mining operations in Antarctica.[188] Today, the World Park proposal appears a more politically viable option than CRAMRA.

Section IV: CRAMRA or a World Park

This article seeks to determine which proposal, CRAMRA or the World Park, is better for the Antarctic environment. At first glance, the obvious answer may seem to be the World Park. By preventing any minerals development, a world park necessarily would result in greater protection. There could be no risk of environmental harm if minerals were not being exploited. Upon a closer look, however, the case is not as clear. Political influences may make the world park idea unworkable. Consequently, it may be better to have a legal system like CRAMRA that could regulate mineral exploitation in the Antarctic. This section will analyze arguments for and against each proposal.

The Argument for CRAMRA

CRAMRA's proponents argue that, absent an agreement like CRAMRA, there will be unregulated exploitation of Antarctica's resources. They base their argument on several assumptions. First, CRAMRA's proponents claim that mineral exploitation currently is permitted under the Antarctic Treaty System. If CRAMRA is not ratified and mineral exploitation occurs, the Antarctic environment will be without protection. Second, even if the Consultative Parties prohibit mineral exploitation, the pressure to drill for oil may become so great that the Consultative Parties will allow oil to be drilled without creating necessary safeguards. Third, CRAMRA proponents argue that failure to enter into a minerals regime similar to CRAMRA may cause a breakdown of the entire Treaty System.

The Antarctic Treaty Permits Exploration

Supporters of CRAMRA argue that failure to ratify CRAMRA will result in unacceptable environmental risks. They argue that the Antarctic Treaty currently permits mineral exploitation activities as long as such activities are consistent with the principles of the Antarctic Treaty.[189] The Treaty is not expensive, and it proscribes only enumerated activities.[190] Since the Treaty does not address mineral development, it does not prevent mineral exploitation in Antarctica.

Forces other than the Treaty, which could prevent a nation from acting unilaterally to exploit Antarctica's minerals, may have limited value. While a fear of causing an international dispute could deter some nations from exploiting Antarctica's minerals, that fear might be outweighed by a nation's substantial demand for scarce resources. Moreover, some nations may believe that their exploitation activities will not be challenged strongly. For example, the official position in the United States is that mineral exploitation activities are permitted as long as they conform to the principles of the Antarctic Treaty System.[191] Thus, in the absence of a minerals convention, the United States might decide to act unilaterally.[192]

Political Pressures Will Result in Exploration

Proponents of CRAMRA have argued that the agreement is necessary to avoid an unregulated scramble of mineral prospecting in Antarctica.[193] Neither the Antarctic Treaty nor the Final Act prevents mineral exploration. A party legitimately could claim that the Final Act was only valid while CRAMRA was being negotiated.[194] Because CRAMRA has not been ratified, the Final Act is no longer valid. Therefore, mineral exploration presently is permitted in Antarctica, and no environmental protections are in place.

Supporters of a minerals regime believe that oil will be discovered in Antarctica soon. Unless a minerals regime is in place before discovery, the pressure to exploit known resources will be tremendous.[195] Supporters argue that some countries may want to develop Antarctic oil fields even if they are not profitable. For example, an energy-poor country like Japan might undertake unprofitable production to obtain an assured source of supply.[196] Additionally, some countries may even try to use mineral exploration and development as a way of bolstering their sovereignty claims.[197] More importantly, as the world's oil demand increases, and as stability in the Middle East decreases, some nations could face petroleum shortages. These nations may view Antarctica's resources as a solution to domestic difficulties caused by oil shortages.

CRAMRA's proponents argue that, as a result of the pressures, the absence of a minerals regime will not prevent exploitation. Some nations will take unilateral actions without consulting the Consultative Parties. Alternatively, the Consultative Parties themselves will feel pressure to allow oil exploitation. If there is a minerals regime in place, however, the Consultative Parties can ensure that the Antarctic environment is protected.

CRAMRA's Defeat May Cause the Treaty's Defeat

A third argument supporting the Convention concerns the future of the Antarctic Treaty itself. In the absence of the Convention, not only will unregulated oil exploration occur, but conflicts over oil could lead to the breakdown of the entire Antarctic Treaty System. Under the terms of the Final Act, all mineral prospecting is prohibited.[198] The prohibition, however, has been largely ignored. Numerous ships currently engaging in "scientific exploration" actually are searching for oil.[199] If an oil field is found before CRAMRA is ratified, the pressure to drill for oil could be substantial. A claimant nation could assert that it has sovereignty over the mineral strike and begin exploiting it. A nonclaimant nation simply could begin exploitation by arguing that the Treaty System does not forbid exploitation. Any unilateral action of this kind could create intense disagreement among Consultative Parties and consequently put the entire Treaty System in jeopardy. The breakdown of the Treaty could result in a return to those elements that were present before the Treaty's negotiation in 1959, namely: the possibility of an arms race in Antarctica, a revival of territorial claims, and the uncertainty of a continent without any rules.[200]

If geologists' theories are correct, one of the exploring nations probably will strike an oil reserve. The results of scientific testing are supposed to be shared with the other Treaty members to prevent the countries from hoarding information or from engaging in illegal pursuits like mineral exploration. This requirement, however, is difficult to enforce. The Japanese Agency of Natural Resources and Energy (ANRE), under the control of the powerful Ministry of International Trade and Industry (MITI), has prospected in the Antarctic under the guise of "scientific research."[201] The Japanese, however, have not published any details of ANRE's work.[202] All of the other Antarctic powers also have been exploring actively for oil in Antarctica.[203] This increased exploration activity suggests that the prospectors think that there is a real possibility of finding a major offshore oil or gas field.

Hence, proponents of the Treaty argue that the Antarctic environment will be protected much more effectively if there is some legal framework governing it. Without a minerals regime, the Consultative

Parties will be unable to control oil exploration, and the entire Treaty System could collapse. Under either scenario, the Antarctic environment would be in trouble.

The Argument for a World Park

To be workable, the World Park proposal needs to answer CRAMRA proponents' concerns about a legal collapse in Antarctica if a minerals regime is not adopted. In addition, the World Park proposal needs to present a viable choice. The proposal must be workable and must protect the Antarctic environment. The following section evaluates the World Park option from these two angles. First, it explains why CRAMRA will fail to protect the Antarctic environment and why a World Park should succeed. Second, it explains why CRAMRA proponents are incorrect in claiming that the absence of CRAMRA will lead to a legal vacuum.

World Park Will Protect Antarctica's Environment

A World Park is needed because of the importance and fragility of the Antarctic environment.[204] It is difficult to imagine any oil regime that would not destroy the fragile Antarctic ecosystem. Even the United States Department of State's environmental impact statement says that "future exploration and exploitation of mineral resources in Antarctica could result in significant harm to its environment."[205] The impact statement recognizes two types of impacts. The first impact is the release of "large amounts" of crude oil into the Southern Ocean from tanker accidents and well blowouts. The second impact is damage to onshore ecosystems from the operation of support facilities. Both of these impacts could overwhelm the fragile Antarctic environment.

Offshore oil drilling may not yet be possible in the harsh Antarctic environment. Therefore, it is impossible to predict all the difficulties that will be encountered.[206] Even if oil operators were to use perfect technology, accidents still could result from human error. A recent United States government study determined that those operating in Arctic and Antarctic regions are virtually certain to have accidents.[207] Furthermore, the Antarctic climate will greatly exacerbate the effects of such accidents.[208] For example, if a blowout were to occur at an offshore well, it would be difficult to stop the flow of oil. This would be especially true during the nine months of the year when the sea is covered with ice.

An oil spill can destroy the local ecosystem. It even may weaken the entire continent's well-being because the Antarctic krill, which form the bottom of the marine food chain, will be contaminated.[209] Spilled oil will be difficult to clean up. Oil takes much longer to degrade in the cold Antarctic temperatures than in warmer climates.[210] The recovery rate on land is also slow. Construction of oil storage facilities, tanker ports, or the exploitation of minerals on the dry land areas of Antarctica would involve permanent environmental disturbances.[211]

Minor oil spills have occurred in Antarctica demonstrating the effects of oil on the continent's ecosystem.[212] The largest oil spill to date in Antarctica occurred when the *Bahai Paraiso* ran into submerged rocks, spilling 170,000 gallons of diesel fuel into the ocean.[213] After this relatively minor spill, about fifty percent of the limpets,[214] the food source for kelp gulls, died.[215] Studies report that the animals most affected by oil spills are those that regularly move in and out of the water.[216] Hence, penguin and seal colonies would be extremely sensitive to even a small isolated spill.[217]

There are other unacceptable consequences of Antarctic oil exploration. Antarctica plays a major role in regulating the global climate. Some scientists fear that a rise in particulate matter caused by pollution associated with oil and mineral development could alter the ability of Antarctica's ice cap to reflect the sun's heat, thus causing the atmosphere to warm.[218] Furthermore, an increase in pollution will ruin Antarctica as a global laboratory for monitoring worldwide pollution levels.[219] In sum, any mineral exploitation in Antarctica will result in significant environmental impacts. Even CRAMRA recognizes environmental hazards by providing for safeguards before oil exploration can begin.[220]

CRAMRA Will Not Protect the Antarctic Environment

CRAMRA's environmental protection provisions will not be able to protect the Antarctic environment properly. CRAMRA is weak because it lacks strong enforcement measures and is ambiguous. Article 4 of CRAMRA ostensibly provides enough environmental safeguards to prevent destruction of the Antarctic.[221] CRAMRA appears to contain relatively strict environmental protection measures.[222] The Commission must vote by consensus to open an area for exploration, and any single Consultative Party can veto exploration.[223] Nevertheless, judging from the Treaty members' past performance,[224] it is unlikely that members will want to create dissension. Throughout the history of the Treaty, the Consultative Parties have hesitated to criticize one another.[225] The lack of criticism when the French injured wildlife while building an airstrip at Dumont d'Urville illustrates this hesitation.[226] Many scientific bases in Antarctica have failed to comply with a number of the Consultative Party regulations.[227] For example, there have been a number of complaints about waste disposal in Antarctica,[228] and areas near research stations are badly polluted.[229]

The Consultative Parties have failed to enforce environmental rules in the past when there was not much economic and political pressure to develop Antarctica's mineral resources. Once oil is discovered, it is doubtful that the Consultative Parties will have the political will to enforce stringent environmental requirements. If the international demand for oil becomes stronger, Commission members may begin to see CRAMRA's requirements as an impediment to their domestic oil demands. Because the interpretation of CRAMRA is up to those states that will benefit from any oil development, they may choose to open areas to exploitation even though such an action will result in substantial environmental damage.

There also may be difficulties enforcing CRAMRA's liability sections. Under the terms of CRAMRA, a multinational corporation can choose which country will be its sponsoring state. Because the sponsoring state is responsible for making sure that an operator complies with CRAMRA's requirements, an operator may try to choose those sponsoring states that interpret CRAMRA leniently. Furthermore, developing nations, hoping to obtain a foothold in Antarctica, may be inclined to pass less strict rules to attract operators. The international community suddenly may find multinational oil companies negotiating deals with cash-starved developing nations to operate joint ventures in Antarctica. The results could be devastating.

In addition to enforcement problems, CRAMRA contains dozens of ambiguous terms. For example, under article 4, no mineral activity is allowed if the activity will cause *significant* adverse effects on air and water quality. Article 4 also states that the Commission should not make decisions about Antarctic mineral resource activities without *adequate* information. Terms such as "significant," "adequate," "reasonably," and "appropriate" are never defined. Instead, the parties are supposed to interpret the terms if a conflict arises. Unfortunately, the terms will be interpreted by Consultative Parties at a time when they themselves will have an interest in exploiting Antarctic oil. At that time, it is improbable that the Commission will interpret the terms in a manner unfavorable to themselves.

Applicability of International Law

Despite CRAMRA's weaknesses, its proponents believe that a minerals regime is the only viable option in light of global geopolitics. CRAMRA proponents claim that, in the absence of the Convention, international law would permit a nation unilaterally to begin exploiting minerals in Antarctica. The following sections discuss why these arguments of political necessity are misguided.

Functional Argument

The first reason nations will refrain from unilaterally exploiting minerals in Antarctica is functional. It is unlikely that any nation or corporation would invest the large amount of capital necessary to fund Antarctic mineral exploitation without a guarantee that their claims could stand up under international law. Nations also might worry that they could lose their investment because of a military confrontation. While most nations have engaged in preliminary prospecting, they have done so thinking CRAMRA would be ratified. Those who have expressed an interest in Antarctic minerals have said that they need a minerals regime in place before they will invest in exploitation. To invest in exploitation without any regime would be far too risky.[230]

Legal Argument

The second reason nations will refrain from unilaterally exploiting minerals in Antarctica is legal. CRAMRA proponents contend that in the absence of a minerals regime, any party legally may drill for oil as long as they abide by the Antarctic Treaty. This argument assumes that no other international law applies in Antarctica. This assumption is mistaken. Antarctica's legal status is controversial because it is unclear whether claims of sovereignty in Antarctica are valid, or whether the continent is outside of any sovereign's jurisdiction. Despite this confusion, there are international laws that apply in each instance. In addition, the entire Antarctic Treaty System is binding on parties to those agreements. Regardless of how the disputed legal issue of sovereignty is resolved, there is a web of international law that will apply.[231]

All generally applicable rules of international law apply to Antarctica in the same way they do elsewhere. International law includes specific international duties that apply to the protection of the environment. The first duty prohibits international environmental interference.[232] This duty prevents a state from causing harmful consequences to the environment of other states, or to areas outside national jurisdiction. This duty is manifested in international agreements. For example, The Stockholm Declaration on the Human Environment (Stockholm Declaration) declares that all states have a duty to prevent harm to the environment.[233] The second duty calls upon the states to cooperate in the duty of preventing and abating international pollution.[234]

If Antarctica is considered an international commons like the deep seabeds or outer space, then mineral activities there would be governed by international law. Because exploring for oil in Antarctica necessarily would involve detrimental environmental impacts, those impacts would be considered a violation of the international duty to prevent environmental degradation of common areas. From the Stockholm Declaration, as well as from other sources in international law,[235] it is reasonable to argue that a country can act to prevent harm to the Antarctic environment before any exploitation occurs, by bringing a case before either the International Court of Justice or the United Nations. Several international court cases have ruled that nations have a duty to prevent environmental degradation outside their national boundaries.[236]

If Antarctica is not an international commons, then those nations with Antarctic claims may assert that international law does not apply because they are operating inside their own jurisdiction. Nevertheless, international law still may apply to their activities. For the past thirty years, Antarctica has been functioning in a legal "twilight zone" between an international commons and state sovereignty. Throughout this period, Antarctica has been subject to the rules of international customary law. Under international customary law, norms first articulated in international agreements can develop into customary international law.[237] Since all the parties that have had contact with Antarctica during the past thirty years have shown their allegiance to the Treaty, it is likely that the treaty has been enveloped by international law. "The process by which [The Antarctic Treaty] gives rise to a norm of customary law establishes new law which is separate from the originating treaty and would not change directly if that Treaty were to be modified or terminated."[238] Hence, in the thirty years since the Antarctic Treaty System was adopted, the nations of the world have conformed to it either as signatories to the Treaty, or tacitly by accepting its rules. As a result, the Treaty System has been adopted as an international custom, and any nation that drilled for oil would be violating international law.

Section V: Conclusion

Although CRAMRA probably has been defeated, its supporters still think that some sort of a minerals convention is needed to establish a regulatory regime in Antarctica. However, regimes like CRAMRA provide little protection. Rather, they provide the framework that multinational companies need to begin drilling for oil. Furthermore, if CRAMRA is not ratified, Antarctic mineral exploitation cannot proceed without violating international law. It is doubtful that any corporation will invest significant capital in oil exploration without the security of international approval.

The World Park proposal, in contrast, is simple and workable. By declaring Antarctica a World Park, the Consultative Parties will dissuade any party from continuing to search for oil. By preventing the discovery of oil, the World Park proposal will reduce the danger of environmental damage that would accompany oil exploitation. Additionally, by creating an Antarctic Environmental Protection Agency, the Consultative Parties would be creating an institution that could enforce international environmental laws effectively.

Notes

1. "Antarctica: Highest, Coldest, Darkest, Driest," *Calypso Log*, Apr. 1989, at 12 [hereinafter *Calypso Log*].
2. See generally Multilateral Antarctic Treaty, Dec. 1, 1959, 12 U.S.T. 794, T.I.A.S. No. 4780, 402 U.N.T.S. 71 [hereinafter Antarctic Treaty]. As of June 1988, 19 nations were voting members of the Antarctic Treaty System. These voting members, referred to as "Consultative Parties," were Argentina, Belgium, Brazil, Chile, China, France, German Democratic Republic, Federal Republic of Germany, India, Italy, Japan, New Zealand, Norway, Poland, South Africa, Union of Soviet Socialist Republics, United Kingdom, United States, and Uruguay.

   In addition to the Consultative Parties, thirteen "Contracting Parties," or "Non-Consultative Parties," initialed CRAMRA. These parties are nations that have agreed to the terms of the Treaty System, but have not done sufficient scientific research to become Consultative Parties. The Contracting Parties were Bulgaria, Canada, Czechoslovakia, Denmark, Ecuador, Finland, Greece, Republic of Korea, Netherlands, Papua New Guinea, Peru, Romania, and Sweden.
3. Convention on the Regulation of Antarctic Mineral Resource Activities,

opened for signature Nov. 25, 1988, 27 I.L.M. 859 [hereinafter CRAMRA].

4. Id., preamble, at 868.

5. See Crawford, "Antarctic Conference Ends in Dismal Failure," *Fin. Times,* Dec. 8, 1990, § 1, at 2.

6. See Hunt, "Campaign for Mining Ban Splits Antarctic Nations," *The Independent,* Dec. 6, 1990, at 15.

7. Id.

8. See Bogart, "On Thin Ice: Can Antarctica Survive the Gold Rush?" *Greenpeace,* Sept.-Oct. 1988, at 7, 8.

9. *U.S. Office of Technology Assessment, Polar Prospects: A Minerals Treaty for Antarctica* 126 (1989) [hereinafter *Polar Prospects*].

10. *U.S. Central Intelligence Agency, Polar Regions Atlas* 35–39 (1978).

11. *Polar Prospects,* supra note 9, at 126.

12. Id.

13. J. May, *The Greenpeace Book of Antarctica* 16 (1988).

14. B. Brewster, *Antarctica: Wilderness at Risk* 5 (1982).

15. 13 *The New Encyclopedia Britannica* 847 (15th ed. 1975).

16. *Polar Prospects,* supra note 9, at 126.

17. J. May, supra note 13, at 16.

18. *Polar Regions Atlas,* supra note 10, at 35.

19. B. Brewster, supra note 14, at 1.

20. *Polar Regions Atlas,* supra note 10, at 36.

21. J. May, supra note 13, at 30.

22. Swithinbank, "The Ice Shelves," in *Antarctica* 202 (T. Hatherton ed. 1965).

23. J. May, supra note 13, at 18.

24. H. King, *The Antarctic* 2 (1969).

25. As early as 1969, the governments of the United States, Australia, and New Zealand were approached by commercial interests for prospecting rights in Antarctica. In 1969, New Zealand received an application for developing a large area for petroleum. In 1970, Texaco asked the United States how it could obtain a license for oil exploration in the Atlantic section of Antarctica. In 1979–1980, Gulf was reported to have had a survey ship working in the South Georgia area, and the company proposed joint surveys between the government and private companies. As a global strategy, Gulf "is raising cash to carry out the huge programme of [Antarctic] exploration that alone will ensure its survival as a leading force in the world's oil supply." B. Brewster, supra note 14, at 90. See also Friedheim & Akaha, "Antarctic Resources and International Law: Japan, the United States, and the Future of Antarctica," 16 *Ecology L.Q.* 119, 133–34 (1989) (reporting that in 1975, Texas Geophysical requested from the United States exclusive rights to explore the Ross and Weddell Seas, but was turned down).

Several nations also have engaged in mineral exploration in Antarctica. The United States, Norway, Germany, Japan, Great Britain, France, the U.S.S.R., and Poland all have been searching recently for oil under the guise of purely scientific research despite a moratorium on commercial exploration for resources. See Luard, "Who Owns the Antarctic," 1984 *Foreign Aff.* 1175. In 1985, the German ship *Polarstern* found evidence that rock just beneath the sea floor contained organic material suggestive of petroleum at lower depths. In late 1986, a New Zealand team drilled into the Ross Sea and found a six-foot-thick layer of sand stained by a waxy hydrocarbon residue indicating that petroleum had existed there in the past. See Mitchell, "Undermining Antarctica: A Pact to Regulate Mineral Exploitation in Antarctica Threatens That Unique Environment," *Tech. Rev.,* Feb.-Mar. 1988, at 48. More recently, the Japanese Agency of Natural Resources and Energy (ANRE) has been exploring for minerals in the seas surrounding Antarctica. See Friedheim & Akaha, supra, at 138.

26. *Polar Prospects*, supra note 9, at 93.

27. See generally Elliot, "Tectronics of Antarctica: A Review," 275A *Am. J. Sci.* 45 (1976).

28. Id.

29. *Polar Prospects,* supra note 9, at 99.

30. For a discussion of the current knowledge of hard mineral wealth in Antarctica, see D. Shapely, *The Seventh Continent: Antarctica in a Resource Age* 134–45 (1985).

31. See id. at 138–39.

32. Id. at 124.

33. Id.

34. Id. at 130.

35. Id.

36. *Polar Prospects,* supra note 9, at 107–09.

37. B. Brewster, supra note 14, at 89.

38. D. Shapely, supra note 30, at 124–25.

39. Id.

40. Id.

41. Id. In 1979, a representative of Gulf Oil stated that the oil potential of the two most likely areas in the Ross and Weddell Seas was in the range of 50 billion barrels, but probably much more. By comparison, the North Slope oilfield of Alaska is believed to contain 8 billion barrels. Id.

42. B. Brewster, supra note 14, at 89.

43. D. Shapely, supra note 30, at 124.

44. B. Brewster, supra note 14, at 93.

45. See F.M. Auburn, *Antarctic Law and Politics* 248 (1982).

46. A. Parsons, *Antarctica: The Next Decade* 91 (1987).

47. Id.

48. Id.
49. Id, at 92.
50. Id.
51. Id.
52. Id. at 93.
53. See infra notes 79–90 and accompanying text.
54. Antarctic Treaty, supra note 2, art. II, 12 U.S.T. at 795, T.I.A.S. No. 4780, at 2, 402 U.N.T.S. at 74.
55. Id. art. III, 12 U.S.T. at 796, T.I.A.S. No. 4780, at 3, 402 U.N.T.S. at 74 (stating that scientific program plans, personnel, observations, and results shall be freely exchanged).
56. Bogart, supra note 8, at 37.
57. B. Brewster, supra note 14, at 37.
58. See *Calypso Log,* supra note 1, at 14.
59. Hall, "The World's Frozen Clean Room," *Bus. Wk.,* Jan. 22, 1990, at 72.
60. B. Brewster, supra note 14, at 37, 39.
61. Id. at 39.
62. Id.
63. Id. at 37.
64. Id. at 47.
65. Id. at 38.
66. See id. at 38–39.
67. "Krill are delicate, transparent, shrimp-like animals, pink or ocher in color, and measuring 3 to 5 centimeters long with knobby eyes and phosphorescent lights about their legs. They tend to swarm near the surface by day appearing as great reddish patches; their nighttime swarms look like twinkling underwater galaxies." For more detailed information and photographs, see J. May, supra note 13, at 80–81.
68. See B. Brewster, supra note 14.
69. Id. at 8.
70. J. May, supra note 13, at 158.
71. See supra note 57 and accompanying text.
72. See supra notes 65–69 and accompanying text.
73. See J. May, supra note 13, at 158.
74. See D. Shapely, supra note 30, at 66–68.
75. Id. at 68.
76. Id.
77. Id. at 67–68, 78–82.
78. Id. at 63–64, 77–82.
79. Id. at 83.
80. See id. at 89.
81. B. Brewster, supra note 14, at 28.
82. Antarctic Treaty, supra note 2, art. I, 12 U.S.T. at 795, T.I.A.S. No. 4780, at 2, 402 U.N.T.S. at 72.

83. Id. art. V, 12 U.S.T. at 796, T.I.A.S. No. 4780, at 3, 402 U.N.T.S. at 76.
84. Article III reads:
    > In order to promote international cooperation in scientific investigation in Antarctica as provided for in Article II of the present Treaty, the Contracting Parties agree that, to the greatest extent feasible and practical: (a) information regarding plans for scientific programs in Antarctica shall be exchanged to permit maximum economy and efficiency of operation; (b) scientific personnel shall be exchanged in Antarctica between expeditions and stations; (c) scientific observations and results from Antarctica shall be exchanged and made freely available.

    Id. art. III, 12 U.S.T. at 796, T.I.A.S. No. 4780, at 3, 402 U.N.T.S. at 74.
85. Id. art. VII, 12 U.S.T. at 797, T.I.A.S. No. 4780, at 4, 402 U.N.T.S. at 76. A "Consultative Party" is a nation that has adopted the Treaty and been acknowledged a voting member because of its "substantial scientific research activity on the continent."
86. Id. art. IV, 12 U.S.T. at 796, T.I.A.S. No. 4780, at 3, 402 U.N.T.S. at 74.
87. D. Shapely, supra note 30, at 94.
88. Antarctic Treaty, supra note 2, art. IX, 12 U.S.T. at 798, T.I.A.S. No. 4780, at 5, 402 U.N.T.S. at 78.
89. See *Polar Prospects,* supra note 9, at 45.
90. Id. at 44. Nearly 150 recommendations have been adopted since the Treaty went into affect. A wide range of activities are now regulated, including:
    —cooperation in meteorology and in the exchange of meteorological data
    —cooperation in telecommunications, including procedures for communicating among stations in Antarctica
    —cooperation in air transport and logistics
    —control of tourism, including development of guidance for visitors to Antarctica
    —a recommended code of conduct for stations in Antarctica and recommendations for developing procedures to assess impacts of operations
    —the preservation of historical sites
91. W.M. Bush, 1 *Antarctica and International Law* 146 (1982).
92. See Convention for the Conservation of Antarctic Seals, opened for signature June 1, 1972, 29 U.S.T. 441, T.I.A.S. No. 8826, 11 I.L.M. 251; see also Siniff, "Living Resources: Seals," *Oceanus,* Summer 1988, at 71–74.
93. Convention on the Conservation of Antarctic Marine Living Resources, May 20, 1980, T.I.A.S. No. 10,240, 19 I.L.M. 841. For comment, see Lagoni, "Convention on the Conservation of Antarctic Marine Living Resources: A Model for the Use of a Common Good?" in *Antarctic Challenge* 93–108 (Wolfrum ed. 1984).
94. G. Triggs, *The Antarctic Treaty Regime* 64 (1987).

95. Antarctic Treaty, supra note 2, art. IX, 12 U.S.T. at 798, T.I.A.S. No. 4780, at 5, 402 U.N.T.S. at 79.

96. Since 1959, the following 10 nations have become Consultative Parties: Poland (1977), Federal Republic of Germany (1981), Brazil (1983), India (1983), People's Republic of China (1985), Uruguay (1985), German Democratic Republic (1987), Italy (1988), Spain (1988), and Sweden (1988). In addition, the following nations have acceded to the Treaty without conducting "sufficient scientific activity" to become a Consultative Party: Czechoslovakia, Denmark, The Netherlands, Rumania, Bulgaria, Papua New Guinea, Peru, Hungary, Finland, Cuba, Republic of Korea, Democratic Peoples Republic of Korea, Greece, Austria, Ecuador, Canada, and Colombia.

It is worth noting that almost all of the acceding members and all of the Consultative Parties did not join until after the oil crisis of 1973 and after "scientific exploration" established that Antarctica probably contains a fairly significant amount of petroleum.

97. *Polar Prospects,* supra note 9, at 45.

98. In recent years, India, Brazil, China, Uruguay, Poland, Italy, West Germany, and East Germany have become Consultative Parties, meaning they now can participate in the decisionmaking process.

99. Bogart, supra note 8, at 11.

100. Id.

101. Id.

102. Id.

103. Hall, supra note 59, at 72.

104. Crawford, supra note 5, at 8.

105. Id.

106. Id.

107. See, e.g., Hunt, supra note 6, at 15.

108. The Independent reports that New Zealand, Australia, and France led a group of 10 nations who support a permanent ban on mineral exploitation; the United States and Norway believe the parties should pass a binding moratorium on mining, followed by a regulatory framework. Id.

109. Hall, supra note 59, at 72.

110. See, e.g., Tetzeli, "Allocation of Mineral Resources in Antarctica: Problems and a Possible Solution," 10 *Hastings Int'l & Comp. L. Rev.* 525, 539–41 (1987); Rich, "A Minerals Regime for Antarctica," 31 *Int'l Comp. L.Q.* 709 (1982). The United States government also argued in favor of CRAMRA. See, e.g., *Polar Prospects,* supra note 9.

111. See infra notes 114–127.

112. Roberts, "International Co-operation for Antarctic Development: The Test for the Antarctic Treaty," 19 *Polar Rec.* 107, 111 (1978).

113. D. Shapely, supra note 30, at 97.

114. Roberts, supra note 112, at 111.

115. D. Shapely, supra note 30, at 158.
116. Id. at 218.
117. Id. at 162.
118. See generally D. Shapely, supra note 30, at 149.
119. The term "The Group of 77" refers to a group of 112 developing nations who were organized at the time of the Third United Nations Conference on the Law of the Sea, which began in 1974 in Caracas, Venezuela.
120. D. Shapely, supra note 30, at 150.
121. Id. at 218.
122. Id. at 150.
123. For a complete discussion of Recommendation IX-1, the recommendation that all Treaty parties restrain from any minerals exploration until a minerals regime is negotiated, see W.M. Bush, 1 *Antarctica and International Law* 343–47 (1982).
124. Id. at 345, para. 8.
125. For the complete text of the Convention, see CRAMRA, supra note 3.
126. CRAMRA defines mineral resources as "all non-living natural non-renewable resources, including fossil fuels, metallic and non-metallic minerals." Id. art. 1, para. 6, 27 I.L.M. at 869.
127. June 2, 1988, 27 I.L.M. 865 [hereinafter Final Act]. Many nations, however, have ignored the "voluntary restraint" agreement by conducting prospecting surveys of the hitherto unexplored Antarctic continental shelf under the guise of scientific studies. See D. Shapely, supra note 30, at 139.
128. Final Act, supra note 127, at 865.
129. CRAMRA, supra note 3, art. 62, para. 1, 27 I.L.M. at 896.
130. Id.
131. Id. art. 18, para. 1, 27 I.L.M. at 876.
132. Id. art. 21, para. 1, 27 I.L.M. at 878–79.
133. Id. art. 21, para 1(d), 27 I.L.M. at 878.
134. Id. art. 21, para 1(b), 27 I.L.M. at 878.
135. Id. art. 21, para 1(c), 27 I.L.M. at 878.
136. Id. art. 21, para. 1(o), 27 I.L.M. at 878.
137. Id. art. 21, paras. 1(p), (q), 27 I.L.M. at 878.
138. Id. art. 21, para. 1(r), 27 I.L.M. at 878.
139. Id. art. 18, para. 2, 27 I.L.M. at 876–77.
140. Id. art. 22, para. 1, 27 I.L.M. at 879.
141. Id. art. 22, paras. 2(a), (c), 27 I.L.M. at 879.
142. Id. art. 22, para. 5, 27 I.L.M. at 879.
143. Id. art. 22, para. 3, 27 I.L.M. at 879.
144. Id. art. 22, para. 1, 27 I.L.M. at 879.
145. Id. art. 29, para. 1, 27 I.L.M. at 882.
146. Id. art. 29, para. 2(c), 27 I.L.M. at 882. A claimant is a nation that has made a claim to a portion of Antarctica.

147. Id. art. 29, para. 2(a), 27 I.L.M. at 882.
148. Id. art. 29, para. 2(b), 27 I.L.M. at 882.
149. Id. art. 29, para. 6(a), 27 I.L.M. at 882–83.
150. Id. art. 29, para. 6(b), 27 I.L.M. at 883. A Management Scheme grants a party an exclusive right to exploration and prescribes the terms and conditions with which the party must comply in order to maintain such rights. Id. art. 47, 27 I.L.M. at 891.
151. Id. art. 31, 27 I.L.M. at 883.
152. Id. arts. 43(3), 47, 27 I.L.M. at 889, 891.
153. Id.
154. Id. arts. 31(1e), 51, 54, 27 I.L.M. at 883, 892–93, 893–94.
155. Id. art. 49, 27 I.L.M. at 892. Article 49 gives the Commission the right to review the Committee's decisions. However, the Commission "shall not assume the functions of the Regulatory Committee, nor shall it substitute its discretion for that of the Regulatory Committee." The Commission may only ask the Regulatory Committee to reconsider a decision. It may not overturn a decision on its own.
156. Id. arts. 23, 28, 33, 27 I.L.M. at 879, 881, 884.
157. Id. art. 28(2), 27 I.L.M. at 881.
158. Id. arts. 28, 40, 27 I.L.M. at 881–82, 888.
159. Id. art 33, 27 I.L.M. at 884.
160. Id. art. 26, 27 I.L.M. at 880–81.
161. Id. art. 23, 27 I.L.M. at 879.
162. Id. art. 1, paras. 7–10, 27 I.L.M. at 869.
163. Prospecting is the initial stage of mineral resource exploitation. CRAMRA defines prospecting as

> activities, including logistic support, aimed at identifying areas of mineral resource potential for possible exploration and development, including geological, geochemical, and geophysical investigations and field observations, the use of remote sensing techniques and collection of surface, sea floor and sub-ice samples. Such activities do not include dredging and excavations, except for the purpose of obtaining small-scale samples, or drilling, except shallow drilling into rock and sediment to depths not exceeding 25 meters or other such depth as the Commission may determine for particular circumstances.

Id. art. 1(8), 27 I.L.M. at 869.
164. For a discussion of the Final Act, see supra text accompanying notes 125–28.
165. CRAMRA, supra note 2, art. 37(3)(a), 27 I.L.M. at 886. For the definition of a sponsoring state, see id. art. 1(12), 27 I.L.M. at 869. Article 8 defines the financial and technical responsibility requirements for an operator. Id. art. 8, 27 I.L.M. at 872–73. Article 8(2) holds an operator strictly liable for: (a) damage to the Antarctic environment; (b)

damage to an established use such as the operation of scientific stations; (c) loss or damage to property of a third party or loss of life; and (d) reimbursement of reasonable costs to anyone who incurred them as a result of necessary response action where mineral activities result in, or threaten to result in, damage to the Antarctic environment. See id. art. 8(2), 27 I.L.M. at 872.

166. A sponsoring state's responsibilities are laid out in article 37(7). Id. art. 37(7), 27 I.L.M. at 886. Article 4(2) states that no mineral activity shall occur until an environmental assessment has been made. Id. art. 4(2), 27, I.L.M. at 871. The environmental assessment shall include a finding that the proposed activity would not cause:

(a) significant adverse effects on air and water quality;

(b) significant changes in atmospheric, terrestrial or marine environments;

(c) significant changes in the distribution, abundance or productivity of populations of species of fauna or flora;

(d) further jeopardy to endangered or threatened species or populations of such species; or

(e) degradation of, or substantial risk to, areas of special biological, scientific, historic, aesthetic or wilderness significance.

167. See supra note 165 for a list of some of the activities for which the operator is held strictly liable. Under article 8(4) an operator is not held liable if the damage was the result of an event constituting a natural disaster of exceptional character that reasonably could not have been foreseen or an armed conflict or an act of terrorism. Id. art. 8(4), 27 I.L.M. at 873.

168. Id. arts. 37(10), 37(12), 27 I.L.M. at 887.

169. Id. art. 37(1), 27 I.L.M. at 886.

170. Id. art. 1(9), 27 I.L.M. at 869.

171. Id. art. 41, 27 I.L.M. at 888.

172. Id. arts. 45–48, 27 I.L.M. at 890–92.

173. Id. art. 53, 27 I.L.M. at 893.

174. Id. art. 1(10), 27 I.L.M. at 869.

175. Id. art. 54(3), 27 I.L.M. at 893.

176. Id.

177. Id. art. 54(5), 27 I.L.M. at 894.

178. J. May, supra note 13, at 158.

179. Note, "Antarctic Resource Jurisdiction and the Law of the Sea: A Question of Compromise," 11 *Brooklyn J. Int'l L.* 65 n.103 (1985).

180. Greenpeace International, the International Union for the Conservation of Nature, Environmental Defense Fund, the Cousteau Society, and the Antarctic and Southern Ocean Coalition all have been active in advocating a World Park regime, and their proposals are all similar.

181. See generally J. May, supra note 13, at 158.

182. Id. at 159.

183. For an overview of the Greenpeace proposal, see id.

184. Id.

185. Id.

186. Lancaster, "U.S.-Backed Antarctic Pact Criticized; Prospecting Could Pave Way to Ecological Disaster, Opponents Say," *Wash. Post,* Sept. 30, 1989, at A17.

187. 135 *Cong. Rec. S11,906–07* (daily ed. Sept. 25, 1989) (statement of Sen. Gore).

188. See The Antarctic Protection Act, H.R. 3977, 101st Cong., 2d Sess., 136 *Cong. Rec. H9605* (1990). The Antarctic Protection Act requires the Secretary of State to negotiate international agreements to prohibit mining and to protect and to protect and preserve the Antarctic environment.

189. Although the Antarctic Treaty does not forbid mineral exploration, it contains several recommendations for protecting the environment. See Antarctic Treaty, supra note 2. The only impediment to minerals exploration in the Treaty System is the Final Act. See Final Act, supra note 127, at 865. However, the Final Act only requires parties to refrain from minerals exploration as long as progress is being made on CRAMRA negotiation. See id.

190. See Antarctic Treaty, supra note 2.

191. W. Westermeyer, *The Politics of Mineral Resources Development in Antarctica: Alternative Regimes for the Future* 28 (1986).

192. See, e.g., id.

193. See, e.g., F. Auburn, *Antarctic Law and Politics* 232 (1982). Yet the same commentator argues that a regime is needed to protect the investments of prospecting nations and corporations. See id. at 251.

194. See supra note 187.

195. Although the United States contends that the world supply of oil is now fairly stable, and that even world oil production could be sustained for about 50 years at the present rate, it still believes that a scramble to exploit oil would ensure if oil were discovered in Antarctica. See J. River, *The World's Conventional Oil Production Capability Projected into the Future by Country* 15 (1987).

196. *Polar Prospects*, supra note 9, at 113.

197. Other countries have used minerals exploration to establish sovereign claims. Before 1925, Svalbard, an archipelago north of Norway, belonged to no country. Several countries entered into a treaty that gave them rights of access to the islands. Partly to consolidate these rights, six countries subsidized mineral development in Svalbard even though they operated at a net loss. See Mitchell, supra note 25, at 55.

198. See Final Act, supra note 127, at 865.

199. D. Shapely, supra note 30, at 139.

200. See A. Parsons, supra note 46, at 14.

201. Friedheim & Akaha, supra note 25, at 143.

202. Id. at 144.

203. See supra note 25.

204. See generally Kindt, "Ice Covered Areas and the Law of the Sea: Issues Involving Resource Exploitation and the Antarctic Environment," 14 *Brooklyn J. Int'l L.* 27 (1988).

205. *U.S. Department of State, Final Environmental Impact Statement on the Negotiation of an International Regime for Antarctic Mineral Resources,* at vii (1982) [hereinafter *Final EIS*].

206. See supra text accompanying notes 43–52.

207. *U.S. Office of Technology Assessment, Oil and Gas Technologies for the Arctic and Deepwater* 163–201 (1985).

208. *National Research Council, Oil in the Sea: Inputs, Fates and Effects* 6 (1985).

209. See supra notes 67–69 and accompanying text.

210. *Central Intelligence Agency, Polar Regions Atlas* 28 (1978).

211. B. Brewster, supra note 14, at 94.

212. Spills in other locations give scientists an idea of how oil contamination will affect Antarctica. See B. Brewster, supra note 14, at 93.

213. See Hall, supra note 59.

214. A limpet is a mollusk of the intertidal regions that adheres to rocks and other shells. W. Amos & S. Amos, *The Audubon Society Nature Guide: Atlantic and Gulf Coasts* (1985).

215. "Alerting the World to Save Antarctica," *Calypso Log,* Apr. 1990, at 4.

216. B. Brewster, supra note 14, at 97.

217. "Penguin colonies along the South African coast were severely distressed by oil spilled in the collision of two tankers in 1977." Id. at 62.

218. *Final EIS,* supra note 205, at 8.

219. Id.

220. CRAMRA, supra note 3, art. 2, para. 4, 27 I.L.M. at 871. This paragraph states:

> No Antarctic mineral resource activity shall take place until it is judged, based upon assessment of its possible impacts on the Antarctic environment and on dependent and on associated ecosystems, that the activity in question would not cause:
>
> (a) significant adverse effects on air and water quality;
>
> (b) significant changes in atmospheric, terrestrial or marine environments;
>
> (c) significant changes in the distribution, abundance or productivity of populations of species of fauna or flora;
>
> (d) further jeopardy to endangered or threatened species or populations of such species; or
>
> (e) degradation of, or substantial risk to, areas of special biological, scientific, historic, aesthetic or wilderness significance.

Id.

221. See id.
222. See id. art. 8, 27 I.L.M. at 872–74.
223. Id. art. 22, 27 I.L.M. at 879.
224. See Bogart, supra note 8, at 11.
225. Id.
226. Id.
227. Id.
228. Several of the management practices used at United States Antarctic research stations would violate United States federal environmental statutes. See Bogart, supra note 8, at 10.
229. Liquid wastes have been observed being released directly into the marine environment at a number of bases. See Friends of the Earth, "Cleanup Needed: Antarctic Bases a Shambles," 48 ECO 5 (May 16, 1988).
230. See, e.g., Tempest, "France Urges Antarctic 'Nature Reserve,'" *L.A. Times,* Oct. 10, 1989, § 1, at 7, col. 1.

> A lot of countries that support ratification raise the specter of an unregulated scramble to the continent. . . . But if you talk to companies, or particularly to bankers, and ask them if they would be willing to finance unregulated exploration, they say no. What they are looking for is a framework that guarantees them the right to be there. That is what the minerals convention gives them.

Id. (quoting James N. Barnes, Executive Director of the Antarctic Project).
231. Charney, "The Antarctic System and Customary International Law," in *International Law for Antarctica* 85 (F. Francioni & T. Scouazzi eds. 1987).
232. Pineschi, "The Antarctic Treaty System and General Rules of International Environmental Law," in *International Law for Antarctica* 188 (F. Francioni & T. Scouazzi eds. 1987).
233. Stockholm Conference on the Human Environment, June 16, 1972, 11 I.L.M. 1466.
234. See, e.g., "World Charter for Nature," G.A. Res. 37–7, art. 21(d), 37 U.N. GAOR Supp. (No. 51) at 17, U.N. Doc. A/RES/37–7 (1982), reprinted in 22 I.L.M. 455 (1983); "Charter of Economic Rights and Duties of States," G.A. Res. 3281, art. 30, 29(1), U.N. GAOR Supp. (No. 31) at 50, U.N. Doc. A/RES/3281 (1974), reprinted in 14 I.L.M. 261 (1975).
235. See, e.g., Lake Lanoux Arbitration (Fr. v. Spain), 24 I.L.R. 101, 129 (1957); Trail Smelter Arbitration (U.S. v. Can.), 3 R. Int'l Arb. Awards 1965 (1941).
236. See, e.g., "Lake Lanoux Arbitration," 24 I.L.R. at 129; "Trail Smelter Arbitration," 3 R. Int'l Arb. Awards at 1965.
237. Charney, supra note 231, at 84.
238. Id. at 85.

20

Antarctica: Whose Continent Is It Anyway?
Daniel and Sally Grotta

*A new treaty helps protect it, but the coldest place on Earth
remains vulnerable to conflicting interests.*

Last February the *World Discoverer*, our cruise ship, slowed and
then stopped directly in front of a seemingly endless, monochromatical-
ly white ice cliff higher than the ship's mast. As flat as Kansas and as
large as France, the Ross Ice Shelf extends unbroken along the Ross
Sea for hundreds of miles. The average depth of this jutting lip of the
Antarctic continent, 500 to 1,500 feet, seems puny compared with that
of the awesome icecap that covers most of Antarctica; it's almost three
miles thick in places and so unimaginably heavy that it actually
depresses the continental bedrock more than 1,900 feet.

We were scheduled to visit such Antarctic highlights as Sir Ernest
Shackleton's hut at Cape Royds on Ross Island, a bleak, uninhabited
rock from which he launched the 1907–1909 expedition that came
within a tantalizing 97 miles of the South Pole; Robert Falcon Scott's
shack at Cape Evans, from which he set off on his fatal trek to the Pole
in 1910–13; the United States' McMurdo Station; and Cape Adare, the
place where, in 1895, man first set foot on the Antarctic continent.

Like the other passengers on our cruise ship paying anywhere from
$12,000 to $25,000 apiece, we had been lured by an irresistible
attraction: the chance to visit the most remote place on Earth, and the
most unusual. The coldest place on Earth is also a fire pit for a blaze
of conflicting interests: scientists, tourists, environmentalists, oil and
mineral seekers—all vying to stake a claim on the only continent never

344

colonized by the human race, where there are only visitors, not inhabitants.

Scientists treasure the unparalleled advantages for research; tourists prize the chance to visit Earth's last frontier; environmentalists fear that increases in both activities will despoil an unsullied haven and jeopardize its fabulous creatures; others contend that preserving Antarctica as a kind of world park will deprive the rest of the world of much needed oil and mineral reserves.

Fears of Antarctica's ruin through commercial exploitation have been partly allayed by last October's 31-nation signing of the Madrid Protocol, which bans oil and gas exploration for the next 50 years. But Antarctica's unique attributes—it is the coldest, driest, and highest continent—will keep it at the focus of conflicting scientific and touristic interests.

Think of a place as remote as the far side of the moon, as strange as Saturn, and as inhospitable as Mars, and that will give some idea of what Antarctica is like. A mere 2.4 percent of its 5.4 million-square-mile land mass (it's 50 percent larger than the United States) is ice-free, and, then, only for a few months a year. Scientists estimate that 70 percent of the world's fresh water is locked away in Antarctica's icecap; if it were ever to melt, sea levels might rise 200 feet, inundating coastal lands together with their major cities. In Antarctica, winds can blow at better than 200 mph, temperatures plummet as low as minus 128.6°F, and icebergs larger than Long Island are calved. There's not a single village or town, not a tree, bush, or blade of grass on the entire continent.

But far from being merely a white wasteland, a useless continent, Antarctica is vital to life on Earth. The continent's vast ice fields reflect sunlight back into space, preventing the planet from overheating. The cold water that the breakaway icebergs generate flows north and mixes with equatorial warm water, producing currents, clouds, and ultimately creating complex weather patterns. Antarctic seas teem with life—from microscopic phytoplankton and tiny krill at the bottom of the food chain to killer whales and leopard seals at the top—making them an important link in the world food chain. The frigid waters of the Southern Ocean that lap the continent's edge—the planet's largest coherent ecosystem representing ten percent of the total extent of the world's oceans—are home to species of birds and mammals that are found nowhere else.

Ironically, despite all the ice, Antarctica is also the driest desert on Earth. Not far from America's McMurdo Base is a region, aptly called the Dry Valleys, where geologists say it hasn't rained or snowed for a million years. Because Antarctica seems to have more in common with outer space than with the rest of the planet, NASA periodically sends astronauts and new technology there for training and testing.

The virtually pristine state of Antarctica and its relative inaccessibility make it an invaluable place for all sorts of scientific research. Unlike Mount Palomar, Mount Wilson, and other astronomical observatories in the United States and elsewhere that have been scientifically compromised by the gradual encroachment of light-polluting civilization, Antarctica is an optical astronomer's dream. It's not just the velvety black 24-hour night skies; a combination of intense cold and high altitude (the South Pole is about 9,300 feet above sea level) put optical telescopes above the rippling lower atmosphere, which lessens blurring. Solar telescopes, on the other hand, can observe the sun for 24 hours a day all through Antarctica's austral summer, giving astronomers an unparalleled opportunity for long-term tracking of the sun's surface oscillations. These "sunquakes" are possible clues to the sun's internal structure.

According to the National Science Foundation (NSF), the government agency responsible for the three permanent and three summer U.S. stations in Antarctica, the South Pole is the best place to study the interaction of the solar wind and Earth's magnetic field. Solar wind particles, normally deflected by the field, can penetrate through openings in the field at the planet's poles. And because of the continent's extreme cold and almost complete isolation, the NSF considers it to be the best place to study and understand such phenomena as plasma dynamics in the upper atmosphere, thermohaline (temperature) circulation in the oceans, unique animal life, ozone depletion, ice zone ecosystems, and glacial history.

Scientists have come to view Antarctica as a planetary bellwether, an early indicator of possibly ominous changes in the entire planet's health. Satellite observations of the Pole, for example, have revealed troubling reductions in the amount of protective ozone in the atmosphere; the ozonosphere acts to shield life on Earth's surface from lethal ultraviolet radiation.

And buried deep in layers of Antarctic ice lie clues to ancient climates, clues such as trapped bubbles of atmospheric gases, which can help predict whether present and future global warming poses a real threat or whether the planet is actually on the verge of a new ice age

["Exploring Earth's Ancient Climate," Aug.]. The ice sheet itself may play a large, very-long-term role in fashioning Earth's future climate.

Until this year, most scientists have accepted as fact that Antarctica has been covered by ice for 40 million to 52 million years and that the present icecap is about 15 million years old. However, a recent discovery of remnants of a beech forest near the head of the Beardmore glacier, approximately 250 miles from the South Pole, provides conclusive proof that Antarctica was both ice-free and much more temperate 2.5 million to 3 million years ago. Furthermore, similar fossil finds made elsewhere indicate that western Antarctica was completely ice-free as recently as 100,000 years ago, a mere blink of the eye in geological terms.

According to Dr. David Harwood, assistant professor of geology at the University of Nebraska at Lincoln and part of the team that discovered the fossilized vegetation, their findings indicate that periodic fluctuations of the icecap seem to be entirely natural, cyclical, and relatively frequent phenomena. "We now take the view that the time of the present ice sheet refrigeration occurred around 2.5 million years ago and that ice sheets could come or go every 1 million to 2 million years. . . . As many as ten ice sheets grew and retreated over the last 40 million years. . . . The present icecap is now much more unstable and capable of collapse," he says.

Dr. Peter Webb, chairman of the department of geological sciences at Ohio State University, leads a team of scientists trying to answer questions about Earth's climate.

"What we're finding is that it is much sounder to accept the fact that there have been many, many ice ages. Right now, we have geological records of the last 40 million years and perhaps beyond that, which gives us a perfect data base for predicting future climate changes. This is where we enter the realm of controversy, because when we look at the geological record, we see it waxing and waning on a scale between 1 million and 3 million years."

While it's far too soon to tell—Webb's group hopes to complete a supercomputer model of Antarctica's climatic history within the next ten years—the unofficial consensus is that we're overdue for the next ice age—and, paradoxically, for the next warming period.

Until scientists began the first serious study of the continent during the 1957–58 International Geophysical Year (IGY), a multi-country cooperative research project, Antarctica was dismissed, as Cook had done, as a vast, useless continent. Robert Falcon Scott, who perished along with his entire expedition in 1912 after losing the race to be the first man at the South Pole to Norway's Roald Amundsen, wrote in his diary: "Great God! This is an awful place."

Since the early 19th century, whalers and fishermen had plied Antarctic waters in search of catches, but because the dangers frequently outweighed the profits, few ventured farther than 65 degrees south. In fact, Antarctica is so formidable that it took 75 years after the continent was first sighted before man actually landed on it; likewise, 44 years passed after the Amundsen and Scott expeditions before another human stood at the South Pole.

Based upon early explorations and questionable land grants, seven countries, including Great Britain, Chile, and Argentina, claim sovereignty over vast tracts of the continent. However, until IGY, none of the countries was capable of or interested in establishing permanent settlements.

As IGY wound down, the question of who owns Antarctica came to a head, with the concern that some of the 12 participating countries might use their bases—there were 67 in all during IGY—to bolster claims of sovereignty instead of simply to conduct scientific research. To tackle this problem, a series of biweekly meetings was held at the NSF offices in Washington, D.C. They culminated in one of the most successful international agreements in history, the Antarctic Treaty, which took effect in June 1961.

Originally signed by 12 voting nations that had had a scientific presence in Antarctica during IGY, the number of signatories has since grown to 26; there are 13 additional nonvoting countries that are without bases but agree to abide by the treaty, making 39 in all. It established Antarctica—actually the area south of 60 degrees south latitude—as a "continent for science and peace," and ensured that there would never be boundaries or borders there. It forbids military activity, nuclear explosions, and the disposal of radioactive waste, and grants to all Treaty parties the right to inspect all of the area. It temporarily sets aside all claims of sovereignty for as long as the Treaty remains in effect. Its de facto consequence was to establish Antarctica as either co-owned by all the signatory nations or not owned by anyone. The Treaty's success has established new international precedents that are often called the ideal model for how the world's nations should deal with a much larger province—outer space. Because a consensus couldn't be reached on such things as tourism, fishing rights, or mineral rights, all major decisions have to be unanimous. The parties "agreed to disagree" and to hammer out those troublesome areas at later meetings.

There have been few rules to govern what any individuals—or governments—might do in Antarctica, apart from those laid down by the Treaty. And the provisions of the Treaty have been binding only on citizens of the 39 countries, representing two-thirds of the world's population. They include the United States, the Soviet Union, China, Japan, the United Kingdom, Australia, Chile and Argentina—but not, for example, Mexico, Iceland, Venezuela, Israel, and Egypt. And because there are no governments or armies at the bottom of the world, the only means of enforcement is one of moral suasion.

The rules of the Treaty meant that as tourists to Antarctica, passengers on our cruise ship needed neither passports nor visas. Except for a handful of SSSIs (sites of special scientific interest), SPAs (specially protected areas) and SMAs (specially managed areas)—such as certain penguin rookeries or patches of land staked out by scientists for observation or experiments—there was nothing to restrict us from wandering anywhere we wanted. We and our fellow passengers were therefore free to move about as if we owned the continent.

Had we gotten trapped in the ice or lost a propeller, however, we would have been completely on our own, because there was no nearby coast guard cutter or friendly fleet of salvage tugs to rescue us. Indeed, Antarctica is not Disney World or the Caribbean, but an unpredictable, desolate, treacherous, and unforgiving region; no tour operator can guarantee the planned itinerary. Every trip down there—cruise ships are the only practical means for most tourists to get to Antarctica, and a record 3,500 went down last season—offers adventure tinged with danger.

Getting in trouble in Antarctica is not a remote possibility, but a relatively common occurrence, as our own experience can attest. For instance, we had hung back in the last group ashore at Cape Royds to photograph the interior of Shackleton's hut. During that extra half-hour, thick pack ice blew onto the shore where the Zodiac boats (small motor craft) had landed, cutting a dozen of us off from the ship. To keep from being stranded, we had to hike to waiting Zodiacs on the other side of the peninsula. On another occasion, at Cape Adare, fast-moving, swirling pack ice suddenly surrounded four Zodiacs tethered together off shore and swept them and the driver miles out to sea. Fortunately, the driver had a walkie-talkie, and the ship was able to find her several hours later.

Over the years, many vessels, including cruise ships, have run aground, struck rocks, been caught and crushed in the ice, sunk, or simply disappeared in the waters. In fact, our February 1991 voyage was delayed because the *World Discoverer* was in a New Zealand dry dock having a rip in the hull repaired from an encounter with an uncharted rock on a previous cruise. And even undersea explorer Jacques Cousteau's famed *Calypso* narrowly escaped destruction twice during its 1972–73 private expedition to Antarctica.

Purpose-built adventure ships like the 3,153-ton *World Discoverer* are shallow-draft, ice-strengthened, double-bottomed passenger vessels specifically designed for polar waters. But two other passenger ships plying the waters of Antarctica, the 4,000-ton *Illiria* and the 12,000-ton *Ocean Princess,* were not built for adventure cruising. Worse yet, from an environmental point of view, the *Ocean Princess* is more than double the size of the largest adventure ship and carries triple the number of passengers.

Some believe that it's only a matter of time before there is a major nautical disaster in Antarctica. "This is a troubling new development," explains Ron Naveen, author of the book *Wild Ice* and head of Oceanites, an organization dedicated to protecting the world's oceans. "Not that there are too many people, but too many large vessels that shouldn't be there. We are also concerned whether the officers and crew have ever been in the area before. An analogy to the *Titanic* is more apt than you would suspect. I'm suggesting that the Antarctic is in fact as dangerous as hell."

Partly because of its dangers, but primarily because of its scientific and ecological importance, many scientists feel that Antarctica should be dedicated to research only. During the Southern Hemisphere summer, there are some 3,500 scientists and support personnel manning 38 bases; only about 10 percent actually winter over. Antarctica is so remote, alien, and empty that, says Antarctic ornithologist Frank Todd, "in all history, probably few people have been there than attend a Saturday afternoon Big Ten football game." By a wide margin, Antarctica has the lowest population density on Earth, and scientists like Todd would like to keep it that way.

While the NSF can't forbid anyone from going down to Antarctica, the agency's unofficial attitude has been that all tourists are unwanted interlopers who siphon off valuable time and resources when visiting the research stations, interfere with experiments or research facilities, or get into trouble and have to be rescued. According to Todd, who has visited

Antarctica every summer for the past 19 seasons, "the NSF's reluctance to accept tourism as a positive thing has probably come about because of the negative impact on our science bases."

There is some validity in the charge that unstructured visits by tourists can interfere with scientists' schedules. With such a short season—most research is done during the austral summer, before the weather turns bad—any undue time away from the lab or the field can mean missed opportunities. An occasional visit by a cruise ship is a welcome break from routine for researchers at the bases, but it can be a burden when cruise ships carrying between 88 and 450 tourists stop twice a week at a place like Palmer Station, a U.S. base that has a maximum summer complement of 45. The tourist stops there became so disruptive to the staff during the 1989–90 season that officials refused to let tourists from some cruise ships into the buildings (a measure that is permitted under the Antarctic Treaty).

Science vs. Tourism

Sometimes the restrictions against nonofficial visitors border on the malicious. Last year, a private five-man Norwegian expedition drove dog sleds to the South Pole along the route Shackleton attempted in his unsuccessful 1908 expedition. From there, three of them intended to be the first men to parachute ski to the coast and were successful. When the Norwegians reached the U.S. Scott-Amundsen Base at the Pole, the NSF, in order to drive home the point that private adventurers and explorers were unwelcome, officially refused them entry inside the base. Thus they lived in tents in subfreezing temperatures for three days while waiting for their chartered plane to pick up the dogs and deliver supplies. (Unofficially, however, base personnel invited them inside for meals and showers.)

On the other hand, the tourist threat to scientific research in Antarctica can be greatly exaggerated. When we first interviewed David Harwood, assistant professor of geology at the University of Nebraska at Lincoln, he complained that souvenir-seeking tourists had removed some extremely important fossils near the Dry Valleys. That didn't sound right, not only because tourists from cruise ships never go into the continent's interior, but because most who visit Antarctica are committed environmentalists who scrupulously adhere to the strict guidelines that cruise ship companies promulgate. (The guidelines cover everything from how to behave around animals to the importance of not removing rocks, bones, or any other objects from the continent.) When we pressed for details, Harwood revealed that what he called "tourists" were actually "distinguished visitors, navy people from helicopters, biologists, others collecting who weren't geologists."

Baden Morris, curator of the Antarctic exhibit at the Canterbury Museum in Christchurch, New Zealand, believes scientists should not be especially favored. "We have to divorce the idea that tourists are visitors and scientists have some God-given right to be present," he says. "The main thing is not to draw this line of demarcation."

Environmental Concerns

Another charge often hurled against tourists is that they wreak havoc on the Antarctic environment. It's been suggested by environmental support groups, such as Greenpeace, that tourists litter beaches, stress animals, and destroy delicate mosses and lichens that will take a century to grow back. Worse yet, a cruise ship accident could cause a catastrophic oil spill that could never be cleaned up. The episode seized on by critics is the 1989 sinking of the cruise ship *Bahia Paraiso* at Palmer Station, and its disastrous effect upon the local bird population.

But according to bird authority Todd, those charges are unfair and misleading. "The *Bahia Paraiso* was claimed by organizations including Greenpeace to be a tourist vessel. The data show that it was an Argentine supply vessel that had tourists on board and would have been in Antarctica whether there were tourists on it or not. Nevertheless, she hit the rocks, sank, and spilled oil. It was widely reported that all the skua chicks perished as a result. Now that's negative, it's hot, and it's going to make headlines. But if they had examined the other rookeries very far away from the oil spill, all the skua chicks died there as well. It was a very bad year for skua chicks all over the Antarctic Peninsula. You have good years and bad years, and in bad years skua chicks die whether or not there are oil spills and whether or not there are tourists."

According to curator Morris, "there is a misconception that tourists do a great deal of damage and scientists do only good. I'm unaware of any pollution problems occasioned by the tourist. If there is a problem at all, it is the permanent visitor."

Until the mid-1980s, virtually all research stations disposed of waste in a haphazard, even cavalier fashion. Former Coast Guard Capt. Dick Taylor, who had been assigned to icebreakers in Antarctica from 1968 through 1990, remembers that "trash was just rolled down the hill. Urine was put into 55-gallon drums, rolled down the hill, and dumped into the sea. One of the jobs of the icebreakers was to break up the ice where the trash was and push it out to sea. Before the cleanup, McMurdo looked worse than a Welsh mining town."

Greenpeace Claims

In 1987, the 4.5 million-member Greenpeace decided that it had a self-appointed mission to keep Antarctica from being destroyed. Greenpeace chose to maintain a year-round five-person "world park base" near Scott's shack at Cape Evans.

The station's leader, Keith Swenson, who once was a diesel mechanic at McMurdo Station, boasts that Greenpeace has "shown what a mess they [the NSF] have left for the 30 years they have been here. At McMurdo they were bulldozing their rubbish into the sea, and that stopped the year Greenpeace came here. It's quite obvious that my co-workers in Greenpeace had a definite impact in stopping that kind of practice."

Ridiculous, counters the NSF. The cleanup, as well as recycling, retrograde disposal (hauling all refuse on ships back to the United States), removing all low-level radioactive waste left over from a dismantled experimental reactor, and other environmentally sound measures, were well under way before Greenpeace showed up. Others privately dispute the NSF's assessment, expressing doubts that there would have been major environmental policy changes if the bases hadn't been dogged by Greenpeace's presence and publicity.

There's little love lost between Greenpeace, the NSF, and the other countries' station chiefs. In the beginning, McMurdo not only barred Greenpeace staffers entry into the buildings, but refused to give their helicopter local weather information. The New Zealanders at Scott Base wouldn't even lend them a key to view Scott's shack. Both bases refused to carry Greenpeace's mail out on navy ships. For its part, Greenpeace snowmobiled to all the stations within a few hundred miles' radius to carry out detailed inspections for Treaty violations and environmental shortcomings. Of course, the staffers photographed and documented all alleged violations.

How valid are Greenpeace's concerns that the Antarctic environment is in danger? On the one hand, it's true that the whale, bird, and krill (the shrimplike crustaceans that are Antarctica's most important link in the food chain) populations have been diminishing for some years. Is this a result of human activity, including tourism and the presence of scientific bases? Or is it a cyclical or other natural phenomenon unrelated to man's presence?

There is little evidence to substantiate either view. But what Greenpeace and other environmentalists overlook is the order of magnitude: The stations may affect dozens or perhaps hundreds of square miles of a 5.4 million-square-mile continent. It is highly improbable that anything short of exploding scores of thermonuclear weapons, establishing hundreds of large cities, or building thousands of factories could make even the slightest dent in the polar icecap. While an oil spill or the accidental death of a thousand penguins or the destruction of a beach in Antarctica would be a local tragedy with possible long-term consequences, it just wouldn't have much ecological significance for the rest of the continent or the planet.

Mineral Exploitation

Recent events have shown that the greatest future threat to Antarctica's integrity may not be tourism or scientific stations, but the worldwide thirst for oil and minerals. With hindsight, it's fortunate that so little was known about Antarctica's resource potential at the time of the Treaty signing, says geologist John Splettstoesser, co-editor of *Mineral Resources Potential of Antarctica* and advocate—along with Greenpeace and the governments of France, New Zealand, and Australia—of making Antarctica a permanently commerce-free world park.

"The reason the Antarctic Treaty was negotiated and went through so quickly," he explains, "is that at the time, relatively few minerals were known to exist there. Mineral rights were deliberately excluded from discussion because if they had been raised as an issue, passage would have been delayed. So the treaty was passed, and everybody was happy."

By the early 1970s, however, there were some indications that there might be gas and oil in Antarctica. Since then, the NSF, sponsored by the U.S. Geological Survey, has taken seismic soundings for oil and gas off the Ross Ice Shelf and Wilkes Land and so has Norway in the Weddell Sea. No oil companies have taken part in these programs, which are nominally purely scientific. But some Brazilian research, as well as Brazilian station operating costs, is being borne by the National Petroleum Co. of Brazil.

The treaty countries, Splettstoesser says, decided to impose a moratorium, a gentleman's agreement, that no commercial companies would be permitted to prospect until some kind of negotiated document was in hand. A commission was set up to look into the matter and began negotiations toward what was ultimately called the Convention for the Regulation of Antarctic Mineral Resources Activities (CRAMRA).

These CRAMRA discussions had been under way for a decade when delegates finally achieved a tentative consensus at the biannual meeting in Madrid last April. Called the Madrid Protocol, it would have barred all prospecting, exploration, and commercial exploitation of natural resources on the continent for the next 50 years. Only after 50 years could the Protocol be abrogated and then only with the agreement of 100 percent of the signatory members.

The CRAMRA negotiations were so heated and acrimonious that some of the signatory nations issued an "all or nothing" ultimatum: Either the Protocol would be signed by all countries by June 23, 1991— the 30th anniversary of the Antarctic Treaty—or they might formally petition that the Treaty itself be set aside. One of the original Treaty provisions states that after 30 years, any signatory nation could make such a request.

By June 23, 38 of the 39 signatory and non-signatory members had signed the Protocol. The solo holdout? The United States.

Sen. Albert Gore, a long-time advocate for a "hands-off" Antarctic policy, blasted "the administration's refusal to move on this treaty," calling it "nothing less than an outrage." He blamed a small group of conservative members of the State and Interior departments and the White House for torpedoing the treaty because they thought the unbreachable moratorium would block any future U.S. oil and mineral interests.

Whose Continent?

Within a few days, however, delegates, prompted by the U.S. intransigence, finally achieved a breakthrough leading to an amended— and diluted—Madrid Protocol. It will ban all prospecting, exploration, or commercial exploitation of natural resources on the continent for the next 50 years. While the 50-year moratorium is intact, the Protocol can be modified after this time period if *two-thirds* of the signatories agree. That new provision, said President Bush, "provides effective protection for Antarctica without foreclosing the options of future generations." On Oct. 4, 1991, this modified version of the Madrid Protocol was ratified by 31 signatory and non-signatory nations, including the United States.

President Bush also said that "this Protocol will ensure the protection of this natural resource for generations. The new environmental measures will protect native species of Antarctic flora and fauna and will place needed limits on tourism, waste disposal, and marine pollution. I strongly support these measures, which are based on a U.S. initiative."

That doesn't automatically guarantee that the Antarctic is safe from oil rigs and strip mines for the foreseeable future. For one thing, the initiative that President Bush referred to resulted in weakening the terms of the moratorium on mineral and oil exploration and exploitation.

Moreover, like the Antarctic Treaty itself, the Madrid Protocol is binding only on the 39 Treaty countries. There's nothing whatsoever to stop non-Treaty countries like Kenya or Bangladesh or Venezuela from establishing commercial bases anywhere on the continent and doing whatever they please. And if an overpopulated, nearly broke signatory country like Brazil feels that it can solve some of its economic problems by striking oil in Antarctica, who's to prevent it from dropping out and going at it alone?

Right now, it is technologically improbable and economically impractical to look to Antarctica as a source of oil and minerals. But in a resource-hungry, nation-eat-nation 21st century, who's to say that Antarctica might not be perceived as the new mother lode?

Where do we go from here? So far, no non-Treaty nation has expressed a serious interest in sailing south and setting up for business in Antarctica. So far, none of the countries claiming sovereignty has moved to formally annex Antarctic territory. Greenpeace, the Environmental Defense Fund, Oceanites, and other environmental organizations will renew their cry to make Antarctica a world park. And more cruise ships than ever will sail south for the short austral summer.

So whose continent is Antarctica, anyway? Gore best expresses the feelings of those of us who have fallen in love with this strange and spectacular land: "I think that it should be held in trust as a global ecological reserve for all the people of the world, not just in this generation, but later generations to come as well."

21

Nature Preservation in the Global South: A Survey and Assessment[1]

Lewis P. Hinchman
Sandra K. Hinchman

The export of tangible things—machinery, computers, Coca Cola—from the industrialized world has caused some wrenching dislocations in developing countries. At least, however, such products have usually proved easy to understand and use, and may even have improved the quality of life for some. By contrast, the "export" of ideas, whether these be religious faiths, constitutional theories, or moral codes, has been far more controversial and difficult. Ideas tend to undergo a transformation almost from the moment they are "received" by an alien culture, since they have to be made intelligible and applied within a quite different context than the one in which they originated. The expectations and purposes that initially accompanied them may not pass unscathed from one cultural milieu to another.

The concepts "national park," "wilderness area," and "nature preserve" would certainly appear to belong in the category of contested ideological exports, since these notions took form and evolved in the peculiar setting of the United States.[2] A few critics have even charged that the national park idea is out-and-out "cultural imperialism" imposed on poor countries by "ecological mandarins" determined to lock up much-needed resources for the benefit of well-heeled ecotourists, if not to prevent the Third World from developing in its own right.[3] Even where the park idea has found support and been widely applied, a host of unforeseen complications has persuaded its most fervent adherents

357

to rethink their assumptions, reinventing the whole notion of nature preservation[4] to fit circumstances in the Global South.

Our goal in this essay is to interpret and support that process of reinventing parks by showing what nature preservation can accomplish in the developing world, what unforeseen problems it has generated, and what measures have been tried to make parks work for nature and people alike. We maintain that it is regrettably necessary, in many cases, for standards of protection appropriate to the wealthy countries of the North to be relaxed considerably when applied to the South, where cultural and economic survival often hang in the balance. For instance, the "multiple use" concept, by which mining, grazing, and logging interests have sought to justify unacceptable incursions into public lands in the U.S., may turn out to be the only feasible way to achieve *de facto* protection of wilderness and wildlife in Zimbabwe or Indonesia, at least in the short term.

Some environmentalists, particularly those of the Deep Ecology school,[5] believe that their movement should not be called upon to solve all the world's problems. In their view, protecting nature should not take a backseat to other, more "anthropocentric" goals, such as development (which they see as inimical to conservation, in any case). They fear that if environmental advocates get sidetracked in this way, their message will be diluted, and no one will remain to speak for nature.

Admittedly, these are understandable and legitimate concerns, and we do sympathize with them to some degree. We share with the Deep Ecologists a commitment to the preservation of nature—of landscapes, species, and entire ecosystems—for its own sake. We recognize that nature yields the resources from which the human artifice is constructed, but we insist that it possesses a dignity and worth all its own and must not be evaluated solely in terms of the number of board feet of timber or kilowatts of power it might be made to produce.

However, we have come to believe that unless environmentalists are willing to tackle larger issues and problems, nature protection—assuming it were to happen at all—would most likely happen only on paper, and would lack efficacy. Committed environmentalists may be able to accept this reasoning on the "half a loaf" principle, or perhaps as an expedient to buy time until nature preservation becomes more practicable.

Why Parks and Nature Reserves?

Although conservation of nature and its resources dates back to times immemorial and has been practiced all over the globe, the United States government can take credit for designating the world's first official national park: Yellowstone, in 1872. The motives behind the creation of Yellowstone (and of Yosemite, created in 1864 but transferred to California) and the meaning of national parks have been much debated. One historian, Alfred Runte, traces the park idea back to Americans' collective inferiority complex vis-a-vis the great cultural and natural monuments of Europe.[6] Americans wanted to have something that would be comparable in grandeur to the Alps or even the Roman Coliseum. Runte and others add that commercial advantage played a large role as well, especially the hope of attracting tourists to ride on the Northern Pacific Railroad[7] on their way to Yellowstone. As we shall see, these early motives for park creation—national pride and economic benefit—have been prominent in the parks movement in developing nations as well.

Such motives might not have prevailed if the United States had not also had so much nearly uninhabited territory (the Native Americans having been removed to reservations) and if that territory had not appeared nearly worthless for agriculture and other extractive uses. Congress carefully excluded any land from the early parks that might conceivably have economic value. And, to be doubly sure, it even permitted mining in some parks and encouraged tourism in the grand style elsewhere. To this day, Congress has created very few parks or wilderness areas on lands really coveted by farmers or miners.

In any case, the idea of preserving nature evolved as American society and culture entered the twentieth century. Two rival schools of thought emerged. The conservation movement spearheaded by Gifford Pinchot led to the designation of millions of acres of land, mostly in the West, as multiple-use "national forests" that were supposed to ensure that we would always have enough timber by restricting cutting and planting new trees. While much acreage was thus set aside for utilitarian reasons, a different view of nature preservation emerged under the influence of Pinchot's contemporary, John Muir, and later writers such as Edward Abbey. On this view, nature offers a sanctuary from overregimentation, bureaucracy, pollution—in short, the "rat race" of modern urban society. Its purity, beauty, and magnificence can ennoble our souls, freeing us from neurotic dependencies and deadening routines. Other writers, like Aldo Leopold, added that the careful study of pristine land can teach us much about the subtle ways in which ecosystems maintain stability and integrity, and how humans might learn to be "plain citizens" rather than lords and masters of nature. The answer to the question, "why do we have parks and ecological or forest preserves?" thus has changed dramatically in the century since the parks movement began. But whatever the reasons, the U.S. has succeeded in putting about 4 percent of its territory into national parks or similar protected categories.[8]

During the last 40 years or so, i.e. roughly since the end of the era of European colonialism, more and more governments in the developing world, too, have adopted the idea that protecting nature is a good thing, and most have created at least a few national parks. Indeed, at last count the world could boast of more than 8 billion acres placed under some form of protected status, and that number increased by 82 percent during the single decade 1974–1984.[9] By one estimate, about 5 percent of the world's natural habitat is now formally protected from development.[10] If one considers the protected acreage and number of parks in some conservation-conscious developing nations, they appear to have outshone the United States by far. Thailand now has 77 parks, with 24 more on the drawing board.[11] Costa Rica has placed fully 27 percent of its land under some form of protected status, about one-third in national parks.[12] In Belize, a poor country on the Caribbean coast of Central America, over 30 percent of all land is held in nature or archaeological preserves.[13] It seems as though the conservation ethic of men like Muir, Pinchot, and Abbey has taken the world by storm.

But the reality on the ground is very different. While federally protected park, forest, and wilderness lands in the U.S. are relatively safe from incursions, protected areas in the developing world are often little more than lines drawn on a map, and have tended to be fair game for every imaginable form of exploitation and development. We can only sample the type and extent of these incursions. Already, 17 percent of the tropical forests in Indonesia's national parks has been logged illegally, and the logging continues.[14] Costa Rica's Corcovado National Park was invaded by gold miners in 1985 and practically ruined.[15] Thailand's national parks have been developed for golf courses, second homes, hotels, and other money-making projects, and the whole park system is now threatened with a takeover by the notorious Tourism Authority, which has already spoiled much of the country's coastal region.[16] Alerce trees, ancient, towering coastal cypresses, are being logged right in the middle of Chile's Alerce Andino National Park; with boards selling for $25 apiece, the wood is a status symbol among wealthy urbanites, and despite legal prohibitions, international sales of alerce products have been brisk.[17] In Ecuador's vast Yasuni National Park, recent petroleum discoveries have led to large-scale development and even an oil spill. To get access to these subsurface riches, the government detached a large portion of the park, in which development of subsoil minerals was forbidden, and "gave" it to the Huaorani Indians (but with the proviso that the Indians not interfere with oil recovery),[18] since development of oil reserves is permitted on reservations.

To understand why parks and nature preservation in the developing world have not lived up to the standards and expectations of the North, we need to review how the idea of nature preservation got exported in the first place, and what happened when it did. Initially, leaders of developing nations expressed interest in creating national parks on the model of Yellowstone and Yosemite: lands held by the government in public trust on account of their ecological value or scenic beauty, in which most forms of development, exploitation, and residence would be barred.[19] But their motives resembled less those of John Muir or Edward Abbey than those of J. Cornelius Hedges, one of Yellowstone's prime movers, who imagined parks designed for well-heeled, genteel tourists. Since the North had parks and nature preserves, the reasoning went, so should developing countries, as a badge of their maturity and token of national pride. As one critic sniped, "national parks are chic."[20] On the other hand, many leaders in the developing world expected that nature preservation ought to have some kind of payoff, especially in generating tourist dollars and thus scarce foreign exchange. One official put it this way: "parks must be seen to contribute to the total economic development process."[21]

These motives, national pride and calculations of economic advantage, did not bode well for the future of parks in the developing world. Even more ominously, many developing nations did not have the blessing of vast uninhabited tracts of land on which to designate nature preserves. Many of the most attractive lands for parks had been inhabited, often for centuries, and usually by either subsistence farmers or traditional peoples or both. Furthermore, where pristine lands did exist, the government's ability to safeguard them was often hampered by a lack of resources.

During the first wave of park creation in the 1960s and '70s, government authorities in nations all over the developing world resolved the potential conflicts between parks and resident peoples in favor of parks. Time after time, locals had to move out of lands that the government desired for new parks, nature reserves, and wildlife sanctuaries. And even when no one was forced to move, the people who lived in or on the periphery of parks had to cease using resources upon which they had long depended: food, medicines, building materials, fuelwood, pasture, and wild game. In some instances these relocations and resource losses devastated entire cultures like that of the Ik in Uganda, who—evicted from their remote valley home—lost their sense of solidarity and dissolved into a Hobbesian war of all against all.[22]

Inevitably, such clashes with the central government led many resident peoples to take a jaundiced view of nature preservation. In any country, including the United States, there will always be those who have grievances against parks and preserves, and the government that sponsors them. But in the developed world most governments possess a fairly high level of legitimacy. Citizens generally believe that government officials have the right to create and operate parks, and—however grudgingly—they obey the orders of the (often highly professional) park officials. But many states in the Global South lack a history of legitimacy, having been created only recently and then often without regard to the loyalties and will of their residents, especially when these latter were considered too "primitive" to consult. Even in long-established nation-states such as those of Latin America, legitimacy is often in short supply: "In Latin American political systems . . . no group has faith in the honesty, impartiality, and efficiency of the government."[23]

As one might expect, impoverished resident peoples in and around parks created by remote and perhaps hardly even known governments will not be inclined to accept limitations on where they should live and what resources they will be permitted to take. They may poach protected game or encroach on park territory, hunting or mining or clearing land. Sometimes, the government will feel that it must react with a show of force to stop these incursions, uphold the law, and assert its tenuous authority. In Tanzania, for example, one consultant attended a celebration at the Serengeti-Ngorongoro reserve that featured goose-stepping park rangers parading past, with automatic weapons at the ready.[24]

At the same time, high government officials in developing nations may grow impatient that the parks they have created seem to demand scarce budget resources without generating enough cash to "justify" their existence. Since, in many officials' minds, the main purpose of nature preservation had been to generate hard currency, it is easy to understand why they would be sorely tempted to excise land from parks for more lucrative ventures like hotels and golf courses, logging, or petroleum drilling. Needless to say, corruption and profiteering by some officials only compound the problem. As several writers have observed, the destruction of tropical rainforests in Asia, both inside and outside of protected areas, may be linked to the top political elites who tacitly or openly benefit from it.[25]

Thus, the circumstances under which the national park idea specifically, and the notion of nature preservation more generally, came to the developing world seemed to presage serious problems for parks and people alike. But both governments and preservationists have begun to rethink the way parks are designated and operated, and even the very rationale for them.

The 1982 World Congress on National Parks

In 1982 the International Union for the Conservation of Nature and Natural Resources sponsored the third in a series of conferences on national parks and protected areas, held in Bali, Indonesia.[26] At its previous conference, in 1972, this influential organization had committed itself to help create more protected areas along traditional lines, i.e. to "insulate a series of wildland pockets from human impact."[27] But the various crises and festering problems with established parks discussed above had evidently made a profound impression on the delegates, many of them professional park planners and managers from all over the world. While no one favored abandoning the American-inspired idea of parks as islands of pristine nature, the IUCN's officials frankly conceded that protected areas had evoked "fear, mistrust and opposition from local inhabitants and organizations," who believed that economic resources would be "locked up" in national parks and reserves. And, they admitted, such fears were often "justified," because parks in the developing world had too slavishly followed the American model and failed to show resident people how nature preservation might benefit them.[28] In part, delegates treated this opposition as a public relations problem, to be resolved by getting their message out more effectively. But the official line took resistance to parks more seriously.

The IUCN announced that the underlying theme of its protected areas policy would henceforth be "the interdependence of conservation and sustainable development."[29] Park managers and advocates would need to emphasize that conservation and development were not only compatible, but actually had the "same goal," namely, to eliminate habitat degradation and overexploitation of resources. In other words, "sustainable" development or "ecodevelopment" would promote economic growth, but with the recognition that one has to conserve the resource base upon which its, and the whole planet's, survival and prosperity depend.

Besides acknowledging that protection of nature would need to have a pro-development component to win converts in the developing nations, the IUCN promoted another innovation of historic significance. It presented a list of ten protected area categories ranging from most restrictive (for example, "scientific research areas" and "national parks") through moderately restrictive ("protected landscapes") to those that tolerated considerable exploitation of natural resources (for example, "multiple use" areas like the U.S. National Forests, and "biosphere reserves," of which we shall say more later). The point of these classifications transcended mere bureaucratic phrase-mongering; as the IUCN's chief, Jeffrey McNeely, remarked, "the stringent protection required for [U.S.-style parks] is not necessarily appropriate for all areas which should be kept in a natural or semi-natural state."[30] The IUCN signaled that its members ought to look for ways to preserve nature that did not exclude the presence of human beings and that made room for at least some forms of resource extraction and use. For an organization dedicated to the Muir/Abbey idea of national parks, that was a big and doubtless painful step, but one that opened the way for the most creative phase of nature preservation in the developing world, one in which the "exported" idea of parks found a niche in its new environment by selective adaptations.

"Paper" Parks and Displaced Residents

Since 1982, park rangers and proponents, as well as sympathetic government officials, have made an effort to review the lessons of nature preservation that have accumulated over three decades. What has been done wrong? What are the success stories? What preconceptions have been shattered by on-the-ground experience? The answers to such questions have started to emerge in a variety of sources: conference proceedings, magazine and newspaper articles, and academic studies. In our view, a sampling of this literature reveals an emerging new paradigm of conservation. We begin with a look at some of the disasters and miscues that have plagued nature preservation since its inception in the developing world.

Perhaps the most morally vexing issues that have surfaced in park management concern "resident" peoples, i.e., those who live in or near nature reserves and depend culturally and economically on their resources. At first, believing that parks and people were incompatible, governments often forced these residents to move out, sometimes with tragic results. The previously mentioned case of the Ik, though extreme, is far from unique. In 1970 Cahuita National Park was established in Costa Rica as a small but beautiful patch of Caribbean littoral with a fringing coral reef. But the government did not have the money to buy out the local people, mostly of Afro-Caribbean stock, so it simply established the park on their land (87 percent of Cahuita is in private ownership) and restricted their right to use the available resources, such as coconuts, in accustomed ways. It promised compensation, but has not, at this writing, provided any. Not unexpectedly, local people resented the park and surreptitiously violated many of its restrictions. When officials tried to stop them, relations worsened. As one observer comments: "a working relationship between park authorities and local people has completely broken down. Not only is the ecological integrity of the park in jeopardy, but many of the basic needs of the local people remain unmet."[31]

The Cahuita case has important ramifications for our inquiry. First, it shows that the goals of nature preservation often cannot be met if resident people do not voluntarily lend a hand. Cahuita is a nesting area for endangered sea turtles, which lay their eggs on the beach. The local populace has long harvested these eggs as a food source, a use that is incompatible with the park's mission. But, given the high-handedness of park officials, their failure to provide compensation for residents' land, and the lack of alternative food sources, what reason did the local populace have to cooperate? Second, the Afro-Caribbean residents of Cahuita had long lived in relative isolation from the rest of Costa Rica and had developed their own peculiar folkways and traditions. While the park might have done something to preserve the natural environment of the coast, it tended to undermine the locals' culture by exposing them precipitously to a plethora of unsuspected problems, not to mention a growing stream of tourists. The Costa Rican government has lately recognized its responsibility and now declares the park to be a "regional center for promoting and perpetuating local cultural values." Cahuita may someday become a park in which culture and nature coexist in harmony, but that will require considerable money and diplomacy, given the damage already done.

In India, another local group, the Maldharis, had traditionally grazed cattle in and around Gir National Park in Gujarat state. At first, officials seemed willing to tolerate the Maldharis inside the new park, but eventually, as the population of lions there began to decline, these stockmen took the blame (unjustly, as it turns out). The state government expelled them and tried to make them farmers, a metier that they had trouble mastering. To this day, they have never really adjusted to their new life. Yet the ecology of the Gir, including the lion population, remains hard-pressed, mainly because the government has left it as a small island of wilderness in a sea of densely settled, cultivated land. As at Cahuita, the decline of a unique culture has not brought a corresponding improvement in the conservation of nature.[32] One Indian scientist caustically remarks that his country's wildlife reserves, though "hailed by the international conservation community as an outstanding success," have involved "a direct transfer of resources from the poor to the rich."[33]

A similar situation prevails throughout much of Africa, where wildlife sanctuaries are often perceived as a continuing legacy of colonialism, existing for the pleasure of the affluent without regard to the needs, interests, and traditions of local peoples. There is clearly some justification for this view. In the Sahel, for example, nomadic pastoralists have been excluded from areas where their herds historically grazed, and are prohibited by law to hunt game that had once sustained them in times of drought.[34] Likewise, in Zambia's wildlife reserves, hunting by local villagers is forbidden, yet park guards may take a certain amount of bush meat, and "even senior staff from Lusaka apparently collect such meat regularly for their home freezers."[35]

Aside from the nutritional value of game animals, many have a significant market value as well, giving added impetus to poaching in eastern and southern Africa. By one estimate, the proceeds derived from selling the tusks of a single elephant "could support an entire African village for a year,"[36] while rhinoceros horn sells for $2,000 per pound on the black market.[37] Local people appear not to be responsible for the most extensive and destructive poaching, which tends to be the work of organized bands using sophisticated weaponry. Sadly, military men and even game park personnel have frequently been implicated in "wildlife massacres."[38] Resident peoples, poor and resentful, lack the means and the will to call a halt to such plunder. Meanwhile, tourism itself—which generates substantial revenues for businesses and governments, but little for local populations—has caused considerable ecological damage in game reserves.[39] And in some areas, habitat destruction caused by a superabundance of large mammals ironically bodes ill for their survival.[40]

Another instructive example of the tension between conservation and resident peoples is provided by Nepal's Sagarmatha National Park, which includes Mt. Everest.[41] The government created this park mainly to preserve the high-elevation environment around Everest and attract more tourists, but its policies produced the opposite effect, at least initially. The land on which Sagarmatha was established had been inhabited for centuries by Sherpas, a people akin to Tibetans. The Sherpas had a long history of relative autonomy, and did not accept the Nepalese government's claim to exercise such broad authority over their territory. Accordingly, they resisted directives to stop cutting down forests; in fact, the rate of deforestation (and subsequent erosion) actually increased as a result of the park. First, the Everest expedition trade brought a flood of cash to the local economy, most of which was invested in the traditional symbol of wealth, yaks, which need open meadow to graze, not forest. Moreover, the increasing stream of foreign trekkers needed fuelwood, and the Sherpas could only provide that by cutting trees. Economic advantage for the Sherpas thus favored deforestation, and the government offered no plausible motive for them to desist from it. The pattern was repeated in the case of food supplies; to meet expeditionary demands, local people brought increased acreage under cultivation, even though doing so was questionable from an ecological point of view.

The Nepalese government learned some valuable lessons from its tense relationship with the Sherpas of Sagarmatha. It has recognized an obligation to help them increase wood supplies by starting tree nurseries and promoting reforestation on denuded slopes. In the longer term it has pledged help in establishing small-scale hydroelectric projects so the villagers can make the transition from fuelwood to electricity. And it now requires foreign climbers to bring their own fuel supplies (expeditions had been consuming on average 8,000 kg. of wood, versus the 5,000 used by a typical Sherpa family in an entire year!). Finally, as we will see, reflection on its disappointments with the Sagarmatha model induced the government of Nepal to try a quite different approach in its more recent venture: the Annapurna Conservation Area.

Though a world away from the Himalayas, Oceania illustrates many of the same dilemmas. There, the most urgent priority of conservationists has been to safeguard the rich and varied marine life of Oceania's countless islands, to protect the marine environment that nurtures it, and to conserve the upland forests that prevent siltation of coral reefs. Most of these islands have been densely settled for centuries. Indeed, the population of Yap used to be eight times greater than it is today. Consequently, resident peoples had surely encountered signs of overuse, resource depletion, and marine pollution long before Europeans arrived. And they learned to cope by devising their own unique strategies for conservation. As one observer remarks, perhaps overstating his case: "programmes of resource management and environmental protection are already in operation wherever indigenous peoples live in traditional settings."[42]

In the early stages of the park and protected area movement, planners in Oceania did not recognize that local people had conservation strategies, because they found no evidence of Western-style nature preserves, open to the public yet regulated by professional staff. So they sought, as elsewhere, to create as many parks as they could. But land-tenure patterns in Oceania, especially Papua-New Guinea, frustrated their designs. About 98 percent of all land on that large island is held communally by villages or by individual clans; one finds much the same system of ownership on other islands like Fiji.[43] Such land generally cannot be sold at all, so it becomes almost impossible to create Yellowstone-style parks in Oceania. Where such parks were set up, they tended to fail in their main missions; some were even abandoned. Sea tenure systems seem to have followed a similar model. The ocean is not a vast "commons," as Western political theorists like Locke have said; it is partitioned among the villages and clans so that each has access only to very specific reefs and fishing grounds.[44]

By the 1982 IUCN conference, virtually every participant from Oceania agreed that traditional national parks were not the answer. The solution to conserving the beauty and ecological bounty of Oceania would involve securing the help and cooperation of indigenous people. That objective could be accomplished in several ways. In one scenario, park proponents could try to persuade local people to reduce their pressure on marine life and forests; but they would have to offer something in return. One IUCN member from Fiji suggested compensating villagers for the revenue they would lose by not cutting down trees in upland forests.[45] Another, from Papua-New Guinea, suggested apportioning some revenue from scuba diving operations to indigenous people whose conservation practices helped keep reefs healthy. In a third instance, the government of PNG has helped introduce the Kiwai people to alternative marine resources (barramundi and crayfish) to make up for what they lost by not exploiting their traditional food source: dugongs or "sea cows."[46]

But the most promising alternative is simply to allow the ancient conservation practices of indigenous peoples to keep working as they always have. Oceania's new nations suffer from the same legitimacy gap as many other developing countries, but the mistrust of public authority is exacerbated by geography: it is nearly impossible for a handful of underfunded park officials to regulate and police conservation areas spread out over thousands of square miles of ocean. Thus, almost the only hope of making conservation work is to gain the support of public opinion, and especially of the village elders who supervise the traditional land and sea tenure systems, so that indigenous people will voluntarily restrict development and exploitation.

How do these traditional systems of conservation work? Sometimes, villages treat certain areas as "taboo," meaning that they are off-limits for fishing, hunting, agriculture or almost any other use. Then, as noted, villages in many parts of Oceania do not permit unrestricted access to the ocean; they limit it to specific villages, clans, or persons, and then only at certain times of the year. It must be emphasized that although these traditional systems can work, they are fragile; they depend on the flourishing of the entire culture in which they are imbedded. Thus, "conservation of the cultural resources may be critical in promoting and achieving conservation of the biological resources."[47] The restraints of traditional cultures depend on the vitality of ancient religious beliefs, the persistence of accustomed forms of life, and the continuing respect accorded to authority figures such as elders and shamans. The trouble is that these traditional beliefs and folkways have not survived everywhere. On some of the islands, notably Palau, Yap, Fiji, and Papua-New Guinea, the old ways are still intact, but in many other places they are in decline, as the market economy and modern consumer culture have made inroads upon once nearly self-sufficient societies. Thus, as one observer suggests, it may be necessary to create "neotraditions" of conservation, making a conscious and deliberate effort to reinvigorate ancient authorities and beliefs.[48]

It would be unfair and misleading to blame the deterioration of conservation areas on resident peoples in the developing world, rather than on the actions of certain Northern and Southern elites or on consumption patterns among the wealthy, worldwide. As noted, many resident peoples are, in their own way, conscientious stewards of their lands and oceans. But even in those cases when local people do "invade" parks or exploit regulated resources, they usually have good reasons. For example, in Corcovado National Park, Costa Rica, the gold panners who moved into the park's river valleys had mostly been employed on banana plantations until those folded in the early 1980s due to falling world prices. Many had no source of income at all, and those who did find work could expect to earn only about $4 a day toiling as agricultural laborers, whereas with even limited skill they could earn perhaps 10 times that much searching for gold.[49]

A glance at the Sierra Club's list of "endangered parks" indicates that many of them face pressure not only from resident people trying to earn a living, but also from large-scale projects such as hydroelectric power dams, commercial logging, or mineral exploration and extraction.[50] Most of these either are sponsored by governments in developing nations or result from specific laws and policies that promote untrammeled development. For example, laws in Thailand favor deforestation, as do those in Brazil.[51] In Ecuador, the government encourages homesteading in the rainforests by granting free land to those who clear it. Indirectly, the government there has promoted a "land rights industry" much like the one that flourished on the American frontier a century or two ago. Settlers move in, clear the forest, and wait for land values to rise, then sell out and relocate deeper into the wilderness, repeating the process.

Although each family is legally entitled to only a 50 hectare plot, many families will file separate claims for every member. Thus, as one critic put it, "rainforest parks are destroyed by greed as well as need."[52] The protection, expansion, and improvement of nature preserves in the developing world evidently will demand not only more attention to the needs and problems of resident peoples, but a more effective defense of preserves' usefulness to political and business leaders, and to the banks that finance their projects.

Models of Success

A review of successes in protecting unique and threatened natural areas in the developing world can be as eye-opening as the long list of disasters. To begin with the treatment of resident peoples and their reaction to protected areas, experience suggests that tact, education, flexibility, participation, and economic support can all help to gain their understanding of and support for preservation.

The case of Kinabalu National Park in Sabah, Malaysia illustrates the way these factors may work. Kinabalu occupies mountainous terrain that had been almost uninhabited prior to the park's 1964 inauguration and never cultivated. Its centerpiece, Kinabalu Mountain, had been a place sacred to the local people, an abode of spirits. Hence, establishing the park did not clash seriously with traditional attitudes and resource exploitation. Then, too, the park entailed immediate, tangible benefits for villagers living on its periphery. It now employs about 200 people, either directly or in park-related tourism. Moreover, it attracts large numbers of visitors from the capital on a new highway (which, of course, may have unfortunate environmental side-effects of its own). Nearly 100,000 visit the park each year, with many making the ascent to Kinabalu's summit. They spend money in the surrounding towns and thus support many more local jobs, while forming a constituency for continued protection in the urban areas. On the whole, surveys reveal that resident people see Mt. Kinabalu Park in an "overwhelmingly positive" light.[53]

Dominica, a lush and rugged but terribly impoverished Caribbean island nation, has had a similar history with its national park, Morne Trois Pitons. Park proponents in and out of government pored over maps before defining the park's boundaries so they could avoid economic and social dislocation. They began with a small demonstration project—a picnic area and trail near a spectacular falls—that immediately attracted tourists and native Dominicans alike. In that way, park planners made sure as many people as possible knew about and enjoyed their new reserve. To create better understanding of its benefits, they encouraged island teachers to tell students about the park and take them to see it, while providing a wealth of literature, films, and trail guides to support this education program. Above all, they tried at every opportunity to explain the park's goals in practical, utilitarian terms: assurance of water quality, tourism revenues, prevention of erosion, and the like. Within six years of its founding, the park had already become a self-sustaining and popular asset to Dominica.[54]

We have mentioned two of Costa Rica's more controversial parks as examples of practices to avoid, but that country has had success stories as well. Volcan Poas protects a volcano of that name near the capital, San Jose. From its inception it has enjoyed strong support from almost everyone, urbanites and local farmers alike. It offers the former a nearby refuge from city life, while the latter benefit from tourist spending and watershed protection. On the Pacific coast, Manuel

Antonio National Park owes its very existence to local initiative. A foreign landowner had purchased a lovely stretch of coast and installed iron gates to keep locals away from "his" beach, which they had been using for years. They successfully petitioned the government to purchase the land and dedicate it as a park.[55] In neighboring Panama, meanwhile, the initiative to create a forest park was taken by the Kuna Indians, who now derive income from tourists and researchers even as they protect their heritage.[56]

The parks and reserves most likely to generate conflict and bitterness generally have been those whose establishment involved removal of resident peoples from their former homes. But even this extreme step has not always resulted in discontent and human suffering. Malolotja National Park in Swaziland was from the outset a favorite project of the king, a highly respected figure. To minimize dislocations, he asked a prince in the area of the proposed reserve to accept monetary compensation for the transfer of his own and his neighbors' land to the country's park service. The point was that winning the cooperation of a local notable, himself a victim of forced relocation, would make the park seem more acceptable in the eyes of residents. Furthermore, the king met personally with all 63 affected families and asked for their cooperation. He promised them better land in a more fertile region that was nonetheless culturally similar to their former home, and he delivered on that promise. Finally, he made certain concessions to the evicted Swazi families and other local people, such as very inexpensive meat from game animals culled by the rangers and special rights to visit areas of the park in which their ancestors had been interred. The king's approach helped minimize the factors that have made park creation traumatic elsewhere: he was recognized as a legitimate authority; he shrewdly used the status of local opinion leaders; and he made sure the park would bring at least some concrete advantages to resident peoples, while minimizing the harm it would do them.[57]

In some instances, protected areas have succeeded because their founders and supporters have made such a powerful case for their economic utility. Recent kings of Bhutan, for example, recognized the importance of conservation, and were able to create greenbelts and wildlife reserves and to nationalize the country's forests as a way of preventing overexploitation.[58] Clearly, not every nature reserve will yield tangible, measurable benefits, but a few, like Canaima, Guatopo, and Yacamb National Parks in Venezuela, do. Guatopo provides excellent quality fresh water to the Caracas metropolitan area, for which the government was willing to remove 4,300 resident families. Yacamb preserves a dense rainforest, and will also serve as a source of irrigation water for a dry, yet fertile area not far away. The largest of the three, Canaima, covers 3 million hectares of rainforest, high mesas, and cataracts, including Angel Falls, but also encompasses part of the Caroni River basin which will eventually supply 20 million watts of hydropower to the country. So far, the hydropower infrastructure has been kept outside of park boundaries. Park officials in Venezuela can make a case for park creation on the grounds that parks are the best way to safeguard supplies of drinking water, and to prevent deforestation and erosion that would clog turbine intakes, dump sediment into reservoirs, and silt up irrigation works.[59] Such arguments do not come easily to supporters of nature conservation, given the ecological damage done by dam-building, irrigation, and hydropower projects in other countries. However, they may be the only arguments that will convince powerful politicians, bureaucrats, and financiers in developing countries to preserve places like Canaima.

A similar benefit accrues to many citizens of Malawi in East Africa from its system of parks and forest reserves. Despite a high population density, 17 percent of the country's territory is legally protected, helping to avert deforestation and its consequences, erosion, flooding, and siltation. At the same time, rural Malawians enjoy clean and inexpensive water from a gravity-fed catchment system. As the system's architect put it, "Instead of fighting against nature, we are allowing nature to do our work for us."[60]

In the African game parks, the emerging consensus seems to be that, as a matter of both justice and utility, local people must benefit more from preservationist policies. As is true elsewhere, the parks will have little chance to succeed without local support. A way of enlisting such support is to make wildlife "show an economic return," where possible, by treating it as a sustainable, "harvestable crop." Several objectives can thereby be accomplished at once: residents' protein deficiencies are remedied; herds are reduced to prevent environmental degradation; and a sense of ownership is conveyed to the populace, inspiring them to defend nearby parklands against unwarranted intrusions.[61]

Reinventing Parks and Preserves for the Global South

Can any broader principles be extracted from the case studies that we have examined? Certainly, it appears that national parks on the

American model may often do more harm than good in developing countries, particularly where they mean hardship for local people, as several IUCN officials admitted at the 1982 conference. For that matter, even the United States generally has not resorted to evictions when desirable parklands included many longtime residents. Canyon de Chelly in Arizona, for example, a deep, beautiful gorge studded with archaeological sites, has long been a summer home for Navajos, and the park service has left it that way, allowing access to nonresidents only under severe restrictions. Clearly, since so many ecologically sensitive and valuable areas in the developing world have resident populations, authorities need to devise models of nature preservation that do not require mass eviction and that provide local people with either tangible benefits or continued opportunities to use resources lying within protected areas. Otherwise, they will not respect park boundaries and rules; poaching, squatting, mineral exploration, and other incursions into protected areas will become more frequent.

The time has come when proponents of parks and preserves need to rethink the purposes of protected areas. Unquestionably, the reasons men like John Muir once gave for establishing new parks still hold true. People in developing countries, like those in the industrialized world, need open space, solitude, and natural beauty. The popularity of parks like Kinabalu and Morne Trois Pitons among citizens of their respective countries attest that parks are not just for "ecomandarins." As these countries do become more prosperous and urbanized, their citizens will doubtless find themselves needing traditional parks even more.

Nevertheless, there has been a change in the way policy elites think about and justify nature preservation, one certainly evident at the IUCN. The ideas of Aldo Leopold and other environmental writers have begun to displace the more romantic, mystical strain of Muir. The declaration of principle of the World National Park Congress now calls protected areas "indispensable" because they maintain essential ecological processes, preserve species diversity and genetic variations, sustain the productivity of ecosystems, safeguard wildlife habitat, and provide opportunities for scientific research and education.[62] Many if not all of these functions can be carried out by preserves that differ from the Yellowstone-type parks of old, and none of them would incontrovertibly require removal of resident peoples or strict curtailment of their activities. In short, the "new" thinking on parks and preserves undergirds the IUCN's efforts to lengthen the list of protected-area types, and to find ways to improve the lives of people in the developing world. Let us briefly consider some of these nontraditional alternatives.

Among the most intriguing innovations promoted by the international parks movement has been the concept of a biosphere reserve. Inspired more by the science of ecology than by the traditional parks idea, a biosphere reserve is meant to protect a representative sample of one of the world's major ecosystems. It would conserve genetically viable plant and animal populations in their natural habitats, provide research and monitoring sites, and—unlike older "insular" parks—contribute to the social and economic development of the surrounding human population. In form, a biosphere reserve resembles a set of concentric circles: the innermost ring remains pristine and unvisited by humankind, except for scientific research; the middle ring is given over to multiple-use, including recreation and tourism (though not usually the intensive and highly commercial type that characterizes U.S. national forests); and the outer ring contains human settlements, but with at least some restrictions on land use and future development.[63] At latest count, 250 biosphere reserves had been established in 65 countries.[64]

Of course, the most difficult and exciting aspect of biosphere reserves is the last: finding ways to help rural families improve their standard of living in "sustainable" ways. La Michilla biosphere reserve in Mexico suggests some concrete benefits that resident people might derive from these innovative protected areas. La Michilla had endured excessive hunting and grazing, to the point where certain species were at the point of disappearing. To reduce pressure on the region, reserve scientists introduced new plant species for forage, brought back white-tailed deer as a food source for local hunters, helped farmers plant new and profitable crops like strawberries, and promoted crafts and skills like beekeeping, woodworking, gem-cutting, and basket-weaving. The net effect has been to raise living standards, take pressure off the reserve, and generate support from local people.[65]

We should point out that the idea of creating buffer zones around parks is hardly new. Several parks in the developing world, such as La Planada in Colombia and Guanacaste in Costa Rica, have pioneered this approach, with some success.[66] At La Planada, park officials set up a zone of influence of about 100,000 hectares around the core reserve, hoping to control destructive practices such as firewood cutting in adjacent areas. But they did not just establish restrictions; they tried to offer alternatives, for example by starting a tree nursery to produce fast-growing species suitable for firewood. What is more, they assisted local

Indians in getting clear title to their land, which otherwise might have been seized by outsiders. They also offered educational help and set up a variety of other projects too numerous to list. They built up so much respect and goodwill that local people, especially the Indians, asked that a biosphere reserve be established at La Planada and contiguous areas of Ecuador.[67]

A slightly different model emerged as the government of Nepal meditated on the troubles at Sagarmatha, mentioned above. In 1986, Nepal established the Annapurna Conservation Area, deliberately designed not to be a traditional national park, but a multi-purpose protected area, encouraging tourism, recreation, forestry, agriculture, medicinal plant gathering, hunting, and grazing. Rather than following the model of concentric circles around a core area, Annapurna features a checkerboard zoning pattern, so that all uses will have their proper, ecologically sound niche. Like Sagarmatha after its initial phase of conflict, Annapurna also offers local residents services ranging from a tree nursery to small-scale hydropower to clean water supplies and sanitary latrines. But its more impressive innovations concern management. It is largely run by a private institution, the King Mahendra Trust for Nature Conservation, and by local villagers, who administer many of its programs. To finance these, Annapurna Conservation Area charges an entry fee of $8 per visitor and returns the money not to the Nepalese treasury, but to the local people.[68] In this way, Annapurna Conservation Area can accommodate a population of some 40,000 and still protect the high mountain ecology to which it was dedicated.

Still another variation has been adopted in Brazil to protect the rainforest and its people. Until the 1960s Brazil's Amazon basin had not been intensively exploited. Of course, indigenous peoples had lived there since time immemorial, some without ever having been contacted by whites. Besides them, the rainforests were the abode of a retiring and resourceful people, the rubber tappers. These tappers, many from northeastern Brazil originally, lived on "seringals," former estates now rented by the tappers and averaging about 750 acres each. The seringals remained in practically virgin condition, altered only by the tappers' extraction of latex (which does not harm the trees) and by their foraging for natural products to eat or sell, such as Brazil nuts. But starting in the 1960s and accelerating in the '80s, would-be ranchers—encouraged by government policies[69]—started arriving in the forests, claiming supposedly open land that was actually in the possession of Indians or tappers, and setting fires to create pasture for cattle. Although rubber tappers tried to halt this onslaught, they had little success until they joined forces with the international environmental movement and stood up not only for their property and way of life, but for the rainforest itself.

Chico Mendes, their leader until his assassination by ranchers in 1989, came up with a plan. The tappers, he suggested, should ask the government to create "extractive reserves" that would guarantee the preservation of the rainforest environment, and yet offer Brazilians a way to earn a living from it. The rubber tappers formed an alliance with the Indians, calling themselves the "peoples of the forest," and garnered much sympathy both in the capital and in international financial circles. Eventually, the government did begin to create extractive reserves (12 as of this writing), although ranchers have not always respected them.[70]

Parks and Development

The story of Chico Mendes and the rubber tappers as well as the other innovative nature reserve ideas we have mentioned point toward some unavoidable questions: Does nature preservation really have an economic payoff? And if so, how great is it? Who gets the benefits of it? For any given area, will purely economic calculations favor preservation, even if in some form of biosphere or extractive reserve? Or would that area generate more wealth if exploited in conventional ways, i.e. as pasture, farmland, timber, commercial fishing grounds, etc.? However imaginative protected area advocates have been in blending conservation and development, resident peoples and government officials probably will not embrace their ideas in the long run if other uses of the land and marine resources appear more economically advantageous.

Clearly, no one can answer such questions in the abstract; everything depends on the characteristics and history of the region under consideration, and what has been done to promote ecodevelopment. But a few generalizations stand out in the literature on protected areas. First, the developing world lies predominantly in tropical and semitropical latitudes. Inevitably, a great deal of the land that has been placed in protected status, or considered for it, is tropical rainforest. Much of the sea contains coral reefs that cannot live in waters under about 64 degrees, Fahrenheit. In countries that have seen massive deforestation, the most common use of cleared land has been for cattle grazing, which supplies (among other customers) the U.S. fast food and dog food industries. For example, in Costa Rica in the year 1950, 65 percent of all lands were still in public ownership, much of that rainforest. Now that figure has dropped to 40 percent, with most of the loss representing the conversion of forest to pasture. But as one observer has pointed out, the conversion "did not result in any notable increase in cultivated area, nor in agricultural production of basic foodstuffs."[71] In other words, although cattle grazing does earn foreign currency, it creates few jobs; it is a low-value exploitation of the land.

What is worse, it is a temporary one at that, because tropical soils typically have low fertility. They only seem fertile because of the complex ecosystem that continually enriches them by recycling organic matter and by trapping moisture that eventually drips to the ground below. Frequently, the cutting of rainforest interrupts the cycle of energy on which soil fertility depends; cleared rainforest soon deteriorates into hardpan and becomes unusable, even for pasture, after just a few years.[72] Thus, one should not be fooled by appearances: land-hungry settlers cannot burn the rainforest and create another Iowa from the cleared land. Their best chance might be to leave the forest intact and try to derive economic benefits from it *as* a rainforest.

At the time Chico Mendes and his allies were pressing Brasilia to create extractive reserves, some calculations were done comparing the relative return from an acre of land held in forest as against its payoff if converted to pasture. In 20 years, an acre of land would yield $15.05 as cattle pasture (though of course it could produce fodder only for the first 10 years, until its fertility had been utterly exhausted). By contrast, it would generate $72.79 if kept as standing forest for the extraction of rubber and other forest products like Brazil nuts. Translating them into human terms, these statistics mean that a rubber tapper family could earn more than $1,250 in an average year by selling rubber and nuts. Beyond that, the people would glean many other valuable products from the forest: manioc, grown in small patches; game animals for food; building materials for their houses; and so on. Reckoning the cash value of these extra benefits would raise the average yearly income of a tapper family to $2,400—not a princely sum, but double what a family in a shantytown might make. And those figures reflect only forest-derived income from a few traditional sources. With help from science and extension services, tappers in extractive reserves could boost rubber production and find many other forest products to market, increasing their incomes still more, to the point at which extractive reserves could contribute significantly to the overall economy.[73]

But rubber and Brazil nuts represent only a tiny fraction of the potential economic bonanza of the tropical forests. As one IUCN scientist admonished, perhaps the most important reason for having protected areas is conservation of genetic resources, and many current parks are vulnerable precisely on that score because the value of these resources has not been sufficiently appreciated. Some experts claim that the value of these genetic resources alone is so great that it justifies the restrictions on development that protected areas enjoin. To cite one example, a species of perennial maize (corn) has recently been discovered growing wild in Mexico. If it could be crossed with currently available species of annual maize, we might get a commercial crop that would never need to be sown; it would simply come up every year from the rootstock, saving billions in costs to farmers for buying and sowing new seed each year.[74]

The rainforest may someday yield a cornucopia of medicines as well. So far medical researchers have studied only about 1 percent of the world's 250,000 flowering plant species, most of which grow in tropical forests. Already, over 120 medicinal chemicals have been extracted from them, including vincristine and vinblastine, both used in cancer treatment, which have sales of over $100 million per year. Next to the value of such discoveries—and there will be far more of them— the economic benefits of cattle grazing on sterile, hardpan tropical soils is laughably small.[75]

Nevertheless, some of that value, paltry though it is, does find its way into the pockets of resident peoples, whereas the fortunes made from rainforest drugs and plant species accrue only to the multinational companies that market them. To give local people an incentive to preserve the forests, we must somehow assure them a cut of the revenues. This is especially true for indigenous peoples who know the forest intimately and have hitherto shared their knowledge with outsiders for free. One conservationist declares that "botanical wisdom stored in collective tribal memories must be given economic value. Otherwise . . . it will continue to disappear."[76] Perhaps local people could be compensated for their knowledge through some form of "intellectual property" rights, similar to patents and copyrights. Or else drug companies and other interested parties could directly subsidize the rainforest and hire local people to protect it, seek out new genetic material, and carry out on-site research.

On the governmental level, conservation of rainforest and other threatened ecosystems might be made more attractive through debt-for-nature swaps, which began in the late 1980s. Here, a group such as The Nature Conservancy, Conservation International, or the World Wildlife Fund will buy a portion of a country's foreign debt at a discount on the bond market, using dollars or some other hard currency. It may then forgive the debt if the country agrees to set aside land for preservation. In a variant, the group may resell the debt to the country in the local currency, stipulating that some of savings be earmarked for environmental protection. Although some Third World leaders have balked at debt swaps, arguing that swaps invite meddling in their nations' internal affairs, the practice has grown increasingly popular. Participating countries have included Costa Rica, Madagascar, and the Philippines, and recently, institutions like the Inter-American Development Bank have also gotten involved.[77]

Finally, and most obviously, many parks and preserves can generate revenue through tourism, especially "ecotourism," in which visitors pay to experience the remote and exotic beauty and adventure of wild places in the developing world. For example, in Kenya, tourism is second only to agriculture as an economic mainstay.[78] Worldwide, tourists do increasingly pay cash to spot a rare quetzal, run an unknown river, dive pristine tropical reefs, or climb snow-covered peaks. But, some development experts caution, we should not exaggerate the worth of tourism to resident people (or, for that matter, ignore the damage tourism can inflict upon cultures and ecosystems alike if not properly regulated).[79] Often, tours are organized by companies in big cities (or even abroad) that capture most of the income, while locals must bear many indirect costs. In extreme cases, such as Ecuador's management of the Galapagos Islands, local people are *de facto* excluded from any role in tourism by strict regulations that they cannot meet.[80]

Governments, park managers, and international development agencies must devise ways to involve resident people in tourism, giving them a stake in the preservation of endangered environments. Sometimes, as in the high Himalayan parks, this has happened, and local people have dramatically improved their standard of living. And we must bear in mind that government officials, who also must be convinced of ecotourism's benefits, will not fail to recognize its contribution to their efforts to accumulate hard currencies which pay for imports. In Costa Rica and Guatemala, for example, "the tourist industry has become one of the biggest earners of foreign exchange . . . a hard fact that translates into political clout."[81]

Certainly, charging users' fees for entry into parks and earmarking them for local development, park salaries and maintenance, and environmental protection, as the Annapurna Conservation Area does, would establish a solid link in the residents' minds between tourism and their own aspirations for a better life. Similarly, Bonaire, a reef-encircled island in the Netherlands Antilles, has instituted a users' fee for divers visiting its marine park. Each diver pays $10 for a tag that must be presented to park rangers on request. The revenue goes to finance the park service's operations, install mooring buoys, fund research, and publicize dive sites. The authors, during a recent trip to the island, heard no complaints from visiting divers about this fee, and indeed noted widespread understanding for its goals.

In a variation on this theme, Costa Rica has resolved henceforth to charge differential entry fees into its parks, with foreigners paying about 10 times more than Costa Rican citizens. The dramatic fee increase for foreigners should improve the revenue picture for the country's cash-strapped park service.[82] If parks do not have enough income to hire rangers, mark boundaries, create new jobs in the community, build infrastructure, and generally present a high profile, they will, as one expert testified, soon be regarded as abandoned land, ripe for squatting and other incursions.[83] Santa Barbara National Park in Honduras, for example, has only one, unpaid ranger. Almost no one knows about the park, and it brings nothing to the nearby village. Not surprisingly, illegal slash-and-burn farming has already begun within park boundaries.[84]

Contemporary Ends, Traditional Methods

The theme of conservation and development that we have been pursuing actually suggests a wider question. The American parks idea, at least in recent times, has presupposed a dichotomy between the nature that parks are meant to preserve and humankind, which has no discernible role in ecosystems other than to foul up natural processes.[85] Signs of human intrusion, even campfire rings, have been strongly discouraged by our Park Service. Any sort of exploitation of park resources would be, it goes without saying, utterly unacceptable. Why is this? Must parks and preserves inherently exclude all traces of human activity, or is this exclusionary attitude a peculiar artifact of Western, specifically American, experience?

We would subscribe to the latter explanation. From Thoreau to Muir and Abbey, nature has been apotheosized as the antithesis of grubby, commercial civilization—in short, of a market economy. What our wilderness prophets have really espoused is that people have some sanctuary from the relentless objectification of the world, its conversion into a potential or actual factor of material production. Abbey, Muir, and the rest wanted to draw a line in the sand proclaiming: "this valley, this canyon is too sublime, too perfect, to be treated as anything but an end in itself; beyond here the values of the marketplace must not pass."

To avoid misunderstanding, we entirely support efforts to minimize human impacts in the American national park system. One must avoid jumping to the conclusion, however, that what is good in an American context is good universally. The dichotomy between human economic activity, human valuing, and nature may be entirely appropriate for the kind of civilization the United States has become but not for many places in the developing world. Although the global market economy is, to be sure, rapidly making inroads there as well, much of the developing world retains beliefs, traditions, knowledge, and values from the preindustrial, precommercial past. In them, we can still catch glimpses of a time when human beings, through long trial and error, had established a degree of rapport and balance with their environment that residents of developed countries can scarcely imagine today. Our Western conservation, by drawing on scientific research, planning, and administrative fiat, tries to approximate the state of ecological balance that some peoples in the Global South achieved unselfconsciously, by following traditions and adapting them slowly when necessary. While eschewing romanticism, we must recognize that local people, in many cases, have an unsurpassed grasp of the ecology of their own region, and may be the best possible guides to and interpreters of it.[86] Three brief examples will illustrate the gulf between Western-style conservation and the "ecology" of some indigenous peoples.

In the rainforests of Amazonia one may still find native people who have had precious little contact with whites. We have already mentioned how potentially valuable their encyclopedic knowledge of their world someday may be for the rest of us. But there is more. They too have had to face the problem of conservation. While they have no conscious, deliberate strategy to protect resources, such as fish, they do have taboos that instill in them awe or fear of certain places: the very ones (so it turns out) that are precisely the most ecologically sensitive and vulnerable, such as fish-spawning habitat. As one observer of these tribes explains it, theirs is an ecological wisdom "intricately woven into the very fabric of their cultures; for the most part it is not an articulated, conscious 'body of knowledge.'"[87]

In India, the government has tried to conserve forest lands, wildlife habitat, and pure, fresh water with the usual methods of Western centralized conservation bureaucracies: laws, fines, park rangers, and so forth. One anthropologist reports that the "forestry agents" of the government have "*no* moral authority whatsoever" in the eyes of villagers whom they fine for illegal wood cutting. However, the villagers do respect one authority: namely, religion in the form of certain groves or glades sacred to the gods. The gods of India delight in flowing water, greenery, birdsong, robust trees and plants: in short, all the components of healthy ecosystems. Most Indians will visit these places to enjoy them, but will rarely take anything. According to legend, those who abuse the sacred places suffer swift punishment from the gods. In this way, "divine conservation" accomplishes far more than textbook conservation, and that is because "in Rajasthan, the gods have not departed; the landscape is alive with spirits and powers."[88] Of course, if Weberian disenchantment proceeds apace, such religiously-inspired conservation practices cannot be expected to have much lasting impact.

Our last example is set in Palau, a Pacific archipelago that shelters vast numbers of fish and other marine species. For thousands of years, the Palauans accumulated knowledge of the oceanic environment as detailed and precise as that which Brazil's indigenous peoples had gathered of their rainforest home. One fisherman in particular, Ngiraklang, had devoted his long life to mastering the traditional lore of Palau's wisest men, and adding to it. By the time he met an American biologist named Bob Johannes, he "could tell by the feeding behavior of seabirds what kind and how big were the fish that swam beneath. Without time charts to clue him, Ngiraklang would note the otherwise imperceptible turning of the tide by watching tiny fish realign themselves in the current."[89] Johannes studied under this aged Palauan for several years and learned much more about the reef and its life than any scientific texts could have taught him.

The Palauans had always had an informal system of conservation that worked well as long as they were limited by traditional fishing technologies. But the coming of a commercial economy brought with it disequilibrium: motorboats capable of traveling farther than traditional canoes, marine pollution, ice coolers to store fish, loss of authority by traditional leaders, and (in consequence) declining fish catches. But, at least in northern Palau, the old knowledge has not entirely vanished. There, local chiefs have revived an ancient custom, the *bul*, a taboo against fishing during certain times of the year; and with their knowledge of fish behavior, the Palauans picked just the right times to allow fish numbers to rebound, which is now starting to happen.

These cases illustrate our argument that the essence of parks and preserves should not simply be to keep humans out, but to preserve a sphere of life exempt from the alienating, objectivizing power of the market economy. And in the developing world, that will often mean treating nature and human culture as interrelated and mutually sustaining. Taboos, sacred places, shamans, and legends are all so many reminders of the world our early ancestors knew and in their own way understood deeply. In countries like the United States, in which nature has been disenchanted almost completely, we need the authority of ecological science, of park rangers, and of visionary writers to protect what little uncommercialized space we have left. But in some parts of the developing world, traditional patterns of knowledge and living may, for a time, provide support for conservation more effective than anything that Western methods could invent.

In conclusion, then, we believe that the IUCN is right to wed development to conservation ("ecodevelopment"), because conservation does have benefits that in many cases exceed the economic value of commercial development, especially in the long run.[90] Assuming that population pressures can be kept in check, and the destabilizing influences of the market economy and Western values can be controlled, we may find that the nations of the developing world will be better guardians of nature than we have been, if only we do not have contempt for their traditional knowledge, religions, and folkways.

Notes

1. The authors would like to thank their colleagues, Dan Bradburd of Clarkson University and Steven White and Ansil Ramsay of St. Lawrence University, for suggesting useful source materials for this project.
2. In making this generalization, we are bracketing out protected areas established by colonial powers during the pre-independence era, such as the game reserves set up by the British in East Africa and South Asia. Since the purpose of these reserves was to allow for sport hunting by Europeans while excluding subsistence activity by locals, their legacy was a bitter one. The effect was to taint the very concept of environmental protection in the eyes of many in the Global South. See Aiken 1994; Guha 1989; Anderson and Grove 1987, part I; F. Kayanja and Iain Douglas-

Hamilton, "The Impact of the Unexpected on the Uganda National Parks," in McNeely and Miller 1984: 87–92; David Western, "Amboseli National Park: Human Values and the Conservation of a Savanna Ecosystem," in McNeely and Miller 1994: 93–100.

3. West and Brechin 1991: xvii and dedication page; see also Harmon 1987, Gunn 1994, Tsuruoka 1992, and Guha 1989. A rebuttal to Guha's position is offered by Johns 1989.

4. In this paper we tend to use "preservation" and "conservation" as equivalent terms, but specialists prefer to keep them analytically distinct. See for example Norton 1986.

5. For an elaboration of the distinction between deep and shallow ecology, see Naess 1973.

6. Runte 1987: 11–32. See also Worster 1983 and Nash 1982.

7. Hughes 1982: 369.

8. Buchanan 1985: 32.

9. McCloskey 1984: 36.

10. World Bank 1992: 37.

11. Handley 1994: 36.

12. Craig MacFarland, Roger Morales, and James Barborak, "Establishment, Planning and Implementation of a National Wildlands System in Costa Rica," in McNeeley and Miller 1984: 592–600 at 592; Gerardo Budowski and Craig MacFarland, "Keynote Address: The Neotropical Realm," in McNeely and Miller 1984: 552–60 at 553.

13. Fayhee 1994: 20.

14. Vatikiotis 1988: 41.

15. Hopkins 1992: 29–38; Buchanan 1985.

16. Handley 1994: 36–37.

17. Cooper 1992.

18. Highum and Parker 1994; James Nations, "Protected Areas in Tropical Rainforests: Five Lessons," in Head and Heinzman 1990: 208–16.

19. Cf. Harmon 1987: 148.

20. Hughes 1982: 369. On the other hand, Cartwright 1991: 359 points out that many among Africa's "urban elite" regard "the presence of large numbers of wild animals and even more the existence of stretches of 'bush' as indications that their country is 'backward.'"

21. James Thorsell, "National Parks from the Ground Up: Experience from Dominica, West Indies," in McNeely and Miller 1984: 616–20 at 619.

22. John Calhoun, "The Plight of the Ik," in West and Brechin 1991: 55–60.

23. Hopkins 1992: 47.

24. Norman Myers, "Eternal Values of the Parks Movement and the Monday Morning World," in McNeely and Miller 1984: 656–60 at 657.

25. See Sricharatchanga 1989; Handley 1994; Scott 1989.

26. At the time we wrote this paper, the proceedings of the fourth IUCN conference were still unavailable.

27. Myers, *op. cit.*, in McNeely and Miller 1984: 657.
28. Keith Garratt, "The Relationship Between Adjacent Lands and Protected Areas," in McNeely and Miller 1984: 65–70 at 68.
29. Lee Talbot, "The Role of Protected Areas in the Implementation of the World Conservation Strategy," in McNeely and Miller 1984: 15–16 at 16.
30. Jeffrey McNeely, "Introduction: Protected Areas Are Adapting to New Realities," in McNeely and Miller 1984: 1–7 at 1.
31. Kurt Kutay, "Cahuita National Park, Costa Rica: A Case Study in Living Cultures and National Park Management," in West and Brechin 1991: 114–29 at 119.
32. Shishir Raval, "The Gir National Park and the Maldharis: Beyond 'Setting Aside,'" in West and Brechin 1991: 68–86.
33. Guha 1989: 75.
34. John Newby, "The Role of Protected Areas in Saving the Sahel," in McNeely and Miller 1984: 130–36; Western, *op. cit.*, in McNeely and Miller 1984: 94.
35. Cartwright 1991: 360.
36. Anne and Paul Ehrlich, "Extinction: Life in Peril," in Head and Heinzmann 1991: 95–105 at 98.
37. Report from Zimbabwe on National Public Radio, "All Things Considered" program, November 13, 1994. The rhinoceros is so severely endangered by poaching that desperate measures have been taken to save it. In Zimbabwe, for example, officials have authorized capturing and tranquilizing the animals, and harvesting their horns—which regenerate—as closely as possible to the skull, in order to halt the slaughter. Currently under debate is a proposal to sell the harvested horn and use the proceeds to finance development and conservation projects. Graham Child, "Managing Wildlife for People in Zimbabwe," in McNeely and Miller 1984: 118–23 at 119, mentions that the Zimbabwean authorities decided to reduce elephant herds in the early 1980s for reasons of plant conservation. Most of the meat was distributed locally, while the ivory and hides were sold on the international market.
38. Newby, *op. cit.*, in McNeely and Miller 1984: 133; Walter Lusigi, "Future Directions for the Afrotropical Realm," in McNeely and Miller 1984: 137–46 at 139; Kayanga and Douglas-Hamilton, *op. cit.*, in McNeely and Miller 1984.
39. Lusigi, *op. cit.*, in McNeely and Miller 1984: 141; Western, *op. cit.*, in McNeely and Miller 1984: 95.
40. Kayanja and Douglas-Hamilton, *op. cit.*, in McNeely and Miller 1984: 88.
41. Will Weber, "Enduring Peaks and Changing Cultures: The Sherpas and Sagarmatha (Mount Everest) National Park," in West and Brechin 1991: 206–14; Bruce Bunting, Mingma Norbu Sherpa, and Michael Wright, "Annapurna Conservation Area: Nepal's New Approach to Protected Area Management," in West and Brechin 1991: 160–72.

42. Bernard Nietschmann, "Indigenous Peoples, Living Resources, and Protected Areas," in McNeely and Miller 1984: 333–43 at 333.

43. Navu Kwapena, "Wildlife Management by the People," in McNeely and Miller 1984: 315–21 at 316.

44. Nietschmann, *op. cit.,* in McNeely and Miller 1984: 341.

45. Birandra Singh, "Keynote Address: The Oceanian Realm," in McNeely and Miller 1984: 310–14 at 313.

46. John Genolagani, "An Assessment on the Development of Marine Parks and Reserves in Papua New Guinea," in McNeely and Miller 1984: 322–29 at 325.

47. Nietschmann, *op. cit.,* in McNeely and Miller 1984: 334.

48. Marjorie Falanruw, "People Pressure and Management of Limited Resources on Yap," in McNeely and Miller 1984: 348–54 at 353.

49. Buchanan 1985.

50. McCloskey 1984.

51. Handley 1994, Scott 1989, and Revkin 1990.

52. Nations, *op. cit.,* in Head and Heinzman 1990: 212.

53. Susan Jacobson, "Resident Attitudes About a National Park in Sabah, Malaysia," in West and Brechin 1991: 250–62 at 257.

54. Thorsell, *op. cit.,* in McNeely and Miller 1984.

55. MacFarland, Morales, and Barborak, *op. cit.,* in McNeely and Miller 1984: 596–97.

56. Jason Clay, "Indigenous Peoples: The Miner's Canary for the Twentieth Century," in Head and Heinzman 1991: 107–17 at 115.

57. Concelia Ntshalintshali and Carmelita McGurk, "Resident Peoples and Swaziland's Malolotja National Park: A Success Story," in West and Brechin 1991: 61–67.

58. Ophuls and Boyan 1992: 263. They contend that Bhutan, "alone among modern countries, practices sustainable development."

59. Jose Rafael Garcia, "Waterfalls, Hydro-Power, and Water for Industry: Contributions from Canaima National Park, Venezuela," in McNeely and Miller 1984: 588–91.

60. A.D.C. Kombe, "The Role of Protected Areas in Catchment Conservation in Malawi," in McNeely and Miller 1984: 115–17 at 117.

61. Edward Ayensu, "Keynote Address: The Afrotropical Realm," in McNeely and Miller 1984: 80–86; Child, *op. cit.,* in McNeely and Miller 1984. Western, *op. cit.,* in McNeely and Miller 1984: 95 calculates that if tourism is factored in, Kenyans can earn 18 times more money from wildlife than from cattle products. Again, though, we must remember that the beneficiaries of these two development strategies may not be the same people. Everything depends upon how the economic gains in each case are distributed.

62. McNeely and Miller 1984: xi.

63. Bernd von Droste zu Huelshoff, "How UNESCO's Man and the Biosphere Programme Is Contributing to Human Welfare," in McNeely and Miller 1984: 689–91.

64. Nations, *op. cit.,* in Head and Heinzmann 1991: 214.

65. von Droste, *op. cit.,* in McNeely and Miller 1984: 691.

66. Hopkins 1992: 49–52; Dennis Glick and Jorge Orejuela, "La Planada: Looking Beyond the Borders, in West and Brechin 1991: 150–59.

67. Glick and Orejuela, *op. cit.,* in West and Brechin 1991.

68. Bunting, Sherpa, and Wright, *op. cit.,* in West and Brechin 1991.

69. According to Ophuls and Boyan 1992: 131, the Brazilian government no longer subsidizes the clearing of tropical forests to create pasture.

70. For sympathetic accounts of Mendes' life and crusade, see Revkin 1990 and Dwyer 1990.

71. MacFarland, Morales, and Barborak, *op. cit.,* in McNeely and Miller 1984: 593.

72. Ophuls and Boyan 1992: 129.

73. Revkin 1990: 219.

74. De Klemm, *op. cit.,* in McNeely and Miller 1984: 661; Brundtland Commission 1987: 155.

75. Wallace 1991.

76. Wallace 1991: 40.

77. Murray 1991. See also World Bank 1992: 169.

78. Fred Pertet, "Kenya's Experience in Establishing Coastal and Marine Protected Areas," in McNeely and Miller 1984: 101–08 at 107.

79. Edington and Edington 1986; Cartwright 1991: 357.

80. Conner Bailey, "Conservation and Development in the Galapagos Islands," in West and Brechin 1991: 187–99.

81. McConahay 1993: 48.

82. David Munro, "Global Sharing and Self-Interest in Protected Areas Conservation," in McNeely and Miller 1984: 672–76 at 674.

83. Marc Dourojeanni, "Future Directions for the Neotropical Realm," in McNeely and Miller 1984: 621–25 at 624.

84. Cahill 1994: 178.

85. For commentary see Grumbine 1994.

86. N.V.C. Polunin, "Delimiting Nature: Regulated Area Management in the Coastal Zone of Malesia," in West and Brechin 1991: 107–13 at 110–11. It is important, however, not to overstate this point. Many indigenous cultures throughout history depleted their environment in significant ways. Plato complains about deforestation in ancient Attica; the aboriginal Hohokam, who overpopulated the area around present-day Phoenix, died off in vast numbers after devastating floods wrecked irrigation systems that they were too weak and malnourished to rebuild.

87. Kenneth Taylor, "Why Supernatural Eels Matter," in Head and Heinzman 1990: 184–95 at 191.

88. Gold and Gujar 1989: 223, 225. Cartwright 1991: 359 observes that this tendency to invest nature and wildlife with spirituality is not part of the African tradition. See also Ophuls and Boyan 1992: 203, who point out that "despite a basic world view profoundly respectful of nature, the Chinese have severely abused and degraded their environment throughout their long history—more, ironically, than the premodern Europeans, who lacked a philosophy expressive of the same kind of natural harmony." Thus, "the right kind of cultural attitudes are not by themselves sufficient" for environmental protection. Lewis 1992: 64 identifies cases in which the religious ideologies of non-Western peoples "prevented the development of a conservation ethos."
89. Stolzenburg 1994: 19.
90. Some economists have pointed out that the price of "amenity services" like unique physical environments will increase over time relative to the price of conventional goods, since the former cannot be "produced" like automobiles or even food: They are "gifts of nature." This means that, in calculating the economic value of a development project versus that of an intact ecosystem, we must figure that the value of the intact ecosystem would actually *increase* every year. Hence, "the increasing relative value of undisturbed environments will reduce the attractiveness of the resource development alternative." Pearson and Pryor 1978: 231.

Bibliography

Adams, W.M., 1990. *Green Development: Environment and Sustainability in the Third World.* New York: Routledge.

Aiken, S. Robert, 1994. "Peninsular Malaysia's Protected Areas' Coverage, 1903–92: Creation, Recission, Excision, and Intrusion." *Environmental Conservation*, vol. 21, no. 1: 49–56.

Athanasiou, Tom, 1992. "After the Summit." *Socialist Review*, vol. 22, no. 4: 57–92.

Beckerman, Wilfred, 1992. "Economic Growth and the Environment: Whose Growth? Whose Environment?" *World Development*, vol. 20, no. 4: 481–96.

Bird, Joan, 1994. "Managing Biodiversity." *Nature Conservancy*, Jan./Feb. issue: 22–27.

Bhasin, Kamla, 1992/93. "Some Thoughts on Development and Sustainable Development." *Women in Action*. Philippines: Isis International: 10–18.

Broad, Robin, 1994. "The Poor and the Environment: Friends or Foes?" *World Development*, vol. 22, no. 6: 811–22.

Brundtland Commission (World Commission on Environment and Development), 1987. *Our Common Future.* New York: Oxford University Press.

Bryant, Raymond, 1992. "Political Ecology: An Emerging Research Agenda in Third World Studies." *Political Geography*, vol. 11, no. 1: 12–36.

Buchanan, Al, 1985. "Costa Rica's Wild West." *Sierra*, July/Aug. issue: 32–35.

Cahill, Tim, 1994. "Welcome to Honduras." *Outside*, vol. xix, no. 11: 78–88, 178–82.

Cartwright, John, 1991. "Is There Hope for Conservation in Africa?" *Journal of Modern African Studies*, vol. 29, no. 3: 355–71.

Cooper, Marc, 1992. "Alerce Dreams." *Sierra*, Jan./Feb. issue: 122–29.

Dwyer, Augusta, 1990. *Into the Amazon: Chico Mendes and the Struggle for the Rain Forest*. Toronto: Key Porter.

Edington, John, and M. Ann Edington, 1986. *Ecology, Recreation, and Tourism*. Cambridge: Cambridge University Press.

Fayhee, John, 1994. "A Gringo Among the Howlers." *Backpacker*, Feb. issue: 16–27.

Gold, Ann Grodzins, and Bhoju Ram Gujar, 1989. "Of Gods, Trees and Boundaries: Divine Conservation in Rajasthan." *Asian Folklore Studies*, vol. 48: 211–29.

Graf, William, 1992. "Sustainable Ideologies and Interests: Beyond Brundtland." *Third World Quarterly*, vol. 13, no. 3: 553–59.

Green, Michael (compiler), 1990. *IUCN Directory of South Asian Protected Areas*. Gland, Switzerland: International Union for Consrvation of Nature and Natural Resources.

Grumbine, R. Edward, 1994. "Wildness, Wise Use, and Sustainable Development." *Environmental Ethics*, vol. 16, no. 4: 227–49.

Guha, Ramachandra, 1989. "Radical American Environmentalism and Wilderness Preservation: A Third World Critique." *Environmental Ethics*, vol. 11, no. 1: 71–83.

Gunn, Alasdair, 1994. "Environmental Ethics and Tropical Rain Forests: Should Greens Have Standing?" *Environmental Ethics*, vol. 16, no. 2: 21–40.

Hackel, Jeffrey, 1990. "Conservation Attitudes in Southern Africa: A Comparison Between KwaZulu and Swaziland." *Human Ecology*, vol. 18, no. 2: 203–09.

Handley, Paul, 1994. "Parks Under Siege." *Far Eastern Economic Review*, Jan. 20 issue: 36–37.

Harmon, David, 1987. "Cultural Diversity, Human Subsistence, and the National Park Ideal." *Environmental Ethics*, vol. 9, no. 3: 147–58.

Hays, Samuel, 1987. *Beauty, Health, and Permanence: Environmental Politics in the United States, 1955–85*. New York: Cambridge University Press.

Head, Suzanne, and Robert Heinzman (eds.), 1990. *Lessons of the Rain Forest*. San Francisco: Sierra Club.

Highum, Erik, and Karen Parker, 1994. "Development, Rights, and the Rainforests." *Peace Review*, vol. 6, no. 3: 285–92.

Homer-Dixon, Thomas, 1991. "On the Threshold: Environmental Changes as Causes of Acute Conflict." *International Security*, vol. 16, no. 2: 76–116.

Hopkins, Jack, 1992. "The Delicate Balance: Conservation and Development in Chile and Costa Rica." *Occasional Paper no. 13, Series on Environment and Development*. Bloomington: Indiana University.

Hughes, Donald, 1982. "Mountains Without Handrails." *Environmental Ethics*, vol. 4, no. 1: 369–71.

Isla, Anna, 1993. "Women, Development, and the Market Economy." *Canadian Woman Studies*, vol. 13, no. 3: 28–33.

Jenkins, M.D. (ed.), 1987. *Madagascar: An Environmental Profile*. Gland, Switzerland: IUCN.

Johns, David, 1990. "The Relevance of Deep Ecology to the Third World: Some Preliminary Comments." *Environmental Ethics*, vol. 12, no. 4: 233–52.

Lewis, Martin W., 1992. *Green Delusions*, Durham: Duke University Press.

Lipske, Michael, 1992. "Racing to Save Hot Spots of Life." *National Wildlife*, Apr./May issue: 40–45.

Lovejoy, Thomas, 1994. "People and Biodiversity." *Nature Conservancy*, Jan./Feb. issue: 28–33.

Matthiessen, Peter, 1991. *African Silences*, New York: Random House.

McCloskey, Michael, 1984. "World Parks." *Sierra*, Nov./Dec. issue: 36–42.

McConahay, Mary Jo, 1993. "Sweet Waist of America." *Sierra*, Jan./Feb. issue: 42–49, 153–57.

McNeely, Jeff, and Kenton Miller (eds.), 1984. *National Parks, Conservation, and Development: The Role of Protected Areas in Sustaining Society*. Washington, D.C.: Smithsonian Institution.

McNeely, Jeffrey, Kenton Miller, Walter Reid, Russell Mittermeier, and Timothy Werner (eds.), 1990. *Conserving the World's Biological Diversity*. Washington, D.C.: IUCN.

McNeely, Jeffrey, and David Pitt (eds.), 1985. *Conservation and Culture: The Human Dimension in Environmental Planning*. London: Croom Helm.

Mies, Maria, 1992/93. "Consumption Patterns of the North: The Cause of Environmental Destruction and Poverty in the South." *Women in Action*. Philippines: Isis International, 19–27.

Murray, Michael, 1991. "Natural Forgiveness." *Geographical Magazine*, Dec. issue: 18–22.

Naess, Arne, 1973. "The Shallow and the Deep, Long-Range Ecology Movement." *Inquiry*, vol. 16: 95–100.

Nash, Roderick, 1970. "Wilderness Values and the Colorado River." *New Courses for the Colorado*, Gary Weatherford and F. Lee Brown (eds.). Albuquerque: University of New Mexico Press: 201–14.

Nash, Roderick, 1982. *Wilderness and the American Mind*, 3d edition. New Haven: Yale University Press.

Nickel, James, and Eduardo Viola, 1994. "Integrating Environmentalism and Human Rights." *Environmental Ethics*, vol. 16, no. 4: 265–73.

Norton, Bryan, 1986. "Conservation and Preservation: A Conceptual Rehabilitation." *Environmental Ethics*, vol. 8, no. 4: 195–220.

O'Connor, James, 1989. "Uneven and Combined Development and Ecological Crisis: A Theoretical Introduction." *Race and Class*, vol. 30, no. 1: 3–11.

Omara-Ojungu, Peter, 1992. *Resource Management in Developing Countries.* New York: Longman.

Ophuls, William, and Stephen Boyan, Jr., 1992. *Ecology and the Politics of Scarcity: The Unraveling of the American Dream.* New York: W.H. Freeman.

Parasuk, Chartchai, 1992. "Greener Growth: Thailand's Road to Sustainable Development." *TDRI Quarterly Review,* vol. 7, no. 2: 10–16.

Pearson, Charles, and Anthony Pryor, 1978. *Environment: North and South.* New York: John Wiley.

Phantumvanit, Dhira, and Claudia Winkelman, 1991. "Designing Environmentally Sound Development Projects." *TDRI Quarterly Review,* vol. 6, no. 2: 9–12.

Pletsch, Carl, 1993. "Regimes of Nature." *The Humanist,* Nov./Dec. issue: 3–8.

Porter, Gareth, and Janet Brown, 1991. *Global Environmental Politics.* Boulder: Westview.

Raven, Peter, 1994. "Defining Biodiversity." *Nature Conservancy,* Jan./Feb. issue: 10–15.

Revkin, Andrew, 1990. *The Burning Season: The Murder of Chico Mendes and the Fight for the Amazon Rain Forest.* Boston: Houghton Mifflin.

Rosse, Steve, 1993. "Thai Forestry Rangers at Work." *Christian Science Monitor,* Aug. 2 issue: 9–11.

Runte, Alfred, 1987. *National Parks: The American Experience,* second ed. Lincoln: University of Nebraska Press.

Sadoff, Claudia, 1992. "The Importance of Accounting for Natural Resources and the Environment." *TDRI Quarterly Review,* vol. 7, no. 2: 17–23.

Santikarn Kaosa-ard, Mingsarn, 1993. "Environment and Development: The Thai Experience." *TDRI Quarterly Review,* vol. 8, no. 4: 13–17.

Santikarn Kaosa-ard, Mingsarn, 1994. "Thailand's Tourism Industry: What Do We Gain and Lose?" *TDRI Quarterly Review,* vol. 9, no. 3: 23–26.

Sawhill, John, 1994. "The Nature Conservancy and Biodiversity." *Nature Conservancy,* Jan./Feb. issue: 5–9.

Scott, Margaret, 1989. "The Disappearing Forests." *Far Eastern Economic Review,* Jan. 12 issue: 34–35, 38.

Shanmugaratnam, N., 1989. "Development and Environment: A View From the South." *Race and Class,* vol. 30, no. 3: 13–30.

Sricharatchanya, Paisal, 1989. "Too Little, Too Late." *Far Eastern Economic Review,* Jan. 12 issue: 40.

Stolzenburg, William, 1994. "The Old Men and the Sea." *Nature Conservancy,* Nov./Dec. issue: 16–23.

Taylor, Jim, 1993. "Social Activism and Resistance on the Thai Frontier: The Case of Phra Prajak Khuttajitto." *Bulletin of Concerned Asian Scholars,* vol. 25, no. 2: 3–16.

Tsuruoka, Doug, 1992. "The Pen and the Saw." *Far Eastern Economic Review,* Aug. 27 issue: 8–9.

Vatikiotis, Michael, 1989. "Tug-of-War Over Trees." *Far Eastern Economic Review*, Jan. 12 issue: 41.

Wallace, Joseph, 1991. "Rainforest Rx." *Sierra*, July/Aug. issue: 36–41.

West, Patrick, and Steven Breslin (eds.), 1991. *Resident Peoples and National Parks: Social Dilemmas and Strategies in International Conservation.* Tucson: University of Arizona Press.

White, Alan, 1988. *Marine Parks and Reserves: Management for Coastal Environments in Southeast Asia.* Manila: International Center for Living Aquatic Resources Management.

White, Rodney, 1993. *North, South, and the Environmental Crisis.* Toronto: University of Toronto Press.

World Bank, 1992. *World Development Report 1992: Development and the Environment.* Oxford: Oxford University Press.

Worster, Donald, 1983. "Review of Stephen Fox, *John Muir and His Legacy*," in *Environmental Ethics*, vol. 5, no. 4: 277–81.

The Environmental Challenge to Outer Space

In 1967 the international community attempted to apply the general principles and rules of international law to outer space by enacting the Outer Space Treaty. Over one hundred countries have signed and ratified the agreement. It prohibits appropriation of outer space, militarization, nuclear weapons, and other weapons of mass destruction in outer space. States are responsible for their activities in space and are liable for actions which cause injury or damage in space-related activities.

Currently there are no specific prohibitions of an environmental nature in space treaty law. One could assert that general principles and rules of customary international environmental law apply to states in space, but there is no general consensus on this matter.

What is required is legislation which sets forth a set of rules which created an environmental regime in both inner and outer space. Current science and technology relentlessly push back the frontiers of outer space and generate activity there. Presently, there are approximately seven thousand earth-orbiting objects, four-fifths of which are classified as "space junk." No legal provisions govern the activities of space stations and manned orbiting satellites concerning space contamination and environmental protection which would be required in space-related activities.

Little is known about the impact that earth-generated pollution, nuclear weapons testing, and ozone depletion have on inner space, the area closest to the earth's atmosphere. At a minimum a protocol to accompany the 1967 Outer Space Treaty should be drafted and opened for signatory. The essence of this protocol would be the application of general rules and principles of customary international environmental law to outer space and that states would be liable for their activities in space.

—RNW

22

Solid, Hazardous, and Radioactive Wastes in Outer Space: Present Controls and Suggested Changes

Major Bernard K. Schafer, U.S.A.F.[*]

Introduction

Pollution of outer space, particularly the region of space in proximity to the earth, is a matter of great concern. Although there is no apparent "ecosystem" in outer space due to the harsh conditions there, there are, nevertheless, several reasons why contamination should be avoided. Although there are both conventional and customary international laws which prohibit the pollution of outer space, these laws have not prevented the considerable amount of pollution which has already occurred. In light of proposed plans to expand operation in space into the area of manufacturing and the threat of further pollution that such activity would pose, a new international regime to control pollution in outer space is proposed. Employed as loose models are the Resource Conservation and Recovery Act (RCRA)[1] and the Comprehensive Environmental Response, Compensation and Liability Act (CERCLA)[2] which are enforced by the U.S. Environmental Protection Agency (EPA). Enforcement of a set of laws like these,

---

The views expressed in this article are those of the author and do not reflect the official policy or position of the United States Air Force, Department of Defense, or the United States Government.

adapted to apply on an international level, could help avoid irreparable contamination of the outer space realm.

Two types of pollution can occur in outer space: (1) back pollution which, though arising in space, adversely affects the surface or atmosphere of earth;[3] and (2) forward pollution, which arises from earth, its atmosphere, or space itself, and which affects the quality of the space environment. This article will focus on this second type of pollution as the environmental effects of pollution on earth have been discussed in detail by others. Little has been written about space pollution despite the likelihood that such pollution will become increasingly visible over the next few decades as commercial exploitation and its accompanying pollution increase, especially in "close" space.

Of the various types of pollution which can occur in space, there are three categories which are of immediate concern, and two that are esoteric. Solid waste[4] is the first category, and it encompasses all forms of debris found in outer space of a nonhazardous nature. This includes chunks of metal, clouds of gas, or even human waste, and the refuse of almost thirty years of space travel and exploration. Aside from the prospect of this solid waste physically crashing into a viable space object, it is really more of a nuisance. The second category is hazardous waste, which includes solid waste which is chemically or physically dangerous, and which can cause serious damage if improperly handled by space travelers (e.g., explosions or toxic contamination of a space station environment may occur if clouds of hazardous waste were to drift in after a space walk). In the third category is radioactive waste. This is the residue of nuclear-powered space objects which exude doses of radiation causing somatic or long-term effects.[5]

The first esoteric category is electromagnetic pollution coming from derelict satellites. Such satellites continue to broadcast unnecessary signals which tie up scarce radio frequencies. The second esoteric category is biological—the contamination of space and celestial bodies by microbes from earth. Both of these categories are called esoteric because the likelihood of harm from them seems rather remote. Wayward satellites need only be incapacitated to stop the harm they cause. Biological contamination, considering the lethality of the space environment, is unlikely, particularly in the vicinity of the earth.[6]

The three categories of pollution which are of immediate concern will be the focus of this article. Specifically:

1. To what extent have solid, hazardous, and radioactive wastes polluted space to date and to what extent do they threaten future pollution?
2. What are the legal regimes which presently exist to control this pollution and how effective are they?
3. What improvements could be made to make the controls on outer space pollution more effective?
4. Why has space become a dumping ground and why are changes in our treatment of the space environment needed?

The Threat of Pollution in Outer Space

Present Pollution: How Much is There?

Today, a significant amount of man-made debris can be found in outer space, principally in the vicinity of the earth. It is located in various orbital paths, the bulk of which can be found approximately 900 kilometers (540 miles) from the earth's surface.[7] It consists of an amazing collection of waste, in a variety of sizes, the detritus of almost thirty years of humanity's exploration of the space frontier.

The larger items include discarded rocket bodies; burned out motors; spent fuel boosters; derelict spacecraft and satellites; pieces of launch mechanisms; and payloads which have gone awry. The smaller items include human wastes, in the form of actual trash bags heaped over the side of spacecraft from previous manned space missions;[8] clouds of urine ice crystals;[9] a lost Hasselblad camera;[10] large quantities of small copper needles placed into orbit 3,600 kilometers (2,300 miles) into space to act as passive radio reflectors;[11] millions of metal shards, the product of some sixty explosions in space resulting from unintentional and intentional destruction of space objects;[12] and finally, clouds of gas molecules such as hydrazide, nitrogen, and hydrogen chloride, the propellants and effluents from spacecraft propulsion systems.[13]

In the area of radioactive debris, there are approximately forty nuclear-powered devices in space, carrying an estimated ton of radioactive material.[14] Although a number of these devices are on deep space probes, the majority are located in the vicinity of the earth and are still operational. The radioactive substances are Plutonium 238, with a half life of 87.5 years, and Uranium 235, with a half life of 713 million years.[15]

The amount of debris in space, excluding the millions of metal fragments mentioned above, ranges from 10,000 to 15,000 objects.

Some of these items, such as the millions of metal fragments, travel at speeds of 22,000 miles per hour as they orbit the earth.[16] For a perspective on the velocity power of even a small object, it is illuminating to realize that an object weighing 10 grams, traveling 40 kilometers per second (24 miles per second or 86,000 miles per hour), upon hitting a spacecraft, has the same impact as two kilograms (4.4 pounds) of TNT.[17] The amount, location, identity, and ownership of this debris is catalogued by the United States Air Force's Space Defense Operations Center (SPADOC). SPADOC has the capability of tracking items as small as four inches by radar. Although this function is performed for national defense purposes, SPADOC also uses the information to advise space users of "launch windows" and safe orbits based on the location of this debris.[18] It is certainly a reflection of the significance of the space pollution when a federal agency of the United States is entrusted with such a mission.

Is this Pollution Really a Threat?

The answer to the question whether man-made pollution is a threat is yes and no. On one hand, there are many arguments against fretting over the environmental state of the heavens. This argument is basically that there is no known ecosystem in space to despoil. Outer space, after all, is a lethal area with incredible extremes of cold and heat, and constant bombardment by radiation.[19] The absence of oxygen and the existence of a vacuum prohibit any sort of biological life from existing. About the only advantages of space as a respite from the earth is the absence of noise pollution and the view. The only ecosystem in space is that of nature in its rawest form, and since none of the traditional earth-bound environmentalist considerations (e.g., purity of air, water, and soil; and protection of human health) are applicable in outer space, it makes no sense to worry about its "contamination."

Further, in relation to the vastness and infinity of space, the amount of debris in orbit is minuscule. As for what does exist, the natural self-cleansing action of the earth's gravity and the friction generated upon entering its atmosphere, or the sun's gravity and heat, will eventually purge space of this debris anyway. Earth-bound incineration of hazardous waste requires temperatures of 1250°C (2282°F),[20] while the reentry heat experienced by a spacecraft can reach 1600°C (2912°F) and the sun's temperature is approximately 6000°C (10,000°F).[21] The bottom line on environmental protection for outer space is, therefore, how can anyone contaminate, pollute, or harm such an inhospitable realm that few people will ever visit?

On the other hand, the argument that man-made pollution is a threat starts with the observation that much of the skepticism voiced above is similar to the skepticism of those who used to question the need to protect the deserts on earth. Skeptics painted the deserts in stark colors, stressing that there was no ecosystem or environmental values to justify protecting them. Today humanity is aware that deserts do have an ecosystem. Tomorrow it may well find an ecosystem in space too, if given a chance to study it in its natural, untainted form. Just as dioxin-contaminated waste oil was simplemindedly sprayed on the roads of Times Beach, Missouri, to control a dust problem (causing this town to become another hazardous waste horror story in the spirit of the Love Canal in Niagara Falls, New York), so too could humanity's dim-witted fouling of space have a traumatic impact on the environment of outer space and the earth, in ways not yet understood.[22] Finally, there is one important and traditional environmental value being championed by those seeking an end to the pollution of space. Human health issues aside, there is the desire to have untrammeled natural vistas, and to protect scenic wonders from disruption, purely for aesthetic reasons. Outer space, a source of wonder and inspiration for centuries, deserves to be preserved in its original pristine state, for its own sake and for future generations to enjoy.

Furthermore, there are four practical arguments for keeping space free of waste. First, it poses a genuine safety hazard to space travelers. An example is an incident in 1984 when the space shuttle Challenger was struck in the windshield by a fast moving piece of debris.[23] Although the object only pitted the glass, it demonstrated that pollution can endanger lives and missions unless better controls are not established. One can also speculate that the debris and clouds of gas could become so prevalent that space-walking astronauts risk returning to their space ships carrying hazardous substances which could incapacitate the crew. Certainly in the case of larger objects which still carry fuel (radioactive or nonradioactive), the risk of harm to passing spacecraft caused by explosions, collisions, or just plain exposure, cannot be ignored.

Second, space experiments require that the pristine nature of space remain intact in order to be effective. During a number of Gemini space flights, for instance, a noticeable amount of contamination occurred in the area of the spacecraft, arising from some of the craft's subsystems such as its fuel cells and water evaporators. Due to an accumulation of debris on the windows of the vessel, star-gazing was impaired.[24]

Third, the various gases given off by space operations may be a threat to the vital ozone layer in the earth's upper atmosphere. Depletion of the ozone layer is of concern because it provides humanity with protection from harmful, cancer-causing, ultraviolet radiation emanating from outer space.[25]

Fourth, the ability of the earth and the sun to purge space of pollution is not as reliable as it may appear. In the case of controlled reentry of space objects, there are no guarantees of complete destruction—the most that can be predicted is when and where the object or its pieces might land within a strip 50 miles wide and 1700 miles long.[26] In addition, uncontrolled reentries are just as likely to happen, as many space objects are used until devoid of the fuel which would be needed to achieve a controlled reentry. The harm of such a reentry is demonstrated by the reentries of Skylab, Cosmos 954, and several U.S.-owned, radioactive powered satellites, which showed that it is practically impossible to predict when, where, or in how many pieces a satellite will land during an unprogrammed reentry. Indeed, the interaction of the earth's gravity and atmospheric friction can be an efficient method of spreading pollution, as in the case of the 1964 uncontrolled reentry of a U.S.-owned, nuclear powered navigation satellite, which smeared 17,000 curies of fine Plutonium 238 dust into the earth's atmosphere.[27]

The uncertainties arising from the laissez-faire approach to pollution control and the practical reasons for trying to control it indicate that man-made pollution should be considered a threat. Given that there is a certain amount of pollution of space, and that it does pose a threat, the threat of future pollution will be examined next.

Is There a Threat of Future Pollution?

The answer to the question whether future pollution will occur is yes, based on humanity's past practice of polluting outer space and the continuation of this practice today. However, there is a special threat of future pollution found in current plans to expand the use of outer space. These plans are to use outer space on a commercial basis to manufacture items which cannot be produced on earth. It is due to these plans that the amount of pollution may increase, and the nature of the substances themselves may become more hazardous than mere orbiting garbage.

Over the last year or so, interest in the commercial exploitation of space has increased significantly.[28] Ironically, the tragic destruction of the space shuttle Challenger[29] has helped accelerate interest in private enterprise launch services. The Reagan Administration has announced that future shuttle missions will be primarily military projects (to make up for the backlog of military payloads caused by the lack of an operational shuttle), and that private enterprise will need to find other providers for launch services for their payloads.[30] In response, several companies have proposed plans to provide not only launch services, but space stations and research labs as well, to be leased or purchased to conduct manufacturing operations.[31] The threat of further contamination of space prompted by this new commercial interest is probably best typified by the plan to put in orbit a drum containing 5,000, 2"-long metal capsules, each containing the cremated remains of a human.[32]

Use of space to manufacture items was tested as far back as 1974, with the U.S. National Aeronautics and Space Administration's (NASA) Skylab project.[33] Subsequent space shuttle missions confirmed the utility of space manufacturing processes.[34] With the joint NASA and European Space Agency (ESA) Spacelab mission of 1983, experimentation in this area reached its zenith.[35] A sampling of some of the intriguing possibilities of the near zero gravity of space[36] resulted in the following observations: air can be whipped into molten metal to create a light but strong metal soufflé; crystals for microchips grow faster and purer in space, particularly gallium arsenide crystal microchips which are faster, require less power, generate less heat than regular silicon crystals microchips, and are very hard to grow on earth; impurities in medicines can be removed more easily and more completely because the electrophoresis process used on earth works far more efficiently in space; and substances such as metals, plastics, and glass can be manufactured more purely and uniformly because electromagnetic forces hold the substances suspended in place during the manufacturing process, eliminating the need for containers.[37] This is important because almost all containers leak impurities into the mixtures, causing the materials to cool and form at uneven rates.[38]

These operations pose a distinct threat of increased pollution because the manufacturing processes described above will undoubtedly have waste by-products. After all, the goal in many of these activities is to remove impurities. Some of these impurities will undoubtedly be hazardous, such as wastes from the creation of gallium arsenide crystals. What will industry do with them? If one looks at its record on earth, the answer is clear—they will be tempted to dump them in space. In the United States alone, as of September 1984, over 17,000 abandoned hazardous waste sites were discovered for possible listing under the Comprehensive Environmental Response, Compensation, and Liability Act (CERCLA), a law passed to clean up such facilities.[39] Since space is something out of sight and out of mind to the average citizen, and since there has been a practice of dumping debris in outer space for the last thirty years, it is easy to see why industry might feel it is acceptable to dump space manufacturing wastes in space, untreated and untended—after all, who will know or care?

One final point should be made. At first, the amount of manufacturing waste will probably not be very large, and may be carried back to earth by spacecraft. This is because of the great cost of putting materials in space—it currently costs $10,000 per kilogram. Once an item is placed in space, manufacturing costs will be even greater. Therefore, only small scale, expensive items, such as medicines and electronics, will be created at first.[40] This is not a reason for the international community to fail to address the pollution issue. There is a danger in bringing such waste back to the earth. The returning spacecraft might crash while landing and spread its hazardous cargo onto the earth. Also, as manufacturing processes in space expand over the next several decades, the amount of waste generated will eventually be too large to pack into valuable cargo space, and will be left in space for disposal purposes. Although this problem will increase very slowly over time, there is an opportunity now for the world community to address the use of space as a dumping ground, and to develop a legal regime for controlling such activity.

Present Controls on Outer Space Pollution

Conventional International Law

There are five international treaties which can be cited as proof that international laws against the pollution of outer space exist. As treaties they comprise that body of international law known as conventional law. Conventional law is binding only on the parties who signed the treaties. The nations of the world who are most involved in space exploration, now and in the foreseeable future, have signed the treaties. These nations are namely the United States; the Union of Soviet Socialist Republics; the European Space Agency (ESA) which is comprised of Belgium, Denmark, France, Great Britain, Ireland, Italy,

Netherlands, Spain, Sweden, Switzerland, and West Germany; Japan; and the Peoples Republic of China (PRC). Chronologically, the treaties are as follows:

Test Ban Treaty of 1963.[41] Entitled the "Treaty Banning Nuclear Weapon Tests in the Atmosphere, in Outer Space and Under Water," the Test Ban Treaty, as it is more commonly known, was the first treaty signed by the "space powers" to limit the abuse of outer space by harmful contamination.

In its Preamble, the treaty's goal is to "put an end to the contamination of man's environment by radioactive substances."[42] In Article I, the parties to the treaty promise "not [to] carry out any nuclear weapon test explosion . . . in the atmosphere; beyond its limits, including outer space."[43] This treaty clearly prohibits contamination of outer space by nuclear materials, although it only addresses contamination by explosion. It does not, for example, cover leaks of radioactive materials from a satellite's nuclear reactor. Although France and the PRC have not signed this agreement, they have apparently acquiesced to it insofar as explosions in outer space are concerned, because they have not conducted such tests.

Outer Space Treaty of 1967.[44] Entitled the "Treaty on Principles Governing the Activity of States in the Exploration and Use of Outer Space, Including the Moon and Other Celestial Bodies," the Outer Space Treaty (OST) or the Principles Treaty as it is also called, addresses space pollution more directly than any other international treaty. This treaty designates the realm of space as a *res communis. Res communis* means that space is an area common to all mankind, used by all but never to be owned.[45] Another label for this concept is that space is the "common heritage of mankind" (CHOM).[46] The U.S. policy is that the two terms are not synonymous.

The CHOM principle is presented in the Preamble, Article I, and Article IX, which state that the treaty recognizes "the common interest of all mankind in the progress of the exploration and use of outer space . . . that the exploration and use of outer space should be carried on for the benefit of all peoples . . . in the interests of all countries, irrespective of their degree of economic or scientific development."[47] These words indicate that no State has the right to foul space as if it were its own territory. The CHOM principle creates a global commons in space.[48]

Other articles explore a State's liability for the harm caused by its space activities. Article VII holds that a State that launches, procures the launch, or allows the launch of an object on its own territory or that of another, is liable for the harm the launched object causes another State. Article VI expands Article VII, and makes clear that a State is liable even if a nongovernment entity causes the harm. The State's responsibility for the activities of these entities requires States to authorize and continually supervise nongovernment activities in space.[49]

Article VIII establishes property rights in space: "Ownership of objects launched into outer space, and of their component parts, is not affected by their presence in outer space." This cuts both ways however, and is interpreted to prohibit a State from disowning a harmful and contaminating item that is placed in space. It creates a responsibility to deal with all of the incidence of ownership of such an item, including the contamination it may cause the space environment.

Finally, Article XI requires parties to notify, to the extent feasible and practicable, the Secretary General of the United Nations, the public, and the international scientific community, of the nature, conduct, locations and results of space activities.

The Rescue and Return Agreement of 1968.[50] "The Agreement on the Rescue of Astronauts, the Return of Astronauts, and the Return of Objects Launched Into Outer Space," commonly referred to as the Rescue and Return Agreement (RRA), expands on Article V of the OST.[51] Article 5, paragraph 4 of the RRA says that "[A] Contracting Party which has reason to believe that a space object or its component parts discovered in territory under its jurisdiction or recovered by it elsewhere, is of a hazardous or deleterious nature, may so notify the launching authority, which shall immediately take effective steps . . . to eliminate the possible danger of harm."[52] Therefore, if a hazardous object is discovered in an area of outer space where another nation is conducting space operations, the finder can demand that the owner (the launching State) do what is necessary to eliminate the problem. Japan and Spain are not parties to this agreement.

The Liability Convention of 1973.[53] Formally entitled "The Convention on International Liability for Damage Caused by Space Objects," the Liability Convention expanded on the guidelines of Articles VI and VII of the OST.[54] The Liability Convention establishes two different standards of liability for damages caused by space activities which are determined by where the harm was experienced. According to Article II, an absolute liability standard applies to harm caused to an aircraft in flight or on the surface of the earth.[55] Article III uses a fault standard for harm caused in outer space.[56] Article XII says that the amount of compensation to be paid is determined "in accordance with international law and principles of justice and equity . . ." which should restore the victim "to the condition which would have existed if the damage had not occurred."[57] Japan has not signed this treaty.

The Registration Convention of 1976.[58] "The Convention on the Registration of Objects Launched Into Outer Space," referred to as the Registration Convention, expands on Article XI of the OST. It establishes a regime for notifying the Secretary General of the United Nations about objects launched into outer space. It also requires a State to report any launch by a private firm.[59] Significantly, Article IV requires that the Secretary General be notified about the general function of the space object as well as its location. Article VI provides a remedy for harm to a State by a space object whose location and nature have not been properly reported to the Secretary General.[60] Taken together, Articles IV and VI require States to declare what they have put into orbit, including any hazardous or potentially polluting aspects of the object, in order to lessen the chance of harming another State party to this treaty. The PRC, Japan, Ireland, and Italy have not signed this treaty.

From this examination of the conventional international law dealing with the pollution of outer space, several observations can be made. There is a requirement that nations respect the CHOM aspect of space just as they do other *res communis* areas, by not polluting space to the detriment or exclusion of other nations. There is a duty to notify the world of dangerous activities in space. Liability will be imposed on nations responsible for causing harm to other nations by their activities in space. General concepts of international law will be applied to gauge a nation's conduct and to determine compensation for harm. And, at the very least, there is a requirement to not explode nuclear devices in outer space.

Although these treaties are binding only on signatories, they are significant because the preeminent space powers, the United States and the USSR, as well as the majority of the members of the ESA, have signed them. Of greater significance is that all of the space powers have signed the OST, the most important space treaty of all. This conventional law effectively controls all activities in space until such time as a nonsignatory makes its appearance on the space scene. One must look to customary international law to determine what controls apply to the activities of nonsignatory nations.

Customary International Law

Independent of conventional international law is a body of law called customary international law. Customary law is "international custom, as evidence of a general practice accepted by law."[61] To prove the existence of an international custom, one must establish two elements: an empirical element, or uniform practice by the world's States; and a psychological element, or *opinio juris*, the opinion of the world community as reflected in its practice and in the writings of experts in the field. The significance of establishing a customary international law against pollution of space is twofold: it acts as a body of law applicable to nonsignatories of treaties, binding them just as if they were signatories; and it bolsters the prohibition of outer space pollution by conventional international law. As noted by the International Court of Justice, conventional international law can generate rules which pass "into the general corpus of international law and [are] now accepted as such by the *opinio juris,* so as to have become binding even for countries which have never, and do not, become parties to the Convention."[62]

There are some things purely in the realm of space law which can be cited as evidence of a general practice against the pollution of space. First, the various treaties discussed above are empirical evidence of a uniform practice by the world against the pollution of space. Second, the psychological element is established by the wide acceptance of these treaties,[63] by the failure of any nation to reserve unto itself the right to pollute, and by the writings of experts who have noted that States have a duty not to pollute outer space.[64] Of course, based on the description of current space pollution made earlier in this article, it is questionable whether the actual practice of the world's space powers has been to avoid space pollution. There is an argument, however, that the pollution which has occurred to date has been a natural, though undesired, by-product of humanity's early steps into space.[65]

The large body of international and domestic law relating to the protection of the earth's environment provides a second form of customary international law against space pollution. Clearly, this body of law is not directed at the space environment, but instead to the surface of the earth and its atmosphere. However, the line separating the earth's atmosphere from space has been difficult to draw legally,[66] as well as environmentally.[67] Therefore, this body of law can be cited as evidence that the world community does not accept pollution of space, any more than it does on earth or in other *res communis* areas, such as the sea. The psychological element is established by the wide acceptance of these earth-based environmental laws, and by the acceptance of basic outer space environmental protection principles by some of the world's nations and experts in the space law field.

Customary International Law: The Empirical Element

International and domestic laws creating customary international law against outer space pollution will be examined by first looking at the empirical element: international environmental treaties, declarations, organizations, cases, and domestic practices.

International Treaties

A number of multilateral and bilateral treaties exist which clarify the responsibility of all States to protect the world's environment:

Antarctic Treaty.[68] Signed in 1959, this treaty establishes the use of Antarctica for peaceful purposes. In the area of environmental protection, it prohibits the disposing of radioactive wastes in Antarctica.

International Convention on Civil Liability for Oil Pollution Damage.[69] This 1969 treaty seeks to protect the oceans from oil pollution by bulk carriers, by creating a system of liability and compensation for harm caused by oil spills. This law stands for the proposition that the world community gives no one the right to spill oil into the *res communis* of the sea with impunity.[70]

Agreement on Cooperation in the Field of Environmental Protection Between the United States of America and the Union of Soviet Socialist Republics.[71] This 1972 bilateral agreement between the world's preeminent space powers is a significant declaration of the environmental values of both countries. Both parties agree to cooperate to prevent pollution, develop the basis for controlling the impact of human activities on nature, and develop new technologies which do not pollute the environment.[72]

Convention on the Prevention of Marine Pollution by Dumping of Wastes and Other Matter.[73] Signed in 1972, this multilateral agreement is undoubtedly one of the most significant expressions of the world's practice and opinion on the environmental protection of the sea. This treaty requires contracting parties to prohibit the dumping of wastes in the oceans by vessels and aircraft, unless the dumping is authorized by a domestically-created permit program.[74]

Convention on the Prohibition of Military or Other Hostile Use of Environmental Modification Techniques.[75] This 1973 multilateral treaty stresses, in Article III, the need to cooperate "[i]n the preservation, improvement, and peaceful utilization of the environment. . . ."[76] Its main thrust is to prohibit the "[m]ilitary or other hostile use of environmental modification techniques having widespread, long-lasting or severe effects as the means of destruction, damage, or injury to another State party. . . ."[77]

Agreement Governing the Activities of States on the Moon and other Celestial Bodies.[78] Known as the Moon Treaty, this 1979 agreement has been signed by only two of the world's space powers—the Netherlands and France. Nonetheless, it is a treaty open for signature to the world's nations, and eleven have chosen to do so.[79] Aside from referring to the moon and other celestial bodies as the common heritage of mankind, this treaty reflects a state of the art appreciation for the need to protect the environment of the moon and celestial bodies.[80]

International Declarations

Stockholm Declaration of the United Nations Conference on the Human Environment.[81] In 1972, a new United Nations organization was established—the United Nations Environmental Programme (UNEP). At a conference in Stockholm, 113 States adopted a declaration containing 26 principles relating to the protection and enhancement of the world's environment.[82] Principle 6 bolsters the sea treaties by stressing the undesirability of dumping substances that the environment cannot handle. Principle 7, viewing the sea as *res communis,* forbids pollution of the sea because of the harm it causes other legitimate users. Principle 24 refers to eliminating "adverse environmental effects resulting from activities conducted in all spheres," and could be interpreted as meaning activities in space. In total, this Declaration is a significant indication of the position of the vast majority of the international community on the issue of environmental protection.

United Nations General Assembly Resolution 3281: Charter of Economic Rights and Duties of States.[83] Article 29 of the resolution accords the seas CHOM status, which was previously conferred on space. This again helps tie in the issue of pollution in space to the issue of pollution in the seas. Article 30 is another iteration of the general principle that States should prevent pollution, particularly pollution that causes damage to other States.

Resolutions of the Organization for Economic Cooperation and Development (OECD). A confederation of European countries (with the exception of Turkey), the OECD is composed of all of the members of the ESA.[84] Of its numerous resolutions, three 1974 resolutions relating to the environment are cited here:

Declaration on Environmental Policy: "The protection and progressive improvement of the environment is a major objective of the OECD Member Countries."[85]

Principles Concerning Transfrontier Pollution: The OECD recommends that member countries should cooperate to develop international law applicable to transfrontier pollution.[86]

The Polluter Pays Principle: This is a "fundamental principle for allocating costs of pollution prevention and control measures."[87] It requires the polluter to bear the expenses of carrying out the necessary measures to ensure the environment is in an acceptable state.[88]

Although these principles are intended to guide the conduct of the nations within the OECD, these nations are nonetheless influential members of both the international community and the space community. These principles also provide a logical approach to the problem of transfrontier pollution. They can be looked to as empirical evidence of the norm against pollution—particularly transfrontier pollution. Any pollution in space can involve transfrontier pollution effects. There can be either back pollution onto the surface of the earth, or forward pollution if a nation's space object or experiment is disrupted by pollution emanating from another nation's space activities. If pollution occurs, these principles have great utility in determining how space activities should be judged.

International Organizations

The activities of three international organizations involved in environmental affairs dictate how the world perceives the issue of pollution. It should come as no surprise that pollution is not condoned by these groups, and that their membership includes the major space powers. All three are affiliated with the United Nations.

The International Law Commission (ILC). Established in 1947, the commission encourages the progressive development and codification of international law.[89] Of the various topics it explores, several involve international environmental law. One topic, the Law of Non-Navigational Uses of International Watercourses, explores the prevention of conflicts between States that share a single watercourse system.[90] In the area of environmental protection, the ILC believes that as a principle of international law, States should refrain from "activities that may cause harm to the interests of other States in the use of such a watercourse, and that States have an obligation not to pollute such streams."[91] The work of the ILC is viewed with interest because it carries weight as a statement of general international law.[92]

The International Atomic Energy Agency (IAEA). Established in 1956, the IAEA is an autonomous, intergovernmental agency, with over 100 members. Its purpose is "to accelerate and enlarge the contributions of atomic energy to peace, health, and prosperity throughout the world."[93] The IAEA, in terms of environmental protection, is primarily concerned with the safe operation of nuclear devices and disposal of radioactive wastes on earth. However, it does have an interest and programs in the area of nuclear safety in space. One of its programs concerns the possibility of contamination of the space environment by the escape of radioactive power supplies.

The United Nations Environmental Program (UNEP). Established in 1972 by a United Nations resolution, UNEP is the pre-eminent international environmental protection body.[94] It is funded by voluntary contributions separate from contributions to the UN. All of the world's space powers are contributors, with the exception of Belgium and Spain.[95] The UNEP charter is the Stockholm Declaration,[96] and under it UNEP is active in many programs to monitor environmental problems of worldwide concern, and to coordinate international cooperation in dealing with these problems. Although it funds environmental protection programs on its own, UNEP acts more as a coordinating clearinghouse, relying on individual States to remedy most of the specific environmental threats.[97] All of the proclamations made by UNEP on the issue of pollution would be too numerous to mention. It is fair to characterize what is has said and done as being against any kind of right to pollute, and in favor of environmental protection.

International Cases

The resolution of international cases or disputes can provide principles of international law. The four cases discussed below are cited for the international environmental law principles they establish, which can be easily applied to space activities.

The Trail Smelter Case. This was an arbitration decision rendered in two parts, in 1938 and 1941.[98] The case involved transfrontier air pollution from a Canadian smelting operation into the United States. The tribunal held Canada liable for damages, stating that "no State has a right to use or permit the use of its territory in such a manner as to cause injury to the territory of another or the persons or property therein when the case is of serious consequence and the injury is established by clear and convincing evidence."[99]

The Corfu Channel Case. This 1946 International Court of Justice (ICJ) case involved the laying of mines by Albania within its territorial waters, which caused damage to British vessels that came in contact with the mines.[100] Albania had not announced the presence of the mines, and as a result the court found Albania at fault. The ICJ held that it "is every State's obligation not to knowingly allow its territory to be used for acts contrary to the rights of other States."[101]

The Lake Lanoux Case. This was an arbitrated decision made in 1957. It involved a lake located in France which discharged into a river and continued for twenty-five kilometers to Spain where it was used for irrigation and drinking water purposes. Although it upheld France's plan to alter the flow of the river for a hydroelectric project on the basis that its project included plans to continue the water flow to Spain by an alternate route, the tribunal noted in passing that "there exists a principle prohibiting the upstream State from changing the waters of a river in their natural condition to the serious injury of a downstream State."[102] As applied to outer space, the case can be cited as meaning that at the very least, no one can foul the sector of space they are operating within if it will impact to the injury of other nations in their use of space.

The Cosmos 954 Case. This was a claim made by Canada against the USSR for the expenses it incurred in searching for and cleaning up the debris of a Soviet satellite which made an uncontrolled reentry into the atmosphere in 1978.[103] The debris included highly radioactive Uranium 235 particles from the satellite's nuclear reactor. Canada's claim was eventually settled by the USSR in the amount of $3,000,000 Canadian dollars. The settlement agreement does not reflect exactly what damages the USSR paid for and this is still a matter of conjecture. Nonetheless, the Soviets were willing to pay.[104] Canada based its claim on the Liability Convention,[105] the Outer Space Treaty,[106] and customary international law. This is the first successful utilization of these treaties to deal with the issue of space pollution (though admittedly of the back pollution variety), and demonstrates the impropriety of pollution in general, even if from a space-based source.

To summarize the first three cases: in the realm of earth-based pollution, it is clear that international environmental law establishes the responsibility of States to control their pollution activities in order to avoid damage to other States. Nations must consider the transfrontier impacts of pollution which arise within their borders.[107] Comparing this principle to the result in the Cosmos 954 incident, it can be concluded that the principle also applies to govern the conduct of States in outer space—whether that conduct causes harm to a State's territory on earth, or its "territory" in space. In light of the jurisdictional rights States exercise over their space objects, these objects are in effect a State's territory. Therefore, States have an obligation not to engage in polluting activities via their space objects, if such activities would harm the space activities and objects (i.e., territory) of other States.

Domestic Practice

Independent of the conduct of the world's nations in the international arena, what are the domestic practices of these nations when it comes to environmental protection and pollution control? Looking at such practices gives an insight into the world's "uniform practices" as a basis for finding customary international law.

The United States. The United States is heavily regulated by a host of domestic laws that attempt to control pollution and protect the environment. Laws such as the CAA, NCA, FWPCA, SDWA, RCRA, CERCLA, TOSCA, and NEPA, attempt to maintain the purity of America's air, water, and soil, all with the goal of protecting human health and the environment.[108] This body of law is mirrored repeatedly on state levels. It is correct to say that the U.S. position on pollution is to avoid and prevent it, and to clean it up when it occurs. The U.S. domestic practice mirrors its involvement in the United Nations Environmental Programme,[109] and its participation in the various international environmental protection treaties discussed earlier.

The Union of Soviet Socialist Republics. The Soviet Union's domestic practice is a reflection of its political system. Since all of the land and natural resources are owned by the State, it is the national government's responsibility to protect the environment. The Soviet Union's environmental protection laws are geared towards controlling the extent and manner to which the environment can be exploited. Of these laws, the Fundamentals of the Legislation of the USSR and Union Republics on Protection of Health (1969) most closely approximates those of the United States. This law contains a provision very similar to NEPA in its requirement to evaluate the environmental effects of activities:

> Managers of enterprises, institutions, design and construction
> organizations, and management boards of collective farms,

must envisage and prevent air, water bodies, underground waters and soil from pollution while planning, constructing, reconstructing and exploiting enterprises. In case they fail to perform their duties they bear the responsibility determined by the legislation of the USSR and the Union Republics.[110]

Actually, this law appears to be more far-reaching than NEPA, since NEPA deals only with major federal government actions. This Soviet law also places controls on the "production, application, storage and transportation, of radioactive, poisonous, and powerful substances."[111] Environmental protection laws are, for the most part, managed on a national level by the Ministry of Health Regulation.[112] It is clear that on the domestic front, the Soviet Union does engage in pollution control and environmental activities, following the uniform practice of States to avoid contamination of the environment.

The Nations of the ESA. The domestic positions of the European Space Agency (ESA) countries on environmental protection are reflected to a certain extent by the OECD's declarations on the environment. Further evidence is found in the regulations, directives, and decisions of the European Community (EC) formerly called the European Economic Community (EEC). These three categories of rules are binding upon member States pursuant to Article 189 of the EEC Treaty.[113] Through these means, the EC "has taken formal action in the areas of air, water, and noise pollution; control of toxic chemical substances; solid and liquid waste disposal; land and natural resource management; protection of flora and fauna; nuclear safety; and international environmental problems."[114] As of March 1, 1984, fifty-eight environmentally related directives were in existence. Pursuant to the EEC Treaty, the EC has the power to serve notices on member States for noncompliance with these directives, issue opinions on the failure of the member States to fully comply with the directives, and bring cases before the International Court of Justice for a member State's failure to fulfill its obligations under these directives. As of March 1, 1984, the EC served 199 notices, rendered 55 opinions, and brought suit on 22 cases.[115]

It is clear from the EC's enforcement of its environmental directives that the ESA States are aware of the need to protect the environment. This desire to pursue environmental quality is shared by the European populace, as revealed in a 1983 survey of EC citizens. The poll showed environmental protection rated second behind unemployment as the most important "socio-political problem" in five of nine member States.[116]

Summary

Various types of empirical evidence show that there is an international uniform practice to protect the earth and its atmosphere from pollution. The evidence indicates that States have a duty to avoid engaging in pollution activities. By interpretation and implication, this practice also applies to activities in outer space. This uniform practice by the world's States comprises the first element of a customary international law against pollution of space.

Customary International Law: The Psychological Element

The second element of customary law, the psychological element, or *opinio juris*, looks to the world's opinion of the law on a given subject. Evidence of this element can be initially established by looking once again at the evidence of the empirical element. The various treaties, declarations, and organizations reflect the opinion of those nations who are signatories or members, and are also proof of the psychological element. This means that the world's opinion is that nations should avoid pollution in general, and specifically pollution which can cause harm to another nation's interests. Furthermore, a nation which causes harm by its transfrontier pollution activities must provide compensation for the harm it causes.

A second form of evidence of *opinio juris* is the writings of experts in the space law field. The focus is to see if these experts agree that there is a norm, principle, custom, or general concept in international space law against the pollution of outer space.

Most of these experts are members of the International Aeronautical Federation's International Institute on Space Law (IISL). Members of this private organization are considered the leading thinkers in the area of space law—most of the major treatises, texts, and law review articles on the issue of space law have been written by them. In a series of articles written for the 1971 Colloquium on the Law of Outer Space, the issue of environmental protection was addressed. Although primarily addressing the issue of back pollution, the principles of international space law discussed are nonetheless illuminating.

Ernest Fasan of Austria noted that international law forbids negligent acts in space which endanger the earth's environment or the life, health, and security of mankind or segments of mankind, independent of the dictates of Article IX of the OST.[117]

Gunter B. Krauss-Ablass of the Federal Republic of Germany, noting the existence of an international principle against actions which "endanger the existence of the entire human race as well as the existence of individual persons of a foreign nation," and of "every State's obligation not to allow knowingly its territory to be used for acts contrary to the rights of other States,"[118] concluded that it is also a principle of international law that "any activities in outer space which cause harmful effects on the territory of another State must be avoided."[119]

Nicholas M. Poulantzas of Greece found that general international law allows a State to ask for compensation for the contamination of its territory caused by another State's activities in outer space. This principle includes the right of a state to demand the activities be stopped for self-preservation purposes, and includes the right of reprisal.[120]

Peter Sand of the Federal Republic of Germany noted that existing international law which protects against the contamination of earth's environment by space activities is very narrow. Nonetheless, he cited the Test Ban Treaty and the OST as evidence of at least some law in this area, although he questioned how well it had been honored by the world's space powers.[121]

The remaining three experts are all Americans. Andrew Ritholz noted the existence of an "internationally accepted ban against contamination of outer space."[122] He concluded that this ban could be construed as including nonfunctioning space debris.

Stephen Gorove, a member of the IISL, examining the meaning of the OST as it relates to space pollution, found the OST to be a reflection of "mankind's concern about the dangers of pollution and contamination" in outer space.[123] He nonetheless recommended a strengthening of the OST via a new international code of conduct dealing with pollution in space.

Carl Christol, also a member of the IISL, examining nuclear power sources in outer space, stated that the general principles of international law prohibit a State from using radioactive materials in space in such a way as to cause harm to another State's interests.[124] In examining pollution in outer space in general, he concluded:

> Harms to the natural environment of outer space, per se, the Moon, and other celestial bodies can result from the intentional and unintentional conduct of juridical and natural persons.

Such activities can produce the legal duty to provide compensation to those who have experienced detriment. Such detriment can be caused by physical debris. It can also be caused by non-physical or intangible contamination pollution.[125]

On the basis of the 1967 Principles Treaty, as well as other relevant international law, the conclusion was reached that States have an affirmative duty to avoid allowing debris, and contaminants, from constituting harmful interferences in the beneficial and peaceful uses of the natural environment of outer space, per se, the Moon, and other celestial bodies.

The consultative provisions of Article 9 of the 1967 Principles Treaty have particular relevance to a procedure whereby this duty can be implemented. Thus, the space environment cannot be treated as an area open to the wholly unregulated conduct of the space-resource States.[126]

Of these experts, Christol most clearly accepts the existence of an international principle against the pollution of outer space. His statements can be interpreted to mean that pollution in outer space includes pollution of space itself, without the need for a specific harm to another nation.

To summarize the psychological element: the opinions of the world's States and its experts oppose pollution in general, and pollution which causes harm in particular, both on earth and in outer space.

Customary International Law: Combining the Elements

When the empirical and psychological elements are combined, a customary international law against pollution can be perceived. The law is in favor of protecting the environment, prohibiting activities in space which cause back pollution, and activities in space which cause forward pollution of a type that causes direct harm to another State's interests (e.g., damage to a State's satellite).

There is also a strong case that this customary law extends to forward pollution where space activities cause contamination of the purity of the space environment, although no one in particular is presently harmed. Such pollution could be prohibited as a potential interference with other States' future use of space. It also amounts to appropriation of that particular area of space by the pollution, particularly in the case of a dumping site. Such conduct is a clear violation of the CHOM principle of space.[127] Independently, it is a violation of the overwhelmingly accepted practice on earth to condemn pollution and protect the environment for its own sake, and not purely for reasons of sovereignty.

Regardless of the parameters of the customary law against pollution in outer space, the area could benefit from clarification. The next section explores a suggested regime to address present and future space pollution.

Suggested Controls on Outer Space Pollution

There are three significant flaws in the present system of international space pollution law. First, the rules primarily relate to pollution which causes harm to another State. Generally speaking, until a piece of space debris hurts somebody, it doesn't become a problem under the law—but by then it is too late. Second, unlike the sea where there is at least the chance for someone to catch the polluter doing its dirty work, the remoteness of space makes it far more difficult to police the waste-handling practices of space manufacturing industries. Third, although the system of compensation for harm caused by space activities is in place,[128] there may in the future be serious proof problems in establishing whose waste caused the harm.[129]

These problems, as well as others, have been pointed out by other authors.[130] It is apparent that they will not be solved by creating some sort of supranational space environmental protection agency to which States would give their allegiance. Historically, States are reluctant to submit to binding arbitration to resolve disputes, so it is unlikely they will give up whatever measure of sovereignty it would take to make such an agency effective.[131] Also, while such an agency would prove of great utility in the realm of ordinary pollution on earth, one has never been created.

What is needed instead is an international agency in the mold of the International Atomic Energy Agency (IAEA),[132] dedicated to the singular issue of pollution in outer space. This agency would be within the United Nations Environmental Programme.[133] For illustration purposes it will be called the Office of Outer Space Environmental Protection (OOSEP). OOSEP would act as a clearinghouse for information relating to research and the space environmental protection activities of other nations; promulgate proposed model treaties, domestic laws, and regulations to establish controls on space pollution; perform inspections of space operations and receive notice from the States on their space activities which involve potential pollution; and perform cleanup activities in outer space of already existing pollution, and of future pollution in the case of accidental releases.

To boost its effectiveness, OOSEP would benefit from a formal declaration by the United Nations, similar to the Stockholm Declaration which initially gave rise to the Nations Environmental Programme.[134] This declaration would establish a world position that contamination of outer space should be regulated as much as the dumping of wastes in the oceans. The declaration would give OOSEP the charter to coordinate world activity to this end. The IAEA is cited as an example because of its somewhat activist approach to the issue of radioactive material safety. In fact, IAEA conducts inspections of nuclear facilities to ensure that minimal guidelines established by IAEA are met (although only at the request of the State who owns the facility).[135] IAEA was even called upon by the Soviet Union after the Chernobyl disaster to help evaluate Soviet handling of the situation, and it is presently considering developing an international convention to resolve damage claims for future nuclear accidents.[136]

OOSEP could benefit from IAEA's example. OOSEP's goal would be to create a regime of space environmental protection laws which the world would want to adhere to based on the scientific reliability of the rules, and the independence and neutrality of its creator. This section will describe the general nature of this regime, the specific regulations to control space pollution, and how cleanup operations should proceed.

The General Nature of the Space Environmental Protection Regime

The proposed regime would have as its most basic principle that no waste created on earth could be put into space, and no waste generated in space could be returned to earth. The purpose of this principle is to prevent the destruction of a spacecraft either on launch or reentry, and to eliminate the risk of wastes (nonhazardous, hazardous, and radioactive) spreading into the atmosphere and onto the surface of the earth. In the future, such flights may become so reliable that this premise can be changed. However, in light of the Challenger disaster,[137] it may take years for this to occur. Another purpose of this principle is to force generators of waste to clean up pollution in the location that it is created, and prevent them from shipping the problem someplace else.

There are seven basic rules which would govern the control of space pollution:
1.   Each State would regulate the activities of its governmental and nongovernmental entities. The model for this approach is the

Convention on the Prevention of Marine Pollution by Dumping of Wastes and Other Matter.[138] This convention envisions each State issuing permits to those who would dump wastes into the sea. As noted earlier, the annexes to the Convention list items which must be carefully reviewed before issuing a permit to dump. OOSEP, in its model treaty, would create the same kind of framework for items dumped in space.

2. The proposed convention on space pollution would limit liability for damage caused in space to a specific dollar amount (subject to upward revision due to inflation). This is similar to Article V of the International Convention on Civil Liability for Oil Pollution Damage.[139] As for back pollution damage to earth, liability limits would also be allowed, but the dollar limit would be higher to account for the greater extent of harm which might occur if an accident happened. As in the International Convention on Civil Liability for Oil Pollution Damage, the polluter would need to post a bond equal to the value of the liability limitation. Such a scheme would encourage prompt settlement of damage claims.

3. States would report the location and extent of the activities by the government and the nongovernmental entities to OOSEP. This would allow OOSEP, acting in its clearinghouse capacity, to provide information to victims of space pollution damage and to help pinpoint the source of harm.

4. OOSEP would inspect generators, transporters, and facilities that store and dispose wastes to ensure safe practices in handling wastes are followed. Although these inspections would be voluntary, it is hoped that OOSEP would command respect in the world community analogous to the IAEA, so that OOSEP inspections and assistance would be willingly sought.

5. Use of the earth and sun to dispose of wastes would not be permitted until OOSEP has an opportunity to determine if these methods are safe, and in what manner they are safe. In the meantime, wastes would be handled in space by treatment, storage, and disposal facilities, with the goal to render the substances harmless.

6. Funding for OOSEP would be voluntary, as in the case with the IAEA and UNEP. OOSEP would have no space resources of its own with the exception of a few spacecraft, already parked in space, to be used in conducting its inspections and research of the

outer space environment. Instead it would rely on state support to put its personnel into space.

7.   OOSEP would have a cleanup function which is explained in detail below.

Regulations of the Space Environmental Protection Regime

Although each State would regulate its own activities in space, OOSEP would create a series of model regulations to help States maintain uniformity, and avoid the pitfalls of national subsidization of polluters which the OECD has recognized in its "Polluter-Pays Principle."[140] This would be consistent with Principles 21, 22, and 25, of the Stockholm Declaration, which holds each State responsible for the pollution activities of its nongovernment entities, and encourages States to allow international organizations like OOSEP to play a role in the protection of the environment.[141]

Under the model regulation of space pollution activities, OOSEP should propose the following rules:

1.   Any nongovernment entity (hereinafter "industry") whose activities in space create waste, would be required to obtain insurance in advance, to indemnify the State.[142] This is a simple recognition of the State's continuing responsibility for the conduct of industry. The amount of liability coverage would vary depending on the type of waste being handled. Simple trash of a nonhazardous nature would require a small amount of coverage, while hazardous and radioactive waste would require greater coverage.

2.   The current philosophy of the Environmental Protection Agency (EPA) on managing wastes would be adopted in a regulation to encourage industry to produce as little waste as possible; to reuse the waste that is produced; and to treat whatever waste is leftover after reuse to render it harmless.[143]

3.   The basic model for the proposed space pollution regulation would be the Resource Conservation and Recovery Act (RCRA)[144] which is managed by the Environmental Protection Agency in the United States. This law was created to deal with the problem of how to safely dispose of solid and hazardous wastes.[145] Although it does not deal with wastes of a radioactive character, for purposes of space pollution it would be expanded to address these substances as well.

4.   The proposed space pollution regulation (for illustration purposes, the Space Resource Conservation and Recovery Act (SRCRA),

would parallel RCRA's categorization of participants in the waste process, and the rules that govern their behavior.

The cast of characters includes:

Generators: These are the individuals who place any type of substance into a space manufacturing facility, laboratory, or other activity, from which they will generate any type of waste material (solid, hazardous, or radioactive) as a by-product of their activity.

Transporters: These are individuals who move wastes from the site of the manufacturing facility, laboratory, or other area to the site of the treatment, storage, or disposal facility which handles the particular type of waste involved.

Treatment, Storage, and Disposal Facility: These are facilities where waste is treated to render it harmless, stored until it can be treated or disposed, or disposed in an environmentally acceptable manner (e.g., using the earth or sun once the safety parameters for doing so are established by OOSEP).

A facility could, of course, contain all three types of operations. Also, a given form of waste could conceivably receive all three forms of handling—it could be initially stored, then treated, and then disposed.

SRCRA would regulate these entities as follows:

Generators, transporters, and treatment, storage, or disposal facilities would need a SRCRA permit to operate in space. A detailed list of substances subject to SRCRA controls would be established. This list would consist of substances whose unmanaged presence in outer space would pose a danger to earth if they were to migrate into its atmosphere (e.g., radioactive wastes and most of the wastes currently deemed hazardous by RCRA). If these substances are generated, transported, treated, stored, or disposed, then manifests would be required to trace the item from "cradle to grave."[146]

Solid wastes would be less rigorously controlled. Solid wastes could not be casually dumped into space, however, if for no other reason that the navigational hazard they would pose to other States. Nonetheless, solid wastes which are celestially-biodegradable could be disposed of by injecting them into space. No report to the state space agency administering the SRCRA regulation would be necessary, as long as OOSEP is certain that such waste could truly be assimilated.

The basic scheme would call for generators who create controllable waste to either reuse the substance, or store it and then treat and/or dispose of it. The generator would have the option to send the items to a central treatment, storage, and disposal facility. The generator could also use the services of a transporter, whose job would be to move these substances in a safe manner to the treatment, storage, and disposal facility.

Under RCRA, generators can store wastes on-site for up to ninety days, without a permit to function as a treatment, storage, or disposal facility.[147] SRCRA would also have time standards, but they would likely be longer. This concession would be due to the remoteness of space, where the risks from the accumulation of large quantities of waste would not be as great as they would be on earth.

Under RCRA there is also a category of small quantity generators, which is allowed to accumulate wastes for up to 180 days, if the amount of waste is less than 100 kilograms of waste per month.[148] In relation to the vastness of space, what constitutes a large amount of waste on earth will likely be a small amount in space. As a result, small quantity generators in space may be more numerous than they are on earth.

If a generator is able to reuse its waste, it would still need a permit. However, it would not need a permit to operate as a treatment, storage, or disposal facility, unless it stored the wastes on site without reusing them beyond the storage standards established by SRCRA.

Inspections conducted without notice under RCRA would need modification under SRCRA. If the inspections are conducted by the State's regulating space agency, then it should be easy to arrange, even in light of the practical need for approaching spacecraft to identify themselves before boarding a space station. If OOSEP conducted the inspection, advance coordination with the state space agency would be necessary to ensure that the facility would honor a request from OOSEP spacecraft to dock for an inspection. Such OOSEP inspections would occur only with the State's consent.

Examining these proposed SRCRA rules, it is apparent that there is little variation from the way RCRA is enforced on earth. This is because the RCRA regime is a fairly straightforward attempt to control the complex problem of solid and hazardous wastes. As such, it is worthy of emulation in the realm of space.

Cleanup Operations in Outer Space

In light of the debris which is presently in outer space and the hazards to navigation it poses, and the danger to space travelers posed by radioactive materials, OOSEP should be charged with responsibility for coordinating the resources of the world to clean up outer space. In addition, an international coordinating agency like OOSEP should be created to respond to accidental releases of wastes into outer space.

On earth, there are no concerted general environmental cleanup operations (e.g., there has been no organized cleanup of the seas). Cleanups occurred case-by-case as the result of specific incidents. And as to these, States have performed the necessary cleanup operation either individually or in concert with the nation of the polluter or neighboring States.

But space, of course, is different. There are no territorial boundaries and no State has the same type of relationship with a region of space as it does to its territorial, contiguous, or continental shelf sea areas. That is why the need for a central agency like OOSEP is greater in the realm of space environmental pollution.

To perform this cleanup function, OOSEP would draft an international treaty, modeled very loosely on the Comprehensive Environmental Response, Compensation, and Liability Act (CERCLA)[149] administered by the Environmental Protection Agency in the United States. CERCLA enables the federal government to respond to abandoned or inactive hazardous waste sites. It creates a "Superfund" composed of taxes on industry and federal funds. This money is used by the EPA to hire contractors to perform the cleanup.[150]

As for future accidental leaks, the OOSEP treaty would have each State perform its own cleanup operations using its own resources. If a State refused, OOSEP would be permitted under the treaty to clean up the waste itself. It would do this exclusively through contractors, and would have no space cleanup resources of its own. Contractors would consist of other States or private industry. The big problem would be funding and indemnification of OOSEP by the recalcitrant State. Since OOSEP's funding will consist of voluntary contributions by the States, the amount of funding must be sufficient to accomplish such a cleanup program, and indemnification would be critical to allow OOSEP to act again. It is hoped that the international opprobrium which would greet such a scofflaw State would force voluntary cleanup, or at least grudging compliance with an indemnification demand.

As for the debris presently in outer space, OOSEP would coordinate a one-time massive cleanup effort of this thirty-year accumulation of junk. Once this is accomplished, and the SRCRA regulations are in place, such an endeavor would theoretically never need to be repeated. Similar plans have been suggested by others.[151] Such a cleanup would occur only after careful research, to ensure that only those objects which are no longer performing an active function are disposed of. Coordination with States of registry would be necessary to ensure appropriate removal. Funding for such a project would be secured by seeking contributions in proportion to the percentage of debris in space for which the State is responsible.

For purposes of a one-time cleanup, this voluntary funding could be passed by the State onto private industry. However, the percentage of such contributions solicited from industry should take account of the great amount of debris resulting from purely governmental space operations. As for cleanup efforts of accidental leakages, private industry contributions should be greater, but at the same time proportional to the amount of insurance coverage they are required to have for such contingencies.

In summary, a regime of treaties and regulations empowered to deal with present and future pollution in outer space is suggested. As with all similar suggestions dealing with the unknown demands of the future, scientific matters in general, and outer space in particular, a great deal of what has been presented can be viewed as fanciful conjecture. Nonetheless, this is the very nature of outer space law, and it is what makes it the unique area of study that it is.

Final Observations

The comparison between those who derided the notion of protecting the deserts, and those who question the need to protect outer space, is useful in making another point. Basically, the treatment of the deserts is similar to the treatment of outer space. In both cases, a trail of trash was left in the wake of early explorers and travelers.

In the quest to tame the West, early settlers made the deserts true "wastelands" by casting off supplies, refuse, and unwanted items to lighten their load and ensure their survival. In space, items are also cast off when they become superfluous to the main objective of simple survival in this equally inhospitable region. Both the deserts and outer space were new and strange to their travelers, and in the end neatness did not amount for much, whereas expediency and survival did.

Today, we know the deserts have a fragile ecology. Cleanup of the deserts has been relatively effortless, because most of the debris was biodegradable. Much of the debris presently in space is also reclaimable by nature, by the friction of earth's atmosphere and the sun. But we stand at a threshold in outer space that we did not face in the early years of our use of the deserts. The plans to begin manufacturing operations in outer space and the resulting wastes which cannot be assimilated by nature pose a threat to the space environment that the deserts did not have to face.

As noted earlier, several years will pass before these manufacturing operations pose such a threat. This time should be used by the world's States to ensure that the legacy of space can be preserved, just as humanity today is attempting to preserve the deserts and other areas. This should be done, if not to preserve the aesthetic quality of outer space, then for the sake of space safety and the protection of the earth.

A side benefit to developing an agency like OOSEP would be to help the world in dealing with terrestrial environmental catastrophes. Most of the environmental emergencies which have occurred in the world have been addressed by those States directly affected. Someday the world may be faced with an environmental problem of such tremendous international scope that no one country or group of countries will have the ability to address it. Only concerted international action could address such a problem—the kind of action that an agency like OOSEP will be designed to muster. An OOSEP prototype for the global environmental problem would save time and limit damages by providing ready access to the environmental protection resources of the world.

OOSEP is an idea whose time has come, both to benefit humanity's future use of space, as well as to provide the earth with an extra measure of security from environmental catastrophes. The world community should work to make such an agency a reality while time is still available.

Notes

1. Resource Conservation and Recovery Act, 42 U.S.C. §§ 6901–87 (1982).
2. Comprehensive Environmental Response, Compensation and Liability Act, 42 U.S.C. §§ 9601–57 (1982).
3. No attempt will be made in this article to address the issue of where the earth's atmosphere ends and outer space begins. However, for general reference purposes, Professor Muyres S. McDougal observes that customary law seems to recognize that outer space begins where artificial satellites move in durable orbit. Gorove, S. "Pollution and Outer Space: A Legal Analysis and Appraisal," 5 *N.Y.J. Int'l. L.* 53–54 (1972).
4. The terms "solid waste" and "hazardous waste" are freely adapted from the definition of these terms used by the Environmental Protection Agency (EPA) in its enforcement of the Resource Conservation and Recovery Act (RCRA), 42 U.S.C. §§ 6901–87 (1982). As defined by the

EPA, a solid waste consists of gases, liquids, semi-solids and solid waste products which are not hazardous wastes. Hazardous wastes are solid wastes which may cause or contribute to an increase in mortal or serious illness, or pose a substantial present or potential hazard to human health or the environment when improperly treated, stored, transported, or disposed. *Office of Solid Waste, Environmental Protection Agency, RCRA Orientation Manual* §§ II–5, III–9 (Jan. 1986).

5.   Somatic effects are those which are immediate, serious, and possibly even life-threatening. In the area of exposure to radiation this encompasses, for example, the potentially fatal suppression of the immune system. Long-term effects are those not realized immediately, but gradually, over a period of years. Again, in the area of radiation, this encompasses maladies such as cancer.

6.   Unanswered for the time being is the effect earth microbes might have on certain planets such as Venus, where natural conditions, though rigorous, might in fact be conducive to the unfettered growth or mutation of these organisms. Gorove, supra note 3, at 55.

7.   Menter, "Legal Regime of International Spaceflight," in *Space Shuttle and the Law* 61–63 (S. Gorove, ed. 1980).

8.   Hall, "Comments on Salvage and Removal of Man-Made Objects From Outer Space," 33 *J. Air L. & Com.* 288 (1967).

9.   M. Freeman, *Space Traveller's Handbook: Every Man's Comprehensive Manual to Space Flight* 40 (1979).

10.   Morrison, "Star Drek," *Envtl. Action*, July 1983, at 10.

11.   Scheraga, "Curbing Pollution in Outer Space," *Tech. Rev.,* Jan. 8, 1986, at 9. This experiment, conducted in 1961 and 1963, was called the West Ford Project. Its impact on the world is still being felt. Because many of the needles are still in orbit, radio astronomers must take them into account when designing their experiments. See also, S. Lay and H. Taubenfeld, *The Law Relating to Activities of Man in Space* 189 (1970).

12.   Examples of intentional destruction are the USSR's practice of blowing up its derelict electronic intelligence satellites to prevent their recovery by the U.S., and the more than 20 anti-satellite experiments the USSR has conducted since 1968. Morrison, supra note 10, at 10–11.

13.   Smith, "A Review of Contamination Issues Associated With An Orbiting Space Station External Environment," *J. Envtl. Sci.,* Jan. 1985, at 53; Christol, "Stratospheric Ozone, Space Objects, and International Environmental Law," 6 *J. Space L.* 23 (1976).

14.   Morrison, supra note 10, at 13.

15.   C. Christol, *The Modern International Law of Outer Space* 765–67 (1982). See also Morrison, supra note 10, at 10–14.

16.   Morrison, supra note 10, at 10; Scheraga, supra note 11, at 8.

17.   M. Freeman, supra note 9, at 155.

18.   Morrison, supra note 10, at 10–11.

19. A hypothetically unprotected astronaut in space would receive (in the absence of solar flares) about 10 rems of radiation per year. In comparison, the average person on the face of the earth receives only about .1 rems of radiation per year from background sources (i.e., from the earth and from space). M. Freeman, supra note 9, at 154.

20. 4 *Toxic and Hazardous Waste Disposal* 177 (R. Bojasek, ed. 1980).

21. D. Shapland and M. Rycroft, *SPACELAB: Research in Earth Orbit* 22, 55 (1984).

22. Boraiko, "Storing up Trouble . . . Hazardous Waste," 167 *Nat'l. Geographic*, Mar. 1985, at 330.

23. Scheraga, supra note 11, at 8. The space shuttle Challenger exploded shortly after launching on January 28, 1986. All seven crew members died in the explosion, which occurred 74 seconds after lift-off, at 11:38 a.m., from Cape Canaveral. On March 21, 1988, NASA officials conceded that the failure of a synthetic rubber O-ring safety sealing at a joint on the right side rocket booster was the probable cause of the explosion. The failure of this seal allowed superheated gases to escape and ignite the fuel in the shuttle's external tank. The rupture of this seal was due to a combination of cold weather experienced at the launch site, and design flaws in the seal itself. *46 Facts on File no. 2358,* Jan 31, 1986, at 49; *46 Facts on File no. 2366,* Mar. 28, 1986, at 210; *46 Facts on File no. 2372,* May 9, 1986, at 334.

24. Smith, supra note 13, at 52.

25. Christol, supra note 13, at 1.

26. Doyle, "Reentering Space Objects: Facts and Fiction," 6 *J. Space L.* 107, 119 (1978).

27. Morrison, supra note 10, at 11.

28. Isikoff, "U.S. Firms Unveil Plan For Space Lab," *Washington Post,* Sept. 30, 1986, at C3, describes plans between Westinghouse Electric Co. and Space Industries Inc. to build the first commercial space research lab. Tucker, "Fairchild Bids to Build First Gas Station in the Heavens," *Washington Post,* Sept. 15, 1986, at Washington Business 3, describes Fairchild Space Company's plans to design a system to refuel satellites and extend their useful lives.

29. The Challenger disaster is discussed supra note 23.

30. Sawyer, "Military Payloads Dominate New Schedule for Shuttle," *Washington Post,* Oct. 1, 1986, at A1; Levine, "Commercialization of Space: Policy and Administrative Issues," *Pub. Admin. Rev.,* Sept. 1985, at 562.

31. Simpson, "Small Space Flight Office Sees Business Taking Off," *Washington Post,* Sept. 17, 1986, at A23; Corrigan, "Space-Age Speculators Plan Orbiting Industrial parks with NASA's Help," *Nat'l. J.,* Sept. 7, 1985, at 1986–87. There are two likely locations for these factories in space: geostationary orbits around the earth, and in deep space

at the Lagrange liberation points. Geostationary orbits are an ideal spot because this will place the factories in a position to be managed more easily by the owners of the project. Also, such a location puts the factory close to the markets on earth where the manufactured products are intended to be used. An alternative location may be those spots in deep space where the gravity of the earth is cancelled by the gravity of the moon, referred to as the Lagrange liberation points. These points may be suitable for the location of space stations due to the congestion of the geostationary orbit locations, the proximity of the points to the natural resources of the moon, and the natural advantage the points offer of reducing the expenditure of energy to maintain a zero gravity status. *National Commission on Space, Pioneering the Space Frontier* 131–32 (1986).

32. *Time*, Sept. 29, 1986, at 59. This is somewhat reminiscent of the West Ford Project. See supra note 11 and accompanying text.

33. Finch and Moore, "Ecospace and Some of Its Legal Implications," 4 *J. Space L.* 117 (1976).

34. E. Finch and A. Moore, *Astrobusiness: A Guide to the Commerce and Law of Outer Space* 6 (1985).

35. Bourely, "The Spacelab Program and Related Legal Issues," 11 *J. Space L.* 27 (1983); Shapland, D., and Rycroft, M. supra note 21, at 186–87.

36. Space gravity is considered near zero because some gravitational disturbances are experienced as a result movements of the astronauts within the spacecraft, the movement of the craft itself, and the influences of the earth's atmosphere and gravitational pull. D. Shapland and M. Rycroft, supra note 21, at 67.

37. *The Economist,* Aug. 4, 1984, at 74.

38. Id.

39. Hill, CERCLA New-Hire Training Information, EPA Memorandum (June 13, 1986) (available at Office of Solid Waste and Emergency Response, Environmental Protection Agency).

40. *The Economist,* Aug. 4, 1984, at 4.

41. Treaty Banning Nuclear Weapon Tests in the Atmosphere, in Outer Space, and Underwater, Aug. 5, 1963, 14 U.S.T. 1313, T.I.A.S. No. 5433, 480 U.N.T.S. 43.

42. Id. at preamble.

43. Id. at art. I.

44. Treaty on Principles Governing the Activities of States in the Exploration and Use of Outer Space, Including the Moon and Other Celestial Bodies, *opened for signature* Jan. 27, 1967, 18 U.S.T. 2410, T.I.A.S. No. 6347, 610 U.N.T.S. 205 [hereinafter OST].

45. *Black's Law Dictionary* 1173 (5th ed. 1979); C. Christol, supra note 15, at 286.

46. See "Agreement Governing the Activities of States on the Moon and other Celestial Bodies," Dec. 5, 1979, G.A. Res. 34/68, 34 U.N. GAOR Supp. (No. 46) at 77, U.N. Doc. A/Res/34/68; Menter, "Commercial Space Activities Under the Moon Treaty," 7 *Syracuse J. Int'l. L. & Com.* 213, 216 (1979).

47. OST, supra note 44, at art. I & IX.

48. C. Christol, supra note 15, at 286. Other articles make this even clearer. Article III provides: "State parties to the treaty shall carry on activities in the exploration and use of outer space including the moon and other celestial bodies, in accordance with international law." OST, supra note 44, at art. III. This suggests that in addition to the body of conventional law created by the OST, customary international law relating to the terrestrial environment, applies as well. See *infra* sec. IIB. Article IX states that parties shall: "pursue studies of outer space, including the moon and their celestial bodies, and conduct exploration of them so as to avoid their harmful contamination and . . . where necessary, shall adopt appropriate measures for this purpose." OST, supra note 44, at art. IX. If a party has "reason to believe that an activity or experiment planned by it or its nationals in outer space . . . would cause potentially harmful interference with the activities of other Parties in the peaceful exploration and use of outer space . . . it shall undertake appropriate international consultations before proceeding with any such activity or experiment." Id. A party "may request consultation concerning the activity or experiment of other Parties, if it has reason to believe the activity or experiment of the other party would cause potentially harmful interference with its activities." Id. This language clearly prohibits the pollution of outer space. It places a duty on potential polluters to notify others of harmful activities by the State or private enterprise. It creates a right for potentially affected parties to request consultation with polluting countries about their harmful outer space activities.

49. Esposito, "The Commercial Exploitation of Space," 25 *A.F.L. Rev.* 159, 160 (1985).

50. Agreement on the Rescue of Astronauts, the Return of Astronauts, and the Return of Objects Launched into Outer Space, opened for signature Apr. 22, 1968, 19 U.S.T. 7570, T.I.A.S. No. 6599, 672 U.N.T.S. 119 [hereinafter Rescue and Return Agreement].

51. Trimble, "The International Law of Outer Space and Its Effect on Commercial Space Activity," 11 *Pepperdine L. Rev.* 521, 536 (1984).

52. Rescue and Return Agreement, supra note 50, at art. 5, para. 4.

53. Convention on International Liability for Damage Caused by Space Objects, Mar. 29, 1972, 24 U.S.T. 2389, T.I.A.S. No. 7762 [hereinafter Liability Convention].

54. Martin, "Legal Ramifications of the Uncontrolled Return of Space Objects to Earth," 45 *J. Air L. Com.* 457, 461 (1980).

55. Liability Convention, supra note 53, at art. II; see also *Space Shuttle and the Law* 15 (S. Gorove ed. 1980).

56. Deem, "Liability of Private Space Transportation Companies," 51 *Ins. Couns. J.* 340, 355 (1984).

57. This suggests that one could look to cases such as the Trail Smelter Arbitration, which deal with environmental issues on an international scale to determine what the fair measure of damages would be in a space environmental pollution case. See Trail Smelter (Can. v. U.S.), Arbitral Tribunal Under the Convention of Apr. 15, 1935, 3 R. Int'l Arb. Awards 1905 (1949).

58. Convention on the Registration of Objects Launched into Outer Space, opened for signature Jan. 14, 1975, 28 U.S.T. 695, T.I.A.S. No. 8480.

59. Id.

60. In such a case, Article VI requires, to the greatest extent feasible, other States to assist the State damaged by a space object either by a collision or by the object's "harmful or deleterious nature." It requires monitoring and tracking assistance and identification of the previously unreported object. N. Matte, *Aerospace Law: From Scientific Exploration to Commercial Utilization* 175 (1977).

61. Statute of the International Court of Justice, as annexed to the Charter of the United Nations, June 26, 1945, 59 Stat. 1055, T.S. No. 993, Article 38(1)(b).

62. The court further noted that "this process is a perfectly possible one and does from time to time occur: it constitutes indeed one of the recognized methods by which new rules of customary international law may be formed." North Sea Continental Shelf (W. Ger. v. Den. & Neth.) 1969 I.C.J. 12, at para. 71, (Judgment Feb. 20, 1969), reprinted in McDougal and Reisman, *International Law in Contemporary Perspective* (1981).

63. The OST in particular, which 84 of 154 countries have signed.

64. C. Christol, supra note 15, at 912. See also infra notes 106–15 and accompanying text.

65. See infra sec. V.

66. Gorove, supra note 3.

67. Id. E.g., the issue of back pollution recognizes that space activities can have an adverse impact on the earth's environment.

68. Antarctic Treaty, Dec. 1, 1959, 12 U.S.T. 794, T.I.A.S. No. 4780. The treaty was signed by 13 nations, including seven space powers: the United States, the U.S.S.R., the United Kingdom, Ireland, Belgium, France, and Japan. Although this treaty divided the use of the Antarctic up among the 13 signatories, it still has a flavor of viewing the Antarctic as *res communis* (though admittedly for a *communis* of 13), and as such, deserving of some environmental protections.

69. International Convention on Civil Liability for Oil Pollution Damage, Nov. 29, 1969, 9 I.L.M. 45, 64 *Am. J. Int'l. L.* 481. The treaty requires

adequate insurance by carriers, and creates a trust fund to pay claims, if an incident has occurred and the carrier wants to limit its liability to treaty-based monetary limits. This agreement has been signed by all of the space powers.

70. Id. at art. XI.

71. Agreement on Cooperation in the Field of Environmental Protection, May 23, 1972, United States-USSR, 23 U.S.T. 845, T.I.A.S. No. 7345, reprinted in *1 International Protection of the Environment: Treaties and Related Documents* 50–57 (B. Ruster and B. Simma eds. 1975).

72. Id. at art. 2. A Joint Committee on Cooperation in the Field of Environmental Protection was established to further these goals. See id. at art. 5. This treaty is a clear sign of the environmental practices of these two significant countries.

73. Convention on the Prevention of Marine Pollution by Dumping of Wastes and Other Matter, Dec. 29, 1972, 26 U.S.T. 2403, T.I.A.S. No. 8165.

74. Id. at art. IV & VI. Specific lists of wastes and the parameters which govern when, where and how these wastes are to be dumped are detailed in annexes to this treaty. Id. at art. I, II & III. Although the Convention does not apply to vessels or aircraft entitled to sovereign immunity, it does require contracting parties to conduct dumping activities in a manner consistent with the purposes of the Convention. Id. at art. VII. The purpose of this Convention is to conduct dumping so as to minimize the likelihood of damage to human and marine life. Id. at art. V. This agreement has been signed by all the space powers.

75. Convention on the Prohibition of Military or Other Hostile Use of Environmental Modification Techniques, May 18, 1977, 31 U.S.T. 333, T.I.A.S. No. 9614.

76. Id. at art. III.

77. Id. at art. I. A loose interpretation of this treaty would prohibit wanton and reckless pollution of outer space if such activity were to modify the environment of another country, and such a degree of recklessness were exhibited that the act could be termed "hostile." With such an interpretation, this treaty could be viewed as a limitation of the kind of behavior that will be tolerated when it comes to pollution in space. All of the space powers have signed this agreement.

78. *Agreement Governing the Activities of States on the Moon and Other Celestial Bodies*, Dec. 5, 1979, G.A. Res. 34/68, 34 U.N. GAOR Supp. (No. 46) at 77, U.N. Doc. A/Res/34/68 [hereinafter *Moon Treaty*].

79. C. Christol, supra note 15, at 912.

80. *Moon Treaty*, supra note 78, art. VII. Article VII states:

        1. In exploring and using the moon, states parties shall take measures to prevent the disruption of the existing balance of its environment whether by introducing adverse changes in such environment, its harmful contamination through the introduction of

extra-environmental matter or otherwise. States parties shall also take measures to prevent harmfully affecting the environment of the earth through the introduction of extraterrestrial matter or otherwise. 2. States parties shall inform the Secretary-General of the United Nations of the measures being adopted by them in accordance with paragraph 1 of this article and shall to the maximum extent feasible notify him in advance of all placements by them of radioactive materials on the moon and of the purposes of such placements. 3. States parties shall report to other States parties and to the Secretary-General concerning areas of the moon having special scientific interest in order that, without prejudice to the rights of other States parties, consideration may be given to the designation of such areas as international scientific preserves for which special protective arrangements are to be agreed in consultation with the competent organs of the United Nations.

These words reflect a deep concern for the ecosystem of space bodies. In contrast to the OST, there is a sophistication here which reflects the growth of environmental awareness in the world. Here there is an affirmative duty to report the environmental protective measures taken. There is even the possibility of creating "wilderness areas" on space bodies, similar to those created in the U.S. This deference accorded environmental protection of the moon, a concededly sterile object is space, is perhaps a reflection about the care to be afforded outer space itself, an equally sterile environment.

81. *Stockholm Declaration of the United Nations Conference on the Human Environment*, June 16, 1972, U.N. Doc. A/Conf. 48/14, 11 I.L.M. 1416 (1972).

82. Christol, supra note 13, at 29. Some of the more significant principles were:

Principle 6. The discharge of toxic substances or of other substances and the release of heat, in such quantities or concentrations as to exceed the capacity of the environment to render them harmless, must be halted in order to ensure that serious or irreversible damage is not inflicted upon ecosystems. The just struggle of the problems of all countries against pollution should be supported.

Principle 7. States shall take all possible steps to prevent pollution of the seas by substances that are liable to create hazards to human health, to harm living resources and marine life, to damage amenities or to interfere with other legitimate uses of the sea.

Principle 21. States have, in accordance with the Charter of the United Nations and the principles of international law, the sovereign right to exploit their own resources pursuant to their own environmental policies, and the responsibility to ensure that activities within their jurisdiction or control do not cause damage to the environment of other States or of areas beyond the limits of national jurisdiction.

Principle 22. States shall cooperate to develop further the international law regarding liability and compensation for the victims of pollution and other environmental damage caused by activities within the jurisdiction or control of such States to areas beyond their jurisdiction.

Principle 24. International matters concerning the protection and improvement of the environment should be handled in a cooperative spirit by all countries, big and small, on an equal footing. Cooperation through multilateral or bilateral arrangements or other appropriate means is essential to effectively control, prevent, reduce and eliminate adverse environmental effects resulting from activities conducted in all spheres, in such a way that due account is taken of the sovereignty and interests of all States.

Principle 25. States shall ensure that international organizations play a coordinated, efficient and dynamic role for the protection and improvement of the environment.

83.   Charter of Economic Rights and Duties of States, G.A. Res. 832 (1975), reprinted in *United Nations Resolutions 300* (D. Djonovich ed. 1984). Adopted in 1974 by a vote of 120 in favor, 6 against and 10 abstentions, there are two significant articles which address environmental issues:

Article 29

The sea-bed and ocean floor and the subsoil thereof, beyond the limits of national jurisdiction, as well as the resources of the area, are the common heritage of mankind. On the basis of the principles adopted by the General Assembly in resolution 2749 (XXV) of 17 December 1970, all States shall ensure that the exploration of the area and exploitation of its resources are carried out exclusively for peaceful purposes and that the benefits derived therefrom are shared equitably by all States, taking into account the particular interests and needs of developing countries; an international regime applying to the area and its resources and including appropriate international machinery to give effect to its provisions shall be established by an international treaty of a universal character, generally agreed upon.

Article 30

The protection, preservation and enhancement of the environment for the present and future generations is the responsibility of all States. All States shall endeavor to establish their own environmental and developmental policies in conformity with such responsibility. The environmental policies of all States should enhance and not adversely affect the present and future development potential of developing countries. All States have the responsibility to ensure that activities within their jurisdiction or control do not cause damage to the environment of other States or of areas beyond the limits of national jurisdiction. All States should cooperate in evolving international norms and regulations in the field of the environment.

84. 2 *Air War College Associate Programs, The European Communities*, ch. 14 (18th ed. 1984).

85. "Declaration on Environmental Policy," Organization of Economic Cooperation and Development, Nov. 14, 1974, O.E.C.D. Doc. A (74) 47.

86. "Recommendations on Principles Concerning Transfrontier Pollution," Organization for Economic Cooperation and Development, Nov. 14, 1974, O.E.C.D. Doc. C (74) 224, at preamble, para. 4. The O.E.C.D. states further: Countries should define a concerted longterm policy for the protection and improvement of the environment in zones liable to be affected by transfrontier pollution. Id. at tit. B, para. 1. In implementing this concerted policy, countries should among other things . . . draw up and maintain up-to-date lists of particularly dangers substances regarding which efforts should be made to eliminate polluting discharges. Id. Countries should, individually and jointly, take all appropriate measures to prevent and control transfrontier pollutions, and harmonize as far as possible their relevant policies. Id. at tit. B, para. 2. Polluters causing transfrontier pollution should be subject to legal or statutory provisions no less severe than those which would apply for any equivalent pollution occurring within their country. Id. at tit. C, para. 4a. Levels of transfrontier pollution entering into the zones liable to be affected by such pollution should not exceed those considered acceptable under comparable conditions and in comparable zones inside the country in which it originates. Id. at tit. C, para. 4b. Prior to the initiation in a country of works or undertakings which might create a significant risk of transfrontier pollution, this country should provide early information to other countries which are or may be affected. Id. at tit. E, para. 6. Countries should promptly warn other potentially affected countries of any situation which may cause any sudden increase in the level of pollution in areas outside the country of origin of the pollution, and take all appropriate steps to reduce the effects of any such sudden increase. Id. at tit. F, para. 9.

87. "Recommendation on the Implementation of the Polluter Pays Principle," Organization for Economic Cooperation and Development, Nov. 14, 1974, O.E.C.D. Doc. C (74) 224, at art. I, para. 1.

88. Id. at art. I, para. 2. "In other words, the cost of these measures should be reflected in the cost of goods and services which cause pollution in

production and/or consumption." Id. "[T]herefore, as a general rule [Member Countries] should not assist the polluter in bearing the costs of pollution control whether by means of subsidies, tax advantages, or other measures." Id. at art. III, para. I.

89. McCaffrey, "The Work of the International Law Commission Relating to the Environment," 11 *Ecology L.Q.* 189, 190 (1983).

90. Id. at 192.

91. Id. at 201, 205.

92. Id. at 191.

93. "International Cooperation in Outer Space: A Symposium Prepared for the Committee on Aeronautical and Space Sciences," S. Doc. No. 92–57, 92d Cong., 1st Sess. 426 (1971).

94. Smith, Lopatkiewicz, and Rothblatt, "Legal Implications of a Permanent Manned Presence in Space," 85 *W. Va. L. Rev.* 857 (1980).

95. 1983 U.N.Y.B. 775, U.N. Sales No. E.86.I.1.

96. See supra notes 81–82 and accompanying text.

97. Buckley, "The United Nations Environment Programme: A Ten-Year Perspective," Quarterly Newsletter of the Standing Committee on Environmental Law 4–6 (Winter 1982–83).

98. Trail Smelter (Can. v. U.S.), 3 R. Int'l Arb. Awards 1905 (1949).

99. See Wetstone and Rosencranz, "Transboundary Air Pollution: The Search for an International Response," 8 *Harv. Envtl. L. Rev.* 89, 121 (1984).

100. Corfu Channel (U.K. v. Albania), 1949 I.C.J. 4, reprinted in McDougal and Reisman, *International Law in Contemporary Perspective* 524 (1981).

101. Id.; see also Wetstone and Rosencranz, supra note 99, at 121.

102. Lake Lanoux (Fr. v. Spain), Arbitrated Decision of Nov. 16, 1957, reprinted in 24 *International Law Reports* 101 (Lauterpacht, E. ed. 1961); 53 *Am. J. Int'l L.* 156 (1959).

103. Dept. of External Affairs, Canada's Claim Against the U.S.S.R. Arising Out of the Cosmos 954 Incident and the Claim's Settlement, Note No. FLA-268 (Jan. 23, 1979).

104. Gorove, "Cosmos 934: Issues of Law and Policy," 6 *J. Space L.* 137, 138 (1978).

105. See supra notes 53–57 and accompanying text.

106. See supra notes 44–49 and accompanying text.

107. Wetstone and Rosencranz, supra note 99, at 121.

108. CAA: Clean Air Act, 42 U.S.C. §§ 7401–7642 (1982). NCA: Noise Control Act, 42 U.S.C. §§ 4901–18 (1982). FWPCA: Federal Water Pollution Control Act, 33 U.S.C. §§ 1251–1376 (1982). SDWA: Safe Drinking Water Act, 42 U.S.C. §§ 300f-j (1982). RCRA: Resource Conservation and Recovery Act, 42 U.S.C. §§ 6901–87 (1982). CERCLA: Comprehensive Environmental Response, Compensation, and Liability Act, 42 U.S.C. §§ 9601–57 (1982). NEPA: National Environmental Policy

Act, 42 U.S.C. §§ 4321–70 (1982). TOSCA: Toxic Substances Control Act, 15 U.S.C. §§ 2601–29 (1982).

109. See supra notes 94–97 and accompanying text.

110. Kolbasov, "Legal Protection of the Environment in the USSR," 1 *Earth L.J.* 51 (1975).

111. Id.

112. Id. On a local level, more than 3,000 standing committees on nature conservation help influence the implementation of these laws. On a private level, there are various environmental awareness groups. Of note is the All-Russia Society for the Conservation of Nature, which has more than 20 million members, and has as its creed: "For the Leninist attitude towards nature."

113. Kelly, "International Regulation of Transfrontier Hazardous Waste Shipments: A New EEC Environmental Directive," 21 *Tex. Int'l. L.J.* 85, 90 (1985). The member States of the EC include all of the ESA States, except Switzerland and Sweden.

114. Id. at 89.

115. Id. at 98.

116. Id. at 90.

117. Fasan, "Legal Problems of the Terrestrial Environment," in *Proceedings of the Fourteenth Colloquium on the Law of Outer Space* 55 (M. Schwartz ed. 1972). Article IX of the OST is described supra notes 47–48 and accompanying text.

118. Krauss-Ablass, "Protection of the Terrestrial Environment in Outer Space: A Principle of International Law," in *Proceedings of the Fourteenth Colloquium on the Law of Outer Space* 72 (M. Schwartz ed. 1972).

119. Id. at 74.

120. Poulantzas, "Legal Problems Arising Out of Environmental Protection of the Earth," in *Proceedings of the Fourteenth Colloquium on the Law of Outer Space* 75 (M. Schwartz ed. 1972).

121. Sand, "Space Programs and International Environmental Protection," in *Proceedings of the Fourteenth Colloquium on the Law of Outer Space* 83 (M. Schwartz ed. 1972). The Test Ban Treaty and the OST are discussed supra notes 41–49 and accompanying text.

122. Ritholz, "International and Domestic Regulation of Private Launching Ventures," 24 *Stan. J. Int'l L.* 135, 150 (1984).

123. Gorove, supra note 3, at 64. The OST is discussed supra notes 44–49 and accompanying text.

124. C. Christol, supra note 15, at 800.

125. Id. at 146.

126. Id. at 147.

127. The CHOM principle is developed in Articles I and IX of the OST. See supra notes 47–48 and accompanying text.

128. See Liability Convention, supra note 53.

129. Wetstone and Rosencranz, supra note 99, at 123.
130. See, e.g., Sand, supra note 121, at 60; Gorove, supra note 3, at 64.
131. Beckstiegel, "Arbitration and Adjudication Regarding Activities in Outer Space," 6 *J. Space L.* 3 (1978); Smith, Lopatkiewicz, and Rothblatt, supra note 94, at 859.
132. See supra note 93 and accompanying text.
133. See supra notes 94–97 and accompanying text.
134. Sand, supra note 121, at 87.
135. 1957 U.N.Y.B. 420. The Stockholm Declaration is discussed supra notes 81–82 and accompanying text.
136. Pincus, "Chernobyl Is Focus of IAEA Session," Washington Post, Sept. 30, 1986, at A22.
137. See supra note 23.
138. See supra notes 73–74 and accompanying text.
139. See supra notes 69–70 and accompanying text.
140. See supra notes 87–88 and accompanying text.
141. See supra notes 81–82 and accompanying text.
142. Esposito, supra note 49, at 26.
143. Pryor, "Getting Some Good Out of EDB," 11 *EPA J.* 22 (1985).
144. 42 U.S.C. §§ 6901–87 (1982).
145. Hinds, "Liability Under Federal Law for Hazardous Waste Injuries," 6 *Harv. Envtl. L. Rev.* 1, 15 (1982).
146. See *Office of Solid Waste, Environmental Protection Agency, EPA Activities and Accomplishments Under the Resource Conservation and Recovery Act: Fiscal Years 1980–1985,* July 1986, at 8–9. These manifests are required by RCRA. Corrigan, "Space-Age Speculators Plan Orbiting Industrial Parks with NASA's Help, *Nat'l J.*, Sept. 7, 1985, at 1986–87.
147. See 42 U.S.C. §§ 6901–87 (1982).
148. Hinds, supra note 145. Macbeth, Superfund: Impact on Environmental Litigation, Quarterly Newsletter of the Standing Committee on Environmental Law, Winter 1982–83, 1–2, 6–7.
149. 42 U.S.C. §§ 9601–57 (1982).
150. Hill, supra note 39.
151. See Desaussure, "Manned Space Stations," 21 *San Diego L.J.* 985, 1000 (1984).

Selected Bibliography

"Agreement Governing the Activities of States on the Moon and other Celestial Bodies," Dec. 5, 1979, G.A. Res 34/68, 34 U.N. GAOR Supp. (No. 46) at 77, U.N. Doc. A/Res/34/68.
Agreement on Cooperation in the Field of Environmental Protection, May 23, 1972, United States-USSR, 23 U.S.T. 845, T.I.A.S. No. 7345, reprinted in

1 *International Protection of the Environment: Treaties and Related Documents* 50–57 (B. Ruster and B. Simma eds. 1975).

Agreement on the Rescue of Astronauts, the Return of Astronauts, and the Return of Objects Launched into Outer Space, opened for signature Apr. 22, 1968, 19 U.S.T. 7570, T.I.A.S. No. 6599, 672 U.N.T.S. 119.

2 *Air War College Associate Programs, The European Communities* ch. 14 (18th ed. 1984).

Antarctic Treaty, Dec. 1, 1959, 12 U.S.T. 794, T.I.A.S. No. 4780.

Beckstiegel, "Arbitration and Adjudication Regarding Activities in Outer Space," 6 *J. Space L.* 3 (1978).

Boraiko, "Storing up Trouble . . . Hazardous Waste," 167 *Nat'l Geographic*, Mar. 1985, at 318.

Bourely, "The Spacelab Program and Related Legal Issues, 11 *J. Space L.* 27 (1983).

Buckley, "The United Nations Environment Programme: A Ten-Year Perspective," Quarterly Newsletter of the Standing Committee on Environmental Law 4–6 (Winter 1982–83).

"Charter of Economic Rights and Duties of States," G.A. Res. 832 (1975), reprinted in *United Nations Resolutions* 300 (D. Djonovich ed. 1984).

Christol, "Stratospheric Ozone, Space Objects, and International Environmental Law," 6 *J. Space L.* 23 (1976).

C. Christol, *The Modern International Law of Outer Space* (1982).

Comprehensive Environmental Response, Compensation, and Liability Act, 42 U.S.C. §§ 9601–57 (1982).

Convention on International Liability for Damage Caused by Space Objects, Mar. 29, 1972, 24 U.S.T. 2389, T.I.A.S. No. 7762.

Convention on the Prevention of Marine Pollution by Dumping of Wastes and Other Matter, Dec. 29, 1972, 26 U.S.T. 2403, T.I.A.S. No. 8165.

Convention on the Prohibition of Military or Other Hostile Use of Environmental Modification Techniques, May 18, 1977, 31 U.S.T. 333, T.I.A.S. No. 9614.

Convention on the Registration of Objects Launched into Outer Space, opened for signature Jan. 14, 1975, 28 U.S.T. 695, T.I.A.S. No. 8480.

Corfu Channel (U.K. v. Albania), 1949 I.C.J. 4, reprinted in McDougal & Reisman, *International Law in Contemporary Perspective* 524 (1981).

Corrigan, "Space-Age Speculators Plan Orbiting Industrial Parks with NASA's Help," *Nat'l J.,* Sept. 7, 1985, at 1986.

"Declaration on Environmental Policy," Organization for Economic Cooperation and Development, Nov. 14, 1974, O.E.C.D. Doc. A (74) 47.

Deem, "Liability of Private Space Transportation Companies," 51 *Ins. Couns. J.* 340 (1984).

Dept. External Affairs, Canada's Claim Against the U.S.S.R. Arising Out of the Cosmos 954 Incident and the Claim's Settlement, Note No. FLA-268 (Jan. 23, 1979).

Desaussure, "Manned Space Stations," 21 *San Diego L.J.* 985 (1984).

Doyle, "Reentering Space Objects: Facts and Fiction," 6 *J. Space L.* 107 (1978).

Esposito, "The Commercial Exploitation of Space," 25 *A.F.L. Rev.* 159 (1985).

Fasan, "Legal Problems of the Terrestrial Environment," in *Proceedings of the Fourteenth Colloquium on the Law of Outer Space* 55 (M. Schwartz ed. 1972).

E. Finch and A. Moore, *Astrobusiness: A Guide to the Commerce and Law of Outer Space* (1985).

Finch and Moore, "Ecospace and Some of Its Legal Implications," 4 *J. Space L.* 117 (1976).

M. Freeman, *Space Traveller's Handbook: Every Man's Comprehensive Manual to Space Flight* (1979).

Gorove, "Cosmos 934: Issues of Law and Policy," 6 *J. Space L.* 137 (1978).

———, "Pollution and Outer Space: A Legal Analysis and Appraisal," 5 *N.Y.J. Int'l L.* 53 (1972).

Hall, "Comments on Salvage and Removal of Man-Made Objects From Outer Space," 33 *J. Air L. & Com.* 288 (1967).

Hill, CERCLA New-Hire Training Information, EPA Memorandum (June 13, 1986) (available at Office of Solid Waste and Emergency Response, Environmental Protection Agency).

Hinds, "Liability Under Federal Law for Hazardous Waste Injuries," 6 *Harv. Envtl. L. Rev.* 1 (1982).

International Convention on Civil Liability for Oil Pollution Damage, Nov. 29, 1969, 9 I.L.M. 45, 69 *Am. J. Int'l L.* 481.

"International Cooperation in Outer Space: A Symposium Prepared for the Committee on Aeronautical and Space Sciences," S. Doc. No. 92–57, 92d Cong., 1st Sess. 426 (1971).

Kelly, "International Regulation of Transfrontier Hazardous Waste Shipments: A New EEC Environmental Directive, 21 *Tex. Int'l L.J.* 85 (1985).

Kolbasov, "Legal Protection of the Environment in the USSR," 1 *Earth L.J.* 51 (1975).

Krauss-Albass, "Protection of the Terrestrial Environment in Outer Space: A Principle of International Law," in *Proceedings of the Fourteenth Colloquium on the Law of Outer Space* 72 (M. Schwartz ed. 1972).

Lake Lanoux (Fr. v. Spain), Arbitrated Decision of Nov. 16, 1957, reprinted in *International Law Reporter* 101 (E. Lauterpacht ed. 1961), 53 *Am. J. Int'l L.* 156 (1959).

S. Lay and H. Taubenfeld, *The Law Relating to Activities of Man in Space* (1970).

Levine, "Commercialization of Space: Policy and Administrative Issues," *Pub. Admin. Rev.,* Sept. 1985, at 562.

Macbeth, "Superfund: Impact on Environmental Litigation," Quarterly Newsletter of the Standing Committee on Environmental Law, Winter 1982–83, 1–2, 6–7.

Martin, "Legal Ramifications of the Uncontrolled Return of Space Objects to Earth," 45 *J. Air L. & Com.* 457 (1980).

N. Matte, *Aerospace Law: From Scientific Exploration to Commercial Utilization* (1977).

McCaffrey, "The Work of the International Law Commission Relating to the Environment," 11 *Ecology L.Q.* 189 (1983).

Menter, "Commercial Space Activities Under the Moon Treaty, 7 *Syracuse J. Int'l L. & Com.* 213 (1979).

Menter, "Legal Regime of International Spaceflight," in *Space Shuttle and the Law* 61 (S. Gorove ed. 1980).

Morrison, "Star Drek," *Envtl. Action,* July 1983, at 10.

National Commission on Space, Pioneering the Space Frontier (1986).

North Sea Continental Shelf (W. Ger. v. Den. & Neth.) 1969 I.C.J. 12 (Judgment Feb. 20, 1969) reprinted in McDougal & Reisman, *International Law in Contemporary Perspective* (1981).

Office of Solid Waste, Environmental Protection Agency, EPA Activities and Accomplishments Under the Resource Conservation and Recovery Act: Fiscal Years 1980–1985, July 1986.

Office of Solid Waste, Environmental Protection Agency, RCRA Orientation Manual (Jan. 1986).

Poulantzas, "Legal Problems Arising Out of Environmental Protection of the Earth," in *Proceedings of the Fourteenth Colloquium on the Law of Outer Space* 75 (M. Schwartz ed. 1972).

Pryor, "Getting Some Good Out of EDB," 11 *EPA J.* 22 (1985).

"Recommendations on Principles Concerning Transfrontier Pollution," Organization for Economic Cooperation and Development, Nov. 14, 1974, O.E.C.D. Doc. C (74) 224.

Resource Conservation and Recovery Act, 42 U.S.C. §§ 6901–87 (1982).

Ritholz, "International and Domestic Regulation of Private Launching Ventures," 24 *Stan. J. Int'l L.* 135 (1984).

Sand, "Space Programs and International Environmental Protection," in *Proceedings of the Fourteenth Colloquium on the Law of Outer Space* 79 (M. Schwartz ed. 1972).

Scheraga, "Curbing Pollution in Outer Space," *Tech. Rev.,* Jan. 8, 1986, at 8.

D. Shapland and M. Rycroft, *SPACELAB: Research in Earth Orbit* (1984).

Smith, "A Review of Contamination Issues Associated With An Orbiting Space Station External Environment," *J. Envtl. Sci.,* Jan. 1985, at 52.

Smith, Lopatkiewicz, and Rothblatt, "Legal Implications of a Permanent Manned Presence in Space," 85 *W. Va. L. Rev* 857 (1980).

Space Shuttle and the Law (S. Gorove ed. 1980).

Statute of the International Court of Justice, as annexed to the Charter of the United Nations, June 26, 1945, 59 Stat. 1055, T.S. No. 993, Article 38(1)(b).

"Stockholm Declaration of the United Nations Conference on the Human Environment," June 16, 1972, U.N. Doc. A/Conf. 48/14, 11 I.L.M. 1416 (1972).

4 *Toxic and Hazardous Waste Disposal* (R. Bojasek ed. 1980).

Trimble, "The International Law of Outer Space and Its Effect on Commercial Space Activity," 11 *Pepperdine L. Rev.* 521 (1984).

Trail Smelter (Can. v. U.S.), Arbitral Tribunal Under the Convention of Apr. 15, 1935, 3 R Int'l Arb. Awards 1905 (1949).

Treaty Banning Nuclear Weapon Tests in the Atmosphere, in Outer Space, and Underwater, Aug. 5, 1963, 14 U.S.T. 1313, T.I.A.S. No. 5433, 480 U.N.T.S. 43.

Treaty on Principles Governing the Activities of States in the Exploration and Use of Outer Space, Including the Moon and Other Celestial Bodies, opened for signature Jan. 27, 1967, 18 U.S.T. 2410, T.I.A.S. No. 6347, 610 U.N.T.S. 205.

Wetstone and Rosencranz, "Transboundary Air Pollution: The Search for an International Response," 8 *Harv. Envtl. L. Rev.* 89 (1984).

Crafting an International Legal System to Protect the Environment

Both the 1972 Stockholm and the 1992 Rio Conferences have made a substantial contribution to the development of international environmental law. UNEP (United Nations Environment Program), created at the 1972 Stockholm Conference, has been a major instrument in expanding environmental law through its regulations, standard setting, and environmental treaties and protocols which have come into force since Stockholm (see appendix). The 1992 Rio Conference on the Environment and Development produced four major documents; the Biodiversity Treaty, the Framework Convention on Climate Change, the Rio Declaration, and Agenda 21. It also set up a continuing body to implement the provisions of the Rio Conference, the Commission on Sustainable Development.

Yet much work remains to be done to expand the scope of environmental law and establish rules for state behavior. Areas such as desertification and land degradation, tropical forests destruction, toxic wastes, outer space regulation, freshwater protection, transboundary pollution, and environmentally sensitive habitats (wetlands, wilderness areas, and savannas) are in need of international protection and regulation. States and international organization have been creative and innovative in the manner of going about creating environmental rules. Beyond treaties, protocols, regional agreements, regulations, and standards set by international organizations and incorporation of state regulations into international agreements have characterized the eclectic approach to environmental rule making at the international level. Progress has been made on air pollution, acid rain abatement, ozone layer protection, and species protection. Equally important international environmental problems await solutions and innovative approaches to resolve them.

—*RNW*

23

Beyond Rio? The Evolution of International Environmental Law*
Jutta Brunnée

Environmental degradation and other threats to sustainability are now clearly global problems and many of them require global responses. So far, from an environmental protection perspective, most of these responses could be called disappointing. Accordingly, the 1992 United Nations Conference on Environment and Development in Rio de Janeiro is widely regarded among environmentalists as a failure that consumed much energy and delivered little substance.[1]

Judged against the pressing needs for immediate global action, the Rio conference and other such international initiatives have indeed been inadequate. Nevertheless, it would be unwise to give up on such approaches and premature to dismiss Rio as a failure merely because it did not yield conventions with specific environmental protection targets.

It is difficult to imagine success in global environmental protection without effective international law. Dissatisfaction with the accomplishments of international environmental protection efforts should be taken as reason to look more carefully at the challenges to be faced and the tools available for facing them.

---

*This paper is an abbreviated version of a presentation to the sixth Canadian Institute of Resources Law (CIRL) Conference on Natural Resources Law held in Ottawa in May 1993. The full paper appears in *Law and Process in Environmental Management*, Steven A. Kennett, ed., published by CIRL.

Certainly the challenges are formidable. Development of effective mechanisms of international environmental law must overcome the fundamental tension between the unity of ecosystems and the fragmentation of an international legal order built upon the rights and obligations of sovereign states. Progress is inevitably slow. Nonetheless, the past decade has seen considerable expansion and innovation in the use of international environmental law mechanisms, beginning with customary international law and proceeding creatively with various forms of international agreements and nonbinding "soft law."

Customary Law

Customary law evolves from the consistent practice of states accompanied by their conviction that they are legally bound to adhere to this practice. Customary international environmental law has its roots in the concept of international neighborhood law, which developed as a response to the conflicting interests of sovereign states.[2] The idea of state sovereignty is central to the international legal order. Initially, environmental problems were simply defined in terms of interferences with the interests of other states. Rules were based on the idea that no state may use its territory, or allow the use of it, in a way that causes serious damage to the territory of another state.[3]

Over the years other customary rules have evolved. Generally, states are subject to "procedural" duties, which derive from an obligation to cooperate in matters of international environmental protection, and include the duty to warn, notify, inform or consult.[4] Unfortunately, all these obligations are connected to the threshold of serious transboundary damage. Serious damage must occur before such rules can be invoked. Only in the context of shared resources has another concept evolved: the equitable use of resources.[5] Originally applied to transboundary water systems, the idea is that states must share common resources fairly with neighboring states.

There are a variety of limitations to the effectiveness of these rules of traditional international environmental law. Conceptually, the rules are often general and vague. Notions such as "serious damage" and "equitable share" are poorly defined, making it difficult to determine when a violation has occurred. It is easy for states to cite "scientific uncertainty" and "lack of proof" to escape responsibility while still claiming to uphold the letter of the law."[6]

This situation is exacerbated by the increasing complexity of environmental problems. Even where there is reasonable scientific agreement about the overall seriousness of global problems such as ozone layer depletion and climate change, the multiplicity of sources, effects and other relevant factors makes it virtually impossible to determine the responsibilities of individual states. In most cases it is at best difficult to satisfy the ideals of scientific certainty, clearly responsible parties and well-identified victims that the current international legal order demands. As a result, customary international rules are perhaps best seen as general guidelines that outline proper behavior but cannot provide the carefully crafted solutions essential to addressing major global environmental problems.

Existing customary norms are also limited by their bias toward the territorial interests of states. For example, the duty not to cause transboundary damage applies to areas beyond the limits of national jurisdiction, but the term "areas" has a geographical connotation.[7] This neglects global issues such as ozone layer depletion and global warming. The only way to provide protection on these issues is to apply the rules indirectly, for example when ozone loss or climate change adversely affects a state's territory. Current international law generally fails to recognize the idea of a global "commons." No state may defend areas or environmental resources beyond the limits of national jurisdiction against even serious damage, unless injury to the "commons" happens to coincide with injury to sovereign interests.

A related problem is that states are reluctant to accept an obligation to preserve certain resources which, while within their territorial jurisdiction, are of importance to other nations or the international community as a whole. A classic example of this is rainforest preservation. Extending the idea of an obligation to protect such resources would present a challenge to deeply held notions of territorial sovereignty, which nations are not ready to tolerate. Developing countries in particular assert their sovereign rights against what they see as "eco-imperialism."

In addition to the "spatial" gaps thus left by customary law, there is also a "temporal" gap of future generations in cases where there is a time lag between human activities and the subsequent negative impacts, or when activities have irreversible impacts.

The conceptual shortcomings of the customary international legal system can be explained, in large part, by the fact that states, as the subjects of international law, are also the lawmakers, enforcers, and adjudicators. As a result, their interests significantly shape the content of rules. With the exception of some cases dealing with localized transboundary problems, states have not pursued pollution incidents, for example through arbitration, to an extent that would have permitted the formation of more specific or further reaching rules. Obviously, the more complex environmental problems become, the more solutions implicate the economic and sovereign spheres of states. States are unwilling to create precedents for fear of undermining control over their affairs and interests.[8] The evolution of generally applicable duties would carve into the sovereign realm of states in a potentially unpredictable range of situations. And given the impossibility of avoiding all transboundary impacts, states are also reluctant to create precedents which might subsequently work to their disadvantage.

The law of state responsibility could potentially serve as an important tool for enforcement of customary law. It is concerned with the consequences of violations of international law by states and determines when and what sanctions or remedies may be appropriate. However, due to the predominant role of states and state interest, the development of this law has proven difficult. Thus even in cases where there are clear violations of international law, such as the nuclear reactor accident at Chernobyl or the Sandoz spill in the Rhine, state responsibility channels have not been pursued.[9] Further limitations are imposed by the reactive nature of the system. The state responsibility approach comes into play only after environmental damage has already occurred, so that it is inadequate for addressing incompensable or irreversible environmental problems. In addition, the underlying principles of the state responsibility approach cannot provide for the necessary planning, cooperation, or proactive management. Finally, the system is inherently confrontational and does not encourage the cooperation that is essential for managing the international environment.[10]

Despite these limitations, customary international law is still an important tool for international cooperation. It defines the thrust of international environmental protection and interacts with other forms of international legal action. Treaties or soft law may complement general rules and ultimately lead to the emergence of conceptually more effective and more demanding customary norms.

International Agreements

International agreements can fill many of the effectiveness gaps left by customary law. Treaties, for example, can be designed to target very specific environmental problems. Within specific treaties, nations may implicitly define concepts like "serious damage" by setting standards as part of the terms of such treaties. In negotiations, states have control over sovereignty sacrifices and can participate in the definition of environmental protection targets. In the development of environmental treaties, states have demonstrated willingness to address transboundary issues, protection of the commons, and stewardship of globally significant resources which are under their exclusive jurisdiction.[11] States fear being labeled "violators of international law" and many are nervous about the potential loss of sovereignty entailed by the state responsibility approach. For them, the treaty approach offers a more acceptable means of agreeing to participate with other states in remedial or preventative efforts.

Treaties can also be useful in addressing other weaknesses of customary international environmental law. They can provide for a proactive approach to problems, more predictability, and a degree of coordination and flexibility not possible with customary rules.

In the last 20 years, the framework treaty has become an increasingly popular method for states to cooperate on international solutions to environmental problems.[12] One important advantage of the framework treaty is that it allows for greater control and maximization of those elements that enhance effectiveness. The initial establishment of general cooperative duties, information exchange, data collection, and technical assistance are gradually broadened to include specific emission reduction targets in "protocols."

The benefit of this format is that it provides a cooperative and inclusive atmosphere, which can help shorten the typically long period between the emergence of international concern over an environmental problem and the adoption of an agreement.[13] Even states concerned about scientific uncertainty or the economic implications of an agreement can participate. The framework creates a win-win situation in which all States claim to cooperate to protect the environment without making demanding commitments at an early stage.

Admittedly, a framework convention lacks firm commitments; however, one should not underestimate its value. The convention process brings together and binds into a cooperative practice a larger number of parties than a more demanding treaty would. In cases where states with widely divergent political and economic interests must cooperate, this trust building is a particularly important function. Another important benefit of the framework convention is the sharing of information and scientific cooperation. This exchange is essential to overcoming scientific uncertainty and clarifying economic implications.

The process of gathering information and negotiating commitments for framework conventions can also provide the time and the inclination for governments and industry to prepare for the necessary adjustments. In the case of the international response to ozone depletion, for example, the fact that producers of ozone depleting substances had been induced by the expectation of international regulation to develop alternative substances and processes, allowed the adoption of the Montreal Protocol only two years after the signing of the Vienna Convention for the Protection of the Ozone Layer.[14]

The subsequent protocol has its own advantages. Because it focuses on specific areas, meaningful commitments are more likely than they are in broadly defined treaties. For example, rather than addressing acid rain or long-range transboundary air pollution by way of vague undertakings in the convention itself, the protocols to the Geneva Convention on Long-Range Transboundary Air Pollution (Geneva Convention) singled out individual pollutants.[15] The first such protocol centered on sulphur dioxide emissions because they were considered the most significant contributor to acid rain and because they were relatively easy to reduce.[16] As more information and technology became available, protocols were developed to deal with nitrogen oxide emissions and volatile organic compounds.[17] When measured on a goal achievement scale, the Geneva Convention, at least with respect to sulphur emissions, has proven effective. Between 1980 and 1990 overall sulphur emissions in Europe decreased by 22 percent. This reduction was a result of emission cutbacks by 24 to the 33 signatory parties to the convention. Twelve countries reduced emissions by at least 30 percent, ten countries are aiming for reductions of more than 50 percent.[18]

Another advantage to the protocol approach is its flexibility compared to a comprehensive treaty. Protocols allow for some "picking and choosing." States can decide, at least in principle, which protocols they sign. A state that might be willing to act on one particular pollutant but not another, would likely not be willing to sign a comprehensive treaty, but may be willing to sign a more narrow protocol. In addition, protocols can be added or amended on an individual basis should our information change. For example, the Montreal Protocol has been amended twice in response to an increasing sense of urgency over ozone depletion and an increased ability to phase out ozone-depleting substances.

Clearly, the framework-protocol approach does not solve all the problems associated with bringing together a large number of diverse groups and interests. One particular difficulty that remains is the need to bring developing countries into these agreements. In this context, two approaches have evolved to bring more equity into global environmental protection. Both knowledge that equity does not always mean equal commitment, but may require asymmetrical obligations and incentives that better reflect differences in the parties' contributions to the problem and their abilities to address it.

The first approach provides for "multi-track obligations" which are phrased to accommodate different economic and technical capabilities.[19] This may mean giving less able parties a longer time frame within which to work, or smaller reduction targets.[20] The second approach focuses on funding mechanisms to give developing countries the financial means to meet treaty obligations. At the urging of developing countries including China and India, the 1990 London amendments to the Montreal Protocol set up the Multilateral Ozone Fund as just such a funding mechanism.[21] However, not all countries have the influence to negotiate this type of clause. Both India and China had a great deal of bargaining power in the ozone negotiations because their participation in the treaty was essential.

Both of these techniques fall under the concept of "common but differentiated obligation." The concept provides a flexible formula encompassing both the need for common action and a recognition of differing contributions to a problem and differing economic and technical capabilities. Technology transfer is a further element of the concept. The Ozone Fund, for example, provides not only financial assistance, but also support for the acquisition of new technology. Thus, the amended Montreal Protocol contains a commitment to ensure prompt transfer of "best available, environmentally safe substitutes and related technologies" recognizing that such assistance will play a large role in determining the effectiveness of the treaty.[22]

All things considered, use of the framework-protocol approach with asymmetrical obligations has proven effective for the ozone issue. Beyond scientific cooperation and information exchange, it has led to significant reductions in consumption and production of controlled substances, has stimulated development and transfer of new technology, and enjoys broad participation by both industrialized and developing countries.[23]

While the treaty approach has a variety of demonstrable advantages, using a binding agreement as a basis for international cooperation has three major limitations. First, the treaty development process tends to be frustratingly slow. Negotiation of binding standards typically takes several years and additional years normally pass before enough ratifications are received for the treaty to come into force. Second, the outcomes of treaty processes tend to be minimum solutions since they must satisfy the self-interest of states with differing, sometimes competing, agendas and commitment. Finally, agreements characteristically lack "teeth." Stringent enforcement mechanisms, which may represent a threat to state sovereignty, are avoided. Instead, environmental protection agreements typically rely on reporting schemes that try to capitalize on the enforcement value of peer pressure and public opinion. Although this approach may be more acceptable, and in the end, more effective than more confrontational or invasive mechanisms, the success of reporting schemes has been mixed. For example, just seven out of thirty-one parties to the Geneva Convention submitted major review reports for 1990.[24] Developing countries in particular, have difficulty meeting requirements.

Soft Law

The use of soft law has become increasingly popular in light of the limitations of customary law and international agreements.[25] Soft law is the term used to describe forms of international cooperation that are not legally binding. Because they are not designed to be enforceable, soft norms avoid the lengthy ratification process to which treaties are typically subject, and agreement is generally reached more quickly than in the case of binding rules or treaties.

Soft law is also more flexible. States are willing to be more innovative when the outcome is not legally binding. New ideas or approaches can be experimented with and refined in a nonbinding setting thus providing immediate benefits while developing a basis for negotiation of binding requirements at a later stage. Two promising soft law approaches are "codes of conduct" and "soft principles."

Codes of conduct can exhibit a variety of characteristics and functions.[26] They may be written to mimic the terms of binding agreements or the cooperative practices of treaties. Alternatively they may aim for the convergence of national standards or practices. This, in turn, may ease the way for later treaty negotiations or eliminate the need for a treaty altogether. Codes of conduct allow states to participate in a cooperative arrangement based on their abilities. This characteristic encourages the participation of states that might avoid binding agreements, due to competing national interests or shortage of the technical or financial means to participate.

One area of success for codes of conduct has been the international trade in ultra-hazardous pesticides to developing countries. Solutions based on customary and treaty law were not practical. Customary law was not applicable because the voluntary import of a substance does not constitute "serious transboundary damage," despite any hazardous effects of the use of those substances.[27] The negotiation of a binding agreement was not a viable option because exporting countries and their chemical industries were reluctant to give up the profitable trade in pesticides, and developing countries considered the importation of hazardous pesticides indispensable and rejected interference with their sovereign rights.[28] At the same time, exporting states were increasingly concerned about the "circle of poison." Banned substances were turning up in imported food and other products. Developing countries were concerned about the lack of information available about imported substances, and about growing evidence that pesticides use did not ultimately sustain crop yields. As a result, there was enough common ground to generate interest in some level of international cooperation.[29]

The response was to develop a code of conduct for exporting and importing states. The United Nations Environment Programme (UNEP), the World Health Organization (WHO), and the international community cooperated to expand the International Registry of Potentially Toxic Chemicals. The registry serves as a system for collecting and storing data on chemical substances for use in risk assessments. The information gathered raised the level of awareness about the risks of pesticides and initiated further cooperation among states.

Under the sponsorship of the Food and Agricultural Organization (FAO), states developed an International Code of Conduct on the Distribution and Use of Pesticides.[30] This code built upon existing domestic export regulations and emerging international practices. The original approach of the code was to require simple notification of the importing state when a shipment was upcoming. Eventually the code's approach was tightened to require "prior informed consent."[31] This requirement was considered the best compromise between those who supported a free flow of hazardous pesticides and those who supported a total ban of exports.

It should be noted, however, that codes of conduct may often be insufficient. There are cases in which binding commitments are necessary. To deal with ozone layer depletion, for example, any package of satisfactory solutions will require states to take actions that are expensive or that may affect their competitiveness. Furthermore, these actions must be undertaken by a large number of states to be effective. In this situation, it makes little sense for any one state to go forward without commitments from other states. Similarly, in cases where some states require financial or technical assistance, binding agreements are indispensable.

Yet in the appropriate circumstances, codes of conduct can be constructive temporary mechanisms or precursors to treaty commitments.[32] They can also aid in the evolution of customary norms. For example, the principle of prior informed consent, has now achieved widespread acceptance and some have argued that it is emerging as a principle of customary law in the area of hazardous substance transfers.[33]

A second soft law approach relies on initially soft principles which, like prior informed consent, can provide a conceptual frame of reference for future agreements, or form part of the crystallization process producing customary law. The crystallization aspect may be the most promising from the point of view of environmentalists. Indeed, soft law has been called the "environmentalists' Trojan horse."[34]

One of these emerging principles, the concept of "common concern of humankind," may allow protection of resources beyond the limits of jurisdiction. The increasingly frequent and prominent use of this term is evidence that states are beginning to acknowledge that state responsibility extends to protecting the environment not just in their own interests, but also in the "common interest of the international community." The need to protect the commons may lead to the recognition that all states are bound by rules of common interest and, perhaps more significantly, each state, even if not directly affected, could demand compliance.[35] Although such developments will take time, international environmental law is progressing beyond the narrow focus of the sovereignty-based "transboundary era" into what may be called the "commons era."

An "intergenerational era" may also be on the horizon. An evolution of the concepts of sustainable development, intergenerational equity and the precautionary principle may fill the temporal gap in customary law. However, at this point, these three concepts are too vague to allow a crystallization into customary law.[36]

Nonetheless, such concepts can provide guidelines for treaty making and chart the course for international cooperation. Already the principles have been incorporated into documents adopted at the United Nations Conference on Environment and Development (UNCED) and, in particular, in the Rio Declaration and the Framework Convention on Climate Change.[37] This is significant for two reasons. First, the principles provide a conceptual justification for international cooperation. Secondly, their acceptance in significant international agreements may eventually contribute to their evolution from soft law into customary law.

International Environmental Law and the Rio Conference

The international environmental legal regime is a dynamic system of interactions and cross-fertilization between different levels of law making. Custom, treaties and soft law each have their strengths and weaknesses. Together they provide an impressive range of options for effective international environmental protection. Viewed in this light, the U.N.'s Rio Conference made important contributions. It is too early to tell whether this conference will ultimately be more successful in halting global environmental decline than its predecessor, the 1972 Stockholm conference. But as a step in the process of international environmental law making, Rio was significant.

The conference generated several complex documents on highly contentious issues in little over two years—a rapid pace for international environmental protection. In integrating soft principles, the Rio Declaration and the Climate and Biodiversity Conventions may contribute to the emergence of customary law and increase the effectiveness of the existing body of rules.[38]

The conference also set in motion processes that will serve to by-pass some of the systemic constraints of international law. While the Climate Convention contains no binding emission reduction targets, it serves as a framework to be complemented by further agreements on emission and reductions. The convention's focus is on national emission inventories, scientific cooperation, promotion of technology transfer, and the adoption of national politics to mitigate climate change. In keeping with previous framework agreements, the general aim is to create cooperative process as a first step of regime building.

However, UNCED's most significant achievement in terms of process is agenda 21, the "blueprint for sustainable development strategies" to guide the world into the 21st century. The document, a product of consensus among 178 states, grapples with many contentious issues including sustainable development, population growth, atmospheric and marine pollution, desertification, and technology transfer. Agenda 21 is the most ambitious soft law process ever initiated in the field of international environment protection. Its success will, in part, depend on the willingness of states to go beyond the only very modest financial commitments made at the Rio conference. It will also hinge on the work of the Commission on Sustainable Development, a high-level body of representatives of the 53 member states of the U.N. Economic and Social Council envisaged in chapter 38 of agenda 21. Along with a strengthened UNEP, the commission is intended to review the implementation of international environmental agreements and their reporting requirements.

It is encouraging that effectiveness of international legal instruments also was a prominent concern at UNCED. Our pathway to a common future will require creative international law making. Given the rich experience of the past 20 years, the international community is well-positioned to choose appropriate legal approaches to take UNCED's results into the realm of true global environmental protection. Yet one should not overstate these accomplishments or downplay the tasks that remain. As Jim MacNeil has observed:

> . . . our leaders always find it easy to embrace environmental rhetoric under the guise of principles, then support continuing processes of conferences, studies, and negotiations under the guise of action. As a political strategy, doing so is a proven success, but as a strategy for transition to more sustainable forms of development or environmental protection it leaves just about everything to be desired.[39]

In light of these comments, the reader may be left to judge the opening statement to the conference, UNCED Secretary-General Maurice Strong.

> The Earth Summit is not an end in itself, but a new beginning. The measures you agree on here will be but first steps on a new pathway to our common future. Thus, the results of this conference will ultimately depend on the credibility and effectiveness of a follow-up. . . .[40]

Notes

1. Jim MacNeill, Canada, *Minutes of Proceedings and Evidence of the Standing Committee on Environment*, Third Session of the Thirty-fourth Parliament, Tuesday, May 11, 1993, Issue No. 67 (Ottawa: Queen's Printer, 1993), 9.
2. Patricia Birnie and Alan Boyle, *International Law and the Environment* (Oxford: Clarendon Press, 1992), 83.
3. See Trail Smelter Arbitration, *United Nations Reports on International Arbitral Awards*, III (1941), 1905.
4. Jutta Brunnée, *Acid Rain and Ozone Layer Depletion: International Law and Regulation* (Dobbs Ferry: Transnational Publishers, 1988), 103–111.
5. Ibid., 98–103.
6. Birnie and Boyle, *International Law* [n. 2], 98, 99.
7. See Principle 21 of the "Declaration of the United Nations Conference on the Human Environment," ("Stockholm Declaration"), reprinted in *International Legal Materials*, 11 (1972), 1416.
8. Birnie and Boyle, *International Law* [n. 2], 159.
9. See Linda Malone, "The Chernobyl Accident: A Case Study in International Law in Regulating State Responsibility for Transboundary Nuclear Pollution," *Columbia Journal of Environmental Law*, 12 (1987), 203; and Anton Schwabach, "The Failure of International Law to Protect the Rhine from Pollution," *Ecology Law Quarterly*, 16 (1989), 443.
10. See Birnie and Boyle. *International Law* [n. 2], 136.
11. For the transboundary context see the "Canada-United States Agreement on Air Quality," reprinted in *International Legal Materials*, 30 (1991), 676. For the "commons" context see the "Vienna Convention for the Protection of the Ozone Layer," *International Legal Materials*, 26 (1987), 1516. For the "exclusive jurisdiction" context see the "Bonn Convention on the Conservation of Migratory Species of Wild Animals," reprinted in *International Legal Materials*, 19 (1980), 15.
12. For an annotated list see *The Effectiveness of International Environmental Agreements: A Survey of Existing Legal Instruments*, Peter Sand, ed. (Cambridge: Grotius Publications, 1992), 501–538.
13. Consider the following examples: acid rain was identified as an international problem in 1972, yet while a general agreement was adopted in 1979, the first binding international document did not enter into force until 1987; see Brunnée, Jutta. *Acid Rain* [n. 4], 9, 176, 183; and *ibid.*, 43, 339, 243: the depletion of the ozone layer due to chlorofluorocarbon emissions was predicted in 1974, yet a general convention was adopted only in 1985 and the first binding commitments did not enter into force until 1989.
14. See Brunnée, *Acid Rain* [n. 4], 249; "Vienna Convention" [n. 11], 1516; and "Montreal Protocol on Substances that Deplete the Ozone Layer," reprinted in *International Legal Materials*, 26 (1987), 1541.

15. "Geneva Convention on Long-Range Transboundary Air Pollution," reprinted in *International Legal Materials*, 18 (1979), 1442.

16. See "Protocol on the Reduction of Sulphur Emissions or Their Transboundary Fluxes by at Least 30 Percent," reprinted in *International Legal Materials*, 27 (1988), 698.

17. "Protocol Concerning the Control of Emissions of Nitrogen Oxides," reprinted in *International Legal Materials*, 28 (1989), 212; and "Protocol Concerning the Control of Emissions of Volatile Organic Compounds or Their Transboundary Fluxes," reprinted in *International Legal Materials*, 31 (1992), 573.

18. See Richard Benedick and Ricardo Pronove III, "Atmosphere and Outer Space, *Effectiveness*, Sand, ed. [n. 12], 132.

19. See article 6 "Geneva Convention" [n. 15].

20. For example, see article 5 of the "Montreal Protocol [n. 14].

21. See article 10, "Montreal Protocol," London amendments and adjustments, reprinted in *International Legal Materials*, 30 (1991), 537.

22. Ibid., articles 10, 10A of the London amendments; in article 5 the parties recognize that ". . . developing the capacity to fulfil the obligations . . . will depend upon the effective implementation of the financial cooperation . . . and transfer of technology . . ."

23. See Benedick and Pronove, [n. 18], 137–138.

24. See "Summary Report on the Survey," *Effectiveness*, Sand, ed. [n. 12], 8, 13–14; and Benedick and Pronove, "Atmosphere" [n. 18], 140–141.

25. On soft law more generally, see Christine Chinkin, "The Challenge of Soft Law: Development and Change in International Law," *International and Comparative Law Quarterly*, 38 (1989), 850.

26. For a detailed discussion see Robert Lutz and George Aron, "Codes of Conduct and their Legal Instruments," *Transferring Hazardous Technologies and Substances: The International Legal Challenge*, Gunther Handl and Robert Lutz, eds. (London: Graham & Trotman, 1989) 129–154.

27. See Gunther Handl, "Environmental Protection and Development in Third World Countries: Common Destiny: Common Responsibility," *New York University Journal of International Law & Politics*, 20 (1989), 603–615.

28. Ibid., 613.

29. See Raymond Hill, "Problems and Policy for Pesticides Exports to Less Developed Countries," *Natural Resources Law Journal*, 28 (1988), 699–704.

30. See "International Code of Conduct on the Distribution and Use of Pesticides," *Food and Agriculture Organization Resolution*, 10/85 (November 28, 1985) reprinted in *International Digest of Health Legislation*, 37:1 (1986), 172; and "FAO International Code of Conduct on the Distribution and Use of Pesticides," amended version (Rome: 1990).

31. Ibid., see article 9.1 of the 1985 code and articles 2 and 9.7 of the 1990 amended version.

32. See Lutz and Aron, "Codes of Conduct" [n. 26], 155.
33. Ibid.
34. See Winfried Lang, "Die Verrechtlichung des Umweltschutzes," *Archiv fur Volkerrecht*, 22 (1984), 283–303.
35. See Birnie and Boyle. *International Law* [n. 2], 154–157.
36. See Gunther Handl, "Environmental Security and Global Change: The Challenge to International Law," *Yearbook of International Environmental Law*, 1 (1990), 3–23, 25–27.
37. "Rio Declaration on Environment and Development," reprinted in *International Legal Material*, 31 (1992), 876; and "Framework Convention on Climate Change," reprinted in *International Legal Materials*. 31 (1992), 822.
38. "Convention on Biological Diversity," reprinted in *International Legal Materials,* 31 (1992), 822.
39. MacNeill, *Minutes* [n. 1].
40. Cited in Peter Haas, Marc Levy and Edward Parson, "Appraising the Earth Summit: How Should We Judge UNCED's Success?" *Environment*, 34 (1992), 7, 26–28.

24

New Ways to Make International Environmental Law

Geoffrey Palmer

Introduction

The purpose of this article is to suggest new ways to make international law for the environment. The existing methods are slow, cumbersome, expensive, uncoordinated and uncertain. Something better must be found if the environmental challenges the world faces are to be dealt with successfully. Nearly twenty years after the Stockholm Declaration, we still lack the institutional and legal mechanisms to deal effectively with transboundary and biospheric environmental degradation.[1] The 1992 United Nations Conference on Environment and Development presents an opportunity to make progress.[2] Unfortunately, my reading of the situation in late 1991 suggests that there is no political will to take decisions that will give us the tools to do the job.

As matters stand today, we lack many of the necessary rules and the means for devising them; we lack institutions capable of ensuring that the rules we have are effective. I do not wish to sound apocalyptic. In fact, the proposals put forward here build on existing international law and institutions. But it will take political courage to take the necessary decisions. Unless we devise a better way to make international law for the environment, future progress is likely to be piecemeal, fitful, unsystematic and even random. If the appropriate steps are not taken now, the manifestly unsatisfactory situation we have will limp along toward crisis. Assuredly, action will be necessary in the end; it will be easier if we start soon.

The justification for taking bold steps now rests on an analysis of three factors: the formidable nature of the environmental issues that must be dealt with; the condition of international organization relating to the environment, particularly the United Nations system; and the methods currently used to make international environmental law. To the first two of these, we will now turn briefly; to the third, a more extended treatment will be given. But, first, a word about a fourth factor that will not be analyzed here. The extraordinary changes in world order that have recently taken place must surely increase the chances of achieving change in the methods of making international environmental law.

The Institutional Gap

The proposition that the world faces serious global environmental problems hardly needs demonstration or rehearsal. It was the reason that led to the establishment of the United Nations Conference on Environment and Development to begin with. Ozone depletion, climate change and biodiversity are the issues that have the most public prominence, but there are many others. They include the quality and supply of fresh water; protection of the oceans; deforestation, desertification and drought; the management of biotechnology; the management of wastes, including toxic chemicals and other hazardous wastes; urban slums; and poor human health conditions.[3] In recent times, the issues have been couched in security terms. Security of adequate food supplies is an obvious one, but the issues of energy can be dealt with from the same angle. As Peter Sand has recently put it,

> if global environmental security is taken to mean security against those risks that threaten our common survival, the focus of collective legal action may indeed be sharpened considerably. A tentative priority list of genuine survival risks would thus, as a minimum, have to include the following essential concerns: climatic security, biological security, chemical security.[4]

A myriad of other issues concern the health of our planet and the capacity to sustain life upon it. The whole question was summed up by the World Commission on Environment and Development as one of sustainable development.[5] To produce the conditions necessary for sustainable development, a great deal more in the way of regulation and prohibition will be required at the international level than we have been prepared to tolerate up to now. In this respect, both developed and developing countries have an interest in resisting change—their freedom of action as nations is likely to be reduced and they know it—hence the lack of enthusiasm for new institutions and methods of international lawmaking.

In truth, the United Nations lacks any coherent institutional mechanism for dealing effectively with environmental issues. Strengthening its capacity and structure should be high on the list of priorities for the 1992 Conference on Environment and Development. The Charter itself provides no environmental organ, an omission that would most certainly be rectified if it were being drafted today. In no respect is the Charter more a product of its times than in its disregard of the environment. Aside from a reference to "good neighbourliness," it contains nothing. At present, environmental responsibilities are divided among a number of the specialized agencies, including the Food and Agriculture Organization, the World Health Organization, the World Meteorological Organization, the International Maritime Organization, the U.N. Educational, Scientific and Cultural Organization and the U.N. Development Programme, with a coordinating and catalytic role assigned to the U.N. Environment Programme (UNEP). UNEP itself is a creature of a mere General Assembly resolution.[6] The Economic and Social Council has the task of coordinating all of these diffuse efforts and it is fair to say that the task has not been accomplished.

UNEP was established to act as a focal point for environmental action and coordination within the United Nations. It lacks any formal powers. Under its Executive Director, Dr. Mostafa Tolba, it points out environmental problems to nations and suggests solutions. In fact, it does much more than its limited powers suggest. It has become an agency that sets out to produce concrete results in terms of treaties negotiated. In my opinion, without UNEP, the system to prevent ozone depletion now in place would not have been developed.

UNEP can push states, probe their policies and plead with them; it cannot coerce them. UNEP lacks teeth. It has no executive authority. Partly for this reason, UNEP has made generous use of "soft law" instruments in the international consensus building that it engages in. All UNEP programs are financed by direct, voluntary contributions from member states. It has a Governing Council composed of representatives of fifty-eight member states. UNEP has access to excellent scientific advice not filtered through nation-states.[7] Given the nature of UNEP's constitution, its achievements are substantial, but it is not an adequate international organization for protecting the world's environment.

Various suggestions have been made to strengthen UNEP. The most important were the recommendations of the World Commission on Environment and Development in 1987. The commission recommended a major reorientation and refocusing of programs and budgets on sustainable development among all U.N. organizations.[8] The commission saw UNEP as the principal source of environmental data, assessment and reporting and as an advocate of change and cooperation. It was to be the lead U.N. agency in restoring, protecting, and improving the ecological basis for sustainable development. Its catalytic role was to be extended.

Recent attempts to improve the coordination of international environmental protection include the System-Wide Medium-Term Environment Programme, an effort to address all the activities in a single document and to provide a framework and strategy.[9] The Committee of International Development Institutions on the Environment, although not part of the U.N. system, offers some opportunities for integrating environmental issues into the plans of financial and developmental organizations.[10] Regional coordination mechanisms do exist and have been effective; but, by definition, these cannot take a global approach.[11] In particular, one finds yawning gaps in the organizational framework for carrying out effective monitoring and assessment regarding such concerns as climate change, ozone layer depletion, water quality, living marine resources, sustainable development in some areas and biodiversity.

Many of these problems are widely recognized, but the logical inference from the facts seems politically unpalatable; the only way to cure the problem is to create a proper international environmental agency within the United Nations system that has real power and authority. At the same time, other environmental components within the U.N. system should be restructured and reorganized. That restructuring needs to be rigorous if resources are to be saved and priorities redirected. With determination the task could be achieved without spending more resources in total than are expended now. They should be regrouped and reorganized.

If we consider the new instruments that have developed the international law for the environment in the last twenty years, we would be pardoned for thinking that the record is a good one. It is certainly substantial. The proliferation of international agreements has been enormous. There are more than a hundred multilateral instruments in force, many of which were negotiated since the Stockholm Declaration. The UNEP register listed 152 as of May 1991.[12] In the years since the Stockholm Declaration, there have been some prodigious achievements in the negotiation of conventions dealing with global environmental problems. The United Nations Convention on the Law of the Sea is an obvious example, although perhaps less successful than the Regional Seas Programme, which was less ambitious.[13] The many famous victories include instruments on long-range transboundary air pollution,[14] notification and assistance regarding nuclear accidents,[15] endangered species,[16] and the movement and disposal of hazardous waste.[17] The Vienna Convention for the Protection of the Ozone Layer and its progeny amount to perhaps the most substantial achievement of all.[18]

Many of these instruments were stimulated by the activities of UNEP, which has launched various initiatives to develop new policies: action plans, a multitude of soft law instruments and framework conventions. UNEP's Montevideo plan set out a comprehensive program for the progressive development of international environmental law that, in 1991, is in the course of being revised for the next ten years.[10]

While the number of instruments is impressive, and some of them will have slowed down degradation, it cannot be assumed that they have led to an improvement in the overall situation. A strong argument can be made that, during the time these instruments were being developed, the environmental situation in the world became worse and is deteriorating further. There is no effective legal framework to help halt the degradation. Furthermore, many international agreements do not necessarily mean many ratifications. Frequently, there appears to be a long lag in securing widespread ratification because of insufficient incentives for nations to sign up. Many other nations simply seem not to address the issues, not regarding them as of sufficient priority compared to domestic concerns. Nor is there any institutional mechanism to provide nations with incentives to comply when they have ratified. Moreover, ratification itself says nothing about whether the agreed standards are being observed. In many instances monitoring is difficult; in some instances it is simply not being done. Sometimes the instruments themselves provide for proper assessment; the Montreal Protocol is the best example.[20] But every time a new instrument is negotiated, fresh machinery has to be devised.

The making and negotiation of the instruments themselves has to start anew each time. No organization commands clear power to coordinate international environmental negotiations. Each negotiation proceeds differently. The ozone negotiations were conducted in a different way and serviced by a different organization from those on climate change. Such an approach carries the grave risk that on each occasion the wheel must be reinvented. Common elements are not necessarily treated the same way.

There is no institutional machinery to evaluate gaps that may be found in the international framework of agreements or to develop means of assigning priorities among competing claims for attention. Nor is there any way of ensuring that environmental issues are effectively coordinated with and integrated into other activities that may be progressing at the international level. Scientific data and input, which are critical on the global issues, need to be assembled and tested before the political decisions are taken. Yet on each occasion the data are assembled in a different fashion. Institutional means need to be devised to channel scientific and technical expertise to the appropriate policy needs.

If an institutional home for the conduct of the negotiations themselves could be devised, it would cut the substantial costs of dealing with the global issues. Instead of having a new group of nations assemble to discuss each problem by holding a series of international meetings at different locations around the world in an effort to hammer out a consensus on the provisions of a multilateral convention, there could easily be a uniform method for bringing the nations together, conveying the relevant scientific information to them and conducting the negotiations. Such procedures offer the possibility of appreciably reducing the cost of all the present diplomatic activity, as well as increasing the coherence of the rules.

One of the biggest obstacles that must be overcome in international negotiations is the rule of unanimous consent.[21] This rule impels each negotiating body to search for the lowest common denominator; it adds to the difficulty of negotiations because sometimes a single nation can resist the development of a common position and demand concessions as the price of securing unanimous consent. While it is doubtful that the rule of unanimous consent can be banished from international global negotiations, the introduction of new institutional mechanisms may provide ways around it, which would speed up the process and result in instruments of greater potency.

What is missing from the present institutional arrangements is the equivalent of a legislature:[22] some structured and coherent mechanism for making the rules of international law. For such an institution to succeed, it must have access to high-quality streams of advice. An effective way of ensuring the availability of appropriate scientific information is essential. To maintain the authority of the rules that are made, international efforts must be devoted to effective monitoring, assessment, and enforcement.

In sum, the methods and techniques now available to fashion new instruments of international law to cope with global environmental problems cannot meet that challenge. The emerging issues are so big and so all-embracing that current ways of doing things will not solve these problems. The institutional mechanisms within the United Nations system are not capable of handling the issues. The time has come for "something more innovative, for a conceptual leap forward in institutional terms."[23]

To succeed, the case for a new way of making international environmental law must show how it is made now and how it has developed. To those issues this article now turns.

The Development of International Environmental Law

Customary International Law

Customary international law does offer some modest protection for the environment.[24] And as the web of treaty law protecting the environment increases, resonances from it enter into customary international law. That development has the effect of tightening the standards by increasing the number of occasions on which a credible argument can be mounted that customary international law has been breached. As environmental consciousness expands, the practice of nations alters to comply with the new norms, which makes it easier to contend that an "international custom, as evidence of a general practice accepted as law," has emerged.[25]

There is a quartet of cases that quite usefully establishes some of the strengths, and also the weakness, of customary international law. The "Corfu Channel" case is authority for the proposition that if a nation knows that harmful effects may occur to other nations from facts within its ken and fails to disclose them, it will be liable to the nation that suffers damage.[26] In other words, every state has a duty not to knowingly allow its territory to be used for acts contrary to the rights of other states. While that principle ought not to be overworked, it is capable of wide application.

One can just conceivably imagine the principle being applied to a nation that allowed the unlimited manufacture and use of chlorofluorocarbons, to the detriment of the ozone layer, even though the nation was not a party to either the Vienna Convention or the Montreal Protocol.[27] It is not necessary to extrapolate from the principles of customary international law very far, if at all, to fit them into some of the circumstances that might arise in relation to pollution of the atmosphere.

The "Trail Smelter" arbitration, which dealt with transboundary air pollution, also has potential application to ozone and climate change.[28] To the extent that the case establishes a principle of good neighborliness, it may be applied to global environmental problems. The principle would be that no state has the right to use its territory in such a manner as to cause injury to the atmosphere by emissions when serious consequences are involved and the injury to the atmosphere is demonstrated by clear and convincing evidence.[29] Indeed, the principle established by the case may go further than this and is certainly capable of extension.[30]

The "Lake Lanoux" arbitration turned on the interpretation of a particular treaty, but it may establish the principle that a state has the duty to give notice when its actions may impair the environmental enjoyment of another state. A nation is not entitled to ignore the interests of another.[31] That principle can have clear and obvious application to situations involving ozone depletion and climate change.

The "Nuclear Tests" cases, brought by Australia and New Zealand in the International Court of Justice, do not establish much, regrettably, because the Court ducked the issue.[32] Nonetheless, some legal inferences can be drawn from the decision. The burden of the complaint was that the nations were entitled to be free from the hazardous increased radiation due to fallout from the Mururoa atmospheric testing atoll. Because France ceased atmospheric testing while the case was before the Court, the judges found it unnecessary to address the issue, attributing "legal effect" to France's public undertaking to halt the testing.[33] Press statements do not often have legal effect at international law, but this one did. The case can be used to argue that there are circumstances in which government declarations can be binding, a prospect pregnant with possibilities.

While customary international law must not be underestimated or ignored, it cannot be said to have sufficient strength to cope with the problems of the global environment. Customary international law has some advantages. It is flexible, although there is an irreducible minimum that must be met for a norm to be counted as part of international law. The principles discussed have their own charm and complexity. They are not without some capacity to impose binding obligations on states regarding the global environment. But, even on the most optimistic view, customary international law can hardly be said to have sufficient scope or content to prevent damage and provide sufficient sanctions to be directed against the perpetrators of the damage when it occurs. Above all, customary international law is not a regulatory system and cannot be turned into one. Yet a regulatory system is required. It should have defined standards, monitoring, exchange of information, and some prohibitions.

One requirement of the test of custom is that a general recognition must be found among nations that a certain practice is obligatory. Even on a more relaxed view of what that test may entail, the body of customary law simply lacks the horsepower to deal with many of the great problems. Professor Ian Bownlie concludes in a survey of the international customary rules of environmental protection that custom "provides limited means of social engineering."[34] To him the limitations of custom evidence the need for the development of new institutions, standards, and localized regimes. He reached that conclusion in 1973. Everything which has happened since then reinforces that conclusion.

The Stockholm Declaration

The new environmental consciousness among nations started with the Stockholm Conference in 1972,[35] not a moment too soon. The Stockholm Declaration of the United Nations Conference on the Human Environment attracted 103 affirmative votes, 12 abstentions, and not a single negative vote.[36] In some respects the declaration was a masterpiece of international drafting. It wove the politics and the principles together in a web so tight it would not unravel. The preambular language was uplifting, and the declarations of principles ringing; but they marched together in matched pairs. The declaration was also a wish list of items that were inconsistent with one another and the overall result was to some extent intellectually incoherent.

The document suggests that we have a right now to a life of dignity and equality in an environment of quality, but that we also have a "solemn responsibility to protect and improve the environment for present and future generations."[37] The declaration does not tell us how these aims, which may be mutually incompatible, are to be achieved. That is left to another day.

Tucked away in the document are most of the main issues of global significance, which have increased in scope in the intervening years. These include:

- sustainability;
- conservation of wildlife and habitat;
- toxic substances;
- pollution of the seas;
- population growth;
- nuclear weapons; and
- the ecological balance of the biosphere.[38]

The problems of global environmental policy and diplomacy have mushroomed in the two decades since Stockholm. Many of them are now viewed with a sense of urgency that could not have reasonably been expected on the basis of the scientific evidence then available. The United Nations Environment Programme to coordinate global environmental assessment and management was established in the wake of the Stockholm Declaration.[39] The sense of urgency dates perhaps from the mid-1980s or even later. Ten years after Stockholm, a meeting was held at Nairobi (UNEP's headquarters) to look at progress.[40] There it became clear that extraneous political issues would intrude into environmental questions and that political advantage could be gained from the way environmental questions were faced in the international arena. The enthusiasm of the large developed countries, which had been such a feature at Stockholm, seemed to be on the wane at Nairobi.[41]

Some of the progress called for at Stockholm was for developments in international law. Principle 22 urged states to "co-operate to develop further the international law regarding liability and compensation for the victims of pollution and other environmental damage caused by the activities within the jurisdiction or control of such States to areas beyond their jurisdiction."[42] That imprecation appears to have been agreed to because of the difficulties that arose over Principle 21, a classical case of matched pairs traveling together:

> States have, in accordance with the Charter of the United Nations and the principles of international law, the sovereign right to exploit their own resources pursuant to their own environmental policies, and the responsibility to ensure that the activities within their jurisdiction or control do not cause

damage to the environment of other States or of areas beyond the limits of national jurisdiction.[43]

Contained within the latter part of that principle are echoes of the customary international law cases discussed above. Indeed, the declaration, with such a massive measure of international support, has a strong claim to be regarded, itself, as a source of customary international law. Read in that way, the declaration would certainly impose duties on states, independently of the treaties, not to engage in activities that, for example, would massively and unreasonably deplete the ozone layer.

The attempt by the International Law Commission to put some flesh on the bones of Principle 21 demonstrates just how hard it is to secure consensus on the core principles of international environmental law. The Commission began dealing with the topic in 1978[44] at the same time as it was engaged in codifying the law of state responsibility. The exercise may have got off on the wrong track at the beginning. It was characterized as "international liability for injurious consequences arising out of acts not prohibited by international law." In the documents generated by the special rapporteurs, the focus has been on the law concerning harm to the environment from an international point of view. But it was never clear how this topic was analytically distinct from state responsibility in general. In any event, the effort turned into an attempt to codify part of international environmental law. One commentator has characterized the effort by writing that "it is liable to seem at best a questionable exercise in reconceptualising an existing body of law, or at worst, a dangerously retrograde step which may seriously weaken international efforts to secure agreement on effective principles of international environmental law."[45]

Perhaps the Experts Group on Environmental Law established by the World Commission on Environment and Development had an easier task than the International Law Commission.[46] They formulated a report on legal principles for environmental protection and sustainable development and for accelerating the development of international law. The group produced elements of a draft convention in 1986, setting out clear principles of liability concerning transboundary interferences. The principle of state responsibility enunciated by the group was:
1. A State is responsible under international law for a breach of an international obligation relating to the use of a natural resource or the prevention or abatement of an environmental interference.

2. In particular, it shall:
    (a) cease the internationally wrongful act;
    (b) as far as possible, re-establish the situation which would have existed if the internationally wrongful act had not taken place;
    (c) provide compensation for the harm which results from the internationally wrongful act;
    (d) where appropriate, give satisfaction for the internationally wrongful act.[47]

Soft Law

Hard law in the international area comes mainly from custom or treaties. Custom takes time and often a lot of state practice before it hardens into a legally enforceable rule. Treaties take a long time to negotiate and nations tend to shy away from the specificity they often involve. A much more politically attractive approach is the "soft law" option.[48] My impression is that this phenomenon is increasingly used precisely because it is so politically convenient.

Resort to soft law leaves large amounts of discretion to states. The standards are often so vague that third-party adjudication would be impossible even if it were provided for.[49] Often the standards themselves are discretionary. What is important about these instruments is not so much the form in which they appear but the manner in which the obligations, if any, created by them are expressed.[50] Frequently, what is expressed is a series of political statements or values. The Stockholm Declaration is a good example.

In international trade law, where soft law norms are used extensively, there is a sizable literature on what soft law is and whether it really is law.[51] What does not appear to have been commented upon to any extent is the burgeoning soft law on the global environment. Whatever the jurisprudential difficulty involved, and I cannot think it is great considering the nature of international law generally, the use of soft law in the environmental area has substantial advantages. The method is particularly helpful in creating a climate that can produce a hard law instrument in the end.

All politicians know the value of ambiguity. It can serve to secure agreement where agreement may otherwise not be achieved. International instruments are frequently drafted with studied ambiguity. Such an approach may have deceptive elements to it and may create wrong impressions, but it promotes feelings of international comity and cooperation that are very valuable. Since political leaders and countries must continue dealing with one another, it is better that those dealings be based on agreement than on disagreement—and soft law solutions produce agreement.

More importantly, soft law solutions change the political thinking on an issue. They alter the circumstances in which an issue is considered; they cause opinion to coalesce. These changes can be a very important catalyst in securing an agreement with a harder edge later. Soft law solutions can thus be useful steps on a longer journey. Soft law is where international law and international politics combine to build new norms. The Helsinki Declaration on the Protection of the Ozone Layer is such an instrument.[52] The purpose was to ensure that the London meeting in 1990 could agree on hard amendments to the Montreal Protocol.[53] The consensus expressed at Helsinki was undoubtedly helpful in that respect.

Political decision makers are influenced by soft law solutions. No political leader wants to endorse an empty declaration. They usually take a lot of care with the language since they have to defend it in the media and other public forums. The political impact of the statement is their prime concern, usually its impact on domestic political opinion. They want to have achieved something that is politically significant. Press statements are taken seriously by the politicians who make them.[54] International instruments involving political leaders from other countries are taken even more seriously. Such soft law documents are often produced by lengthy negotiations simply because the statement is perceived to have political consequences of a serious sort. The Langkawi Declaration on the Environment of 1989 is an example of soft law in which the Commonwealth heads of government committed themselves to a fairly explicit program of action.[55] No doubt, they did not expect to be held legally liable in respect of the undertakings, but they were no less sincere and serious for that. And when it came to lining up support in other forums such as the United Nations, being able to point to a signature on the Langkawi Declaration was a great help. It meant, for example, that New Zealand and other Pacific countries of the commonwealth were able to rely on Commonwealth support for the United Nations resolution stopping driftnet fishing in the South Pacific.[56]

Considering that the system is somewhat short of means for establishing norms, it would be a great mistake to get too excited from an analytical point of view about the dangers of soft law. It has the capacity to make an important contribution and in the global environmental area it has already done so. Soft law is a concept of both range and flexibility. It ranges from material that is not law at all, through a long spectrum to material so close to being hard law as to be indistinguishable from it. Environmental soft law needs to be kept as far as possible toward the high end of the spectrum. It is a vital part of the continuous process of building norms.

Treaty Law and the Rule of Unanimous Consent

There are about 160 coequal sovereign states in the international community. At the moment, it is not possible to arrive at a system that includes legislation, enforcement, and third-party adjudication unless all the nations agree. In their strongest form, arguments about sovereignty are used unhesitatingly by political decision makers to tell decision makers of other nations to keep out of matters that are not their business. What Brierly called the "incubus" of sovereignty still sits heavily upon the body of international law. As Brierly said, it stands "for something in the relations of states which is both true and very formidable."[57] But it does not stand for everything. It is not an absolute. It cannot mean a state of international lawlessness, or a condition of permanent paralysis.

In international law sovereignty casts a long shadow. Consider Professor Ian Brownlie's formulation in the latest edition of his treatise: "The sovereignty and equality of states represent the basic constitutional doctrine of the law of nations, which governs a community consisting primarily of states having a uniform legal personality."[58] From that principle Brownlie deduces several consequences, the most important of which for present purposes concerns consent. He points out that the

> jurisdiction of international tribunals depends on the consent of the parties; membership of international organizations is not obligatory; and the powers of the organs of such organizations to determine their own competence, to take decisions by majority vote, and to enforce decisions, depend on the consent of member states.[59]

These are the features that pose an obstacle to the development of an international law to deal effectively with environmental problems. They must be overcome through the acceptance of an international set of rules for this particular purpose that can be applied universally.

Political decision makers in the international arena dwell little on theory and even less on jurisprudence. They want something practical that works. If they can be convinced that a broadly acceptable regime can be worked out that will offer the prospect of solving the problems, they will not quibble about the surrender of some sovereignty. The greater challenge is to design a regime that will satisfy them and meet their very real political needs.

The ordering of the affairs of nations in their relationships with one another has steadily eroded the power of nations to please themselves. The complexity of the modern world and the plethora of intricate treaties, sometimes on highly specialized subjects, that constitute the basis of most international obligations today have whittled away sovereignty. Political decision makers most assuredly do not think of themselves as inhabiting a world where they can take any actions they choose regardless of the consequences to other nations and people. They may choose to defend their actions on the basis of sovereignty, but they understand increasingly their mutual interdependence. So much international business between nations is transacted over the telephone or facsimile transmission machines or by personal visits and international meetings that this reality is inescapable. These conditions greatly affect the context in which the instruments of international law function. The formal rules tend to lag behind the contemporary reality. We need lawmaking methods that recognize the new reality.

Conventional international law takes time to develop. It is frequently cumbersome. Treaties have first to be negotiated, then ratified. This process can sometimes be so slow and time-consuming that events overtake the convention. Such was the fate of the Convention on the Regulation of Antarctic Mineral Resource Activities, which was agreed to in 1988 but will not enter into force because of the widespread conviction that its provisions do not sufficiently protect the Antarctic environment.[60] Negotiations on the convention began in about 1982, and in the end public opinion advanced quicker than the negotiations. Now a different protocol has been negotiated.[61]

Yet the number of parties negotiating on the Antarctic comprised only the Antarctic Treaty partners, a small segment of the international community.[62] The difficulties are greatly multiplied when virtually every country in the world is involved. Multilateral conventions will always be difficult to negotiate—they require extensive multilateral diplomacy. Nothing can change that. But the essential difficulty in making treaty law lies elsewhere. It is in the requirement of unanimous consent.

The whole structure and content of treaty law is based on the principle of consent, usually quite specific content. The Vienna Convention on the Law of Treaties deals with the subject of consent explicitly.[63] Article 11 provides: "The consent of a State to be bound by a treaty may be expressed by signature, exchange of instruments constituting a treaty, ratification, acceptance, approval or accession, or by any other means if so agreed."[64] There follow a number of articles spelling out when consent is present or when it can be inferred. The law is rooted in the requirement of consent. Indications that a state can be bound without its consent do not appear in the Vienna Convention, but some limited exception to the rule of unanimous consent is afforded under Article 41, which makes provision for agreements to modify multilateral treaties between certain parties only.

This clear feature of treaty law bothered one of the leading writers on the subject, Lord McNair. He recognized the "underlying principle that no State can be bound by any treaty provision unless it has given its assent, and [that] that principle is applicable equally to all types of treaty."[65] Obviously, there has been an enormous growth in multilateral treaties which have an almost legislative character about them. These treaties often regulate matters in detail. The changing character of international treaty law, however, has not been followed by sufficient changes in the rules about how a nation becomes bound.

In his discussion of the revision of treaties, Lord McNair made the following observation:

> [W]e touch here one of the weakest spots in the now existing system of States, and it must be admitted that no national society which is not equipped with legislative and administrative machinery for effecting changes could hope to hold together for long. International society is clearly groping its way towards the creation of some escape from the present effect of the rule requiring the consent of all the parties affected by a change, and some of the attempts to mitigate that rule should be noted.[66]

Lord McNair noted that some technical multilateral treaties contain provisions by which, within certain narrowly defined limits, the parties agreed to permit modifications by majority vote. Many years earlier, in 1934, Lord McNair had made some observations about the need to develop an international legislative process—a means of making binding rules for everyone.[67]

Since he wrote, there have been developments in the way some international organizations create norms. In some cases, the world is well on the way toward having the international legislative process Lord

McNair thought so necessary. Consequently, it is now possible for nations that do not agree with a particular norm to be bound by it. Unanimous consent is not required. This development has been achieved by a process of prolepsis.

Procedures for the creation of norms are agreed upon. Those procedures include a provision that in respect of certain rules or in certain circumstances unanimous consent is not required. The norms created by using the procedures did not necessarily receive unanimous consent but are binding on any nation that did not consent because they were created by agreed procedures. Nations thus consent in advance to be bound by norms whose content is unknown at the time of the consent.

Frederic Kirgis, Jr., has analyzed these "nontraditional" rule-making techniques of several international organizations, including the International Labour Organisation, the Universal Postal Union, the World Health Organization, the International Civil Aviation Organization, and the International Maritime Organization. He finds that the use of such a supertreaty system is most advanced in the case of the ILO. But he also finds that "[t]he constituent instruments of most specialized agencies contain amendment procedures that bind all members if some fraction—often two-thirds—of the total membership adopts and ratifies the amendment."[68] For example, for nonstate aircraft over the high seas, binding rules are made by a two-thirds majority in a representative ICAO body.

Another increasingly used procedure requires only tacit consent to the creation of new norms. Rules are adopted subject to being disallowed if a specified percentage of the membership blocks them. There is often an escape procedure for individual members as well. For example, the ICAO Council, which has thirty-three members, adopts international standards and recommended practices covering a wide range of matters relating to safety in the air. Standards become effective when adopted by two-thirds of the Council, unless in the meantime a majority of member states disapprove. While states that find it impracticable to comply may opt out, they will face considerable peer pressure to comply. The standards are in fact widely complied with.[69]

Professor Kirgis's analysis points out just how far some of these agencies have moved from the traditional model and how effective these untraditional techniques are in developing new norms that change the conduct of the members. While it cannot be said these developments presage the imminent establishment of world legislature, they do have clear applicability to global environmental problems. There is ample precedent for developing institutions with the power to make rules after following established procedures that are binding on the members of the organization. These developments are neither fresh nor novel. They have been going on for years and nations appear to feel comfortable with them. The organization whose constitution and procedures appear to have the most to offer for the environment is the ILO, which is discussed in more detail in the next section of this article.

The proleptic method of avoiding the rule of unanimous consent has already been employed in the environmental sphere in the Montreal Protocol on Substances that Deplete the Ozone Layer of 1987. Some little-noticed innovations were made that certainly go beyond the technical and change the rule of unanimous consent in dramatic ways.

To understand the nature and quality of the achievement, we need to review the general history of the ozone issue. It took some time and quite a lot of scientific research before the ozone problem was fully revealed. In 1974, when the first reports began to appear that there was a problem, the industry that produced the depleting substances contested the evidence and warned against precipitate action.[70] The chlorofluoro-carbons industry persisted in that stance for some years: We need more evidence, was the refrain. The argument that policy makers should wait until the scientific evidence is clear and compelling is a recurrent theme; it is both reasonable and persuasive. It can also be fundamentally wrong, as it was in the ozone case, and as is now accepted by the chlorofluorocarbons industry. Scientific disagreement can always be found and much can be made of the uncertainty. Arguments based on uncertainty often succeed with political decision makers; doing nothing is a policy option that succeeds more than most.

In the three years preceding the conclusion of the Vienna Convention for the Protection of the Ozone Layer in 1985, the evidence was strongly contested and conflicting studies were published about it. As a result, the Vienna Convention was very much a framework convention; that is, it did not decide anything specific about reductions in the use of substances that deplete the ozone layer but, rather, established mechanisms to study the question and voiced some general obligations to cooperate.[71] The Convention provided for a secretariat and a conference of the parties,[72] as well as a dispute settlement mechanism.[73] This technique of slicing the salami thinly was the key to success regarding the ozone problem. Although the specifics could not be agreed upon, a process was established that led progressively to the 1987 Montreal Protocol and the London agreement.[74]

By 1987 fresh scientific discoveries about the ozone hole over Antarctica spurred the movement to curb the emission of ozone-depleting substances. Indeed, the science was changing so fast that it was hard for the policy makers to keep up. Hardly was the ink dry on the Montreal Protocol, which required a 50 percent reduction in the production and use of ozone-depleting substances by 1999 (calculated on 1986 base figures), than it became evident that the reductions would not be sufficient. That led, in turn, to the Helsinki Declaration and the London Amendments of 1990, which should result in the virtual elimination of emissions of ozone-depleting substances by January 1, 2000.[75]

The Montreal Protocol requires an assessment and review of the control measures beginning in 1990 and "at least every four years thereafter."[76] Parties must convene panels of experts and the secretariat must report the conclusions of these experts to the parties. On the basis of those assessments, the parties are to decide whether adjustments to the ozone-depleting potentials of the controlled substances should be made and "what the scope, amount and timing of any such adjustments and reductions should be."[77] If adjustments are proposed, six months' notice must be given. All of that seems quite unexceptional until Article 2(9)(c) is reached:

> In taking such decisions, the Parties shall make every effort to reach agreement by consensus. If all efforts at consensus have been exhausted, and no agreement reached, such decisions shall, as a last resort, be adopted by a two-thirds majority vote of the Parties present and voting representing *at least fifty per cent of the total consumption of the controlled substances of the Parties.*[78]

The next provision makes it explicit that the decisions taken are binding on all the parties. This provision, however, applies only to adjustments in ozone-depleting substances mentioned in the annex to the Montreal Protocol. To add new substances, as the London conference did, requires application of the ordinary rule.

This most instructive departure from the unanimous consent rule was further fine-tuned in the 1990 London Amendments to the Montreal Protocol. The developing countries objected to the weighting provisions, which gave power to those representing 50 percent of the combined total consumption of the substances[79] (which meant that a few large chlorofluorocarbon-producing countries could block a new agreement). The final sixteen words of the provision above were deleted and the following words substituted: "a majority of the Parties operating under paragraph 1 of Article 5 present and voting and a majority of the Parties not so operating present and voting."[80] In effect, this new provision gives a veto to both developed and developing countries. A two-thirds majority is required and it must include a simple majority of each group. Future adjustments should be easier to achieve than before.

The issue obviously arises as to what a nation will do if it does not agree with an adjustment made in accordance with the foregoing rule. The country is bound if it is a party to the Protocol. Withdrawal under the Vienna Convention itself is permitted at any time after four years from the date on which the Convention entered into force, which was September 22, 1988.[81] Withdrawals can take effect one year after receipt of written notification. As amended in London in 1990, the Protocol now provides that any party may withdraw from it at any time after four years of assuming the obligations of reducing the consumption of controlled substances.[82] The withdrawal takes effect one year after giving notice. Consequently, while there are fetters on the withdrawal of nations that do got get their own way, the system is nonetheless vulnerable to withdrawal.

On the other hand, there are provisions prohibiting nations that are parties to the treaty system from exporting controlled substances to nations that are not parties, or importing from them.[83] These prohibitions may in time be extended to trade in products produced with controlled substances but not containing them. While these measures will certainly tend to discourage nations from trying to thwart the system, they are not certain to prevent it.

The ozone system is also vulnerable because of the nations that do not join. While arguments about customary international law and "jus cogens"[84] may eventually be available to induce compliance, it is wholly impractical for nations to be able to please themselves about the production of ozone-depleting substances when great effort has been made to put a fair and balanced international system into place. It renders the entire enterprise open to subversion. The ozone example demonstrates that, while a framework treaty can be used to set standards later by means that do not involve unanimous consent, the consequences of the rule of consent cannot be avoided altogether.

The argument is strengthened by considering the record of ratification of the Montreal Protocol. As of September 1991, there were eighty countries that had ratified the Vienna Convention, seventy-three the Montreal Protocol, and only five the London Amendments.[85] Conspicuous omissions from the Montreal Protocol were India and China, which nevertheless indicated after the 1990 London meeting that they would ratify when agreement was made for a financial mechanism, including a multilateral fund that would facilitate compliance by developing countries.[86] In fact, legislation passed by the United States Congress makes the level of funds appropriated for this purpose contingent upon ratification by India and China.[87] China has ratified the Protocol as amended but not the Protocol itself. Certainly, incentives should be provided for countries to sign, but what if the incentives do not work? Large countries with the capacity to frustrate the system of reductions may be inclined to do so. There are any number of reasons why nations may see an advantage in not complying with the general will.

The most persuasive analogy is with the power of acquisition the state has over land for public works in domestic law. If the power does not exist, the state must rely on private contracts. Large sums of money go to holdouts. Those who sell early may only get the market price. Those who hang on to the end will demand extraordinarily high prices for selling. That sort of behavior cannot be tolerated in the international sphere, where the future of the planet is in issue.

A means of overcoming the problems that flow from this analysis must be found, and the best means lies in the creation of a new international organization. Such an organization provides the best context in which to employ the proleptic technique of creating norms. It can also create strong incentives to point the behavior of nations in the appropriate direction and keep them bound to the rules.

There is more support for getting rid of the rule of unanimous consent than may be thought. That attitude was strikingly in evidence at the International Summit on the Protection of the Global Atmosphere, held at The Hague in March 1989.[88] The twenty-four nations that signed the Hague Declaration laid down some new principles that would constitute a new approach to making international rules and enforcing them.[89] Of course, the instrument that put them forward is of a soft law character.

For a document containing such far-reaching principles, the Hague Declaration was not difficult to negotiate, primarily because the drafters took care to stay at the level of general principle. Details on these issues could well have spawned substantial disagreement. Heads of government met to consider a draft that had been put together. I doubt that it took longer than five hours for the text to be amended and debated. As international negotiations go, it was a very easy one.

The conference had been organized as a joint initiative by the Prime Ministers of France, the Netherlands, and Norway. It was held a week after the London conference on the ozone layer sponsored by British Prime Minister Thatcher. In political terms it could be seen as something of a competitor with that conference, although the approach was far different and the subject matter much broader. In some respects the two conferences highlighted the differences between the British and continental ways of doing things. The delegates to the British-run conference relished dealing with a practical problem to which there were known solutions. What was needed was concerted and clear action. Exposing government environmental leaders to well-presented scientific evidence and giving them an opportunity to debate the solutions and arrive at a consensus had the advantage of ensuring that the subsequent London conference of 1990 could reach agreement to tighten the standards in the Montreal Protocol.

The Hague conference stood in stark contrast. The concern was with high principle. Detail and specifics were not appropriate. A conference of heads of government, it was attended by such leaders as the President of France and the Chancellor of Germany. In addition to being an interesting group, the selection of countries was representative enough to raise the range of problems threatening the global environment, including the tensions between North and South. The caution of the heavily industrialized countries, especially Japan, was evident. Brazil, which occupies a position of importance in relation to some of the issues raised by climate change, particularly deforestation, was an active participant.

The Hague Declaration calls for the "development of new principles of international law including new and more effective decision-making and enforcement mechanisms."[90] Since the problems are planet-wide, solutions can only be devised on a global level. In designing the solutions, the different levels of development of nations must be taken into account. The declaration states that most of the emissions affecting the atmosphere originate in industrialized countries. Special obligations will have to be undertaken to assist developing countries. In concrete terms the nations that signed the declaration acknowledged several principles and undertook to promote them. What they undertook to do by a soft law method was to promote a new species of hard law. The first casualty was to be the rule of unanimous consent. They thus pledged themselves to promote

> [t]he principle of developing, within the framework of the United Nations, new institutional authority, either by strengthening existing institutions or by creating a new institution, which, in the context of the preservation of the earth's atmosphere, shall be responsible for combating any further global warming of the atmosphere and shall involve such decision-making procedures as may be effective even if, on occasion, unanimous agreement has not been achieved.[91]

In terms of traditional international law, this statement is radical. It is the embryo of a legislative system for international environmental issues. Nations that do not agree with a rule and will not consent to its inclusion in a treaty may be obliged to follow the rule anyway. This principle opens up the opportunity for the creation of a new organization with the ability to create norms by special majorities. If state sovereignty is the foundation of international law, the Hague Declaration may be the first nail in its coffin.

The statement leaves a good many questions unanswered. When will it be judged that effective decision making requires the suspension of the rule of unanimous agreement? What sort of procedures must be followed to reach that conclusion? What sort of majority is sufficient to make a rule binding on a state that has refused to accept it? Furthermore, there is a troublesome first-principles question of how to get there from here. If the existing rule is unanimous consent and unanimous consent to changing the rule does not exist, how can it be changed? These issues were not addressed and they were not addressed deliberately.

For twenty-four nations to accept a principle that involves the abolition of the unanimous consent rule is surely a significant and novel event in the life of international law. Some of the nations that espoused this principle are powerful and influential actors in international politics. France is a permanent member of the Security Council. Germany and Japan are among the foremost industrial powers on the planet. India is the most populous democracy.

Acceptance that nations can be bound without their consent opens the door to a quite different legal context from that in which international law has developed. It offers the prospect of fashioning an international legislative process for global environmental issues. It offers the practical means of securing the higher standards that may be required by an objective assessment of the scientific evidence, however politically inconvenient a particular measure may be for an individual country. The search for the lowest common denominator in environmental matters, as in others, can be a grinding and laborious diplomatic search that hungrily consumes energies and time—both of which are too scarce. Nations that do not want to change can sit tight and avoid change. A recurring theme at international conferences is the last-minute effort to persuade one country or another to go along. Language is softened, material is removed, and much of substance is lost. Herein lies a fundamental difference between the legislative and the diplomatic process. With legislation everyone is bound by the outcome, including those who do not agree. With treaties those who do not agree simply do not become bound.

A New Institution

The weakness of the international machinery has not escaped comment. The Hague signatories wanted new institutional authority that would "develop instruments and define standards to enhance or guarantee the protection of the atmosphere and monitor compliance."[92] In 1988 a Canadian-sponsored conference in Toronto called for a comprehensive framework convention and protocols to protect the atmosphere,[93] and experts did quite a lot of work in framing a convention. Taking a different tack, in 1988 the President of the World Federation of United Nations Associations proposed that the Trusteeship Council be revitalized and given a new mission to exercise trusteeship over the "planetary systems on which our security and survival depends, as well as [over] the global commons."[94]

Relying explicitly on the Hague Declaration, New Zealand advanced a proposal in the 1989 General Assembly debate for a new United Nations institution, an Environmental Protection Council. The proposal was developed in the following way:

> In New Zealand's judgment, the traditional response of international law, developing international legal standards in small incremental steps, each of which must be subsequently ratified by all countries, is no longer appropriate to deal with the highly complex environmental problems of the future.

The time has come for something more innovative, for a conceptual leap forward in institutional terms. And we see the need for the establishment of a new organ in the United Nations system—perhaps it would be called the "Environmental Protection Council". . . . I have no doubt that if the Charter were being drawn up today, there would be widespread support for including among the organs of the United Nations a body empowered to take binding decisions on global environmental issues. In our view, nothing less than an institution with this status will command the necessary respect and authority to achieve what is required.

Perhaps the most effective way to achieve this would be the inclusion in the United Nations Charter of a new Chapter dealing with the environment.

The missing institutional link, however, is the equivalent of a legislature. We would envisage the new Environmental Protection Council becoming the point in the United Nations system which links the streams of economic and environmental advice. It would perform the function that currently falls between the cracks in the mandates of all existing organizations. It would have responsibility for taking coordinated decisions on sustainable policies for global environmental protection. It would be empowered to take binding decisions. And if decisions are to be binding, the membership of the Council may need to be very wide— perhaps including all members of the United Nations. But the key thing is that it should have power to act—not just talk.[95]

There are basically four policy options in the institutional area. First, things could be left as they are. Second, UNEP could be strengthened and given formal responsibilities. Third, the secretariat approach of the Vienna Convention could be embroidered upon and developed so that a series of secretariats operate for separate environmental issues. At present, that is the way things are heading. The fourth broad option is to create a new international institution.

To take the high road now will require considerable political commitment, but it is likely to ensure that there will be less trouble later on. International norms gain legitimacy from the process by which they are arrived at. An enduring institutional framework in which the processes are thorough and based on solid scientific data, and in which there is plenty of opportunity for refinement and debate, is likely to serve the world best in the long run.

What form should a new institution take? The most ambitious course is to create a new organ in the United Nations by amending the Charter. It would be the best possible outcome of the 1992 Conference on Environment and Development. But the procedures for changing the Charter are by no means easy, and the permanent members of the Security Council have a veto. Although I favor creating a new U.N. organ, it is not the only option. An easier choice to achieve, and one that could provide a workable institutional framework, would be to create a new specialized U.N. agency.

Of course, it would be possible to expand and develop the United Nations Environment Programme, negotiate a charter for it, and charge it with some extra responsibilities. Or such bodies as the General Agreement on Tariffs and Trade and the International Monetary Fund could serve as models for a new environmental organization. But, to my mind, the most useful model is the one that has been developed over many years by the International Labour Organisation.[96]

One feature of the ILO's approach is the direct involvement of nongovernmental organizations in setting the standards. The ozone work demonstrated that environmental decisions have enormous impact on the business community. Widespread consultation with industry is necessary at the domestic level both to provide information about the problem and to work through the practical difficulties of compliance. In New Zealand the Ministry for the Environment was able to implement a tough policy without objections from industry as a result of such consultation.[97]

In addition, many environmental organizations have more expertise on some global environmental issues than governments. Governments of smaller countries, in particular, often lack the background and manpower to develop the necessary expertise. The better course is to share information and hold consultations with environmental NGOs so that the approaches to be taken at international conferences can be worked out on the basis of the best available knowledge and judgment.

The International Labour Organisation is the most advanced supertreaty system in terms of providing legislative outcomes of any of the international agencies. Borrowing loosely from the ILO Constitution, a new International Environment Organization could be established with the following features.[98]

1. A General Conference comprising all members, to be called together annually and more often if the Governing Council so

decides. The conference shall consist of four representatives from each member; two shall be government delegates and the two others shall represent business and environmental organizations, respectively.

2. A Governing Council of forty people—twenty representing governments, ten representing business organizations and ten representing environmental organizations.

3. The ability of the conference to set international environmental regulations by a two-thirds majority of the votes cast by delegates present. The regulations would become binding without further action. There would also be provision for recommendations to be made to members.

4. A Director-General and staff of the International Environment Office, to have explicit international responsibilities for educating people about the global environmental problems and what they can do to help.

5. The office to have defined functions for gathering information and monitoring compliance, including verification of compliance with the regulations. There should be regular reviews of the environmental policies of member states and their compliance with the regulations.

6. A thorough preparatory process, in which there are ample notice, thorough scientific and technical preparation, and consultation before regulations are made.

7. Formal provision for authoritative and widely representative scientific advice and papers to be available to the organization.

8. Detailed requirements for nations to report annually on action taken to implement agreed regulations. The environment and business representatives would be required to report separately from governments.

9. Provision, for any member to be able to submit complaints regarding nonobservance in respect of any other member to the International Environment Office.

10. Discretion of the council to refer such complaints to a commission of inquiry for a full report. The commission shall consist of three appropriate experts of recognized impartiality and be chaired by a lawyer. The commission is to make findings of fact and rule on the steps to be taken to deal with the complaint and the time by which the steps must be taken. Refusals by governments to accept these findings are to be referred to the full conference.

11. Authority for the council to recommend measures to the conference to secure compliance when it is lacking.

A word needs to be said here about the last feature, on measures to secure compliance. For them to be effective, there must be some strong incentives to join the organization and stay in it. For many countries these will probably reside in technical assistance, information, advice, technology transfer, and even financial assistance for dealing with environmental problems. From a practical point of view, the sanctions should include the withholding of benefits by the organization and of direct contacts with delinquent governments, and the mobilization of the politics of shame. Few nations like to be regarded as international pariahs and shame as a sanction ought not to be underestimated.

The great advantage of creating a new international organization of the type outlined is that it allows the technique of prolepsis to be used to arrive at rules that are binding, without the requirement of unanimity. It maximizes the prospects of observance of those rules by mandating explanation for their adoption and monitoring for compliance with them. It establishes a dispute settlement mechanism that is part of the institutional structure and not remote from it. What it does not do is overcome the need for consent by a nation to join the organization and remain a member. The incentives for that will have to be supplied by peer pressure and political means. But I do not regard it as unrealistic to think that we will reach the point where the norms are binding on every nation in the international community. It may happen quite quickly.

Many nations, particularly the most powerful and certainly the United States, are likely to be opposed to the creation of such an organization. There appears to be a broad consensus among governments that the creation of new institutions should be avoided when possible. In some quarters those sentiments derive from the ponderous nature of some U.N. structures and the impenetrable bureaucratic thickets surrounding them. Many nations reshape and reorganize their domestic agencies periodically. Such an effort ought to be made at the U.N. level. If the position is taken that the total outlay for bureaucratic resources must not exceed what it is now, great and beneficial restructuring could be achieved. It would involve cutting away existing overlaps in international agencies. Without a new institution, progress will be too slow and unsystematic. How much better it would be to have a coherent set of procedures and institutions for creating the norms. The ability to respond to the global challenges we face will be greatly reduced unless a new organization with clean lines of jurisdiction and new powers is created.

Conclusion

The global environmental problems make up a classic case of the tragedy of the commons. The author of that thesis tells us that "[r]uin is the destination toward which all men rush, each pursuing his own best interest in a society which believes in the freedom of the commons. Freedom in a commons brings ruin to all."[99] International society is only slowly waking up to the consequences of its own actions toward the global commons. The challenge is how to legislate temperance using the only means at our disposal, international law.

International law has never been confronted with a set of problems of the nature and quality of the global environmental problems. To meet the challenge, a new approach is needed, one that builds on the international law and institutions we have. The thesis advanced is that in those ways that international law seems different from municipal law, there will have to be changes. To deal effectively with the global problems, a form of legislative capacity is essential. Rules that are binding on nations will have to be made by means other than unanimous consent.

Some of the disputes that may lie ahead could be difficult indeed; the rules will have to ensure that fair and binding adjudication can be held between nations. Some inspection and enforcement will be inevitable. The stakes are so high that slippage in meeting the standards will be intolerable. The actions of one nation could render nugatory the actions of all the others to preserve the global environment.

The global environmental problems pose three specific challenges: setting the rules, monitoring and verifying compliance, and providing an authoritative and binding method of settling disputes. Each of these goals could be better achieved if a new organ of the United Nations were created or a new United Nations organization established. A new U.N. organization called the International Environment Organization could be established at the 1992 meeting in Brazil. It should look to the procedures of the International Labour Organisation as a model for establishing norms, monitoring compliance and settling disputes. The rest of the international machinery touching on the environment should be restructured to avoid duplication and waste.

The argument here is not for some utopian system of world government. It is merely for a limited extension of the existing institutions of international law so that the law can cope effectively with a new problem. The proposal does require nations to surrender some sovereignty. It is palpably in their self-interest to do so. The politics of it are good. Most members of the global public consider preservation of life here a sound idea.[100]

There is a political imperative driving environmental diplomacy. It is the rising level of consciousness among people everywhere of the serious nature of the global environmental problems. One can feel it in the air at the increasingly numerous international conferences held on the subject. Governments are eager to be seen as taking a constructive stance. It is time to translate that attitude into action.

Notes

1. Stockholm Declaration on the Human Environment, adopted by the U.N. Conference on the Human Environment at Stockholm, June 16, 1972, Section I of Report of the United Nations Conference on the Human Environment, U.N. Doc. A/CONF.48/14 and Corr. 1 (1972), reprinted in 11 ILM 1416 (1972) (adopted with no roll-call vote recorded) [hereinafter Stockholm Declaration]. See also *Basic Documents in International Law and World Order* 691, 943 (B. Weston, R. Falk and A. D'Amato 2d ed. 1990).

2. See United Nations Conference on Environment and Development, GA Res. 44/228, 44 U.N. GAOR Supp. (No. 49) at 151, U.N. Doc. A/44/49 (1989) [hereinafter UNCED resolution].

3. See id.

4. P. Sand, "International Law on the Agenda of the United Nations Conference on Environment and Development" 15 (unpublished paper on file, Victoria University of Wellington). The paper is based on a background report prepared for the Aspen Institute International Environmental Policy Meeting, July 1991.

5. *World Commission on Environment and Development, Our Common Future* 320 (1987).

6. Institutional and Financial Arrangements for International Environmental Co-operation, GA Res. 2997, 27 U.N. GAOR Supp. (No. 30) at 43, U.N. Doc. A/8730 (1972), reprinted in *International Organisation and Integration* 460 (L. Sohn, ed. 1986). For a detailed account of the formation of UNEP, see L. Caldwell, *International Environmental Policy* 19–34 (1984). For a complete collection of official documents relating to UNEP, see *UNEP, Compendium of Legislative Authority* (1978).

7. Gray, "The United Nations Environment Programme: An Assessment," 20 *Envt. L.* 291 (1990).

8. *World Commission on Environment and Development*, supra note 5.

9. GA Res. 32/197, 32 U.N. GAOR Supp. (No. 45) at 121, U.N. Doc. A/32/45 (1977); UNEP, *The United Nations System-Wide Medium-Term Environment Programme, 1990–1995*, U.N. Doc. UNEP/GC/DEC/SS.1/3 (1988).

10. The Declaration of Environmental Policies and Procedures relating to Economic Development was made in 1980 by the World Bank, the Asian Development Bank, the African Development Bank, the Organization of American States, the Arab Bank for Economic Development, the Caribbean Development Bank, the Inter-American Development Bank, the Commission of the European Communities, the United Nations Development Programme, and the United Nations Environment Programme. From this beginning, they formed the Committee of International Development Institutions on the Environment (CIDIE). See *CIDIE Secretariat, Action and Interaction: The Role and Potential of CIDIE* (1988).

11. UNEP's Regional Seas Programme—now known as the Ocean and Coastal Affairs Programme—which extends to 10 regions, is perhaps the best example. See further note 13 infra.

12. Register of International Treaties and other Agreements on the Environment, U.N. Doc. UNEP/GC.16/Inf.4 (1991). See also *International Environmental Law—Primary Materials* (Molitor, M. ed. 1991).

13. United Nations Convention on the Law of the Sea, opened for signature Dec. 10, 1982, U.N. Doc. A/CONF.62/122, reprinted in *United Nations, Official Text of the United Nations Convention on the Law of the Sea with Annexes and Index*, U.N. Sales No. E.83V.5 (1983), 21 *ILM* 1261 (1982). The Convention will replace the 1958 Geneva Law of the Sea Conventions upon entry into force (12 months after the 60th acceptance) for the parties. For details of the Regional Seas Programme, see P. Sand, *Marine Environment Law* (1988). See also Barcelona Convention for the Protection of the Mediterranean Sea against Pollution, Feb. 16, 1976, reprinted in 15 *ILM* 285 (1976).

14. Convention on Long-Range Transboundary Air Pollution, Nov. 13, 1979, reprinted in 18 *ILM* 1442 (1979).

15. Convention on Early Notification of a Nuclear Accident, Sept. 26, 1986, reprinted in 25 *ILM* 1370 (1986); Convention on Assistance in Case of a Nuclear Accident or Radiological Emergency, Sept. 26, 1986, reprinted in id. at 1377.

16. Convention on International Trade in Endangered Species of Wild Fauna and Flora, Mar. 6, 1973, 27 UST 1087, TIAS No. 8249, 993 UNTS 243, reprinted in 12 *ILM* 1085 (1973).

17. Convention on the Control of Transboundary Movements of Hazardous Wastes and Their Disposal, with Annexes, Mar. 22, 1989, reprinted in 28 *ILM* 649 (1989).

18. Vienna Convention for the Protection of the Ozone Layer, Mar. 22, 1985, U.N. Doc. UNEP/IG.53/Rev.1, *S. Treaty Doc. No. 9*, 99th Cong., 1st Sess. (1985), reprinted in 26 ILM 1529 (1987) (entered into force Sept. 22, 1988) [hereinafter Vienna Convention]; Protocol on Substances That Deplete the Ozone Layer, with Annex A, Sept. 19, 1987, reprinted in 26 *ILM* at 1550 (entered into force Jan. 1, 1989) [hereinafter Montreal Protocol]; Helsinki Declaration on the Protection of the Ozone Layer, May 2, 1989, reprinted in 28 *ILM* 1335 (1989) (see Conference Report: U.N. Doc. UNEP/Ozl.Conv.1/5 (1989) [hereinafter Helsinki Declaration]; and Adjustments to the Montreal Protocol on Substances That Deplete the Ozone Layer, June 29, 1990, reprinted in 30 *ILM* 537 (1991) [hereinafter London Amendments]. See also J. Brunnée, *Acid Rain and Ozone Layer Depletion* (1988); A. Miller and I. Mintzer, *The Sky Is the Limit: Strategies for Protecting the Ozone Layer* (1986); Nanda, "Stratospheric Ozone Depletion: A Challenge for International Environmental Law and Policy," 10 *Mich. J. Int'l L.* 482 (1989).

19. UNEP, Montevideo Programme for the Development and Periodic Review of Environmental Law, ad hoc meeting of senior government officials expert in environmental law (Nov. 6, 1981); UNEP Governing Council Decision 10/21 (May 31, 1982).

20. Montreal Protocol, supra note 18, Art. 6.

21. A. McNair, *The Law of Treaties* 162 (1961).

22. Id. at 534.

23. Rt. Hon. Geoffrey Palmer, General Debate Statement of New Zealand Government, U.N. Doc. A/44/PV.15, at 61, 76 (1989) [hereinafter Palmer Statement].

24. Brownlie, "A Survey of International Customary Rules of Environmental Protection," 13 *Nat. Resources J.* 179 (1973).

25. Statute of the International Court of Justice, Art. 38(b), 59 Stat. 1031, TS No. 993, 1976 U.N.Y.B. 1052.

26. Corfu Channel (UK v. Alb.) 1949 *ICJ Rep.* 4 (Judgment of Apr. 9). One would have supposed that the principle applied to the Chernobyl accident, but the timidity of nations with nuclear installations of their own appears to have made them leery of bringing claims.

27. See note 18 supra.

28. Trail Smelter (U.S. v. Can.), 3 R. Int'l Arb. Awards 1905 (1938 and 1941).

29. Id. at 1965.

30. See Kirgis, "Technological Challenge to the Shared Environment: United States Practice," 66 *AJIL* 290, 290–94 (1972).

31. Lake Lanoux Arbitration, 12 R. Int'l Arb. Awards 281, 315–16 (1957) (citing the Treaty of Bayonne, Dec. 1, 1856; Apr. 14, 1862; and May 26, 1866; Additional Act, May 26, 1866, Arts. 8–19).

32.   Nuclear Tests (Austl. v. Fr.; NZ v. Fr.), Interim Protection, 1973 *ICJ Rep.* 99 and 135 (Orders of June 22); 1974 *ICJ Rep.* 253 and 257 (Judgments of Dec. 20).

33.   1974 *ICJ Rep.* at 474.

34.   Brownlie, supra note 24, at 180.

35.   Report of the United Nations Conference on the Human Environment, supra note 1, at 3.

36.   Stockholm Declaration, supra note 1. See *Basic Documents in International Law and World Order*, supra note 1, at 943. Ambassador George Bush led the United States delegation.

37.   See Stockholm Declaration, supra note 1, Principle 1.

38.   See Stockholm Declaration, supra note 1, passim. A number of issues were underemphasized in the Stockholm Declaration, including chemical and biological weapons, carbon dioxide production and global warming, ozone depletion (which was unknown at the time), and biological diversity. For a recent account of the overall crisis, see P. Raven, *We're Killing Our World—The Global Ecosystem Crisis* (1987).

39.   See GA Res. 2997 (XXVII), supra note 6.

40.   Nairobi Declaration, 37 U.N. GAOR Supp. (No. 25) at 49, U.N. Doc. A/37/25 (1982).

41.   "Ten Years After Stockholm—International Environmental Law," 77 *ASIL Proc.* 411, 413 (1983) (introductory remarks by Ved Nanda to panel discussion).

42.   Stockholm Declaration, supra note 1, Principle 2.

43.   Id., Principle 21. See also World Charter for Nature, Oct. 28, 1982, GA Res. 37/7, 37 U.N. GAOR Supp. (No. 51) at 21, U.N. Doc. A/37/51 (1982).

44.   The ILC established the Working Group on International Liability for Injurious Consequences Arising out of Acts Not Prohibited by International Law at its 1502d meeting on June 16, 1978, and Robert Q. Quentin-Baxter was appointed special rapporteur. [1978] 1 *Y.B. Int'l L. Comm'n* at 150, U.N. Doc. A/CN.4/SER.A/1978. The tortuous history of the Commission's efforts can be traced in the "Yearbooks" of the ILC. After Professor Quentin-Baxter's death, Ambassador Julio Barboza took over as special rapporteur.

45.   Boyle, "State Responsibility and International Liability for Injurious Consequences of Acts Not Prohibited by International Law: A Necessary Distinction?", 39 *Int'l & Comp. L.Q.* 1, 1 (1990).

46.   See *World Commission on Environment and Development, Experts Group on Environmental Law, Environmental Protection and Sustainable Development* (1987).

47.   Id. at 32.

48.   See generally, Chinkin, "The Challenge of Soft Law: Development and Change in International Law," 38 *Int'l & Comp. L.Q.* 850 (1989); Wellens

and Borchardt, "Soft Law in European Community Law," 14 *Eur. L. Rev.* 267 (1989); "A Hard Look at Soft Law," 82 *ASIL Proc.* 371 (1988); Riphagen, "From Soft Law to Jus Cogens and Back," 17 *Victoria U. Wellington L. Rev.* 81 (1987); Gamble, "The 1982 United Nations Convention on the Law of the Sea as Soft Law," 8 *Houston J. Int'l L.* 37 (1985); Carlson, "Hunger, Agricultural Trade Liberalization, and Soft International Law: Addressing the Legal Dimensions of a Political Problem," 70 *Iowa L. Rev.* 1187 (1985); Gruchalla-Wesierski, "A Framework for Understanding 'Soft Law,'" 30 *McGill L.J.* 37 (1984); Gold, "Strengthening the Soft International Law of Exchange Agreements," 77 *AJIL* 443 (1983).

49. Gruchalla-Wesierski, supra note 48, at 44–45.
50. Id. at 52–55.
51. See "A Hard Look at Soft Law," Wellens and Borchardt, Carlson, and Gold, all supra note 48.
52. Helsinki Declaration, supra note 18.
53. London Amendments, supra note 18.
54. The "Nuclear Tests" cases make this a more powerful argument. See text at note 33 supra.
55. Commonwealth Heads of Government, Langkawi Declaration on the Environment, Oct. 29, 1989, reprinted in "Selected Legal Materials," 5 *Am. U.J. Int'l L. & Pol'y* 589, 590, para. 8 (1990). The declaration was drafted to address environmental problems that transcend national boundaries, such as global warming, depletion of the ozone layer, acid rain, marine pollution, land degradation, and the extinction of plant and animal species. The declaration stressed that environmental protection measures must take account of the need to promote "economic growth and sustainable development, including the eradication of poverty." The heads of the Commonwealth, representing a quarter of the world's population, agreed to develop policies to help achieve sustainable development, strengthen funding of environmental protection, back ways to improve energy conservation and efficiency, phase out substances depleting the ozone layer, promote afforestation, help protect low-lying countries from sea-level rise, discourage and restrict driftnet fishing, and curb marine pollution and ocean dumping of toxic wastes. See "Commonwealth Concerned about Deterioration in Environment" (Oct. 21, 1989) (NEXIS, Reuters library, Omni file).
56. Large-scale Pelagic Driftnet Fishing and Its Impact on the Living Marine Resources of the World's Oceans and Seas, GA Res. 44/225 (Mar. 15, 1990), reprinted in 29 *ILM* 1556 (1990).
57. J. Brierly, *The Law of Nations* 47 (6th ed. 1963).
58. I. Brownlie, *Principles of Public International Law* 287 (4th ed. 1990).
59. Id. at 287–88.

60. Convention on the Regulation of Antarctic Mineral Resource Activities, June 2, 1988, reprinted in 27 *ILM* 860 (1988).

61. Protocol on Environmental Protection to the Antarctic Treaty, June 21, 1991, reprinted in 30 *ILM* 1461 (1991). See the Current Developments Note by Blay, infra p. 377.

62. The 12 original members of the Treaty were Argentina, Australia, Belgium, Chile, France, Japan, New Zealand, Norway, South Africa, the Soviet Union, the United Kingdom, and the United States. The eight recent entries are Poland, the Federal Republic of Germany, Brazil, India, the People's Republic of China, Uruguay, the former German Democratic Republic and Italy.

63. Vienna Convention on the Law of Treaties, May 23, 1969, 1155 UNTS 331, reprinted in 8 *ILM* 679 (1969).

64. Id. Art. 11.

65. A. McNair, supra note 21, at 162.

66. Id. at 534.

67. McNair, "International Legislation," 19 *Iowa L. Rev.* 177 (1934).

68. Kirgis, The Promulgation of International Norms in the U.N. System by Nontraditional Methods 13 (unpublished manuscript, on file at the University of Iowa College of Law) [hereinafter Nontraditional Methods]; see also Kirgis, Aviation, and Kirgis, Shipping (unpublished manuscripts, both on file at University of Iowa College of Law). All of the preceding manuscripts will appear in the forthcoming book *The United Nations and the International Legal Order* (C. Joyner and O. Schachter eds.).

69. Kirgis, Nontraditional Methods, supra note 68.

70. Kindt and Minifee, "The Vexing Problem of Ozone Depletion in International Environmental Law and Policy," 24 *Tex. Int'l L. Rev.* 261, 271 (1989).

71. Vienna Convention, supra note 18, Arts. 2, 3, 4.

72. Id., Arts. 6, 7.

73. Id., Art. 11.

74. See note 18 supra.

75. See Helsinki Declaration, supra note 18.

76. Montreal Protocol, supra note 18, Art. 6.

77. Id., Art. 2(9)(a)(ii).

78. Id., Art. 2(9)(c) (emphasis added).

79. R. Benedick, *Ozone Diplomacy—New Directions in Safeguarding the Planet* 178 (1991).

80. London Amendments, supra note 18, Ann. II, sec. H.

81. Vienna Convention, supra note 18, Art. 19.

82. London Amendments, supra note 18, Ann. II, sec. X.

83. Montreal Protocol, supra note 18, Art. 4.

84. See I. Brownlie, supra note 58, at 512–15.

85. For a complete list of signatories to the Vienna Convention and the Montreal Protocol as of January 22, 1991, see U.N. Doc. UNEP/Ozl.Pro./WG.1/5/Inf.1 (1991). Later information is contained in a letter from the Policy Adviser to the Executive Director of UNEP to the author (Sept. 9, 1991) (on file, Victoria University of Wellington).

86. See *Int'l Env't Rep.* (BNA), July 1990, at 275.

87. Clean Air Act Amendments of 1990, Pub. L. No. 101–549, §617, 104 Stat. 2399, 2670 (1990).

88. Hague Declaration on the Environment, Mar. 11, 1989, reprinted in 28 *ILM* 1308 (1989).

89. The signatories to the Hague Declaration were the Federal Republic of Germany, the Ivory Coast, Australia, Egypt, Brazil, Spain, Canada, France, Hungary, India, Indonesia, Italy, Japan, Jordan, Kenya, Malta, Norway, New Zealand, the Netherlands, Senegal, Sweden, Tunisia, Venezuela, and Zimbabwe.

90. Hague Declaration, supra note 88, 28 *ILM* at 1309.

91. Id., para. (a), 28 *ILM* at 1310.

92. Id., para. (b), 28 *ILM* at 1310.

93. Toronto Conference Statement, The Changing Atmosphere: Implications for Global Security (July 5, 1988), reprinted in "Selected Legal Materials," supra note 55, at 515, 520, paras. 16–17.

94. Zaelke and Cameron, "Global Warming and Climate Change—An Overview of the International Legal Process," 5 *Am. U.J. Int'l L. & Pol'y* 249, 280 (1990). Among the suggestions made have been the creation of an Environmental Authority; the creation of an Environmental Security Council within the United Nations; modifying the Trusteeship Council to deal with environmental issues; and the establishment of a committee of the General Assembly to deal with environmental questions.

95. Palmer Statement, supra note 23, at 76–77.

96. For material on the International Labour Organisation and international legislation, see F. Kirgis, Jr., *International Organizations* 212–26, 290–338 (1977); D. Bowett, *The Law of International Institutions* 127–39 (1975). See also Y. Ghebali, *The International Labour Organisation: A Case Study on the Evolution of U.N. Specialised Agencies* (1989); E. Luard, *International Agencies: The Emerging Framework of Interdependence* 133–52 (1977); E. Yemin, *Legislative Powers in the United Nations and Specialized Agencies* (1969); I. Detter, *Law Making by International Organizations* 207–28 (1965).

97. See G. Palmer, *Environmental Politics—A Green Print for New Zealand* 56 (1990). See also Resource Management Act 1991, 1 N.Z. Stat., No. 69. The Act, which is 382 pages long, sets up a system of sustainable management of natural and physical resources in New Zealand.

98. All the features summarized in the next piece of text can be found in the *Constitution of the International Labour Organisation and Standing*

Orders of the International Labour Conference (International Labour Office, Geneva, 1955).

99. Hardin, "The Tragedy of the Commons," 162 *Science* 142 (1968), reprinted in *Economics, Ecology, and Ethics* 100, 104 (H. Daly ed. 1973).

100. The idea of a duty to future generations is fully developed in E. Brown Weiss, *In Fairness to Future Generations* (1989).

25

International Environmental Law: Contemporary Issues and the Emergence of a New World Order

Edith Brown Weiss

In 1972 international environmental law was a fledgling field with less than three dozen multilateral agreements. Today international environmental law is arguably setting the pace for cooperation in the international community in the development of international law. There are nearly nine hundred international legal instruments that are either primarily directed to international environmental issues or contain important provisions on them.[1] This proliferation of legal instruments is likely to continue. Therefore, it is important to assess what we have done and explore where we are headed.

The History of International Environmental Law[2]

Prior to 1950

Before 1900 there were few multilateral or bilateral agreements concerning international environmental issues.[3] Relevant international agreements were based on unrestrained national sovereignty over natural resources and focused primarily on boundary waters, navigation, and fishing rights along shared waterways, particularly the Rhine River and other European waterways. They did not address pollution or other ecological issues. The dramatic exception to this pattern emerged in 1909 in the United States-United Kingdom Boundary Waters Treaty,[4] which provided in Article IV that water "shall not be polluted on either side to the injury of health or property on the other."[5]

In the early 1900s, countries began to conclude agreements to protect commercially valuable species. These agreements include the 1902 Convention for the Protection of Birds Useful to Agriculture,[6] the 1916 Convention for the Protection of Migratory Birds in the United States and Canada,[7] and the Treaty for the Preservation and Protection of Fur Seals signed in 1911.[8] Only one convention focused on wildlife more generally: the 1900 London Convention for the Protection of Wild Animals, Birds and Fish in Africa.[9]

By the 1930s and 1940s, states recognized the importance of conserving natural resources and negotiated several agreements to protect fauna and flora generally. These include the 1933 London Convention on Preservation of Fauna and Flora in Their Natural State[10] (focused primarily on Africa), and the 1940 Washington Convention on Nature Protection and Wild Life Preservation[11] (focused on the Western Hemisphere). During this period, states also concluded the well-known International Convention for the Regulation of Whaling,[12] as well as other conventions concerned with ocean fisheries and birds.[13]

In the first half of this century there was little development and application of customary international norms to environmental issues. The classic Trail Smelter Arbitration between Canada and the United States,[14] which affirmed Canada's responsibility for the damage from copper smelter fumes that transgressed the border into the state of Washington, was the notable exception. The language of the Arbitral Tribunal has been cited widely as confirming the principle that a state is responsible for environmental damage to foreign countries caused by activities within its borders, even though in this case Canada's liability for the damage was determined in the compromise establishing the Tribunal.[15] One of the most important aspects of the Arbitration is the Tribunal's decision that if there is a threat of serious continuing harm, the state must cease the harmful conduct (which implies that damages would not be sufficient). The Tribunal required the parties to effectuate the monitoring regime to ensure that further damaging pollution did not occur. Because the Trail Smelter Arbitration is a rare example of international environmental adjudication in this early period, it has acquired an unusually important place in the jurisprudence of international environmental law.

1950–1972

During the 1950s and early 1960s, the international community was concerned with nuclear damage from civilian use (a by-product of the

Atoms for Peace Proposal[16]) and marine pollution from oil. Thus, countries negotiated agreements governing international liability for nuclear damage and required measures to prevent oil pollution at sea.[17]

In the 1960s, environmental issues began to emerge within countries, Rachel Carson published her famous book *Silent Spring*,[18] and comparable books were published in European countries. In the United States, this new environmental awareness led to the adoption of the first major piece of federal environmental legislation, the National Environmental Policy Act of 1969,[19] which initiated the environmental impact statement. In 1971 the U.S. Council on Environmental Quality and the U.S. Environmental Protection Agency were formed.[20]

Internationally, during the 1960s, multilateral international environmental agreements increased significantly. Conventions were negotiated relating to interventions in case of oil pollution casualties, to civil liability for oil pollution damage, and to oil pollution control in the North Sea.[21] The African Convention on the Conservation of Nature and Natural Resources was concluded in 1968.[22]

1972 and Beyond: The Modern Era of International Environmental Law

Modern international environmental law dates to approximately 1972 when countries gathered for the United Nations Stockholm Conference on the Human Environment, and the United Nations Environment Programme (UNEP) was established.[23] Many important legal developments took place in the period surrounding the Conference, including negotiation of the Convention on International Trade in Endangered Species,[24] the London Ocean Dumping Convention,[25] the World Heritage Convention,[26] and the first of the UNEP regional seas conventions.[27] Since then, there has been a rapid rise in international legal instruments concerned with the environment, to the point that we are concerned today with developing new means for coordinating the negotiation and implementation of related agreements, in particular their administrative, monitoring, and financial provisions.

Since 1970, hundreds of international environmental instruments have been concluded. Including bilateral and multilateral instruments (binding and nonbinding), there are close to nine hundred international legal instruments that have one or more significant provisions addressing the environment.[28] Within the last two years alone, there have been about a dozen highly important multilateral negotiations occurring more or less in parallel.[29]

Historical Developments: The Changing Themes and Focus of International Environmental Law Agreements

The subject matter of international environmental agreements now bears little resemblance to that in agreements concluded in the first half of this century, which focused on boundary rivers, fishing rights, and protection of particularly valued animal species. Today there are agreements to control pollution in all environmental media, conserve habitats, protect global commons, such as the high-level ozone layer,[30] and protect resources located within countries that are of concern to the international community. Moreover, the U.N. Conference on Environment and Development held last June in Rio de Janeiro, Brazil, suggests that we are entering a new phase in international environmental law in which environmental and economic issues will be joined.

The scope of international agreements has expanded significantly since 1972: from transboundary pollution agreements to global pollution agreements; from control of direct emissions into lakes to comprehensive river basin system regimes; from preservation of certain species to conservation of ecosystems; from agreements that take effect only at national borders to ones that restrain resource use and control activities within national borders, such as for world heritages, wetlands, and biologically diverse areas. The duties of the parties to these agreements have also become more comprehensive: from undertaking research and monitoring to preventing pollution and reducing certain pollutants to specified levels. Notably, there is no example in which the provisions of earlier conventions have been weakened; rather, they have been strengthened or their scope has been expanded.

The international community is increasingly aware that it is important not only to monitor and research environmental risks, but also to reduce them. Thus states have moved from international agreements that mainly address research, information exchange, and monitoring to agreements that require reductions in pollutant emissions and changes in control technology. The Protocol on Sulphur Dioxide to the United Nations Economic Commission for Europe (U.N.-ECE) Convention on Long-Range Transboundary Air Pollution[31] calls for a thirty percent reduction in national annual sulphur emissions or their transboundary fluxes by 1993,[32] and the Montreal Protocol on Substances That Deplete the Ozone Layer,[33] including the 1990 Adjustments and Amendments,[34] requires that chlorofluorocarbons and halons, except for essential uses, be phased out by the year 2000.[35] This emphasis on preventing pollution is likely to continue as we appreciate that the capacity of our environment to absorb the by-products of production and consumption is limited.

The last seven years, from 1985 to 1992, illustrate the increasingly rapid development of international environmental law. During this period, countries have negotiated a surprisingly large number of global agreements. These include the Vienna Convention on the Protection of the Ozone Layer;[36] the Montreal Protocol on Substances that Deplete the Ozone Layer with the London Adjustments and Amendments;[37] the Protocol on Environmental Protection (with annexes) to the Antarctic Treaty;[38] the Basel Convention on the Transboundary Movements of Hazardous Wastes and Their Disposal;[39] the two International Atomic Energy Agency (IAEA) Conventions on Early Notification of a Nuclear Accident[40] and on Assistance in the Case of a Nuclear Accident or Radiological Emergency;[41] the International Convention on Oil Pollution Preparedness, Response and Co-operation;[42] the Framework Convention on Climate Change;[43] the Convention on Biological Diversity;[44] the principles on forests;[45] the nonbinding legal instrument of the Arctic Environmental Protection Strategy;[46] and the London Guidelines for the Exchange of Information on Chemicals in International Trade.[47]

Developments at the regional level have proceeded at a similar rate. Member states of the United Nations Economic Commission for Europe[48] have negotiated three protocols to the U.N.-ECE Convention on Long-Range Transboundary Air Pollution:[49] a protocol providing for a thirty percent reduction in transborder fluxes of sulphur dioxides,[50] a protocol freezing the emissions of nitrogen oxides,[51] and a protocol controlling emissions of volatile organic chemicals.[52] These countries have also concluded agreements on environmental impact assessment, transnational industrial accidents, and transboundary fresh waters and lakes.[53]

As part of the United Nations Environment Programme's regional seas program, countries have negotiated the South Pacific Resource and Environmental Protection Agreement[54] with two protocols, one on dumping[55] and the other on emergency assistance.[56] Under the UNEP Caribbean Regional Seas Convention,[57] parties have concluded a protocol on protected areas[58] and are considering negotiation of a protocol on land-based sources of marine pollution.

There have been similar advances in legal instruments to safeguard freshwater resources. States concluded an unusually comprehensive agreement to protect the Zambezi River Basin.[59] In 1987, Canada and the United States agreed to a protocol to their 1978 Great Lakes Water Quality Agreement,[60] which addresses groundwater contamination affecting the Great Lakes and the airborne transport of toxics into the Great Lakes.[61] Amazon Basin countries issued the Declaration of Brasilia[62] and provided for the establishment of two new commissions under the auspices of the Amazon Pact,[63] one to conserve the fauna and flora and the other to protect indigenous peoples. In Asia, members of the Association of Southeast Asian Nations (ASEAN) concluded the Convention on the Conservation of Nature, which provides ecosystem protection and controls on trade in endangered species.[64] And in Africa, the Bamako Convention on Hazardous Wastes bans the importation of hazardous wastes and creates a strict regimen for moving such wastes within the African continent.[65]

In Europe, the Single European Act[66] now provides clear authority for the European Community to act on environmental and natural resource issues.[67] The Community has already issued many directives and regulations aimed at controlling pollution and protecting the environment, and more are under consideration. The European Court of Justice has assumed an important role in ensuring that measures adopted by individual nations conform with Community directives. A new European Environment Agency is being established as part of the institutional framework of the European Community.[68]

At the bilateral level, many international environmental legal instruments have been concluded during this period. In North America, the United States has signed bilateral agreements with Canada and Mexico on the transport of hazardous wastes.[69] An agreement between Mexico and the United States addresses urban air pollution problems in Mexico City.[70] In 1991, Canada and the United States concluded an agreement to control acid precipitation.[71] In Latin America, Brazil and Argentina concluded an agreement that provides for consultation in case of nuclear accidents in either country.[72]

Most of these agreements were considered impossible ten years ago; some were thought impossible only months before they were concluded. The provisions in the new agreements are generally more stringent and detailed than in previous ones, the range of subject matter broader, and the provisions for implementation and adjustment more sophisticated. This history is encouraging because it suggests that the international community's learning curve as reflected in international environmental law is surprisingly steep. This should give us hope that we may be able, with some success, to address the immense challenges of global environmental change and to meet the urgent need for environmentally sustainable development.

The Lessons Learned

In reviewing the past forty years in international environmental law, it is apparent that countries have learned much about both the process of negotiating international environmental agreements and the desirable substantive content of the agreements.

For purposes of this analysis, learning can be defined as social evolutionary progress. Most learning is unconscious, unsystematic, and more or less constant. It takes place through negative and positive feedback to action. States and other organizations, just like individuals, naturally adjust their approaches and procedures to emulate successes and avoid past mistakes.

Some factors seem to facilitate learning: ready access to information, monitoring, prompt feedback, and political pressures for change. Other factors constrain it. Constitutional provisions and other domestic legal instruments may limit available options. Rigid political controls imposed because of tensions among participants may prevent adjustments that experience would otherwise suggest as prudent. An established record of success may delay change even when circumstances are altered, and the old ways no longer correspond to current needs. Similarly, lack of time to explore new approaches, and vested interests in the status quo or in positions that have already been cleared with relevant authorities may make it difficult to change established diplomatic positions.

It is difficult to assess scientifically the learning capacity of the international community in its ability to address environmental issues. To do so would require a learning methodology, which would indicate the factors to be considered and the units of measurement.[73] While such a comprehensive effort would be a worthwhile undertaking, this analysis stops short of such a goal. Rather this article sets forth preliminary insights built upon a review of state behavior in negotiating and implementing international environmental agreements over the last forty years.[74]

Skill and Rapidity in Negotiating International Agreements

Contrary to popular myth, the international community has become very skilled at negotiating international agreements. Countries negotiated nine years (from December 1973 to December 1982) to conclude the Law of the Sea Convention,[75] which admittedly was a herculean effort to conclude a comprehensive, detailed, and definitive agreement, which would in part codify the rules relating to the various uses of the oceans. By contrast, countries today are negotiating complicated agreements in only a few years, often developing entirely new areas of law.[76] Countries negotiated the complex Climate Framework Convention[77] in fifteen months (from February 1991 to May 1992). Negotiations for the Environmental Protocol to the Antarctic Treaty[78] (which includes four detailed annexes) and for the Biological Diversity Convention[79] required less than two years, as did the complex agreements on industrial accidents[80] and volatile organic chemicals[81] under the auspices of the U.N.-ECE. It is now rare for countries to need more than two years to negotiate even complicated, detailed international agreements. Agenda 21,[82] a nonbinding instrument, offers perhaps the most striking evidence of the skill of the international community in achieving these ends. In less than two years, countries negotiated an approximately 850-page text setting forth strategies for the multiple and complex issues raised by environment and development.[83] Thus, countries have evolved a negotiating process in the international environmental field that leads to rapid conclusion of agreements.[84]

Changes in Design and Content of Agreements

International agreements have become increasingly detailed and operational. The provisions of the 1940 Western Hemisphere Convention on the Conservation of Nature[85] and the World Heritage Convention[86] are broad and general. By contrast, the provisions included in the Biological Diversity Convention,[87] the ASEAN Agreement on the Conservation of Nature and Natural Resources,[88] or the Protected Areas Protocol to the Caribbean Regional Seas Convention[89] are more detailed even if still somewhat general. Recent agreements controlling transboundary pollution have become much more specific and operational than previous efforts. The early U.N.-ECE Protocol on Sulphur Dioxide to the U.N.-ECE Long-Range Transboundary Air Pollution Convention[90] sets forth a general obligation to reduce transboundary fluxes by thirty percent,[91] while the new Protocol on Volatile Organic Chemicals[92] provides far more detailed and specific reduction requirements.[93] Similarly, very detailed obligations appear in the Montreal Protocol on Substances That Deplete the Ozone Layer[94] and in the Basel Convention,[95] which controls the transboundary shipment of hazardous wastes, both concluded in the last five years.

The design of agreements has also evolved. In contrast to the traditional practice of negotiating a single agreement for an issue, such as use of boundary waters, or negotiating comprehensively all of the issues in an international environmental matter,[96] countries experimented in the first UNEP Regional Seas Convention in 1976[97] with adopting a framework convention complemented by at least one accompanying comprehensive protocol. This approach has been followed in all subsequent UNEP regional seas conventions. This more open-ended framework allowed countries to begin to take coordinated actions to conserve regional seas but avoided premature negotiations on more complicated issues in the region. This piecemeal negotiation strategy was adopted by the countries of the U.N.-ECE[98] in 1979 when they concluded the Convention on Long-Range Transboundary Air Pollution,[99] which set forth a general framework for monitoring and exchanging information on air pollution in the region. This was followed by protocols among the U.N.-ECE countries establishing a monitoring system and controlling emissions of certain chemicals.[100] Countries adopted a similar negotiating process to address the problem of global ozone depletion: first the Vienna Convention for the Protection of the Ozone Layer,[101] which set forth a general framework for monitoring, exchanging information, and facilitating scientific research, followed by a more detailed Montreal Protocol[102] setting forth a complex regime for controlling chemical depletion of the ozone layer.

In the case of regional seas, countries agreed that the framework agreement could only go forward if they had also concluded at least one protocol to accompany it. This meant that states had to demonstrate serious intent to participate in the arrangements to protect the regional seas in order to become a party to the framework agreement. On the other hand, this requirement broke the management scheme into individual pieces, so that states could develop the protocols over time and become parties to some but not others. By contrast, in the context of controlling transboundary air pollution, protecting the ozone layer, and managing climate change countries have concluded the framework agreement before reaching agreement on, and often before negotiating, any detailed substantive protocols. In such cases, if countries agree to participate in the framework convention, they may become sufficiently engaged that they can subsequently agree upon supplementing protocols.

Adjustments to Changes in Scientific Understanding

Scientific uncertainty is inherent in all international environmental law. We do not have a full understanding of the natural system or of our interactions with it. Our scientific understanding is always changing, as is our technological knowledge and know-how. Consequently, those who draft international agreements have had to design instruments and implementation mechanisms that have sufficient flexibility in order to allow parties to adapt to changes in our scientific understanding and technological abilities.

Early agreements had no special processes for adjusting to changes in the scientific understanding of the problem. Even if there were schedules attached to the agreements, they could be amended only by the traditional process of establishing a negotiating forum, agreeing upon the changes, adopting them, and then obtaining the number of ratifications required by the treaty for them to enter into force. This traditional procedure has proved to be too cumbersome to address rapid scientific advances. Later agreements have eased the process by providing for periodic meeting of the parties, for the formulation of technical changes by experts or international secretariats subject to confirmation by the parties, and entry into force by agreement of the parties without ratification. For example, the Montreal Protocol on Substances that Deplete the Ozone Layer[103] provides for parties to meet at regular intervals to respond to new scientific findings,[104] for regular technical assessments to be made available to parties before a meeting,[105] and for simplified adjustment procedures by which parties can agree to reduce consumption of listed chemicals faster and further than provided in the text without having to use formal and time consuming amendment procedures.[106]

In an effort to promote flexibility the new Climate Framework Convention[107] provides for a standing body to provide scientific and technological advice on a timely basis.[108] This body will provide scientific assessments of climate change and its effects, and the impact of implementing measures under the Convention. It will also identify relevant new technologies, assist in building local capacity for scientific research and assessment, and respond to scientific inquires of the parties.[109] In sum, this body established a process for integrating scientific and technological advances into the operation of the Climate Framework Convention. In so doing, it reflects the experience of the negotiators to the Intergovernmental Panel on Climate Change, which helped to generate the scientific consensus among governments to move forward to negotiate the Convention.

All environmental issues involve scientific uncertainty and hence risks. A major challenge to policymakers is to identify, assess, and manage the risks inherent in scientific uncertainty. This calls for systems for monitoring, providing early warning, and prioritizing risks because there are always limited resources available to address these risks. Recent international agreements, such as those on climate and on biological diversity, include at least some provisions along these lines.

The precautionary principle, or precautionary approach, in international environmental law is one response to the recognition that we are faced with the necessity to act in the face of scientific uncertainty about future harm. The principle lowers the burden of proof required for taking action against proposed or existing activities that may have serious long-term harmful consequences. There is no agreement on the content of this principle, or even as to whether an actual principle has emerged or only an approach to address a problem.[110] Nevertheless, countries have begun to develop precise and useful formulations of the principle in specific contexts, such as implementation of the London Ocean Dumping Convention.[111]

A Systems Focus

As our understanding of the environment has grown, we have recognized that agreements need to be directed to conserving ecological systems, not only to controlling specific pollutants or conserving particular species. This insight has been increasingly reflected in international instruments.

For example, the ASEAN Convention on the Conservation of Resources[112] addresses the conservation of ecosystems and habitats as a central means of conserving endangered species.[113] The new Biological Diversity Convention[114] focuses on the conservation of ecosystems and habitats in full recognition that many of the species that should be conserved are microorganisms or other species about which we know little or nothing.[115] The 1978 Great Lakes Water Quality Agreement[116] modified language in the 1972 Agreement to include reference to basin-wide ecosystems in the Great Lakes.[117] The 1987 Protocol to the Agreement[118] includes annexes that explicitly address ground water pollution and atmospheric transport of pollutants as sources of Great Lakes contamination.[119] The change reflects the recognition that what feeds into lakes through the air and ground water is as relevant as direct discharges into the lake in determining its quality. Similarly, in marine pollution the focus is no longer primarily on specific commodities that are dumped into the marine environment, but also on maintaining ecosystems as a whole. This is reflected in new protocols to protect designated areas in regional seas and to control land-based sources of marine pollution.[120] The latter has become a subject of global concern, raised in part in Agenda 21.[121]

Attention to Nonparties

Because the global environmental system ignores political boundaries, it is important for countries that have an impact on the global environment not to remain outside the convention system and defeat the purposes of the agreement. It is necessary to include in international environmental agreements all those states that are essential for the agreement to be effective.

Traditionally, multilateral agreements usually did not include explicit incentives to join an agreement, although there may have been outside pressures to join. In the environmental agreements reached in the last two decades, in contrast, states have increasingly offered incentives in the agreement in the form of technical assistance or other positive inducements.[122] The Montreal Protocol, the Climate Framework Convention, and the Biological Diversity Convention provide such incentives as technical assistance, technology transfer, or building national capacity to implement the agreement.[123]

A less common way of providing incentives is the use of negative inducements in the form of a ban on trade in the controlled substances with nonparties. As early as the 1973 Washington Convention on International Trade in Endangered Species of Wild Fauna and Flora (CITES),[124] countries recognized that if agreements were to be effective, they needed to ensure that nonparties did not become havens for circumventing the agreements. The CITES agreement limits trade in the covered species with nonparties.[125] This strategy has recently been revived and strengthened in the environmental agreements directed to controlling transboundary shipments of hazardous waste and to preventing ozone layer depletion, both of which include provisions prohibiting trade with nonparties.[126] The Montreal Protocol provisions are punitive because they prohibit the parties from subtracting exports of controlled substances to nonparties from their national consumption calculations of controlled substances.

Parties to the General Agreement on Tariffs and Trade (GATT)[127] are now considering in the GATT Environment Working Group whether the use of negative inducements by limiting trade is consistent with the GATT. Data on the effectiveness of such a provision in the CITES agreement is scattered and mainly anecdotal, but suggests that the negative inducement trade limitation has had little effect on the behavior of countries.[128] However, because it is easier to monitor trade in ozone-depleting chemicals and in hazardous wastes, trade ban provisions relating to these items may prove to be more effective.

Negative inducements in international environmental agreements also address another issue that relates to nonparties: the free-rider problem, in which a state obtains the benefits of the agreement without ever joining and incurring the costs the agreement might impose. For example, a country that declined to join an air pollution agreement or climate convention could receive the benefits of cleaner air or a stabilized climate without incurring the costs of achieving it.[129] Trade prohibitions and positive incentives to join the agreement are also relevant to controlling this phenomenon, and the international community is increasingly recognizing this.

Participation of Nongovernmental Organizations

Nongovernmental organizations (NGOs) have assumed an increasingly important role in the negotiation, ratification, implementation, and enforcement of international environmental agreements. They are a primary link between the public and national governments; they let individuals try to influence the international environmental agreement process.

The presence of NGOs at official negotiations of international environmental agreements has become routine. At the Climate Convention[130] negotiations, for example, a wide array of NGOs monitored the negotiations, distributed material, lobbied delegations, and otherwise tried to influence the negotiators. Representatives of NGOs also are appearing on official country delegations, as in the negotiations for the Environmental Protocol to the Antarctic Treaty.[131] In the Climate Convention negotiations, an NGO, the Foundation for International Environmental Law and Development based in London, provided advice to a group of island states and served as members of their delegations.[132]

Although NGO participation on official delegations may be increasing, there is not yet widespread acceptance of the practice nor any systematic pattern of representation. For example, the United States delegation to the Organization for Economic Cooperation and Development (OECD) joint meetings of the Trade and Environment Working Groups at first included representation from both environmental NGOs and the business community, but the practice was not sustained.

The process of interaction among NGOs, governments, and intergovernmental organizations is complicated. NGOs try to influence national governments directly and indirectly by increasing public awareness and public pressures on national legislatures. Governments, on the other hand, use NGOs to convey positions to the public. Ministries or agencies within governments may use NGOs to strengthen their views in relation to other parts of the bureaucracy by keeping them well-informed about issues and providing venues for them to express their views to various parts of the bureaucracy. NGOs provide intergovernmental organizations with important, independent communication links with national governments; and NGOs rely on intergovernmental organizations to provide information and insights that are useful in influencing national governments.[133]

In a few instances, NGOs have been integrated into the international institutional structure for implementing agreements. Two decades ago in the World Heritage Convention,[134] states gave three NGOs official status in the agreement as advisors and provided that the World Heritage Committee could call upon these organizations "for the implementation of its programmes and projects."[135] The organizations have assumed important roles in evaluating proposed sites for inclusion on the World Heritage List.

A Critique of International Environmental Law Today

Given the rapid proliferation of international environmental legal instruments and the emergence of rules of customary international law, it is important to examine these efforts critically using an established framework. Countries are devoting considerable time and financial resources to the negotiation of legal instruments. Are the instruments effective, efficient, and equitable? Are they adequate to the tasks for which they were negotiated? These are the issues addressed below.

Effectiveness

Although countries have become skilled in negotiating international agreements, they are still much less skilled at making the agreements operate effectively. Some of the problems of effectiveness arise immediately after the agreement is negotiated. While countries may now be able to negotiate complicated environmental agreements in less than two years, the normal period between the time that negotiations are concluded and the agreements enter into force is likely to be three or more years.[136] This means that it is important to accelerate the process of ratification and provide interim or provisional measures that will enable the parties to further the objectives of the convention even before it comes into effect.[137] Ratification could be accelerated by providing assistance to countries, as needed, in translating treaty texts, preparing commentaries for legislative and other decison making bodies, assisting in the preparation of implementing legislation or regulations, and providing important background information to decision makers.[138] Both intergovernmental and nongovernmental organizations could undertake such projects to facilitate ratification.

Implementation and compliance with agreements at the national level involves a dynamic, several-stage process with important feedback loops. As an initial step, lawyers correctly ask whether there is a need for national legislation or regulations to implement the agreement, and whether such national measures on their face fully correspond to the obligations assumed under the convention. But this is only one part of the process. Even if these measures technically fulfill the obligations under the agreement, if governments, industries, or other private actors do not comply with such measures, the agreement cannot be effective. It is important to determine whether the targeted behavior is being changed in response to the agreement. This process of compliance is dynamic; compliance likely becomes more effective over time.[139]

Sadly we have little data on the successful implementation and overall effectiveness of international environmental agreements. There have been two notable governmental efforts to address this question: the United States Government Accounting Office, which concluded that the agreements they examined were not well-monitored for effectiveness,[140] and the intergovernmental report prepared for the United Nations Conference on Environment and Development, which provided a broad overview of agreements and identified several specific problems.[141] The small number of legal studies that have been done on national implementation of particular agreements, which have focused primarily on the Convention on Trade in Endangered Species,[142] have not been based on systematic empirical research, although they have yielded insights into the difficulties of implementing agreements.[143] Thus, there is an urgent need for further empirical research to determine whether, as Professor Louis Henkin has declared for public international law generally, "almost all nations observe almost all principles of international law and almost all of their obligations almost all of the time."[144] Data is needed on implementation and compliance with both binding and nonbinding (soft law) legal instruments.

Making agreements effective, specifically at the national and local levels, should be a high priority of the international community; consequently it is important to identify the factors that influence compliance at the national and subnational levels. These factors include a country's economic and social culture, as well as the structure and operation of its bureaucracy and communication among these bureaucracies; the availability of technical expertise and local technical capacity; ready access to information; the role of nongovernmental organizations; the functions and powers of the secretariat established by the agreement; whether the country participated in the negotiation of the agreement; the influence of other parties to the convention; the incentives in the agreement to encourage compliance; and the provisions for monitoring and reviewing country performance under the agreement.[145] By increasing our understanding of the compliance process and the impact of these factors, we should be able to structure agreements, followup measures, and assistance so as to enhance the likelihood of more effective implementation and compliance.[146]

Efficiency: The Treaty Congestion Problem

Because the international community will always have limited resources to address difficult issues, it is important that the system of negotiating, monitoring, implementing, and complying with international environmental agreements function relatively efficiently. Ironically, the success that countries have had in negotiating a large number of new international environmental agreements has led to an important and potentially negative side effect: treaty congestion. This affects the international community as a whole, particularly international institutions, as well as individual governments that may want to participate in the negotiation and implementation of agreements but have scarce professional resources.[147]

One of the characteristics of the treaty congestion problem is operational inefficiency. It is not yet clear that we will be able to make the new system of international agreements function efficiently.

Moreover, efficient operation is, in part, a function of risk assessment and presently there is no generally accepted system for assessing risks, and even more importantly, none for prioritizing them.

The transaction costs in negotiating international agreements are high. A normal negotiation may require four or five intergovernmental negotiating sessions of one to two weeks each during a period of eighteen months to two years. The Climate Convention negotiations required six sessions of two weeks each in less than sixteen months, in addition to regular meetings of the Intergovernmental Panel on Climate Change and various other informal meetings involving subsets of countries. Despite this very full and expensive schedule of negotiations, the Climate Convention negotiations were only one of more than a half dozen global or regional environmental agreement negotiations occurring more or less at the same time. During this period there were also important international negotiations for the conclusion of nonbinding legal instruments, such as the Arctic Protection Strategy,[148] the Rio Declaration on Environment and Development,[149] Forest Principles,[150] and Agenda 21.[151]

Many countries, especially those with limited resources, have complained about the demands these negotiations place on them for staffing and funding in order to participate in the negotiations. While the industrialized countries have provided some assistance to developing countries to participate in certain negotiations, such as the Climate Convention, such assistance has been insufficient to allow many developing countries to participate with fully staffed delegations, or sometimes to participate at all in particular sessions.

Moreover, the international community has not developed a systematic process for coordinating the negotiations. As Sir Geoffrey Palmer notes,

> The making and negotiation of the instruments themselves has to start anew each time. No organization commands clear power to coordinate international environmental negotiations. Each negotiation proceeds differently. . . . Such an approach carries the grave risk that on each occasion the wheel must be reinvented. Common elements are not necessarily treated the same way.[152]

The opposite problem also arises from treaty congestion—the tendency to take language from one treaty and transfer it to another because it has already received clearances from home governments, even though a different approach, or different language, might be more appropriate. There is sometimes little attention devoted to examining anew what the best approach or language might be for the special circumstances in the agreement under negotiation.

To induce coordination in the system, Palmer proposes a common institutional home for international environmental agreements.[153] But whether it would necessarily be efficient to have such a centralized arrangement is questionable; it would depend in good part on the efficiency of the structure and the operations in the institutional home. It may be possible to induce greater efficiency into the present system through more effective and widespread use of advances in information technology and other coordination measures.

With such a large number of international agreements, there is great potential for the additional inefficiency of overlapping provisions in agreements, inconsistencies in obligations, significant gaps in coverage, and duplication of goals and responsibilities. This issue was recognized during the simultaneous negotiations for the climate[154] and biological diversity conventions[155] and forest principles.[156] All three legal instruments, for example, affect the management of forests. Informal efforts were made to ensure that the obligations were consistent with each other. In particular, the Convention on Biological Diversity addresses the issue of consistency with other agreements explicitly, by including a separate article entitled "Relationship with Other International Conventions."[157]

In still other cases, issues arise that require analyzing the intersection between provisions of different agreements, such as those between the London Ocean Dumping Convention[158] and the Basel Convention on Controlling Transboundary Shipments of Hazardous Waste.[159] Both Conventions address the use and shipment of hazardous wastes that may be ultimately intended for marine disposal. Similarly, there are important legal questions arising from the intersection of the Antarctic Treaty[160] and the Law of the Sea Convention.[161] The intersection of issues is likely to become more frequent as countries conclude ever increasing numbers of agreements, which must be interpreted in conjunction with existing international obligations.

Treaty congestion has also created significant inefficiencies in implementing international agreements. Normally there are separate secretariats, monitoring processes, meetings of parties, sources of scientific advice and presentation of scientific material, financing mechanisms, technical assistance programs, and dispute resolution procedures for each treaty. At a minimum there is a need for coordination of agreements. Agenda 21,[162] which was prepared for the U.N. Conference on Environment and Development, suggests the colocation of secretariats.[163] While this may be desirable, housing the secretariats under one jurisdictional roof does not necessarily guarantee coordination. Although several agreements are located in the United Nations Environment Programme (UNEP), the secretariats are not located in the same place, nor is there necessarily greater coordination as a result of housing the agreement under one jurisdictional roof. It may be possible to address the coordination problem at the international level in a less centralized way, at least initially, by encouraging regular meetings of secretariats or by increasing use of the rapid advances in information technology. The information revolution can assist by making communication easier and less costly and by facilitating the gathering, analysis, and dissemination of data.

As we look to the future, it is evident that more needs to be done to mitigate the inefficiencies in implementing international agreements. In the provisions for financing implementation of the agreements, industrialized countries favor making the Global Environmental Facility (GEF),[164] located at the World Bank, the funding mechanism for new international environmental agreements, in particular for the climate and biological diversity conventions. This proposal, which would promote efficiency, has encountered strong opposition from developing countries who argue it is inequitable unless the governing structure of the GEF is altered to give them a substantial voice in the Facility.[165] Others are wary of the concentration of power this would bring. This particular conflict highlights the larger equity versus efficiency dilemma, which is both ancient and widespread throughout national and international legal systems.[166] This dilemma will likely arise repeatedly as countries attempt to bring greater efficiency into the current system of implementing international environmental agreements.

Finally, treaty congestion leads to overload at the national level in implementing the international agreements. A country needs sufficient political, administrative, and economic capacity to be able to implement agreements effectively. Today a large number of international environmental institutions, including most pointedly the numerous secretariats servicing international environmental agreements, have some claim on the administrative capacity of national states. Even industrialized states with well-developed regulatory mechanisms and bureaucracies show signs of being overwhelmed. As attention shifts to the importance of implementing and complying with the agreements that have been negotiated, this burden on the administrative capacity of states will become even more acute. Attention must be given to developing local capacity within countries to implement and comply with international environmental agreements effectively and efficiently. New technologies will be useful, but cannot substitute for other capacity-building measures, such as the training of personnel, development of economic resources, and restructuring of institutions for accountability.

Equity: The Source of Conflict

Increasingly, notions of equity or fairness are the focus of pointed conflict in the negotiation and implementation of international environmental instruments. For equity to have meaning, it must be defined. The traditional notion of equity that has formed the basis of numerous environmental accords is one of national sovereign rights to exploit resources within a country's jurisdiction or control, combined with rights to shared or common resources (whether for natural resources or for pollution emissions) on a first-come, first-served basis. However, this traditional equity ethic has been deteriorating, and a new ethic is in the process of emerging. The search for a consensus on a new definition of equity is likely to be one of the major factors shaping international environmental accords in the future.

The controversy over the definition of equity lay at the heart of the U.N. Conference on Environment and Development debates. The Rio Declaration on Environment and Development,[167] a nonbinding legal instrument, explicitly reflects this concern with equity. Among other things, the Principles of the Declaration address obligations intended to "decrease the disparities in standards of living and better meet the needs of the majority of the people of the world";[168] provide for priority treatment to "the special situation and needs of developing countries, particularly the least developed and those most environmentally vulnerable";[169] and recognize that "[i]n view of the different contributions to global environmental degradation, States have common but differentiated responsibilities."[170] By contrast, twenty years earlier the U.N. Stockholm Declaration on the Human Environment[171] referred only to the need to consider "the systems of values prevailing in each country and the extent of the applicability of standards which are valid for the most advanced countries but which may be inappropriate and of unwarranted social cost for the developing countries,"[172] and, as was also expressed in the Rio Declaration, the need for financial and technical assistance.[173]

In international environmental law, the two issues that have given definition to equity are the allocation of natural resources and the responsibility and liability for pollution. Both have traditionally been based on rights acquired on a first-come, first-served basis, subject to increasing demands for equitable sharing of the burden of conserving natural resources and controlling pollution.

The right of countries to control the exploitation and use of natural resources within their own jurisdiction or control has been repeatedly reaffirmed in international legal instruments.[174] Traditionally states have also claimed the right to exploit resources outside national borders in commonly held areas on the basis of a first-come, first-served ethic in the absence of agreement to the contrary. This method of exploiting resources is reflected in the initial allocations of the geostationary orbit, the radio frequency spectrum, international waterways, fisheries, marine mammals, birds, and ocean mineral resources. Most international agreements have at least implicitly started from this ethical presumption. Countries have then voluntarily agreed to constraints on their operational behavior affecting these shared or common resources. The two notable international agreements that did not begin with this first-come, first-served presumption, but rather started from a notion of shared responsibility for the resources at issue, are the Convention on the Law of the Sea[175] and the Wellington Convention on Antarctic Mineral Resources,[176] both of which resulted in complicated allocation schemes that have never gone into effect. Increasingly, however, areas once considered to be *res nullius* or belonging to no one are treated as part of the "global commons."

The second primary focus of international environmental legal instruments has been on controlling pollution. Again, states have traditionally asserted the right to pollute at self-determined levels. International instruments have limited these rights. In practice this has meant that states that were able to industrialize first, or those that have vast territories, have been able to establish pollution levels quite independently of other countries.

In instances of transborder pollution, states have the responsibility under Principle 21 of the Stockholm Declaration to ensure that "activities within their jurisdiction or control do not cause damage to the environment of other States or of areas beyond the limits of national jurisdiction."[177] But increasingly the effects of pollution are felt on a regional basis, which means that more detailed, regionally focused control arrangements are needed. Countries have found it difficult to reach consensus on the base-line year for establishing acceptable pollution levels. The problem is that countries that are beginning to industrialize and trying to reach parity with more industrialized countries do not want to be burdened with an early base-line year, and those industrialized countries that have already started controlling pollution want to receive appropriate credit in the selection of the base-line year. In the regional context of the U.N.-ECE, the concern is not only with equitably allocating acceptable levels of pollution for those countries that are still industrializing, but also with treating equitably those countries that have already reduced pollution levels significantly in advance of the target base year.[178]

The equity issues that are most controversial in the international community concern responsibility for the prevention of harm to global resources and liability for their damage. The Rio Declaration addresses these issues in its reference to "common but differentiated responsibilities" arising from "the different contributions to global environmental degradation,"[179] and in its concern with liability issues and the polluter pays approach in internalizing environmental costs.[180]

The controversial issues in defining equity with regard to pollution control are multiple: whether to establish common or differentiated pollution control standards (as in the per capital chemicals consumption base-line standard for developing countries in the Montreal Protocol[181]), what flexibility there should be in the timeframe for meeting standards (as in the ten-year delay permitted for developing countries in meeting Montreal Protocol chemical phase-out requirements[182]), the extent to which countries should be held responsible for activities that contributed to global environmental degradation in the past (for example, liability for effects of ozone depletion on inhabitants of the southern hemisphere), the extent to which a group of countries should be held responsible to particular countries who may suffer harm tomorrow from actions taken globally today (for example, the claims of island countries that industrialized countries establish a trust fund today to cover the costs of the rise of ocean levels due to global warming tomorrow), and the more general question of the responsibility of the present generation to future generations for the care and use of the planet.[183]

In developing a new definition of equity for environmentally sustainable development, several factors and issues must be noted and addressed. First, the global environment knows no political boundaries; its components are spatially and temporally interdependent. This means that no one country or even group of countries has the capability to protect the environment over time by its own isolated efforts. Consequently, there is an incentive for all countries to reach consensus on an equitable and effective basis for allocating responsibility for maintaining the planet.

Second, developing countries have control over resources that are important to the industrialized world, just as the industrialized world has always had control over resources needed by the developing world. The debates during the Biological Diversity Convention reflect this fact; the developing countries realized that the best reserves of biological diversity lie within their boundaries. In some ways this gave them bargaining power in the negotiations.

Third, developing countries are likely to suffer most from environmental degradation. This is both because poverty is a primary source of environmental degradation and because when rapid, human-induced global environmental change occurs, these countries have the least capacity to adapt.

Finally, future generations are, in my view, becoming a party to debates about equity. Sustainable development is inherently intergenerational, as are the agreements we negotiate. Yet future generations' interests have not been identified and adequately represented in the negotiations, the implementing measures, or in the compliance mechanisms of international environmental agreements. The present generation obviously has a built-in bias in favor of itself. Indeed the instruments that we have developed in the marketplace to consider environmental effects on future generations, namely externalities and discount rates, start from the perspective of the present generation. Thus, as we consider the future, it will be important to develop an international consensus on the definition and outlines of the concept of intergenerational equity.

Emerging Directions in World Environmental Law and Order

In June 1992, 178 countries met in Rio de Janeiro, Brazil, for the United Nations Conference on Environment and Development, which was the twentieth anniversary of the United Nations Stockholm Conference on the Human Environment. The Rio Conference was an occasion to consider how far we had come in the last twenty years, and how far we need to go in the next twenty. As we look ahead to the future, it is clear that new directions in the environmental world order are emerging. These trends can be categorized both in immediate, and somewhat narrow terms, and in long-range, broader terms.

The Immediate Trends

In the next two decades, the joining of environmental protection and economic development will grow. The burgeoning new field of environment and trade reflects this linkage. While trade law has operated under the relatively unified and broad framework of the General Agreement on Tariffs and Trade[184] for more than forty years, fledgling international environmental law still consists only of many separate and disparate legal instruments. It is not surprising then that most environment and trade issues are discussed almost exclusively within the GATT context. The environment and trade issues move in two directions: environmental protection practices affect trade, and trading practices affect environmental conservation. Thus, it will be important to move to a *modus vivendi* in which environmental and trade concerns are accorded comparable legitimacy, and both are viewed as important elements of sustainable development.[185]

More generally, in the quest for environmentally sustainable development, the focus will likely move to considering environmental concerns at the front end of the industrializing process, so as to prevent pollution, minimize environmental degradation, and use resources more efficiently. This should mean an increasing concern with making the whole system of production environmentally sound. If so, international environmental law will reflect this emphasis by focusing on standards and procedures for preventing pollution and minimizing environmental degradation, rather than on liability for damage, and on providing incentives to companies to use environmentally sound processes.

Second, the formulation of nonbinding legal instruments, or "soft law," is likely to increase more rapidly than the negotiation of formal international conventions. This is because when the instrument is nonbinding, agreement is normally easier to achieve, the transaction costs are less, the opportunity for detailed strategies to be set forth are greater, and the ability to respond to rapid changes in our scientific understanding of environment and development issues are more vast.

Third, the growing adoption of new approaches, duties, and procedures in international environmental accords is likely to continue.

These include the precautionary principle or approach and the duties to consult with affected states, to prepare an environmental impact assessment before undertaking certain projects, to provide emergency assistance for environmental accidents or disasters, to monitor activities, and to make relevant information available.

Finally, UNCED[186] and the 1992 Rio Declaration[187] may be viewed as legitimizing the importance of public participation in environmental decision making and of public access to relevant information.[188] The international institutional system in which environmental legal instruments are imbedded is likely to continue to become more diverse and to include increasingly larger numbers of nongovernmental organizations of various kinds. While four decades ago we could speak of an international system focused almost exclusively on nation-states and their subunits, today the system includes national governments (and local governments), intergovernmental organizations, and nongovernmental organizations as essential components constantly interacting. NGOs are likely to continue to expand their influence in the negotiation, implementation, and compliance process of international environmental legal agreements. The information revolution should greatly facilitate this increased role of NGOs in international environmental decision making.[189]

The Broader Perspective

The concept of national interest, which has long been used to address foreign policy decisions, is not a very useful construct for analyzing global environmental problems in the long-term.[190] National interest can be defined as national preferences, or the preferences of a country's decision makers. On the global scale these interests are often considered in terms of a zero-sum gain. The implicit assumption is that one country's national interest is necessarily opposed to another's. But when addressing global environmental issues the interest is a common one: the overall maintenance of the world's environmental systems. This becomes apparent as we look into the future because no community today can by itself conserve the planet for even its own descendants.

The physical setting in which all peoples are locked together in a common global environment for the foreseeable future means that it is increasingly futile to posit national interests that over the long term can be opposed to another country's national interest in the environment. The rapid advances in international cooperation, as demonstrated in international environmental law, suggest countries are implicitly beginning to recognize this need to coordinate long-term interests.

The international environmental agreements negotiated during the last two decades reflect a commonality of interests. In many international legal instruments, states have agreed to constrain "operational sovereignty,"[191] while continuing to retain formal national sovereignty. The conventions on ozone depletion, transboundary shipments of hazardous waste, air pollutants such as nitrogen oxides and volatile organic chemicals, and the Antarctic environment illustrate this constraint. In other agreements, states have arguably strengthened their operational sovereignty by focusing on national plans and actions and dissemination of these documents to other parties to the agreements. The recent Framework Convention on Climate Change and the Convention on Biological Diversity reflect this approach. Nonetheless in these instances, states have set up an international process for monitoring the health of the environment and for providing other benefits to parties. In the climate change convention, the international procedures are sophisticated and far-reaching,[192] and they could lead to substantial international consideration and evaluation of national measures to mitigate climate change. Thus, the international environmental agreements examined in this article point in the same direction—a recognition of the benefits of international cooperation and an increased willingness to agree to obligations directed to protecting the environment.

While countries may share a commonality of interests in maintaining the robustness and integrity of our planet, there are deep differences among them over the equitable allocation of burdens and benefits in doing so. These were vividly displayed at the Rio Conference meeting and are reflected in more recent agreements. Moreover, states do not agree on priorities—whether to satisfy immediate needs to alleviate poverty and local environmental degradation or longer-term needs to protect the robustness and integrity of the biosphere. The clashes extend to communities and groups at the local and transnational levels. These clashes could intensify in the next two decades, as countries (and communities) try to reach consensus on what is equitable in the context of environmentally sustainable development. Unless resolved, they could lead to inefficient and ineffective outcomes that are inadequate to the task of conserving our global environment and ensuring sustainable development for future generations.

Notes

1. See Edith Brown Weiss et al. *International Environmental Law: Basic Instruments and References* ix (1992) (noting the existence of approximately 885 different environmentally oriented legal instruments).
2. This section is based on the author's Introductory Chapter in *Environmental Change and International Law: New Challenges and Dimensions* (Edith Brown Weiss, ed., 1992). For a general overview of international environmental law, see Alexandre Kiss and Dinah Shelton, *International Environmental Law* (1991); Oscar Schachter, *International Law in Theory and Practice*, 362–88 (1991).
3. For details, see Edith Brown Weiss, "Introductory Comments to Panel at American Society of International Law Annual Meeting," in 85 *American Society of International Law, Proceedings of the Annual Meeting* 401 (1991).
4. Treaty Relating to Boundary Waters Between the United States and Canada, Jan. 11, 1909, U.S.-Gr. Brit., 36 Stat. 2448 [hereinafter 1909 Boundary Waters Treaty].
5. Id. art. IV, 36 Stat. at 2450.
6. Convention for the Protection of Birds Useful to Agriculture, Mar. 19, 1902, 102 B.F.S.P. 969 (entered into force May 11, 1907).
7. Convention for the Protection of Migratory Birds, Aug. 16, 1916, U.S.-Gr. Brit., 39 Stat. 1702.
8. Treaty for the Preservation and Protection of Fur Seals, Feb. 7, 1911, U.S.-Gr. Brit., 37 Stat. 1538.
9. London Convention for the Protection of Wild Animals, Birds and Fish in Africa, May 19, 1900, 4 *International Protection of the Environment: Treaties and Related Documents* 1605 (B. Ruster et al., eds., 1983).
10. Convention on the Preservation of Fauna and Flora in Their Natural State, Nov. 8, 1933, 172 L.N.T.S. 241.
11. Convention on Nature Protection and Wild Life Preservation in the Western Hemisphere, Oct. 12, 1940, 56 Stat. 1354, 161 U.N.T.S. 193.
12. Convention for the Regulation of Whaling, Sept. 24, 1931, 49 Stat. 3079, 155 L.N.T.S. 349.
13. See, e.g., Convention for the Northwest Atlantic Fisheries, Feb. 8, 1949, 1 U.S.T. 477, 157 U.N.T.S. 157; Convention for the Protection of Migratory Birds and Game Mammals, Feb. 7, 1936, U.S.-Mex., 50 Stat. 1311.
14. Trail Smelter Arbitration (U.S. v. Can.), 3 R.I.A.A. 1911, 1933 (1938) (granting damages for agricultural and timber losses); 3 R.I.A.A. 1938, 1966 (1941) (establishing environmental controls to eliminate future injurious emissions). See generally, Arthur K. Kuhn, Comment, "The Trail Smelter Arbitration—United States and Canada," 32 *Am. J. Int'l. L.* 785 (1938).

15. The Arbitral Tribunal noted:
     [U]nder the principles of international law, as well as of the law of
     the United States, no State has the right to use or permit the use of
     its territory in such a manner as to cause injury by fumes in or to
     the territory of another or the properties or persons therein, when
     the case is of serious consequence and the injury is established by
     clear and convincing evidence.
     Trail Smelter Arbitration, 3 R.I.A.A. at 1965.

16. See President Dwight D. Eisenhower, United States "Atoms for Peace"
     Proposal, Address Before the General Assembly (Dec. 8, 1953), in 1
     Dep't St., Documents on Disarmament—1945-1959, at 393, 399 (1960)
     (calling for joint contributions of fissionable material to develop peaceful
     uses of nuclear power).

17. See, e.g. Convention on Third Party Liability in the Field of Nuclear
     Energy, July 29, 1960, 956 U.N.T.S. 251; International Convention for the
     Prevention of Pollution of the Sea by Oil, May 12, 1954, 12 U.S.T. 2989,
     327 U.N.T.S. 3.

18. Rachel Carson, *Silent Spring* (1963).

19. 42 U.S.C. § 4321 (1988).

20. 40 C.F.R. § 1500 (1991) (implementing Pub. L. No. 91–190, 42 U.S.C.
     4321); 40 C.F.R. § 1.1 (1991) (implementing Reorganization Plan No. 3
     of 1970), reprinted in 5 U.S.C. app. at 1343 (1988).

21. See, e.g., Convention Relating to Intervention on the High Seas in Cases
     of Oil Pollution Casualties, Nov. 29, 1969, 26 U.S.T. 765, 970 U.N.T.S.
     211; Convention on Civil Liability for Oil Pollution Damage, Nov. 29,
     1969, 12 U.S.T. 2989, 3 U.N.T.S. 3; Agreement for Cooperation in
     Dealing with Pollution of the North Sea by Oil, June 9, 1969, 704
     U.N.T.S. 3.

22. Convention on the Conservation of Nature and Natural Resources, Sept.
     15, 1968, 1001 U.N.T.S. 3 (attempting to conserve renewable resources
     including soil, water, flora, and fauna in Africa).

23. Report on the United Nations Conference on the Human Environment at
     Stockholm, 11 I.L.M. 1416 (1972).

24. Convention on International Trade in Endangered Species of Wild Fauna
     and Flora, Mar. 3, 1973, 27 U.S.T. 1087, 993 U.N.T.S. 243 [hereinafter
     CITES].

25. Convention on the Prevention of Marine Pollution by Dumping of Wastes
     and Other Matter, Dec. 29, 1972, 26 U.S.T. 2403, 1046 U.N.T.S. 120
     [hereinafter London Ocean Dumping Convention].

26. Convention for the Protection of World Cultural and Natural Heritage,
     Nov. 23, 1972, 27 U.S.T. 37, 1037 U.N.T.S. 151 [hereinafter World
     Heritage Convention].

27. The United Nations Environment Programme initiated the Mediterranean Action Plan in 1975 to control marine and coastal pollution. This led to the Barcelona Convention for the Protection of the Mediterranean Sea Against Pollution, Feb. 16, 1976, 15 I.L.M. 290, and the two accompanying protocols, Barcelona Protocol Concerning Cooperation in Combating Pollution of the Mediterranean Sea by Oil and Other Harmful Substances in Cases of Emergency, Feb. 16, 1976, 15 I.L.M. 306, and Barcelona Protocol for the Prevention of Pollution of the Mediterranean Sea by Dumping from Ships and Aircraft, Feb. 16, 1976, 15 I.L.M. 300.

28. Weiss et al., supra note 1, at ix.

29. From 1990–1992, these included the negotiations for the environmental protocol and annexes to the Antarctic Treaty; the Framework Convention on Climate Change; the Convention on Biological Diversity; the United Nations Economic Commission for Europe (U.N.-ECE) agreements on environmental impact assessment, industrial accidents, volatile organic chemicals, and freshwaters and lakes; the treaty on oil pollution preparedness, response, and cooperation; the draft agreement on marine transport of hazardous and noxious substances; the draft protocol on liability to the Basel Convention on transboundary movements of hazardous waste; the forest principles; the arctic protection strategy; the UNCED Agenda 21; and the Rio Declaration on Environment and Development.

30. See, e.g. Convention for the Protection of the Ozone Layer, Mar. 22, 1985, S. Treaty Doc. No. 9, 99th Cong., 1st Sess. 22 (1985), 26 I.L.M. 1529 (entered into force Sept. 22, 1988); Montreal Protocol on Substances that Deplete the Ozone Layer, Sept. 16, 1987, S. TREATY DOC. NO. 10, 100th Cong., 1st Sess. 2 (1987), 26 I.L.M. 1550 (entered into force Jan. 1, 1989) [hereinafter Montreal Protocol] (attempting to reduce harmful emissions that deplete the ozone layer and adversely affect human health).

31. Protocol to the 1979 Convention on Long-Range Transboundary Air Pollution or the Reduction of Sulphur Emissions on Their Transboundary Fluxes by at Least 30 Percent, July 8, 1985, 27 I.L.M. 707 (entered into force Sept. 2, 1987) [hereinafter 1985 Helsinki Protocol].

32. Id. art. 11, 27 I.L.M. at 708.

33. Montreal Protocol, supra note 30.

34. Report of the Second Meeting of the Parties to the Montreal Protocol on Substances That Deplete the Ozone Layer, U.N. Environment Programme, 2d Sess., Annex 1, Agenda Item 5, U.N. Doc. UNEP/OzL.Pro. 2/3 (1990).

35. Montreal Protocol, supra note 30, art. II, S. Treaty Doc. No. 10, at 2–3, 26 I.L.M. at 1552–53.

36. Convention for the Protection of the Ozone Layer, supra note 30.

37. Montreal Protocol, supra note 30; Adjustments and Amendments to the Montreal Protocol on Substances that Deplete the Ozone Layer, June 29, 1990, 30 I.L.M. 537, 539–41 [hereinafter Adjustments and Amendments

to the Montreal Protocol].

38. Treaty Respecting the Antarctic, Dec. 1, 1959, 12 U.S.T. 794, 402 U.N.T.S. 71; Protocol on Environmental Protection to the Treaty Regarding the Antarctic, June 21, 1991, *S. Treaty Doc. No. 22*, 102d Cong., 2d Sess. (1992), 30 I.L.M. 1455.

39. Convention on the Control of Transboundary Movements of Hazardous Wastes and Their Disposal, Mar. 22, 1989, *S. Treaty Doc. No. 5*, 102d Cong., 1st Sess. (1991), 28 I.L.M. 657 [hereinafter Basel Convention].

40. Convention on Early Notification of a Nuclear Accident, Sept. 26, 1986, *S. Treaty Doc. No. 4*, 100th Cong., 1st Sess. (1987), 25 I.L.M. 1370.

41. Convention on Assistance in the Case of a Nuclear Accident or Radiological Emergency, Sept. 26, 1986, *S. Treaty Doc. No. 4*, 100th Cong., 1st Sess. (1987), 25 I.L.M. 1377 (entered into force Oct. 27, 1986).

42. Convention on Oil Pollution Preparedness, Response and Cooperation, Nov. 30, 1990, 30 I.L.M. 733.

43. Framework Convention on Climate Change, May 9, 1992, 31 I.L.M. 849.

44. Convention on Biological Diversity, June 5, 1992, 31 I.L.M. 818.

45. Statement of Principles for a Global Consensus on the Management, Conservation and Sustainable Development of All Types of Forests, June 13, 1992, 31 I.L.M. 881 [hereinafter Forest Principles].

46. Arctic Environmental Protection Strategy, June 14, 1991, 30 I.L.M. 1624.

47. London Guidelines for the Exchange of Information on Chemicals in International Trade (Amended 1989), U.N. Environmental Programme, 15th Sess., at 15–26, *U.N. Doc. UNEP GC/DEC/15/30* (1989).

48. As of 1992, the U.N.-ECE included the following countries: Albania, Austria, Belarus, Belgium, Bosnia-Herzegovina, Bulgaria, Canada, Croatia, Cyprus, Czech and Slovak Federal Republic, Denmark, Estonia, Finland, France, Germany, Greece, Hungary, Iceland, Ireland, Israel, Italy, Latvia, Liechtenstein, Lithuania, Luxembourg, Malta, Netherlands, Norway, Poland, Portugal, Romania, Russian Federation, San Marino, Slovenia, Spain, Sweden, Switzerland, Turkey, Ukraine, United States, United Kingdom, and Yugoslavia.

49. Convention on Long Range Transboundary Air Pollution, Nov. 13, 1979, T.I.A.S. No. 10, 541, 18 I.L.M. 1442 (entered into force Mar. 16, 1983).

50. 1985 Helsinki Protocol, supra note 31, art. II, 27 I.L.M. at 708.

51. Protocol to the Convention on Long-Range Transboundary Air Pollution, Oct. 31, 1988, art. II, cl. 1, 28 I.L.M. 212, 216 (entered into force 1991) [hereinafter Sofia Protocol].

52. Protocol to the 1979 Convention on Long-Range Transboundary Air Pollution Concerning the Control of Emissions of Volatile Organic Compounds or Their Transboundary Fluxes, 31 I.L.M. 573 (1991) [hereinafter LRTAP VOC Protocol].

53. See, e.g., Convention on Environmental Impact Assessment in a Transboundary Context, Feb. 25, 1991, 30 I.L.M. 800; United Nations, Economic Commission for Europe, Convention on the Protection and Use of Transboundary Watercourses and International Lakes, Mar. 17, 1992, 31 I.L.M. 1312; United Nations, Commission for Europe, Draft Convention on the Transboundary Effects of Industrial Accidents, Mar. 17, 1992, 31 I.L.M. 1330 [hereinafter U.N.-ECE Convention on Transboundary Industrial Accidents].

54. Convention for the Protection of the Nautical Resources and Environment of the South Pacific Region, Nov. 25, 1986, 26 I.L.M. 38 (entered into force Aug. 22, 1990).

55. Protocol for the Prevention of Pollution of the South Pacific Region by Dumping, Nov. 25, 1986, 26 I.L.M. 65 (entered into force Aug. 22, 1990).

56. Protocol Concerning Co-Operation in Combating Pollution Emergencies in the South Pacific Region, Nov. 25, 1986, 26 I.L.M. 59 (entered into force Aug. 22, 1990).

57. Convention for the Protection and Development of the Marine Environment of the Wider Caribbean Region, Mar. 24, 1983, T.I.A.S. No. 11,085, 22 I.L.M. 227 (entered into force Oct. 11, 1986).

58. Protocol Concerning Specially Protected Areas and Wildlife, Jan. 16, 1990, 19 *Envtl. Pol'y L.* 224 (1990) (not in force).

59. Agreement on the Action Plan for the Environmentally Sound Management of the Common Zambezi River System, May 28, 1987, 27 I.L.M. 1109 (entered into force upon signature).

60. Agreement on Great Lakes Water Quality, Nov. 22, 1987, Can-U.S., 30 U.S.T. 1383.

61. Protocol Respecting Great Lakes Water Quality, Oct. 16, 1987, Can-U.S., T.I.A.S. No. 10,798.

62. Declaration of Brasilia, Mar. 31, 1989, 28 I.L.M. 1311.

63. Treaty for Amazonian Cooperation, July 3, 1987, 17 I.L.M. 1045.

64. Agreement on the Conservation of Nature and Natural Resources, July 9, 1985, 15 *Envtl. Pol'y & L.* 64 (1985) [hereinafter ASEAN Conservation Agreement]. It should be noted that this agreement is not yet in effect. The ASEAN countries include Brunei, Darussalam, Indonesia, Malaysia, Philippines, Singapore, and Thailand.

65. Bamako Convention on the Ban of Import into Africa and the Control of Transboundary Movement of Hazardous Wastes Within Africa, Jan. 29, 1991, 30 I.L.M. 773 [hereinafter Bamako Convention).

66. Single European Act, Feb. 17, 1986, 25 I.L.M. 503 (entered into force July 1, 1987).

67. Id., § II, § VI, title VII. art. 130R, cl. 4, 25 I.L.M. at 515.

68. Council Regulation 1210/90 of 7 May 1990 on the Establishment of the European Environment Agency and the European Environment Information and Observation Network, 1990 O.J. (L120) 1.
69. See, e.g., Agreement Concerning the Transboundary Movement of Hazardous Waste, Oct. 28, 1986, Can-U.S., T.I.A.S. No. 11,099; Agreement of Cooperation Regarding Transboundary Shipments of Hazardous Wastes and Hazardous Substances, Nov. 12, 1986, U.S.-Mex., Annex III, 26 I.L.M. 25 (entered into force Jan. 29, 1987).
70. Agreement on Cooperation for the Protection and Improvement of the Environment in the Metropolitan Area of Mexico, Oct. 3, 1981, U.S.-Mex., 29 I.L.M. 25 (entered into force Aug. 22, 1990).
71. Agreement on Air Quality, Mar. 13, 1991, Can-U.S., 30 I.L.M. 676.
72. Declaration Conjunta Sobre Politica Nuclear, Dec. 10, 1986, Arg-Braz., Integracion Latinoamericana, 12 (122), Apr. 1987, 70. The Agreement was concluded contemporaneously with the two IAEA agreements on notification and provision of emergency assistance in case of nuclear accident.
73. For an attempt to develop this methodology, see Edward A. Parson and William C. Clark, Learning to Manage Global Environmental Change: A Review of Relevant Theory (1991) (unpublished discussion paper, on file with the Center for Science and International Affairs, Cambridge, Mass.).
74. For an excellent brief inquiry into the learning patterns of international institutions concerned with issues such as nuclear energy, see Paul C. Szasz, "Restructuring the International Organizational Framework; Annex: The Learning Capacity of International Organizations," in *Environmental Change and International Law: New Challenges and Dimensions* 340, 377–84 (Edith Brown Weiss ed., 1992).
75. Convention on the Law of the Sea, Dec. 10, 1982, 21 I.L.M. 1261 (not in force). For a history of the prenegotiations in the preceding five years, see Ann L. Hollick, *U.S. Foreign Policy and the Law of the Sea* 196–239 (1981).
76. Paul C. Szasz has observed that it may be easier to negotiate agreements in new fields because there is less existing law to be considered. The negotiation for the Law of the Sea Convention was in part an exercise in codifying existing norms, which was a contentious process. Letter from Paul C. Szasz, former Deputy Legal Counsel and Director of the General Legal Division at the United Nations, to Professor Edith Brown Weiss, Georgetown University Law Center (Nov. 18, 1992).
77. Framework Convention on Climate Change, supra note 44.
78. Protocol on Environmental Protection to the Treaty Regarding the Antarctic, supra note 38.
79. Convention on Biological Diversity, supra note 44.

80. U.N.-ECE Convention on Transboundary Industrial Accidents, supra note 53.

81. LRTAP VOC Protocol, supra note 52.

82. United Nations Conference on Environment and Development, Agenda Item 21, U.N. Doc. A/Conf. 151/PC/100/Add. 1 (1992) [hereinafter Agenda 21].

83. Countries have also demonstrated skill in concluding agreements quickly in other areas, as evidenced by the successful negotiation of the North American Free Trade Agreement between Canada, Mexico, and the United States, which required slightly over a year to conclude. North American Free Trade Agreement, Dec. 17, 1992 (Sept. 8, 1992 released edition) (implementing legislation necessary to ratify the agreement is likely to be introduced in Congress in 1993).

84. For a chronology of principal developments in international legislation regarding the atmosphere, see Paul C. Szasz, "International Norm-making: Annex," in *Environmental Change and International Law: New Challenges and Dimensions* 41, 75–80 (Edith Brown Weiss ed., 1992).

85. Convention on Nature Protection and Wild Life Preservation in the Western Hemisphere, supra note 11.

86. Convention for the Protection of World Cultural and Natural Heritage, supra note 26.

87. Convention on Biological Diversity, supra note 44.

88. ASEAN Conservation Agreement, supra note 63.

89. Protocol Concerning Specially Protected Areas and Wildlife, supra note 58.

90. 1985 Helsinki Protocol, supra note 31.

91. Id. art. 6, 27 I.L.M. at 709.

92. LRTAP VOC Protocol, supra note 52.

93. See, e.g., id. at 575–80, 583–611.

94. See, e.g., Montreal Protocol, supra note 30, art. 2, *S. Treaty Doc. No. 10*, at 2, 26 I.L.M. at 1552 (requiring parties to meet annual control measures with regard to the specific consumption levels of certain controlled substances, defined as national production plus imports minus exports of the controlled substance on an annual basis); id. art. 3, *S. Treaty Doc. No. 10*, at 4, 26 I.L.M. at 1554 (determining how to calculate these levels of consumption).

95. See, e.g., Basel Convention, supra note 39, art. 4(5), *S. Treaty Doc. No. 5*, 102d Cong., 1st Sess. at 10, 28 I.L.M. at 662 (prohibiting parties from exporting hazardous wastes to nonparties).

96. Convention on the Law of the Sea, supra note 75, which took eight years to negotiate, illustrates this all-encompassing approach. This approach has obvious drawbacks, the most obvious of which is that the more ambitious the goals, the more issues upon which the participating countries must reach agreement. Delay and lengthy negotiations become

the rule, rather than the exception, in these settings.

97. Barcelona Convention for the Protection of the Mediterranean Sea Against Pollution, supra note 27; Barcelona Protocol Concerning Cooperation in Combating Pollution of the Mediterranean Sea by Oil and Other Harmful Substances in Cases of Emergency, supra note 27; Barcelona Protocol for the Prevention of Pollution of the Mediterranean Sea by Dumping from Ships and Aircraft, supra note 27.

98. See supra note 48 (listing the members of U.N.-ECE).

99. Convention on Long-Range Transboundary Air Pollution, supra note 49.

100. See Protocol on Long-Term Financing of the Co-Operative Programme for Monitoring and Evaluation of the Long Range Transmission of Air Pollutants in Europe, Sept. 28, 1984, 24 I.L.M. 484 (providing a funding mechanism for the monitoring system); 1985 Helsinki Protocol, supra note 31, 27 I.L.M. at 707 (limiting sulphur emissions); Sofia Protocol, supra note 51, 28 I.L.M. at 212 (limiting nitrogen oxides emissions).

101. Convention for the Protection of the Ozone Layer, supra note 30.

102. Montreal Protocol, supra note 30, art. III, *S. Treaty Doc. No. 10*, at 4, 26 I.L.M. at 1554 (regime establishing limits based on multiplication of annual production of each controlled substance by its ozone depleting potential). Countries were unable to agree upon the Protocol during the negotiations for the Vienna Convention.

103. Montreal Protocol, supra note 30.

104. Id. art. 11, *S. Treaty Doc. No. 10* at 7, 26 I.L.M. at 1557–58.

105. Id. art. 6. *S. Treaty Doc. No. 10*, at 6, 26 I.L.M. at 1556 (calling for assessment of the control measures of Art.2 at least every four years and for expert panels to report their conclusions to the parties within one year prior to the parties being convened).

106. Id. arts. 2(9), 2(10), *S. Treaty Doc. No. 10*, at 4, 26 I.L.M. at 1553–54. Thus, the adjustments agreed to by the parties to fully phase out chlorofluorocarbons by the year 2000 and all but essential uses of halons came into effect in March 1991. Adjustments and Amendments to the Montreal Protocol, supra note 37, at 539–41. The Amendments, which put new chemicals on the list of regulated substances, did not come into effect until August 1992. Id. at 541–53. For an account of the effect of scientific uncertainty on the negotiation of the Montreal Protocol, see generally Richard Benedict, *Ozone Diplomacy* (1991).

107. Framework Convention on Climate Change, supra note 43.

108. Id. art. 9, 31 I.L.M. at 863.

109. Id.

110. For an analysis of the precautionary principle, see Daniel Bodansky, "Scientific Uncertainty and the Precautionary Principle," 33 *Env't* 4 (1991) (providing a skeptical analysis); M.P.A. Kindall, "UNCED and the Evolution of Principles of International Environmental Law," 25 *John Marshall L. Rev.* 19, 23 (1991) (suggesting elements to include in a

precautionary approach); James Cameron and Jacob D. Werksman, The Precautionary Principle: A Policy for Action in the Face of Uncertainty (paper presented at the Centre for International Environmental Law, Kings College, London (Jan. 1991)).

111. See London Ocean Dumping Convention, supra note 25. At the fall 1991 meeting of the parties to the London Ocean Dumping Convention, countries agreed to be guided by a "precautionary approach" in implementing the Convention. They would take preventive action when there is reason to believe the dumped material is likely to cause harm even when there is no conclusive evidence to prove a causal link to certain effects, and they would be guided by certain specific measures in carrying out this approach. "The Application of a Precautionary Approach in Environmental Protection Within the Framework of the London Dumping Convention," *IMO Assembly Res. LDC* 44(14) (Nov. 1991 14th Consultative meeting) (on file with author); P.J. Taylor and T. Jackson, The Precautionary Principle and the Prevention of Marine Pollution. Paper presented at the International Ocean Pollution Symposium, Puerto Rico (Apr. 1991).

112. ASEAN Conservation Agreement, supra note 63.

113. See id. arts. 3-9; 15 *Envtl. Pol'y & L.* at 64-65 (calling for specific measures to conserve and protect habitats, prevent changes in ecosystems, preserve vegetation cover, prevent soil erosion, and conserve underground and surface water resources as a means of preserving genetic diversity).

114. Convention on Biological Diversity, supra note 44.

115. See id. pmbl., art. 2, 31 I.L.M. at 822, 824 (noting that the conservation of ecosystems and natural habitats is necessary for the conservation of biological diversity, that lack of full scientific certainty should not postpone the implementation of measures, and defining "ecosystem" to include all animal and "micro-organism" communities).

116. Agreement on Great Lakes Water Quality, supra note 60.

117. See id. pmbl., 30 U.S.T. at 1383, 1384.

118. Protocol Respecting Great Lakes Water Quality, Nov. 18, 1987, U.S.-Can., reprinted in Weiss et al., supra note 1, at 419.

119. See Protocol Amending the 1978 Agreement between the United States of America and Canada on Great Lakes Water Quality, Annex 15 (Airborne Toxic Substances), Annex 16 (Pollution from Contaminated Groundwater) Oct. 16, 1983 (on file with *The Georgetown Law Journal*).

120. See, e.g., Protocol Concerning Specially Protected Areas and Wildlife to the Convention for the Protection and Development of the Marine Environment of the Wider Caribbean Region, Jan. 18, 1990, 34 Int'l Envtl. Rep. (BNA) 3261; Protocol for the Protection of the Mediterranean Sea Against Pollution from Land-Based Sources, May 17, 1980, 19 I.L.M. 869; Protocol for the Protection of the South-East-Pacific Against Pollution From Land-Based Sources, July 23, 1983, UNEP Reg. at 199.

121. See Agenda 21, supra note 82, at ch. 17, ¶ ¶ 18–29.
122. Agreements in other areas have also done this. See, e.g., Treaty on the Non-Proliferation of Nuclear Weapons, July 1, 1968, 21 U.S.T. 483, 729 U.N.T.S. 161. Under the treaty, nuclear weapons states agreed to assist nonnuclear states in the development of peaceful uses of nuclear energy. Id. art. v, 21 U.S.T. at 490, 729 U.S.T.S. at 173.
123. See Montreal Protocol, supra note 30, art. 10, *S. Treaty Doc. No. 10*, at 7, 26 I.L.M. at 1557 (calling on parties to cooperate in promoting technical assistance in order to facilitate participation in the Protocol); Framework Convention on Climate Change, supra note 43, art. 4(c), 31 I.L.M. at 855 (calling on parties to transfer technology and cooperate in other ways "to reduce or prevent anthropogenic emissions of greenhouse gases not controlled by the Montreal Protocol"); Convention on Biological Diversity, *supra* note 44, art. 16, ¶ 1, 31 I.L.M. at 829 (calling on parties to facilitate access to and transfer of technologies "that are relevant to the conservation and sustainable use of biological diversity"); *id.* art. 18, ¶ 1, 31 I.L.M. at 829 (requiring parties to "promote international technical and scientific cooperation").
124. CITES, supra note 24.
125. Id. art. x, 27 U.S.T. at 1104, 993 U.N.T.S. at 251.
126. See Montreal Protocol, supra note 30, art. 4. *S. Treaty Doc. No. 10*, at 5, 26 I.L.M. at 1554–55 (providing that parties shall ban the import of controlled substances from nonparty states); see also Basel Convention, supra note 39, art. 4, ¶ 5, *S. Treaty Doc. No. 5*, at 10, 28 I.L.M. at 662 (providing that parties shall ban the import and export of hazardous wastes from nonparty states).
127. General Agreement on Tariffs and Trade, Oct. 30, 1947, T.I.A.S. No. 1700, 55 U.N.T.S. 187 [hereinafter GATT].
128. For a particularly astute analysis of the effects of a CITES ban on elephant ivory trade, see Michael J. Glennon, "Has International Law Failed the Elephant?" 84 *Am. J. Int'l. L.* 1, 17–22 (1990).
129. The opposite phenomenon could also occur, namely that some countries could control greenhouse gas emissions at great cost and receive little benefit unless other countries that emit large amounts also joined the agreement.
130. Framework Convention on Climate Change, supra note 43.
131. See Protocol on Environmental Protection to the Treaty Regarding the Antarctic, supra note 38, 30 I.L.M. at 1460 (stating that representatives of "international governmental and non-governmental organizations attended the Meeting as observers").
132. At the time, the organization was called the London Centre for International environmental Law (CIEL). The group of island states is known formally as the Alliance of Small Island States.

133. See *Institutions for the Earth* (Peter M. Haas et al., eds., forthcoming 1993).

134. World Heritage Convention, supra note 26.

135. Id. art 13, ¶ 7, 27 U.S.T. at 44, 1037 U.N.T.S. at 157; see also id. art. 8, ¶ 3, 27 U.S.T. at 42, 1037 U.N.T.S. at 155, and art. 14, ¶ 2, 27 U.S.T. at 44, 1037 U.N.T.S. at 157–58 (providing for advisory roles for the International Centre for the Study of the Preservation and the Restoration of Cultural Property, the International Council of Monuments and Sites, and the International Union for Conservation of Nature and Natural Resources).

136. See, e.g., Basel Convention, supra note 39 (concluded in March 1989, but not entered into force until May 1992). The Montreal Protocol, supra note 30, is a notable exception to this general practice. The Protocol was concluded in September 1987 and entered into force in January 1989. The Amendments to the Protocol were concluded in June 1990 and entered into force in August 1992.

137. For a discussion of issues related to delayed entry into force, see Peter H. Sand, *Lessons Learned in Global Environmental Governance* (1990). The new Climate Convention provides a special article on interim arrangements, Article 21, which addresses issues of an interim secretariat, interim scientific advice, and interim financial arrangements. Framework Convention on Climate Change, *supra* note 43, art. 21, 31 I.L.M. at 870. Some of the concern with interim arrangements relates to how the convention can be made effective before the parties have agreed on particular modalities.

138. See Paul C. Szasz, "International Norm-making," in *Environmental Change and International Law: New Challenges and Dimensions* 41 (Edith Brown Weiss, ed., 1992).

139. There is an emerging literature on compliance with international environmental agreements. See, e.g., Kenneth Hanf and Arild Underal, *Domesticating International Commitments: Linking National and International DecisionMaking* (July 1991) (on file with author); Abram Chayes and Antonia H. Chayes, *On Compliance* (1992) (on file with author); Ronald Bruce Mitchell, *From Paper to Practice: Improving Environmental Treaty Compliance* (doctoral dissertation chapter, on file with author) (study of compliance with the London Convention for the Prevention of Pollution by Ships). See generally, Oran R. Young, *Compliance and Public Authority: A Theory with International Applications* (1979); Jesse H. Ausubel and David G. Victor, "Verification of International Environmental Agreements," 17 *Ann. Rev. Energy Env't* 1 (1992).

140. See generally, U.S. General Accounting Office, GAO/RECD 92–43, *International Environment: International Agreements Are Not Well Monitored* (1992); see also U.S. General Accounting Office, GAO/RECD

92–188, International Environmental Agreements (1992).

141. Preparatory Comm. for the U.N. Conference on Environment and Development, Survey of Existing Agreements and Instruments and its Follow-up, U.N. GAOR, 4th Sess., Agenda Item 2, U.N. Doc. A/Conf. 151/PC/WG.III/L.32 (1992) [hereinafter UNCED]. The summary and the background papers have been published in *The Effectiveness of International Environmental Agreements* (Peter H. Sand, ed., 1992).

142. CITES, supra note 24.

143. See generally, Kathryn Fuller et al., "Wildlife Trade Law Implementation in Developing Countries: The Experience in Latin America," 5 *B.U. Int'l L.J.* 289 (1987); Laura Kosloff and Mark Trexler, "The Convention on International Trade in Endangered Species: Enforcement Theory and Practice in the United States," 5 *B.U. Int'l L.J.* 327 (1987); Eric McFadden, "Asian Compliance with CITES: Problems and Prospects," 5 *B.U. Int'l L.J.* 311 (1987).

144. Louis Henkin, *How Nations Behave* 47 (1979).

145. See Harold K. Jacobson and Edith Brown Weiss, "Implementing and Complying with International Environmental Accords: A Framework for Research" (American Political Science Association, 1990) (unpublished manuscript, on file with *The Georgetown Law Journal*).

146. Under the auspices of the Social Science Research Council, a multidisciplinary international team of scholars has begun an empirical study of national implementation of and compliance with five international environmental agreements in nine countries. The International Institute of Applied Systems Analysis in Laxenburg, Austria held a small workshop on the subject in October 1992 and has proposed a major initiative in this area.

147. This does not necessarily mean that we should slow down the process for developing international norms; rather it means that we must try to make the process more efficient and manageable for all countries.

148. Arctic Environmental Protection Strategy, supra note 46.

149. Rio Declaration on Environment and Development, June 13, 1992, 31 I.L.M. 874 [hereinafter Rio Declaration].

150. Forest Principles, supra note 45.

151. Agenda 21, supra note 82.

152. Geoffrey Palmer, "New Ways to Make International Environmental Law," 86 *Am. J. Int'l. L.* 259, 263 (1992).

153. Id. at 264. The United Nations Environmental Programme, for example, might be designated as the home for international environmental agreements, which would mean that the secretariats would be located there.

154. Framework Convention on Climate Change, supra note 43.

155. Convention on Biological Diversity, supra note 44.

156. Forest Principles, supra note 45.

157. Convention on Biological Diversity, supra note 44, art. 22, 31 I.L.M. at 832. This article provides that the Convention does not affect the rights and obligations of state parties to other international agreements, "except where the exercise of those rights and obligations would cause a serious damage or threat to biological diversity." Id. The article further provides that the Convention is to be implemented consistently with the Convention on the Law of the Sea. Id. The Basel Convention addresses the relationship of the global convention to regional and bilateral agreements. Article 11 stipulates that parties may enter into regional and bilateral agreements provided that the provisions are "not less environmentally sound than those provided for by this Convention in particular taking into account the interests of developing countries." Basel Convention, supra note 39, art. 11, 28 I.L.M. at 668. If countries have already entered into such agreements at the time they become parties to the Basel Convention, the provisions of the Convention do not affect movements of waste pursuant to these agreements "provided that such agreements are compatible with the environmentally sound management of hazardous wastes and other wastes as required by this Convention." Id.

158. London Ocean Dumping Convention, supra note 25, art. I, 26 U.S.T. at 2406, 1046 U.N.T.S. at 140.

159. Basel Convention, supra note 39.

160. Treaty Respecting the Antarctic, supra note 38.

161. Convention on the Law of the Sea, supra note 75. The 1982 Law of the Sea Convention is not in force because it has not been ratified by the required number of countries. However, the United States has claimed that most of its provisions, with the notable exception of the seabed provisions, constitute customary international law, so the intersection of the two agreements is still a timely issue.

162. Agenda 21, supra note 82.

163. See id.

164. The Global Environmental Facility (GEF) was established to fund projects on global warming, pollution of international waters, destruction of biological diversity, and depletion of the ozone layer. It is a three-year experiment administered by the World Bank that provides grants for investment projects, technical assistance, and to a lesser extent, research to assist developing countries in protecting the global environment and to transfer environmentally safe technologies to them. Countries with per capita income of less than $4,000 a year (as of October 1969) are eligible.

    The GEF is an umbrella for three distinct funds: the so-called "core fund" or global environmental trust fund (GET); the associated cofinancing arrangements, which are available on grant or highly concessionary terms; and the Montreal Protocol Fund to help developing countries comply with the provisions of the Protocol. The Montreal

Protocol Fund, while under the umbrella of the GEF, is administered separately from the other two by the United Nations Environment Programme under the auspices of a fourteen-country executive committee.

The World Bank, U.N. Development Programme (UNDP), and the UNEP have coresponsibility for the GEF. The World Bank administers the Facility, acts as the repository of the Trust Fund, and is responsible for investment projects. The UNDP provides technical assistance, helps identify projects, and will run the small-grants program for NGOs. The UNEP provides the secretariat for the Scientific and Technical Advisory Panel to the GEF and provides environmental expertise.

165. The Framework Convention on Climate Change designates the Global Environmental Facility (GEF) to serve as the financial mechanism on an interim basis and notes that the GEF "should be appropriately restructured and its membership made universal to enable it to fulfill the requirement of Article 11 (Financial Mechanism)." Framework Convention on Climate Change, *supra* note 43, art. 21, 31 I.L.M. at 870. The failure to designate the GEF as the interim financial mechanism in the Convention on Biological Diversity was indicated as one of the principal points of concern to the United States when it considered whether to sign the agreement.

166. See generally, A. Dan Tarlock, "Environmental Protection: The Potential Misfit Between Equity and Efficiency," 63 *U. Colo. L. Rev.* 871 (1992).

167. Rio Declaration, supra note 149.

168. Id. princ. 5, 31 I.L.M. at 877.

169. Id. princ. 6, 31 I.L.M. at 877.

170. Id. princ. 7, 31 I.L.M. at 877.

171. Declaration of the United Nations Conference on the Human Environment, June 16, 1972, 11 I.L.M. 1416 [hereinafter Stockholm Declaration].

172. Id. princ. 23, 11 I.L.M. at 1420.

173. Id. princ. 12, 11 I.L.M. at 1419. The Rio Declaration deliberately does not use the term "technical assistance," which some countries view as unnecessarily narrow in scope and possibly condescending. Rather, the relevant article focuses on cooperation and provides that "[s]tates should cooperate to strengthen endogenous capacity-building for sustainable development by improving scientific understanding . . . and by enhancing the development, adaptation, diffusion and transfer of technologies, including new and innovative technologies." Rio Declaration, supra note 149, princ. 9, 31 I.L.M. at 877.

174. For example, Principle 21 of the Stockholm Declaration on the Human Environment begins by explaining that "states have, in accordance with the Charter of the United Nations and the principles of international law, the sovereign right to exploit their own resources pursuant to their own environmental policies." Stockholm Declaration, supra note 171, princ.

21, 11 I.L.M. at 1420. The Rio Declaration repeats this statement in Principle 2, and adds "and developmental" to environmental policies. Rio Declaration, *supra* note 149. The Stockholm principle has been commonly regarded as reflecting customary international law, and hence being binding on all states. Stockholm Declaration, supra note 171, princ. 21, 11 I.L.M. at 1420.

175. See Convention on the Law of the Sea, supra note 75, Part XI, 21 I.L.M. at 1293 (chapter on seabed minerals).

176. Convention on the Regulation of Antarctic Mineral Resource Activities, June 2, 1988, 27 I.L.M. 859 [hereinafter Wellington Convention]. The Wellington Convention will be shelved for at least fifty years when the new Protocol on Environmental Protection to the Antarctic Treaty enters into force. The Antarctic Environmental Protocol prohibits any activity related to mineral resources, except for scientific research; the prohibition can only be lifted by the parties after fifty years if "there is in force a binding legal regime on Antarctic mineral resource activities that includes an agreed means for determining whether, and, if so, under which conditions, any such activities would be acceptable." Protocol on Environmental Protection to the Antarctic Treaty, Oct. 4, 1991, arts. 7, 25, 30 I.L.M. 1455, 1470.

177. Stockholm Declaration, supra note 171, princ. 21, 11 I.L.M. at 1420.

178. The negotiations for the U.N.-ECE protocols controlling sulphur dioxide and nitrogen oxide reflected this. The United States has never joined the Protocol on Sulphur Dioxide, in part because of concern that it would not be given appropriate credit for the reductions it had made prior to the conclusion of the Protocol. 1985 Helsinki Protocol, supra note 31. See Protocol to the 1979 Convention on Long-Range Transboundary Air Pollution Concerning the Control of Emissions of Nitrogen Oxides or Their Transboundary Fluxes, Oct. 31, 1988, 28 I.L.M. 214 (1989), to which the United States did become a party.

179. Rio Declaration, supra note 149, princ. 7, 31 I.L.M. at 877. This principle was formulated initially with the belief that the developed countries should have the "main responsibility" for combating pollution because they have contributed the most to pollution. The initial draft of the Rio Declaration by the Group of 77, an informal group of developing countries, contained a principle entitled "Main Responsibility." This principle declared:

> The major historical and current cause of the continuing deterioration of the global environment is the unsustainable pattern of production and consumption, particularly in developed countries. Thus, the responsibility for containing, reducing and eliminating global environmental damage must be borne by the countries causing such damage, must be in relation to the damage caused and must be in accordance with their respective responsibilities.

Moritaka Hayashi, Differentiated Responsibilities of "Unequal" Parties to International Environmental Agreements. Paper presented at the Conference on Environmental Inequality, Harvard University (Nov. 14, 1992) (on file with *The Georgetown Law Journal*). Hayashi argues that the principle of common but differentiated responsibilities is accompanied by the "concept of different obligations," by which he means that states with less capacity to fulfill an agreement are accorded special treatment, as in the ten-year delay period for compliance with the Montreal Protocol, and those states with greater capacities have the duty to assist those in the former group. Id. at 3–4.

180. Rio Declaration, supra note 149, princs. 13 and 16, 31 I.L.M. at 878–79. The Rio Declaration prudently treats the question of liability in a separate principle from the polluter-pays approach and appropriately refers to the polluter pays as an approach rather than as a principle.   Within the international legal and policy community, there have been efforts to promote the polluter-pays approach as a principle of legal liability. The problem is that the principle of polluter pays was developed to ascribe responsibilities of individual firms to "bear the expenses of carrying out the [pollution control] measures. . . . [and reflect them] in the cost of the goods or services which cause pollution."   Recommendation of the Council on the Implementation of the Polluter-Pays Principle, Nov. 14, 1974, 14 I.L.M. 234. This is not appropriate as a principle of liability between states, nor was it intended as such. Liability in international law has been traditionally concerned with compensating for damage, although it is nearly impossible to compensate states fully for environmental damage.   Moreover, if the goal of those who argue for a polluter-pays liability principle is to discourage polluting behavior, the amount needed to deter such behavior is unlikely to be the same as that needed to compensate for damage.   Moreover, the polluter-pays principle as an economic approach suggests that a party could be liable only for negligent behavior, not strictly liable, in international law. Finally, the emphasis on liability is questionable.   There is virtually no instance in public international law when states have admitted liability for environmental damage to another country in the absence of treaty provisions. Indeed the trend has been directly opposite—some countries have paid for the installation of proper pollution control in polluting countries because the costs of doing so were less than the costs of continuing to suffer pollution damage. See Edith Brown Weiss, Remarks, "World Climate Change—Greenhouse Effect," in 84 *American Society of International Law, Proceedings of the Annual Meeting* 356, 359–60 (1990).

181. Montreal Protocol, supra note 30, art. 5, *S. Treaty Doc. No. 10*, at 1555, 26 I.L.M. at 1555.

182. Id.

183. For presentation and analysis of issues of intergenerational equity, see Edith Brown Weiss, *In Fairness to Future Generations: International Law, Common Patrimony, and Intergenerational Equity* (1989). For legal analysis of equity issues and developing countries, see Daniel Barstow Magraw, "Legal Treatment of Developing Countries: Differential, Contextual, and Absolute Norms," 1 *Colo. J. Envtl. L. & Pol'y* 69 (1990); Cheng Zheng-Kang, "Equity, Special Considerations, and the Third World," 1 *Colo. J. Envtl. L & Pol'y* 57 (1990).

184. GATT, supra note 127.

185. See generally, Edith Brown Weiss, "Environment and Trade as Partners in Sustainable Development: A Commentary," 86 *Am. J. Int'l L.* 728 (1992). For an analysis of environmental issues in the context of trade law, see John H. Jackson, "World Trade Rules and Environmental Policies: Congruence or Conflict?" 49 *Wash. & Lee L. Rev.* 1227 (1992); Thomas J. Schoenbaum, "Free International Trade and Protection of the Environment: Irreconcilable Conflict?" 86 *Am. J. Int'l. L.* 700 (1992).

186. UNCED, supra note 141.

187. Rio Declaration, supra note 149, princ. 10, 31 I.L.M. at 878.

188. Principle 10 provides in part that "[e]nvironmental issues are best handled with the participation of all concerned citizens, at the relevant level. At the national level, each individual shall have appropriate access to information." Id.

189. While the information revolution offers a powerful tool for ensuring global environmental health and for empowering the public, it may also promote fragmentation and make management more difficult. In some cases, governments may find it more challenging to address problems in the face of the information revolution because widely disparate groups will have access to powerful information technologies to persuade constituencies, whom once persuaded, may be hard to change.

190. For an excellent overview of different attitudes toward the general validity of national interest, see Stephen D. Krasner, *Defending the National Interest* 1–30 (1978).

191. *Institutions for the Earth*, supra note 133, at 21. Lynton Caldwell notes that states have in some instances agreed to modify their asserted freedom to act as they please in relation to their natural resources, industrial practices, and the environment. Lynton Caldwell, *International Environmental Policy: Emergence and Dimensions* 311 (2d ed. 1990). Internationally agreed limits on pollution and use of natural resources constrain operational sovereignty.

192. Framework Convention on Climate Change, supra note 43, art. 4, 31 I.L.M. at 855–59.

26

International Environmental Law from Stockholm to Rio: An Overview of Past Lessons and Future Challenges

*A.O. Adede**

Introduction

The objectives of this seminar on international environmental law are two-fold: first, to enable the participants to have more than a glimpse of the scope and nature of the major legal and related instruments, which the international community has developed, as frameworks for international responses to the problems of environment and development, during the past twenty years. It also offers, in this connection, an assessment of the efforts which have been made towards progressive development and codification of international environmental law since the United Nations Conference on Human Environment in Stockholm 1972. Secondly, the seminar is intended to indicate the pathway which the international community has chosen towards achieving concrete results at the United Nations Conference on Environment and Development (UNCED) now called the Earth Summit, in Rio de Janeiro, June 2–12, 1992. The decision by the United Nations

The views expressed are those of the author and do not necessarily represent those of the United Nations. (All rights reserved.)

The trip to Moi University to conduct the three-day seminar was financed from the funds received as part of the 1990 Elizabeth Haub Gold Medal Award on International Environmental Law, received by the author. (See Environmental Policy and Law, (1991), vol. 21, 222.)

to hold the Earth Summit twenty years after Stockholm has presented the opportunity, through the preparatory process towards the 1992 Rio Summit, for taking stock of what needs to be done on the basis of past lessons and in light of new challenges ahead.

Consistent with the objectives of the seminar as just outlined, it is useful to recall here briefly that the main results of the 1972 Stockholm Conference on Human Environment[1] were the establishment of the United Nations Environment Programme (UNEP) and the adoption of an Action Plan for the Human Environment. UNEP has, since its establishment, continued to discharge admirably its mandate[2] of coordinating, within the United Nations system, international responses to the first generation environmental issues: namely, pollution of water, air, and soil, resulting both from industrial activities and from activities associated with poverty and underdevelopment.[3]

In the meantime, the second generation environmental issues entered the scene. They are global warming (climate change), acid rain, and the depletion of the stratospheric ozone layer. This group of issues, to which the problem of exploitation of environment as a weapon in times of armed conflict was most recently added, began to receive closer attention of the international community. The problems which they raised brought into focus the need to initiate additional processes for public education and consciousness-raising in order to enable the international community to take effective and timely measures, both internationally and nationally, in response thereto. Such measures would require appropriate legal frameworks which may need to be either strengthened or established.

The assessment of the impacts of these new issues, indeed, leads to the realization of the fact that, although the linkage between environment and development was recognized as far back as the 1972 Stockholm Conference, "all too little progress [has been] made toward actual integration of environmental dimensions into development policies and practices."[4] The establishment of the necessary modalities for integrating more fully environmental dimensions into development policies is the task presently assigned to the Preparatory Committee of the United Nations Conference on Environment and Development. To this end, UNCED is working on the so-called "Agenda 21," with specific components for adoption at Rio and for subsequent action. As will be shown later, the road to UNCED in Rio and beyond is paved with a number of new challenges which must be identified. The means for meeting the new challenges effectively must also be established. It should, in this connection, be pointed out further that the road map to Rio, which is now being improved by UNCED's preparatory process was, since Stockholm, re-charted by the World Commission on Environment and Development (WCED) which, in 1987, produced its report—*Our Common Future*—in which the concept of "sustainable development," among others, was revitalized.[5]

The current process of devising appropriate means for addressing environment and development issues in an integrated manner has thus underscored the need for a truly interdisciplinary approach to the task. It clearly demonstrated the necessity of bringing together, for example, scientists, lawyers, economists, development strategists, ecologists, policymakers and administrators, from both the public and the private sectors, to exchange views concerning appropriate responses to the identified problems of environment and development, and on the necessary international framework for undertaking the agreed measures. The process has also underscored the need to find more effective ways for encouraging and ensuring full participation of the developing countries in the various international conferences and meetings negotiating legal and related instruments which States would be called upon to implement, nationally and internationally towards the achievement of the commonly shared goals.

Although geared predominantly towards the discussion of the legal aspects of the issues, efforts are made in this background paper to raise also the issues which are of interest to non-lawyers among the participants in the seminar, thus clearly demonstrating the multidisciplinary approach to the tasks at hand. A sample of such issues are randomly and briefly offered below:

1. In connection with issues such as those concerning the fight against global warming, acid rain, desertification, and deforestation; the preservation of biological diversity; and the protection of the stratospheric ozone layer, law meets science and economics right at the threshold, raising thereby, a number of preliminary and controversial questions. It is therefore necessary to distinguish genuine gaps in the scientific knowledge or genuine lack of knowledge about possible economic consequences of suggested preventive or corrective measures, from false claims of the existence of such gaps in knowledge. This is to guard against the use of the false claims of gaps in knowledge as a convenient pretext for inaction or rejection of efforts towards the putting into

place of the necessary legal frameworks for international response to these identified problems.

2. In connection with the question of transfer of technology, the legal framework for bringing this about should recognise a number of basic views: one emphasises the fact that technology is an indispensable ingredient of economic growth. Thus, the developing countries which lack adequate capital for acquiring environmentally sound technologies for supporting environmental protection strategies, need assistance. They need adequate financial, institutional and professional capacities for choosing and using technologies which are best suited to their needs; developed and adapted to fit local conditions; and integrated with traditional technologies and experience.[6] There is also the suggestion that the best place for the lawyers, working on the problem of transfer of technology, to start is to look, for example, at the treaties governing patents, intellectual property rights, trade, with full knowledge that the basic questions of transfer of the technology and the additional fund resources linked to the process is to be answered by other experts.[7] The question is whether such technologies should be transferred to developing countries on preferential and non-commercial terms, as suggested by them, or on the basis of straight market value as argued by the industrialized countries emphasizing the proprietary nature of technology. Due regards should be given to the implications of the current efforts towards "globalization of technology" to develop technology without borders.

3. In addressing the questions of prevention of deforestation and desertification, it is necessary to develop new and innovative incentives or trade-offs that would guide the conduct of individuals (natural or juridical persons) whose activities have adverse effects on the forests: the individuals who use the forest for survival as the source of firewood (energy) which they need for preparing their daily meals; those who clear the forest to make room for agricultural activities for subsistence; and those who cut down forest trees as the source of timber for which exist local or international lucrative markets. This use-oriented approach to the forests, for the benefit of human beings, is to be balanced and integrated with the approach of preservation of the tropical rain forests as indispensable carbon sinks and as the home of species of fauna and flora which need to be preserved.

4. In the process of integrating environmental dimensions into development policies and practice, it is essential to avoid pursuing this goal to the extent of turning it into one of the means of introducing new forms of conditionality for the allocation of aid or development financing to developing countries.

5. In devising appropriate measures for responding to the identified problems, it is necessary to continue keeping in perspective the environmental problems of poverty for which development as such would provide the answer and the environmental problems arising from the process of development and industrialisation for which other measures are necessary.

6. While focusing on the problems of environment and development, it is necessary to assess and address the impact of the burgeoning population growth in the developing countries and its link to the causes of urban and rural poverty, through increasing and staggering demand upon various natural resources. This would be balanced with the equal concern about the patterns of production and consumption in the industrialized countries which also have impact upon certain finite natural resources.

7. In recognizing the new grounds being broken by international law through the development of new concepts, it is necessary to evaluate the impact of the application of such concepts in both the North and the South. The new concepts are, for example, (1) intergenerational responsibility and intergenerational equity; (2) shared but differentiated responsibilities; (3) common concern of mankind; (4) precautionary principle; (5) resource transfer; (6) cost internalization; (7) the global commons; (8) polluter pays principle; and (9) sustainable development. The degree of application of these concepts will depend on agreement as to which among them are amenable to precise definitions which generate concrete legal obligations to be included in legally binding instruments and those which continue to defy such definitions and are therefore destined to remain in the realm of general guidelines or statements of aspirations.

8. When putting into place appropriate national legal instruments for responding to problems of environment and development, it is necessary to recognize the rights and the proper roles of individuals (natural or juridical persons) as well as those of nongovernmental organizations, in bringing to the attention of governmental authorities certain cultural, social, and other values that need to be

protected for the benefit of the society, which should not be easily sacrificed on the altar of development.

9. In devising new legal instruments for international response to the identified problems of environment and development, care must be taken to strengthen or establish, as appropriate, institutional mechanisms or arrangements that would ensure the monitoring of compliance with the international obligations contained in the instrument in question to achieve their effective implementation, as well as the mechanisms for updating the instruments expeditiously to enable them to correspond to new realities.

10. In the current exercise, it is necessary for the international community to adopt the policy of taking preventive actions without waiting for a disaster or a crisis in connection with the pollution or degradation of a specified area of the environment, recognizing adverse environmental effects which are across the boundary of States and those which concern the global commons. This would enable the international community to supplement or even replace the practice of "react and correct" by the policy of "forecast and prevent," relying upon exchange of information, collected through the process of monitoring of environmental activities, as may be stipulated under appropriate international legal instruments.

11. In adopting the policy of "forecast and prevent," it is necessary for the international community also to establish or strengthen emergency preparedness and contingency plans for taking effective remedial measures in case of environmental disasters.

12. In an effort to reduce areas of international friction arising from activities relating to problems of environment and development, it is necessary to encourage the process of exchange of pertinent information and the collaboration in the research for obtaining the necessary information. Together with this, efforts should be made to accept, in the appropriate international instruments, effective mechanisms for the *avoidance* of environmental disputes, and those for the *settlement* of such disputes. The mechanism should be flexible enough to allow for those ranging from resort to informal non-adjudicatory procedures, to the formal adjudicatory such as arbitration, including resort to judicial settlement by the International Court of Justice.

The foregoing list of issues is certainly not exhaustive. It is merely illustrative of the point made here that the current process of negotiating international legal instruments for dealing with the problems of environment and development requires a multidisciplinary approach. It is the approach that would enable the international community to continue addressing effectively the first generation environmental issues as well as the second generation problems as briefly identified in this introduction. With this in mind, we may now pass to the analysis aimed at demonstrating that international environmental law has tended to develop, since the Stockholm Conference, in a piecemeal way and that the time has now come to put into place an appropriate multilateral legal instrument dealing comprehensively with environment and development issues in an integrated manner, in light of past lessons and directing attention to new challenges, taking into account the interest and concern of the developing countries.

The Piecemeal Approach to Treaty Making in the Environmental Field: Past Lessons

Areas, Issues, and Activities Addressed by the Existing Treaties

A survey of the existing treaties in the field of environment shows that, since 1972, the following broad areas or issues have been the subject of multilateral treaties (global or regional): protection of marine environment; prevention of air pollution; protection of spheres of fauna and flora and related issues; prevention of pollution of rivers and lakes; protection of the environment from radiological emergencies from peaceful uses of nuclear emergencies and from chemical and toxic substances including hazardous wastes; and protection of the environment from military and related activities. This section will give a synopsis of the existing legal instruments.

It may be shown, for example, that the question of elaborating legal instruments for international responses to issues of environment and development was approached more boldly by some experts groups[8] and too cautiously by others,[9] hampered by the scientific evidence controversy already mentioned. Thus, it is initially unclear whether in a particular case, what is needed or what is achievable is an umbrella/framework convention for the protection of the environment in general; for the protection of the atmospheric environment as a whole, or for addressing only the problems of climate change. There was also the question as to what should come first: framework conventions in these areas, or specific protocols dealing with the control and elimination of particular sources of pollution and environmental degradation or specific issues.

Relying upon the existing examples of efforts since Stockholm, the following may be pointed out concerning the approach to the task of elaborating appropriate legal instruments.[10] In the protection of the marine environment for example, specific regimes were put in place before general regimes by framework conventions were established. This was illustrated by the 1972 London Dumping Convention and the 1973 IMO Convention on Pollution from Ships (both specific), which preceded Part XII of the 1982 United Nations Convention on the Law of the Sea (in general framework convention). But the reverse had also occurred. The most recent example was the 1985 Vienna Convention on the Protection of the Ozone Layer (global framework agreement), negotiated under the auspices of UNEP, which was later followed by its 1987 Montreal Protocol (specific and reduction of CFCs). The same was true in the case of the 1979 ECE Long-Range Transboundary Air Pollution (regional framework agreement) later followed by its 1987 Helsinki protocol (specific control and reduction of SO_2) and the 1989 Sofia Protocol (specific control and reduction of NO_x). It is generally recognized that one approach does not exclude the other, since it is possible to undertake simultaneous drafting of a framework agreement and a technical annex to it, addressing a particular issue, which can lend itself readily to such treatment.

Instruments for the Protection of the Marine Environment

In connection with the question of protection of the marine environment, it is noteworthy that the international community had the political will to conclude, soon after Stockholm, a number of multilateral global instruments dealing with particular sources of marine pollution. The earliest ones were the 1972 London Convention on the Prevention of Marine Pollution by Dumping of Wastes and other Matter (LDC)[11] and the 1973 International Convention for the Prevention of Pollution from Ships (MARPOL).[12]

The 1972 London Dumping Convention (LDC) dealt with the problem of deliberate disposal at sea of wastes or other matter from vessels, aircrafts, platforms or other man-made structures at sea and covered all marine areas except internal waters. Under the Convention, the parties assumed obligation to prohibit the dumping of the type of wastes contained in the "black list" (Annex I) and obligation to seek permits for the dumping of the wastes contained in the "grey list" (Annex II) and permits for the dumping of all other wastes. The technical lists were subject to amendment as appropriate. Guidelines, in the form of nonbinding legal instruments,[13] were later developed by the parties to assist them in implementing the Convention.

The 1973 MARPOL Convention was deliberately restricted to pollution from ships in order to deal with the issues which are within the competence of the International Maritime Organisation (IMO). With the establishment of UNEP after Stockholm, the question of distribution of competence between organizations and bodies within the United Nations system to deal with problems of the environment became necessary. Thus UNEP acquired competence over land-based sources of marine pollution,[14] while IMO dealt exclusively with marine pollution from ships—a fact which was to be emphasized even in the title of the IMO convention in question. MARPOL Convention accordingly addresses pollution releases such as any escape, disposal, spilling, leaking, pumping, emitting, or emptying of pollutants from ships. The convention included several annexes dealing with pollution problems associated with oil; noxious liquid substances in bulk; harmful substances carried by sea in package forms, or in freight containers, portable tanks, or on road and rail tank wagons, sewage, and garbage. Furthermore, MARPOL Convention accepted a number of innovations introduced by the shipping industry such as the load-on-top system and segregated ballast oil tankers. The Convention also provides for obligation of cooperation between the parties concerning certificates, special rules on inspection of ships, enforcement mechanisms, and detection of violations.

It is important to point out here that these two specific regimes for the protection of the marine environment were indeed put in place by States before they could agree on a comprehensive general regime which they later achieved in Part XII of the 1982 United Nations Convention on the Law of the Sea (UNCLOS).[15] As the umbrella framework Convention, UNCLOS addressed six sources of pollution in a series of treaty provisions some of which constituted a codification of international customary rules,[16] while others reflected progressive development of international law.[17] The six sources of pollution dealt with in the generally accepted Part XII of UNCLOS are pollution from: land-based sources; sea-bed activities within national jurisdiction; sea-bed activities beyond national jurisdiction; dumping; vessels; and atmosphere. Thus, in their efforts to develop legally-binding instruments to guide their conduct in the area of protection of the marine environment, States chose to put in place specific regimes first then followed them with a general and comprehensive regime. But as will be shown in connection with similar efforts of States to develop legally-binding instruments for the prevention of air pollution (the protection of the atmospheric environment), quite the opposite occurred.

Apart from the above-mentioned multilateral *global* conventions for the protection of the marine environment and other multilateral instruments negotiated under IMO, dealing with particular issues such as liability for marine pollution damages and compensation as well as other remedial and preventive measures,[18] a number of multilateral conventions were also concluded after Stockholm to deal with environmental issues in specific regions, or in specific areas, through *regional* or *global* instruments.[19] The bulk of the regional conventions were, however, the direct results of UNEP's Regional Seas Programme which encouraged States to conclude regional treaties for dealing with environmental concerns identified by them.[20]

Some of the common features of such regional conventions for the protection of the marine environment may serve as examples of standard treaty provisions for the protection of the marine environment.

Instruments for the Prevention of Air Pollution (Preservation of the Atmospheric Environment)

With respect to the question of protection of the atmospheric environment (prevention of air pollution) the first decade after Stockholm produced only one multilateral regional treaty. This was the Convention on Long-Range Transboundary Air Pollution (LRTAP) concluded in Geneva on 13 November 1979 under the auspices of the Economic Commission for Europe (ECE). LRTAP was aimed primarily at the problem of acid rain and was a general framework convention containing basic obligations for dealing with long-range transboundary air pollution described as "air pollution whose physical origin is situated wholly or in part within the area under jurisdiction of another State and which has adverse effects in the area under national jurisdiction of one State at such distances that it is not generally possible to distinguish the contribution of individual emission sources or groups of sources." The Convention does not, however, apply to pollution affecting the areas beyond national jurisdiction and explicitly excludes provisions dealing with the important question of liability which the conventions for the protection or the marine environment, by contrast, attempted to address to a varying degree as illustrated in this chapter.[21]

But, as the problem of acid rain received added attention, it became one of the three interrelated environmental issues of the second decade after Stockholm mentioned above. The 1979 Long-Range Transboundary Air Pollution, as a regional framework convention, was later supplemented by protocols dealing with control and reduction of emission of specific gases and concrete international actions to combat acid rain.[22] Efforts are accordingly being made to put in place a global framework convention for dealing with LRTP. When the international community, through UNEP, turned its attention to the question of protection of the stratospheric ozone layer, the result was that a general framework convention was negotiated first then followed by a specific protocol reducing emission of specific gases associated with the depletion of the ozone layer.[23] Thus, unlike the experience in the development of legal instruments for protection of the marine environment where, as indicated above, specific regimes preceded the general regime, in the case of protection of the atmosphere, the opposite occurred: the framework conventions preceded the specific protocols.

The success of the LRTP and the ozone layer conventions and their specific protocols has encouraged the international community to strive towards establishing similar legal regimes for the protection of the atmosphere in general or for tackling the problem of climate change in particular. A definite call upon the international community to take concrete steps towards negotiating an umbrella/framework convention for the protection of the atmosphere was made at the June 1988 Toronto Conference on the Changing Atmosphere.[24] The momentum for this exercise was carried to the February 1990 Ottawa Meeting of Experts on Environmental Law and Policy, where the idea of producing a convention on climate change rather than an umbrella convention for the protection of the atmosphere as a whole was vigorously pursued. Following further specific steps taken by both UNEP and WMO, through the work of the International Panel on Climate Change (IPCC), which the two United Nations bodies jointly created in 1988, earnest work on the negotiation of a convention on climate change continued. The conclusion of such an instrument became part of the preparatory work for the Second World Climate Conference in November 1990 and also remained one of the goals for the 1992 United Nations Conference on Environment and Development, as further discussed in Section III below.

From the point of view of lessons for treaty-making techniques, it is important to observe at this juncture that the latter approach (framework conventions first, followed by specific protocols) becomes unavoidable in situations where the international community is being called upon to conclude a multilateral treaty for dealing with a problem with respect to which some States feel reluctant to address questions of detail (specific reduction of pollutants), claiming lack of conclusive scientific evidence or asking for further studies and in-depth assessment of economic and other implications of the treaty being contemplated. Accordingly, the approach may indeed be an evidence of genuine gaps in knowledge, generally recognized, and permitting only the conclusion of a framework convention embodying general principles as the first realistic step to be followed by specific protocols. But the choice of this approach may also be an evidence of lack of political will, on the part of some States, to take concrete actions through binding instruments, because of hidden reasons, while stressing on an apparent gap in knowledge (or controversy over scientific facts for example) as a convenient explanation for their unwillingness to proceed with the negotiation of a multilateral instrument committing them to specific actions.

Instruments for the Protection of Species of Fauna and Flora and Related Issues

With respect to the question of environmental problems addressed through the protection of species of fauna and flora or by the preservation of global or regional natural, and cultural heritage as well as the maintenance of ecological balance and biological diversity, a handful of legal instruments were concluded after Stockholm. Concluded a few months after Stockholm was the November 1972 Convention for the Protection of the World Cultural and Natural Heritage,[25] which was negotiated under the auspices of the United Nations Educational, Scientific and Cultural Organisation (UNESCO). The Convention applied to natural features consisting of physical and biological formations of outstanding universal value from an aesthetic and biological point of view. Then came the 1973 Washington Convention on International Trade in Endangered Species of Wild Fauna and Flora (CITES) which was mainly the work of the International Union for Conservation of Nature and Natural Resources (IUCN). CITES is a protectionist instrument which operates under a system of permits to regulate international trade in wild fauna and flora listed in the three appendices of the Convention. Trade in the species threatened with extinction (Appendix I) is prohibited. Trade in species not yet threatened with extinction but which may soon become so threatened (Appendix II) is exceptionally permitted but strictly limited to the level that would not endanger the survival of the species therein listed. Appendix III provides a mechanism by which a Party may, by domestic legislation, regulate the export of species not listed in Appendix I or Appendix II, and request the other parties to CITES to enforce the domestic legislation in question. The appendices are subject to amendments from time to time. Three other multilateral conventions were later concluded: the 1973 Geneva International Tropical Timber Agreement,[26] the 1979 Convention on the Conservation of Migratory Species of wild Animals,[27] the 1982 World Charter for Nature, adopted by the United Nations General Assembly.[28] As to the regional instruments in this area, the forerunner was the 1968 African Convention on the Conservation of Nature and Natural Resources.[29] Since Stockholm, the following instruments were adopted: the 1976 Convention on Conservation of Nature in the South Pacific;[30] the 1976 Convention on the Protection of the Archaeological, Historical and Artistic Heritage of the American Nations;[31] the 1979 Convention of European Wild Life and Natural Habitats;[32] the 1980 Convention on the Conservation of Antarctic Marine Living Resources;[33] the 1982 Benelux Convention on Natural Resources and Landscape Protection;[34] the 1985 Protocol Concerning Protected Areas and Wild Fauna and Flora in the East African Region,[35] and the 1985 ASEAN Agreement on the Conservation of Natural Resources.[36]

These efforts in the area of protection of species of fauna and flora and for the preservation of natural resources were later supplemented during the second decade after Stockholm with the concern over the preservation of biological diversity. UNEP took the lead in bringing to the attention of the international community the need for a multilateral convention on this topic, having regard also to the work that was being done by the IUCN. Thus the negotiation and conclusion of such an instrument became one of UNEP's urgent activities which coincided with those of the Preparatory Work for the 1992 United Nations Conference on Environment and Development, as further noted in Section III below.

Instruments for the Prevention of Pollution of Rivers and Lakes

A study of an impressive number of international treaties concerning international cooperation on the utilization and management of international rivers, in the period before the Stockholm Conference, disclose that such instruments dealt primarily with the question of allocation of rights and obligations of the parties in respect of their shared natural resources. Very little attention was paid to the environmental consequences of the utilization of international watercourses either for navigation or for non-navigational purposes. However, the riparian States soon became aware of the negative environmental consequences of such uses of the rivers and lakes. They thus began to conclude treaties creating, among others, river basin commissions aimed at studying environmental and other problems and suggesting appropriate preventive and remedial measures.[37]

The efforts to deal comprehensively and exclusively with the problem of pollution of international watercourses from specific sources received impetus after Stockholm. Thus, there was the 1976 Convention for the Protection of the Rhine Against Chemical Pollution,[38] and the 1976 Convention for the Protection of the Rhine from Pollution by Chlorides.[39] The best example of a comprehensive regime is the 1987 Agreement on the Action Plan for the Environmentally Sound Management of the Common Zambezi River system,[40] negotiated under the auspices of UNEP, representing a unique effort to develop and preserve the Zambezi River system. Such a comprehensive effort is being promoted by the Economic Commission for Europe in its "Ecosystem approach to water management," which considers the utilization of the atmosphere, water, soil, and living resources as affecting a single ecosystem which should be protected through balanced international measures aimed at preserving each of the elements of the single ecosystem. This is the approach taken by the International Law Commission of the United Nations which adopted, at first reading, a set of draft articles on the law of the non-navigational uses of international watercourses, as presented in its report of the 46th session of the General Assembly Supp. No. 10 (A/40/10). (See also article on page 66.)

Instruments for the Protection of the Environment from Radiological Emergencies Arising from Peaceful Uses of Nuclear Energy, or from Chemical and Toxic Substances, or from Hazardous Wastes

With respect to the question of notification or assistance in case of nuclear accident or radiological emergencies, there was a mosaic of bilateral agreements concluded between a number of countries during the first decade after Stockholm and before the Chernobyl nuclear accident of 1986. Although some of the bilateral instruments primarily addressed issues of nuclear safety and rules and regulations concerning installation of nuclear plants along the boarders, some of the agreements focused attention on environmental consequences of such nuclear activities.[41] It is evident, therefore, that States had already recognized the need to deal with the threats of transboundary environmental damage arising from accidental radiological emergencies from civilian nuclear activities. These bilateral agreements thus laid a firm foundation for the negotiation of two important multilateral conventions: the 1986 Convention on Early Notification of a Nuclear Accident,[42] and the Convention on Assistance in Case of a Nuclear Accident or Radiological Emergency,[43] which the International Atomic Energy Agency (IAEA) concluded immediately after the Chernobyl nuclear accident of April 26, 1986.

These two conventions which were generally recognized as landmarks in the history of treatymaking,[44] were tailored to address the specific issues among those exposed by the Chernobyl accident with respect to which the IAEA Member States believed international legal instruments were achievable as a matter of urgency. In the notification convention, the Member States of the IAEA singled out the need to establish a treaty obligation to notify a nuclear accident with potential transboundary effects: who to notify, how to notify, and the information to be notified. The emphasis was on the early warning following a nuclear accident that might have transboundary consequences, alerting States likely to be affected and thus enabling them to take some precautionary measures addressing, in that connection, the special needs of the developing countries. In the assistance convention the IAEA also singled out the need to establish a multilateral legal framework for providing prompt emergency assistance: how to request the assistance, how to render it, the modalities for undertaking an assistance mission itself having regard to the applicable bilateral arrangements, the question of equipment, personnel, and also the financial aspects of assistance.

The post-Chernobyl era also witnessed an equally large number of bilateral agreements dealing with some specific details relating to questions of notification and assistance, as envisaged under the two IAEA conventions, and, covering also matters concerning aspects of nuclear safety.[45]

With respect to multilateral instruments addressing the problem of pollution of the environment by chemical or toxic substances, attention is recalled first to the relevant provisions and annexes of the 1972 London Convention for the Prevention of Marine Pollution from Ships and Aircrafts,[46] those contained in the 1972 London Convention for the

Prevention of Marine Pollution by Dumping of Wastes and Other Matters;[47] those found in the 1974 Convention for the Prevention of Marine Pollution from Land-Based Sources as amended in 1986,[48] those covered under the 1985 Ozone Layer Convention on the 1979 Long-Range Transboundary Air Pollution including their relevant protocols,[49] and the two 1976 conventions for the protection of the Rhine from chemical pollution and from pollution by chlorides.[50] Two global conventions were also concluded to deal specifically and comprehensively with environmental pollution from other particularly hazardous substances. One of them was the 1976 Geneva Convention concerning safety in the use of asbestos,[51] negotiated under the auspices of the ILO, and the 1989 Basel Convention on the Control of Transboundary Movements of Hazardous Wastes and their Disposal,[52] negotiated under the auspices of UNEP. The Basel Convention was found unacceptable by the African countries on the grounds that its premise of permitting and simply regulating the transboundary movement of such wastes exposed them to constant peril. The African countries preferred complete prohibition of transboundary movement of hazardous wastes and produced the African Convention on the Control of Transboundary Movement and Disposal of Hazardous Waste, Bamako, 1991.

Instruments Addressing Problems of Interference with the Environment by Military and Related Activities

Apart from the multilateral treaties which, as can be seen above, addressed specific areas of the environment, there had been other efforts to deal with interference with the environment in general. Such efforts produced, for example, the 1977 Convention on the Prohibition of Military or Any Other Hostile Use of Environmental Modification Techniques (ENMOD).[53] It may be further noted that, before Stockholm, several multilateral treaties had been concluded which, although primarily dealing with the problem of nuclear testing in the effort to reduce the nuclear arms race, had clear environmental implications, owing to radioactive pollution associated with the specific activities they were intended to prohibit or control.[54] Specific mention must also be made here of the 1977 Protocol I Additional to the Geneva Conventions of 12 August 1949 and relating to the Protection of Victims of International Armed Conflict (Articles 35(3) and 55), concluded under the auspices of the International Red Cross in its efforts to develop international humanitarian law. Taken together, these legal instruments illustrate the concern and success of the international community to put in place binding legal instruments to guide their conduct in their military and related activities with clear potentials of adversely affecting the environment in general. The assessment of the adequacy of the ENMOD legal regime and of the international humanitarian law regime contained in articles 35(3) and 55 of the above-mentioned Additional Protocol I is the subject of current discussions, as mentioned below.

The foregoing list has been intended to illustrate the areas of the environment and subject matters, with respect to which States have been able to conclude binding legal instruments after Stockholm. It also indicates that international environmental law has largely developed through specific treaties dealing with specific issues arising from human activities at a given period. Thus, there is the need to undertake the elaboration of treaties which deal comprehensively with issues of environment and development so as to generate general principles of international law to guide the conduct of the actors in this field. Such an effort was originally made by the legal experts convened under the above-mentioned World Commission on Environment and Development, the Bruntland Commission. The most recent effort to produce another instrument, dealing comprehensively with issues of environment and development is, however, the Covenant on Environment Conservation and Sustainable Use of Natural Resources, drafted by the Group of Legal Experts convened by the Commission on Environmental Law (CEL) of the World Conservation Union (IUCN). These drafts, prepared by experts in their individual capacities and in a nongovernmental setting, should provide useful bases for the work of governmental experts who may be called upon to consider the question of such a comprehensive environmental treaty. The IUCN draft has already been submitted to the Preparatory Committee of UNCED as document A/CONF.151/AC/WG.III/4/ of 28 August 1991, for information, pending further developments after the Earth Summit. (See also Environmental Policy and Law, (1991), vol. 21, 221.)

The Anatomy of Environmental Treaties: a Survey of Standard Clauses

A survey of environmental treaties concluded since Stockholm indicates that there are certain provisions which have almost become standard. Accordingly, those seeking to identify the gaps in the substantive law of the environment, particularly the treaty-law,[55] may wish to consider the following profile which presents the anatomy of an environmental treaty.

The duty of States to conduct activities under their jurisdiction or control in such a manner as not to cause environmental damage to other States, or to areas beyond their national jurisdiction, as was stated in the nonbinding Principle 21 of the Stockholm Declaration,[56] has now become a well-settled, binding obligation based on treaty law, beyond the customary international law which inspired it.[57] The clearest treaty provision on the scope of this duty is contained in article 193 and article 194, paragraph 2, of the 1982 United Nations Convention on the Law of the Sea, which respectively recognize that "States have the sovereign right to exploit their natural resources pursuant to their environmental policies and in accordance with their duty to protect and preserve the marine environment" and the obligation to "take all measures necessary to ensure that activities under their jurisdiction or control are so conducted as not to cause damage by pollution to other States and their environment, and that pollution arising from incidents or activities under their jurisdiction or control does not spread beyond the areas where they exercise sovereign rights in accordance with (the) Convention."

In all the environmental treaties containing provisions along the lines of the above-mentioned articles of the Law of the Sea Convention, adapted to suit the subject-matter or scope of the particular instrument, some other related provisions are also usually found. The checklist includes provisions on:[58]

1. Recognition of the sovereign rights of States to exploit their natural resources pursuant to their environmental policies and the corresponding duty to protect and preserve the environment.

2. Obligation of States to take measures to prevent, reduce, and control pollution of the environment with the best practicable means at their disposal.

3. Obligation of States to ensure that, in taking the said measures to protect the environment, they do not transfer directly or indirectly, damage or hazards from one area of the environment to another, or transform one type of pollution into another.

4. Obligation of States to ensure that, in taking the said measures to prevent, reduce, and control pollution, they refrain from unjustifiable interference with the activities carried out by other States in the area of environment and development in conformity with the rights and obligations under the instrument in question.

5. Obligation of each State to notify promptly other States in case of activities or events in its territory likely to cause environmental damage to other States.

Another set of provisions found in environmental treaties, also adapted to suit the subject-matter and scope of a particular instrument, establish the general obligation of States parties to cooperate directly or through an appropriate global or regional organization in specific activities relating to the instrument. The checklist in this set includes provisions on obligation of State parties to:

1. Undertake research and systematic observation (monitoring) necessary for the implementation of the instrument in question;
2. Exchange information on scientific, technical socioeconomic, commercial, and legal matters relevant to the particular instrument;
3. Undertake the development and transfer of environmentally sound technology necessary for meeting specific obligations assumed under the treaty in question;
4. Encourage the conclusion of additional international instruments or the harmonisation of domestic policies and legislation consistent with the aims and purposes of the convention in question;
5. Undertake environmental impact assessment of planned activities and prior notice to and consultations with parties likely to be affected by such activities;
6. Provide assistance in case of environmental emergencies, in accordance with the legal framework established for requesting and receiving such assistance and for undertaking contingency plans;
7. Take into account special interests and needs of developing countries;
8. Address the question of liability and compensation in case of environmental harm;
9. Establish procedures and mechanisms for reviewing the effectiveness of the legal regime of the treaty in question, including those relating to its revision or amendment and for speedy entry into force of such revisions or amendments;
10. Establish procedures and mechanisms for settlement or avoidance of environmental disputes;
11. Establish appropriate institutional and financial arrangements for the implementation of the convention in question.

The degree of generality or specificity with which any of the issues in the checklist are treated in each instrument will, no doubt, depend upon the nature of the instrument in question: whether a framework convention or a specific protocol, or/and upon the subject-matter or scope of the instrument.

The anatomy of environmental treaties just outlined is admittedly not exhaustive of all the possible treaty provisions, and was intended to offer illustrations of clauses which treaty makers have succeeded to formulate for the protection of the environment between 1972 after the Stockholm Conference and 1990 when the international community decided to hold another conference in 1992 to address new issues of environment and development.

As discussed in Section III below, the Preparatory Committee of UNCED adopted in its decision 3/25, Annex II, thirty-two criteria for analyzing the effectiveness of the existing multilateral treaties in this field in a search for the gaps in both the substantive or procedural law which need to be filled or areas of weaknesses which need to be strengthened. The forthcoming section is also illustrative of these issues.

Materials and Instruments Other than Treaties as Frameworks for International Responses to Problems of Environment and Development

The experience of UNEP, as the United Nations body with responsibility for coordinating the work of the Organisation in the environment field since Stockholm, and the efforts which the international community has continued to make through the work of the other United Nations system organizations and bodies dealing with problems of environment and development within their competence, provide solid evidence of the usefulness of materials and instruments other than treaties ("soft law") in this field.

The materials and instruments other than treaties, are divided into three broad categories.[59] In one category are the guidelines or principles embodied in non-legally binding instruments recommended to states to take into account when negotiating agreements, enacting legislation, or formulating environmental policies on the issues concerned,[60] or adopted initially as a first step towards negotiation and conclusion of legally binding obligations, thus providing a basis for a treaty regime.[61] In the other category are guidelines or principles prepared by State parties to a particular treaty or convention to provide the necessary specific details for facilitating effective implementation of the treaty or convention in question.[62] In yet another category are the guidelines adopted by certain United Nations system organizations and bodies, or by other international organizations, global or regional, to implement environmental policies established by them.[63]

The specific examples of the materials and instruments other than treaties illustrate the different techniques followed by the international community in responding to problems of environment and development, indicating also issues with respect to which only such non-legally binding instruments could be adopted, and circumstances in which such materials were later developed into legally binding instruments or conventions. As observed elsewhere "such non-binding instruments are easier to adopt than conventions and are immediately applicable by States."[64]

The Road to Rio and Beyond

Towards the Emphasis Upon Integration of Environment and Development Policies

As mentioned briefly above, it is indeed WCED that brought into focus once again the issues concerning environmental survival under the concept of "sustainable development" described in WCED's report as "Development that meets today's needs without compromising the ability of future generations to meet their own needs." Discussions on some aspects of these issues have also been conducted through the debate in the General Assembly of the United Nations (upon the initiative of the Government of Malta) leading to the adoption of resolution 43/53 calling for "Protection of global climate for present and future generations of mankind."[65] Lastly, the issues were taken up in the context of the 1992 United Nations Conference on Environment and Development (UNCED) and its substantive preparatory process which began in March 1990.

On the basis of the identified environment and development issues and the stated objectives to be addressed by UNCED[66] the following have been singled out for specific attention: (1) protection of the atmosphere by combating climate change, depletion of the ozone layer and transboundary air pollution; (2) protection and management of land resources by, *inter alia*, combating deforestation, desertification and drought; (3) conservation of biodiversity; (4) environmentally sound management of biotechnology; (5) protection of the oceans and all kinds of seas, including enclosed and semi-enclosed seas and of coastal areas and the protection, rational use and development of their living resources; and (7) environmentally sound management of wastes, particularly hazardous wastes, environmentally sound management of toxic chemicals, and prevention of illegal traffic in toxic and dangerous products and wastes. The Preparatory Committee of UNCED later established Working Group I to deal with the issues 1–4 above, Working Group II to handle issues 5–7 and Working Group III to deal with legal, institutional, and all related matters.[67]

In the process of elaborating appropriate legal instruments for international responses to these issues, the government representatives taking part in the negotiation of such instruments have been reminded by UNCED of the following: they "should ensure an integrated approach to environment and development questions, taking into account matters such as the patterns of consumption and production, access to and transfers of environmentally sound technology, financial resources requirements, human resources development, economic instruments, attainment of food security in the context of a sustainable development of agriculture, institutional arrangements, the improvement of the living and working environment of the poor in urban slums and rural areas, through eradicating poverty, *inter alia*, by implementing integrated rural and urban development programmes, as well as taking other appropriate measures at all levels necessary to stem the degradation of the environment, protect human health conditions and improve the quality of life."

To make the preparatory work of UNCED more manageable, the Secretary-General of the Conference suggested and the Preparatory Committee accepted that the issues to be addressed by the United Nations Conference could indeed be organized in six principle components as follows:

1 An "Earth Charter," a non-legally binding declaration of basic principles for the conduct of nations and peoples in respect of environment and development;

2 Agreements on specific legal measures, e.g. an umbrella convention on climate change and a convention on biological diversity which would be negotiated prior to the Conference and signed or agreed to at the Conference;

3. An agenda for Action, "Agenda 21," establishing the agreed work programme of the international community for the period beyond 1992 and into the 21st century with respect to the issues to be addressed by the Conference, with priorities, targets, cost estimates, modalities and assignments of responsibilities plus the means to implement this agenda;

4. New additional financial resources;

5. Transfer of technology;
6. Strengthening of institutional capacities and processes of the multilateral system.

With respect to the new problems of global warming (Climate Change), acid rain, depletion of the ozone layer, and the problem of deforestation and its link to the issues of climate change and to the question of conservation of biodiversity, it may be recalled here that the law meets science and economics right off the bat and in a complementary way towards the solving of the identified problems. Thus threshold questions arose which needed to be settled at the outset: whether or not there is indeed a "global warming" and what exactly are its effects; whether or not there is sufficient scientific evidence upon which the international community may take international measures through appropriate international legal instruments to combat global warming, to deal with the problems of acid rain, to prevent further depletion of the stratospheric ozone layer, to preserve biological diversity and to combat desertification through the protection of tropical rain forests, taking into account the interdisciplinary approach mentioned in the introduction.

As a result of the pioneering work of UNEP and WMO and now through the preparatory process of UNCED, these questions have been amply answered as can be seen through the actions already being taken to develop appropriate legal instruments in response to the identified problems. Thus, for example, the Intergovernmental Negotiating Committee established by the General Assembly in resolution 45/212 of December 21, 1990 is proceeding full speed with the drafting of a convention on climate change; UNEP is also continuing its efforts to elaborate a convention on biodiversity. (See also article on page 81.) The Food and Agricultural Organisation (FAO), for its part, has also put in motion the process of elaborating, but with little success, a global convention on the protection of tropical forests. Other instruments are also being negotiated in response to the demands of updating of provisions to address problems of environment and development. For example, there is a Convention on the prevention of industrial disaster being negotiated by the International Labour Organisation (ILO) to be ready by 1993; the Economic Commission for Europe (ECE) is also elaborating a convention on protection and uses of Transboundary watercourses to be completed by 1992; ECE is similarly working on a revision of the 1985 Protocol on SO_2 under the 1979 Long-Range Transboundary Air Pollution Convention; and a revision of the 1958

ECE Motor Vehicle Agreement; The Council of Europe is working on a draft convention on liability for damage resulting from activities dangerous to the environment, to be ready by 1992. Printed in Environmental Policy and Law, (1991), vol. 21, 270. There is also work under way for a revision of the 1974 Baltic Marine Environment Convention; possible merger of the 1972 Oslo and 1974 Paris Conventions on marine pollution in the North Sea, new protocols on offshore mining and on hazardous wastes under the 1976 Mediterranean Convention, and on land-based marine pollution, both under the 1981 West African Convention and the 1983 Caribbean Convention.

While UNCED itself is not the forum for the actual negotiation of the text of these instruments just mentioned, participants in the work of the said United Nations bodies receive suggestions from the preparatory process of UNCED about the kind of issues of environment and development which should be taken into account in drafting the specific legal instruments foreseen. Some of these instruments are thus expected to be completed and ready for formal adoption and signature at UNCED. The decision makers are indeed being told that, on balance, it may be unwise to simply sit by and wait for that day when the scientists will be able to pronounce, with the degree of certainty they demand, their final verdict on, for example, the question of "global warming." That day of complete scientific certainty may not come but if it does, the opportunity to take preventive action may have been lost. Accordingly, negotiations on a climate change convention had to proceed.

It may also be observed that, in the wake of the severe environmental damage caused by Iraq during the Gulf conflict, particularly the oil spills in the Persian Gulf and the burning of Kuwaiti oil wells, Jordan proposed the inclusion of a new item entitled "Exploitation of the environment as a weapon in times of armed conflict and the taking of practical measures to prevent such exploitation" in the agenda of the 46th session of the General Assembly of the United Nations.

During the debate in the Sixth Committee, to which this item was allocated, two main trends emerged. Some States considered the existing body of international law dealing with the protection of the environment in times of armed conflict to be adequate,[68] but stressed the need for greater adherence to and compliance with the existing legal instruments. Other States believed that recent events had demonstrated the inadequacy of the relevant existing rules of international law and supported their strengthening and the elaboration of new rules.

There was a general agreement to await the results of the 26th International Conference of the Red Cross and the Red Crescent which was to be held in late November 1991 and that the Secretary-General of the United Nations would report to the 47th session of the General Assembly on the results of the Conference. However, the Red Cross Conference was suddenly postponed indefinitely. Consequently, the Secretary-General of the United Nations was requested to report to the 47th session of the General Assembly on the activities of the International Red Cross on this issue. The item was accordingly placed on the agenda of the 47th session of the General Assembly.[69]

Several expert groups had also taken up the question of protection of environment in times of armed conflicts, making proposals for encouraging wider acceptance and implementation of the existing treaty-law on this issue and suggesting further development of the law in this area.[70]

Contribution of the Legal Working Group of the Preparatory Committee of UNCED

Working Group III on legal, institutional, and related matters, established by the Preparatory Committee of UNCED, commenced its work at the third session of the Committee when it was given concrete terms of reference.

According to the terms of reference, the Working Group was to:

1. Prepare an annotated list of existing international agreements and international legal instruments in the environmental field, describing their purpose and scope, evaluating their effectiveness, and examining possible areas for the further development of international environmental law, in the light of the need to integrate environment and development, especially taking into account the special needs and concerns of the developing countries;

2. Examine the feasibility of elaborating principles on general rights and obligations of states and regional economic integration organisations, as appropriate, in the field of environment and development, and consider the feasibility of incorporating such principles in an appropriate instrument/charter/statement/declaration, taking due account of the conclusions of all the regional preparatory conferences;

3. Consider the legal and institutional issues referred to it by Working Group I, Working Group II and the plenary of the Preparatory Committee, including the legal and institutional aspects of cross-sectoral issues dealt with by the Preparatory Committee that have been identified in relevant General Assembly resolutions;

4. Review ways and means of strengthening the cooperation and coordination between the United Nations system and other intergovernmental and non-governmental, regional and global institutions in the field of environment and development;

5. Review the role and functioning of the United Nations system in the field of environment and development and make recommendations on ways and means of further enhancing coordination and cooperation on environment and development issues in the United Nations system;

6. Examine and consider strengthening institutional arrangements required for the effective implementation of the Conclusions of the United Nations Conference on Environment and Development in the United Nations system.[71]

The contribution of Working Group III of the Preparatory Committee of UNCED is the main subject of analysis in this section, aimed at indicating the efforts of the international community to encourage the development of appropriate legal instruments for responding to problems of environment and development. It is important to describe here at some length, the contributions of Working Group III, in order to provide a concise legislative history of the final legal instruments which are to emerge from the Earth Summit.

The first order of business for Working Group III was, therefore, the preparation of a list of existing international agreements and international legal instruments to be evaluated and the criteria for undertaking such evaluation. A list of 100 instruments was prepared and became the basis of the work of Working Group III.[72] The 100 instruments, some of which have been the subject of analysis in the section of Section II above, dealing with the anatomy of environmental treaties, include treaties concluded before 1972 Stockholm Conference.

The Working Group then adopted 32 specific criteria for evaluating the effectiveness of instruments in terms of six broad considerations, namely: (1) objectives and achievements, (2) participation in the instruments in question, (3) implementation of the instrument, (4) information requested under the instruments, (5) operation, review, and adjustment of the instruments, and (6) codification programming contained in them. Given the importance of the useful exercise of evaluating the effectiveness of the existing legal instrument in the field of environment, in order to identify the gaps in both the substantive and procedural law, the thirty-two criteria are outlined below:[73]

Objectives and Achievement

1. What are the basic objectives formulated in the international agreements and instruments evaluated, and how do these objectives relate to the effective integration of environment and development?
2. In the case of regional agreements and instruments, what is their actual and potential bearing on global environmental protection and sustainable development?
3. Do these agreements or instruments take into account the special circumstances of developing countries?
4. To what extent have the basic objectives (environmental/developmental) formulated in international agreement and instruments been met, and how is goal achievement measured?

Participation

5. Is membership limited or open-ended?
6. Are reservations possible, and to what extent have they been used?
7. What is the current geographical distribution of membership in existing environmental agreements and instruments, especially as regards developing countries?
9. Which incentives (e.g. financial, trade, technology benefits) are available to encourage participation and facilitate implementation by developing countries?
10. Which measures have been taken to promote and support the effective participation of developing countries in the negotiation and operation of international agreements or instruments, including technical and financial assistance and other available mechanisms for this purpose?
11. Which factors influenced the participation, especially of developing countries, in the agreement or instrument? For example:
    (a) Financial resources required and available for participation in the agreement or instrument;
    (b) Technical assistance required and available for participation in the agreement or instrument;
    (c) Scientific assistance required and available for participation in the agreement or instrument.

(d) Information on the (operation of the) agreement or instrument to Governments, parliaments, press, NGOs, industries and the general public;

(e) Role of parliaments, press, NGOs, industries and public opinion in general;

(f) Availability of reservations.

Implementation

12. To what extent has the implementation of agreements or instruments been constrained or accelerated by provisions regarding their entry into force?

13. What are the commitments imposed on parties by these agreements and instruments, and how is compliance by parties with their commitments monitored and measured?

14. How do parties report on their performance in implementing agreements and instruments, and to what extent have they been met by the parties?

15. Which are the specific requirements (if any) of data supply and data disclosure, and to what extent have they been met by the parties?

16. Which possibilities exist to promote compliance and to follow up on non-compliance, and to what extent have they been used?

17. Which mechanisms are available to deal with disputes over implementation and to what extent have they been used?

18. Which factors influenced the implementation? For example,

(a) Financial resources required and available for implementation of the agreement or instrument;

(b) Technical assistance required and available for implementation of the agreement or instrument;

(c) Scientific assistance required and available for implementation of the agreement or instrument;

(d) Information on the (operation of the) agreement or instrument to Governments, parliaments, press, NGOs, industries and the general public;

(e) Role of parliaments, press, NGOs, industries and public opinion in general;

(f) International supervisory or implementing bodies;

(g) Obligations to report on compliance and/or to supply and disclose data;

(h) Non-compliance procedures and procedures for settlement of disputes (including fact-finding procedures).

Information

19. In which form and in which languages are the texts of existing agreements and instruments published and disseminated?
20. How is current information on the operation and implementation of international agreements and instruments made available to Governments, to the industries concerned and to the general public?
21. What additional materials are available to provide guidance for the implementation of international agreements and instruments at the national level?
22. To what extent is the above information used in international and national training and education programmers?

Operation, Review and Adjustment

23. Which are the institutional arrangements for international administration of existing agreements and instruments?
24. What are the annual (1990) costs of international administration (secretariat, meetings, programmes) of agreements and instruments, and how are they financed?
25. Which are the main benefits and the main cost elements of national participation in existing agreements and instruments, and which possibilities exist to reduce participation cost for developing countries?
26. Which mechanisms are available to ensure that scientific knowledge and advice is taken into account in policy-making decisions under these agreements and instruments?
27. How do these arrangements and mechanisms ensure the effective participation of (a) national authorities, especially from developing countries; and (b) non-governmental participants, including the industries concerned and the scientific community?
28. Which mechanisms are available to ensure periodic review and adjustment of international agreements and instruments in order to meet new requirements, and to what extent have they been used?

Codification Programming

29. Which new drafts, or draft revisions of existing agreements and instruments, in the environmental field are currently under preparation or negotiation?

30. To what extent and through which mechanisms is drafting coordinated with related work regarding other agreements and instruments?
31. Which are the remaining gaps that need to be covered by legal provisions?
32. To what extent are mechanisms other than formal agreements or instruments contributing to the development of international law in the field of the environment?

On the basis of the above criteria for evaluating the effectiveness of the existing agreements in the environmental field, the Secretariat of UNCED prepared a survey of the 100 instruments which were evaluated and included suggestions for follow-up actions.[74] The assessment of the agreements contained in the survey, confirmed, *inter alia*, what has been underscored here earlier, about the piecemeal approach to environmental treaty making and the need to integrate more fully development dimensions into environmental policies in response to the 1987 report of the World Commission on Environment and Development recalling the concept of "sustainable development," and taking into account the interest and concern of the developing countries. The verdict was that most of the existing agreements have too generalized objectives, usually buried in the preambles. Agreements should have more precisely stated objectives; avoid excessive use of reservation clauses which affect the level of participation; contain provisions encouraging speedy entry-into-force to allow for implementation; establish more flexible procedures for settlement of disputes; require the circulation of information regarding implementation; include more expeditious procedures for amendments; contain provisions encouraging further development of the law in the subject matter covered by the instrument through additional protocols; provide for mechanisms for monitoring compliance and for periodic review of the treaty regime relying upon, where appropriate, streamlined, harmonized, or combined administrative or supporting services and institutions; and improve upon the negotiating process of the instruments.

Apart from its assessment of the existing multilateral treaties in the field of environment, Working Group III also undertook discussions on the institutional aspects of such treaties aimed at strengthening the multilateral system for integration of environment and development policies. It received certain proposals in that regard.[75] Whether the solution was to be found in re-establishment of a completely new international institution, in the strengthening of an existing institution such as UNEP or in the maintenance of an existing process such as UNCED, remained a troublesome issue. On the basis of a preliminary discussion in the Working Group III of the Committee, the following eight points were recommended for consideration of this issue towards an appropriate solution.[76]

Some reform of United Nations institutions in the field of environment and development is needed, taking into account general efforts for restructuring and revitalization of the United Nations in the context of General Assembly resolution 45/264.

Working Group III must take into account decisions with institutional implications originating from Working Groups I and II and the Plenary.

Proliferation of institutions at the global level must be avoided.

There is a need to work out mechanisms to promote coordination, both at the intergovernmental level and at the level of the Secretariat and United Nations specialized agencies and programs involved with environment of development.

Existing international institutions at the global and regional levels in the field of environment and development, including UNEP and UNDP, should be adapted to changed circumstances in order to support sustainable development. There was consensus that UNEP must be strengthened.

Among the goals of institutional reform at the global and regional levels should be an enhancement of the capacity of institutions at the national level, especially in developing countries, to ensure the full integration of environment and development.

Institutions and organizations outside the United Nations system, including the nongovernmental sector, have an important role in this process.

The Working Group, at the fourth session of the Preparatory Committee, will have to consider the need for institutional arrangements, both at the intergovernmental and secretariat levels for the implementation and continuous review of Agenda 21.

The analysis or the views of participants at the UNCED Preparatory Committee commenting on some of the above specific points indicate,[77] as noted above, that the whole question was destined to remain a controversial one.

In addition to its work on institutional aspects, the Legal Working Group was also charged with the duty to prepare the draft *Earth*

Charter or the Rio Declaration on Environment and Development, which is one of the important components of "Agenda 21," as mentioned earlier. Specific suggestions for inclusion in the Earth Charter were submitted by a number of States and have been consolidated into one document dealing with principles on general rights and obligations. On the basis of preliminary discussions in Working Group III of the Preparatory Committee, the discussion on this issue was to proceed bearing in mind the following five points:[78]

1. The charter or declaration containing the principles should be short and concise;
2. The text should be closely integrated with Agenda 21;
3. The text should be appealing and inspiring, with a view to enhancing public awareness of environment and development issues;
4. Its language and style, while ensuring legal precision of commitments, should be easily understood by the general public;
5. The charter or declaration should, in a forward-looking manner, build on existing principles contained in documents such as the 1972 Declaration of the United Nations Conference on the Human Environment.

It was also agreed that the proposals for specific provisions concerning Principles on General Rights and Obligations would address the following issues:[79] Principle 1, Integration of environment and development; Principle 2, Common but differentiated responsibility; Principle 3, Individual and group rights; Principle 4, Responsibility to present and future generations; Principal 5, Sovereignty and responsibility to others; Principle 6, Precautionary principle and prior assessment; Principle 7, Cooperation; Principle 8, Special needs of developing countries; Principle 9, Environment and world trade; Principle 10, Peace and security; Principle 11, Production and consumption patterns; Principle 12, Information and education; Principle 13, Cost internalisation; Principle 14, Liability for damage and dispute settlement; Principle 15, Public participation and democracy; Principle 16, Poverty; Principle 17, Resources transfer.

Working Group III also examined possible areas for further development of international environmental law in accordance with the now well-established standard of review, namely the need to integrate environment and development, especially taking into account the needs and concerns of developing countries. Certain objectives were identified in the Survey,[80] along the lines described and expanded below.

Future Objectives and Challenges

Coming back to the objectives of the seminar, and taking into account the evidence presented here concerning the approaches to environmental lawmaking in light of the lessons learned since Stockholm 1972, while looking forward to Rio de Janeiro in 1992 and beyond, the following should be borne in mind, as recognized in UNCED studies.[81]

The overall present and future objective of UNCED is to promote the integration of environment and development policies through effective international agreements and instruments[82] especially taking into account the needs and concerns of the developing countries. To that end, effort must be made in the legal field to:

1. Set priorities for future lawmaking at the appropriate level, incorporating environmental and development concerns in a balanced manner;

2. Promote and support, in more concrete ways, the effective participation of developing countries in the negotiation and implementation of international agreements or instruments. Such support should include assured financial assistant to cover the necessary travel expenses to meetings and access to the necessary information and scientific-technical expertise on preferential terms.

3. Ensure effective implementation and compliance, regular assessment and timely review and adjustment of agreements or instruments by the Parties concerned. In addition, to monitor and review domestic legal instruments giving effect to international agreements on environment and development, with a view to promoting compliance and harmonization;

4. Improve on the substantive scope of international environmental agreements by including more effective provisions on, *inter alia*, environmental emergencies preparedness and contingency plans for assistance in case of such emergencies; environmental impact assessment by planned projects with procedures for allowing effective participation of individual citizens and nongovernmental organizations; more concrete rules on liability and compensation; and equal access of governments to local judicial or administrative procedures;

5. Improve the effectiveness of institutions, mechanisms, and procedures for administration of international environmental agreements and instruments;

6. Assist developing countries and economies in transition in their national efforts at modernizing and strengthening the legal and regulatory framework of governance for sustainable development, having regard to local social values and infrastructures;

7. Disseminate information on effective legal and regulatory innovations in the field of environment and development, including noncoercive instruments and compliance incentives, with a view to encouraging their wider use and adaptation at the national and local level;

8. Promote and resolve environmental disputes including potential conflicts between environment and development/trade agreements or instruments, combining options for resort to informal, non-compulsory procedures which provide for adjudication by *ad hoc* arbitral tribunals or judicial settlement by pre-constituted courts such as the International Court of Justice. Two proposals were submitted in this connection: one seeking to establish a comprehensive instrument for the settlement of all types of environmental disputes[83] while the other deals with the establishment of an independent enquiry commission.[84] They will form the basis of further discussions on this important issue. Whether the establishment of a comprehensive system reflected in the above pentagonal countries' proposals would be the preferred approach is still one of the issues to be settled. Certain governments have expressed doubts about such a system.

The *Earth Summit* in Rio will, as emphasised by the Secretary-General of the Conference,[85] be about environment and development. But there is a primary emphasis on development and economic change. For it is through the development process that we carry out activities with impact upon the environment. It is also through fundamental changes in our economic behavior, in lifestyles and in management or development processes that we can effect the positive synthesis between the environment and development that will produce life that is sustainable, both in economic and environmental things. The challenge is that we have to make the necessary efforts towards the transit on to sustainable development.

The transition to sustainability, he further observed, requires much more effective use of resources and accountability for the environmental as well as economic impacts of such use. This must depend primarily on the provision of the necessary incentives to change rather than over reliance on regulating measures. The challenge is that the system of incentives and penalties through which Governments create conditions that motivate our economic life must be re-examined and re-oriented to provide the necessary incentives for transition to sustainability in both our industrial and individual behavior.

What is called for at Rio, as stated by the Secretary-General of the Conference, is nothing less than "eco-industrial revolution, namely, one that will not only preserve and extend the benefits created by the industrial revolution, but also create a whole new generation of economic opportunity and redress the gross imbalance between the rich and the poor. The challenge is how to redress concretely the imbalances which are incompatible with sustainable development as they are with justice and equity.

Admittedly, traditional patterns of technical assistance which often deepen dependence on foreign experts are simply not adequate. What is needed, the challenge for us to meet, is a sustainable commitment to building indigenous human and institutional capacity. Surely, the key to self-reliance is the fostering of a pool of indigenous talents that can adapt and innovate in a world where knowledge is the primary basis of competitiveness.

As we strive towards putting into place appropriate legal frameworks, for international responses to problems of environment and development, we have to keep in mind the following: the concept of national sovereignty has been an immutable and a most sacred principle of international law. There is no need for wholesale retreat from the principle. The present challenge is for us to recognize that, in many fields, particularly in the environmental field, it is simply not feasible for sovereignty to be exercised unilaterally by individual States, however powerful. Global environmental and economic security requires global cooperation which implies the willingness of States to give up, in appropriate legal instruments, a little of their sovereignty, in the interest of the international community-at-large.

Owing to the increased publicity, environment and development issues are moving to grass roots in a growing number of countries. There is much proliferation of new citizens groups and voluntary organizations which are becoming more important agents of action as well as sources of political pressure. Some of them need, however, to be scrutinized in order to ascertain if they do not have hidden or separate agenda from the Rio mainstream. But, on the whole, most of the citizens' groups simply insist on opportunities for greater participation in the decisions which affect them and for more effective accountability of the decisions and actions by the Governments.

On the pervasive concept of sustainable development the following need to be underscored: sustainable development cannot be imposed by external pressure, it must be noted in the culture, the values, the interests, and the priorities of the people concerned. Developing countries cannot be denied their right to grow, nor to choose their own pathways to growth. Nor should that right be constrained by new conditions on financial flows or trade imposed in the name of environment. The challenge is how to tap the necessary support of the international community and reverse the outflow of resources that has stifled the economic growth of developing countries.

It has been acknowledged in the UNCED documents addressing the question of integration of environment and development in decision making,[86] that laws and regulations are among the most important instruments to transform environment and development policies into action—not only through "command and control" methods but also as a normative framework for economic planning and market instruments. Yet although the volume of legal texts in this field is steadily increasing, much of the lawmaking has been *ad hoc* and piecemeal, or has not been endowed with the necessary institutional machinery and authority for enforcement and timely adjustment. The legal process, which ought to facilitate progress towards sustainable patterns of development, is often ill-adapted to the scale and pace of economic and social change—and to the degree of public participation and transparency of decision-making—required for this purpose.[87]

The UNCED document also notes that, while there is continuous need for law reform in all countries, developing countries have been particularly affected by the shortcomings of laws and regulations often dating back to the colonial period. In order to ensure timely adjustment, technical support is needed both for the drafting of new or revised legal instruments and for their practical implementation, including the appropriate institutions and remedies. Technical cooperation requirements in this field include legal information, advisory services and specialized training and institutional capacity-building.

The document further emphasizes that the enactment and enforcement of laws and regulations (at a national/state/provincial or local/municipal level) is also essential for the implementation of most international agreements in the field of environment and development, as illustrated by the frequent treaty obligation to report on legislative measures. The survey of existing agreements undertaken in the context of UNCED preparations has indicated serious problems of compliance in this respect, and the need for improved monitoring and related technical assistance.

Conclusion: Focus upon Financial Resources as a Fundamental Issue

From the ongoing discussion within the Preparatory Committee for UNCED, in Working Groups I and II, and as demonstrated by the efforts of Working Group III, conclusion is inescapable that a lot more work is still to be done towards the fulfillment of the objectives such as outlined in this section. Thus, what seems readily achievable at the Rio Summit in June, is the formal acceptance of specific commitments by the governments, on the basis of the results achieved by the three working groups, to continue pursuing, within an established period of time after Rio, the further elaboration of appropriate international legal frameworks for concrete actions for implementing "Agenda 21."

Lurking behind all these is the need for a general understanding of the fact that developed and developing countries will have to reach agreement on how to distribute responsibilities for global environmental damage already caused and traced to activities in the industrial countries and those traced to the activities in the developing countries.

There also needs to be an understanding on the part of the countries of the North that they will not divert the funds already earmarked for developments in the South and use such funds for dealing with newly identified environmental problems. Additional resources must thus be made available for dealing with environmental issues of "Agenda 21" as adopted at the Earth Summit in Rio. In this connection, it is necessary to keep in mind the existing *Global Environment Facility* (GEF) which has been billed as an experiment offering a way to pursue development while meeting global environmental concerns. To encourage wider dissemination of the facts about GEF and the evaluation of its role beyond the Earth Summit, its concise description, prepared by the World Bank, United Nations Development Programme, and United Nations Environment Programme, merits inclusion here:

The Global Environment Facility is a U.S. $1 billion-plus program providing grants to developing countries to help them carry out programs to relieve pressures on global ecosystems. The GEF is jointly managed by the World Bank, the United Nations Development Programme (UNDP) and the United Nations Environment Programme, and is funded by both industrialized and developing countries. With experience gained since its founding in November 1990, the facility is poised to play a role in helping regions and nations of the world reach agreements at the United Nations Conference on Environment and Development in June of 1992.

Working closely with each developing country, the GEF acts in four main areas: to reduce global warming; to preserve biological diversity; to protect international waters; and to prevent further depletion of the ozone layer. These activities, however, must be consistent with a country's national development priorities; it is the responsibility of all three managing agencies to ensure that the facility enhances the potential for long-term sustainable development. Specialized agencies and nongovernmental organizations (NGOs) help to assess impact on local populations, advise on project design and implement projects.

To qualify for GEF financial support, both the beneficiary country and the project itself must meet strict criteria. Countries must have per capita gross domestic product (GDP) of U.S. $4,000 or less. The project must protect the global environment in a cost-effective, technologically sound way while respecting the interests of the country's people. While most of the GEF funding goes for investment projects, other activities include technical assistance, technology transfer, and training. Funds support activities which, while they benefit the environment of the world as a whole, would not otherwise be economically viable for that country. The funds are not meant to substitute for existing program or project support, but to provide additional resources. Money has been earmarked for 53 specific projects totaling $470 million so far. Projects currently underway include a $4.8 million project in cooperation with the World Meteorological Organization to monitor greenhouse and ozone-depleting gases by setting up monitoring stations in developing countries. Projects nearing approval include a $10 million East African regional project to support the protection of biodiversity in the area and a biomass gasification program for Brazil with an initial planning and design phase of $7 million, and calling for private sector participation.

In addition to big projects costing millions of dollars, the GEF has created a small-grants program. This provides support for innovative small-scale activities by community groups, NGOs and NGO networks in amounts up to $50,000 each for community and national projects and $250,000 each for subregional, regional, or interregional projects. It is funded initially at $5 million and is managed by UNDP.

Each of the GEF partners—the World Bank, UNDP, and UNEP—has a distinct role to play. The World Bank administers the trust fund and is responsible for investment operations. It undertakes identification, appraisal, and supervision of investment projects with the participation of UNDP and UNEP.

UNEP provides scientific and technological guidance in identifying and selecting projects, and coordinates research and data collection. It convenes a Scientific and Technical Advisory Panel of both industrialized and developing-country experts to provide criteria and priorities for GEF funding.

UNDP coordinates and manages the financing and execution of technical assistance and pre-investment activities. Through its 112 field offices, UNDP plays a central role in identifying projects, communicating with recipient governments and coordinating with donors at the country level. Both UNEP and UNDP help governments to make GEF programs fit with other environment and development activities in beneficiary countries.

The availability of the necessary financial resources for the implementation of Agenda 21 on the basis of legal frameworks for addressing problems of environment and development, through appropriate international or national institutions, remains one of the central issues for which an affective solution must be found. The GEF experiment must therefore be critically evaluated, its shortcomings identified and possibly remedied.

Notes

1. See UN Doc. A/CONF.48/14/Rev.1. L. Sohn, "The Stockholm Declaration on the Human Environment," *Harvard International Law Journal*, vol. 14 no. 3, 1973.
2. See General Assembly resolution 2997 (XXVII) of December 15, 1972.
3. For a synopsis of UNEP's legal instruments, see *Environmental Law in UNEP* (UNEP Environmental Law No. 1, 1991). See also "International Conventions and Protocols in the Field of the Environment," U.N. Doc. A/C.2/46/3.
4. Observation by Maurice F. Strong, Secretary-General, United Nations Conference on Environment and Development, see "From Stockholm to Rio: A Journey Down a Generation," *An Earth Summit Publication: Number one* 1991, 2.
5. Established pursuant to U.N. General Assembly resolution 38/161 of 19 December 1983, WCED was chaired by Gro Harlem Brundtland (then Prime Minister of Norway). The Commission submitted its report to the General Assembly, doc. A/42/427, through the Governing Council of

UNEP. The report was later published under the title: *Our Common Future* (Oxford University Press, 1987).

6. Strong, supra note 4 at 6.

7. Observation by Mustafa K. Tolba, Executive Director, United Nations Environment Programme, made at the Symposium on Developing Countries and International Environmental Law, Beijing, August 12, 1991. See, e.g., U.N. Doc. A/C.6/46/4.

8. See, e.g., the Proposed Legal Principles for Environmental Protection and Sustainable Development, prepared by the group of Legal Experts convened by the World Commission on Environment and Development (WCED) (the Brundtland Commission) in *Our Common Future*, Annex I (1987); draft by the group of Legal Experts on Long-distance Transboundary Air Pollution convened by the International Environment Institute in Aix-les-Bains, 1988 (in the present author's file); draft of the Working Group of Legal Experts on Environmental Law convened by the Commission on Environmental Law and of the International Union for Conservation of Nature and Natural Resources (IUCN, Bonn, April 29, 1991 (in the present author's file). For the texts of these instruments see A.O. Adede, *A Digest of Materials and Instruments for International Responses to Problems of Environment and Development.* (Draft publication of the International Environment Institute (IEI), in progress.)

9. See, e.g., the results of the Toronto meeting, 27–30 June 1988, *The Changing Atmosphere: Implications for Global Security*, infra note 24, and the Ottawa Meeting of Legal and Policy Experts, February 20–22, 1990, U.N. Doc. A/C.2/44/2.

10. For a survey of environmental treaties for the purposes of UNCED, see doc. A/CONF.151/PC/103 and Add. 1 described further paras 51–56 infra.

11. LDC was adopted on December 29, 1972 at a diplomatic conference convened and hosted by the Government of the United Kingdom of Great Britain and Northern Ireland. See 11 *International Legal Materials* (hereinafter, ILM), 1294. Prior to the Stockholm Conference there was the 1972 Convention for the Protection of Marine Pollution by Dumping from Ships and Aircrafts, 11 *ILM*, 262.

12. MARPOL was adopted on November 2, 1973 at a diplomatic conference convened by the International Maritime Organisation. See 12 *ILM*, 1319.

13. See London Guidelines for the Exchange of Information on Chemicals in International Trade. UNEP Publication, Environment Law Guidelines and Principles.

14. See, e.g., the 1974 Convention on the Prevention of Marine Pollution from Land-Based Sources, 13 *ILM*, 352 (1974). The implementation of this convention was to be facilitated by the Montreal Guidelines for the Protection of the Marine Environment from Land-Based-Sources, no. 7 of UNEP's publication on Environmental Law Guidelines and Principles.

15. Opened for signature at Montego Bay, Jamaica, December 10, 1982, not yet in force, see *The Law of the Sea*, UN pub. Sales No. E 83.V.5 (1983).
16. See, e.g., articles 192, 193, and 197 of the Convention.
17. See, e.g., articles 217–220 of the Convention.
18. See, e.g., 1973 "Protocol Relating to Intervention on the High Seas in Case of Pollution by Substances Other than Oil," *ILM* Vol.; 1971 International Convention on the Establishment of an International Fund for Compensation for Oil Pollution Damage, *ILM* Vol.; 1974 International Convention for the Safety of Life at Sea, *ILM* Vol.; and 1976 Protocol to the International Convention on Civil Liability for Oil Pollution Damage, *ILM* Vol.
19. See, e.g., 1973 Convention on Fishing and Conservation of the Living Resources in the Baltic Sea and Belts, 12 *ILM* 1972 (1973); 1974 Nordic Environmental Protection Conventions 11; 1980 Convention on the Conservation of Antarctic Marine Living Resources, 19 *ILM* 841 (1980); 1988 Convention on the Regulation of Antarctic Mineral Resources Activities, 27 *ILM* (1988).
20. See, e.g., 1976 Barcelona Convention for the Protection of the Mediterranean Sea Against Pollution, 15 *ILM* 240 (1976); 1976 Barcelona Protocol Concerning Co-operation in Combating Pollution of the Mediterranean Sea by Oil and Other Harmful Substances in case of Emergency 11; 1978 Kuwait Regional Convention for Co-operation on the Protection of the Marine Environment, 17 *ILM* 511 (1978); 1981 Abidjan Convention for Co-operation in the Protection and Development of the Marine and Coastal Environment of the West and Central African Region, 20 *ILM* 746 (1981); 1981 Lima Convention for the Protection of the Marine Environment and Coastal Areas of the South East Pacific, UNEP pub. (1984); 1982 Jeddah Regional Convention for the Conservation of the Regional Environment of the Sea and the Gulf of Aden, UNEP Pub. (1984); 1983 Cartagena Convention for the Protection and Development of the Marine Environment of Wider Caribbean Region, 20 *ILM* 227 (1983); 1985 Nairobi Convention for the Protection, Management and Development of the Marine and Coastal Environment of the Eastern African Region, UNEP Pub. (1986); and 1986 Noumea Convention for the Protection of Natural Resources and Environment of the South Pacific Region, 26 *ILM* 30 (1987).
21. See paragraphs 22–23 below.
22. See the 1985 Protocol to the 1979 Convention on Long-Range Transboundary Air Pollution on the Reduction of Sulphur Emissions or their Transboundary Fluxes by at least 30 percent. Helsinki, July 8, 1985, and the 1988 Sofia Protocol on the Control of Emissions of Nitrogen Oxides or their Transboundary Fluxes.
23. See the 1985 Vienna Convention for the Protection of Ozone Layer, 26 *ILM* 1516 (1987) and the 1987 Montreal Protocol on the Reduction of the Chlorofluorocarbons (CFCs), 26 *ILM* 1550 (1987).

24. The Conference was hosted by the Government of Canada and was co-sponsored by United Nations Environment Programme (UNEP) and World Meteorological Organization (WMO). More than 300 scientists and policy makers from 48 countries, United Nations and related international organizations and relevant nongovernmental organizations participated in the sessions of the Conference. See *The Changing Atmosphere: Implications for Global Security—Conference Statement*, July 5, 1988 version (hereinafter referred to as *Conference Statement*). The Conference urged the international community to "initiate the development of a comprehensive global convention as a framework for protocols on the protection of the atmosphere. The convention should emphasize such key elements as the free international exchange of information and support of research and monitoring, and should provide a framework for specific protocols for addressing particular issues, taking into account existing international law." This was vigorously pursued at the international workshop on law and policy held in Ottawa early in 1989, and at the Second World Climate Conference, Geneva, June 1990, with a view to having the principles and components of such a convention ready for consideration at the United Nations Conference on Environment and Development in 1992.

25. See 11 *ILM* 1358 (1972). Just prior to this before Stockholm, was the 1971 Ramsar Convention on Wetlands of International Importance Especially as Waterfront Habitat, 11 *ILM*, (1976).

26. See 673 *UNTS* 63.

27. See 19 *ILM* 11 (1979).

28. See GA/RES/37/7 of October 28, 1982.

29. 1001 *UNRA*, 4.

30. See *International Protection of the Environment*, 10359.

31. 56 UKT5. Cmnd 8738.

32. 15 *ILM* 736 (1971).

33. 19 *ILM* 837 (1980).

34. See *Environmental Law Multilateral Agreements* (W.E. Burhenne Ed. 1982), 43.

35. See *New Directions in the Law of the Sea, New Series* (K.R. Simmonds, ed. 1986).

36. Ibid.

37. For a collection of earlier treaties relating to the utilization of international watercourses, see *United Nations Legislative Series*, ST/LEG/SER.H/12.

38. 16 *ILM* 242 (1977).

39. 16 *ILM* 265 (1979).

40. 540 UNTS 587.

41. Eighty-five bilateral treaties on aspects of nuclear activities in the pre-Chernobyl era existed. See generally, "Bilateral, Regional, and Multilateral

Agreements Relating to Co-operation in the Field of Nuclear Safety," IAEA Pub. Leg. Ser. No. 15 (1990).

42. See IAEA doc. INFCIRC/335; 25 *ILM* 1369 (1986) opened for signature September 26, 1986.

43. See IAEA doc. INFCIRC/336; ibid., opened for signature September 26, 1986.

44. The two conventions were negotiated and concluded simultaneously in a single forum, sitting in one session lasting only four weeks. Having been concluded in September 1986, three months following the Chernobyl accident, both conventions entered into force in record time: Notification Convention, one month from the date of signature and Assistance Convention six months from the date of signature. For a legislative history of the conventions, see A.O. Adede, *The IAEA Notification and Assistance Conventions in Case of a Nuclear Accident* (1987).

45. Sixty-two bilateral treaties addressing aspects of civilian nuclear activities in the post-Chernobyl era have been recorded. See IAEA Pub. Leg. Ser. n. 15 supra note 31.

46. 11 *ILM* 262 (1972).

47. 11 *ILM* 1294 (1972).

48. 13 *ILM* 32 (1974).

49. Supra note 12.

50. Supra notes 28 and 29.

51. 16 *ILM* 88 (1977).

52. 28 *ILM* 649 (1977).

53. See 16 *ILM* 85 (1977).

54. Such treaties include the 1963 Treaty Banning Nuclear Weapons Tests in the Atmosphere, in Outer Space and Under Water, 880 UNTS, 385; 1967 Treaty on Principles Governing the Activities of States in the Exploration and Use of Outer Space Including the Moon and the Celestial Bodies, 610 UNTS, 205; 1971 Treaty on the Prohibition of the Emplacement of Nuclear Weapons and Other Weapons of Mass Destruction in the Sea-Bed and the Ocean Floor, 13 UKTS.

55. See in this connection the background papers prepared for consideration of Working Group III of UNCED, UN Doc. A/CONF.151/PC/36; ACONF.151/PC/77 to 80; A/CONF.151/PC/WG.III.L.1. to 7.

56. Principle 21 of the Stockholm Declaration provides that "States have, in accordance with the Charter of the United Nations and the principles of international law, the sovereign right to exploit their own resources pursuant to their own environmental policies, and the responsibility to ensure that activities within their jurisdiction or control do not cause damage to the environment of other States or of areas beyond the limits or national jurisdiction."

57. It may be recalled that the dictum of the International Court of Justice in the *Corfu Channel* case to the effect that it is "every State's obligation not

to allow knowingly its territory to be used for acts contrary to the rights of other States (ICJ Reports, 1949, 4) has been cited as a case in point, along with classical *Trail Smelter* arbitration (3 UNRAA, 1905); *Island of Palmas* case (2 ibid., 281) and *Lac Lanoux "Whitman Digest of International Law"* (262–65). These series of cases have often been cited as standing for the proposition that States have a duty under customary law not to cause transboundary environmental damage and that the violation of this duty entails international responsibility of States under international law.

58. For detailed analysis of specific examples of the treaty provisions outlined in this connection, see *A Digest of Materials and Instruments for International Responses to Problems of Environmental Development 1972–1992.* A.O. Adede (Draft Publication of the International Environment Institute, IEI, Institut de l'Environment International, in progress by the author, 15–72.

59. For a detailed analysis of salient provisions of such nonlegally binding instruments, addressing certain issues of environment and development, and presenting relevant texts, see The Digest, op. cit., note 58, 75–127.

60. See, e.g., Principles of Conduct in the Field of the Environment for the Guidance of States in the Conservation and Harmonious Utilisation of Natural Resources Shared by Two or More States, Decision of the Governing Council of UNEP of May 19, 1978, reproduced in UNEP's Environmental law Guidelines and Principles, Series No. 2 (hereinafter cited as UNEP's Environmental Law Series); Conclusions of the Study of Legal Aspects Concerning the Environment Related to Offshore Mining and Drilling within the limits of National Jurisdiction, Decision 10/14/VI of the Governing Council of UNEP of May 31, 1982, in UNEP's Environmental Law Series No. 4; Cairo Guidelines and Principles for Environmentally Sound Management of Hazardous Waste, Decision 14/30 of the Governing Council of UNEP, of June 17, 1989, in UNEP's Environmental Law Series No. 8; Goals and Principles of Environmental Impact Assessment, Decision 14/25 of the Governing Council of UNEP, of June 17, 1987, in UNEP's Environmental Law Series No. 9; and London Guidelines for Exchange of Information on Chemicals in International Trade, Decision 14/27 of the Governing Council of UNEP, of June 17, 1987, in UNEP's Environmental Law Series No. 10; and FAO Code of Conduct on the Distribution and Use of Pesticides (1985).

61. See the 1983 IAEA Guidelines for Mutual Emergency Assistance Arrangements in Connection with a Nuclear Accident or Radiological Emergency, Doc. INFCIRC/310, and the 1984 IAEA Guidelines on Reportable Events, Integrated Planning and Information of Exchange in a Transboundary Release of Radioactive Materials, Doc. INFCIRC/321. These two guidelines were the basis of the two IAEA conventions concluded after the 1986 Chernobyl nuclear accident, namely: the 1986

Convention on Early Notification of a Nuclear Accident, INFCIRC/335 and the 1986 Convention on Assistance in Case of Nuclear Accident or Radiological Emergency, INFCIRC/336.

62. See, e.g., Interim Guidelines for the Implementation of paragraphs 8 and 9 of Annex I to the 1972 London Dumping Convention, in 10 *New Direction in the Law of the Sea* 23–30 (1978); Montreal Guidelines for the Protection of the Environment Against Pollution from Land-based Sources, Decision 13/18/II of the Governing Council of UNEP of May 24, 1985, in UNEP's *Environmental Law Guidelines and Principles* Series No. 7, adopted in relation to the Paris Convention for the Prevention of Marine Pollution from Land-based Sources; the Helsinki Convention on the Protection of the Marine Environment of the Baltic Sea Area; the Athens Protocol for the Protection of the Mediterranean Sea Against Pollution from land-based Sources, and Part XII of the United Nations Convention on the law of the Sea; the Provisions for Co-operation Between States in Weather Modification Decision 8/7/A of the Governing Council of UNEP, of April 29, 1980, in UNEP's *Environmental Law Series* No. 3, adopted in relation to the Convention on the Prohibition of Military or Any Hostile Use of Environmental Modification Techniques.

63. See, e.g., the 1989 World Bank Operational Directive 4.00. Annex A on Environmental Assessment; the 1990 Guidelines for Environmental Management and Sustainable Development; 1989 FAO's Code of Conduct on the Distribution and Use of Pesticides: Introduction of the "Prior Informed Consent" (PIC) Clause; and the 1989 Council of Europe's Directive on Civil Liability for Damage and Injury to the Environment Caused by Wastes, decision of the Commission of August 3, 1989, CJ-EN (89)9.

64. See Conclusions of the Sienna Forum on International Law of the Environment, UN Doc. A/45/666, Recommendation 5, 4.

65. See General Assembly resolution 43/53 of December 6, 1988, entitled "Protection of global climate for present and future generations of mankind," agenda item 143 (A.43/905). See also Doc. A/45/696 and Add.1.

66. See General Assembly resolution 44/228 of December 22, 1989, convening the United Nations Conference on Environment and Development, Part I, para. 12 and para. 15, respectively.

67. See these specific issues as originally included in the mandate of the two Working Groups established by the Preparatory Committee for the United Nations Conference on Environment and Development; First session, New York. March 5–16, 1990, doc. A/44/48, para. 56, point 9, 14, and as later reformulated in the report of the Working Groups at the end of the sessions of the Preparatory Committee of UNCED. For the latest report see UN Doc. GAOR supp. 48 (A/46/48), vols. I and II.

68. In particular, Protocol I Additional to the Geneva Conventions of 12 August 1949 and relating to the Protection of Victims of International Armed Conflicts of June 10, 1977 and the Convention on the Prohibition of Military or Any Other Hostile Use of Environmental Modification Techniques of May 18, 1977.
69. General Assembly Decision A/46/C.6/L./13, as recommended by the Sixth (Legal Committee) and as amended by the General Assembly Plenary on December 9, 1991, in document A/46/L.39 recognizing the postponement of the Red Cross Conference.
70. See, e.g., Conference of experts on the use of the environment as a tool of environmental warfare, Ottawa, July 10–12, 1991 [copy of executive summary on authors file]; London Conference on "A Fifth Geneva" Convention on the Protection of the Environment in Times of Armed Conflict, June 3, 1991 (copy of executive summary on author's file), and consultation on the Law Concerning the Protection of the Environment in Times of Armed conflict, convened by the International Council of Environmental Law, Munich, December 13–15, 1991 (copy of recommendations on author's file). Also published in Environmental Policy and Law, (1992), vol. 22, 63.
71. See A/46/48, Vol. I, decision 2/3.
72. See A/CONF.151/PC/103/Add.1.
73. See A/CONF.151/PC/77, Sec. II, 12–16; A/CONF.151/PC/94 (Annex II).
74. For details, see A/CONF.151/PC.103/ and Add.1.
75. See, e.g., A/CONF.151/PC/WG.III/L.19; A/CONF.151/PC/102.
76. See A/CONF.151/PC/WG.III/L.10.
77. These views also took into account General Assembly resolution 44/229, requesting the Secretary-General to submit a report on the structure and responsiveness of the United Nations in dealing with major environmental issues.
78. See A/CONF.151/PC/WG.III/L.13.
79. See, e.g., A/CONF.151/PC/WG.III/L.8/Rev. I and Add.1.
80. See A/CONF.151/PC/102 para.40. Cf para. 60 infra.
81. See ACONF.151/PC/103 and Add.1.
82. See generally, Integration of Environment and Development in Decision Making, Doc. A/CONF.151/PC/100 Add.8.
83. See A/CONF.151/PC/L.29, submitted by the pentagonal countries (Austria, the Czech and Slovak Federal Republic, Hungary, Italy and Yugoslavia), and Poland.
84. See A/CONF.151/PC/WG.III/L.1, submitted by the above pentagonal countries and Poland.
85. See, Maurice F. Strong, supra note 4.
86. See Part B of document A/CONF.151/OC/100/Add.8, paras 14–16.
87. See these issues as further developed in Agenda 21 for Rio.

Notes on Contributors

A.O. Adede, LLB, Ph.D., is Deputy Director for Research and Studies, Codification Division, Office of Legal Affairs, United Nations Secretariat, New York.

Carlo A. Balistrieri is a sole practitioner specializing in CITES and endangered species law in Oconomowoc, Wisconsin.

Wolfgang E. Burhenne is a legal adviser to IUCN.

Jutta Brunnée is an assistant professor in the Faculty of Law at McGill University. She teaches environmental law, international environmental law, and comparative law.

Sharon L. Camp is Vice President of the Population Crisis Committee in Washington, D.C.

Harlan Cleveland is a political scientist and public affairs executive. He is a graduate with high honors from Princeton University; he has been professor emeritus at the University of Minnesota since 1988.

Colin Deihl is an associate of Faegre and Benson, Denver, Colorado. He received a B.A. from the University of Vermont in 1984 and a J.D. from Harvard Law School in 1990.

Beverly Nelson Glode received a B.A. from Chicago State in 1979, an M.B.A. from DePaul in 1985, and a J.D. from the University of Bridgeport School of Law in 1991.

Mark L. Glode received a B.S. from Southern Connecticut in 1974 and a Master's in Civil Engineering from the University of Wisconsin-Milwaukee in 1992. He has a background in environmental science, working as an environmental consultant, hazardous waste manager, and safety officer.

Daniel and Sally Grotta are publishers and freelance writers from Boyertown, Pennsylvania.

Sandra Hackman is the managing editor of *Technology Review*.

Lewis P. Hinchman is Associate Professor of Government at Clarkson University, Potsdam, New York. Author of *Hegel's Critique of the Enlightenment* (1984) and co-editor of *Hannah Arendt: Critical Essays* (1994), he has also written on individuality and autonomy, environmental political theory, Native American water rights, and the philosophy of Alasdair MacIntyre.

Sandra K. Hinchman is Professor of Government at St. Lawrence University, Canton, New York. Co-editor of *Hannah Arendt: Critical Essays* (1994), she has done work on environmental political thought and on political theory through literature. Together with Lewis Hinchman, she is currently preparing a volume on the idea of "narrative" in the human sciences.

M. Hirsch is a member of the Law Faculty of The Hebrew University of Jerusalem, Mount Scopus, Jerusalem, Israel.

D. Housen-Couriel is a member of the Law Faculty of The Hebrew University of Jerusalem, Mount Scopus, Jerusalem, Israel.

B. Jessiman is an employee of Health Canada.

Suzanne Keller is Professor of Sociology at Princeton University. She received a Ph.D. from Columbia University in 1955. Professor Keller is an expert in local community organization.

Nicholas Lenssen researches energy, climate, and ocean issues at the Worldwatch Institute.

Nicole Massignon is in charge of technical assistance, urban development, and agriculture in the OECD Development Co-Operation Directorate.

Norman Myers, Ph.D., is a consultant in Environment and Development and a Visiting Fellow of Green College, Oxford University. He was the first, through his 1979 book *The Sinking Ark*, to identify and delineate the mass extinction of species underway. More recently, he has served with the Biodiversity Task Force under the World Bank; and he is an Expert Adviser on Global Environment Facility funding for Biodiversity.

Sir Geoffrey Palmer, P.C., K.C.M.G., A.C., is Professor of Law, Victoria University of Wellington; Ida Beam Distinguished Visiting Professor of Law, University of Iowa; and 1991 Laureate, United Nations Environment Programme Global 500 Roll of Honour. He is a former Prime Minister, Deputy Prime Minister, Attorney-General, and Minister for the Environment of New Zealand.

Sandra Postel is Vice President for Research at Worldwatch Institute. She has written extensively on land, water, and forestry issues, and is co-author of *State of the World 1994*.

R. Raphael is an employee of Health Canada.

G.A. Sarpong, LL.B. (Ghana); LL.M. (Bri. Col.); Lecturer Faculty of Law, University of Ghana; Visiting Fellow, Leiden University (fall, 1992).

Major Bernard K. Schafer, U.S.A.F., is Chief of the Environmental Law Division, Civil Law Directorate, Office of the Staff Judge Advocate, Headquarters Tactical Air Command, Langley Air Force Base, Virginia. He received a B.A. from Michigan State University, a J.D. from Wayne State University, and a Master of Laws in Environmental Laws, Highest Honors, from George Washington University.

Robert G. Skinner is the Director of the Office of Long-Term Cooperation and Policy Analysis of the International Energy Agency, OECD, 2 rue Andre-Pascal, 75775 Paris Cedex 16, France.

Jerome K. Vanclay is professor of tropical forestry in the Department of Economics and Natural Resources, Royal Veterinary and Agricultural University, Copenhagen. His research focuses on sustainable management of tropical moist forests, and much of his work has addressed information systems to assist better forest management. He was previously senior principal scientist with the Queensland Forest Service, where he gained 10 years experience in inventory and yield prediction in natural forests. He has also worked in Southeast Asia and the Pacific. Dr. Vanclay holds a DSc.For. from the University of Queensland and an MSc from the University of Oxford.

Edith Brown Weiss is Professor of Law, Georgetown University Law Center.

R. Whittle is an employee of Health Canada.

Glossary

Acid Rain — Caused by the burning of fossil fuels which emits sulfur dioxide, nitrogen compounds, and particulates into the air. These compounds react and form sulfuric and nitric acid that fall in precipitation on the Earth, killing trees and stunting plant growth.

Air Pollution — The major air pollutants are carbon monoxide, hydrocarbons, nitrogen compounds, particulates and sulfur dioxide. Automobiles and the burning of fossil fuels are the principle causes.

Air Quality Standard — The acceptable level of pollutants in the air that should not be surpassed.

Aquifers — Large permeable areas under the Earth's surface that serve as storage tanks for groundwater. These sources are being depleted by increased water consumption patterns.

Bhopal, India — The location of a December 4, 1984 industrial accident in which methyl isocyanate gas escaped from a Union Carbide chemical plant, killing over 3,700 people and injuring 300,000.

Biodegradable — Through biological processes, this material can be broken down into simple compounds.

Biodiversity — The variety and quantity of species in an ecosystem and the recognition of the importance of each species.

Biomass — The dry weight of organisms, used to describe the quantity of certain groups of organisms in an ecosystem. Also used to describe plant matter that can be used as an energy source.

Biota — The flora and fauna of a specific area.

588

Carbon — Among the most common elements, carbon is found in all living systems.

Carrying Capacity — The term used to describe the limit to how many individuals the natural resources of a defined area, or the planet Earth, are able to support.

Carbon Dioxide — A gas making up .03 percent of the Earth's atmosphere. It is used by plants during photosynthesis and is a product of the respiration of plants and animals. Increased levels of carbon dioxide lead to global warming and are the result of the burning of fossil fuels and of deforestation.

Carcinogen — A cancer-causing substance.

Chlorofluorocarbons — A greenhouse gas which, when broken down by sunlight, destroys the ozone layer. These gases are commonly used in air conditioners, refrigerants, and as propellants in aerosol cans.

Clean Air Act Amendments — Passed in 1990, these amendments required the halving of sulfur dioxide emissions by the year 2000. They also created a free market emissions trading system.

Clean Water Act — Law mandates that each state adopt water quality standards, restrict industrial and municipal waste, and protect wetlands.

Conservation — The management of natural resources to avoid destruction, misuse, or exploitation.

DDT — A chlorinated hydrocarbon-type of insecticide. It was banned in the U.S. in 1972, after it caused a dramatic decline in bird populations; however, it is still being used in many countries.

Deforestation — Destruction of the world's forests, especially the tropical rain forests. Loss of forests causes air pollution and global warming, along with loss of species as habitats vanish. Forests are being destroyed at a rate of 40–50 acres annually.

Earth Summit, Rio de Janeiro — The United Nations Conference on
Environment and Development (UNCED). This world summit on
environmental issues was based on five main documents: The
Treaty on Biological Diversity, Convention on Climate Change,
Forestry Principles, The Rio Declaration, and Agenda 21.

Ecology — The science of the relationship between organisms and their
environment.

Ecosystem — Organisms of a specified area and the way they function
as a unit.

Endangered Species — Organisms whose population is small enough
that extinction is possible if an effort is not made to protect them.

Endangered Species Act, 1973 — This act gave the Federal
Government jurisdiction over the management of endangered
species. It stated that no government agency could perform any
activity that would lead to the extinction of a species.

Erosion — Progressive destruction of an area due to contact with wind
and water.

Estuary — The location where streams or rivers enter the ocean.

Fauna — The animal life of a specific area.

Flora — The plant life of a specific area.

Food Chain — The sequence of organisms in an ecosystem. Each
organism uses the source below it in the sequence as a source of
food energy.

Fossil Fuel — Fuels derived from formerly living organisms. They
consist of coal, oil, and natural gas and are nonrenewable sources
of energy.

Greenhouse Effect — The effect created when shortwave solar
radiation is converted to longer wave radiation, trapping heat in the
atmosphere. Among the gases that contribute to this effect are

carbon dioxide, methane, ozone, nitrous oxide, chlorofluorocarbons, and hydrogenated chlorofluorocarbons.

Greenpeace — An organization of four million members worldwide that promotes awareness of environmental problems, particularly in marine ecosystems.

Groundwater — Water stored in aquifers in the Earth's crust. Groundwater makes up only .5 percent of all water on the Earth but supplies most of our drinking water.

Habitat — The natural environment of a specific plant or animal.

Hazardous Waste — Substances that pose a threat to the health and well being of humans or the environment. The EPA classifies these wastes on the basis of ignitability, corrosiveness, reactivity, and toxicity.

Hydrogen Sulfide — An air pollutant composed of hydrogen and sulfur.

Incineration — Method of solid waste disposal that burns garbage to reduce its volume. The volume is reduce between 60–90 percent. Incineration can be a source of air pollution through the smokestacks and hazardous waste from ash left after burning.

Lake Baikal — The world's largest, deepest, and oldest lake. It contains one-fifth of the planet's fresh water and remains relatively clean, since it is located in remote Siberia. It has recently been threatened by dumping of industrial waste.

Landfill — Waste is dumped into these sites, which are lined to prevent polluted fluids called leachates, from escaping. The waste is capped when the landfill is full. Eighty percent of municipal solid waste in the U.S. goes into landfills.

Montreal Protocol — Signed in 1987 by 24 nations, this document pledges to phase out use of all CFCs by 1999.

Natural Resources Defense Council (NRDC) — Organization dedicated to protecting air, water, and food supplies. The group led the fight against acid rain and has pushed for enforcement of the Clean Air Act.

Natural Selection — The process by which organisms possessing positive adaptive traits produce more offspring than those without such traits. It is part of the evolutionary process.

Nitrogen Oxides — An air pollutant composed of nitrogen and oxygen. A product of the combustion of automobiles that contributes to smog and acid rain.

Nuclear Power — An alternative energy source. By 1989, 110 nuclear power plants were functioning in the United States. Advantages to nuclear power include no air pollution nor greenhouse gases and limited water pollution. Disadvantages include safety, cost, and disposal of nuclear waste.

Ocean Pollution — One-half of all the world's people live on ocean coasts. There are three causes of pollution: point source, pollution traced to a specific source; non-point pollution, pollution with many sources such as fertilizers and pesticides; and municipal solid waste.

Ozone — Serves as a shield for the Earth from ultraviolet radiation, it is a molecule of oxygen composed of three oxygen atoms that breaks down as it absorbs the UV rays.

Pesticide — Poison that kills unwanted organisms. Two million tons are used each year. Side effects of pesticide use are the contamination of drinking water and the poisoning of mammals, birds, and fish.

Pollution — The contamination of air, water, or soil.

Polychlorinated Biphenyls (PCBs) — A poisonous chemical that belongs to the halogenated hydrocarbon group, which has been responsible for many environmental disasters.

Radioactive Waste — Radioactive by-product of nuclear reactors or nuclear processes.

Recycle — The restructuring and reuse of manufactured goods taken from the wastestream.

Smog — Formed by a reaction between nitrogen oxides, caused by burning fuel. The chemicals react in the air to form a brown haze. The main component of smog is ozone.

Solid Waste — Unwanted solid materials from industrial or consumer use.

Sulfur Dioxide — One of the five primary air pollutants. It is released when fossil fuels containing sulfur are burned and is found in industrial smog and acid rain.

Superfund — The Comprehensive Environmental Response, Liability, and Compensation Act (CERCLA) set aside a trust fund to clean up the most dangerous hazardous waste sites. Over 1,200 sites are on the list and less than 60 have been cleaned up.

Sustainable Development — Development that meets the needs of the current population without depleting resources for future generations.

Treaty of Biological Diversity — Signed at the Earth Summit of 1992, the treaty required participating countries to inventory plant and animal species and protect the endangered species. It also calls for the sharing of resources and technology to maintain biological diversity. The U.S. was the only country at the Summit that did not sign.

Water Pollution — Degradation of aquatic ecosystems due to the destruction of the quality of water. Occurs when chemicals such as pesticides, oil, fertilizers, industrial waste, sewage, etc., are added to water.

Wildlife — Nondomesticated animals and uncultivated plant life in a certain area.

Bibliography[*]

General

Annual Editions: Environment. Guilford, CT: Dushkin Publishing Group, 1982–.

Boo, Elizabeth. *Ecotourism: The Potentials and Pitfalls*. Washington, DC: World Wildlife Fund-U.S., 1990.

Caldwell, Lynton Keith. *International Environmental Policy: Emergence and Dimensions*. Durham, NC: Duke University Press, 1984.

De Koning, H.W. *Setting Environmental Standards: Guidelines for Decision Making*. Geneva: World Health Organization, 1987.

Demko, George, and Ramakrishna, P.S. *Global Environmental Change and International Governance*. Hanover: Dartmouth University Press, 1991.

Hughes, Barry B., et al. *Energy in the Global Arena: Actors, Values, Policies and Futures*. Durham, NC: Duke University Press, 1985.

Lacey, Michael J., ed. *Government and Environmental Politics: Essays on Historical Developments since World War II*. Washington, DC: Woodrow Wilson Center Press, 1991.

McCormick, John. *Reclaiming Paradise: The Global Environmental Movement*. Bloomington: Indiana University Press, 1989.

Nash, Roderick. *American Environmentalism*, 3rd ed. New York: McGraw-Hill, 1990.

Pahlke, Robert C. *Environmentalism and the Future of Progressive Politics*. New Haven: Yale University Press, 1989.

Petulla, Joseph M. *Environmental Protection in the United States*. San Francisco: San Francisco Study Center, 1987.

---

*This bibliography is topically organized and each topic is subdivided into documents, books, and articles on the environment. Topics are: Air Pollution, Antarctica, Climate, Environmental Values, Forests, Land Degradation, Population, (Outer) Space, Species, Toxics, Water/Oceans, Urbanization.

Renner, Michael. *National Security: The Economic and Environmental Dimensions.* Washington, DC: Worldwatch Institute, 1989.

Rifkin, Jeremy. *Biosphere Politics.* New York: Crown, 1991.

Sand, Peter H. *Lessons Learned in Global Environmental Governance.* Washington, DC: World Resources Institute, 1990.

Schneider, Jan. *World Public Order of the Environment: Towards an Ecological Law and Organization.* Toronto: Books Demand, 1979.

Switzer, Jacqueline Vaughn. *Environmental Politics: Domestic and Global Dimensions.* New York: St. Martin's Press, 1994.

Air Pollution
Documents

Canada

Canada-United States Acid Rain. Canadian Embassy Report, December 1988.

Hilborn, J., and Still, M. *Canadian Perspectives on Air Pollution.* S.O.E. Report No. 90–91. Ottawa: Environment Canada, 1990, 81.

United Nations

World Health Organization. *Air Quality Guidelines for Europe.* Regional Publication European Series No. 23. Copenhagen: WHO Regional Office for Europe, 1987.

United Nations. *Assessment of Long-Range Transboundary Air Pollution.* New York: United Nations Air Pollution Series No. 7, 1991.

———. *Transboundary Air Pollution Effects and Control.* New York: United Nations, 1987.

United States

Committee on Energy and Commerce, Subcommittee on Health and the Environment, U.S. House of Representatives, 98th Congress, 2nd Session. *Acid Rain: A Survey of Data and Current Analyses.* Washington, DC: U.S. Congressional Research Service, 1984.

Parker, Larry. *Acid Precipitation: Current Issues.* U.S. Library of Congress. Congressional Research Service Report 1b 83016, March 31, 1983.

Other

Acid Rain and Air Pollution. World Wildlife Fund International Report, 1988.

Novotny, Vladimir. *Non-point Pollution—An International Problem.* AWRA Surface and Groundwater Quality Symposium. Cleveland, OH, Feb. 24–27, 1991, 145.

Articles

"Atmosphere: The Fate of Our Air," *UN Chronicle*, v. 29, June 1992, 50–51.

Bishop, Kevin. "Acid Rain, Rational Policy-Making and Apocalyptic Environmentalists," *Ecos.*, v. 8, no. 2, spring 1987, 27.

Bucholtz, Barbara K. "Cause and the Control of Transboundary Pollution: The Sale of Hydroelectricity Under the United States Canada Free Trade Agreement of 1988," *Boston College Environmental Affairs Law Review*, v. 18, winter 1991, 279–317.

Carroll, John C. "The Acid Rain Issue in Canadian-American Relations," in John C. Carroll, ed. *International Environmental Diplomacy*, Cambridge: Cambridge University Press, 1988, 141.

Cowling, E. "Acid Precipitation in a Historical Perspective," *Environmental Science and Technology*, v. 16, no. 2, 1982.

Dockner, Engelbert J., and Long, Ngo Van. "International Pollution Control: Cooperative versus Noncooperative Strategies," *Journal of Environmental Economics and Management*, v. 25, July 1993, 13–29.

"Environment: The Rain that Nobody Wants," *Africa*, v. 170, October 1985, 40.

Gibson, Robert. "Acid Rain as a Political Dilemma," *Alternatives*, v. 11, no. 2, winter 1983, 3.

Glode, Mark L., and Glode, Beverly N. "Transboundary Pollution: Acid Rain and United States-Canadian Relations," *Boston College Environmental Affairs Law Review*, v. 20, no. 1, 1993, 1.

Golich, Vicki L. "Resolution of the United States-Canadian Conflict Over Acid Rain Controls," *Journal of Environmental Development*, v. 2, no. 1, 1993, 63.

Hahn, R.W. "The Politics and Religion of Clean Air," *Regulation*, Winter 1990, 21–30.

Hartman, Joan. "What Do the Clean Air Amendments of 1990 Portend for the Future of Environmental Law," *Environmental Law*, v. 21, no. 4:II, 1991, i.

Hinruchsen, Dan. "Like First World, Like Third World," *Amicus Journal*, v. 10, no. 1, winter 1988, 5.

Howe, C.W. "An Evaluation of U.S. Air and Water Policies," *Environment*, September 1991, 10.

"An International Perspective," *EPA Journal*, v. 12, June/July 1986, 19–20.

Irving, Patricia M. "NAPAP: Where Does It Go From Here?", *Forum for Applied Research in Public Policy*, v. 8, no. 2, summer 1993, 74.

Irwin, Alan. "Acid Pollution and Public Policy: The Changing Climate of Environmental Decision-Making," in *Environmental Management Series. Atmospheric Acidity: Sources, Consequences and Abatement*. New York: Elsevier, 1992, 549.

Knopman, Debra S., and Smith, Richard A. "Twenty Years of the Clean Air Act," *Environment*, v. 35, January/February 1993, 17.

Leaf, Dennis. "Acid Rain and the Clean Air Act," *Chemical Engineering Progress*, v. 86, no. 5, May 1990, 25.

Martz, Clyde O. "A Clean Air Alternative: Balancing Correction and Accommodation," *Environmental Law and Policy*, v. 2, no. 1, winter 1991, 25.

Menz, Fredric. "Transboundary Acid Rain: A Canadian-U.S. Problem Requiring a Joint Solution," in *Tensions at the Border: Energy and Environmental Concerns in Canada and the U.S.* New York: Praeger Press, 1992, 45.

Mills, Mike. "Ozone Pact Ok'd, But Some Say Its Not Enough; New Studies Raise Concerns," *Congressional Quarterly Weekly Report*, v. 46, March 19, 1988, 706.

———. "Ratification of Ozone Pact Recommended; But Some Say 'Too Little Too Late,'" *Congressional Quarterly Weekly Report*, v. 46, February 20, 1988, 370.

"Ozone Loss: Fast, Irreversible and Dangerous," *UN Chronicle*, v. 25, June 1988, 46.

Park, Chris. "Trans-Frontier Air Pollution: Some Geographical Issues," *Geography*, v. 76, January 1991, 21–35.

Rose, David J. "Air Pollution and International Law: A Subject Important to Nuclear Power," *Nuclear Science and Engineering*, v. 90, no. 4, August 1985, 475.

Rosencranz, Armin. "The Acid Rain Controversy in Europe and North America," in John C. Carrol, ed. *International Environmental Diplomacy*, Cambridge: Cambridge University Press, 1988.

598 LAW, VALUES, AND THE ENVIRONMENT

Sand, P. "Air Pollution in Europe: International Policy Responses," *Environment*, v. 29, no. 10, December 1987, 16.

Scott, Wayne. "Acid Rain: What We Know, What We Did, What We Will Do," *Archives of Environmental Contamination and Toxicity*, v. 18, no. 1–2, January-April 1989, 75.

Soroos, Marvin S. "The Evolution of Global Regulation of Atmospheric Pollution," *Policy Studies Journal*, v. 19, no. 2, 1991, 115–125.

"Taking the Air in Antarctica," *The Economist*, v. 299, June 28, 1986, 86.

Trisko, Eugene M. "Alternative Approaches to Acid Rain Control," *Environmental Forum*, v. 3, no. 12, April 1985, 18.

Vaahtoranta, Tapani. "Atmospheric Pollution as a Global Policy Problem," *Journal of Peace Research*, v. 27, May 1990, 169–176.

Valiante, Marcia, and Muldoon, Paul. "Annual Review of Canada-United States Environmental Relations–1991," *International Environmental*, v. 4, no. 3, summer 1992, 254–263.

Waxman, Henry A. "An Overview of the Clean Air Act Amendments of 1990," *Environmental Law*, v. 21, no. 4:II, 1991, 1721.

Welsch, Heinz. "An Equilibrium Framework for Global Pollution Problems," *Journal of Environmental Economics and Management*, v. 25, July 1993, 64–69.

Woods, Frank W. "The Acid Rain Question: Making Decisions Today for Tomorrow," *The Futurist*, v. 21, January/February 1987, 34–37.

Books

Benedick, Richard E. *Transboundary Air Pollution*. Current Policy Series no. 723, July 1985. Washington, DC: U.S. Department of State, Bureau of Public Affairs, 1985.

Bridgman, Howard. *Global Air Pollution: Problems for the 1990s*. Grand Rapids, MI: CRC Press, 1991.

Brunnée, Jutta. *Acid Rain and Ozone Layer Depletion*. Ardsley-on-Hudson, NY: Transnational, 1988.

Carroll, John E. *Acid Rain: An Issue in Canadian-American Relations*. Toronto: C.D. Howe Institute, July 1982.

Fishman, Jack, and Kalish, Robert. *Global Alert: The Ozone Pollution Crisis*. New York: Plenum Press, 1990.

French, Hilary F. *Clearing the Air: A Global Agenda*. Washington, DC: Worldwatch Institute, 1990.

Gibson, Mary. *To Breathe Freely: Risk, Consent and Air*. Berkeley, CA: Rowan, 1985.

Grant, L. et al., eds. *Health and Environmental Hazards from Toxic Chemicals in Air*. Princeton, NJ: Princeton Science Publishers, 1990.

Heck, Walter W., Taylor, O. Clifton, and Tingery, David T. *Assessment of Crop Loss from Air Pollutants*. New York: Elsevier, 1988.

Howells, Gwyneth Parry. *Acid Rain and Acid Waters*. New York: E. Horwood, 1990.

Lee, Dwight. *The Next Environmental Battleground: Indoor Air*. Dallas: National Center of Policy Analysis, 1992.

Loiy, Paul J., and Daisey, Joan M. *Toxic Air Pollution*. Chelsea, MI: Lewis Publishers, 1987.

Luoma, Jon R. *The Air Around Us: An Air Pollution Primer*. Raleigh, NC: Acid Rain Foundation, 1989.

MacKenzie, James J. *Air Pollution's Toll on Forests*. New Haven: Yale University Press, 1990.

MacKenzie, James J., and El-Ashry, Mohamed T. *Air Pollution's Toll on Forests and Crops*. New Haven: Yale University Press, 1992.

Majumdar, S.K., et al., eds. *Air Pollution: Environmental Issues and Health Effects*. Penn Science, 1991.

Mathy, P., ed. *Air Pollution and Ecosystems*. Norwell, MA: Klewer Ac., 1987.

McCormick, John. *Acid Earth: The Global Threat of Acid Pollution*. Washington, DC: International Institute for Environment and Development, 1985.

Miller, E. Willard, and Miller, Ruby M. *Environmental Hazards: Air Pollution*. Santa Barbara, CA: ABC Clio, 1989.

Mintzer, Irving M., et al. *Protecting Our Ozone Shield: Strategies for Phasing Out CFC's During the 1990s*. Washington, DC: World Resources Institute, 1989.

Park, C.C. *Acid Rain: Rhetoric and Reality*. New York: Methuen and Co., 1987.

Postel, Sandra. *Air Pollution, Acid Rain, and the Future of Forests*. Washington, DC: Worldwatch Institute, 1984.

Ross, R. *Air Pollution and Industry*. New York: Van Nos Reinhold, 1992.

Schmandt, Jurgen, Clarkson, Judith, and Roderick, Hilliard, eds. *Acid Rain and Friendly Neighbors: The Policy Dispute between Canada and the United States*. Durham, NC: Duke University Press, 1988.

Urban Air Pollution in Megacities of the World: Earthwatch: Global Environmental Monitoring System. Cambridge, MA: Blackwell Publishers, 1992.

Wark, Kenneth, and Warner, Cecil F. *Air Pollution: Its Origin and Control.* New York: Harper Collins, 1990.

Wellburn, Alan. *Air Pollution and Acid Rain: The Biological Impact.* New York: Wiley, 1988.

Zeavin, Edna, and Parker, Diane. *Breath Taking—Stopping the Plunder of Our Planet's Air.* San Jose, CA: R & E Publishers, 1992.

Antarctica
Documents

United States

Committee on Antarctica Policy and Science, Polar Research Board, Commission on Geosciences, Environment and Resources, National Research Council. *Science and Stewardship in Antarctica.* Washington, DC: National Academy Press, 1993.

U.S. Congress, Office of Technology Assessment. *Polar Prospects: A Minerals Treaty for Antarctica.* Washington, DC: U.S. Government Printing Office, September 1989.

U.S. House Committee on Science, Space and Technology. *The Antarctic Environmental Protection Act of 1992: Hearing February 23, 1993.* 1993 iii+ (103rd Congress, 2:103/21).

Other

IUCN. *A Strategy for Antarctic Conservation.* Gland, Switzerland: IUCN-The World Conservation Union, 1991.

Articles

Beck, Peter J. "Antarctica: A Case for the U.N.?" *The World Today,* v. 40, April 1984, 165–172.

———. "The Antarctic Treaty after 25 Years," *The World Today,* v. 42, November 1986, 166–169.

———. "A New Polar Factor in International Relations," *The World Today,* v. 45, April 1989, 65–68.

Beeby, Chris. "Development and Conservation of Antarctica's Minerals," *Far Eastern Economic Review,* v. 139, February 11, 1988, 22–23.

Blay, S.K.N. "New Trends in the Protection of the Antarctic Environment: The 1991 Madrid Protocol," *American Journal of International Law*, v. 86, April 1992, 377–399.

Bogart. "On Thin Ice: Can Antarctica Survive the Gold Rush?" *Greenpeace*, September/October, 1988, 7.

Burgess, J.S., Spate, A.P., and Norman, F.I. "Environmental Impacts of Station Development in Larsemann Hills, Princess Elizabeth Land, Antarctica," *Journal of Environmental Management*, December 1992, 287.

Canmann, Mary Lynn. "Antarctic Oil Spills in 1989: A Review of the Application of the Antarctic Treaty and the New Law of the Sea to the Antarctic Environment," *Colorado Journal of International Environmental Law and Policy*, v. 1, no. 1, summer 1990, 211.

Carvallo, Maria Luisa. "Antarctic Tourism Must Be Managed, Not Eliminated," *Forum for Applied Research and Public Policy*, v. 9, spring 1994, 76–79.

Cleveland, Harlan. "The Global Commons," *The Futurist*, v. 27, no. 3, May-June 1993, 9.

Dalziell, Janet, and Goldworthy, Lyn. "World Park Antarctica: Does It Have a Future," *Forum for Applied Research and Public Policy*, v. 9, spring 1994, 71–75.

"Dawn at the End of the Earth," *The Economist*, v. 328, September 25, 1993, 95–97.

Deihl, Colin. "Antarctica: An International Laboratory," *Boston College Environmental Affairs Law Review*, v. 18, spring 1991, 423–456.

Dingwall, P.R. "The Madrid Protocol: Antarctica's Protector," *Forum for Applied Research and Public Policy*, v. 9, spring 1994, 80–82.

Draggan, Sidney. "Environment on the Rise as Antarctic Priority," *Forum for Applied Research and Public Policy*, v. 9, spring 1994, 88–92.

"Fact Sheet: Protecting the Antarctic Environment," *U.S. Department of State Dispatch*, October 14, 1991, 771.

"First Committee Reviews Question of Antarctica for Third Time, Three Text Adopted," *UN Chronicle*, v. 23, February 1986, 68–73.

"Frozen Waste," *The Economist*, v. 319, April 20, 1991, 46.

Gist: Protection of the Antarctic Environment," *U.S. Department of State Dispatch*, October 19, 1992, 782.

Herber, Bernard P. "The Common Heritage Principle: Antarctica and the Developing Nations," *The American Journal of Economics and Sociology*, v. 50, October 1991, 391–406.

Hofman, D.J., Oltmans, S.J., et al. "Observation and Possible Causes of the New Ozone Depletion in Antarctica in 1991," *Journal of Nature*, April 15, 1993, 621–623.

Horstmeyer, Steven L. "A Trip to the Ice," *Weatherwise*, June/July 1993, 26–33.

"Ice-Picking Antarctica," *The Economist*, v. 307, May 28, 1988, 46.

Jaffe, Daniel A., Leighton, Elizabeth and Tumeo, Mark A. "Environmental Impact on the Polar Regions," *Forum for Applied Research and Public Policy*, v. 9, spring 1994, 65–70.

James, Colin. "The Fragile Continent: Australia and France Push Antarctic Treaty Alternative," *Far Eastern Economic Review*, v. 144, June 8, 1989, 40.

―――. "Out of the Freezer: Treaty Breakdown Feared After Minerals Accord Fails," *Far Eastern Economic Review*, v. 147, March 22, 1990, 27.

―――. "Thaw on a Mineral Regime," *Far Eastern Economic Review*, v. 139, February 11, 1988, 20+.

Joyner, Christopher C. "Antarctica and the Law of the Sea: An Introductory Overview," *Ocean Development and International Law Journal*, v. 13, no. 3, 1983, 277.

―――. "The Antarctica Minerals Negotiation Process," *American Journal of International Law*, v. 81, October 1987, 888–905.

―――. "The Evolving Antarctica Legal Regime," *American Journal of International Law*, v. 83, July 1989, 605–626.

Kennicutt, Mahlon C. "Grounding of the Bahia Paraiso at Arthur Harbor, Antarctica," *Environmental Science and Technology*, March 1992, 509.

Kriwoken, Lorne K. "Antarctic Environment and Joint Protection," *Forum for Applied Research and Public Policy*, v. 9, spring 1994, 86–88.

Luard, Evan. "Who Owns the Antarctic?" *Foreign Affairs*, v. 62, summer 1984, 1175–1193.

Lucas, P.H. "International Agreement on Conserving the Antarctic Environment," *Ambio.*, v. 11, no. 5, 1982, 292.

Marks, Beth C., and Barnes, James N. "The Future of Antarctica Under the Environmental Protocol," *Journal of Environmental Development*, v. 2, no. 2, summer 1993, 169.

Monastersky, Richard. "Science on Ice," *Science News*, April 10, 1993, 232–235.

"Question of Antarctica Reviewed for Fourth Time: Assembly Adopts Three Texts," *UN Chronicle*, v. 24, February 1987, 94.

"The Question of Antarctica: Second Round of Assembly Debate," *UN Chronicle*, v. 21, September 1984, 45–52.

Ram, Mohan. "Non-Aligned on Ice," *Far Eastern Economic Review*, v. 132, May 15, 1986, 30–31.

Roucek, Joseph S. "The Geopolitics of the Antarctic: The Land is Free for Scientific Work But Its Wealth of Minerals Has Excited Imperialistic Claims," *The American Journal of Economics and Sociology*, v. 45, January 1986, 69–77.

Rudback, Goran T. "Proper Protocol in Antarctica," *Forum for Applied Research and Public Policy*, v. 9, spring 1994, 83–85.

Schatz, Gerald S. "Protecting the Antarctic Environment," *Oceanus*, v. 31, no. 2, summer 1988, 101.

Tenebaum, Ellen S. "A World Park in Antarctica: The Common Heritage of Mankind," *Virginia Environmental Law Journal*, v. 10, no. 1, fall 1990, 109.

"Three Ring Circus," *The Economist*, v. 293, December 8, 1984, 38.

"U.S. Signs Environmental Protocol to Antarctic Treaty," *U.S. Department of State Dispatch*, October 19, 1992, 782.

Books

Beck, Peter. *The International Politics of Antarctica*. New York: St. Martin's Press, 1986.

Bonner, W.N., and Walton, D.W.H. *Antarctica*. Tarrytown, NY: Pergamon Press, 1985.

Chester, Jonathan. *Antarctica: Beauty in the Extreme*. Philadelphia: Courage Books, 1991.

Cook, Grahame. *The Future of Antarctica*. New York: St. Martin's Press, 1991.

———. *The Future of Antarctica: Exploitation vs. Preservation*. London: Manchester University Press, 1991.

Kerry, K.R., and Hempel, G. *Antarctic Ecosystems: Ecological Change and Conservation*. New York: Springer-Verlag, 1990.

Laws, R.M. *Antarctic Ecology*. San Diego: Academic Press, 1984.

Parsons, Sir Anthony. *Antarctica: The New Decade: Report of a Study Group*. New York: Cambridge University Press, 1987.

Shapley, Deborah. *The Seventh Continent: Antarctica in the Resource Age*. Washington, DC: Resources for the Future, Inc., 1985.

Climate
Documents

Australia

Intergovernmental Panel on Climate Change. *Climate Change: The IPCC Impacts Assessment.* Canberra, Australia: Australian Government Publishing Service, 1990.

United Nations

Intergovernmental Panel on Climate Change. *Formulation of Response Strategies. Report of Working Group 3, Intergovernmental Panel on Climate Change.* Geneva: WMO/UNEP, 1990.

————. *Potential Impacts of Climate Change. Report of Working Group 2, Intergovernmental Panel on Climate Change.* Geneva: WMO/UNEP, 1990.

————. *Scientific Assessment of Climate Change: The Policymakers' Summary of the Report of Working Group 1, Intergovernmental Panel on Climate Change.* Geneva: WMO/UNEP, 1990.

United Nations Environment Programme. *Montreal Protocol on Substances That Deplete the Ozone Layer.* Nairobi: UNEP, 1989.

WMO. *Atmospheric Ozone, 1985, Assessment of Our Understanding of the Processes Controlling the Present Distribution and Change, Report No. 16, 3 Volumes.* Geneva: WMO, 1986.

————. *Proceedings from Second World Climate Conference.* Geneva: WMO, 1991.

————. *Report of the International Ozone Trends Panel: 1988. Report No. 18, 2 Volumes.* Geneva: WMO, 1986.

————. *WMO and Global Warming.* Publication no. 741. Geneva: WMO, 1990.

United States

Bureau of Oceans and International Environment and Science Affairs, Office of Global Change. *National Action Plan for Global Climate Change.* Washington, DC: Government Printing Office, 1992.

Pratner, M.J., and Ad Hoc Theory Panel. *Model Predictions of Future Ozone Change. Present State of Knowledge of the Upper Atmosphere, 1988: An Assessment Report.* NASA Reference Publication 1208.

Synthesis Panel Staff, National Academy of Science, National Academy of Engineering, Institute of Medicine, eds. *Policy Implications of*

Greenhouse Warming. Washington, DC: National Academy Press, 1991.

United States Environmental Protection Agency. *Policy Options for Stabilizing Global Climate*. Washington, DC: U.S. EPA, 1989.

Other

International Energy Agency. *Climate Change*. Paris: IEA, 1992.

Organization for Economic Cooperation and Development Staff. *Climate Change Evaluating the Socio-Economic Impacts*. Washington, DC: OECD, 1991.

Shen, Sinyan. *Global Warming: Proceedings of the First International Conference*. Woodridge, IL: Supcan International, 1992.

Articles

"A Kinder, Gentler Greenhouse Effect? Some Aspects May Be Positive, Says Climatologist," *The Futurist*, v. 26, September/October 1992, 53.

Abelson, P.H. "Agriculture and Climate Change," *Science*, v. 257, July 3, 1992, 9.

Babbit, B.E. "The World After Rio," *World Monitor*, v. 5, June 1992, 28–31.

Beckerman, Wilfred, and Malkin, Jesse. "How Much Does Global Warming Matter?," *The Public Interest*, v. 114, winter 1994, 3–16.

Brown, Neville. "The 'Greenhouse Effect': A Global Challenge," *The World Today*, v. 45, April 1989, 61–64.

Brown, Noel. "Global Change and Global Warming: Framing the Issues," *Colorado Journal of International Environmental Law and Policy*, v. 1, no. 1, summer 1990, 11.

Bryner, Gary. "Implementing Global Environmental Agreements," *Policy Studies Journal*, v. 19, no. 2, 1991, 103–114.

Cairncross, Frances. "Everybody's Atmosphere," *The Economist*, v. 323, May 30, 1992, 17–18.

———. "The Warming Globe," *The Economist*, v. 312, September 2, 1989, 12–14.

Christie, Ian. "Social and Political Aspects of Global Warming," *Futures*, v. 24, January/February 1992, 83–90.

Churchill, Anthony A., and Saunders, Robert J. "Global Warming and the Developing World," *Finance and Development*, v. 28, June 1991, 28–31.

"Climate Convention Negotiations Face Difficulties, But 1992 Target Feasible, Chairman Says," *UN Chronicle*, v. 28, June 1991, 56–57.

Colglazier, E. William. "Scientific Uncertainties, Public Policy, and Global Warming: How Sure is Sure Enough?" *Policy Studies Journal*, v. 19, no. 2, 1991, 50–60.

"Combatting Global Warming," *Challenge*, v. 33, July/August 1990, 28–32.

"Confronting Climate Change; No 'Quick Fix' Seen for Reducing Greenhouse Gases and the Threat of Global Climate Change," *The Futurist*, v. 25, May/June 1991, 56.

DeCanio, Stephen J., and Lee, Kai N. "Doing Well by Doing Good: Technology Transfer to Protect the Ozone," *Policy Studies Journal*, v. 19, no. 2, 1991, 140–151.

Eyckmans, Johan, Proost, Stef, and Schokkaert, Erik. "Efficiency and Distribution in Greenhouse Negotiations," *Kyklos*, v. 46, no. 3, 1993, 363–397.

"Global Warming: The Experts Speak," *The Economist*, v. 319, April 13, 1991, 26.

"Green Diplomacy: A Cool Look at Hot Air," *The Economist*, v. 315, June 16, 1990, 17–18+.

Grubb, Michael. "The Greenhouse Effect: Negotiating Targets," *International Affairs*, v. 66, January 1990, 67–89.

Grubb, M.J., Victor, D.C., and Hope, C.W. "Pragmatics in the Greenhouse," *Nature*, v. 354, 348–350.

Hempel, Lamont C. "Greenhouse Warming: The Changing Climate in Science and Politics," *Political Research Quarterly*, v. 46, March 1993, 213–239.

Hulme, Mike, and Kelly, Mick. "Exploring the Links Between Decertification and Climate Change," *Environment*, v. 35, n. 6, July-August 1993, 4.

"It's Getting Hot: The Planet May Turn Into A Gigantic Greenhouse," *UN Chronicle*, v. 25, June 1988, 44–45.

Jacobson, Jodi L. "Holding Back the Sea; Rising Sea Levels in Response to Global Warming Represent an Environmental Threat of Unprecedented Proportion," *The Futurist*, v. 24, September/October 1990, 20–27.

Jones, Tom. "The Economics of Climate Change," *OECD Observer*, n. 179, December 1992-January 1993, 22.

Kempton, Willett. "Lay Perspectives on Global Climate Change," *Human and Policy Dimensions*, v. 1, no. 3, 1991, 183.

Kirgis, Frederic L. Jr. "Standing to Challenge Human Endeavors that Could Change the Climate," *American Journal of International Law*, v. 84, April 1990, 525–530.

Krutilla, Kerry. "Unilateral Environmental Policy in the Global Commons," *Policy Studies Journal*, v. 19, no. 2, 1991, 126–139.

Lambright, W. Henry, and O'Leary, Rosemary. "Governing Global Climate Change: Can We Learn From the Past in Designing the Future?" *Policy Studies Journal*, v. 19, no. 2, 1991, 50–60.

Lave, Lester B. "The Greenhouse Effect: What Government Actions are Needed?" *Journal of Policy Analysis and Management*, v. 7, spring 1988, 460–470.

Le Houerou, H.N. "Climatic Change and Desertification," *Impact of Science on Society*, v. 166, 1992, 183–210.

"Living in the Greenhouse," *The Economist*, v. 310, March 11, 1989, 87–88+.

McFarland, M. "Chlorofluorocarbons and Ozone," *Environmental Science and Technology*, v. 23, no. 10, 1989, 1203–1208.

Mintzer, Irving. "Living in a Warmer World: Challenges for Policy Analysis and Management," *Journal of Policy Analysis and Management*, v. 7, spring 1988, 445–459.

Morrisette, Peter M. "The Montreal Protocol: Lessons for Formulating Policies for Global Warming," *Policy Studies Journal*, v. 19, no. 2, 1991, 152–161.

Morrisette, Peter M., and Plantinga, Andrew J. "Global Warming: A Policy Review," *Policy Studies Journal*, v. 19, no. 2, 1991, 167–172.

Munasinghe, Mohan, and King, Kenneth. "Accelerating Ozone Layer Protection in Developing Countries," *World Development*, v. 20, April 1992, 609–618.

Nangle, Orval E. "Stratospheric Ozone: United States Regulation of Chlorofluorocarbons," *Boston College Environmental Affairs Law Review*, v. 16, spring 1989, 531–580.

Newman, Peter W.G. "Greenhouse, Oil and Cities," *Futures*, v. 23, May 1991, 335–348.

Orr, David W. "Agriculture and Global Warming," *Agriculture, Ecosystems, and Environment*, v. 46, no. 1–4, September 1993, 81.

Owen, Oliver S. "The Heat is On: The Greenhouse Effect and the Earth's Future," *The Futurist*, v. 23, September/October 1989, 34–40.

Parsons, E.A. "A Summary of the Major Documents Signed at the Earth Summit and the Global Forum," *Environment*, v. 34, October 1992, 12–15.

Patersoron, Matthew, and Grubb, Michael. "The International Politics of Climate Change," *International Affairs*, v. 68, April 1992, 293–310.

"A Quick Fix on Ozone," *The Economist*, v. 325, November 28, 1992, 50.

Ray, Dixy Lee. "The Greenhouse Blues: Keep Cool About Global Warming," *Policy Review*, v. 49, Summer 1989, 70–72.

Rubin, E.S. "Realistic Mitigation Options for Global Warming," *Science*, v. 257, July 10, 1992, 148–149.

Sanderson, George F. "Climate Change: The Threat to Human Health," *The Futurist*, v. 26, March/April 1992, 34–38.

Schelling, Thomas C. "Some Economics of Global Warming," *The American Economic Review*, v. 82, March 1992, 1–14.

Skolnikoff, B. "The Policy Gridlock on Global Warming," *Foreign Policy*, v. 79, summer 1990, 73–93.

Solomon, S. "The Earth's Fragile Ozone Shield," in R.S. Defries and T. Malone, eds., *Global Change and Our Common Future: Papers from a Forum*, Washington, DC: National Academy Press, 1989.

Soroos, Marvin S. "The Evolution of Atmospheric Pollution," *Policy Studies Journal*, v. 19, no. 2, 1991, 115–125.

Stevenson, Mark, and Gooden, Victor. "Global Warming and Sustainable Environment," *Journal of Business Ethics*, v. 10, August 1991, 641–645.

Stewart, Richard B., and Wiener, Jonathan B. "A Comprehensive Approach to Climate Change: Using the Market to Protect the Environment," *The American Enterprise*, v. 1, November/December 1990, 75–80.

Stone, Christopher. "Beyond Rio: 'Insuring' Against Global Warming," *American Journal of International Law*, v. 86, July 1992, 445–488.

Sun, Marjorie. "A Clean Act," *Far Eastern Economic Review*, v. 150, November 29, 1990, 74.

Tans, Pieter P. "Greenhouse Gases, Ozone, Acid Rain, Ecosystems, and Society," *Colorado Journal of International Environmental Law and Policy*, v. 1, no. 1, summer 1990, 23.

Titus, James G. "Strategies for Adapting to the Greenhouse Effect," *Journal of the American Planning Association*, v. 56, summer 1990, 311–323.

"UN Global Study of 'Greenhouse Effect,'" *Futures*, v. 20, December 1988, 706–707.

Wirth, David A. "Climate Chaos," *Foreign Policy*, v. 74, spring 1989, 3–22.

Books

Abrahamson, Dean Edward. *The Challenge of Global Warming*. Washington, DC: Island Press, 1989.

Agarwal, Anil, and Narain, Sunita. *Global Warming in an Unequal World: A Case of Environmental Colonialism*. New Delhi: Centre for Science and Environment, 1991.

Allaby, Michael. *Living in the Greenhouse: A Global Warming*. San Francisco: Throsons SF, 1991.

Balling, Robert C., Jr. *The Heated Debate: Greenhouse Predictions vs. Climate Reality*. San Francisco: PRIPP, 1992.

Barth, Michael C., and Titus, James G. *Greenhouse Effect and Sea Level Rise: A Challenge for this Generation*. New York: Van Nostrand Reinhold, 1984.

Benarde, Melvin A. *Global Warning . . . Global Warming*. New York: Wiley, 1992.

Benedick, Richard Elliot. *Ozone Diplomacy: New Directions in Safeguarding the Planet*. Cambridge: Harvard University Press, 1991.

Bolin, Bert, et al., eds. *The Greenhouse Effect, Climate Change and Ecosystems*. New York: Published on Behalf of the Scientific Committee on the Problems of the Environment of the International Council of Scientific Unions by Wiley, 1986.

Bouwman, A.F., ed. *Soils and the Greenhouse Effect: The Present Status and Future Trends Concerning the Effect of Soils and Their Cover on the Fluxes of Greenhouse Gases, the Surface Energy Balance and the Water Balance*. New York: Wiley, 1990.

Boyle, R.H., and Oppenheime, M. *Dead Heat: The Race Against the Greenhouse Effect*. New York: Basic Books, Inc., 1990.

Brower, Michael. *Cool Energy: The Renewable Solution to Global Warming: A Report by the Union of Concerned Scientists*. Cambridge, MA: Union of Concerned Scientist, 1990.

Bryner, Gary C., ed. *Global Warming and the Challenge of International Cooperation*. Provo, UT: Kennedy Center for International Studies, 1992.

Christensen, John O. *Greenhouse Effect and Public Policy: A Selective Bibliography of Recent References*. Monticello, IL: Vance Bibliographies, 1991.

Churchill, Robin. *International Law and Global Climate Change: International Legal Issues and Implications*. Norwell, MA: Kluwer Ac., 1992.

Cline, William R. *The Economics of Global Warming*. Washington, DC: Institute for International Economics, 1992.

Cogan, Douglas. *Stones in a Glass House: CFC's and Ozone Depletion*. Washington, DC: Investor Research Center, 1988.

Cumberland, John H., Hibbs, James R., and Hoch, Irving. *The Economics of Managing Chlorofluorocarbons: Stratospheric Ozone and Climate Issues*. Washington, DC: Resources for the Future; Baltimore, MD: Distributed by The Johns Hopkins University Press, 1982.

Dornbusch, Rudiger, and Poterba, James M. *Global Warming: Economic Policy Response*. Cambridge: MIT Press, 1991.

Duraiappah, Anantha K. *Global Warming and Economic Development: A Holistic Approach to International Policy Co-Operation and Co-Ordination*. Norwell, MA: Kluwer Ac., 1993.

Edgerton, Lynne T. *The Rising Tide: Global Warming and the World Sea Levels*. Washington, DC: Island Press, 1991.

Epstein, Joshua M. *Controlling the Greenhouse Effect: Five Global Regimes Compared*. Washington, DC: Brookings Institution, 1990.

Fisher, David E. *Fire and Ice: The Greenhouse Effect, Ozone Depletion and Nuclear Winter*. New York: Harper and Row, 1990.

Flavin, Christopher. *Slowing Global Warming: A Worldwide Strategy*. Washington, DC: Worldwatch Institute, October 1989.

Goss-Levi, Barbara, Hafemeister, David, and Scribner, Richard. *Global Warming: Physics and Facts*. New York: American Institute of Physics, 1992.

Grubb, Michael. *The Greenhouse Effect: Negotiating Targets*. London: Royal Institute of International Affairs, 1989.

Idso, Sherwood B. *Carbon Dioxide and Global Change: Earth in Transition*. Tempe, AZ: IBR Press, 1989.

Kasperson, Roger E. *Climate Change, the Media and Public Awareness*. Managing Water Resources in the West Under Conditions of Climatic Uncertainty. Conference Paper, 1991.

Kimball, B.A., ed. *Impact of Carbon Dioxide, Trace Gases and Climate Change on Global Agriculture*. Madison, WI: American Society of Agronomy, 1990.

Kiner, Uner, ed. *Ecological Change: Environment, Development and Poverty Linkages*. New York: United Nations Publications, 1992.

Krause, Florentin. *Energy Policy in the Greenhouse*. New York: Wiley, 1992.

Laird, W. *Scientists and Agenda Setting: Advocacy and Global Warming*. Discussion Paper Prepared for the Association for Public Policy Analysis and Management Annual Meeting, Bethesda, Maryland.

Leggett, Jeremy. *Global Warming: The Greenpeace Report*. Oxford: Oxford University Press, 1990.

Lyman, Francesca. *The Greenhouse Trap: What We're Doing to the Atmosphere and How We Can Slow Global Warming*. Boston: Beacon Press, 1990.

McKibben, Bill. *The End of Nature*. New York: Doubleday, 1990.

Mintzer, Irving, M. *A Matter of Degrees: The Potential for Controlling the Greenhouse Effect*. Washington, DC: World Resources Institute, 1987.

Mitchell, George J. *World on Fire: Saving an Endangered Earth*. New York: Macmillan, 1991.

Morris, Beryl, et al. *The Greenhouse Effect: Exploring the Theory*. Portland, OR: International Specialized Book Service, 1989.

Nance, John J. *What Goes Up: The Global Assault on Our Atmosphere*. New York: Morrow, 1991.

National Academy of Sciences. *Policy Implications of Greenhouse Warming*. Washington, DC: National Academy Press, 1991.

Nilsson, Annika. *Greenhouse Earth*. New York: Wiley, 1992.

Nordquist, Joan. *The Greenhouse Effect, a Bibliography*. Santa Cruz: Reference and Research Service, 1990.

Ominde, S.H., and Juma, Calestous eds. *A Change in the Weather: African Perspectives on Climatic Change*. Nairobi: ACTS Press, African Centre for Technology Studies, 1991.

Oppenheimer, Michael. *Dead Heat: The Race Against the Greenhouse Effect*. New York: Basic Books, 1990.

Peters, Robert L., and Lovejoy, Thomas E. *Global Warming and Biological Diversity*. New Haven: Yale University Press, 1992.

Read, Peter. *Responding to Global Warming: The Technology, Economics and Politics of Sustainable Energy.* Atlantic Highlands, NJ: Humanities, 1993.

Revkin, Andrew C. *Global Warming: Understanding the Forecast.* New York: Abbeville Press, 1992.

Roan, Sharon L. *Ozone Crisis: The Fifteen Year Evolution of a Sudden Global Emergency.* New York: Wiley, 1989.

Schmandt, Jurgen, and Clarkson, Judith. *The Regions and Global Warming.* New York: Oxford University Press, 1992.

Schneider, Stephen Henry. *Global Warming: Are We Entering the Greenhouse Century?* San Francisco: Sierra Club Books, 1989.

World Resources Institute. *Greenhouse Warming: Negotiating a Global Warming.* Washington, DC: World Resources Institute, 1991.

Wyman, Richard L., ed. *Global Change, Climate and Life on Earth.* New York: Routledge, Chapman and Hall, 1991.

Environmental Values
Articles

Allison, Lincoln. "Rival Philosophies of the Earth," *The World and I,* v. 7, no. 7, July 1992, 55.

Bennett, David H. "Triage as a Species Preservation Strategy," *Environmental Ethics,* v. 8, no. 1, spring 1986, 47.

Brown, Donald. "Superfund Cleanups, Ethics, and Environmental Risk Assessment," *Boston College Environmental Affairs Law Review,* v. 16, no. 2, winter 1988, 181.

Bullis, Connie A., and Kennedy, James J. "Value Conflicts and Policy Interpretation: Changes in the Case of Fisheries and Wildlife Managers in Multiple Use Agencies," *Policy Studies Journal,* v. 19, no. 3–4, 1991, 542–552.

Caldwell, Lynton K. "The Contextual Basis for Environmental Decisionmaking: Assumptions are Predeterminants of Choice," *Environmental Professional,* v. 9, no. 4, 1987, 302.

Grove-White, Robin. "Getting Behind Environmental Ethics," *Environmental Values,* v. 1, no. 4, Winter 1992, 285.

"Growing Greener—Corporations Come Round to the Environmental Cause," *Conservation Exchange,* v. 7, no. 3, Washington, DC, 1989.

Hammond, John L. "Wilderness and Heritage Values," *Environmental Ethics,* v. 7, no. 2, summer 1985, 165.

Hayes, Denis. "Proposing a Global Priority: Earth Day 1990," *EPA Journal*, v. 14, no. 7, November/December 1988, 34.

Keller, Suzanne. "Ecology and Community," *Boston College Environmental Affairs Law Review*, v. 19, no. 3, spring 1992, 623.

McQuillan, Alan G. "Cabbages and Kings: The Ethics and Aesthetics of New Forestry," *Environmental Values*, v. 2, no. 3, autumn 1993, 191.

Norton, Bryan. "New Directions in Environmental Ethics," *The World and I*, v. 7, no. 7, July 1992, 73.

Papaioannou, John G. "'New Ethics' and the Environment," *Ekistics*, v. 58, May/June-July/August 1991, 247–264.

Pezzey, John. "Sustainability: An Interdisciplinary Guide," *Environmental Values*, v. 1, no. 4, winter 1992, 321.

Rolston, Holmes. "Valuing Wildlands," *Environmental Ethics*, v. 7, no. 1, spring 1985, 23.

Shrader-Frechette, Kristin. "Ethics and the Environment," *World Health Forum*, v. 12, no. 3, 1991, 311.

Stern, Paul C., Dietz, Thomas, and Kalof, Linda. "Value Orientations, Gender, and Environmental Concern," *Environment and Behavior*, v. 25, May 1993, 322–348.

Wellman, J.D. "Foresters' Core Values and Cognitive Styles: Issues for Wildland Recreation Management and Policy," *Policy Studies Review*, v. 7, no. 2, winter 1987, 395.

Weston, Anthony. "Beyond Intrinsic Value: Pragmatism in Environmental Ethics," *Environmental Ethics*, v. 7, no. 4, winter 1985, 321.

Worsley, Anthony, and Worsley, Andrea J. "Naturalistic and Technological Values in the Modern World," *Psychological Reports*, v. 64, June 1989, 1192–1194.

Books

Bramwell, A. *Ecology in the Twentieth Century*. New Haven: Yale University Press, 1989.

Callicott, J.B. *In Defence of the Land Ethic: Essays in Environmental Philosophy*. Albany: State University of New York Press, 1989.

Devall, Bill, and Sessions, George. *Deep Ecology: Living as if Nature Mattered*. Salt Lake City: Peregrine Smith Books, 1985.

———. *Deep Ecology*. Salt Lake City: Gibbs Smith, 1985.

Hays, Samuel P. *Beauty, Health and Permanence: Environmental Politics in the US 1955–1985.* Cambridge, England: Cambridge University Press, 1987.

McCormick, John. *Reclaiming Paradise: The Global Environmental Movement.* Bloomington: Indiana University Press, 1989.

Naess, A., and Rothenberg, D. *Ecology, Community and Lifestyle.* Cambridge: Cambridge University Press, 1989.

Nicholson, E.M. *The New Environmental Age.* Cambridge: Cambridge University Press, 1987.

Parkin, Sara. *Green Parties: An International Guide.* London: Heretic Books, 1989.

Pepper, David. *The Roots of Modern Environmentalism.* London: Croom Helm, 1984.

Rolston, H. *Environmental Ethics: Duties to and Values in the Natural World.* Philadelphia: Temple University Press, 1988.

Scarce, Rik. *Eco-Warriors: Understanding the Radical Environmental Movement.* Chicago: Noble Press, 1990.

Singer, P. *Animal Liberation: A New Ethics for Our Treatment of Animals.* New York: Avon Books, 1977.

Forests
Documents

United Nations

F.A.O. *Protection of Land Resources: Deforestation.* Prep Comm. UNCED, 2nd Session, Doc. A/Conf. 151/PC/27, 1991.

Tropical Forests: A Call for Action. Report of the International Task Force Convened by the World Bank and the United Nations Development Program. Washington, DC: The Institute, 1985.

UNCED. *Combatting Deforestation. UN Conference on Environment and Development Agenda 21. Rio Declaration. Forest Principles,* v. 2, May 1, 1992, 27.

World Bank. *Forest Sector Policy.* Washington, DC: World Bank, 1991.

United States

Office of Technology Assessment. *Technologies to Sustain Tropical Forest Resources.* Washington, DC: Congress of the United States, Office of Technology Assessment.

U.S. Department of State. *Humid Tropical Forests: AID Policy and Guidance*. Washington, DC: U.S. Department of State Memorandum. Government Printing Office, 1985.

Other

World Resources Institute, World Bank and the United Nations Development Programme. *Tropical Forests: A Call for Action*. Washington, DC: World Resources Institute, 3 vols., 1985.

Articles

Allen, J.C., and Barnes, D.F. "The Causes of Deforestation in Developing Countries," *Annals of the Association of American Geographers*, v. 75, 1985, 163–184.

Anderson, Anthony B. "Smokestacks in the Rainforest: Industrial Development and Deforestation in the Amazon Basin," *World Development*, v. 18, September 1990, 1191–1205.

Ayers, Jose Marcio. "Debt-for-Equity Swaps and the Conservation of Tropical Rainforests," *Trends in Research in Ecology and Evolution*, v. 4, no. 11, November 1989, 331–335.

Bowonder, B., and Prasad, S.S.R. "Global Forests: Another View," *Futures*, v. 19, February 1987, 43–53.

Brazee, Richard J., and Southgate, Douglass. "Development of Ethnobiologically Diverse Tropical Forests," *Land Economics*, v. 68, November 1992, 454–461.

Cairncross, Frances. "A Treasure Trove in the Trees," *The Economist*, v. 312, September 2, 1989, 10–12.

Carrier, J.G., and Krippl, E. "Comprehensive Study of European Forests Assesses Damage and Economic Losses From Air Pollution," *Environmental Conservation*, v. 17, 1990, 365–366.

Dunning, A., Denniston, D., Ryan, J.C., and Brown, R., et al. "Four Views of Deforestation," *World Watch*, v. 7, March/April 1994, 34–36.

"Environmental Problems and Developing Countries," *Finance and Development*, v. 29, June 1992, 22–23.

Fearnside, Philip M. "The Rate and Extent of Deforestation in Brazilian Amazonia," *Environmental Conservation*, v. 17, no. 3, Autumn 1990, 213–226.

"Forests: The Lungs of Our Planet," *UN Chronicle*, v. 29, June 1992, 54–55.

Fuller, Kathryn S. "Debt-for-Nature Swaps," *Environmental Science and Technology*, December 1989, 1450.

Grainger, Alan. "Rates of Deforestation in the Humid Tropics: Estimates and Measurements," *The Geographical Journal*, v. 159, March 1993, 33–44.

Guppy, Nicholas. "Tropical Deforestation: A Global View," *Foreign Affairs*, v. 62, spring 1984, 928–965.

Hackman, Sandra. "After Rio: Our Forests, Ourselves," *Technology Review*, v. 95, no. 7, October 1992, 32–40.

Harvey, L.D.D. "A Commentary on Tropical Deforestation and Atmospheric Carbon Dioxide," *Climatic Change*, v. 19, 1991, 119–121.

Hecht, Susanna, and Cockburn, Alexander. "Defenders of the Amazon: Deforestation is Not Just About Ecological Destruction but Social and Political Injustice," *New Statesman and Society*, v. 2, June 23, 1989, 16–21.

Heibert, Murray. "Mountains of Dust," *Far Eastern Economic Review*, v. 155, April 23, 1992, 26–27.

Hurrell, Andrew. "The Politics of Amazonian Deforestation," *Journal of Latin American/American Studies*, v. 23, February 1991, 197–215.

Hyde, William F., and Sedjo, Roger A. "Managing Tropical Forests: Reflections on the Rent Distribution Discussion," *Land Economics*, v. 68, August 1992, 343–350.

Johnson, Stanley. "Reactions to Rio: Rio's Forest Fiasco," *The Geographical Magazine*, v. 64, September 1992, 26–28.

Jukofshy, Diane, and Wille, Chris. "They're Our Rain Forests Too," *National Wildlife*, April-May 1993, 18.

Kottak, Conrad P., and Costa, Alberto C.G. "Ecological Awareness, Environmentalist Action, and International Conservation Strategy," *Human Organization*, v. 52, winter 1993, 335–343.

"Last Stand for Many Species: Population Growth Threatens Biological Diverse Areas," *The Futurist*, v. 26, September/October 1992, 53–54.

Marshall, George. "FAO and Tropical Forestry," *Ecologist*, March-April 1991, 66.

Mather, A.S. "Global Trends in Forest Resources," *Geography*, v. 72, January 1987, 1–15.

"Meanwhile in the Rainforest . . . ," *UN Chronicle*, v. 30, June 1993, 67.

Millikan, Brent H. "Tropical Deforestation, Land Degradation, and Society: Lessons from Rondonia, Brazil," *Latin American Perspectives*, v. 19, winter 1992, 45–72.

Moran, Emilio F. "Deforestation and Land Use in the Brazilian Amazon," *Human Ecology*, v. 21, March 1993, 1–21.

Postel, Sandra. "Forests in a Fossil-Fuel World," *The Futurist*, v. 18, August 1984, 39+.

Ramakrishnan, P.S. "Tropical Forests: Exploitation, Conservation and Management," *Impact of Science on Society*, v. 166, 1992, 149–162.

Repetto, Robert. "Deforestation in the Tropics," *Scientific American*, v. 262, no. 4, April 1990, 36.

Rudel, Thomas K. "Population, Development, and Tropical Deforestation," *Rural Sociology*, v. 54, fall 1989, 327–338.

Sandler, Todd. "Tropical Deforestation: Markets and Market Failures," *Land Economics*, v. 69, August 1993, 225–233.

Scott, Margaret. "The Disappearing Forests: Race Against Time to Salvage the Region's Natural Heritage," *Far Eastern Economic Review*, v. 143, January 12, 1989, 35–35+.

Sedjo, Roger A. "A Global Forestry Initiative," *Resources and Resource Future*, no. 102, fall 1992, 16.

Sharma, Narendra and Rowe, Raymond. "Managing the World's Forests," *Finance and Development*, v. 29, June 1992, 31–33.

Sher, Michael S., Ropes and Gray. "Can Lawyers Save the Rainforest? Enforcing the Second Generation of Debt for Nature Swaps," *Harvard Environmental Law Review*, v. 17, no. 1, 1993, 151.

Sioli, Harald. "The Effects of Deforestation in Amazonia," *The Geographical Journal*, v. 151, July 1985, 197–203.

Smith, N.J.H., and Schultes, R.E. "Deforestation and Shrinking Crop Gene-Pools in Amazonia," *Environmental Conservation*, v. 17, 1990, 227–234.

Southgate, Douglas, and Whitaker, Morris. "Promoting Resource Degradation in Latin America: Tropical Deforestation, Soil Erosion, and Coastal Ecosystem Disturbance in Ecuador," *Economic Development and Cultural Change*, v. 40, July 1992, 787–807.

"Tropical Deforestation: Its Impact on Indigenous Peoples," *The Futurist*, v. 19, February 1985, 66–67.

Tyler, Charles. "Laying Waste," *The Geographical Magazine*, v. 62, January 1990, 26–30.

————. "The Sense of Sustainability," *The Geographical Magazine*, v. 62, February 1990, 8–13.

Vanclay, Jerome K. "Saving the Tropical Forest: Needs and Prognosis," *Ambio.*, v. 22, no. 4, June 1993, 225.

Vatikiotis, Michael. "Malaysian Forests: Clearcut Mandate," *Far Eastern Economic Review*, v. 156, October 28, 1993, 54–55.

Walker, Robert, and Smith, Tony E. "Tropical Deforestation and Forest Management Under the System of Concession Logging: A Decision-Theoretic Analysis," *Journal of Regional Studies*, v. 33, August 1993, 387–419.

Wheelwright, Julie. "The Rainforest Myth," *The Geographical Magazine*, v. 61, April 1989, 22+.

Williams, M. "Forests," in B.L. Turner II et al., eds. *The Earth as Transformed by Human Action*, New York: Cambridge University Press, 1991.

"World Bank Launches Action Programme to Combat Deforestation in Africa," *UN Chronicle*, v. 23, August 1986, 112.

Books

Adams, Patricia. *Odious Debts, Loose Lending, Corruption and the Third World's Environmental Legacy*. London: Earthscan Publishers, 1991.

Anderson, Anthony B. *Alternatives to Deforestation: Steps Toward Sustainable Use of the Amazonian Rain Forest*. New York: Columbia University Press, 1990.

Collins, Mark, ed. *The Last Rain Forests: A World Conservation Atlas*. New York: Oxford University Press, 1990.

Collins, N.M., Sayer, J.A., and Whitmore, T.C. *The Conservation of Tropical Forests: Asia and the Pacific*. London: Macmillan, 1991.

Dietrich, William. *The Final Forest: The Last Great Trees of the Pacific Northwest*. New York: Penguin, 1993.

Forsyth, A., and Miyata, K. *Tropical Nature: Life and Death in the Rainforests of Central and South America*. New York: Scribners, 1984.

Gedicks, Al. *The New Resource Wars: Native and Environmental Struggles Against Multinational Corporations*. Boston: South End Press, 1993.

Goodland, Robert, ed. *Race to Save the Tropics*. Washington, DC: Island Press, 1990.

Gradwohl, Judith, and Greenberg, Russell. *Saving the Tropical Forests.* Washington, DC: Island Press, 1988.

Harns, L.D. *The Fragmented Forest.* Chicago: University of Chicago Press, 1984.

Hecht, Susanna, and Cockburn, Alexander. *The Fate of the Forest.* New York: Verso, 1989.

Hemming, John. *Change in the Amazonian Basin.* Manchester: Manchester University Press, 1985.

Hunter, Malcolm L. *Wildlife, Forests and Forestry: Principles of Managing Forests for Biological Diversity.* Englewood Cliffs, NJ: Prentice Hall, 1990.

Hurst, Philip. *Rain Forest Politics: Ecological Destruction in Southeast Asia.* Atlantic Highlands, NJ: Zed Books, 1990.

Johnson, Brian. *Responding to Tropical Deforestation.* Washington, DC: World Wildlife Federation, 1991.

Jordan, Carl F., ed. *Amazonian Rain Forests: Ecosystem Disturbance and Recovery.* New York: Springer-Verlag, 1987.

Ives, J., and Pitt, D.C. *Deforestation: Social Dynamics in Watersheds and Mountain Ecosystems.* London: Routledge, 1988.

Kimmins, J.P. *Balancing Act: Environmental Issues in Forestry.* Vancouver: University of British Columbia Press, 1992.

Mahar, Dennis J. *Government Policies and Deforestation in Brazil's Amazon Region.* Washington, DC: World Bank, 1989.

Mather, A.S. *Global Forest Resources.* London: Belhaven Press, 1990.

Myers, Norman. *The Primary Source: Tropical Forests and Our Future.* New York: W.W. Norton and Co. 1984.

Newman, Arnold. *Tropical Rainforest: A World Survey of Our Most Valuable and Endangered Habitat with a Blueprint for its Survival.* New York: Facts on File, 1990.

Plotkin, Mark, and Famolare, Lisa, eds. *Sustainable Harvest and Marketing of Rain Forest Products.* Washington, DC: Island Press, 1992.

Poore, D., ed. *No Timber Without Trees.* London: IIED/Earthscan, 1989.

Repetto, Robert. *The Forest for the Trees?* Washington, DC: World Resources Institute, 1988.

Repetto, Robert, and Gillis, Malcolm. *Public Policies and the Misuse of Forest Resources.* New York: Cambridge University Press, 1988.

Revkin, Andrew. *The Burning Season: The Murder of Chico Mendes and the Fight for the Amazon Rain Forest.* Boston: Houghton Mifflin, 1990.

Richards, John F., and Tucker, Richard P. *World Deforestation in the Twentieth Century*. Durham: Duke University Press, 1988.

Rudel, Thomas K. *Tropical Deforestation: Small Farmers and Land Clearing in the Ecuadorian Amazon*. New York: Columbia University Press.

Rush, James. *The Last Tree*. New York: Asia Society, 1991.

Shands, William E., and Hoffman, John S. *The Greenhouse Effect, Climate Change and U.S. Forests*. Washington, DC: Conservation Foundation, 1987.

Shiva, Vandana. *Forestry Crisis and Forestry Myths*. Penang: Rainforest Movement, 1987.

Southgate, D., and Runge, C.F. *The Institutional Origins of Deforestation in Latin America*. Minneapolis: Department of Agricultural and Applied Economics, University of Minnesota, 1990.

Westoby, J. *Introduction of World Forestry*. Oxford: Blackwell, 1989.

Whitmore, T.C. *An Introduction to Tropical Forests*. Oxford: Clarendon Press, 1990.

Whitmore, T.C., and Sayer, J.A. *Tropical Deforestation and Species Extinction*. New York: Chapman and Hall, 1992.

Land Degradation
Documents

United Nations

ISRIC/UNEP. *Guidelines for General Assembly for the Status of Human-Induced Soil Degradation*. Working Paper 88/4. Wageningen, The Netherlands: ISRIC/UNEP, 1988.

UNCED. *Managing Fragile Ecosystems: Combatting Desertification and Drought*. UN Conference on Environment and Development Agenda 21. Rio Declaration. Forest Principles (Rio de Janeiro, Brazil), May 1, 1992, v. 2, 46.

United Nations Environmental Programme. "Land Degradation," in *The World Environment: 1972–1992: Two Decades of Challenge*. New York: Chapman and Hall, 1992, 131.

———. *Status of Decertification and Implementation of the United Nations Plan of Action to Combat Desertification*. Nairobi: UNEP, 1991.

———. *World Atlas of Desertification*. Baltimore: Edward Arnold, 1992.

Other
International Conference on Drought, Desertification and Food Deficit in Africa. *Environmental Crisis in Africa: Scientific Response: Proceedings of the International Conference on Drought, Desert and Food Deficit in Africa.* African Academy of Sciences, Nairobi, Kenya, June 3–6, 1986. Nairobi: Academy of Sciences Publications, 1989.

Articles

Barraclough, Declan. "The Earth Taken For Granted," *The Geographical Magazine*, v. 62, March 1990, 36–38.

Braden, John B., and Uchtmann, Donald L. "Soil Conservation Programs Amidst Environmental Commitments and the 'New Federalism,'" *Boston College Environmental Affairs Law Review.*

Coxhead, Ian, and Jayasuriya, Sisira. "Technical Change in Agriculture and Land Degradation in Developing Countries: A General Equilibrium Analysis," *Land Economics*, v. 70, February 1990, 20–37.

Dregen, H.E. "Erosion and Soil Productivity in Africa," *Journal of Soil and Water Conservation*, v. 45, no. 4, July/August 1990, 431.

Dregen, H.E., and Tucker, C.J. "Desert Encroachment," *Desertification Control Bulletin*, no. 16, 1986, 16–19.

Ervin, David E., and Dicks, Michael R. "Cropland Diversion for Conservation and Environmental Improvement: An Economic Welfare Analysis," *Land Economics*, v. 64, August 1988, 256–268.

"Fighting Soil Erosion," *The Futurist*, v. 22, July/August 1988, 61.

Franchito, Sergio H. "Climatic Change Due to Land Surface Alterations," *Climate Change*, v. 22, September 1992, 1.

Hellden, U. "Desertification—Time for an Assessment," *Ambio.*, v. 20, 1991, 372–383.

Hulme, Mike, and Kelly, Mick. "Exploring the Links Between Desertification and Climate Change," *Environment*, v. 35, no. 6, July/August 1993, 4.

Kaul, Sumedh. "Causes and Consequences of Desertification," *Energy and Environment Monitor*, v. 6, no. 2, September 1990, 35.

Le Houerou, H.N. "Climatic Change and Desertization," *Impact of Science on Society*, v. 166, 1992, 183–201.

Malik, Michael. "Fighting the Arid Land: Good Land Management Can Save Exhausted Soil," *Far Eastern Economic Review*, v. 141, September 22, 1988, 84–85.

Nortcliff, Stephen. "A Basis for Change," *The Geographical Magazine*, v. 62, September 1990, 46–48.

Pearce, Fred. "Mirage of Shifting Sands," *New Scientist*, v. 136, no. 1851, December 12, 1992, 38.

Southgate, D. "The Causes of Land Degradation on 'Spontaneously' Expanding Agricultural Frontiers in the Third World," *Land Economics*, v. 66, 1990, 93–101.

Turner, B.L., and Meyer, William B. "Land Use and Land Cover in Global Environmental Change: Considerations for Study," *International Social Science Journal*, v. 43, November 1991, 669–679.

Books

Ahmad, Yusuf J. *Desertification: Financial Support for the Biosphere*. West Hartford: Kumarian Press, 1987.

Anderson, Anthony B. *Alternatives to Deforestation: Steps Toward Sustainable Use of the Amazonian Rain Forest*. New York: Columbia University Press, 1990.

Blaikie, P.M. *The Political Economy of Soil Erosion in Developing Countries*. London: Longman, 1985.

Blaikie, Piers, and Brookfield, Harold. *Land Degradation and Society*. London: Methuen, 1987.

Freemuth, John C. *Islands under Siege: National Parks and the Politics of External Threats*. Lawrence: University of Kansas Press, 1991.

Glantz, Michael H. *Desertification: Environmental Degradation In and Around Arid Lands*. Boulder: Westview Press.

Gradwohl, Judith, and Greenburgh, Russell. *Saving the Tropical Forests*. Washington, DC: Island Press, 1988.

Graf, William L. *Wilderness Preservation and the Sagebrush Rebellions*. Savage, MD: Rowman and Littlefield, 1990.

Hemming, John. *Change in the Amazonian Basin*. Manchester: Manchester University Press, 1985.

Hunter, Malcolm L. *Wildlife, Forests and Forestry: Principles of Managing Forests for Biological Diversity*. Englewood Cliffs, NJ: Prentice Hall, 1990.

Hurst, Philip. *Rainforest Politics: Ecological Destruction in Southeast Asia*. Atlantic Highlands, NJ: Zed Books, 1990.

Ives, J., and Pitt, D.C. *Deforestation in Watersheds and Mountain Ecosystems*. London: Routledge, 1988.

Jordan, Carl F., ed. *Amazonian Rainforests: Ecosystem Disturbance and Recovery*. New York: Springer-Verlaq, 1987.

Kusler, Jon A., and Kentula, Mary E. *Wetland Creation and Restoration*. Washington, DC: Island Press, 1990.

Lal, R., and Steward, B.A. *Soil Degradation*. New York: Springer-Verlaq, 1990.

Revkin, Andrew. *The Burning Season: The Murder of Chico Mendes and the Fight for the Amazon Rain Forest*. Boston: Houghton Mifflin, 1990.

Mainguet, Monique. *Desertification: Natural Background and Human Mismanagement*. New York: Springer-Verlaq, 1991.

Oldeman, L.R., Hakkeling, R.T.A., and Sombroek, W.G. *World Map of the Status of Human Induced Soil Degradation, An Explanatory Note*. Wageningen, The Netherlands: ISRIC/UNEP, 1990.

Sheridan, David. *Desertification of the United States*. Washington, DC: Council on Environmental Quality.

Population
Documents

United Nations

Mahar, D.J., ed. *Rapid Population Growth and Human Carrying Capacity: Two Perspectives*. Working paper no. 690. Washington, DC: World Bank, 1985.

United Nations. *World Population Policies*. New York: Martinus Nijhoff, 1992.

———. *Population Distribution, Migration and Development*. New York: United Nations, 1990.

———. *Report on the International Conference on Population*. New York: United Nations, 1984.

———. *World Population Prospects, 1988*. New York: ST/ESA/SER.A/106, United Nations, 1989.

UNCED. *Combatting Poverty, Changing Consumption Patterns and Demographic Dynamics and Sustainability*. A/Conf.151/PC/100/Add2. Discussed in the Fourth Session of the Preparatory Committee for the United Nations Conference on Environment and Development. New York, March 2–April 3, 1992.

United Nations Department of International Economic and Social Affairs. *World Population Monitoring, 1989*. New York: United Nations Population Studies, no. 113, 1990.

United Nations Development Programme. *Human Development Report, 1991*. New York: Oxford University Press, 1991.

———. *Human Development Report, 1992*. New York: Oxford University Press, 1992.

———. *A World in Balance—State of the World Population, 1992*. New York: UNFPA, 1992.

United Nations Population Division. *Long-Range Population Projections*. New York: ST/ESA/SER.A/125, UN, 1991.

———. *Revision of World Population Prospects: Computerized Data Base and Summary Tables*. New York: United Nations Department of International Economic and Social Affairs, 1990.

United Nations Population Fund. *Population and the Environment: The Challenges Ahead*. UN Population Fund Report, 1992.

United Nations World Food Council. *The Global State of Hunger and Malnutrition and the Impact of Economic Adjustment on Food and Hunger*. Beijing: World Food Council, Thirteenth Ministerial Session, 1987.

World Bank. *The Population, Agriculture and Environment Nexus in Sub Saharan Africa*. Washington, DC: World Bank, Africa Region, December, 1991.

———. *World Bank Development Report, 1990*. Washington, DC: Oxford University Press, 1990.

Other

Human Needs and Nature's Balance: Population, Resources, and the Environment. Population Reference Bureau Report, October 1987.

"Land," in *State of the Environment*. Paris: OECD, 1991, 95.

Tiffen, M. *Population Profile*. ODI Working Paper 57. London: ODI, 1991.

Articles

Aldington, T.J., and Zegarra, F. "The State of the World Food and Agriculture," *World Resource Review*, v. 2, no. 1, 1990, 7.

Baron, Liz. "Setting the Stage for Cairo," *ZPG Report*, v. 25, no. 4, August 1993, 1.

Berle, Peter A. "On the Road to Cairo and Beyond," *Audobon*, v. 95, July/August 1993, 6.

Brown, Lester. "Feeding Six Billion," *World Watch*, v. 2, no. 5, September/October 1989, 32.

Brown, Lester R., Kane, Hal, and Ayres, Ed. "Agricultural Resource Trends," *Vital Signs 1993: The Trends That Are Shaping Our Future.* Washington, DC: Worldwatch Institute, 1993, 39.

Camp, Sharon. "Population, Poverty and Pollution," *Forum of Applied Research in Public Policy*, v. 6, no. 2, summer 1991, 5.

Clavijo, Hernando. "Population Summit: Developing Countries Hope for Action," *Population Today*, April 1994, 5.

Cleaver, Kevin, and Schreiber, Gotz. "Population, Agriculture, and the Environment in Africa," *Finance and Development*, v. 39, June 1992, 34–35.

Crosson, Pierre R. "Sustainable Agriculture," *Resources—Resources for the Future*, no. 106, winter 1992, 14.

Daily, Gretchen C. "Population, Sustainability, and Earth's Carrying Capacity," *BioScience*, v. 42, no. 10, November 1992, 761.

Daly, Herman E. "Towards an Environmental Macroeconomics," *Land Economics*, v. 68, May 1992, 241–245.

De Sherbinin, Alex, and Kalish, Susan. "Population-Enviornment Links: Crucial but Unwieldy," *Population Today*, January 1994, 1–2.

Farshad, A., and Zinck, J.A. "Seeking Agricultural Sustainability," *Agricultural Ecosystems and Environment*, v. 47, no. 1, October 1993, 1.

Fox, Robert W. "The Population Explosion: Threatening the Third World's Future," *The Futurist*, v. 26, January/February 1992, 60.

Freedman, Ronald. "Family Planning Programs in the Third World," *The Annals of the American Academy of Political and Social Sciences*, July 1990, 33–43.

Goodland, Robert, Daly, Herman, and Kellenberg, John. "Burden Sharing in the Transition to Environmental Sustainability," *Futures*, v. 26, March 1994, 146–155.

Henderson, Conway W. "Population Pressures and Political Repression," *Social Science Quarterly*, v. 74, June 1993, 322–333.

Hitzhusen, Fred J. "Land Degradation and Sustainability of Agricultural Growth: Some Economic Concepts and Evidence from Selected Developing Countries," *Agricultural Ecosystems and Environment*, v. 46, no. 1–4, 69.

Holdgate, Martin W. "The Environment of Tomorrow," *Environment*, v. 33, no. 6, July/August 1991, 14.

Holdren, John P. "Population and the Energy Problem," *Population and Environment*, v. 12, no. 3, spring 1991, 231.

Hollingsworth, William G. "World Population: An Unwishful Assessment, A Hopeful Proposal," *Boston College Environmental Affairs Law Review*, v. 10, no. 4, May 1983, 853.

Kates, Robert W. "The Human Environment: The Road Not Taken, The Road Still Beckons," *Annals of the Association of American Geographers*, v. 77, December 1987, 525–534.

Keyfitz, Nathan. "Population Growth Can Prevent the Development that Would Slow Population Growth," in Mathews, Jessica T. ed. *Preserving the Global Environment: The Challenge of Shared Leadership*. New York: W.W. Norton, 1991.

————. "Population and Sustainable Development: Distinguishing Fact and Preference Concerning the Future Human Population and Environment," *Population and Environment*, v. 14, no. 5, May 1993, 441.

Lamm, Richard D. "The Future of the Environment," *The Annals of the American Academy of Political Science*, v. 522, July 1992, 57–66.

Lopez, Ramon. "Environmental Degradation and Economic Openness in LDC's: the Poverty Linkage," *American Journal of Agricultural Economics*, December 1992, 1138.

Luten, Daniel B. "Population and Resources," *Population and Environment*, v. 12, no. 3, spring 1991, 311.

Maeda, Hiroshi, and Murakami, Shuta. "Population's Urban Environment Evaluation Model and Its Application," *Journal of Regional Science*, v. 25, May 1985, 273–290.

McNamara, Robert S. "The Population Explosion: High Population Growth is Making Poor People Poorer, the Hungry Hungrier, and an Already Fragile Environment Too Weak to Support its Proliferating Inhabitants," *The Futurist*, v. 26, November/December 1992, 9–13.

Merrick, Thomas W. "World Population in Transition," *Population Bulletin*, v. 41, no. 2, 1989.

Ness, Gayl D. "Population, Development and Global Change," *Population*, v. 18, no. 1, March 1991, 24.

Norse, D. "Population and Global Climate Change," in J. Jager and H. L. Ferguson eds. *Climate Change: Science, Impacts and Policy: Proceedings of the Second World Climate Conference*. Cambridge, England: Cambridge University Press, 1991.

Olsson, Lennart. "Desertification and Land Degradation in Perspective," Aarhus University Proc. 2nd Danish Sahel Workshop, Sandbjerg Manor, Denmark, January 1990, 5.

Orr, David W. "The Challenge of Sustainability," *Phytophathol.*, v. 83, no. 1, January 1993, 38.

Parikh, J., and Parikh, K. "Role of Unsustainable Patterns and Population in Global Environmental Stress," *Sustainable Development*, v. 1, no. 1, 108–118.

"Population and Environment: Experts Explore Linkages," *Conservation Foundation Letter*, no. 3, 1988, 1.

"Population, Resources, Environment and Development," *UN Chronicle*, v. 21, June 1984, xxiv–xxv.

Postel, Sandra. "Land's End," *World Watch*, v. 2, no. 3, May-June 1989, 12.

Repetto, Robert. "Population, Resources, Environment: An Uncertain Future," *Population Bulletin*, v. 42, no. 2, 1989.

Riche, Martha Farnsworth. "How Far is it to Cairo?," *Population Today*, April 1994, 3.

Ridker, Ronald G. "Population Issues," *Resources-Resources for the Future*, no. 106, winter 1992, 11.

Salas, Rafael M. "Slowing Population Growth: A Decade of Progress," *UN Chronicle*, v. 21, June 1984, xviii–xix.

Shaw, R.P. "Rapid Population Growth and Environmental Degradation: Ultimate versus Proximate Factors," *Environmental Conservation*, v. 16, 1989, 199–208.

Skinner, Robert G. "World Energy Future: The Demand Side Challenge," *Natural Resource Forum*, v. 17, no. 3, August 1993, 181.

Stutz, Bruce. "The Landscape of Hunger," *Audobon*, v. 95, no. 2, March-April 1993, 54.

Tellier, L.N. "Demographic Growth and Food Production in Developing Countries: A Non-Linear Model," *Ekistics*, v. 313, 1985, 383–385.

Ticknell, Crispin. "The Human Species: A Suicidal Success?" *The Geographical Journal*, v. 159, July 1993, 219–226.

United Nations Fund for Population Activities. "New Contraceptive Methods for Developing Countries," *The Futurist*, July/August 1990, 56.

Wirth, Timothy E. "U.S. Statement on Population and Development," *U.S. Department of State Dispatch*, v. 4, May 31, 1993, 397–8.

Books

Abernathy, V.D. *Population Politics: The Choices that Shape Our Future*. New York: Plenum, 1993.

Arowolo, O., and Ekanow, C. *Population and Development Planning: An Integrated Approach*. New Rochelle, NY: Okapaku Communications, 1992.

Back, Kurt W. *Family Planning and Population Control: The Challenges of a Successful Movement*. New York: Macmillan, 1989.

Bratton, Susan P. *Six Billion and More: Human Population Regulations and Christian Ethics*. Louisville, KY: Westminster/John Knox, 1992.

Bulatao, Rodolfo A., Bos, Eduard, Stephens, Patience W., and Vu, My T. *World Population Projections, 1989–1990*. Baltimore: The Johns Hopkins University Press for the World Bank, 1990.

Davis, Kingsley, and Bernstam, Mikhail S. *Resources, Environment, and Population: Present Knowledge, Future Options*. New York: Oxford University Press, 1991.

Dixon-Mueller, Ruth. *Population Policy and Women's Rights: Transforming Reproductive Choice*. Greenwood: Praeger Publishers, 1993.

Durning, Alan B. *Poverty and Environment: Reversing the Downward Spiral*. Worldwatch Paper No. 92. Washington, DC: Worldwatch, 1989.

Gilbert, A.J., and Brast, L.C. eds. *Modeling for Population and Sustainable Development*. New York: Routledge, 1991.

Hill, Anne M., and King, Elizabeth M. eds. *Women's Education in Developing Countries: Barriers, Benefits, and Policies*. London: Johns Hopkins University, 1993.

Jacobson, Jodi L. *Planning the Global Family*. Washington, DC: Worldwatch Institute, 1987.

Kates, R.W., et al. *The Hunger Report: 1988*. Providence, RI: Brown University Alan Shawn Feinstein World Hunger Program, 1988.

Lee, Ronald D., et al., eds. *Population, Food and Rural Development*. New York: Oxford University Press, 1992.

Leonard, H. Jeffrey, ed. *Environment and the Poor: Development Strategies for a Common Agenda*. New Brunswick: Transaction Books, 1990.

Mahadevan, K., ed. *Ecology, Development and Population Problem: Perspectives from India, China and Australia*. Colombia, MO: S. Asia, 1992.

Meadows, D.C., Meadows, D.L., and Randers, J. *Beyond the Limits: Global Collapse or Sustainable Future*. London: Earthscan Publications, 1992.

Myers, Norman. *Population, Resources and the Environment: Critical Challenges*. New York: UN Population Fund, 1991.

Reid, Ann C., ed. *Population Change, Natural Resources, and Regionalism*. Milford, PA: Grey Towers Press, 1986.

Roberts, Godfrey ed. *Population Policy: Contemporary Issues*. Westport, CT: Greenwood, 1990.

Sadik, Nafis. *State of World Population 1990*. New York: UN Fund for Population Activities, 1990.

Salas, Rafael M. *Reflections on Population*. New York: Pergamon, 1984.

Van Imhoff, E., et al. *Population, Environment and Development*. Bristol, PA: Taylor and Francis, 1992.

Wattenberg, Ben, and Zinmeister, Karl eds. *Are World Population Trends a Problem?* Washington, DC: American Enterprise, 1985.

Space
Documents

United States
Orbiting Debris: A Space Environmental Problem. Washington, DC: Congress of the United States Office of Technology Assessment, 1990.

Articles
Baca, K.A. "Property Rights in Outer Space," *Journal of Air Law and Commerce*, v. 58, Summer 1993, 1041–1085.

Baker, H.A. "Protection of the Outer Space Environment: History and Analysis of Article IX of the Outerspace Treaty," *Annals of Air and Space Law*, v. 12, 1987, 143–173.

Bockstiegel, K.H. "Space Law Past and Future: The Challenges of the XXIst Century," *Annals of Air and Space Law*, v. 17, 1992, 15–28.

Booth, Nicholas. "Cleaning Up the Cosmos," *The Geographical Magazine*, v. 61, April 1989, 32–34.

Bosco, J.A. "International Law Regarding Outerspace—An Overview," *Journal of Air Law and Commerce*, v. 55, spring 1990, 609–651.

Cleveland, Harlan. "The Global Commons," *Futurist*, v. 27, no. 3, May-June 1993, 9.

"Earthly Goals for Mission in Space," *Futurist*, v. 22, no. 5, September-October 1988, 29.

Field, G.B., Rees, M.J., and Spergel, D.N. "Is the Space Environment at Risk," *Nature*, v. 336, December 22/29, 1988, 725–726.

Goldman, Nathan C. "Advances in Domestic Space Law," *Trial*, v. 26, July 1990, 28–30+.

———. "American Space Law; International and Domestic," *Science*, v. 246, October 6, 1989, 132–133.

Gore, Albert, Jr. "Outer Space, the Global Environment and International Law: Into the Next Century," *Tennessee Law Review*, v. 57, winter 1990, 329–337.

Griffiths, Robert J. "From the Ocean Floor to Outer Space: The Third World and Global Commons Negotiations," *Journal of Third World Studies*, v. 9, fall 1992, 375–389.

Jakhu, R.S. "Space Debris in the Geostationary Orbit: A Major Challenge for Space Law," *Annals of Air and Space Law*, v. 17, 1992, 313–323.

Jasentuliyana, N. "Space Law and the United Nations," *Annals of Air and Space Law*, v. 17, 1992, 137–155.

Kayser, V. "Commercial Exploitation of Space: Developing Domestic Regulation," *Annals of Air and Space Law*, v. 17, 1992, 187–197.

Marko, D.E. "A Kindler, Gentler Moon Treaty: A Critical Review of the Current Moon Treaty and a Proposed Alternative," *Journal of Natural Resources and Environmental Law*, v. 8, 1992/93, 293–345.

McDermott, B.L. "Outerspace: The Latest Polluted Frontier," *A.F.L. Review*, v. 36, 1991, 163–198.

"1987 Achievements in Space Lauded by UN Committee," *UN Chronicle*, v. 25, September 1988, 44–46.

Perek, Lubos. "Outer Space: Mankind's Fourth Environment," *Mazingira*, v. 7, no. 2, 1983, 56.

Reibel, D.E. "Environmental Regulation of Space Activity: The Case of Orbital Debris," *Stanford Environmental Law Journal*, v. 10, 1991, 97–136.

Ren, Zhengde. "For Equal Use of Space and Sea," *Beijing Review*, v. 28, September 16, 1985, 12–13.

Roberts, Darryl. "Space and International Relations," *The Journal of Politics*, v. 50, November 1988, 1075–1090.

Schafer, B.K. "Solid, Hazardous, and Radioactive Wastes in Outer Space: Present Controls and Suggested Changes," *Cal. W. International Law Journal*, v. 19, 1988/89, 1–46.

Smith, Gar. "Space as Wilderness," *Earth Island Journal*, winter 1987, 2.

"Trashing the Final Frontier: An Examination of Space Debris from a Legal Perspective," *Tulane Environmental Law Journal*, v. 6, summer 1993, 369–395.

Wassenbergh, H.A. "The Law Governing International Private Commercial Activities of Space Transportation," *Journal of Space Law*, v. 21, 1993, 97–121.

Books

Hargrove, Eugene. *Beyond Spaceship Earth: Environmental Ethics and the Solar System*. San Francisco: Sierra Club Books, 1986.

Napolitano, L.G. *Space: Mankind's Fourth Environment vol. II*. New York: Pergamon, 1983.

Tascione, Thomas F. *Introduction to the Space Environment*. 2nd ed. Melbourne, FL: Krieger, 1994.

Species
Documents

United Nations

United Nations Environment Programme. "Biological Diversity," in *The State of the World Environment*. Nairobi: UNEP, 19–26.

WRI/UNEP/IUCN. *Global Biodiversity Strategy*. New York: WRI/UNEP/IUCN, 1992.

United States

National Forum on Biodiversity. *Biodiversity*. Washington, DC: National Academy Press, 1988.

Office of Technology Assessment Task Force. *Technologies to Maintain Biological Diversity*. New York: Science Information Resource Center.

U.S. Agency for International Development. *U.S. Strategy on the Conservation of Biological Diversity: An Interagency Task Force Report to Congress*. Washington, DC: U.S. Agency for International Development, 1985.

Other

World Conservation Monitoring Center. *Biodiversity Status Report.* WCMC: Cambridge, 1992.

World Conservation Monitoring Centre. Brian Groombridge, ed. *Global Biodiversity: Status of Earth's Living Resources: A Report.* New York: Chapman and Hall, 1992.

Articles

Andressen, Steinar. "The Effectiveness of the International Whaling Commission," *Arctic*, v. 46, no. 2, June 1993, 108.

Balistrieri, Carlo A. "CITES: The ESA and International Trade," *Natural Resources and Environment*, v. 8, no. 1, summer 1993, 33.

"Biodiversity: Variety is the Spice of Life," *UN Chronicle*, v. 29, June 1992, 52–53.

Brown, J.H. "On the Relationship Between Abundance and Distribution of Species," *American Naturalist*, v. 124, no. 184, 255–279.

Burhenne, Wolfgang E. "Biodiversity: The Legal Aspects," *Environmental Policy Law*, v. 22, no. 5–6, December 1992, 324.

"Buying Diversity," *The Economist*, v. 329, October 2, 1993, 18.

Chokor, Boyowa A. "Environmental Pressure Groups and Habitat Protection in the Developing World: The Case of Nigeria," *Environmentalist*, v. 12, no. 3, autumn 1992, 169.

Colwell, R.R. "Biodiversity—An International Challenge," *The FASEB Journal*, September 1993, 1107.

"Conserving and Managing Our Genetic Resources," *Impact of Science on Society*, v. 158, 1990, 95–184.

Cross, Andrew. "Species and Habitat: The Analysis and Impoverishment of Variety," v. 62, June 1990, 42–47.

"The Crowded Brink of Extinction," *The Futurist*, v. 24, May/June 1990, 54–55.

DiCastri and Younes, T. "Ecosystem Function of Biological Diversity," *Biology International*, Special Issue no. 22, 1990, 1–20.

Ehrlich, Paul R., and Ehrlich, Anne H. "The Value of Biodiversity," *Ambio*, v. 21, no. 3, May 1992, 219.

"Food Crops and Genetic Diversity," *The Futurist*, v. 25, March/April 1991, 53.

Gadgil, Madhav. "Indigenous Knowledge for Biodiversity Conservation," *Ambio*, v. 22, no. 2–3, May 1993, 151.

Goudie, Andrew. "Environmental Uncertainty," *Geography*, v. 78, April 1993, 137–141.

Grassle, J.F. "Species Diversity in Deep-Sea Communities," *Trends in Ecology and Evolution*, v. 4, 1989, 12–15.

Hawkes, J.G. "What are Genetic Resources and Why Should They Be Conserved?" *Impact of Science on Society*, v. 158, 1990, 97–106.

Huston, Michael A. "Biological Diversity and Human Resources," *Impact of Science on Society*, v. 166, 1992, 121–130.

Hill, Kevin D. "The Endangered Species Act: What Do We Mean By Species?" *Boston College Environmental Affairs Law Review*, v. 21, December 1993, 1931–1945.

Margulies, Rebecca L. "Protecting Biodiversity: Recognizing International Intellectual Property Rights in Plant Genetic Resources," *Michigan Journal of International Law*, v. 14, winter 1993, 322–356.

Myers, N. "The Biodiversity Challenge: Expanded Hot Spot Analyses," *The Environmentalist*, v. 10, no. 4, 1990, 245–256.

———. "Biodiversity and the Precautionary Principle," *Ambio*, v. 22, no. 2–3, May 1993, 74.

Pearce, D.W. "Saving the World's Biodiversity," *Environment and Planning A*, v. 25, June 1993, 755–757.

Roughgarden, J. "The Structure and Assembly of Communities," in Roughgarden, J., May R., and Levin S. eds., *Perspectives in Ecological Theory*, Princeton, NJ: Princeton University Press, 1989.

Schwarz, Adam. "Biological Resources: Banking on Diversity," *Far Eastern Economic Review*, v. 156, October 28, 1993, 55+.

Slocombe, D. Scott. "CITES, the Wildlife Trade and Sustainable Development," *Alternatives*, v. 16, no. 1, March-April 1989, 20.

Solbrig, Otto T. "The Origin and Function of Biodiversity," *Environment*, v. 33, no. 5, June 1991, 16.

"Species Galore," *The Economist*, v. 320, September 1991, 17.

Swaney, James A., and Olson, Paulette I. "The Economics of Biodiversity: Lives and Lifestyles," *Journal of Economic Issues*, v. 26, March 1992, 1–25.

Tickell, Crispin. "The Diversity of Life," *Geography*, v. 78, October 1993, 374–380.

Weitzman, Martin L. "On Diversity," *The Quarterly Journal of Economics*, v. 107, May 1992, 363–405.

Wilson, E.O. "The Biological Diversity Crisis: A Challenge to Science," *Issues in Science Technology*, v. 2, 1985a, 20–29.

Books

Abramovitz, Janet. *Investing in Biological Diversity.* Washington, DC: World Resources Institute, 1991.

Adams, Douglas, and Carwardine, Mark. *Last Chance to See.* New York: Harmony Books, 1990.

Akerle, O., Heywood, V., and Synge, H. *The Conservation of Medicinal Plants.* Cambridge: Cambridge University Press, 1991.

Barker, Rocky. *Saving All the Parts: Reconciling Economics and the Endangered Species Act.* Washington, DC: Island Press, 1993.

Beatley, Timothy. *Habitat Conservation Planning: Endangered Species and Urban Growth.* Austin: University of Texas Press, 1994.

Caufield, C. *In the Rainforest.* New York: A.A. Knopf, 1985.

Clewis, Beth. *Biological Diversity: A Selected Bibliography.* Monticello, IL: Vance Bibliographies, 1990.

Cook, Lawrence M. *Biological and Ecological Diversity.* New York: Chapman and Hall, 1991.

Davis, George D. *Biological Diversity: Saving All the Pieces.* Elizabethtown, NY: Adirondack Council, 1988.

Ehrlich, Paul, and Ehrlich, Anne. *Extinction: The Causes and Consequences of the Disappearance of Species.* New York: Random House, 1981.

Eldredge, Niles. *The Miner's Canary: Unraveling the Mysteries of Extinction.* New York: Prentice Hall Press, 1991.

————. *Systematics, Ecology, and the Biological Diversity Crisis.* New York: Columbia University Press, 1992.

Ereshefsky, Marc. *The Units of Evolution: Essays on the Nature of Species.* Cambridge: MIT Press, 1992.

Faure, David S. *International Trade in Endangered Species.* Dordrecht, The Netherlands: Martinus Nijhoff, 1989.

Fiedler, Peggy L., and Jain, Subodh K., eds. *Conservation Biology: The Theory and Practice of Nature Conservation, Preservation, and Management.* New York: Chapman and Hall, 1992.

Harf, James E., and Trout B. Thomas, eds. *The Politics of Global Resources: Energy, Environment, Population and Food.* Durham, NC: Duke University Press, 1986.

Jones, G.E. *The Conservation of Ecosystems and Species.* New York: Routledge, Chapman and Hall, 1987.

Kaufman, Les, and Mallory, Kenneth. *The Last Extinction.* Cambridge: MIT Press, 1993.

Kingsland, Sharon E. *Modelling Nature: Episodes in the History of Population Ecology.* Chicago: University of Chicago Press, 1988.

Kohn, Kathryn A., ed. *Balancing on the Brink of Extinction: The Endangered Species Act and Lessons for the Future.* Washington, DC: Island Press, 1990.

Kohn, Kathryn A. *Balancing on the Brink of Extinction: The Endangered Species Act and Lessons for the Future.* Washington, DC: Island Press, 1991.

Lal, K.M. *Population Settlements: Development and Planning.* Colombia, MO: S. Asia, 1988.

Lyster, Simon. *International Wildlife Law.* Cambridge: Grotius Publications, 1985.

McNeely, Jeffrey A. *Conserving the World's Biological Diversity.* Washington, DC: International Union for Conservation of Nature and Natural Resources, World Resources Institute, Conservation International, World Wildlife Fund-U.S. and the World Bank, 1990.

―――. *Economics and Biological Diversity: Developing and Using Incentives to Conserve Biological Resources.* Gland, Switzerland: International Union for Conservation of Nature and Natural Resources, 1988.

McNeely, Jeffrey A., et al. *Conserving the World's Biological Diversity.* New York: International Union for Conservation of Nature, 1990.

Miles, Edward L. *Management of World Fisheries: Implications of Extended Fisheries Jurisdiction.* Seattle: University of Washington Press, 1990.

Nilsson, Greta. *The Endangered Species Handbook.* Washington, DC: Animal Welfare Institute, 1986.

Norton, Bryan G., ed. *The Preservation of Species: The Value of Biological Diversity.* Princeton, NJ: Princeton University Press, 1986.

Ogden, P.E. *Migration and Geographical Change.* Cambridge: Cambridge University Press, 1989.

Oldfield, Margery L. *The Value of Conserving Genetic Resources.* Washington, DC: National Park Service, U.S. Department of the Interior, 1984.

Oldfield, Margery L., and Alcorn, Janis B. *Biodiversity: Culture, Conservation and Ecodevelopment.* Boulder, CO: Westview Press, 1991.

Pimm, Stuart L. *The Balance of Nature?: Ecological Issues in the Conservation of Species and Communities.* Chicago: University of Chicago Press, 1991.

Reid, Walter, V.C. *Keeping Options Alive: The Scientific Basis for Conserving Biodiversity.* Washington, DC: World Resources Institute, 1989.

Ricklefs, Robert E., and Schluter, Dolph, ed. *Species Diversity in Ecological Communities: Historical and Geographical Perspectives.* Chicago: University of Chicago Press, 1993.

Ryan, John C. *Life Support: Conserving Biological Diversity.* Washington, DC: Worldwatch Institute, 1992.

Shiva, Vandana. *Biodiversity: Social and Ecological Consequences.* Atlantic Highlands, NY: Humanities, 1993.

Solbrig, O.T., and Nicolis, G. *Perspectives on Biological Complexity.* Paris: International Union of Biological Sciences, 1991.

Teitel, Martin. *Rainforest In Your Kitchen: The Hidden Connection Between Extinction and Your Supermarket.* Washington, DC: Island Press, 1992.

Thorne-Miller, Boyce. *The Living Ocean: Understanding and Protecting Marine Biodiversity.* Washington, DC: Island Press, 1991.

Whitmore, T.C., and Sayer, J.A. *Tropical Deforestation and Species Extinction.* New York: Chapman and Hall, 1992.

Wilson, Edward Osborn. *The Diversity of Life.* Cambridge: Harvard University Press, 1992.

World Resources Institute. *Global Biodiversity Strategy: Guidelines for Action to Save, Study, and Use Earth's Biotic Wealth Sustainably and Equitably.* Washington, DC: WRI, 1992.

Toxics
Documents

Canada
Whittle, R., Jessiman, B., and Raphael, R. "Hazardous Waste Management: An International Perspective Summary Report," in Environment Canada et al. *Toxic Substances 5th Conference.* Montreal, Quebec, April 1–2, 1992, 151.

United Nations
UNCED. *Environmentally Sound Management of Hazardous Wastes, Including Prevention of Illegal International Traffic in Hazardous*

Wastes. United Nations Conference on Environment and Development Agenda 21. Rio Declaration. Forest Principles. Rio de Janeiro, Brazil, May 1, 1992, v. 2, 237.

————. *Environmentally Sound Management of Toxic Chemicals, Including the Prevention of Illegal International Traffic in Toxic and Dangerous Products.* United Nations Conference on Environment and Development Agenda 21. Rio Declaration. Forest Principles. Rio de Janeiro, Brazil, May 1, 1992, v. 2, 217.

International Atomic Energy Agency. *The International Chernobyl Project: An Overview: Assessment of Radiological Consequences and Evaluation of Protective Measures.* Vienna: International Atomic Energy Agency, 1991.

ILO. *Major Hazards Control.* Geneva: ILO, 1988.

Lucas, Robert E.B., Sheeler, David and Hettige, Hemamala. *Economic Development, Environmental Regulation and the International Migration of Toxic Industrial Pollution: 1960–1988.* World Bank Discussion Paper 159: International Trade and the Environment, 1992, 67.

World Bank/World Health Organization/United Nations Environment Programme. *Safe Disposal of Hazardous Wastes: The Special Needs and Problems of Developing Countries.* Geneva: World Bank/WHO/UNEP, 1989.

World Health Organization. *Public Health Impact of Pesticides Used in Agriculture.* Geneva: WHO, 1990.

United States

Aidala, James. *The Accident in Bhopal, India: Implications for U.S. Hazardous Chemical Policies.* Washington, DC: U.S. Library of Congress Congressional Research Service Report Ib85022, March 6, 1986.

Hinman, Keith, Schwartz, Donald, and Soffer, Eileen. *Analysis of Risks from Exposure to Air Toxics.* Washington, DC: EPA Office of Policy Planning and Evaluation Revised Stage 1 Report, May 30, 1986, 3–1.

————. *Analysis of Risks from Toxics in Drinking Water.* Washington, DC: EPA Office of Policy Planning and Evaluation Revised Stage 1 Report, May 30, 1986, 4–1.

Lee, Martin. *Toxic Waste Incineration At Sea.* Washington, DC: U.S. Library of Congress Congressional Research Service Report Ib85131, April 14, 1986.

Other

Organization for Economic Cooperation and Development. *Transfrontier Movements of Hazardous Wastes.* Paris: OECD, 1985.

Toxics in the Air: Reassessing the Regulatory Framework. Conservation Foundation Report, 1987.

Articles

Anderson, John E. "The Toxic Danger," *American Demographics*, v. 9, January 1987, 45.

Brown, Donald A. "Superfund Cleanups, Ethics, and Environmental Risk Assessment," *Boston College Environmental Affairs Law Review*, v. 16, winter 1988, 181–198.

Calmet, D.P., and Bewers, J.M. "Radioactive Waste and Ocean Dumping," *Marine Policy*, v. 15, no. 6, November 1991, 413.

Cannon, Joseph. "The Regulation of Toxic Air Pollutants: A Critical Review," *APCA Journal*, v. 36, no. 5, May 1986, 561.

Christoffel, Tom. "Grassroots Environmentalism Under Legal Attack: Dandelions, Pesticides, and a Neighbors Right to Know," *American Journal of Public Health*, v. 75, May 1985, 565–567.

Fernie, John, and Openshaw, Stan. "Where to Dump?" *The Geographical Magazine*, v. 58, May 1986, 214–216.

Fleming, India, O'Keeffe, Mary K., and Baum, Andrew. "Chronic Stress and Toxic Waste: The Role of Uncertainty and Helplessness," *Journal of Applied Social Psychology*, v. 21, December 1, 1991, 1889–1907.

Foegen, J.H. "Contaminated Water: The Trickle-Down Problem That's Welling Up Fast," *The Futurist*, v. 20, March/April 1986, 22–24.

Galvin, David, and Toteff, Sally. "Toxics on the Homefront," *Sierra*, September-October 1986, 44.

Goldberg, Marion Zenn. "Lawn Chemicals: Is Greener Grass Worth It?" *Trial*, v. 27, June 1991, 12.

Grossman, Karl. "From Toxic Racism to Environmental Justice," *E. Magazine*, v. 3, May-June 1992, 28–35.

"Hazardous Waste: No Dumping," *The Economist*, v. 313, February 18, 1989, 43–44.

"International Toxicity Update," *Dangerous Properties of Industrial Materials Report*, v. 6, no. 3, May-June 1986, 27.

Kean, Tom. "Dealing with Toxic Air Pollutants: New Initiatives," *Issues in Science and Technology*, v. 11, no. 4, summer 1986, 19.

Kraft, Michael E., and Clary, Bruce B. "Citizen Participation and the NIMBY Syndrome: Public Response to Radioactive Waste Disposal," *The Western Political Quarterly*, v. 44, June 1991, 299–328.

Kumar, Sehdev. "The Three Legacies of Bhopal," *Alternatives*, v. 13, no. 4, November 1986, 3.

LaDou, Joseph. "Deadly Migration: Hazardous Industries' Flight to the Third World," *Technology Review*, v. 94, no. 5, July 1991, 46.

Lake, R.W., and Disch, L. "Structural Constraints and Pluralistic Contradictions in Hazardous Waste Regulation," *Environment and Planning*, v. 24, May 1992, 663–681.

MacKenzie, Debora. "If You Can't Treat It, Ship It," *New Scientist*, v. 122, no. 1658, April 1, 1989, 24.

Mank, Bradford C. "The Two Headed Dragon of Siting and Cleaning Up Hazardous Waste Dumps: Can Economic Incentives or Mediation Slay the Monster?" *Boston College Environmental Affairs Law Review*, v. 19, winter 1991, 239–285.

Meacham, Edith D. "Is it Safe to Sell Banned Pesticides Overseas?" *EPA Journal*, v. 11, January-February 1985, 12–13.

Miceli, Thomas J., and Segerson, Kathleen. "Regulating Agricultural Groundwater Contamination: A Comment," *Journal of Environmental Economics and Management*, v. 25, September 1993, 196–200.

Mitchell, Robert Cameron, and Carson, Richard T. "Property Rights, Protest, and the Siting of Hazardous Waste Facilities," *The American Economic Review*, v. 76, May 1986, 285–290.

Moise, Evdokia. "International Regulations on Radioactive and Toxic Waste: Similarities and Differences," *Nuclear Law Bulletin*, no. 47, June 1991, 10.

Mpanya, Mutombo. "The Dumping of Toxic Waste in African Countries: A Case of Poverty and Racism," in *Race and the Incidence of Environmental Hazards: A Time for Discourse*, New York: Westview Press, 1992, 204.

Murphy, Sean D. "Prospective Liability Regimes for the Transboundary Movement of Hazardous Wastes," *American Journal of International Law*, v. 88, January 1994, 24–75.

Nakamura, Robert T., Church, Thomas W., and Cooper, Philip J. "Environmental Dispute Resolution and Hazardous Waste Cleanups: A Cautionary Tale of Policy Implementation," *Journal of Policy Analysis and Management*, v. 10, spring 1991, 204–221.

Nanda, Ved P. "For Whom the Bell Tolls in the Aftermath of the Bhopal Tragedy: Some Reflections on Forum Non Conveniens and Alternative Methods of Resolving the Bhopal Dispute," *Denver Journal of International Law and Policy*, v. 15, no. 2–3, winter-spring 1987, 235.

Panasewich, Carol. "Protecting Ground Water from Pesticides," *EPA Journal*, v. 11, September 1985, 18–20.

Patrick, David R. "Protecting the Public from Toxic Air Pollutants," *EPA Journal*, v. 11, June 1985, 24–27.

Pearce, Hannah. "Dump and Run," *New Stateman and Society*, v. 6, February 5, 1993, 37–38.

"The Peril of Pesticides," *Africa*, v. 176, April 1986, 59.

Pryor, Margherita. "Tackling Toxics from Motor Vehicles," *EPA Journal*, v. 11, September 1985, 28.

"Reducing Pesticide Use," *The Futurist*, v. 21, July-August 1987, 52–53.

Renner, Michael G. "Military Victory, Ecological Defeat," *World Watch*, v. 4, no. 4, July-August 1991, 27.

Ross, John. "Dangers in Paradise," *Sierra*, v. 77, no. 4, July-August 1992, 44.

"The Rows Behind Ecology," *The Economist*, v. 299, April 26, 1986, 92–93.

Russell, Milton, Colglazier, E. William and Tonn, Bruce F. "The U.S. Hazardous Waste Legacy," *Environment*, v. 34, July-August 1992, 12–14, 34–39.

Schissel, Howard. "The Deadly Trade: Toxic Waste Dumping in Africa," *Africa Report*, v. 33, September-October 1988, 47–49.

Segerson, Kathleen. "Liability for Groundwater Contamination from Pesticides," *Journal of Environmental Economics and Management*, v. 19, November 1990, 227–243.

Simmons, James R., and Stark, Nancy. "Backyard Protest: Emergence, Expansion, and Persistence of a Local Hazardous Waste Controversy," *Policy Studies Journal*, v. 21, no. 3, 1993, 470–491.

Stehr-Green, Paul A., and Lybarger, Jeffrey A. "Exposure to Toxic Waste Sites: An Investigative Approach," *Public Health Reports*, v. 104, January-February 1989, 71–74.

Teclaff, Ludwig A., and Teclaff, Eileen. "Transboundary Toxic Pollution and the Drainage Basin Concept," *Natural Resources Journal*, v. 25, 1985, 581–612.

Thrupp, Lori Ann. "Pesticides and Policies: Approaches to Pest-Control Dilemmas in Nicaragua and Costa Rica," *Latin American Perspectives*, v. 15, fall 1988, 37–70.

"Toxic Chemicals and Hazardous Wastes" in UNEP et al. *The World Environment: 1972–1992: Two Decades of Challenge*. New York: Chapman and Hall, 1992.

"Toxic Waste: Paying for the Past," *The Economist*, v. 322, February 29, 1992, 80.

"Toxics in the Water: A Hidden Threat," *EPA Journal*, v. 11, September 1985, 2–20.

Truaz, Hawley. "The Toxic Waste Trade," *Environmental Action*, v. 20, no. 3, November-December 1988, 23.

"Twenty-Third Conference of the FAO Adopts Pesticide Code, Food Security Compact," *UN Chronicle*, v. 23, January 1986, 61.

"The United Nations Environment Programme Activities in Hazardous Waste Management," *Industry and Environment*, v. 11, no. 1, January-March 1988, 32–33.

Uva, Mary Deery, and Bloom, Jane. "Exporting Pollution: The International Waste Trade," *Environment*, v. 31, no. 5, June 1989, 4.

Books

Bradshaw, A.D., Southwood, R., and Warner, F. *The Treatment and Handling of Wastes*. London: Chapman and Hall, 1992.

Bull, David. *A Growing Problem: Pesticides and the Third World Poor*. Oxford: OXFAM, 1982.

Cassels, Jamie. *The Uncertain Promise of Law: Lessons from Bhopal*. Toronto: University of Toronto Press, 1993.

Center for Investigative Reporting and Bill Moyers. *Global Dumping Ground: The International Traffic in Hazardous Waste*. Cabin John, MD: Seven Locks Press, 1990.

Denison, Richard A., ed. *Recycling and Incineration: Evaluating the Choices*. Washington, DC: Island Press, 1990.

Gallagher, Carole. *American Ground Zero: The Secret Nuclear War*. Cambridge: MIT Press, 1993.

Handl, Gunther, and Lutz, Robert E. *Transferring Hazardous Technologies and Substances: The International Legal Challenge*. Norwell, MA: Kluwer Ac., 1990.

Keeble, John. *Out of the Channel: The Exxon Valdez Oil Spill in Prince William Sound*. New York: Harper Collins, 1991.

Mazmanian, David, and Morrell, David. *Beyond Superfailure: America's Toxics Policy for the 1990s*. Boulder, CO: Westview Press, 1992.

Morehouse, Ward, and Subramaniam, M. Arun. *The Bhopal Tragedy*. New York: Council on International and Public Affairs, 1986.

Pollock, Cynthia. *Mining Urban Wastes: The Potential for Recycling*. Washington, DC: Worldwatch Institute, 1987.

Ramade, Francois. *Ecotoxicology*. New York: John Wiley and Sons Ltd., 1987.

Schweitzer, G.E. *Borrowed Earth, Borrowed Time: Healing America's Chemical Wounds*. New York: Plenum Press, 1991.

Sheail, John. *Pesticides and Nature Conservation*. Oxford: Clarendon Press, 1985.

Tait, Joyce, and Napompeth, Banpot. *Management of Pests and Farmers' Perceptions and Practices*. Boulder: Westview Press, 1987.

Trager, Oliver, ed. *Our Poisoned Planet: Can We Save It?* New York: Facts On File, 1989.

Turner, R.K. *Towards an Integrated Waste Management Strategy*. London: British Petroleum, 1991.

Water/Oceans
Documents

England/United Kingdom

United Kingdom. *Ministerial Declaration, Second International Conference on the Protection of the North Sea*. London: Department of the Environment, 1988.

United Nations

Arnaudo, R. "The Problem of Persistent Plastics and Marine Debris in the Oceans," in *GESAMP: Technical Annexes to the Report on the State of the Marine Environment. UNEP Regional Seas Reports and Studies No. 114/1:1–20*. Nairobi: UNEP.

GESAMP. *The State of the Marine Environment*. UNEP Regional Seas Report, no. 115, 1990.

UNCED. *Protection of the Oceans, All Kinds of Seas, Including Enclosed and Semi-Enclosed Seas, and Coastal Areas and the Protection, Rational Use and Development of their Living Resources*. United Nations Conference on Environment and

Development Agenda. Rio Declaration, Forest Principles, May 1, 1992, v. 2, 134.

————. *Protection of the Quality and Supply of Freshwater Resources: Application of Integrated Approaches to the Development, Management and Use of Water Resources.* United Nations Conference on Environment and Development Agenda 21. Rio Declaration. Forest Principles, May 1, 1992, v. 2, 174.

United Nations Environment Programme. "Availability of Fresh Water," in *The World Environment: 1972–1992: Two Decades of Challenge.* New York: Chapman and Hall, 1992, 87.

————. "Sustainable Water Development: A Synthesis," *International Journal of Water Resource Development*, v. 5, no. 4, 225–251.

WMO/UNESCO. *Report on Water Resource Assessment.* Paris: UNESCO, 1991.

Articles

"All Countries Asked to Sign and Ratify Sea Law," *UN Chronicle*, v. 20, February 1983, 31–33.

Allott, Philip. "Mare Nostrum: A New International Law of the Sea," *American Journal of International Law*, v. 86, October 1992, 764–787.

Batisse, M. "Probing the Future of the Mediterranean," *Environment*, v. 32, 1990, 4–9, 28–34.

Bodansky, Daniel. "Protecting the Marine Environment from Vessel-Source Pollution: UNCLOS III and Beyond," *Ecology Law Quarterly*, v. 18, no. 4, 1991, 719.

Broadus, James M. "Oceanus Magazine," v. 34, no. 2, summer 1991, 14.

Brown, E.D. "'Neither Necessary nor Prudent at This Stage:' The Regime of Seabed Mining and Its Impact on the Universality of the UN Convention on the Law of the Sea," *Marine Policy*, v. 17, no. 2, March 1993, 81.

Burt, Tim, and Haycock, Nick. "Farming and Nitrate Pollution," *Geography*, v. 76, January 1991, 60–63.

Caminos, Hugo, and Molitor, Michael R. "Progressive Development of International Law and the Package Deal," *American Journal of International Law*, v. 79, April 1985, 347–372.

Caponera, Dante A. "Patterns of Cooperation in International Water Law: Principles and Institutions," *Natural Resources Journal*, v. 25, 1985, 564–587.

Downey, Terrence J., and Mitchell, Bruce. "Middle East Water: Acute or Chornic Problem?" *Water International*, v. 18, no. 1, March 1993, 1–4.

Duanzhi, She. "Rallying Around Common Interests," *Beijing Review*, v. 29, September 22, 1986, 12.

Earney, Fillmore C. "Law of the Sea, Resource Use, and International Understanding," *Journal of Geography*, v. 84, no. 3, May-June 1985, 105.

Elliot, Michael. "The Global Politics of Clean Water," *American Enterprise*, v. 2, September/October 1991, 26–31.

———. "Water Wars," *The Geographical Magazine*, v. 64, May 1991, 28–30.

Falkenmark, Malin. "Global Water Issues Confronting Humanity," *Journal of Peace Research*, v. 27, May 1990, 177–190.

Falkenmark, Malin and Widstrand, Carl. "Population and Water Resources: A Delicate Balance," *Population Bulletin*, v. 47, November 1992, 1–36.

"The First Commodity," *The Economist*, v. 322, March 28, 1992, 11–12.

"Fresh Water: None for the 1.2 Billion People," *UN Chronicle*, v. 29, June 1992, 60.

"General Assembly Calls on All States to Become Parties to Convention on the Law of the Sea," *UN Chronicle*, v. 23, February 1986, 66–67.

Glassner, Martin Ira. "The Political Geography of the Sea," *The Canadian Geographer*, v. 37, fall 1993, 271–279.

Gleick, Peter H. "Water and Conflict: Fresh Water Resources and International Security," *International Security*, v. 18, no. 1, summer 1993, 79–81+.

———. "Water Resources: A Long-Range Global Evaluation," *Ecology Law Quarterly*, v. 20, no. 1, 1993, 141.

Gunn, J.M. and Keller W. "Biological Recovery of an Acid Lake After Reductions in Industrial Emmissions of Sulfur," *Nature*, v. 345, 431–433.

Hindson, James. "Fieldwork on the Farm," *The Geographical Magazine*, v. 61, September 1989, supp. 4–6.

Hirsch, M., and Housen-Couriel, D. "Aspects of the Law of International Water Resources," *Water Science Technology*, v. 27, no. 7–8, 1993, 213.

Hutchings, Vicky. "Green Gauge," *New Stateman and Society*, v. 6, July 23, 1993, 31.

"Impact of Water Supply and Sanitation Programs on Community Health and Organization," *Ekistics*, v. 49, September/October 1982, 405–407.

Jin, Di, and Grigalunas, Thomas A. "Environmental Compliance and Energy Exploration and Production: Application to Offshore Oil and Gas," *Land Economics*, v. 69, February 1993, 82–97.

Kimball, L.A. "International Law and Institutions: The Oceans and Beyond," *Ocean Development and International Law*, v. 21, no. 2, 1990, 147.

Kindt, John W. "Particulate Pollution and the Law of the Sea," *Boston College Environmental Affairs Law Review*, v. 12, no. 2, winter 1985, 273.

Kovacs, Gyorgy. "Are Groundwater Resources Sufficiently Protected?" *Impact of Science on Society*, v. 1, 1983, 35–47.

Kwiatkowska, Barbara. "Ocean Affairs and the Law of the Sea in Africa: Towards the 21st Century," *Marine Policy*, v. 17, no. 1, January 1993, 11.

"Law of the Sea Convention: Ten Years Later," *UN Chronicle*, v. 30, March 1993, 87.

"Lenssen, Nicholas. "The Ocean Blues," *World Watch*, v. 2, no. 4, July/August 1989, 26.

Leopold, L.B. "Ethos Equity and the Water Resource," *Environment*, April 1990, 16.

Levenson, Howard. "Estuaries and Coastal Waters Need Help," *Environmental Science and Technology*, November 1987, 1052–1054.

"Managing Freshwater Resources," *Impact of Science on Society*, v. 1, 1983, 3–123.

Marx, Wesley. "Great Water Bodies at a Watershed: Pollution Prevention and a Regional Approach are Needed," *EPA Journal*, v. 18, no. 4, September-October 1992, 45–48.

McCaffrey, Stephen C. "The Law of International Watercourses: Some Recent Developments and Unanswered Questions," *Denver Journal of International Law and Policy*, v. 17, no. 3, spring 1989, 505.

McManus, Roger. "Pollution at Sea is a Luxury We Can't Afford," *Forum for Applied Research and Public Policy*, v. 9, spring 1994, 46–48.

McNeill, Desmond. "The Appraisal of Rural Water Supplies," *World Development*, v. 13, October/November 1985, 1178–1178.

Michaelides, G., and Young, R.J. "Rainwater Harvesting for Domestic Use in Rural Areas," *Ekistics*, v. 50, November/December 1983, 473–476.

Milne, Roger. "Pollution and Politics in the North Sea," *New Scientist*, v. 116, no. 1587, November 19, 1987, 53.

Morrisey, Siobhan. "Estuaries: Concern over Troubled Waters," *Oceans*, June 1988, 23–26.

Niemczynowicz, Janusz. "Water Management and Urban Development: A Call for Realistic Alternatives for the Future," *Impact of Science on Society*, v. 166, 1992, 131–147.

"Now What? The Environment," *Human Ecology Forum*, v. 21, winter 1993, 20–23.

"Of Wets and Water," *The Economist*, v. 330, March 26, 1994, 17.

Okun, D.A. "Realizing the Benefits of Water Reuse in Developing Countries," *Water Environment and Technology*, v. 2, 1990, 78–82.

———. "The Value of Water Supply and Sanitation in Development: An Assessment," *American Journal of Public Health*, v. 78, November 1988, 1463–1467.

Oxman, Bernard H. "United States Interests in the Law of the Sea Convention," *American Journal of International Law*, v. 88, January 1994, 167–178.

Petts, Geoff. "Mighty Torrents and Mankind," *The Geographical Magazine*, v. 59, September 1987, 436.

Postel, Sandra. "The Politics of Water," *World Watch*, v. 6, no. 4, July-August 1993, 10–18.

———. "Water for the Future: On Tap or Down the Drain?," *The Futurist*, v. 20, March/April 1986, 17–21.

Ren, Zhengde. "For Equal Use of Space and Sea," *Beijing Review*, v. 28, September 16, 1985.

"Research, International Law and the Sea in Man's Future," *Impact of Science on Society*, v. 3–4, 1983, 247–504.

Roundy, Robert W. "Clean Water Provision in Rural Areas of Less Developed Countries," *Social Science and Medicine*, v. 20, no. 3, 1985, 293–300.

Sankovitch, Nina. "Ocean is No Place to Put Our Waste," *Forum for Applied Research and Public Policy*, v. 9, spring 1994, 45–49.

Sarpong, G.A. "WEST AFRICAN STATES: The Marine Pollution Problem: Some Lessons from UNCLOS," *Environmental Policy and Law*, v. 33, no. 2, April 1993, 87–102.

"Sea Convention Not Yet in Force, But its Impact is Already Felt," *UN Chronicle*, v. 22, no. 2, 1985, 36–39.

Shiklomanov, L.A. "Global Water Resources," *Nature and Resources*, v. 26, 1990, 34–43.

Smith, William. "Sustainable Use for Water in the 21st Century," *Ambio*, v. 18, no. 5, 1989, 294.

Sorokin, A.Z. "International Cooperation in Aquaculture: Legal Aspects," *Marine Policy*, v. 16, no. 2, March 1992, 99.

Stokes, Bruce. "Water Shortages: The Next 'Energy Crisis,'" *The Futurist*, v. 17, April 1983, 37–41.

Swanson, R.L., Schubel, J.R., and West-Valle, A.S. "Are Oceans Being Over Protected From Pollution?" *Forum for Applied Research and Public Policy*, v. 9, spring 1994, 38–44.

Vallarta, Jose Luis. "Protection and Preservation of the Marine Environment and Marine Scientific Research at the Third United Nations Conference on the Law of the Sea," *Law and Contemporary Problems*, v. 46, spring 1983, 147–154.

Verner, Joel G. "Changes in the Law of the Sea: Latin American Contributions and Rationales," *Social and Economic Studies*, v. 30, June 1981, 18–44.

Viessman, Warren Jr. "A Framework for Reshaping Water Management," *Environment*, May 1990, 10.

————. "Water Management: Challenge and Opportunity," *Journal of Water Resources Planning and Management-ASCE*, v. 116, no. 2, March-April 1990, 155.

Waldichuk, Michael, Department of Fisheries and Oceans. "The Contamination of Seas," in Environment Canada et al. *Toxic Substances Fourth Conference*, Montreal, April 4–5, 1990, 1.

Ward, Colin. "Fringe Benefits," *New Stateman and Society*, v. 6, May 14, 1993, 27.

"Water: A Thirsty Planet," *U.N. Chronicle*, v. 25, June 1988, 48.

"A Well Running Dry: Study Shows that Water Supplies May Not Last Forever," *The Futurist*, v. 27, May/June 1993, 56–57.

"Women's Rights and Clean Water: Essentials for Survival," *UN Chronicle*, v. 22, no. 2, 1985, x–xi.

Books

Agricultural Chemicals and Groundwater Protection: Emerging Management and Policy. Wayzata, MN: Freshwater Foundation, 1988.

Albaiges, J., ed. *Marine Pollution*. New York: Hemisphere, 1989.

Ashworth, William. *The Late, Great Lakes*. New York: Knopf, 1986.

Bulloch, David K. *The Wasted Ocean*. New York: Lyons and Burford, 1989.

Calabrese, Edward J., Gilbert, Charles E., and Pastides, Harris, eds. *Safe Drinking Water Act: Amendments, Regulations and Standards*. Chelsea, MI: Lewis Publishers, 1989.

Churchill, R.R. *The Law of the Sea*. Dover, NH: Manchester University Press, 1985.

Davidson, Art. *In the Wake of the Exxon Valdez*. San Francisco: Sierra Club Books, 1990.

Day, John W. *Estuarine Ecology*. New York: John Wiley and Sons, 1989.

Falkenmar, Malin, and Lindh, Gunnar. *Water for a Starving World*. Boulder, CO: Westview Press, 1976.

Feldman, David Lewis. *Water Resources Management*. Baltimore: Johns Hopkins University Press, 1991.

Fisher, Diane, et al. *Polluted Coastal Waters: The Role of Acid Rain*. Environmental Defense Fund, 1988.

Haas, Peter M. *Saving the Mediterranean: The Politics of International Environmental Cooperation*. New York: Columbia University Press, 1990.

Hinrichsen, D. *Our Common Seas: Coasts in Crisis*. London: Earthscan Publications Ltd., 1990.

Johnston, Douglas. *The Environmental Law of the Sea*. Gland, Switzerland: International Union for Conservation of Nature and Natural Resources, 1981.

Jones, R. Russell, and Wigley T. *Ozone Depletion and Health*. New York: Wiley, 1989.

Jorgensen, Eric P., ed. *The Poisoned Well: New Strategies for Groundwater Protection*. Washington, DC: Island Press, 1989.

Kennish, Michael J. *Ecology of Estuaries: Anthropogenic Effects*. London: CRC Press, 1992.

Lammers, J.G. *Pollution of International Watercourses*. Norwell, MA: Kluwer Ac., 1984.

Laws, Edward S. *Aquatic Pollution: An Introductory Text, 2nd ed.* New York: Wiley, 1993.

Leggett, Denis. *Troubled Waters.* North Bellmore, NY: Marshall Cavendish, 1991.

Leonard, Nelson. *Stream, Lake, Estuary, and Ocean Pollution.* New York: Van Nostrand Reinhold, 1991.

Mason, C.F. *Pollution.* New York: John Wiley and Sons, 1991.

Mele, Andre. *Polluting for Pleasure.* New York: W.W. Norton and Company, 1993.

Maybeck, Michel, et al., eds. *Global Freshwater Quality: A First Assessment.* Cambridge, MA: Blackwell Publishers, 1990.

Mishra, P.C. *Fundamentals of Air and Water Pollution.* Colombia, MO: S. Asia, 1990.

Nemerow, Nelson L. *Stream, Lake, Estuary and Ocean Pollution.* New York: Van Nos Reinhold, 1991.

Okun, D.A., and Lauria, D.T. *Capacity Building for Water Resources.* New York: UNDP, 1991.

Richardson, Jacques G., ed. *Managing the Ocean: Resources, Research, Law.* Mt. Airy, MD: Lomond, 1985.

Sambasiva, B. *Water, Ecology, Pollution and Management.* Colombia, MO: S. Asia, 1991.

Snodgrass, M.E. *Environmental Awareness: Water Pollution.* Marco, FL: Bancroft-Sage, 1991.

Soons, Alfred H. *Implementation of the Law of the Sea Convention Through International Institutions.* Honolulu: Law of the Sea Institute, 1989.

Solbe, J.F., ed. *Effects of Land Use on Fresh Waters: Agriculture, Forestry, Mineral Exploitation, Urbanisation.* New York: Halsted Press, 1986.

Suter, Glen W. II, and Lewis, Michael A., eds. *Aquatic Toxicology and Environmental Fate. vol. II.* Philadelphia: ASTM, 1989.

Thanh, N.C., and Biswas, Asit K. *Environmentally Sound Water Management.* Oxford: Oxford University Press, 1990.

Thatcher, P.C. *Sea Pollution: The Mediterranean—A New Approach to Marine Pollution.* Paper prepared for International Institute for Applied Systems Analysis (IIASA). September 29, 1990. Washington, DC: World Resources Institute, 1990.

Thorne-Miller, Boyce, and Catena, John G. *The Living Ocean: Understanding and Protecting Marine Biodiversity.* Washington, DC: Island Press, 1990.

Weller, Phil. *Fresh Water Seas*. Ontario: Between the Lines, 1990.

Urbanization
Documents

United Nations
UNCHS. *Global Report on Human Settlement, 1986*. Nairobi: UNCHS, 1986.
————. *Shelter and Urbanization*. Nairobi: UNCHS, 1990.
————. *Sustainable Cities Programme*. Nairobi: UNCHS, 1990.
WHO. *Environmental Health in Urban Development*. WHO Technical Report Series no. 807. Geneva: WHO, 1991.
WHO/UNEP. *Urbanization and its Implications for Child Health*. Geneva: WHO, 1988.

Articles
Axelbank, Jay. "The Crisis of the Cities," *Population*, v. 15, no. 4, December 1988, 28.
Bell, Judith Kjellberg. "Women, Environment and Urbanization in a Third World Context: A Guide to the Literature," *Women and Environments*, v. 13, spring 1992, 12–17.
Harpham, T., and Stephens, C. "Urbanization and Health in Developing Countries, *World Health Statistics Quarterly*, v. 44, 1991, 62.
Homer-Dixon, Thomas F., Boutwell, Jefferey, H., and Rathjens, George. "Environmental Change and Violent Conflict," *Scientific American*, v. 268, no. 2, February 1993, 38.
Kasarda, J., and Rondinelli, D.A. "Mega-Cities, the Environment and Private Enterprise," *Environmental Impact Assessment Review*, v. 10, 1990, 393.
Plpadwala, Porus, and Goldsmith, William W. "The Sustainability of Privilege: Reflections on the Environment, the Third World City, and Poverty," *World Development*, v. 20, April 1992, 627–640.
Massignon, Nicole. "The Urban Explosion in the Third World," *OECD Observer*, no. 182, June/July 1993, 18.
Smith, David, and London, Bruce. "Convergence in World Urbanization? A Quantitative Assessment," *Urban Affairs Quarterly*, v. 25, no. 4, 574.
Sumka, Howard J. "Global Urbanization: Mobilizing International H/CD Partnership," *Journal of Housing*, v. 46, no. 5, September/October 1989, 221.

"The Year 2000 and Beyond: An Agenda of Priority Issues," *Ekistics*, v. 53, September/October-November/December 1986, 266–370 and v. 54, July/August-November/December 1987, 215–347.

Books

Krupnick, A.J. *Urban Air Pollution in Developing Countries.* Washington, DC: Resources for the Future, 1991.

Index

Abidhjan Convention, 100–101
Acid rain: affecting U.S./Canadian relations, 240–244, 249–251; Air Quality Agreement, U.S./Canadian, 251–253; Canadian vulnerability to U.S. emissions, 243–244; chemical processes, 233–234; Convention on Long-Range Transboundary Air Pollution, 237–238, 547; environmental effects, 47–48, 234–235, 251; health effects, 235; impact on tropical forests, 52–53; as industrialization product, 232; origin of term, 233; treaties, 547–548
Action Plan for the Human Environment, 539
Activism, *see* Political activism
Adede, A. O., 538–583
Africa: decline in food production, 188; poaching of wildlife, 366–367; urban population growth, 204t; wildlife sanctuaries, 366. *See also* West and Central African Action Plan
African Convention on the Conservation of Nature and Natural Resources, 497
Agriculture: cropland loss, 173–174, 272; and deforestation, 141, 148–149, 192; mismanagement and land degradation, 175t; pasture and range land loss, 174–175, 191; research needs, 282–283; technological advances, 178; water supply

affecting, 179
Air pollution: abatement procedures: Canada, 249; Great Britain, 236; bibliography, 595–600; in Brazil, 163; clean air legislation: Canada, 245, 250; England, 233; United States, 245–246, 251–253, 253–256; fossil fuels, 211; *New York v. Thomas,* 246–248; North American agreement, 500; Stockholm Declaration, 236–237; transboundary, 231, 242–244, *see also* Convention on Long-Range Transboundary Air Pollution; treaties, 547–549; table, xiii; U.S./Canadian, 244–245, 251–253, 253–256
Air Quality Agreement, U.S./Canadian (1991): addressing acid rain concerns, 253; creation of, 253–254; dispute resolution process, 254; obligations of parties, 255; review mechanisms, 254; role of International Joint Commission, 253–255; time frame, 255–256
Alaska, oil spills, 71
Alerce Andino National Park, Chile, 360
Algae blooms, toxic, 70–71
Amazon region, environmental issues, 158
Annapurna Conservation Area, 376, 380
Antarctic Mineral Resources Com-

652